INTRODUCTION TO
TRANSGENDER STUDIES

HARRINGTON PARK PRESS

NEW YORK, NY • USA

INTRODUCTION TO
TRANSGENDER STUDIES

ARDEL HAEFELE-THOMAS

WITH THE PARTICIPATION
OF THATCHER COMBS

Illustrations by Cameron Rains

Harrington Park Press
Box 331
9 East 8th Street
New York, NY 10003

http://harringtonparkpress.com

Library of Congress Cataloging-in-Publication Data

Names: Haefele-Thomas, Ardel, author.
Title: Introduction to transgender studies / Ardel Haefele-Thomas ; with the
        participation of Thatcher Combs ; illustrations by Cameron Rains.
Description: New York : Harrington Park Press, [2019] | Includes
        bibliographical references and index.
Identifiers: LCCN 2018035468 (print) | LCCN 2018037860 (ebook) |
        ISBN 9781939594280 (ebook) | ISBN 9781939594273 (pbk. : alk. paper)
Subjects: LCSH: Gender nonconformity—Study and teaching. | Transsexualism. |
        Transgender people. | Transsexuals.
Classification: LCC HQ77.9 (ebook) | LCC HQ77.9 .T496 2019 (print) |
        DDC 306.76/8-—dc23
LC record available at https://lccn.loc.gov/2018035468

In Memory of

James Miranda Barry
Frances Thompson
Louis Graydon Sullivan
Marsha P. Johnson
Sylvia Rivera
Leslie Feinberg

In Honor of

Miss Major Griffin-Gracy
TGI Justice

Dedicated to

Lisa Haefele
Jalen Haefele-Thomas
Austin Mantele

CONTENTS

DETAILED CONTENTS

CHAPTER 5
Navigating Binary Spaces: Bathrooms, Schools, Sports   170

CHAPTER 8
Four Historical Figures Who Cross-Dressed:
The Adventurer, the Ambassador, the Surgeon, and the Seamstress

268

CHAPTER 9

Cross-Dressing and Political Protest: Parasols and Pitchforks **320**

CHAPTER 11

Trans Literature, Performing Arts, Music, and Visual Arts: **382**
The Art of Resistance/The Art of Empowerment

PREFACE

Introduction to Transgender Studies is the first introductory textbook to the field of transgender (trans) studies. While numerous outstanding books are available in the rapidly growing field of trans studies, they often focus on theory, with an intended audience of graduate students; or they are autobiographical or biographical and thus look at only one person; or they explore only one topic, such as health care, legal systems, history, or coming out as trans to family and friends. In contrast, *Introduction to Transgender Studies* is the first full-length textbook to introduce trans studies as a rich field of study that encompasses and connects global contexts, intersecting identities, historic and contemporary issues, literature, history, politics, art, and culture. Each of its twelve chapters includes key concepts, original artwork by Cameron Rains, never-before-published essays by trans people and allies from around the world, an extensive list of film and television of interest, numerous topics for student discussion, in-class and out-of-class activities, and ideas for writing and research that range from informal reports to formal research projects.

Intended Audience

The intended audience for *Introduction to Transgender Studies* is undergraduates in courses ranging from introductory gender studies courses and introductory LGBTQ+ studies courses to more specific classes focusing on the expanding field of transgender studies. This text can also be used in graduate courses focusing on pedagogical practices in gender studies, feminist studies, LGBTQ+ studies, and transgender studies.

The Need for This Book

The seeds for this book came from my own teaching in the writing program at Stanford University, where I taught feminist rhetoric and queer rhetoric, as well as my teaching at City College of San Francisco in the LGBT Studies Department and Berkeley City College in the Women's Studies Department. In all these settings, undergraduates were eager to learn about contemporary transgender issues as well as the rich global history of gender diversity through the ages. Textbooks published for courses in LGBTQ+ studies often have minimal focus on transgender issues and experiences. More broadly, in women's studies, feminist studies, and gender studies, most textbooks highlight women's issues and women's lived experiences; more to the point, they tend to focus on cisgender

Haefele-Thomas, Ardel, *Introduction to Transgender Studies*
dx.doi.org/10.17312/harringtonparkpress/2019.01.itts.00a
© 2019 by Harrington Park Press

women and rarely consider the experiences of trans women. Even the feminist and gender studies texts that now include masculinity studies often do not consider trans studies or the expansion of gender beyond the binary. When trans issues are introduced, they are often discussed within the context of a person transitioning and crossing the gender binary from one pole to another. While *Introduction to Transgender Studies* honors trans people who identify along a male/female binary, it is also mindful of ancient cultures that honored gender diversity with third-, fourth-, and fifth-gender identities as well as contemporary nonbinary, agender, and gender-expansive identities.

A Welcoming, Student-Centered Approach

Introduction to Transgender Studies takes a student-centered approach. In my women and gender studies, feminist philosophy, LGBT studies, and transgender studies classes, I have often found that students experience a good deal of anxiety, trepidation, and confusion when studying issues pertaining to sex and gender, gender identity, gender expression, and sexual orientation. Even students who identify within the gay, lesbian, bisexual, transgender, queer, intersex (or differences of sex development)+ community often find it difficult to distinguish among sexual orientation, gender identity, and gender expression. I wrote this book to create a safe space for the full spectrum of undergraduate students, ranging from those who have never thought about gender issues to students who identify as transgender, trans, nonbinary, agender, and/or gender expansive.

In short, the language and the artwork in this book are meant to be welcoming. They invite the reader and the instructor to find ways to discuss gender issues and gender identities and issues in a safe and comfortable way. I have tried to make the text welcoming to newcomers who may not have thought about trans issues, as well as to gender-expansive students who have. Often, these students sit side by side in the same classroom. The text promotes dialogue, communication, and mutual respect.

Class-Tested

The first two chapters of this book were piloted with great success among undergraduates in a wide range of institutions of higher learning, including community colleges, public state universities, and private colleges and universities. At the University of Colorado in the United States and at the University of Exeter in the United Kingdom, these chapters were successfully piloted in graduate courses, with the goal of students' considering the material in light of their own pedagogical practices in teaching.

Writings from the Community

As one person living in the United States and as a nonbinary trans white person, I have been aware that my voice is unable to capture the wealth of diversity regarding trans issues around the world. Thus, each chapter concludes with brief contributed "Writings from the Community" essays. The majority of the writings were specifically commissioned for this textbook and relate to the overall chapter theme. Each piece allows students to hear the voices of people from different parts of the world; most of the contributors identify as trans, and all have thought deeply about gender identity, intersecting identities, intersecting oppressions, and their own lived experience.

The writings include not only Andrea Jenkins's poem "Blues for SOGI" and her essay explaining the importance of the Transgender Oral History Project at the Tretter Collection at the University of Minnesota but also a recounting of Eileen Chester's experiences as a Two-Spirit person from the Nuu-chah-nulth Nation in British Columbia attempting to find a recovery center that will be open to a person who is Indigenous and Two Spirit. (Andrea Jenkins is an award-winning poet and the first out African American transgender woman elected to a city government in the United States. Eileen Chester is a returning community college student who works two full-time jobs while attending college.) The Ugandan LGBTQI+ activist and educator John (Longjones) Abdallah Wambere discusses the climate for trans people in his home country. Two of the essays are written by a mother and her trans teenage son, and two other essays written by medical doctors focus on points of access to medical care for trans people (one written by a cisgender ally, the other written by a trans man).

Content and Organization

The first two chapters of *Introduction to Transgender Studies* focus on definitions in the context of people's personal stories, which help to underscore and explain each definition. Chapter 1 looks at primary and secondary sex traits, differences of sex development (also known as intersex), gender identity, gender expression, diverse gender possibilities, and the differences between gender and sex. Various terms under the trans umbrella are defined and explored, including the term *cisgender*. Chapter 2 explores sexual orientation and considers how gender identity and gender expression are often conflated with sexual orientation. Heterosexuality, homosexuality, and bisexuality are defined and considered within contemporary and historic contexts. Asexuality and pansexuality are also defined and examined. The chapter concludes by considering contemporary terminology and slang relating to sexual orientation.

Chapter 3 examines nineteenth-century sexology to illuminate why Western culture sometimes seems obsessed with gender-identity and sexual-orientation labels. In examining historical sexological taxonomies that are today considered homophobic and transphobic, the chapter also explores early outcries against these narratives of disease and disorder. The chapter concludes by looking at the work of present-day individuals and clinics working to make sexology inclusive of all people.

Chapter 4 focuses on riots, protests, and rebellions for trans rights in the mid- to late twentieth century. The chapter also explores why, in the United States, we often see a split between the LGB and the T communities. The chapter concludes with a look at Georgina Beyer, a Maori trans woman who became the first known transgender person in the world to become a member of parliament.

Chapters 5 and 6 examine twenty-first century issues, including bathroom access, education, sports, legal identification, and health care. They consider various countries around the world as well as individual states within the United States.

Chapters 7, 8, 9, and 10 focus on various trans histories. Chapter 7 looks specifically at global Indigenous cultures that not only accepted but also revered gender diversity. The groups studied range from ancient India and the third-gender identity group known as the *Hijras* (who have existed for over four thousand years) to the third-, fourth-, and fifth-gender identities known as *Nádleeh* in Navajo culture. In general, Chapter 7 considers the history before colonization as well as the ways that colonial violence attempted to erase gender diversity. The chapter ends with a discussion of current de-colonial recovery projects.

Chapter 8 focuses on four historic figures who cross-dressed in order to fully embody their gender identity: Catalina/Don Antonio de Erauso of Spain, Le Chevalier/La Chevalière d' Éon of France, Dr. James Miranda Barry of England, and Frances Thompson of the United States. While this chapter focuses on individuals, it also raises important questions about the ways that historians gather history and make assumptions about their subjects. Several archival newspaper accounts help enliven this chapter.

Chapter 9 focuses on cross-dressing as a form of protest from the seventeenth century to the twenty-first. The chapter examines cross-dressing and troubling the gender binary as means of protest in the Enclosure Riots, the Luddite Riots, the Rebecca Riots, the 1990s antiwar protests in the United States, and the current #meninhijab protests against restrictive laws enforced on women in Iran.

Chapter 10 considers trans-related ancient art and artifacts from India, Nepal, and Egypt; it also focuses on Pharaoh Hatshepsut and the Chinese legend of General Mulan. The chapter then explores religious icons that were dual-gendered as well as the story of Joan of Arc.

Chapter 11 considers trans art and culture from the nineteenth century to the twenty-first. Musicians ranging from Billy Tipton (jazz) and Little Axe Broadnax (gospel) are discussed alongside the Canadian Two-Spirit artist Iceis Rain (rap/rock) and the San Francisco icon Shawna Virago (rockabilly/punk/folk). Visual artist Jess T. Dugan's trans elders photo project is also presented in this chapter as well as three other chapters, along with a one-time South African trans arts collective show. Authors and characters who embrace gender diversity are also explored, along with important novels, media, film, and television.

Finally, Chapter 12 looks to transgender archives and the necessity of uncovering and safeguarding trans histories around the world. The book closes with suggestions for further research at several of the online trans archives.

Instructors' Resources

Introduction to Transgender Studies is accompanied by instructors' resources intended to support the book's use in a class setting. The resources are available to confirmed adopters. To request the resources, contact coursematerials@columbiauniversitypress.com or bcohen@harringtonparkpress.com. The resources include sample syllabi for various course configurations in transgender studies and gender studies classes. For each chapter, instructors can access key teaching points with further discussion questions, in-class activities, research projects, and tips for using the book's film and television suggestions. The resources also include a brief description of various approaches to teaching the material in each chapter. PowerPoint presentations for each chapter (including approximately twenty-five to thirty slides per presentation) are also available.

Acknowledgements

I am so fortunate in that I have never been truly alone at any point in the process of writing this book. I would like to thank Bill Cohen at Harrington Parkress for believing in this project and for his unwavering support. I also thank Steven Rigolosi, who laughed when I called him the God of Editing. But he is. Thanks also to Ann Twombly for the third round of edits. And thank you to Patrick Ciano for his incredible eye for detail and layout.

Thank you to Susan Stryker, historian, filmmaker, and professor of gender and women's studies and the director of the Institute for LGBT Studies at the University of Arizona. Susan was an incredible supporter of this project even before I had written one word. Her encouragement from the beginning has meant so much to me. To Jo Clifford, a Scottish playwright and international advocate for trans rights through art—aside from being lulled into a sense of calm and "it will all be all right" as my family and I sat in the front row of your play, *Eve*, at the Edinburgh Fringe Festival—I want to thank you for your generous spirit. I would also like to thank Aaron H. Devor, Research Chair in Transgender Studies at the University of Victoria, along with the entire group at the University of Victoria who coordinate the Moving Trans History Forward conference. Your conference has been key to this book. And to all of the people at the University of Victoria library who kept bringing me box after box and helping me with the Transgender Archives there, a huge thank-you.

I offer a very special thank-you to Paisley Currah, professor of political science and women's and gender studies at Brooklyn College and the Graduate Center of the City University of New York. Paisley was a valued reader for this project, and his in-depth comments on each chapter have made this a much stronger text.

Thank you to all of my students past and present who have participated in reading and giving feedback on various drafts of this book. Thanks to Thatcher Combs for participating in the early stages of this book. Thank you to the professors and their students who piloted early drafts of Chapters 1 and 2: Molly Merryman, Regenia Gagnier, Emmanuel David, and Susan Rose Galle-Boyko. And thank you to Logan Barsigian for reading early drafts, giving comments, and culling all the comments from various pilots.

To all the people who have shared their stories in this book and to all the contributors to "Writings from the Community," I am forever in your debt. You have all made this book what it is. Your voices all together are strong and beautiful: Jess T. Dugan and Vanessa Fabbre (and the four people of focus from *To Survive on This Shore*: Tasha, Bobbi, Chris, and Gloria), Charlie Manzano, Lorenzo, Andrea Jenkins, Austin Mantele, T. J. Gundling, Paulina Angel, Jesus Coronado, Luke, Hanne, Jules Chyten-Brennan, Mat Kladney, Veronika Fimbres, Dallas Denny, Eileen Chester, John (Longjones) Abdallah Wambere, Ms. Bob Davis, Rhian E. Jones, Cheryl Morgan, Sean Dorsey, Shawna Virago, Jamison Green, Aaron H. Devor, and Harrison Apple.

The librarians at Stanford University deserve a huge thank-you for helping me locate obscure articles and for delivering older books and journals from campus library storage. A big thank-you, too, to Stanford Special Collections for help with one of the images of the Rebecca Riots and the first-edition novel about the Luddite Riots.

Barbara Rudlaff, a dear friend in Colorado who has known me since 1984, said this when I came out to her as nonbinary trans a few years ago: "You've always been." Thank you for seeing me. And thank you for making the special trip to the

Boulder Daily Camera newspaper archive to get me the wonderful images for Chapter 9 and Ladies in Support of the President.

Thank you to my coach Osabemiye Tyehimba for always talking intersecting identities and critical theory with me between deadlift sets. And, on that same note, thank you to Chris Morgan and Charlotte Wareing and everyone in the LGBT International Powerlifting Federation, all of whom have been so incredibly supportive of full inclusion for trans athletes across and beyond the binary. To be able to come out of retirement as a powerlifter who can register in a nonbinary gender category thrills me.

Regenia Gagnier, professor of English at the University of Exeter, has been my mentor for over twenty-five years. I would not be where I am now without her support, and I am honored that she piloted early drafts of Chapters 1 and 2 with her graduate students.

My colleague Breana Bahar Hansen has been a superb reader of this book, giving me outstanding feedback for the discussion questions and group activities.

Thank you to Cameron Rains, my former CCSF student, who has devoted so much time to making the artwork in this book warm, inviting, and humorous. Their images create a safe space for all of us to discuss gender.

Austin Mantele, my former CCSF student who is now working on his MFA at Columbia University, read every draft of every chapter of this book. His comments have truly shaped each and every chapter. When I was on deadline, he also worked alongside Lisa Haefele to make sure that all the contributors to the "Writings from the Community" had everything they needed.

Thank you, Lisa Haefele, for being my life partner, my co-parent, and my strength every single day. Thank you for finding ways to give me room to work on this project over the past three years. Thank you for reading all the drafts, working with all the contributors to "Writings from the Community," and being willing to talk with me endlessly about history, gender, intersecting identities, and global politics. I am forever in your debt.

Finally, I want to thank my students. You have all been my role models and have shown me the way to be fully out as my authentic nonbinary trans self. Your courage and your strength have changed my life.

Ardel Haefele-Thomas

FOREWORD

Susan Stryker

At a moment in history when so many things seem to be getting worse the whole world over, it's nice to see some things moving in a direction that feels better. Ardel Haefele-Thomas's *Introduction to Transgender Studies* is one of those better-feeling things.

Ardel and I both hail from Oklahoma, both felt the genders we were assigned at birth didn't quite fit, both turned the curiosity our gender-questioning inspired in us toward careers in education, and both wound up making long-time homes in the San Francisco Bay Area. Reading this book felt like hanging out with a friend and having a conversation about things we share and care about. I trust it's a conversation you'll feel welcome and at home in, too.

I wish I'd had something like this book when I was growing up in Oklahoma in the 1960s and 1970s. I'd felt trans my whole life but kept my mouth shut and my head down about it. I learned the word *transsexual* from reading a "Dear Abby" column in my hometown newspaper when I still was a preteen, but I had a hard time finding information that rang true with me—the only books I could find in the card catalogue of the Carnegie Public Library of Lawton, Oklahoma, about the kind of people I thought I was were textbooks of abnormal psychology.

I was mesmerized when the early 1970s trans film *I Want What I Want* played at the Diana, a sort of sleazy second-rate movie theater downtown, because it was the first time I'd encountered visual media depicting a trans person. By the time I was in high school, Renée Richards, the trans woman who was a professional tennis player, was all over the news, and the ridicule and resistance she encountered let me know I'd been wise to stay silent about my own trans feelings. Still, I learned from all that sensationalistic coverage that Richards was the most notable transsexual since Christine Jorgensen in the 1950s, which was my first clue that folks like me had a history.

By the time I got to college at the University of Oklahoma in 1979, there were still only two books on trans topics in the university library: the psychiatrist Robert Stoller's *Perversion: The Erotic Form of Hatred* and Janice Raymond's notorious *Transsexual Empire,* the mother lode of transphobic feminist rhetoric, tropes, and discourse. One spring break, I found a copy of the lesbian feminist anthropologist Esther Newton's remarkable study of drag performers, *Mother Camp,* in a secondhand bookstore in Austin, Texas, which was the first time I'd seen anything trans-related treated in a smart, morally neutral, non-stigmatizing manner.

Haefele-Thomas, Ardel, *Introduction to Transgender Studies*
dx.doi.org/10.17312/harringtonparkpress/2019.01.itts.00b
© 2019 by Harrington Park Press

Even after I'd started graduate school in U.S. history at UC Berkeley in 1983, I had a hard time finding trans resources in one of the best research libraries in the world, though I did encounter there Carol Riddell's *Divided Sisterhood,* a transfeminist rebuttal of Raymond's hateful bilge. My people had a politics, it seemed, as well as a history.

Mostly, though, I learned about being trans simply by being trans. It was a seat-of-the-pants, hem-of-the-skirt sort of education. There was little in the way of affirming literature to read, or positive media representation to watch, in the 1980s. I had the good fortune of living in an urban area where, when it became really clear to me that I needed to transition if I wanted to live a life that felt worth living, I could snoop around the dark corners of the city and find interesting people to talk to, learn from, and be myself with—most of whom were constrained in their life circumstance because of their gender, some of whom were broken by their circumstances, but all of whom were fierce. Still, it was a furtive and underground sort of existence.

It still didn't seem possible, into the early 1990s, for me to both be trans and do the kind of work I was being trained to do. And when I finally flamed into public visibility just as I was finishing my degree, it in fact did turn out to be not possible to work in my profession and be openly, unapologetically trans. The financial hardships of the following years, the kind of marginalization and stigma that I lived through, are what stoked in me an unquenchable desire to use my academic training to change not just *what* people knew of trans, but *how* they knew it.

A cliché about universities is that they are "knowledge factories." There's a truth in that cliché, because what universities in fact do is produce what could be called "legitimated knowledge": not just what Uncle Donnie tweeted yesterday while scratching his keester and drinking a beer, but knowledge drawn from research and cogent thinking, grounded in other research and cogent thinking, ad infinitum. My goal as a trans academic working outside the academy was to make a different kind of knowledge about trans people, drawn as much from what we all knew from living in our bodies in the world as it was from what my grandmother called "school-book learnin'," and to get that knowledge into circulation, both on the streets and in the so-called ivory tower. The practice of making that different body of knowledge about trans people is what I think of as "transgender studies."

I feel very fortunate that I was eventually able to use my work in transgender studies to gain a university professorship, and that transgender studies has indeed helped produce a more affirming kind of knowledge about trans lives, both within and beyond the formal classroom, that can help people think differently about themselves, their world, and of the varieties of transness to be encountered therein. I see this book as a welcome addition to that expansive project. It offers a useful place to start thinking about basic concepts like sex and gender, sexual orientation, and identity. It offers, too, an opportunity to reflect on how best to acknowledge that human cultures throughout time and around the world have concocted a great many gender systems, without therefore assuming that all that diversity can be squeezed into the three little syllables of "transgender," or that everybody who has ever lived a life at odds with currently dominant forms of Eurocentric gender categorization can properly be referenced by that perpetually fraught pronoun, *we*.

I love that this book has such a strong historical focus, not just because I'm a history nerd, but because I think we can learn a lot about what's possible—what *can* be—by learning more about what already *actually has existed*. The past offers a kind of testimony that how things are is not how they've always been, which bears the sly implication that the future can be different from the present, too. Change is the only reality. And I love, too, that what counts as knowledge in these pages is not just what cisgender experts have to say about trans lives, but what trans people—those with formal expertise and scholarly training as well as those who went to the school of embodied experiences—have to say for themselves, about themselves. As the "Writings from the Community" sections of the book make clear, we are the best experts on our own lives.

Back in Oklahoma, I now have a young trans nephew who came out while he was still in high school, served as president of his school's Gay-Straight Alliance, and socially and hormonally transitioned before his twenty-first birthday. I have friends and colleagues who have gender-nonconforming, nonbinary, and trans-identified kids, who support their children's creative gender exploration at earlier and earlier ages. Something profound is shifting in our culture's understanding of what gender means and does, and what we call "transgender" now is but a window into that deeper transformation.

Though gender's change is a welcome one, that change also distances the experiences of "kids today" from the experiences of their trans elders, among whom I now number myself. Books like this *Introduction to Transgender Studies* thus play a vital role in transmitting intergenerational knowledge. As you undoubtedly will see as you read the pages that follow, Ardel Haefele-Thomas has done a commendable job presenting what *transgender* has meant up to our present moment, thereby giving the rising generation a generous gift to use as they see fit for the ongoing project of creating a less straitjacketed, more expansive sense of what a human life can be.

INTRODUCTION

Jo Clifford

I grew up in a very conventional family in England in the 1950s. I had no way to understand myself, and my family had no way to understand me.

It is hard to imagine, now, just how cut off from the basic information it was possible to be before the Internet.

I would look in the mirror and not truly recognize the boy I saw. This made me so afraid. I knew I could tell no one. I could only do my best to ignore it.

I would so badly want to play with girls' toys and wear girls' clothes, and, because I had no sisters and was brought up in all-male environments, this was mostly impossible.

But sometimes I could wear girls' clothes and openly imagine myself as a girl. This was when I was acting girls' parts in the all-male school I was forced to attend.

These experiences filled me with great joy and the greatest terror. Changing gender seemed utterly impossible at that time; and the desire to do so felt like something disgusting.

I was so ashamed of myself that I truly felt that if anyone knew the truth about me I would die of shame.

It seemed at the time that all I could do was hide my female self away and hope that no one would notice her.

What made it all far, far worse was that there were no words to describe myself. Words like *transgendered* simply did not exist.

So I considered myself unspeakable.

Unspeakably bad. Unspeakably alone.

I left school at eighteen and worked as a volunteer in a psychiatric hospital. I met a psychiatrist there who lent me a book called *Childhood and Society*.

It was written by a psychoanalyst called Erik Erikson, who was exploring, among other things, the different ways different societies bring up their children.

I was reading the chapter on Native American cultures when I read to my amazement about how adolescent boys were encouraged to pay attention to their dreams because a dream could tell an adolescent entering adulthood who they truly were.

A boy might dream of the moon holding in one hand a bow and arrow, the symbols of manhood, and in another a burden strap, a symbol of womanhood.

The boy had to choose.

Haefele-Thomas, Ardel, *Introduction to Transgender Studies*
dx.doi.org/10.17312/harringtonparkpress/2019.01.itts.00c

And if at the end of the dream he found himself holding the symbol of womanhood, he could go to the elders of the tribe, tell them of the dream, and renounce the identity of manhood.

He could wear women's clothes and perform women's tasks and be honored and respected for doing so.

Finding that information was such an important moment for me.

I so longed to be able to tell my parents, and my friends, that in some way I could understand my identity seemed to be female.

And I longed even more to be able to live openly as I felt myself to be.

And even though I also knew such a thing was utterly impossible in the place and time in which I found myself, the understanding that there had been places where this happened, and perhaps still did . . . this so profoundly helped me.

In fact, I think it saved my life.

Because I knew I was no longer alone.

Ever since then I have been passionately interested in trans and queer history, and it makes me so honored and happy to write this introduction to Ardel Haefele-Thomas's groundbreaking and profoundly important *Introduction to Transgender Studies*.

A book like this matters to everybody. The more I speak and perform as a trans artist, the clearer it becomes to me that everyone suffers from the painful and damaging belief that there are only two genders in the world.

In that way it is so helpful for everyone to be reminded that ever since human beings began to organize themselves into societies there have existed different genders and sexualities outside the heterosexual norm.

And it helps all of us who identify as queer or trans to understand that we are not alone in the world.

That we all have a history to which we can proudly belong.

Jo Clifford
Buenos Aires, October 2018

A NOTE ON LANGUAGE

Dear Reader:

Welcome to *Introduction to Transgender Studies,* and welcome to numerous ideas and discussions about gender and intersecting identities throughout time and around the world.

As you begin to explore the chapters of this text, please remember that language is constantly changing. For example, when I first began researching and writing this book, the shortened umbrella term for all people under the "transgender" umbrella was trans*. Today, trans* is no longer in use, and the truncated term *trans* has become predominant. So, when I refer to historic people, places, and time periods before the word *transgender* was coined and became widely adopted, I will often use the umbrella term *trans*.

As a nonbinary trans person myself, I have taken great pains in all cases to be as respectful with my language as possible. By the time you have this book in your possession, however, the language will most likely have changed again. Like any one piece of writing, this book offers the best practices for this moment in time as I submit the final draft to the publisher.

Near the end of each chapter in this book, I have included a section called "Writings from the Community." These contributions have been written by different people from around the world and from all walks of life. Each contributor has their/his/her own preferred vocabulary and ways of seeing the world. The language that the contributors use may be different from mine, but their words are part of their voices and their reality. Out of respect, I present their writing the way they have presented it to me.

INTRODUCTION TO
TRANSGENDER STUDIES

CHAPTER 1

Sex and Gender
Stories and Definitions

Key Questions

1. What are the differences between sex and gender?

2. How many options are available for sex and gender?

3. At what age did you begin to understand your gender identity?

4. We are all made up of many identities. Which of your identities feels most important to you? What are some things that make you you?

5. What aspects of your identity link you to a community of other people who are like you in some way?

6. When you get dressed to leave your home for the day, how much do your choices express your identity? As you get dressed, do you consider where you are going and the ways you would like others to see you?

Chapter Overview

Welcome to *Introduction to Transgender Studies*! The first two chapters of this book introduce you to definitions and concepts about sex, gender, gender expression, gender identity, and sexual orientation that will be used throughout this book. As you read, it is useful to remember that definitions can change quickly and may vary by geographic region, community, and larger social and cultural contexts. Historical context also becomes important as you consider these issues. You will encounter stories from a diverse group of people who give voice to these definitions; the stories of their lived experiences and intersecting identities will help you see how rich, nuanced, and interesting explorations of identity can be.

This first chapter explores the definitions and differences between sex and gender, two separate concepts that are not synonyms. After learning about the differences between sex and gender, you will also look at contemporary cultural assumptions about gender as a *binary*—that is, the idea that one is either a man or a woman. Gender identity and gender expression, however, often move beyond

Haefele-Thomas, Ardel, *Introduction to Transgender Studies*
dx.doi.org/10.17312/harringtonparkpress/2019.01.itts.001
© 2019 by Harrington Park Press

the binary. As the book progresses, you will encounter historical definitions of sex, gender, and sexual orientation around the world, gaining insight into the ways that different cultures and societies have understood, valued, and given meaning to these aspects of identity.

Introduction: How Did You Express Your Gender Today?

When you are getting ready to go out in public, how do you choose what you are going to wear? How are you going to present yourself to the world? Some of you may not give much thought to the matter. You dig through the laundry pile and throw on sweats, a T-shirt, and flip-flops, and you're ready to face the day. Others may spend more time thinking about what they want to wear and how they want to look. As you get ready, how often does your gender dictate the way you want to present yourself? Do any cultural or religious considerations affect the way you will express your gender in a public space? Are there specific social "rules" regarding how you should look? Did you even think about your gender as you were getting ready?

These questions may seem odd if you did not consciously think about your gender identity or your gender expression today. For some, however, these questions are serious considerations each and every day because, for many different reasons, they may always be very aware of their gender identity and gender expression. One final question: Did you *express* your gender in the same way you *identify* your gender?

Defining Sex: Is It a Boy or a Girl?

Do you know someone who is pregnant or who has had a baby recently? What is the first question people tend to ask about the baby? Do they ask about the baby's health? Hair color? Ethnicity? Weight? Length? In the United States and many other societies, the first question is usually: Is it a boy or a girl? Even if the babies are twins or triplets, that first question is about the infants' **sex**. "Boy or girl?" may seem like a simple question, but sex is made up of intricate parts comprising chromosomal makeup and various sex characteristics.

Genitalia

In many parts of the world, if the expecting parent has access to medical care, the answer to the "boy or girl?" question can often be found in an early obstetrical ultrasound. From the moment the child's sex is determined—based on a visual scan of the fetus's genitalia—almost everyone, whether intentionally or not, begins to make assumptions about the baby's gender.

The choices for a baby's sex are set up as either male or female, thus creating a **binary** of only two options. Generally speaking, we think of the two categories—male and female—as opposites between which there is no middle ground. In many languages, there are only two pronoun choices for an individual: *he* or *she*. Some languages have numerous pronoun choices, which we will explore in more depth later. In English, many *think* there are only two pronoun choices. The language does have room for multiple possibilities, however, which you will read about later in this chapter.

Chromosomal Makeup and Differences of Sex Development (DSD)

Most of us understand our sex based on genitalia and the reproductive organs. A baby born with a penis and testicles gets labeled *male,* while a baby born with a vulva and ovaries gets labeled *female.* But what happens if either on the ultrasound or right after birth, the baby's external genitalia do not clearly indicate male or female? Depending on geographic location and the level of medical support, further testing at the level of the chromosome may be conducted.

In human biology, babies with two X chromosomes are labeled female, and babies with one X chromosome and one Y chromosome are labeled male. Most babies do not undergo chromosomal testing unless there is a possibility that the baby might have **differences of sex development (DSD)**. DSD refers to people with a sex chromosomal makeup that varies from XX or XY, and/or people who have hormonal levels that do not fit neatly in a male/female binary, and/or people who have genitals that are usually associated with both the male sex and the female sex. As you may already know from your science courses, there are numerous chromosomal variations, such as XXY (also known as Klinefelter syndrome), XYY (also known as Jacob syndrome), and XXX (triple X or trisomy X), which suggests that sex is not binary. Sex is defined not only by genitalia, as many of us assume, but also by an individual's hormonal, chromosomal, and genital makeup.

Historic Terms and Healthcare Issues for People with DSD

Over the past century, there have been different terms used to label people who have differences of sex development. The term **hermaphrodite,** which comes from Greek mythology, was one of the first words used to describe people who have DSD. Hermaphroditus was the child of Hermes (the male Greek god of commerce and a messenger to the other gods) and Aphrodite (the female Greek goddess of love and beauty). Classical Greek sculptors and poets depicted Hermaphroditus as a person with both a penis and breasts. Greek mythology is not alone in depicting gods and other powerful and mystical beings as embodying male and female attributes. Ancient Egypt, Rome, India, and Mesopotamia also embraced figures who were understood to be simultaneously female and male.[1]

Historically, *hermaphrodite* is an important term. It will appear in later chapters that explore historical contexts and the ways that various cultures tried to name and identify people who could not be placed precisely in one or another of a sex binary. In many of those cultures, possessing male and female attributes was considered a gift, often a spiritual gift. Today the term *hermaphrodite* should be used only in a historical context (unless you are someone who has DSD and chooses to self-label this way) because it is no longer considered a respectful designation.

In the twentieth and twenty-first centuries, the word **intersex** has been and still continues to be used as a term for people with DSD. Generally speaking, though, intersex is not a self-determined definition, but rather a label applied to persons by Western medicine. If you begin to research DSD, you might find that it also stands for *disorders of sex development*. Many people find this term offensive, too, because a "disorder" sounds as though the person being described is sick. As the historian Susan Stryker points out in her definitions found at the beginning of *Transgender History: The Roots of Today's Revolution,* the terminology that people with differences of sex development might use varies from person to person depending on each person's own sense of being within a sex minority community.[2] For example, people who do not have differences of sex development should not use the term *hermaphrodite;* however, for people within that community, it may be empowering to use this historic terminology.

In an essay entitled "Hermaphrodites with Attitude," the activist and scholar Cheryl Chase writes that "the insistence on two clearly distinguished sexes has calamitous personal consequences for the many individuals who arrive in the world with sexual anatomy that fails to be easily distinguished as male or female."[3] Chase writes about the ways that a forced sex binary has had painful consequences in her own life. When Chase was born with "ambiguous genitals," the first set of doctors determined that she was a boy. A year later, however, a different set of doctors encouraged removal of her penis because it was "too short to mark masculine status effectively or to penetrate females."[4] When she was eighteen months old, Chase's penis was removed, the family relocated to another town, relatives were told to forget there was ever a boy, and a new life was started. Several surgeries were performed on Chase during her childhood, but her family never told her that she had DSD. Like many people with DSD whose family members and doctors treat sex difference as something shameful that should be kept secret, as an adult Cheryl Chase began noticing she was physically different from other women, and she began to research medical journals and explore what all her childhood surgeries might really have been about. Once she began to get a sense that all her surgical interventions had nothing to do with her stomach, which her parents had told her, but were, instead, procedures to clean out gonadal material, Chase petitioned her former doctors and finally got answers. In 1993 she started a support network called the Intersex Society of North America (ISNA).[5] Through her work with ISNA, Chase also began to realize that people with differences of sex development are quite common. As a result of the work of ISNA and numerous other global organizations, since the 1990s there has been a major shift in the ways that babies with differences of sex development are treated.

In a 2016 article on intersex babies, a London-based journalist wrote: "'Normalising' surgery to make very young children look more typically male or female has been standard practice for decades. Malta became the first country to outlaw non-consensual medical interventions on intersex people (including those too young to give informed consent) in 2015."[6] This was a huge victory for people with differences of sex development, who had been arguing for decades that the surgery was, regardless of intent, genital mutilation.

Social scientists have been doing important work when looking at the ways that Western medicine has in the past constructed sex through surgical intervention on children with DSD. They point to these interventions as examples of the ways that a sex binary is imposed, whereas sex variations beyond the binary are not only natural but quite common. We live in a diverse world where numerous people have sex chromosomes that are not XX or XY. This is why, in its mission statement, the Intersex Society of North America (which is no longer an operating organization) stated that it was "devoted to systemic change to end shame, secrecy, and unwanted genital surgeries for people born with an anatomy that someone decided is not standard for male or female."[7] As Thea Hillman writes in the short essay "Privates": "I'm not going to tell people about my genitals anymore. It's no one's business what my genitals look like. And it doesn't make a difference."[8] For Hillman, this is an empowering statement about personal space and reclaiming a body that has been examined and probed endlessly by doctors.

The variations in chromosome pairings for people and their medical resolution point to the ways in which society forces natural human variation into a binary of male and female through medicine. Unlike previous understandings of sex (something biological and inherent), Western science and medicine, which do eventually affect culture, are now beginning to understand the complex possibilities of chromosomal differences beyond XX and XY. Past scientific misreadings and misunderstandings, however, which have helped construct cultural and societal biases against people outside the XX and XY binary, can be very difficult and slow to change for the better. The idea of a sexed binary male/female world is *constructed*.

In her book *Making Sense of Intersex: Changing Ethical Perspectives in Biomedicine*, Ellen K. Feder asks about the ethics of surgeons insisting to parents that their atypically sexed baby needs to have immediate surgery to make the baby fit into *either* a male *or* a female category. She argues that instead of making people with differences in sex development a problem, the field of medicine—and more broadly culture and society—needs to see that "atypical sex anatomy is not some exceptional difference, but an ordinary matter of our humanity."[9]

This book uses *DSD* and *intersex* interchangeably because many people who are DSD use the word intersex as part of their self-definition.

Secondary Sex Traits

As a society, we often determine someone's sex through **secondary sex traits.** Generally speaking, these traits do not necessarily inform which box—male or female—gets checked off when a baby is born. They do inform the ways that an individual's sex gets read by others in society. Secondary sex traits are often connected to variations in hormone levels, which often do not begin to become noticeable until puberty. Secondary sex traits include hair, body fat, hip and shoulder width, and breasts. Typical expectations for secondary sex characteristics are that women have smooth faces and that men's pectorals are flat. Some women have facial hair, however, and some men have breasts. This does not necessarily mean that they have a chromosomal makeup that varies from XX or XY. It is important to remember that within each XX and XY there can be multiple nuances and differences.

Take a moment and think about how you felt as you went through puberty. Quite often, just going through this life phase can be jarring enough. But how would you have felt if you lived in a culture that has (for example) very specific ideas about who should and should not have a certain amount of body hair? How are people who have different, unusual, or unexpected secondary sex traits treated?

Along with secondary sex traits, other social and emotional traits are also tied to hormone levels. These include **libido** (the sexual drive) and aggression. What is most important to remember here is that there is a tremendous range of human sex variation based on external genitalia, chromosomal makeup, secondary sex traits, and social and emotional traits associated with hormone levels. Regardless of all this diversity, many people—lay people and scientists alike—operate as if there is only the binary.

Defining Gender: Is the Baby Male or Female?

Like sex, gender has numerous variations. In our contemporary culture and society, though, gender is often presented to us *only* as a binary. Think about any sort of form you had to fill out recently that asked for your gender, whether it was a credit card application, a new mobile phone plan, or some other form. Chances are, your choices were *either* male or female. Those terms are then associated with being masculine or feminine. Culturally, many people define specific attitudes, feelings, and behaviors that are socially acceptable according to which side of the binary a person falls on. In short, while *sex* is often defined as biological (male or female), **gender** is often defined as the ways culture and society reinforce what is masculine to go with the male sex and what is feminine to go with the female sex. This definition of gender may sound straightforward, but, like sex, it is not, because there are many people who do not identify solely as male or female.

When viewing an ultrasound, what happens if a doctor looks at a fetus and does not see any evidence of a penis or testicles? Usually, the doctor tells the expectant parent, "It's a girl!" From this moment on, if the expectant parent shares this news (in U.S. culture at least), pink teddy bears and princess diapers start arriving for the forthcoming baby girl. But what does it *mean* to be a girl? What does it *mean* to be a boy? Think about your own childhood. What did being a girl mean to you, or what did being a boy mean to you? What if you, like so many people, never quite felt comfortable within this binary, yet you were still expected to act either male *or* female? Were you encouraged to do certain activities based on your being male or female? Were you encouraged *not* to do other activities based on your being male or female?

In many contemporary cultures, gender is often confused with sex; people tend to use the two terms as though they were one. As we've seen, sex and gender still do go together in the moment a baby's sex is determined (if it is determined). Gender stereotypes of what is male and therefore supposedly masculine, or what is female and therefore supposedly feminine, are already being heaped on infants whether they are out of the womb or not.

Think of all the plans that begin to revolve around the ways the child will be raised according to the definitions of what is a *boy* and *male*, and what is a *girl* and *female*. Listen to the comments made by someone who is pregnant. If the baby is a boy, you may hear "what a strong kick he has" in the womb. Or, if the baby is a girl, you may hear comments about how gentle her kick is or how sweet her face looks on the ultrasound.

In the United States, the ever-growing popularity of ultrasounds and the appeal of finding out a baby's sex have combined to create an industry of ultrasound lab technicians with mobile machines who are willing to come to a *gender reveal* house party, in which expectant parents "reveal" the baby's sex to their friends and family.[10] Note that even the medical experts (incorrectly) use *sex* and *gender* synonymously because they call these parties *gender reveal parties*, when they should be calling them *sex reveal parties*.

These parties have become so popular partly because knowing the baby's sex helps loved ones know what to purchase for the baby, as well as how they are supposed to interact with the child. For infants' clothing and toys, much of what you can purchase is color-coded pink for girls/females and blue for boys/males. Commercially speaking, stores quite literally bank on consumer demand dictated by this binary. Interestingly, though, this "tradition" has not always existed. In fact, until the early twentieth century in the United States, pink was the chosen color for boys because it was bold and bright; blue was for girls because it was calm and gentle.[11]

Once the baby is born, the stereotypes surrounding the gender binary become even stronger. Think about the last conversation you heard, or took part in, about newborns. How were the babies being discussed? For example, say two parents are comparing their newborn son and newborn daughter. About the daughter they say, "See how pretty her eyes are," or "Look at her delicate little hands"; about the boy they say, "Wow, he's already so big and strong, I bet he's going to be a football player," or "Listen to his strong cry." The babies could, actually, weigh the same, be the same length, and even look about the same, but gender roles and stereotypes are already being placed on them, along with societal expectations of masculinity and femininity. What is clear is this: neither newborn will be playing football any time soon.

Gender Roles

A **gender role** is a cultural set of behavioral expectations assigned to individuals on the basis of their sex. A person's biological sex becomes the marker for the ways that culture and society will reinforce gender roles. For example, a girl's family may encourage her to play with dolls, speak softly, and wear feminine clothes, such as pastel-colored dresses. The girl's family did not invent these expectations of what their baby daughter should play with, act like, and wear. Rather, they have been deeply influenced by what society and our culture—in the form of other people's direct comments, magazines, television shows, advertisements, and other media—inform them are the proper choices for girls. Of course, some girls prefer to play with trucks and dress like a pirate. And some boys prefer to play with dolls and dress like a princess. These two examples show us children who are not following strict and stereotypical *socially and culturally constructed* gender roles.

Gender Norms, Stereotypes, and Intersecting Identities

A **norm,** or something that is seen as *normal,* connotes something that is typical, maybe even something that is average or statistically prevalent. Something that is not statistically prevalent often gets understood as outside the norm or less acceptable, less proper, or even less healthy. Concepts that you may have always considered completely *normal* (for example, that boys will want to play with trucks and that girls will want to play with dolls) get confused with what is *natural.* If you go to a preschool class on dress-up day, you will see that some of the boys gravitate toward the princess dress and some of the girls want the pirate costume. What message might these kids receive if the adult in charge gets upset and demands that the little girl wear the princess dress or that the boy put on the pirate suit? In contrast, what message might these kids receive if the adult in charge is happy that they are all playing dress-up in whatever costume they choose? The adults' reactions are crucial because they signal whether it is safe for the child to explore diverse gender play or whether it is actually dangerous, physically or emotionally, for the child to explore gender possibilities. It is normal for children to have fun and play around with gender; however, adults often get panicky in these situations. Why?

Gender norms and stereotypes become even more complex if you add in other stereotypes about race and ethnicity, socioeconomic status, or education. Each individual is composed of multiple identities—race, ethnicity, language, culture, place of origin, physical ability, religion, and socioeconomic background, to name a few. The concept of **intersecting identities** means that to truly understand people, it is important to take all their identities into consideration. These intersecting identities can also inform gender stereotypes.

For example, if you go to a toddler park or indoor play area in a mall and observe the ways that people in public talk to or react to two little girls from different ethnic and/or racial backgrounds, what might you observe? If you watched the ways people react to two little boys who are clearly from different religious backgrounds, what might you observe? These toddlers may not be aware of it yet, but cultural stereotypes about race *and* gender, or about religion *and* gender, are already influencing the ways adults and other children treat them. At what point do the external influences also begin to affect each child internally?

In short, many behaviors and identities that we may think are inherent in our nature are instead culturally or socially constructed.

A Note on Privilege

Often, if we do not need to think about an aspect of our identity, there is a cultural assumption or even a privilege attached to that identity. **Privilege** is not something that you ask for, but rather is something socially and culturally given. Think about the ways that you move about from place to place in your daily life. Where do you go? What do you do there? How are you treated by others? When you go shopping, do the shop clerks follow you around because they believe you might shoplift? When you go through an airport security line, are you one of the lucky people who never gets pulled out of the line and frisked?

If you have complete freedom of movement in your day-to-day life and do not worry about getting from point A to point B without encountering some sort of problem, then you may be enjoying privilege. As an example, for those of you who do not use a wheelchair, a walker, or a cane, think about someone who does. Now, picture your daily routine and where you go. Can someone using a walker get to the same place in the same way you did? Are there stairs? Is there a working elevator? What about that snack shop you like to visit in the afternoon to grab a quick bite? Can a person in a wheelchair easily access the front door? The aisles? The shelves? Many of us have the simple privilege of being *able-bodied* people who have relative physical freedom of movement, which means we do not have to think about full access. It is important to remember that although someone may *look* able-bodied, many physical disabilities are not visible. Now, to bring the idea of privilege back to babies: able-bodied people who are new parents often suddenly realize how inaccessible the world is when they are trying to get that baby stroller in and out of places.

Gender Identity

GREG identifies as a fifty-three-year-old Caucasian Italian American man and a former police officer who now teaches in the police cadet program at a community college: "I have always identified my gender as male. Gender identity was never a point of wonder or confusion for me."

CAMERON R. identifies as a twenty-eight-year-old artist who is Spanish, Mexican, and Cherokee. "My identity has always presented difficulties for me. From the moment you are assigned a gender based on your genitalia, you are expected to play a role. I never felt as though I were a woman. Or a man for that matter."

Gender identity is someone's deeply felt sense of their own gender—their own masculinity, femininity, a combination of the two, or something else less tied to the gender binary. But even for those who are more tied to the gender binary, each of them figures out what masculine or feminine means on a personal level. In other words, there is no one specific way of being masculine or feminine, although there certainly are social expectations that depend on family, culture, geographic location, school peer groups, friends, religious communities, athletic teams, and numerous other factors. As already mentioned, most contemporary cultures link gender identity to sex at birth, so it is assumed that a person will act a certain way according to the sex that was assigned at birth. For some people, like Greg, defining gender identity does not feel like a struggle; for Cameron, it does. In your experience, what happens when people cross the line of gender norms? Is a woman's experience of crossing this line different from a man's? If so, why and how?

Rafael's story explores the ways that masculinity and femininity were thought of in his home as he was growing up.

RAFAEL is in his late twenties and is a social worker with a nonprofit agency that helps low-income people get access to medical care: "I identify as Nicaraguan and Cuban. I was raised in a Spanish-speaking household with a very macho ideology. Boys wore blue and played with tools, and girls wore pink and cooked and cleaned. I was the youngest in my family, raised with lots of girls. Naturally, there was more cleaning, cooking, and playing with dolls in my house. The boys would make fun of me for never playing sports and for always hanging out with girls. Then, my great-grandmother became really ill. She was bedridden and needed to be fed, bathed, and changed. Being very close to her, I did a great deal of bathing, changing, and feeding. Up until her death I was changing her diapers. I bring this story up because this is where I get a sense of my manhood. My masculinity, or manhood, is in my character, and realizing this set me free. The paradigm of gender norms that I grew up with were broken."

Rafael talks about the **paradigm** (a model or a standard) of masculinity and femininity in his family. He also talks about crossing gender norms when he realized that his masculine gender identity could include being a nurturing caretaker for his great-grandmother. What is even more important is that Rafael is able to be comfortable and happy defining his maleness in ways that his family, his culture, and larger parts of our society might not. In this way, he helps expand what it means to be a man. Note, too, that Rafael considers his own intersecting identities in this situation. He is a Nicaraguan and Cuban Spanish-speaker who, as a child, preferred to cook, clean, and play with dolls. As he grew into adulthood, he developed his own sense of masculinity, which was vastly different from what many people in his family thought was masculine, by caring for his bedridden great-grandmother.

Up to this point, the focus has been on gender identity within the binary. However, many people, like Cameron R., identify outside this male/female binary. People who reject the gender binary may modify, mix, or reject gender norms and expectations, refusing the constraints of a culture that often seems to insist that everyone be *either* masculine *or* feminine. Here are some terms that people who embrace a gender identity outside the binary might use: *nonbinary, non-gender, third gender, gender variant, gender fluid, androgynous, andro, agender, gender expansive, genderqueer, gender nonconforming, Two-Spirit.* These terms, which describe someone who does not feel *either* male *or* female, help illustrate that all gender identities are simultaneously very personal, situated in time and space, and complex.

 **JAMAL** is in his forties and identifies as an African American chef who loves the outdoors: "The older I get, the less I know what all those gendered terms mean. I just know what it feels like to be me. Ultimately, I think that gender is a deeply personal and also interactive way of expressing oneself (with huge social implications!). We all have genders."

Jamal makes the point that every person has multiple genders, not just a single gender. What Jamal says is not something new, but rather something that numerous ancient cultures have honored throughout time. In a historical context, the gender binary is the new kid on the block.

 **EILEEN** is in her forties and of the Nuu-Chah-Nulth First Nations of the West Coast of the Vancouver Islands: "When I first came out I really wanted to seek out different ways that people express themselves: Transgender, Transsexual, Cross-Dresser, Drag Queen, Transvestite, Female Impersonator. Before I came to be myself, a very sweet man came right up to my face in a very kind way. He stated out loud that I am Two-Spirited. Back then I was not even out as Eileen. Since then, I have learned about and done research on Two-Spirit people where I go to school now."

As the Indigenous poet, professor, and theorist Qwo-Li Driskill writes: "The term 'Two-Spirit' is a contemporary term being used in Native communities to describe someone whose gender exists outside of colonial logic. It is an umbrella term that references Indigenous traditions for people who don't fit into rigid gender categories."[12] We will explore **Two-Spirit** identities in more depth in Chapter 7, but the important point to remember now is this: the term purposefully rejects the binary gender system because that system has proven harmful to Indigenous populations.

The term *Two-Spirit* should be used only by Indigenous people. Non-Indigenous people who use this term are appropriating a part of Indigenous culture. **Appropriation** occurs when a dominant culture decides to adopt something for itself that has been empowering to another culture that has often been marginalized through imperialism and colonialism. **Imperialism** is the takeover of a country or a culture through political, religious, and/or military force. **Colonialism** is the continuing occupation, exploitation, and erasure of the culture and the people affected by the imperial takeover.

For a visual representation of gender possibilities, see Cameron Rains's illustration "The Gender Run" (figure 1.1).

The Problem with Pronouns

As we've seen, the English language (and many other languages) include only two singular personal pronouns: *he* and *she*. Now that you have been introduced

FIGURE 1.1 "The Gender Run," by Cameron Rains. Ski slopes don't offer just one or two ways down the mountain. If we think of gender as a series of ski runs, we can begin to envision a multitude of paths crisscrossing the slope.

to the idea of people who identify their gender outside the binary, let's look at language and pronouns. Language both shapes culture and is changed by culture. For example, in the English language in the past, *thou* was singular and *you* was plural. It would sound really silly now if you went around saying "Hey, thou!" But there was a time in the past when people resisted *you* to indicate both singular and plural. The idea that language always evolves is one to remember in the context of the relationship between gender identity and pronouns.

If you step back into the past and find an older textbook from the 1940s or 1950s in the library, you will probably see that the pronoun used for all people in the singular is *he*. An author uses this *universal he* or *general he* when referring to all people. In a magazine article that discusses the debate about trying to find a **gender-neutral pronoun**, which is a pronoun that is not specifically *she* or *he* but a pronoun that resists the gender binary, Patricia T. O'Conner and Stewart Kellerman note some interesting history about English pronouns and their traditional usage.

Specifically, the universal *he* was not something invented by one man or a group of men to exclude women from the language, although that is the story many of us have heard. Instead, the universal *he* came from Anne Fisher, an eighteenth-century English schoolteacher who wrote one of the first books on English grammar. Anne Fisher was an independent, intellectual woman who ran a business on an equal footing with her husband, which was extremely unusual at that time. When she wrote her book on grammar, she was putting forth a universal singular pronoun because *they* and *their* had been used as both singular and plural in the English language since the medieval era. As O'Conner and Kellerman note, though, "In swapping *he* for *they*, Fisher replaced a number problem with a gender problem."[13]

Since the 1970s, many scholars have argued that the universal *he* upholds *social hierarchies* in which men are viewed as above or more important than women. Certainly, if a job ad describes the ideal candidate with the phrase "he will be hardworking," it seems safe to assume that the job is not open to women. After the 1970s, and at the urging of many feminist scholars, a majority of textbooks, newspapers, and magazines began writing *he or she*, *him or her*, or *s/he* instead of the universal *he*.

This relatively new use of paired pronouns has made it crystal clear that both men and women are welcome and included. Here again, however, we may have swapped one pronoun problem for another. What happens when someone does not identify with *she* or *he*?

Over the past thirty years, some writers have begun to experiment with or invent new pronouns that are not within the binary. Leslie Feinberg's words **ze** and **hir** offer excellent examples of pronouns outside the gender binary. While *ze* and *hir* are used enough to have an entry in the online Urban Dictionary, they are not very well known to the general public. So you have to be "in the know" to have these words in your vocabulary.[14] (Here's an example of how these pronouns work: Yesterday, Alex went to the store. Ze went there because hir special order had come in.)

One solution is to go back to the past. If we return to the time before Anne Fisher decided that a universal *he* could stand as a singular for all people, we find two very old and traditional English words that are completely gender neutral: *they* and *their*. It is always important to respect each individual's pronoun. So when you are unsure of a person's pronoun, a good practice is to use *they* and *their*.

How Do You Look? Gender Expression

Let's return to some of the questions at the beginning of this chapter: When you went out in public today, what were you wearing? How did you style your hair? Did you wear makeup? How much did you think about where you needed to go before you got ready to go out in public? If you are a woman, were you wearing pants? If you answered yes to this last question, did you know that seventy-five years ago you could have been arrested in California, New York, and Pennsylvania (among other places) for cross-dressing? The police officers who arrested you would probably have labeled you a transvestite, which was seen as not only illegal but also deviant. All the topics discussed in this section have one thing in common: they all refer to people's **gender expression**—that is, their outer appearance in public, which often focuses on clothing choices, cosmetics, hairstyle, and gender identity.

Cross-Dressing

Cross-dressing is a modern term that has mostly replaced the older term **transvestism.** Definitions have varied over time, but simply put, cross-dressing means dressing in clothing deemed appropriate for a different gender. For example, a man wearing a skirt (unless it is seen as culturally specific such as a kilt, *longyi,* or sarong) may be said to be cross-dressed. Historically, the term *transvestite* was used by legal and medical authorities to police and restrict cross-dressers (although, as you will learn in Chapter 3, the term was originally used as a legal label so that the authorities would not harass transvestites).

Terms like *transvestite, transvestism,* and *cross-dressing* are sometimes confused with the words *transsexual, transgender,* and *trans.* There is good reason for this, historically, because words and language relating to gender diversity have continued to evolve. For example, when Dr. Magnus Hirschfeld (whom you will read about in Chapter 3) first coined the term *transvestite,* he was referring to people who would probably have been known in the mid-twentieth century as transsexual and now in the twenty-first century are known as transgender or trans. One easy way to remember the difference is to note the word *vest* in the middle of trans*vest*ite. Because a vest is something you can wear, you can remember that a transvestite's choices usually concern clothing. The difference between cross-dressing and transgender depends heavily on historical context as well as intent. Before we had our current definitions of transsexual, transgender, and trans, transvestism was often the only way that those whose gender identity did not align with their assigned sex at birth had of being themselves.

Cross-dressing as a concept still depends on the gender binary because it involves a *crossing* of gender categories understood to be masculine or feminine. The person's intent behind cross-dressing is important to consider. Are they having a bit of fun with friends? Are they doing it for a photo shoot? Or are they cross-dressing in an attempt to pass as a different gender? In other words, cross-dressing can be a totally humorous and flagrant crossing of the line, an attempt to cross the binary and pass relatively well, or something in between. Cross-dressing can have different meanings for the cross-dresser and for the culture or observer.

Let's take an example of Halloween day at many U.S. high schools. How many times has one of the boys on the football team exchanged outfits with a cheerleader for the day? Is the male football player embracing a trans identity for the day? Is the female cheerleader embracing a trans identity for the day? Generally speaking, the answer is probably no. But even if cross-dressing is "just for fun," there may still be a bit of a transgression and experimentation involved.

What if, instead, one of the male cheerleaders opted to wear the female cheerleading outfit? What if one of the football players exchanged his helmet and pads for the male cheerleading outfit? Both of these cases draw a more complex gray area. Already, at least within U.S. culture, male cheerleaders are looked at cautiously in much the same way male ballet dancers are. The perceptions have nothing to do with athleticism, because cheerleading and ballet can be just as physically demanding (perhaps more so) as playing American football, which incorporates a protective helmet and pads. Meanwhile, there is no protection for ballet dancers or cheerleaders. Ballet and cheerleading are usually seen as "girls' activities," which implies the specific and opposite understanding that they are *not* boys' activities. Underneath these assumptions lies the idea that activities done by girls or women have lower status than men's activities. **Sexism** perpetuates stereotypes and cultural ideas that promote the lower status of women in all areas of society, including work, sports, math, and the sciences.

Drag

Drag is distinguished from cross-dressing because drag is purposefully done as a performance, and the manner of dress exaggerates the gender expression. Through this exaggerated gender performance, drag illustrates how ridiculous and constraining gender norms can be; in fact, drag helps show us that we all perform gender on a daily basis. Drag, however, is usually specifically tied to performing for a crowd. In short, cross-dressing occurs mostly offstage, within private spheres, whereas drag is a performance for a specific audience.

Transgender: Across *and* beyond the Binary

You have probably heard the words *transsexual* and *transgender,* which are often used as synonyms. According to the scholar Susan Stryker, **transsexual** came into popular use in the 1950s, when the sexologist Dr. Harry Benjamin used the term to describe people like Christine Jorgensen who wanted to surgically change their bodies, as opposed to people who did not do body modification but rather remained transvestites.[15] In this mid-twentieth-century definition, being transsexual was tied to being able to afford body modification. The term was also tied to purposefully crossing the gender binary. Although *transsexual* is now considered an "old-school" term, it is important to note that some people still prefer this identity *and* that it no longer necessarily means any type of body modification has taken place, because such modification is expensive, and/or people have medical conditions that prevent body modification, and/or they do not think that body modification needs to happen in order to cross the gender binary.

Transgender, as Stryker notes, "implies movement away from an assigned, unchosen gender position. . . . It usually meant a person who wanted . . . to change their social gender in an ongoing way through a change of habits and gender expression, which perhaps included the use of hormones, but usually not surgery."[16] This term, however, continues to undergo shifting definitions. In the late twentieth century, *transgender* became synonymous with being a gender renegade. In other words, it was embraced by people who rejected the gender binary altogether; but now, in the twenty-first century, Stryker writes that "some people have begun to use the term transgender to refer *only* to those who identify with a binary gender other than the one they were assigned at birth—which is what *transsexual* used to mean."[17] So, clearly, the definitions of *transsexual* and *transgender* continue to shift. Generally speaking, *transgender* in its broadest sense can encompass "the widest imaginable range of gender-variant practices and identities."[18] Throughout this textbook, you will see the word *transgender* used in this broadest sense as an umbrella term. You will also see the word **trans,** which is also used as an umbrella term to note gender diversity in the broadest sense.

Some older terminology that you might see regarding trans people is MTF (male to female) and FTM (female to male). MTF and FTM denote people who have crossed the gender binary; it is crucial not to assume that the person has necessarily had any hormones or surgery. Some people have and some people have not. In some cases, people may not even identify as transgender or transsexual, but instead solely as the gender they transitioned to or moved to. For example, James was assigned female at birth. At the age of two, James began to identify as a boy. Now, as a teenager who is undergoing medical intervention to delay puberty, he identifies as a young man rather than as a young trans man. MTF and FTM are used less and less as the language regarding gender diversity changes rapidly. It is important, however, to honor and respect each individual's choice of words and identifiers for themselves.

CERRIDWYN identifies as a white woman who is a college student in her twenties. She has a genetic condition that affects hormone levels and has differences of sex development: "I AM part of the disabled community as someone who has a rare metabolic, genetic disability called Prader Willi syndrome. I AM a trans woman because I have never identified with what is associated with the male gender that I was assigned at birth. I AM a transsexual because I feel trapped in my own body that does not conform to how I feel inside."

Cerridwyn specifically uses the word *transsexual* for herself and associates it with the feeling of being trapped in the wrong body. Cerridwyn's experience is much like that of the famous 1950s celebrity Christine Jorgensen; both Cerridwyn and Christine did not feel that their bodies matched their gender identities. Note, too, that Cerridwyn's intersecting identities as someone who has differences of sex development (DSD) and is differently abled also inform her identity. It is important to note that people who have differences of sex development do *not* always identify as transgender. There are some people who have DSD, like Cerridwyn, who are trans, just as there are some people without DSD who are trans. There is often a misperception that being intersex or having DSD means that a person is transgender. They are not the same.

Even now, with the word *transgender* in full use, we can find that the terms are constantly evolving and that people use them differently. For instance, if you go online and listen to various podcasts about or interviews with Caitlyn Jenner as she came out as a *trans woman* (a shortened term for either a transsexual or transgender woman), you will hear the press refer to her in several different ways. Some say transsexual, some say trans woman, and others say transgender. Most important, Caitlyn Jenner refers to herself as transgender, so this is the term that is most respectful of her identity. In the United States, transgender is abbreviated as the "T" in the LGBT (lesbian, gay, bisexual, and transgender) movement. It is a predominantly Western, late twentieth- and early twenty-first-century word. In terms of laws and public policies, *transgender* and *trans* are the broadest words that people use to be respectful.

 **PAULINA** identifies as a Hispanic trans woman and musician in her twenties: "My family is very loving, but traditional Hispanics, so you can imagine it was very hard trying not to show any signs of difference around them. I was raised primarily by my Grandma. I knew at the age of four or five that I was different. I didn't know what it was called or how to explain it to anyone what I was, but I knew that I wasn't like the rest of the kids in my family or at school. When I came out as transgender, my dad's first reaction: go see a priest. Like a priest was going to change the way I was feeling inside. My grandma knew I was feeling this way, she just didn't want to believe it. Today, my mom accepts me 100 percent due in large part to the Caitlyn Jenner story, which must have struck a chord in her."

Although Paulina is from a small and socioeconomically impoverished community in the rural high desert of southern California, it is interesting to note that Caitlyn Jenner's story helped her family understand her. Socioeconomically, racially, ethnically, and culturally, Caitlyn Jenner has nothing in common with Paulina and her family, yet her story was still able to help Paulina's relationship with her family.

MIA identifies as a white transgender woman who grew up in a low-income family in Texas. She is in her twenties. Mia felt alienated growing up: "I didn't even know that transgender people existed until I saw Marci Bowers on Oprah, but even then transitioning only felt possible for rich white people in California. My feminine gender expression was always scrutinized, but when I moved to California at eighteen I felt comfortable enough to start presenting as female full-time and was blessed to have a community in San Francisco that has supported me for who I am."

Note Mia's idea that transitioning is expensive. In many countries and situations, transitioning often involves an expensive medical intervention that is not covered by insurance. There are many reasons that trans people might not be able to afford a full transition, and some may have health issues that prevent them from attaining full gender-affirmation procedures. In other cases, a trans person may have personal reasons for not pursuing medical intervention. These people are not any less transgender or trans than people who have medical help, however. As you will see in later chapters, some of the most acclaimed trans pioneers were never able to afford medical intervention.

Mia's story is a common one for people who identify as transgender, especially for people growing up where the LGBT community is less visible or accepted. The support for a young transgender person may depend on the location and size of the community where they are raised, but their experiences probably depend most heavily on family, friends, and other local cultural influences. The experiences of a transgender person growing up in Huntsville, Arkansas, may be very different from the experiences of a transgender person growing up in Chicago, Illinois. However, we should be careful not to stereotype. A small town in the Ozarks may be more welcoming to transgender people than a large city.

Think about the first time you heard the term *transgender*. Was being transgender described in the way that Cerridwyn writes about being trapped in a body that she does not identify with? That is probably the most common way that being transgender is explained in popular culture and contemporary society. The notion of being trapped in or born into the wrong body is relatively easy to understand; many transgender people feel this way. It is certainly part of the story in the popular U.S. television show *Transparent*. The same feeling is common to some celebrities who have come out as transgender, including Laverne Cox, Chaz Bono, and Caitlyn Jenner.

Some people (although not all) who feel trapped in the wrong body decide to transition from one side of the gender binary to the other. For example, from her interviews, we know that Caitlyn struggled for decades feeling trapped in a male body when, in fact, she always felt like a woman on the inside. It is crucial to remember that for many transgender people, transition is a *need,* and the prospect of transitioning across the gender binary and aligning their bodies with their most deeply felt sense of self represents a profound and often life-or-death necessity.

For many other transgender people, though, being transgender does not necessarily mean feeling trapped in the wrong body. *Transgender* or *trans* is a much broader umbrella term for many different ways to identify both within and outside the gender binary. The following stories illuminate other ways that transgender individuals understand their gender identities. You have already met Jamal, Mia, and Eileen:

JAMAL identifies as a trans man: "I wasn't trapped in the wrong body. There were just parts of it I wanted to change—I wanted to be bigger and hairier. Testosterone feels so right in my body. That's me. I like my testosterone, and it makes me way more emotional and I cry and laugh more. And I like that too. Feeling more. And feeling more myself."

MIA "Transitioning from male to female has given me a greater in-depth understanding of what it's like to live life in the margins, as a freak, as a gender renegade. I do not feel trapped in my body. I feel trapped in a society that excludes people like me from textbooks and bathrooms, and perpetuates harmful stereotypes that breed fear."

EILEEN "I made a decision to keep my body the way my body came into our world we share. No hormones. No breast implants. Not to have my penis removed. This is 'as is,' the way God made me, and I am happy with myself—a Two-Spirited and proud feminine cross-dresser."

KELLY KELLY is fifty years old and a returning college student. She volunteers with a transgender legal group and hopes to be able to go to law school: "I'm a white, third-gender transwoman. After a long spiritual journey and a prolonged period of soul-searching, I received a revelation that I was NOT a man. Then I thought I must be all woman. But I'm not that binary. So I finally settled on the term third-gender, and I prefer to utilize the she/her pronouns because that feels closest to my deepest sensibilities."

Though Jamal, Mia, Eileen, and Kelly Kelly all identify as transgender, their experiences of their identities vary. All four have chosen to stick with either male or female pronouns, but they have done so in the face of a culture that still, on almost all legal forms, gives people only two choices for sex or gender: male or female. And though Jamal, Mia, Eileen, and Kelly Kelly have each chosen a male or female pronoun, you can see that they have also been very thoughtful about the gender binary and its limitations. Of them, Eileen has the most flexibility because the word *Two-Spirit* allows room for gender flexibility.

Transgender and *trans* have evolved into umbrella terms for people who want to opt out of the gender binary. The *transgender* and *trans* categories can therefore include individuals who embrace a genderqueer, nonbinary, gender-variant, gender-expansive, or agender identity. In recent years, *trans* has been used to indicate the full complexity of gender and to acknowledge that gender identity does not fall into a neat binary. *Trans* is an overarching term that includes transgender, transsexual, nonbinary, and multiple gender identities.

CAMERON R. "I fit into neither male nor female definitions. I don't think of myself as more male because I wear pants, have short hair, and like to build things—the binary says pants, short hair, and building are male. I don't think of myself as more female because I wear makeup—society says that's female. I have quite a bit of body hair. Every time I go to a pool or hot tub, I get so many looks. I have pretty tough skin when it comes to that—courtesy of a decade of confused looks, but the pool area is especially difficult to shrug off. A happy trail and a sports bra aren't exactly a subtle combination. It became such an issue that I considered top surgery. A happy trail and a flat chest is less confusing to the majority of people."

"Then I thought more about it. I don't identify as male, so why would I want to modify my body in order to present as male so that men at the pool are more comfortable around me? No. Once I realized that anything having to do with my gender expression that doesn't appear in media/advertisement is a radical act; for me, this is where I find my validation—standing on the shoulders of those who were also told that they were wrong to be themselves. The bravest thing you can do is be yourself."

Cameron R. has chosen not to have *top surgery* (a double mastectomy, which is the removal of the breast tissue) that some trans people opt for in order to feel more right in their bodies. Jamal chooses to use testosterone because it feels so good and so right in his body. Both Cameron R. and Jamal have thoughtfully and actively chosen what feels right to them.

Cisgender

You may be wondering if there is a word for someone who does not identify on the transgender spectrum—a word for someone who thinks of their gender as being in line with the sex they were assigned at birth. In the 1990s the word **cisgender** was developed to define a person whose gender identity is in line with their assigned sex at birth. The prefix *cis-* means "on the same side as," and *trans* means "on the opposite side of." The term *cisgender* has come into wider use in popular culture.

In the contemporary United States, identifying as cisgender is a point of cultural privilege because our society is still based on the assumption that all people who are assigned male/female are simultaneously masculine/feminine as well as man/woman. Those who do not fit into this social construct often face hardships such as being bullied, physically assaulted, and even murdered.

EMILY identifies as a thirty-two-year-old southern cisgender woman. She is a counselor and teacher at a community college: "My ancestry is Eastern European and Cherokee. I grew up poor—working class and identify most with these cultural values. As a woman who passes with cisgender privilege, I never have to worry about what bathroom to use, or if someone is going to mis-gender or mis-pronoun me. This is a privilege I take very seriously."

Emily works comfortably with the cisgender label for herself, and she is keenly aware of her privilege as a cisgender, or cis, person. Emily is also acutely aware that *cissexism*, which is the assumption that all people are or should be cisgender, can be hurtful and transphobic. **Transphobia** is the fear of and/or dislike of anyone who is trans.

Some people whose gender identity, for the most part, does line up with their assigned sex at birth, do not like the term *cisgender*.

 **DEIRDRE** is a fifty-two-year-old white woman who has returned to graduate school as a student of anthropology: "I am an American, mostly of Western European ancestry, in a female-identified body. I will very grudgingly answer to 'cis' if it makes a trans person I'm talking to more comfortable, but it makes me uncomfortable. The first time I learned the term, I thought, 'Oh great, here's yet another binary I don't fit in.' I've always been very happy in my female-identified body but very aware, since childhood, of the boy and man who could have been here. He's in me. The label 'cis' pinches me like an ill-fitting shoe—it's supposed to be my size, but the shape is wrong."

Emily and Deirdre both move through their daily lives with cisgender privilege, but their stories help illustrate the point that any gender identity, whether cisgender, transgender, or some other, is always personal and complex, and sometimes in flux. None of us knows what might be going on in someone else's head and heart.

Throughout this chapter, you have heard stories about sex and gender from numerous people. You may have noticed that they are all adults between the ages of twenty and fifty-five. In the following "Writings from the Community," you will find a story from Tasha, who is in her sixties, and stories from Charlie and Lorenzo, who are both in their late teens.

WRITINGS FROM THE COMMUNITY

TASHA

The following story is from Jess T. Dugan and Vanessa Fabbre's collaborative project To Survive on This Shore: Photographs and Interviews with Transgender and Gender Non-Conforming Older Adults. *Jess T. Dugan's art explores "issues of gender, sexuality, identity, and community."*[19] *Dugan received an MFA in photography from Columbia College Chicago and an MA in museum studies from Harvard University. Vanessa Fabbreis a professor in the Women, Gender, and Sexuality Studies Departmen at Washington University in St. Louis, Missouri. Her research focuses on gender identity and aging.*

Tasha, 65, Birmingham, AL, 2013.
Photo by Jess T. Dugan.

I was born in Childersburg, Alabama. When I was growing up, I knew that something about me was different. I knew that I liked the guys. I pretty much today live as a gay man that lives just like a woman, because I see from Day One, from that day to this day, I've always felt like a woman born in a man's body. And that's the way I live. I live as a woman today. I didn't get to the place of where I'm so all right with this until later in life—at a young age I would've had a sex change. But today, I'm so all right with me it doesn't even cross my mind.

I have never been a case of being in the closet. I've always been wide open. And back in that time of the civil rights movement, I still didn't have any problem. I was still wide open. I participated in the marches and stuff. I was arrested, wet up with the hoses, all that stuff.

Whether you say, "Yes, ma'am," or "Yes, sir," I'm all right. I don't let nothing like that bother me. At times it was kinda rough growing up when you had to hear guys call you all kinda names, such as freaking fag and all this kinda stuff. It used to hurt me and make me angry. But as I got into the church and started letting the verse of John 3:16 register in me, a whole lot of stuff changed.

It said, "For God so loved the world that whosoever will, let them come." And after that, I felt like I was one of the "whosoevers." And knowing that I was gay and knowing what people were saying, I stopped getting mad. I stopped fighting and just be who I am—and just be me. Now, I am real respected in my neighborhood as Tasha because a lot of people don't even know my real name. I'm Tasha to everybody. And most of the children say, "Miss Tasha." But when I come upon situations where children are curious and ask, "Are you a man or a lady?" I don't lie to them. I just tell them I'm a man that lives as a woman. And then I have no problems with them. If you don't say anything to me, I'm not going to say anything to you, although I have some eyes that can talk to you where I won't have to say anything. But, all in all, I feel that I done had a good life. I'm just happy with me today, real happy.

CHARLIE MANZANO

Five Foot Five

Charlie Manzano is a student from the San Francisco Bay Area. He is a cocreator of the Transgender Cancer Patient Zine at transcancerzine. He wrote this piece in his junior year of high school as a way of coming out; he hopes that his story strikes a chord with people who have been through similar experiences. He would like to dedicate this piece to Ryn McWhirter.

I tell myself that I'm actually five foot five. It may sound ridiculous to lie about an inch, but sometimes it's the only thing that gets me through the day. Height, an insignificant aspect of most people's lives, has become one of the most distressing parts of mine. When I pass by taller people in the hallways, which is a good 90 percent of the time, all I can focus on is how short I am in comparison. I compare my height to others' in a convoluted daily ritual, constantly trying to figure out who I'm taller than in a room, when I honestly should be focused on something else entirely. So why do I care about height? After all, I am "the height of the average girl." Well, it's true: I am the average height for a girl. And that wouldn't necessarily be bad, if I were a girl. But I'm not a girl. I never was a girl, and I never will be a girl. I am a boy, and for a boy, I'm short.

The majority of transgender people struggle with their height in one way or another. It is a harsh reality that we have to face, and it affects me personally every day. Height, for me, is a matter of body image. The way I see myself in my head does not reflect what I see in the mirror. I struggle with dysphoria, or not being able to feel content with myself (in my case, my appearance). Lying to myself about how far I am off the ground helps me cope.

I've gotten off the bus, driven home, and find myself once again sitting at my desk looking up "short male celebrities." Apparently their version of short is five foot eight (where the list starts) to around five foot five (where the list stops). I now realize that this must be where I got the idea that five foot five is the height I should aspire to be. Because as long as I can be on that list, I am safe, I can still be attractive and respected in society's eyes. After all, Daniel Radcliffe is five foot five—he's on the list. I can own being five foot five knowing Daniel Radcliffe and I are in the same boat, even if it is the very end of the list.

Another illusion I cling to is the possibility of growing. Chances are I won't, and hormones aren't going to do anything to increase that likelihood. The other day, after telling a friend about my height dysphoria, she made a point of saying, "Well I heard of this one guy who grew four inches on testosterone." I didn't have the heart to tell her it was likely he grew because of a predetermined growth spurt, not the testosterone. Even knowing the facts, I convince myself I could grow. If I just believe, then certainly I could. Shouldn't putting in the effort of believing reward me with something? There's nothing a person can do to help them gain height. But I try everything I see on the Internet, whether it's good for me or not. In the past, I've convinced myself that drinking milk daily, stretching compulsively, and having extremely good posture are all ways I can dramatically increase my stature. The reality is they do virtually nothing at all.

I think my height is the one part of me that gives me away the most in terms of passing as male. This, more than my voice, my face, and my hips. It's one of the most anxiety-producing things I have to deal with in my life. Knowing that I am as tall as I will ever be and that my girlfriend "towers" over me certainly doesn't help. In the days leading up to prom, I worried she would wear heels and make our height difference even more apparent. When she walked up to me in Converse sneakers, I was overwhelmingly relieved. She wasn't taller than I am. But even with the help of a pair of dress shoes, I still wasn't taller.

It's weird that, being transgender, the part that often bothers me the most about my body is something as arbitrary as height. I realize that I don't have it that bad even if I don't make it onto the list of "short male celebrities." It's probably not a great idea to focus on it so much. After all, there are plenty of cisgender short guys, and some are probably even shorter than me. But by being ashamed of my height, I am actually putting other guys down. I realize not all guys are tall, or fit society's ideal mold of what is physically attractive, but a part of me has always wanted to fit in at least one of these areas. I have convinced myself that being taller always gives you an advantage, that you're automatically more attractive, strong, healthy, and respectable. That's not true at all. As cliché as it is to say, height is not what makes a person. It determines neither a person's attractiveness nor their gender identity. I cannot allow my self-worth to be dictated by height. So, it's time to be honest with myself:

I am not five foot five. I am five foot four, and I am a boy.

LORENZO

GUTS, or Growing Up Trans in Secret

Lorenzo is an eighteen-year-old dance student living in San Francisco. He moved to the United States from Argentina in 2001 and grew up transgender in the Southern California dance and circus community.

I still remember the first time someone ever asked me, "Are you a boy or a girl?" That was long before I knew this question would follow me throughout life. I was in the fifth grade. A week or so earlier I'd convinced my mother to chop my dark hair short.

"A pixie cut," the lady who bleached her hair had called it around a mouthful of chewing gum. "Like Halle Berry."

The night of the haircut, I heard my father's car pull into the driveway. I ran out to meet him, my bare feet slapping on the front porch.

"Who's this boy?" he asked in Spanish, ruffling my hair. I was ten years old and didn't bother wondering why his question brought a gap-toothed grin out of me.

"Are you a boy or a girl?" The question came on the bus to a field trip I've long since forgotten, from a younger kid I didn't recognize. Eyes wide and leaning over the back of their seat, they stared at me expectantly. I froze for a second—no one had ever actually *asked* me before—everyone in my life had simply *told* me, so confidently, that I was a girl."

I smiled and piped back, "I'm a boy!"

There was a snicker from the seat next to me. My classmate scolded, "Don't tease the little kids." I sank back in my seat, dejected and humiliated, and the inquisitor turned back around, having lost interest. That question followed me consistently from that moment on, but for many years I answered it differently and, in retrospect, incorrectly.

I grew up in the mountains of Southern California, an area that proudly boasts its status as "The Most Urbanized Mountain Community in North America!" Urban is relative. Tucked smack in the center of California's largest, very red county, my community consisted of 10,000 people. There were no public parks in my neighborhood, but the shooting range was a short walk from my house. I was thirteen years old before I heard the word *transgender* somewhere online. It immediately struck a chord with me, and I began to do research in secret.

It took another two years before I told my parents. I don't remember how the conversation went—perhaps I've blocked it out over time—but I remember their tight-lipped discomfort. I've always thought of my parents as politically leaning toward the left—my father was something of a revolutionary in junta-run Argentina—but their coldness and distance whenever the subject came up left me uneasy. They rejected the idea off the bat, and I have yet to hear them use the correct name or pronouns with me. But to be fair, I stopped pushing pretty quickly. When gender wasn't involved, my parents could be supportive, even warm, working hard to keep me involved as a circus performer, even driving me thirty miles to practice five nights a week. I tried to make that enough, I did.

I stopped bringing the topic up. I even grew my hair long and dressed in a way I thought they'd prefer for the rest of high school. It cut me like a knife to do it, but I would've done anything to escape their stern disapproval. My gender and, by extension, my life felt like a burden I had unleashed upon my family. They had worked so hard to make a life for us in the United States, had supported me in my circus career, and struggled and fought to make it happen—and I had pushed this upon them. I felt selfish. I wanted to make them proud. We never talked about gender. It was taboo.

When I stopped trying with my parents, I stopped trying at school too. None of my classmates or teachers had been overly supportive to begin with, and the general population seemed to breathe a sigh of relief at the realization that they could dismiss the whole ordeal as a teenage phase and rid themselves of the discomfort. They didn't have to make an effort, and I wouldn't say anything to correct them. It blew over more easily than I had expected. At home, at school, I lived a lie, but I was able to be myself in two places: small online communities and with Tita and Jack.

I started circus classes at the gym where Tita taught when I was fourteen, freshly out of the closet to my family, hair once again clipped above my ears. On my first day, a whirlwind of choppy bangs and Halloween socks plopped next to me as I stretched and extended a hand. I learned years later that Tita had seen me across the gym and had asked to join the class specifically to talk to me. I met Jack, their husband, a few months later, and over the years they became my family. They were the first older trans people I ever met and, in a lot of ways, they were living like me—forced into a lie until their daughter, who was my age, graduated from high school. Tita had me help train their classes, and Jack spotted me during each show I performed in. Between classes or during nights around the firepit in their backyard, we talked about all the things I couldn't with my biological parents. They helped keep me alive.

I moved out of my parents' house at seventeen, a month after I graduated from high school, into a house in the Sunset District of San Francisco with nine other people, most of them queer and trans. I had one of them cut off my grown-out hair before I'd even unpacked, and I started hormones that same week. I didn't break that news to my parents until three months in—over Skype. It was the first time we had acknowledged my transness in years. I told my mother first. The way she froze and grimaced sent me right back to being a fourteen-year-old in the mountains. She had questions of course, and they came panicked through clenched teeth. When we hung up, it was the last we spoke of it. It was as though the conversation hadn't happened, but from that moment on, she made it a point to tell me what a beautiful girl I was every time she saw me. I answered "thank you" in the full depth of my new testosterone-molded voice. The "compliment" cut deeper than it would have before. It seemed calculated, weaponized.

I spent this New Year's back in Southern California at Tita and Jack's house. Jack was two days post-op from top surgery, so it was a quiet night. None of us are really hiding anymore. When it struck midnight, we stood on the front porch and let off dollar-store confetti poppers in the rain. Tita gave me a tattoo of a moth that night—not a butterfly, but easily mistaken for one. Jack gave me a dose of testosterone. I have a long way to go still. Most days I get more "miss" and "she" from strangers than "sir" or "him," my parents still haven't said my name out loud, and a lot of days feel like a WWE fight (me vs. my body).

I've added on to my family too. My older brother calls me "hermanito" on the phone now. And when little kids ask me, "Are you a boy or a girl?" most of the time I answer truthfully now. It's a start.

Key Concepts

appropriation (p. 14)

binary (p. 4)

cisgender (p. 25)

colonialism (p. 14)

cross-dressing (p. 17)

difference of sex development (DSD) (p. 4)

drag (p. 19)

gender (p. 8)

gender expression (p. 17)

gender identity (p. 12)

gender-neutral pronoun (p. 16)

gender role (p. 9)

hermaphrodite (p. 4)

imperialism (p. 14)

intersecting identities (p. 10)

intersex (p. 5)

libido (p. 8)

norm (p. 10)

paradigm (p. 13)

privilege (p. 11)

secondary sex traits (p. 7)

sex (p. 3)

sexism (p. 19)

trans (p. 20)

transgender (p. 19)

transphobia (p. 26)

transsexual (p. 19)

transvestism (p. 17)

Two-Spirit (p. 14)

ze, hir (p. 17)

Activities, Discussion Questions, and Observations

1. Tasha often gets asked, "Are you a man or a lady?" And Lorenzo often gets asked, "Are you a boy or a girl?" How does each answer these questions? How do their intersecting identities (including age, ethnicity, and geographic location) become part of their answers?

2. Some religions can be very harsh to LGBT people. Yet Tasha truly becomes comfortable with herself in the face of bigotry by reading the Bible. Discuss the ways that Christianity helps her embrace her gender identity.

3. Lorenzo and Charlie both write about very different experiences as young trans men. What parts of their stories caught your attention and why? How are set ideas about gender identity and the gender binary discussed in their narratives? What is the tone of their narratives? If you had a chance to ask Charlie and Lorenzo one question each, what would it be?

4. Get ready to go shopping! Don't worry, this activity does not require you to spend money. You need only to go into a store and make some observations. Go to any large chain store that carries babies' and children's items, such as

Walmart, Target, Sam's Club, Ikea, or Costco. If you live somewhere that has boutique-style stores, you can choose one of those instead. Then complete one of the following activities:

a. Think about shopping for a newborn, but instead of going for blue or pink, look for something that is more neutral. What can you find that is not relegated to the boy/girl binary? You may have to ask one of the store clerks to help you in your quest. If you do speak to someone at the store, gauge the person's reaction when you ask for something neutral. How does the store's location affect the clerk's response?

b. If you would rather do the opposite, go into the store of your choice and purposefully seek out something specifically intended for either a boy or a girl. What options are available for boys and girls? What do you see on the shelves? Are the boy and girl items in the same aisle? Are they in different aisles? Is there any mixing between the two? If you ask the clerk to help you find an item for a baby boy or a baby girl, note the clerk's reaction. How does the clerk respond to your asking about something for either a boy or a girl? Write up your observations and bring them to share during class discussion. What did you expect from your trip to the store? Did any part of the experience surprise you?

5. Write about an experience growing up. The following is Austin's story.

> I remember the first time I'd ever felt crushingly defeated by something I couldn't explain—or see. . . . I was roughly five at the time. I stood there in a skirt and bra I had made out of construction paper. . . . When you give a child a pair of scissors and paper with no perceivable rules about the world and "how it works," you will see the human spirit in its true form. The eyes of teachers, a school counselor, and parents stared down at me in my construction paper bikini that I had crafted. Fear beamed through their eyes like shiny scissors and started cutting the bikini off of my young body, desperate to turn it into "board shorts" or something "appropriate." Except the scissors emotionally cut through me instead, leaving a scar that reminds me of what truly commands situations: gender rules. What's a boy to do in a construction paper bikini or dress? Run into the shadows—perhaps forever, if the scissors cut that deep. This was the first moment I became conscious of gender in its crushing reality, and also the first instance I experienced heartbreak.

For this activity, you will be writing about an experience in your past. Think back to a time when someone with authority in your life told you that your attire (even if it was a costume) was not appropriate, that "you cannot wear that" or "you cannot go out like that." The "inappropriate" clothes might have had nothing to do with gender expression (or they might have); it could be that you were not wearing something "patriotic enough" or that you wore the jersey for the "wrong" soccer team.

Describe the outfit, perhaps including jewelry, that was "not okay." Why do you think you were told it was not okay? Were you supposed to be dressed for a specific occasion? If so, what was the occasion? Were you about to leave for school and stopped from leaving the house because of your clothing?

Why do you remember this particular experience? What reason did the person in authority give for the unacceptability of your attire? And now, as you think about it more, what do you think were the underlying reasons you were asked (or told) to change your clothes? Was the authority figure worried about your safety if you went out in public in your clothes, makeup, and jewelry of choice? Was the authority figure worried that the world would view you in a stereotypical way? Was the authority figure worried about how your look would reflect on them?

Take a few moments to write about this experience and how it made you feel about yourself. How did it make you feel about the person who asked you to go change?

Conversely, if you never had this experience, think about an occasion where an authority figure complimented your clothing highly, and think about all the above questions in this situation.

6. Throughout this chapter, several people discussed either their privilege or their struggles. In some cases, a person struggled with their race, ethnicity, or religion. In other cases, the person's gender identity or sexual orientation was the point of the struggle, while their race or ethnicity gave them privilege. Think about your identities. What gives you privilege in our culture? What parts of your identity do you not have to think about, worry about, or even monitor? What parts of your identity are a struggle for you? What makes you feel marginalized or left out? What parts of your identity (if any) do you try to hide or hope do not get pointed out?

7. This is an in-class writing or discussion question. This chapter focuses on definitions and labels. *Many* definitions and labels. What are your thoughts about these terms? Why are they important? As you were reading, what were

you thinking or what were you feeling? Did you find yourself wanting to learn more about the various identities? Did you find that reading any part of this chapter made you anxious? What are some of the core assumptions you had about yourself and our culture as you began reading this chapter? How are you feeling now? Sometimes the best classroom discussions arise from a sense of discomfort, so be honest about your thoughts as you were reading.

Film and Television of Interest

Apache 8 (2011, U.S., 57 minutes)
This documentary film focuses on a group of women from the White Mountain Apache Tribe who fight wildland fires throughout the United States. The film explores intersecting identities and gender stereotypes. Although there is no trans content in this film, it is an excellent look at binary gendered expectations for women.

Ascendance: The Angels of Change Documentary (2015, U.S., 75 minutes)
Focusing on youth and mentors from the Center for Trans Youth Health and Development at Children's Hospital LA, this documentary explores the 2014 Angels of Change show. This positive film shows the connections between trans elders and trans youth as they work together to be completely visible as trans people not only on the runway during the show, but in life as they embrace true gender diversity.

Becoming Chaz (2011, U.S., 80 minutes)
Chaz Bono, the adult child of the stars Cher and Sonny Bono, made headlines when he came out as a trans man. This documentary film follows his transition and includes interviews with family and friends.

Bikini (2008, Sweden, 7 minutes)
Lasse Persson from Stockholm, Sweden, creates a charming animated video about a young trans person taking a risk by wearing a bikini to the beach. This is a lighthearted short film that was shown in numerous LGBTQ+ film festivals around the world.

Boy I Am (2006, U.S, 72 minutes)
Many trans documentaries focus on people as they transition. This film explores the nuances and complexities found within a lesbian feminist community in New York when some of their members come out as trans men.

But I'm a Genderqueer (2011, U.S., 12 minutes)
A short film that explores a genderqueer identity.

The Christine Jorgensen Story (1970, U.S., 98 minutes)

This sensationalized dramatization of Christine Jorgensen's actual autobiography shows the ways that her story was presented in the press. In the 1950s Jorgensen became an overnight sensation when the story of her gender-affirmation surgery in Denmark became public knowledge.

The Cockettes (2002, U.S., 100 minutes)

Hippies, flower children, and acid freaks converge in this documentary on San Francisco in the late 1960s and early 1970s. The performing group known as the Cockettes became famous for their gender-expansive shows that melded together Broadway musicals and U.S. politics. Early followers of the Cockettes were the filmmaker John Waters, the actor Divine, and the Beat poet Allen Ginsberg.

Deep Run (2015, U.S., 75 minutes)

The setting for this film is rural North Carolina, where conservative Christianity is seen as the only religion. The focus of *Deep Run* is on Cole, a young trans man, who is rejected by his family, bullied at school, and shunned in his church. Ashley, Cole's girlfriend, also struggles with being queer and being rejected by the church. An outstanding film that looks at social and religious pressure to conform to cisgender and heterosexual expectations.

Different for Girls (1996, U.K., 92 minutes)

Starring Rupert Graves and other mainstream British actors, this feature-length film follows the story of a friendship between two boys at public school who lose touch after graduation. Over a decade later, they run into each other again, and one of them is now a transgender woman. An intelligent and entertaining love story.

Finding Phong (2015, Vietnam, 92 minutes)

This film works within two genres as a documentary and a video diary that explores a year in the life of Phong, a trans woman in Vietnam, as she begins her journey to transition. Phong's biggest challenge is coming out to her large family living in a small village.

A Florida Enchantment (1914, U.S., 63 minutes)

Sidney Drew directed this early Hollywood silent film that explores gender stereotypes. A young woman swallows some mysterious seeds and turns into a man. A young man swallows the same seeds and turns into a woman. The film has some very problematic racial stereotyping (there are people in blackface) and gender stereotyping about men and women. It is a very early film depiction of the ways that society finds women trading up on the gender power pole to be amusing while men who trade down on the gender power pole are ridiculed and physically violated.

Freak Show (2017, U.S., 91 minutes)

Billy is a gender-nonconforming teenager who gets sent to a small southern high school where the majority of the students uphold the belief in the gender binary, often violently. Despite being bullied, Billy still strives to become homecoming queen. This comedy looks at the serious bullying that goes on with gender policing while also managing to be uplifting.

From This Day Forward (2015, U.S., 79 minutes)

There are numerous documentary films about young people coming out as trans, but fewer about parents who come out as trans. In this award-winning documentary, the filmmaker explores her father's coming out as trans and her parents' desire to remain together and keep their family completely intact. In a reversal of many trans narratives in which children must gain their parents' acceptance, in this film a grown child is the person who must come to terms with her rigid thinking.

Gendernauts: A Journey through Shifting Identities (Eine Reise durch die Geschlechter) (1999, U.S., Germany, 87 minutes)

The director Monika Treut focuses this documentary on a group of trans people in San Francisco. This is one of the first films to explore trans identities both within and outside the gender binary.

Georgie Girl (2001, New Zealand, 69 minutes)

Georgina Beyer, who is Maori and lives in New Zealand, became the first openly transgender elected member of Parliament in the world. This award-winning documentary film follows her life and her groundbreaking work in politics as an advocate for equity and access for all people.

Girl Inside (2007, Canada, 70 minutes)

Three years in the life of Madison, a trans woman, are documented in this Canadian film. Madison's relationship with her eighty-year-old grandmother and their conversations about gender, femininity, and the definition of "woman" are the focus of this film.

Girl Unbound: The War to Be Her (2016, Pakistan, Canada, 80 minutes)

Maria Toorpakai, an outstanding squash player, was assigned female at birth but as a youth passed as a boy in order to play squash in a region of Pakistan controlled by the Taliban, who do not allow girls to go to school, much less play sports. This is a beautiful documentary about a gender-fluid squash player on the international stage whose biggest support comes from family in a region controlled by conservative religious ideals and laws.

Hit and Miss (2012, television, U.K., 6 episodes)

This is a quirky British thriller that focuses on Mia, a trans woman, who is also a contract killer. She moves to rural England to find her ex-girlfriend, only to become a stepparent to the children. Meanwhile, to make money, Mia continues as a contract killer.

Intersexion (2012, New Zealand, 68 minutes)
This award-winning documentary film presented by an intersex person from New Zealand explores stories of intersex people around the world. It is a very engaging and accessible film that looks at the intersections of sex, gender, race, and socioeconomics along with various issues and concerns about Western medical interventions.

Junk Box Warrior (2002, U.S., 5 minutes)
Marcus Rene Van is a trans African American slam poet who critiques the gender binary in this experimental short film.

Just Call Me Kade (2002, U.S., 26 minutes)
An international award-winning documentary, this short film follows the story of a four-teen-year-old as he transitions from female to male. Kade and his family live in Arizona; his family is loving and supportive of his transition.

Kumu Hina (2015, U.S., 77 minutes)
Hinaleimoana Wong Kalu (Hina) is a cultural icon and teacher (kumu) in Hawai'i. She is Māhū and has spent her life battling against the leftovers of colonial transphobia and homophobia. Kumu Hina teaches Indigenous Hawai'ian values at a public school. This film is an in-depth documentary that delves into her life.

Man's Favorite Sport? (1963, U.S., 121 minutes)
Rock Hudson and Paula Prentiss star in this comedy about a sports shop clerk who is supposed to be an expert sportsman, particularly in the area of competitive fishing; however, he actually dislikes sports in general and fishing in particular. Paula Prentiss loves sports and has to teach Rock Hudson how to be a real sportsman. Gender role reversals highlight gender stereotypes in this romantic comedy.

Mind If I Call You Sir? (2004, U.S., 30 minutes)
This is a documentary about Latinx trans men. (Latinx or Latin@ are now often used instead of Latino or Latina, which are rooted in the gender binary. The "x" or the "@" leaves room for gender diversity.) It is one of the few existing documentaries that explores trans issues within Latinx culture.

More Than T (2017, U.S., 54 minutes)
This documentary film looks at intersecting identities and explores the ways that trans people are often defined only by their gender identity. The trans people in this film are from all walks of life: Asian/Pacific Islanders, African Americans, Two-Spirit people, AIDS survivors, and spiritual leaders.

Orange Is the New Black (2013–ongoing, television, U.S.)

This award-winning and popular television show about women in prison features Laverne Cox as an African American trans woman. Film and television often use cisgender actors to play the roles of trans people. *Orange Is the New Black* is important because Laverne Cox is a trans woman and a trans advocate.

Orchids: My Intersex Adventure (2010, Australia, 56 minutes)

This documentary, which won several Australian film awards, follows the filmmaker Phoebe Hart on a journey across Australia as she interviews other intersex people like herself. Phoebe learned in her adolescence that she was born with forty-six XY (male) chromosomes. This documentary questions and explores the sex binary and the gender binary.

Outlaw (1994, U.S., 26 minutes)

Alisa Lebow's documentary film features Leslie Feinberg, the famous gender outlaw, historian, writer, and activist. Feinberg speaks about hir experiences in a binary gender culture in this video manifesto.

Paris Is Burning (1990, U.S., 76 minutes)

Jennie Livingston's iconic and controversial documentary won numerous film awards, including Sundance's Grand Jury Prize and the National Society of Film Critics Award. It appears on most Top 10 LGBTQ+ film lists. The film documents the lives of African American and Latinx drag performers in New York City. Some of the people in the film identify as transgender; all the people in the film embody intersecting identities and identify outside a rigid gender binary. An outstanding film that considers race, class, sexual orientation, and gender identity in late twentieth-century America.

Passing: Profiling the Lives of Young Transmen of Color (2015, U.S., 23 minutes)

An outstanding short documentary that explores what it feels like for these trans men of color to completely pass and be presumed to be cisgender in their day-to-day lives. An excellent look at the intersections of race and masculinity.

A Place in the Middle: A Strength-Based Approach to Gender Diversity and Inclusion (2015, U.S., 25 minutes)

Taking the part of the documentary *Kumu Hina* that focuses on a middle-school youth who identifies outside the gender binary, this award-winning film looks at intersecting identities and ways to combat bullying and bring about inclusion.

She's a Boy I Knew (2007, Canada, 70 minutes)

The filmmaker Gwen Haworth focuses the camera on herself, her family, and her friends as she transitions. Haworth uses family videos and animation as part of this very personal look at the ways she and her community work with her coming out as a trans woman.

Three to Infinity: Beyond Two Genders (2015, U.S., 84 minutes)

This is a documentary film that explores people who identify as trans outside a gender binary. The film depicts gender and gender difference as something to be celebrated.

Tomboy (2008, U.S., 5 minutes)

Donna Carter's experimental short film looks at a young African American tomboy who is athletic and works to become self-confident in a gender-rigid world.

Two-Spirit People (1992, U.S., 20 minutes)

One of the first films to explore Indigenous cultures in the Americas and the gender diversity embraced in many of those cultures before European colonization.

What's the T? (2012, U.S., 70 minutes)

This documentary focuses on intersecting identities as it follows five trans women in the San Francisco Bay Area as they go about their daily lives in a culturally diverse urban area.

XXY (2007, Spain, Argentina, France, 86 minutes)

This film won awards at the Cannes and Edinburgh film festivals. It is a drama about a teenager who is intersex and the ways the teen's family works with nonbinary sex in a world that expects a binary.

NOTES

1. See the Lilith Gallery of Toronto, Canada, website: www.lilithgallery.com/. For "The Legend of Salmacis and Aphroditus," see the portion of the website that also gives a part of Ovid's account of the love that bound them together as one person who was both sexes for all eternity, www.lilithgallery .com/library/hermaphroditus/ (accessed 11 July 2017).

2. Susan Stryker, *Transgender History: The Roots of Today's Revolution,* rev. ed. (New York: Seal Press, 2017), 29.

3. Cheryl Chase, "Hermaphrodites with Attitude: Mapping the Emergence of Intersex Political Activism," *GLQ: A Journal of Lesbian and Gay Studies — The Transgender Issue* 4.2 (1998): 189.

4. Ibid., 193.

5. Ibid., 197.

6. Jenny Kleeman, "Being Both," *Guardian,* 7 February 2016, 19.

7. Intersex Society of North America (ISNA), http://isna.org/.

8. Thea Hillman, "Privates," in *Intersex (For Lack of a Better Word)* (San Francisco: Manic D Press, 2008), 108.

9. Ellen K. Feder, *Making Sense of Intersex: Changing Ethical Perspectives in Biomedicine* (Bloomington: Indiana University Press, 2014), 210.

10. Nellie Bowles, "Ultrasound Parties — Wombs with a View," *SFGate,* 10 May 2013, www.sfgate.com/style/article/Ultrasound -parties-wombs-with-a-view-4506767 .php (accessed 10 July 2017).

11. Terynn Boulton, "The Surprisingly Recent Time Period When Boys Wore Pink, Girls Wore Blue, and They Both Wore Dresses," *Today I Found Out: Feed Your Brain*, 17 October 2014, www.todayifoundout.com/index .php/2014 /10/pink-used-common-color-boys-blue-girls/ (accessed 10 July 2017).

12. Qwo-Li Driskill, *Asegi Stories: Cherokee Queer and Two-Spirit Memory* (Tucson: University of Arizona Press, 2016), 5.

13. Patricia T. O'Conner and Stewart Kellerman, "All-Purpose Pronoun," *New York Times Magazine,* 21 July 2009, www.nytimes .com/2009/07/26/magazine/26FOB-onlanguage-t.html?_r=0 (accessed 6 July 2015).

14. Leslie Feinberg, *Transgender Warriors: Making History from Joan of Arc to RuPaul* (Boston: Beacon Press, 1996).

15. Stryker, *Transgender History,* 38.

16. Ibid., 36–37.

17. Ibid., 37.

18. Ibid., 38.

19. Jess Dugan, "Artist Statement," http://www .jessdugan.com/statements/ (accessed 27 March 2018).

BIBLIOGRAPHY

Association for X and Y Chromosome Variations. www.genetic.org/About. Accessed 7 January 2016.

Boulton, Tarynn. "The Surprisingly Recent Time Period When Boys Wore Pink, Girls Wore Blue, and They Both Wore Dresses." *Today I Found Out: Feed Your Brain,* 17 October 2014. www.todayifoundout.com/index.php/2014/10/pink-used-common-color-boys-blue-girls/. Accessed 10 July 2017.

Bowles, Nellie. "Ultrasound Parties—Wombs with a View." *SFGate,* 10 May 2013. www.sfgate.com/style/article/Ultrasound-parties-wombs-with-a-view-4506767.php. Accessed 10 July 2017.

Chase, Cheryl. "Hermaphrodites with Attitude: Mapping the Emergence of Intersex Political Activism." *GLQ: A Journal of Lesbian and Gay Studies—The Transgender Issue* 4.2 (1998): 189–211.

Driskill, Qwo-Li. *Asegi Stories: Cherokee Queer and Two-Spirit Memory.* Tucson: University of Arizona Press, 2016.

Feder, Susan K. *Making Sense of Intersex: Changing Ethical Perspectives in Biomedicine.* Bloomington: Indiana University Press, 2014.

Feinberg, Leslie. *Transgender Warriors: Making History from Joan of Arc to RuPaul.* Boston: Beacon Press, 1996.

Hida. "How Common Is Intersex? An Explanation of the Stats." *Intersex Campaign for Equality,* 1 April 2015. http://oii-usa.org/2563/how-common-is-intersex-in-humans/. Accessed 10 July 2017.

Hillman, Thea. *Intersex (For Lack of a Better Word).* San Francisco: Manic D Press, 2008.

Intersex Society of North America (ISNA). www.isna.org. Accessed 10 July 2017.

Jorgensen, Christine. *Christine Jorgensen: A Personal Autobiography.* San Francisco: Cleis Press, 1967.

Kleeman, Jenny. "Being Both." *Guardian,* 7 February 2016, 16–24.

Lilith Gallery of Toronto, Canada. www.lilithgallery.com/. For "The Legend of Salmacis and Aphroditus," see the portion of the website that also gives a part of Ovid's account of the love that bound them together as one person who was both sexes for all eternity: www.lilithgallery.com/library/hermaphroditus/.

O'Conner, Patricia T., and Stewart Kellerman. "All-Purpose Pronoun." *New York Times Magazine,* 21 July 2009. www.nytimes.com/2009/07/26/magazine/26FOB-onlanguage-t.html?_r=0. Accessed 6 July 2015.

Stryker, Susan. *Transgender History: The Roots of Today's Revolution.* Revised edition. New York: Seal Press, 2017.

CHAPTER 2

Sexual Orientation
Stories and Definitions

Key Questions

1. Considering everything you read about gender identity and gender expression in Chapter 1, what are your ideas about sexual orientation and its relationship to gender identity and gender expression?

2. Think about yourself and where you grew up. How have your cultural surroundings influenced your thoughts and ideas about sexuality and sexual orientation? Have you considered the ways that other cultures might think about sexual orientation?

3. Now, when you think about sexuality and sexual orientation, what words and definitions come to mind?

4. In what situations do you think sexual orientation becomes important?

Chapter Overview

Chapter 2 builds on the definitions of and stories about sex, gender, gender identity, and gender expression from Chapter 1. In this chapter, you will focus on exploring how sex and gender are related to a person's sexual orientation. You have already learned that gender often is discussed within a binary. In numerous mainstream contemporary cultures, many people also think of sexual orientation within a strict *heterosexual/homosexual binary*. You may have already studied gender and sexual orientation within different historical or cultural contexts, or your personal experiences may have taught you that sexual orientation does not adhere to this binary. The early part of this chapter explores the ways that *heterosexual* and *homosexual* become set against one another and defined (incorrectly) as the only two possibilities for sexual orientation. You will learn how these labels, and the preconceptions that accompany them, become very limiting. Then you will explore numerous sexual orientations and the ways that sexual orientation intersects with other identities, including gender, race, socioeconomic status, culture, religion, and geographic location, in the twenty-first century.

Haefele-Thomas, Ardel, *Introduction to Transgender Studies*
dx.doi.org/10.17312/harringtonparkpress/2019.01.itts.002
© 2019 by Harrington Park Press

Introduction: Sexuality and Sexual Orientation

What are the differences among sexuality, sexual orientation, and sexual preference? In casual conversation, they are often used interchangeably. Each carries different nuances, however, so it is important to explore each term in more detail.

Sexuality encompasses the behaviors you enjoy sexually; it is what gives you erotic or sexual pleasure, so it is very personal. You may experience a fluctuation in your sexuality over time. For example, what you enjoy erotically/sexually when you are nineteen may not give you pleasure when you are forty-two.

Sexuality is often confused with **sexual orientation,** which very broadly defined refers to the persons (if anyone) to whom you are attracted sexually, romantically, and/or emotionally. Sexuality and sexual orientation are experienced as important parts of each person's identity. Like sexuality, sexual orientation can evolve and change over time. This chapter focuses on the intersections of gender identity, sexual orientation, and cultural context.

You have probably noticed that *sexual preference* and *sexual orientation* are often used interchangeably. There is a difference between the two, however, because *preference* implies a choice that can, more or less, be changed *easily*. For example, you may prefer peppermint ice cream, but your favorite ice cream shop is out of it today, so you order chocolate chip instead. Chocolate chip is good, but you still prefer peppermint. For ice cream flavors, preference works well, but for sexual orientation, it does not.

An orientation, as opposed to a preference, is an inherent part of your identity. *Orientation* implies that you turn in a certain direction—like a compass point. It may be fixed and permanent, *or* it may be experienced as fluid and changing over time, but it is not a simple choice.

The Homosexual/Heterosexual Binary

In February 2014 the government of Uganda passed the Anti-Homosexuality Act (originally titled "Kill the Gays Bill"), which calls for lifetime imprisonment of anyone involved in same-sex relations.[1] Later that same year, Uganda's Constitutional Court annulled the law, although there is a constant threat that the law will be put in place again.[2] Ugandans fighting against this law included Sexual Minorities Uganda (SMUG), which is based in Uganda and fights for justice and equality, and Amnesty International, which held a Global Day of Action in protest.[3] Members of SMUG appeared on global news networks asking for support from other countries around the world.

The following year, in 2015, the U.S. Supreme Court also made global headlines when it voted to legalize same-sex marriage in all fifty states. In retaliation against the Supreme Court decision, Kim Davis, a court clerk in Kentucky, refused to marry same-sex couples on moral grounds; she briefly went to jail for her actions.[4] Just as SMUG members' pleas were seen on the international stage, so, too, was Kim Davis's protest. She even captured the pope's attention.[5] Although the U.S. Supreme Court ruled in 2015 that same-sex marriage in all fifty states is legal, in January 2018 this same court upheld the Mississippi state law that allows businesses to discriminate against gay and lesbian couples.[6] And, starting with reports in 2017, the world has become aware of the brutal beatings and murders of gay men in Chechnya as that government tries to eradicate homosexuality.[7] These situations in Uganda, the United States, and Chechnya underscore the perception that, like masculine/feminine, *heterosexual* and *homosexual* exist within a strictly *opposing* binary.

Homosexual refers to someone who is romantically and/or sexually attracted to a person of the same sex.[8] The prefix *homo-* comes from the Greek *homos,* which means "same."[9] Before the rise of **sexology,** the scientific study of sexual practices and sexual orientations, the word *homo* was used for all people as a shortened version of *Homo sapiens* (which refers to the human species). Shakespeare's *Henry IV, Part 1* refers to all men as "homo," and as late as the mid-nineteenth century, writers often referred to the human race as homo. The prefix and the word match each other.

The word *homosexual* is not typically used by people attracted to others of the same sex or gender. Why? Over the past 150 years, the word *homosexual* has been used by doctors and psychiatrists as a diagnosis for a physical and/or mental sickness. (See Chapter 3 for a history of sexology and classifications of sexual orientation and gender identity.) In 1973 the American Psychological Association (APA) removed homosexuality from the list of mental illnesses published in the *Diagnostic and Statistical Manual of Mental Disorders* (DSM).[10] Even today some psychologists carry out what they call *reparative therapies* that attempt to change a homosexual into a heterosexual.[11] There are currently nine U.S. states, along with the District of Columbia, that have banned reparative therapy; in the forty-one states where it is still legal, there are cities and towns that have also banned this practice.[12]

The continued underlying assumption that homosexuality is a sickness is one of the reasons the term *homosexual* is not used within contemporary lesbian, gay, bisexual, and transgender (LGBT) culture. In fact, if you conduct some quick online research, you will find that the word *homosexual* usually comes up in reference to people who still believe (1) that homosexuality should be classified as an illness, a crime, or a sin, and (2) that people who have same-sex/same-gender partners need to be cured, imprisoned, or sent to church. If a cure, whether medical or religious, is sought, then the underlying goal is to move the person across the perceived binary and make the person heterosexual.

Heterosexual refers to someone who is romantically and/or sexually attracted to a person of the opposite sex.[13] The prefix *hetero-*, however, does not mean opposite; rather, it signifies *other* or *different*.[14] Take a moment to think about the distinction between something that is opposite and something that is different. For example, the opposite of hot is cold; hot and cold are also different. But hot and warm are *not* opposite temperatures, although they are different.

Words, the feelings and ideas they convey, and the subtle changes in the ways they are used and understood affect all of us on a daily basis, even if we do not stop to think about them constantly. So it is interesting to emphasize here that the prefix *hetero-* in *heterosexual* does not mean opposite but, rather, *different*. "Opposite" as part of the assumed definition of heterosexual depends on a strict gender binary without room for a spectrum of gender identity because homosexual and heterosexual are often understood to be in opposition to each other.

Think again about the Ugandan Anti-Homosexuality Act of 2014. Or think of the leaders in Chechnya who have demanded the eradication of gay men. Or think about the fact that businesses in Mississippi can discriminate against gay and lesbian people on religious grounds. Underneath all three of these arguments and pieces of legislation, there is a pro-heterosexual argument. The binary set up here, as is true of the gender binary, is a combative one. Not only are *heterosexual* and *homosexual* opposite, they are at war. Even if many of us do not think in terms of battle, the implication is there.

The homosexual/heterosexual binary differs from the gender binary because, although we have all seen various examples of the "battle of the sexes," being a cisgender woman is not necessarily seen as abnormal or unnatural, although several countries still have laws that discriminate against cis women simply because they are women. (You can probably think of several ways that cis women might not be treated equally within the gender binary. For example, how long did it take women to be able to vote in various countries? Are there places in the world where women are still treated as men's property?) The homosexual/heterosexual distinction is different from the gender binary because one pole (heterosexual) is valued to the absolute exclusion of the other pole (homosexual). Alongside this exclusion is the idea that heterosexuality is traditional, normal, and natural, while homosexuality is nontraditional, abnormal, and unnatural.

As you learned in Chapter 1, binaries regarding gender identity can categorize and limit self-expression, but **cultural norms** are fixed ideas and judgments about what is right and normal. Cultural norms result in part from strict social constructions about binaries. The construction of the homosexual/heterosexual binary *depends on the control of a gender binary*. Gender identity and sexual orientation are not the same, but they are monitored socially and culturally in many of the same ways. For example, in Uganda the heterosexual/homosexual binary is strictly policed, and there are dire legal consequences if someone crosses over the binary from the heterosexual side to the homosexual side. In the United States, the heterosexual/homosexual binary may not mean the difference between life in and out of prison; however, deep cultural stereotypes and assumptions continue to uphold the binary.

Boy Meets Girl: Heterosexual = Normal?

Remember the examples of the ways that people talk about newborns in Chapter 1? Now imagine the possible conversation between the parent of a baby assigned female at birth and the parent of a baby assigned male at birth while they sit on a park bench on a summer afternoon. You might hear them planning out the Saturday afternoon football games featuring the boy as the star quarterback and the Sunday afternoon ballet performances with the girl as the prima donna in *Swan Lake*. Alongside the expectations about their developing masculinity and femininity, we can also listen for another assumption. Imagine these statements: "He's going to be quite a ladies' man!" "Wow, she's going to have all the boys following her around." You might even hear this comment: "They are so adorable! Don't you think they will make beautiful babies together?" Keep in mind that these babies are less than three months old. Neither of them is going on a date with anyone anytime soon.

The parents of the newborns are planning the children's future, which is something most parents do. They are also making specific assumptions about the formation of their baby's gender identity *and* sexual orientation. Without thinking that either child might wind up identifying as something other than cisgender and heterosexual, the parents are making a *cissexist* and *heterosexist* assumption. In short, **heterosexism** is the societal idea that heterosexuality is the preferred, normal sexual orientation.[15] Generally speaking, society holds the notion that everyone is heterosexual unless they *come out*—that is, reveal what is not necessarily obvious (in this case, something other than heterosexuality).

The product of heterosexism is the social and cultural pressure embodied in **heteronormativity,** which is the notion that the only normal and natural sexual and romantic relationships are those between cisgender people who are romantically/sexually attracted to people of the opposite sex. Heteronormativity creates the following: (1) the binary construction of sex and gender: there is only female and male, where male equals man and female equals woman; (2) men and women must follow *gender roles,* or expected behaviors and self-presentations; and (3) the norm for sexual behavior sits on one side or the other of a rigid gender binary. But heteronormativity goes well beyond personal relationships to become a cornerstone of many social and cultural institutions, including government, law, religion, medicine, and marriage.

There have been many historic legal debates about the definition of "normal" sexual behavior. For example, until the historic 2003 U.S. Supreme Court decision in *Lawrence et al. v. Texas,* several states (including Arkansas and Texas) had laws that made certain heterosexual sexual acts between consenting adults, even in the privacy of a person's own home, illegal. These same states made all homosexual sex acts between consenting adults illegal.[16] Homosexuality is still illegal in over seventy countries, including the United Arab Emirates, Tonga, Ethiopia, and Jamaica. In Russia homosexuality is not technically illegal, but the country's "anti-homosexual propaganda law" makes it illegal to write or say anything *positive* about homosexuality.[17]

We are all presented with examples of heterosexuality as the norm every day, so much so that most of us do not even notice them. Think back to your own childhood, the people in your family, and people out in the community in places such as school, church, and the grocery store. Did the people in your life make assumptions about whom you would fall in love with and marry? If so, how old were you when you started to notice these comments? What was the gender identity of the person they imagined you marrying? If everyone assumed you were heterosexual and would marry someone of the opposite sex, then you have experienced, firsthand, heterosexism and heteronormativity. If you identify *outside* the heterosexual box, what kinds of pressure do heteronormative expectations place on you? If you identify *within* the heterosexual box, what kinds of pressure do heteronormative expectations place on you?

Diverse Heterosexualities

We have already discussed the definition of heterosexual, but let's go back again and reconsider the prefix *hetero-* as meaning something *other* or *different.* The word *heterosexual* itself points away from rigid definitions, and yet, culturally and socially, we are often taught that there are very specific ways to be heterosexual: (1) A relationship must consist of one cisgender woman and one cisgender man, usually of the same racial, ethnic, and/or religious background; (2) this couple needs to enter into a monogamous marriage; (3) this marriage needs to create children; (4) this monogamous marriage with children means that everyone lives in one place together. This set of assumptions constitutes what we think of in the United States as the typical nuclear family. Culturally, we stereotype the nuclear family as not only the best type of family structure, but also the *normal* type of family structure. The United States is rich in immigrant history, however, so depending on socioeconomic factors, cultural and familial background, and location (urban or rural), a household might be composed of an extended family living under one roof. This extended family could include grandparents, aunts, uncles, and cousins. In other countries and cultures, heterosexuality may include polygamous marriages, but the creation of children is still emphasized. Think for a moment about cultural judgments we make about other models of heterosexuality that do not fit this image.

For example, how do we view a married heterosexual couple that chooses not to have children? How do we view an interracial heterosexual married couple? How do we view interfaith heterosexual couples? How do we view heterosexuals within a group like the Fundamentalist Church of Jesus Christ of Latter-Day Saints, who often feel the need to live in isolation because they believe in polygamy? How do we view older kinship family systems like those found in Indigenous communities before European colonization? How do we view people who identify as transgender and heterosexual? As you begin to think about these questions, you can see that heterosexuality is much more diverse and rich than our stereotypes of it.

In the three stories below, you can see expansive and diverse understandings of heterosexuality.

OSABEMIYE identifies himself as a cisgender man: "My name is Osabemiye. I am a married forty-four-year-old African American man of Egyptian descent. I am heterosexual. I work as a personal trainer and group fitness director. I grew up between Birmingham, Alabama, and Morganfield, a small town in Kentucky. I served in the United States Army for nearly twelve years, and I am a parent. I believe that being a heterosexual man lends itself to certain privileges, but I am careful about not allowing those to become a trap. Because I am heterosexual, it does not mean I am the enemy of anyone who isn't."

KELLY KELLY "I'm sexually attracted to masculine men. Most men I've dated have self-identified as straight, even though they are having sex with me, a non-op trans female."

VERONIKA identifies as an African American trans woman: "I identify as a trans woman, though I am a woman who happens to be trans. I am a heterosexual woman, though I was always open to trying new things if the chemistry was right. I have slept with men, women, and a masculine trans woman. I can still say that I am heterosexual, or maybe just sexual, but I do prefer men."

At the age of forty-four, Osabemiye has just entered into his first marriage. Culturally, he is considered "old" for someone tying the knot for the first time. Also note that Osabemiye describes himself as a parent, which means that he did not follow the script of marriage and then children; rather, he had a child and then much later got married. His being a responsible and loving parent has nothing to do with his being married.

If you recall from her story in Chapter 1, Kelly Kelly identifies as third gender but uses *she* pronouns and dates men. In her description of the men she dates, Kelly Kelly uses the informal term *straight* to mean heterosexual. Kelly Kelly is very open about the fact that she has not had any surgical intervention in her process as a trans woman; she identifies as heterosexual because her gender identity does not hinge on medical intervention, and the people she desires are masculine cisgender men. Veronika, who is a trans woman, makes it clear that she is open to sexual relations with people of different gender identities; she also makes it clear that she prefers cisgender men and identifies as heterosexual. For Veronika, her sexual orientation is heterosexual because that is how she has defined herself; *heterosexual* is her self-determination.

Osabemiye, Kelly Kelly, and Veronika might not fit into a narrow heterosexual model for very different reasons. They do, however, exemplify a spectrum of heterosexuality that goes beyond the definitions of heterosexual found within the traditional binary.

FIGURE 2.1 Alfred Kinsey, by Cameron Rains. Dr. Alfred Kinsey was an American sexologist who, along with Drs. Wardell Pomeroy and Clyde Martin, developed the Heterosexual-Homosexual Rating Scale, more commonly known as the Kinsey Scale. This scale was first published in *Sexual Behavior in the Human Male* in 1948.

Identities beyond the Homo/Hetero Binary: Bisexual, Pansexual, and Asexual

As you were reading the above descriptions of the homosexual/heterosexual binary, you may have been thinking, "Hey, what if I don't completely fit one side or the other?" Guess what? If that is how you feel, you are actually in the *majority of the population!*

In 1948 the American scientist and sexologist Alfred Kinsey (figure 2.1), along with his colleagues Wardell Pomeroy and Clyde Martin, created a scale to measure people's sexual orientation when they realized that many people did not fit neatly onto the homosexual/heterosexual binary.

When the Heterosexual-Homosexual Rating Scale, more popularly known as the Kinsey Scale, was first administered anonymously in the United States, the results were very surprising. Kinsey's original scale was broken down along a heterosexual/homosexual binary because his questions asked people to note if they were "predominantly," "exclusively," or "equally" heterosexual *or* homosexual. This scale ranged from 0 (which indicated a person was exclusively heterosexual in thoughts, feelings, and sexual practices) to 6 (which indicated that a person was exclusively homosexual in thoughts, feelings and sexual practices).[18] Guess where the majority of the respondents landed on the scale? If you guessed between the numbers 2 and 4, you are correct. In other words, the majority of respondents fell into a category of not strictly heterosexual *or* homosexual, but

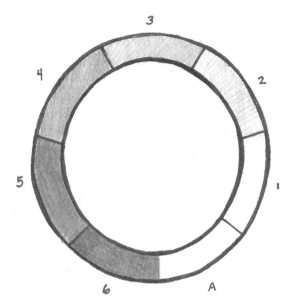

FIGURE 2.2 Circular Kinsey Scale, by Cameron Rains. Though Kinsey envisioned his scale as a linear progression from 1 (completely heterosexual attraction) to 6 (completely homosexual attraction), this version by Cameron Rains depicts the gradations as more continuous and includes categories (such as asexual) that the original Kinsey Scale did not.

rather open to intimacy with either sex (note that in the original study, sex was seen as either male or female). The findings from Kinsey's study helped the term **bisexual** emerge in the popular imagination. In popular culture, sexual orientation was no longer seen as only a heterosexual/homosexual binary.

Take a moment and think about Veronika's story. She defines herself as heterosexual; however, she is also clear that she is open to various possibilities. So, on Kinsey's scale, she might fall into the 2 or 3 category because bisexuality covers the widest range within the scale. Note, though, that the word *bisexual* and the Kinsey Scale both equate sex and gender, and they both assume that there are only two choices (because the prefix *bi-* means just that: two). Also, because even though Veronika would technically be a 2 or 3 on the Kinsey Scale, she clearly does not identify herself as bisexual, but as heterosexual. Also important to remember is that Kinsey's original research did not consider trans people and their sexual orientation, so both Veronika and Kelly Kelly would most likely have been mislabeled, which is often the problem with labels—they are constricting. If you look to Cameron Rains's interpretation of the Kinsey Scale in figure 2.2, you will see that it has been drawn as a circle with gradations between white and black. The circular figure is meant to portray the fluidity of the scale. In the 1800s *bisexual* meant that a single person, plant, or animal had the sex traits of both male and female. In very rare instances, bisexual could also mean *hermaphrodite*, which as you know, is the historic term for people with DSD.[19]

Culturally, sexual orientation is often still discussed, inaccurately, in terms of the homosexual/heterosexual binary—even by people who have given a lot of thought to issues concerning gender identity and sexual orientation. For example, let's listen to Deirdre's story about growing up and the ways that she understood sexual orientation.

 **DEIRDRE** "I grew up with gays and lesbians in my life as family friends. I felt that if people were brave enough to love who they wanted to in the face of massive societal pressure to do otherwise, they were living proof that you really could do and be whatever you wanted. I was boy crazy from a very early age and I thought you were either homosexual or heterosexual, so I knew there was no way I could be a lesbian. Then, when I was twelve years old, my best friend told me about bisexuality, and I felt like my head was going to explode. I knew right away, that was what I wanted to be."

When she was a child, Deirdre's family had friends who were gay and lesbian, so she already knew that there was a sexual orientation other than heterosexual; but reread what she says here. Deirdre was boy crazy and thought that she had to be *either* heterosexual or homosexual until her friend told her about bisexuality.

Historically, it has sometimes been assumed that people go through a bisexual phase but ultimately come out as gay or lesbian. For this reason (and others), bisexual people often feel they do not fit into heterosexual communities and are also rejected within gay and lesbian communities. It is true that some people who identify and exist at an extreme of the homosexual/heterosexual binary are suspicious of bisexuals, and yet, according to the Kinsey Scale, bisexuality truly embraces the majority of people.

The term *bisexual* exists within a binary and often still assumes that everyone is cisgender, so you might be wondering: How do people who are romantically and/or sexually attracted to people of all gender identities identify? **Pansexual** refers to people who are open to relationships with people of all gender identities and sexual orientations. The ancient Greek prefix *pan-* means "all."[20] Although the word *pansexual* has been in use since the early twentieth century, it has only recently come into popular use.

Let's look at the rest of Deirdre's story.

DEIRDRE "Nowadays, I will use the term 'pansexual' because it resists the gender binary, but I do feel a certain nostalgic loyalty to my old 'bi' identity, because it has faced so much political backlash and invisibility over my lifetime."

For Deirdre, it is not so much that her sexual orientation has changed over time, but rather that the term *pansexual* has come into popular use. Deirdre feels it best describes her sexual and romantic openness to people of all gender identities and sexual orientations. At the same time, she also embraces a *bisexual* identity.

In recent years, a new category has been added to the Kinsey Scale. The category term **asexual** refers to someone who, generally speaking, has very little or no desire to be with anyone sexually. There is some controversy in the social and behavioral sciences about whether asexuality is a sexual orientation at all. Asexual communities, however, argue that asexuality (like homosexuality, bisexuality, and pansexuality) is a marginalized sexual orientation that scientists have attempted to study as a *pathology* (disease or problem). This book considers asexuality as a sexual orientation—one that is often misunderstood and marginalized. Figure 2.2 shows asexuality added to the Kinsey Scale and labeled as "A."

Asexuality, Sexual Abstinence, and Celibacy

Sexual abstinence is the choice not to act on sexual feelings. For example, some people decide to remain sexually abstinent until marriage. Most of the discussion about sexual abstinence makes both cisgender and heterosexual assumptions about marriage. How do you think the 2015 U.S. Supreme Court ruling that allows same-sex marriage in all fifty states will affect education about and choices regarding sexual abstinence? What kinds of discussions about sexual abstinence will take place in schools, community groups, churches, synagogues, mosques, temples, and other public forums?

Sexual abstinence is not the same as asexuality, and neither is **celibacy,** which is sexual abstinence that is typically tied to religious beliefs. Celibacy within religious orders is a global phenomenon that has existed for thousands of years. Buddhist monks and nuns embrace celibacy, as do Catholic nuns and priests, Jainist monks, some Taoist priests, and some schools of Hinduism.

Everyday people who have chosen not to engage in sexual activity sometimes use the word *celibate* to describe themselves. Like sexual abstinence, celibacy is a choice. In contrast, asexuality is a sexual orientation.

Asexual people may date and seek or find romance; some do, some do not. Asexual people can also identify emotionally as heterosexual, homosexual, bisexual, or pansexual. In other words, their personal experiences of attraction and love are just as diverse as those of anyone else. Thus, an asexual person may still fall in love with someone and still bond with people emotionally and physically, but not sexually.

Here is how Cameron D. explains what being asexual means to them.

CAMERON D. identifies as Canadian, Chinese-Irish, and genderqueer. They are also asexual: "I've always identified with asexuality, starting when I was eleven. The words, and the particular type of asexuality, didn't come until I was nineteen. This was in part from the research I did and in my developing understanding of my gender identity. I am panromantic. As a person of color, and as someone made invisible by my ethnic, gender, and sexual identities, I try to spend my time with people who are politically and socially aware and who are supportive of me."

Cameron uses the word *panromantic*, which means they are open to romance with someone of any gender identity. In other words, being asexual does not necessarily mean living without romance. Note, too, how Cameron's intersecting identities often create a situation where they may not feel understood, so they are perhaps more cautious in establishing friendships than other people might be.

Alternatives to the Term *Homosexual*

Though many social and behavioral sciences, legal documents, and medical practices still use the term *homosexual,* for most people who identify as a 5 or a 6 on the Kinsey Scale, the word still feels like a bad diagnosis or something illegal. The question, then, is: What respectful and positive terms can we use for people who are homosexual? In the 1980s in Denver, Colorado, there was a gay bookstore named Category Six Books, after Kinsey's scale. "Category Six" was coded language in that people aware of Kinsey's scale would understand that it was a gay bookstore. "Category Six" was a great name for a bookstore, but *category sixers* does not feel like an identity that people would want to embrace. In this section you will learn about the two most commonly used and embraced identities for category 5 and 6 people: the G and the L in LGBTQ+.

Gay

Have you heard the Christmas carol "Deck the Halls"? Here is one of the lines from it: "Don we now our gay apparel." Have you seen *West Side Story* on film or on the stage? Maria sings, "I Feel Pretty," which includes the lyrics "I feel pretty and witty and gay!" These lyrics elicit a chuckle from many of us because the way these songs use the word *gay* is not how the word is currently used.

Gay generally refers to men who find other men romantically and/or sexually attractive. That said, many women also use the term *gay* for themselves; in English-speaking countries it is often the most-used word. For example, the London bookshop Gay's The Word is an all-inclusive bookstore for the entire LGBTQ+ community. If you research its *etymology* (the history of a word), you will learn some interesting information about the word *gay*. Let's go back to our two songs. "Deck the Halls" was originally written in Wales in the sixteenth century as a song for New Year's Eve. The Welsh title was "Nos Galan," and the song was not translated into English until 1862.[21] According to the *Oxford English Dictionary, gay* meant "bright looking" or "dressed in finery."[22] Because this was a folk holiday song for the new year that is now associated more with the yuletide, we can guess that the people who are putting on their "gay apparel" are dressing up for the festivities.

"I Feel Pretty" is much more recent. In 1957 Leonard Bernstein and Stephen Sondheim wrote the musical *West Side Story*. In the song Maria's singing that she is "gay" means that she is happy and full of joy. Interestingly, by 1957 *gay* was in use as a *euphemism* (a socially and publicly more acceptable word or phrase) for *homosexual*.

In her 1922 short story "Miss Furr and Miss Skeene," Gertrude Stein, an expatriate American author who lived in Paris with her lifetime woman partner, Alice B. Toklas, uses the word *gay* playfully as a *double entendre,* which is a word or phrase that has a second underlying meaning that is often sexual. It is clear from her repetition of the word *gay* that Stein was playing with the language and playing with the meaning, which she often did in her Modernist writing.[23] Stein was gay, so we can see the ways that the word *gay* begins to be used by people who self-identify as homosexual, but who might reject the negative term *homosexual* and move toward a more empowering term.

By the 1960s the word *gay* specifically meant homosexual. Although it has been used positively (think of "gay pride"), it can also be used negatively. Let's read what Greg, a college professor and retired police officer, has to say about growing up and the ways the word *gay* felt negative.

GREG "I realized my attraction to other males at a conscious level in seventh grade. The words 'gay' and 'queer' were both very negative terms—about on the same level as 'fag.' Once I realized that I was sexually attracted to men, I kept that part of my identity a deeply hidden secret, so I never had a need or the occasion to use a term to identify my sexual orientation. Throughout my life, I considered and wondered if my attraction to men would change, but as I moved through my twenties, it became very clear to me that I was 'gay.' This was the term that I eventually accepted for myself and shared with others at the age of forty. Being gay was a great point of shame for me until I came out at age forty. Both the reality of being attracted to men and the associated label prevented me from sharing this part of my identity with anyone. The identity that I associated with being 'gay' for most of my life was that of an effeminate man, who was flamboyant and overly sexual. I never saw myself as having feminine characteristics, so the word didn't work for me. More so, it was the shame associated with identifying as gay that I had to get over."

Greg held several stereotypes about gay men being effeminate, which underscores two different issues: misogyny and homophobia. **Misogyny** is a hatred of women, but more broadly, it is a hatred of what is feminine. The stereotype of gay men being effeminate denigrates them as feminine, and so it is misogynous. Greg's fear also points to his own internal **homophobia,** which is both a fear and a hatred of homosexuality. Homophobia can be the fear of homosexuality within the self, but it is also supported on a cultural level where anything seen as homosexual is denigrated. In contrast, heterosexuality is expected and even mandated, whether through subtle cultural cues or through laws prohibiting homosexuality.

Many people still believe that male police officers need to be very masculine, and that if you are gay, you are automatically not masculine. So you can see why the stereotypes of gay men would get in Greg's way. You can also see the ways that *gay* and *transgender* might overlap in someone's mind, too. Because sexual orientation is understood as a binary, in the same way that gender is understood as a binary, many people assume that if two men are in a relationship, one must be "the woman" and the other must be "the man." So, even here, homosexuality gets stereotyped as a form of heterosexuality, which is still viewed as the norm.

These views of masculinity, femininity, and being gay permeate our culture. Mia, whose story you read in Chapter 1, writes about her coming out.

MIA "I originally came out as gay because growing up in a small town in Texas if you were assigned male and acted feminine, that meant you were gay."

Mia's experience is not unusual. Because of a combination of gender stereotyping, misogyny, and homophobia, people often assume that a little boy acting feminine is a child who is going to be gay. In reality, it could mean many things, but panic that the child could be gay is often the first reaction. In the "Writings from the Community" at the end of this chapter, you will find Austin's short story, "Deb," which asks you to consider the ways that worries about sexual orientation and gender identity become intertwined.

Today *gay* is the term most commonly used for men who have romantic and/or sexual attachments to other men, but it can also be used as an *umbrella term* that can encompass numerous ideas and identities. In fact, many cultures that do not use the terms within LGBTQ+ often have one word that covers all sexual orientations that are not heterosexual and all gender identities that are not cisgender. In a recent book, *A Little Gay History* by R. B. Parkinson, the author explores ancient artifacts from around the globe that illuminate the fact that all cultures through time have included people of various sexual orientations and gender identities and expressions.[24] The book's title includes the word *gay*, but, as the author uses it, the word refers to people who identify as LGBTQ+. (The Q stands for *queer*, which we discuss later in this chapter.)

Lesbian

You might hear women use the word *gay* to describe themselves and their sexual orientation rather than the term *lesbian*, which sometimes takes on political connotations or is seen as culturally white and not welcoming to women of color. A **lesbian** is a woman who is romantically and/or sexually attracted to other women. The word comes from the Greek island Lesbos, or Lesvos, which is located in the northeastern Aegean Sea, very close to the coast of Turkey. You may be wondering how a Greek island's name came to be associated with women who love women. One of the most famous residents of the island was Sappho (610–570 BCE), the famous Greek lyric poet who was known to have romantic and sexual relationships with women. Her love of women lives on in her poetry. Interestingly, she almost surely had relationships with men. History, however, has all but forgotten that she was probably bisexual by today's definition. The word *Sapphist* became associated with Sappho, and this word was and still is used to denote a lesbian. **Sapphic** is also in common parlance as another word for lesbian, but in scholarly circles the term applies to the exact poetic meter used by Sappho in her poems.

How does *lesbian* become a political term if its etymology refers to an ancient Greek island and the poet Sappho? The 1960s and 1970s in the United States were marked by several radical political struggles: the Civil Rights movement, the United Farmworkers' movement, the American Indian Movement, the women's movement (also known as the feminist movement), the peace movement, and the beginning of the LGBTQ+ movement. Many of the participants in these movements worked within more than one of them, and sometimes within all of them. You have probably studied at least one of these political movements. The women's movement, which we also think of as the second wave of feminism (the first wave happened in the early twentieth century in Great Britain and the United States and centered on women's right to vote), included many lesbian activists. The convergence of the feminist movement and the beginning of the modern LGBTQ+ movement helped solidify the idea of a lesbian as someone who is political as a feminist and also political as a woman who loves women. Here is Betsy's story of coming out as a lesbian, going back to college in her thirties as a single mother, and living in Amherst, Massachusetts, in the 1980s. Betsy is now in her sixties, and she and her wife have a close relationship with her grown children and are helping raise her grandchildren.

BETSY "Coming out in 1984, in my thirties, after a heterosexual marriage was the hardest thing I've ever done. Was I crazy? Going through a 'phase'? Of course I sought professional help. One therapist suggested I was having a 'delayed adolescence.' My divorce attorney advised me to have no contact with lesbians whatsoever, no phone calls, nothing. The message was clear: if I wanted to keep my children, I had to keep a secret, deny my very SELF, and go into hiding. But there was no denying my feelings. I felt I was on a runaway train, setting into motion changes in my life for which there was no stopping, and no turning back. I worried constantly about how these changes would affect my children. I briefly thought of suicide, but the impact that would have on my children was unconscionable. I could never leave them with that legacy. Once I cleared myself of the darkness I feared would surely envelop me, there was only one choice: to be a good mother, I had to be a happy woman. And what made me happy, what completed the missing pieces of me, was to be true to myself. I am a lesbian."

Betsy was raised in a strict Catholic environment and did what was expected by her family and by our culture. In her early twenties she married a man, and they had three children. In her thirties she finally came out as a lesbian. Betsy's story shows the difficulty and the triumph of her experience of fully embracing her lesbian identity over the past thirty years. For Betsy's generation, it was difficult to come out of the closet and to live their lives fully. A huge worry for Betsy was the ever-present danger that her children would be taken away from her because she was a lesbian. This would have been completely legal in the 1980s, even in a relatively liberal place like Amherst, Massachusetts. Even now, thirty years after Betsy struggled with coming out, it can still be very difficult for a person to come out of the closet.

Betsy is cisgender and lesbian. Remember, though, that someone who identifies as transgender can also identify as a lesbian. Do you remember Cerridwyn from Chapter 1? She wrote about her experience of being transsexual as feeling stuck in the wrong body. Here she continues to write about her sexual orientation: "I am a lesbian because I am a woman attracted to women." Cerridwyn is a transgender woman who comfortably embraces the term lesbian.

Some genderqueer, trans, transgender, and other gender-nonconforming people, however, have a problem with the perceived gender binary that gay and lesbian identities can appear to uphold. Some cisgender and trans people perceive the terms *gay* and *lesbian* as too white (Anglo-European). For some people who do not live in a Western cultural context, these terms, along with *bisexual* and *transgender,* feel "too American" or "too European." In the next two sections you will examine various alternative terms, the ways they are used, and who tends to use them.

Reclaiming Labels

Imagine that you run into a deli to pick up some lunch. As you wait for your sandwich, you gaze up at the flat-screen television on the wall just in time to see the national news footage of an LGBTQ+ Pride Parade that took place the day before. The words scrolling on the bottom of the screen tell you that the "Dykes on Bikes" opened the festivities. You have your sandwich and are going to get on with your day. Is it okay for you, now that you've seen this story on the national news, to use the word **dyke**? The answer to the question is: it depends. If you identify with this label, then, yes, you can use it. If you do not identify with this label, then in most cases, it is not okay for you to use it unless you are referring to the news story and mention that you saw the footage about "Dykes on Bikes." At this point, you may be confused, so consider this explanation.

In 2014 Brian Taylor, an Australian football (soccer) commentator, referred to a football player as a *poofter,* a British derogatory term for a gay man. Some people were outraged, and others wondered why Taylor's use of the term was so awful because some gay men use the word *poofter* to refer to themselves. The journalist Nic Holas addressed the issue: "The 'reclaiming' of derogatory slurs by minorities is a longstanding coping mechanism. It's something we do to rid those words of their power, a power that is held over us by anyone who uses them. Every time we take back that word and use it in a positive way to collectively describe ourselves, it waters down the negative effects."[25] Not only does reclaiming a slur help reduce the negative effect, it can actually *empower* or help individuals or a community feel that they are able to take control and make the derogatory word their own.

The words you will explore in this section are just a few of the terms that people within the LGBTQ+ community have, as marginalized people, taken back. As you study these terms, it is important to understand their etymology and why they can still do great harm to someone. A reclaimed word used by someone outside the community can still feel uncomfortable, even if the intention is not to be hurtful. And, of course, these reclaimed words can still be used in purposely hurtful ways as hate speech.

Fairy

Have you seen or read *Peter Pan?* Even if you haven't, you're probably familiar with the story of the boy who never wanted to grow up. You probably also remember Tinker Bell, who is a fairy. The oldest definitions of *fairy* referred to people with supernatural or magical powers. By the 1600s Shakespeare was using *fairy* to denote a woman who is a powerful enchantress. By 1895, though, the *Journal of American Psychology* used *fairy* negatively to mean an effeminate gay man.[26] Note that this sudden negative connotation not only took power away from fairies, but also assumed that gay men must be feminine.

The term **fairy** has been reclaimed within part of the LGBTQ+ community, specifically the counterculture group called the Radical Faeries, who have a global network of members; they focus on spirituality and empowerment. Radical Faerie culture was particularly proactive during the first decade of the AIDS epidemic in the United States. The Radical Faeries held support groups and published articles on the need for kindness, love, and compassion for people who were suffering with AIDS.[27] Outside the LGBTQ+ community, though, *fairy* is still a hurtful word.

Dyke

Outside the LGBTQ+ community, the word *dyke* is often used as a derogatory term for lesbians or women who are seen as "too masculine"—that is, women who are not following societal rules about femininity. The origins of this meaning of *dyke* are obscure; however, an actual dyke or dike refers to a ditch or a wall.

The LGBTQ+ community has embraced *dyke* in several ways. Alison Bechdel's cartoon strips following a group of friends entitled *Dykes to Watch Out For* became a huge hit in the LGBTQ+ community in the 1980s. In 2003 the San Francisco chapter of Dykes on Bikes, which is famous for starting off the San Francisco Pride Parade, sued a Wisconsin woman who was attempting to trademark the name "Dykes on Bikes" for a new clothing company. The San Francisco–based chapter went to court to trademark the phrase "Dykes on Bikes" so that it can be used only as it was originally created. The lawsuit was a success, and now you will see the phrase trademarked as Dykes on Bikes®. Please note, however, that when someone outside the community shouts "Dyke!" at a person, the word can feel like an attack.[28]

Beyond Dykes on Bikes®, the word *dyke* has often been reclaimed by women of color, particularly African American women who prefer women romantically and/or sexually. As I mentioned earlier, some people are uncomfortable with the word *lesbian* because it feels too political. For many women of color, *lesbian* also feels too white and *exclusionary* (that is, it makes people feel unwelcome). Even though the early feminist movement was very homophobic, lesbians were still an integral part of the movement, which often excluded women of color and working-class women of all ethnic and racial backgrounds. In contrast, *dyke,* when reclaimed, can be a strong, powerful, and empowering word.

Even words or terms that are meant to be inclusive and empowering can be perceived as exclusionary. For example, some people avoid using the Western-centric abbreviation LGBTQ+ because it excludes and underscores long and deep histories of colonial and imperial violence. For example, here is what Valerie Mason-John, a woman of African descent who grew up in England, writes about the word *lesbian:* "I felt repulsed. It was like someone was saying I had a disease. The word looked so clinical. . . . I soon became a dyke—I liked that term. . . . Dyke derived from the American word 'bulldyke,' and . . . the word probably came from the African American culture because the word appeared in blues songs of the 1930s."[29]

Queer

As we've seen, LGBTQ+ people have reclaimed some of the derogatory words that are hurled at them. Meanwhile, other words are so horrible and hurtful that many still feel that they cannot be reclaimed. One reclaimed word that causes great confusion is *queer*. For some people, it is still offensive and hurtful. For others, it feels defiant and empowering. In some places, queer studies is an academic discipline. Despite the reclaiming, the word can still be thrown around in a violent way, so proceed with caution.

Queer in its historic context means "odd" or "weird." Perhaps in one of your literature courses in high school or college you had to read something from the nineteenth century, and it is very likely that you stumbled on the word *queer*. In that context, it meant something was "different" or "not normal." For example, a "queer-looking" carriage simply meant that the carriage appeared different or odd compared to other carriages. However, you can probably also see the ways that the word, when used to describe people, evolved into an adjective used to describe homosexuals. *Queer* goes back to the homosexual/heterosexual dichotomy, where heterosexual equals "normal" and homosexual means "odd," "different," or "queer."

Within the LGBTQ+ community, *queer* elicits strong feelings, and there is ongoing debate within the community about the term. Remember Greg, the retired police officer and college professor? Here is what he says about "queer."

GREG "'Queer' had such a negative connotation when I was young that I've never been comfortable with it."

Greg's sentiment is not unusual, especially for people who were taunted and tortured by bullies who called them queer. Very often the verbal insult was followed by physical violence.

You might hear someone say that the use and acceptability of *queer* depends on the age of the person—that there is a generational difference. This statement, however, is not necessarily true. For example, let's see what Matt, who, like Greg, is also a college professor in his fifties, has to say about it.

MATT "I no longer feel 'gay' in a mainstream social-political-sexual context. 'Queer' works best for me now as a widely embracing identity."

Matt and Greg belong to the same generation; in fact, Matt is a few years older than Greg. So they were both tortured by being called queer growing up. Greg and Matt are both gay men. Greg finds the term *gay* comfortable at this point in his life, but Matt finds it too confining and prefers the reclaimed word *queer* for its expansive possibilities.

In 1990 a group of political activists (many of them college students, professors, and activists) got tired of the ways that LGBTQ+ people were treated as second-class citizens throughout much of the United States. During that summer, several unusual protests were staged all over the country by a new group, Queer Nation, which formed out of another political group, AIDS Coalition to Unleash Power (ACT UP). Queer Nation sponsored several *be-ins* where people reclaiming the term *queer* went out in public in groups acting visibly queer. For example, in Los Angeles, a large group went to the Beverly Shopping Center wearing homemade Queer Nation T-shirts and made themselves visible by walking around and holding hands. In other cities, other groups of people, also with homemade T-shirts, had kiss-ins in public spaces. The idea was to become visible, to be queer and loud and proud. The people at the original be-ins probably had no idea about the ways that this form of empowerment would catch on fire.

By 1992 various colleges and universities in Europe and North America began offering classes entitled "Queer Literature" and "Queer Political Movements." One of the big reasons that the word *queer* appealed to so many was that it could be used as an umbrella term for anyone and everyone who identified as gay, lesbian, bisexual, and/or transgender, and even for heterosexual allies who did not feel "straight" in a narrow sense. *Queer* pushed beyond the bounds of structural and institutional binaries and became a revolutionary way of theorizing and learning. To this day, particularly in Great Britain, Europe, and parts of North America, queer studies is a respected field of academic inquiry. Numerous scholars and professors who are not gay or lesbian work in the field.

Let's look at three stories that help exemplify the expansiveness of this reclaimed and empowering term. First, let's read a bit more about Mia's identity. She is the trans woman who grew up in the small Texas town where everyone assumed that because she was feminine and because she was assigned male at birth, she must be gay.

 **MIA** "I identify as a queer and trans young white woman. When I went to speak in public comment at City Hall in San Francisco for the first time as a homeless queer and trans youth, I wore a dress, red lipstick, with a dash of facial hair that I left visible to make a statement that people should be respected whatever their gender expression."

Mia's queerness is part of her rejection of the gender binary and the homosexual/heterosexual binary. It gave her a source of strength that helped her advocate for herself when she was homeless. At this time, Mia is working on a master's degree in public health at a small liberal arts college; she was recently awarded a prestigious scholarship that will cover all her schooling. Her being out as a queer trans woman has given her strength to be herself, and her goal is to help other disadvantaged urban youth.

Remember Deirdre? She is in her fifties and discussed her identity as a bisexual woman who now feels the term *pansexual* fits better. For the past twenty years, Deirdre has been in a committed relationship with a man. Here is what she says about being queer.

 DEIRDRE "It's my openness to possibility that I want to wear on my sleeve, not who I actually have sex with. Because even in my current state as a functionally monogamous partner in a heterosexual (but not heteronormative) relationship, I am still queer."

Mia and Deirdre discuss the term *queer* as one that they each personally embrace; let's examine the ways that Austin explores *queer* both as an individual experience and as a broad unifying identity.

 AUSTIN "I originally came out as a gay male in my early teens, but then began identifying as queer in my early twenties. There is no pre-scribed experience of being queer; however, a lot of the truth about identity lies in the shared experiences of the community. Queerness is about a collective identity that brings together those who don't fall into normative identities or sexual categories. It gains power through togetherness. I have been to too many gay bars that vilify lesbians, women, or trans people; I have been to too many lesbian bars that vilify men or trans people. Under the queer umbrella, rather than approaching a safe space as a zone of exclu-sion based on differences, we need to understand that we are sharing an overarching experience based on sexual identity in a world that already vilifies us enough."

Austin points to the ways that the word *queer* can be empowering and notes that the use of the term can go beyond binaries and toward community building.

As we move through the twenty-first century, perhaps *queer* will become the truly positive and empowering umbrella term that Austin envisions. At this moment, though, we need to remember that a person's geographic location plays an important role in our understanding of the word *queer*. Just as most of the Queer Nation be-ins in the 1990s were in urban centers, at least in the United States, it still holds true that *queer* is viewed in a very different light in Boise, Idaho, or Lexington, Kentucky, from the way it is in San Francisco or New York. And even in San Francisco and New York there is still a sense of unease with using *queer* as an umbrella term; it is also important to note that many trans people do not feel comfortable with the term *queer*.

Reclaiming Identities: Global Contexts and Problems with LGBTQ+ as Western Eurocentric

In the 1996 Indian film, *Fire*, Sita and Radha, two women married to men in arranged marriages, are thrown together by circumstance. They fall in love with each other. Sita and Radha know they are in love, but they also talk to each other about the fact that there is no specific word that describes their kind of love.[30] As you read this paragraph, you may be thinking that Sita and Radha are bisexual or lesbian. But these words often do not feel comfortable to people outside a Western (Anglo-European and U.S.) context. Yet LGBTQ+ is the global acronym. What is important about global language? What is the problem with it?

We often think of LGBTQIQAA (Lesbian, Gay, Bisexual, Transgender, Queer, Intersex (DSD), Questioning, Asexual, and Ally) as the most universal and all-encompassing way to discuss people whose gender identity and/or expression and/or sexual orientation are in a minority. You might often see this "alphabet soup" simplified to LGBT, LGBTI, LGBTQ, LGBTQ+ (the current and most commonly used acronym), particularly in the United States, or LGBTQ2+, particular to Canada and honoring Two-Spirit people.

Have you seen the rainbow flag, which is generally known around the world as a symbol of LGBTQ+ pride? Did you know it was created by a group of people in San Francisco?[31] While something related to LGBTQ+ pride coming from San Francisco might not be a surprise to you, what you might find remarkable is walking into Gin Gin's LGBTQ+ bookstore in Taipei and seeing rainbow flags. If you look at the LGBTQ+ groups struggling to make change in Uganda, you will see that they also use the rainbow flag. Truly, the rainbow flag has come to indicate LGBTQ+ safe spaces around the world.

If there is a global symbol or global abbreviation (LGBTQ+), then everyone must be happy with it, right? The answer depends on context. As an example, let's look at a true story. In February 2014 John Abdallah Wambere (his nickname is Longjones—pronounced "Long Johns") traveled to the United States as an invited guest to give several talks about healthcare issues in Uganda. Longjones was a cofounder of Spectrum Uganda Initiatives, which is an LGBTQ+ rights group focused on health education. In his beloved home country of Uganda, the umbrella term that people use among themselves is not queer or LGBTQ+ but rather **kuchu,** which encompasses anyone and everyone who is not a cisgender heterosexual person. Uganda has some strict antihomosexuality laws that target LGBTQ+ people; the law may be anti*homosexual,* but it also includes anti-transgender policies. Family members who are not LGBTQ+ but who do not turn in a loved one who is LGBTQ+ can also be prosecuted under Ugandan law. At home, Longjones uses the word *kuchu,* but on his tour of the United States, he needed to use LGBTQ+ because of his audience. In the United States people may not have known what *kuchu* means. Beyond this issue of ideas that can get "lost in translation," something else completely unexpected and life-changing happened to Longjones.

One morning in Boston, Longjones woke up and found several text messages from friends and colleagues in Uganda. The message was clear: if he came back to Uganda, he was going to be killed because of his work in the HIV/AIDS-prevention clinics and with Spectrum Uganda. At that moment, Longjones's life forever changed. He needed to seek *asylum* in the United States—that is, he had to ask for permanent refuge in a country that is not his home country because his life would be in danger upon returning home. Longjones's safety depended on his knowing a universal LGBTQ+ language (including the meaning of the symbolic rainbow flag) to help him find immediate legal help and begin the legal process of seeking asylum.

In September 2014 Longjones was granted asylum in the United States. Indeed, one of his close Ugandan friends, David Kato, who had also been active in LGBTQ+ (*kuchu*) rights work, had been murdered because he was *kuchu*.[32] Do you think Longjones's story has a happy ending? How will he experience life in the United States as a gay man who is African? How will he cope with the fact that he will never be able to go back home and see his daughter or his friends? In "Writings from the Community" at the end of Chapter 7, you will read the answers in his own words.[33]

Why does Uganda have such strict laws that criminalize LGBTQ+ people? You might be wondering if that is "just the way it is," or if intolerance is an innate part of Ugandan culture. It is not; however, a complex and violent history accounts for the Ugandan government's treatment of people who are *kuchu*. **Colonialism** refers to a situation in which a group of people move into a place that is not their country or culture of origin. Instead of moving in and becoming part of the existing culture, though, the colonizers take over the local culture through imperialism. **Imperialism** refers to a policy of extending a country's power and influence through force and sometimes (but rarely) diplomacy. Imperialism ultimately attempts to eradicate the original culture. Under colonialism and imperialism, many of the original inhabitants are killed or imprisoned. Over generations, native cultural practices, religions, laws, and languages are made invisible and often nearly forgotten.

The strict anti-*kuchu* laws in Uganda are not originally African laws or Ugandan laws. Great Britain colonized Uganda and turned it into part of the vast British Empire. Starting in 1862, British explorers became interested in eastern Africa and the area that we know today as Uganda. Officially, the British fully colonized the area from 1888 to 1962.[34] Today Uganda is its own country. The British have been successfully kicked out. Interestingly, though, the old British laws that criminalized LGBTQ+ people are still followed in Uganda—*even though modern laws in Great Britain are much more accepting of LGBTQ+ people.* But when Great Britain tried to step in and argue against Uganda's Anti-Homosexuality Act, the Ugandan government did not listen because of the country's long history of being violently abused at the hands of the British colonial government. This explanation does not help people like Longjones, David Kato, or anyone else in the *kuchu* community; however, it does provide a historical context. You will have an opportunity to explore these historical global issues surrounding imperialism and colonialism in Chapter 7.

People in other countries that have been victimized by violent imperialism often find that LGBTQ+ still feels too "English" or "American." They are suspicious because the last time they had significant interactions with Western cultures, they lost their own rich cultures, many of which openly embraced people of various sexual orientations and gender identities. At the end of this chapter, you will find a list of words that come from diverse cultures. These words, like *kuchu,* are either newly invented words that are used instead of LGBTQ+ or ancient terms that were used for people outside a gender binary and across the sexual orientation spectrum, including various modes of heterosexuality. In many places the ancient terms are being reclaimed. As you learn about these words, keep in mind that many cultures did not have distinct terms for gender identity, gender expression, and sexual orientation. Rather, there was often one umbrella word like *kuchu.* The use of one word can be confusing because it is not clear whether it is being used to denote someone who is transgender or someone who is gay, or someone who is gay and transgender or heterosexual and gender nonconforming.

In Chapter 3 we will turn our focus to the *sexologists,* scientists who wanted to classify everyone and everything. For now, please read on for Andrea Jenkins's poetic take on sexual orientation and gender identity in her poem "Blues for SOGI," and Austin Mantele's short story "Deb," which depicts a creative nine-year-old.

WRITINGS FROM THE COMMUNITY

ANDREA JENKINS

Blues for SOGI [35]

In 2017 Andrea Jenkins became the first African American transgender woman to be elected to the city council of a major city. She now proudly represents Ward 8 of Minneapolis, Minnesota. Andrea is an artist-activist and award-winning poet and writer. She has been awarded fellowships from the Bush Foundation, Intermedia Arts, and the Playwrights Center and has won writing and performance grants and scholarships from the Givens Foundation, Intermedia Arts, the Loft, the Napa Valley Writers Conference, and Pillsbury House Theater. Andrea is the cocurator of Queer Voices at Intermedia Arts (the longest-running series of its kind in the nation) and, in 2018, completed several years' worth of work collecting oral histories from hundreds of people in the upper Midwest transgender community as an oral historian in the Jean-Nickolaus Tretter Collection in Gay, Lesbian, Bisexual, and Transgender Studies.

Andrea is the author of three chapbooks of poems and a full-length book of poetry, The "T" Is NOT Silent: New and Selected Poems. *She has been published in several anthologies, including* Gender Outlaws Two: The Next Generation; When We Become Weavers: Queer Female Poets on the Midwestern Experience, *edited by Kate Lynn Hibbard;* The Naked I: Wide Open *and* The Naked I: Inside Out, *edited by 20% Theater; and most recently* Gay, Lesbian, Bisexual, and Transgender Civil Rights: A Public Policy Agenda for Uniting a Divided America, *edited by Wallace Swan. She was also a contributor to the widely acclaimed anthology* Blues Vision, *edited by Alexs Pate, Pamela Fletcher, and J. Otis Powell! (Minnesota Historical Society Press, 2015), as well as the anthology* A Good Time for the Truth, *edited by Sun Yung Shin (Minnesota Historical Society Press, 2016). To learn more about her, visit http://andreajenkins.webs.com.*

> Dear SOGI,
>
> How they mistreated you
> In a time that at the time was considered magical
>
> Enlightened even,
> But you and I know different

The tired debate
Marriage is between a man and a woman

SOGI, cultural weaver, soul talker
Digital alchemist, always taking the temperature

Looking for the right moment
To strike the iron while it's

Hot, it's always hot SOGI
I love you for that . . .

Make moves, make it happen SOGI
You didn't dare dream this

Forty years ago, darkened windows
At Stonewall, coded movies where you were always the villain

Buggery laws, unveiled threats
Against life and limb,
Shocked by the therapy

What up,   Son?
The boys on the block believed you were one of them

You knew different, you knew truth telling
Would become the characteristic you'd

Become closely associated with
But before that it was "be careful who you associate with"

That one dude, went on the road to HOWL[36]
Him and a couple of other cats

Frank O'Hara[37] kept it real cool
Langston[38] too, we cried for you yesterday

In a workshop where we discussed identity politics
And Black Feminist Freedom Fighters
Oh Audre[39]—where did the power come from
Love was never about easy,

But doesn't it supposed to feel good
Entertaining angels after midnight

Now you're wounded, spent up
Perhaps you should have been a legend
A martyr, maybe you should have done more than survived?

AUSTIN MANTELE

Deb

Austin Mantele is a writer living in New York City working on a novel and a television series. After years of scraping rock bottom, he got his act together while working at vintage stores in San Francisco and attending City College of San Francisco. After deciding to pursue his academic interests full-time, he moved to Manhattan to complete his bachelor's degree at Columbia University. He is currently enrolled in their creative writing MFA program and is also teaching undergraduate academic writing.

As a nine-year-old boy, I used to play "Deb"—a fortysomething diner waitress with hairspray-glazed tresses and a scratchy Long Island twang. Deb was sassy, boisterous, tenderly crude. I reveled in her unapologetic candor, her immunity to others' glares.

Deb's garments were finely constructed from pastel-colored paper, glitter, and glue. The suburban California classroom was her diner—Your Friend Deb's Place. Bubble-gum pink countertops, black-and-white tiled floors, mint green booths, and matching jukeboxes replaced the classroom's beige desks and tables every afternoon during arts and crafts. With a notepad in hand, she asked her valued customers whether they wanted a tuna melt or a vanilla milkshake adorned with a cherry. Some classmates would answer in laughter; most would ignore her. She eventually settled on a simpler name for the diner—Deb's Joint—after several customers complained that they did not consider Deb a "friend."

"Ya want fries with that, hon?" Deb asked a classmate with a buzz cut one afternoon. I had spent the morning constructing a new uniform for her shift. A construction paper skirt of bone shapes and spidery threads hung from her waist. Her loose-fitting paper bra was covered in pools of dried glue and streaks of silver glitter. Buzz Cut didn't answer as she hovered around his seat. He refused to look up at her: a personal pet peeve of Deb's. She leaned over, tapping her fingers near his box of crayons.

"No," Buzz Cut muttered, scowling as he resumed coloring. Deb looked down to see a brightly colored drawing of a brawny soldier tearing off another soldier's arm. "Go away."

"We don't have all day," Deb tapped her fingers faster, imagining the sound of long acrylic nails clacking on the table's surface. "I'm tryin' to run a business here, toots."

Buzz Cut leaned over to another classmate—a boy in a blue baseball cap—and whispered something. They both laughed.

"Can you believe these kids, Sam?" Deb asked her only friend and employee, Samantha. "They come to a diner and don't know if they want our world-famous fries!"

Samantha was at the opposite side of the craft table, taking orders in a paper uniform almost identical to Deb's. There were more orders scribbled on her notepad—the customers loved Samantha's service.

"My dad said you shouldn't talk to us," Buzz Cut announced to Deb as he continued to color. She looked down to see blood pouring from his illustrated soldiers. "He told us not to hang out with you."

"Not like we would anyway," Ball Cap added.

"I don't know your Pop," Deb laughed, pretending to loudly chew gum. "Bet he's a real charmer."

The two boys looked up, leering at Deb like a stubborn grease stain that refused to be scrubbed clean from her diner apron. Deb looked around to see customers staring. Pointed conversations quietly erupted around the craft table. Teacher rose from her desk.

"Everyone knows there's something wrong with you," Ball Cap blurted out, baring his remaining baby teeth as he spoke. "The parents talk about it after baseball practice."

"That's why you're not allowed to our houses!" Buzz Cut jeered.

Teacher began walking toward Deb.

"Listen to how you talk," Ball Cap added. "And who plays waitress?"

"Are they giving you trouble again, Deb?" Samantha shouted from across the table.

I stared down at Buzz Cut's drawing of guns, explosions, mangled soldiers, and bloody entrails as customers began to laugh. My face became flushed, pricked with embarrassment. Laughter ripped across the table as more joined in, pointing at Deb with crayons, chewed pencils, and craft scissors. Buzz Cut grabbed at her skirt. Ball Cap pulled at her bra strap.

"Not in my damn diner!" Deb shouted as she slapped Ball Cap across the face with her notepad.

Teacher asked Deb to stay after school for a conference. Parents were called.

Held captive in her own restaurant, she watched as Teacher wiped the dusty chalkboard, opened the blinds, and rearranged chairs. Deb stared at posters on the wall of determined rock climbers, celebratory track stars, and a terrified cat clinging to a lonely branch. Quotes like "Be Anything You Want!" and "Hang in There, Baby!" accompanied the images. Counselor arrived, instructing Deb to sit down in a plastic blue desk in the center of the room. Parents rushed in. Everyone sat in a circle around my desk. Everyone stared in dismay at the paper scraps exquisitely draped from Deb's body. Everyone hated Deb.

"We need to talk about Deb," Teacher announced, gripping my shoulder. "Again."

"We've gone over this," Counselor sighed. "Do we need to take away the construction paper?"

"No!" Deb pleaded, staring past the adults and into the eyes of the struggling cat on the branch. "Deb isn't just construction paper. She just happens to look good in it."

"Honey," Mother chimed in. "Remember what we told you last week when you made a bikini?"

"We just want what's best," Counselor interrupted. "Boys don't play 'waitress' or wear bikinis." Deb imagined the branch cracking, splintering from existence under the cat's claws.

"Have you considered football?" Teacher asked both parents. "Or baseball?"

Father took a deep breath. "He's enrolled in both."

Counselor stood up and walked toward the chalkboard. Teacher approached the desk. Deb watched as Teacher opened the desk drawer, removing a pair of scissors. Chalk pierced the blackboard as Counselor drew a thick line down the center.

"We should also talk about . . ." Counselor paused, continuing to drag the white stick down the black surface. "Speech classes."

"We've discussed that." Father took a deep breath. "The kids at baseball give him a hard time about sounding too feminine."

Teacher fondled a pair of scissors. "A speech class before puberty would help."

The parents nodded at Teacher and Counselor, refusing to look at Deb. I felt a searing flush blossom across their faces, a deep burn upon their cheeks. Everyone was ashamed of Deb.

Counselor turned around at the chalkboard, staring through Deb and into me. Teacher circled her finger across the tip of the scissors. Father placed his arm around Mother.

"I'm going to name some things and I want you to tell me what side you think they go on. Everything on the right side is encouraged for a boy your age," Counselor said as she tapped the right side of the chalkboard. "Everything on the left is not."

"Okay," Deb resumed her gravelly East Coast accent. "Sure, hon."

"Stop that!" Mother snapped at Deb. "Please."

"I'm sorry." A dense silence hung in the air.

"Ready?" Counselor continued. "Where do you think construction paper bikinis go?"

Deb watched as Teacher slid her thumb and index finger into the scissor rings, opening and shutting the blades repeatedly. Deb kneaded her bra anxiously.

"Where?" Counselor's tone grew sharper.

"Nowhere," I replied.

Counselor's glance cut deep from across the room. "No," she sighed. "Bikinis—paper or otherwise—always go on the left side." Deb watched as she wrote "bikinis" on the left side of the impenetrable chalk line.

"What about playing 'waitress'?" Teacher asked from her seat. She moved her finger along the scissor's outer blade while scanning the meticulously trimmed lines of Deb's bra. "Which side is that on?"

"I don't know." I fidgeted with Deb's bra. Sweat dripped from my fingers, wilting the straps. The once-vibrant pastel-colored paper dampened into a sickly gray.

"Yes, you do!" Father shouted.

Deb watched as Counselor wrote "waitress" on the left side of the board. She went over the stiff, straight letters repeatedly, the chalk crumbling slowly against the stubborn black surface. A loud snap cut through the room as the chalk broke in two.

"What should we do about him?" Father asked Teacher. "We're at a loss."

"Last month, we bought him roller blades to play hockey," Mother interrupted. "But he ended up playing 'figure skater' with Samantha."

"He was playing figure skater here too," Counselor sighed, returning to her seat in the circle. "In a paper tiara."

"The boys won't spend time with him," Teacher added. "We've tried encouraging them to be a good influence."

"We know," Mother replied.

"Have you taken him to see someone?" Counselor asked. Everyone began speaking as if I wasn't there.

"Yes," Father answered. "But he wasn't on our side."

"Well." Counselor quickly stood up. "What should we do?"

"I know a boarding school that has been known to help cases like his," Teacher announced, lightly tapping the scissors against her chair. "It might be worth considering."

A bead of cold sweat dripped down my forehead. Deb was under siege. The adults fired barbed glances at Deb as they discussed military school and therapy. I imagined Deb as one of Buzz Cut's soldiers—mutilated, torn limb from limb, innards spilling on the diner floor.

"What do you want to do about this?" Father sharply turned his head toward me. A disdainful smile emerged on the adults' faces as they collectively turned to Deb. Teacher's scissors continued to tap faster against the chair like machine gun fire.

Deb's bra flitted through my fingers. My breathing became more hurried, disjointed. Would we have this meeting every year? I asked myself. Every class?

For how long? I pictured foam forming in the corners of the adults' curled mouths, threats seething between their lips.

"Deb!" I envisioned Teacher standing up, pointing her pair of scissors at the beloved waitress. "Get Deb!"

"Get her!" I imagined a chorus of classmates' parents shouting as they stormed the diner. I could hear a mob gather outside. Buzz Cut, Ball Cap, and the other students crowded the window. Eager faces fought to breathe on the glass and write "Kill Deb!" with their fingers.

An image of everyone rising in unison—scissors in hand, fiery eyes, thin strands of saliva hanging from their teeth as they smiled—slowly unfurled through my mind. They approached Deb from each side, gliding their shears across her chest and legs.

"Kill Deb!" everyone chanted—their voices becoming louder, more unified in purpose. "Kill Deb!"

Visions of steel blades cutting through the construction paper, grazing my bare skin underneath ambushed my thoughts. Blades furiously sliced up into Deb's bra straps, sliding back down to her skirt. Inner shears tore through her voice, puncturing her accent. Uneven strands of Deb's hair fell to the ground in jagged clumps. Thumbs and fingers jutted through the scissor eye rings, carving away at Deb's frame. Shreds of her clothes dropped to the diner floor. Classmates swung baseball bats, smashing the diner windows. Streams of gasoline coated the black-and-white tile as everyone began emptying cans inside. Deb's Joint burst into careless conflagration, flames devouring the jukeboxes, booths, tables, and menus.

I began to perspire, gripping the soggy edges of Deb's clothing. I walked backward toward the chalkboard. Mother, Father, and Counselor rose from their chairs in confusion. Teacher soon followed, leaving her scissors on the desk. Everyone approached me—tentatively, as if walking on a blanket of broken diner glass. I continued to step backward until the back of my head hit the chalkboard.

"What's wrong, buddy?" Father asked, cautiously extending his hand. "We're just trying to help."

Counselor nodded, "We're just looking out for you!"

Shards of chalk rolled under my palms as I grasped the ledge of the board. My eyes darted around the room, afraid they would begin dismantling Deb—thread by thread, limb from limb. Visions of Deb retired on a provincial porch somewhere in the woods—voluminous gray hair, uneven lipstick, unshaven legs, frayed glitter bra—materialized when I closed my eyes. I imagined Deb waving good-bye as the surrounding shrubbery consumed her hideaway.

"Honey?" Mother said, reaching for my shoulder. "Talk to us."

Deb's clothing shook between my fingers as I began tugging at the seams. I dug my fingers into Deb's damp bra, tearing the straps from my body. They can't kill Deb, I thought. I won't let them. The sound of torn paper filled the room as I hurled the discarded fragments of her uniform to the floor. I pulled her skirt from my hips, nails sinking into the sodden paper. My hands trembled as I shredded the garment into paltry, unrecognizable pieces. Glitter, glue, food orders, fragments of waistbands, bra straps, necklines floated to the classroom floor. A pile of Deb's remains sat at my feet. I buried my face into my clammy, chalk-covered hands.

I felt Mother's hand caress my shoulders. Father wanted a high five. Counselor cracked a smile. I raised my head to see that I surrendered—sweating, shaking—on the right side of the chalkboard line.

Key Concepts

asexual (p. 55)
bisexual (p. 53)
celibacy (p. 55)
colonialism (p. 69)
cultural norms (p. 48)
dyke (p. 62)
fairy (p. 63)
gay (p. 57)
heteronormativity (p. 49)
heterosexism (p. 48)
heterosexual (p. 47)
homophobia (p. 58)
homosexual (p. 46)
imperialism (p. 69)
kuchu (p. 68)
lesbian (p. 60)
misogyny (p. 58)
pansexual (p. 54)
queer (p. 64)
sapphic (p. 60)
sexology (p. 46)
sexual abstinence (p. 55)
sexuality (p. 45)
sexual orientation (p. 45)

Activities, Discussion Questions, and Observations

1. Both Andrea Jenkins and Austin Mantele use a creative forum to explore the intersection and blending of gender identity and sexual orientation. Andrea refers to several historic moments and people in her poem. Pick something or someone from her poem that you are not familiar with and research their importance in the poem as well as in LGBTQ+ culture.

2. Austin's story ends with "Deb" crossing over the chalkboard line. How do you interpret what happened to the nine-year-old? The parents and the school authorities seem to be quite worried about "Deb." What do you think is at the heart of their concern? Have you witnessed an incident like this in your past? Have you had this happen to you? Have you been like the boys who make fun of "Deb"? Have you been like the one friend who sticks by "Deb"?

3. For this exercise, think about your childhood. Whom did you live with as you were growing up? Whom do you consider your family? Think about any discussions you had concerning sexuality or sexual orientation as you were growing up. Was the subject approached in your home? If so, how was it approached? Were certain assumptions made? Did you ask questions? If so, what kinds of questions did you ask? (This can be a private journal exercise, an in-class writing exercise that is submitted to the instructor, or a small-group discussion.)

4. This is a small-group, in-class presentation. Students are in small groups of three or four. You will either choose a country together or pick one randomly. As a group, you will research the country's laws concerning LGBTQ+ people. Is it illegal or legal to be LGBTQ+ in the country? What legal protections are afforded to LGBTQ+ people? Are LGBQ people treated differently under the law than trans and/or people with DSD? You will want to consider marriage laws as well as adoption laws in your chosen country. Each group will give a ten-minute presentation to the class at a "Model United Nations."

5. Choose an advertisement from a magazine or a commercial on television. What assumptions about people are being made? Did you see any links being made between sex, gender, sexuality, and sexual orientation?

6. As part of a journal activity, write about a time when you had to come out to friends, family, or loved ones about something that you felt afraid/ashamed/worried/different about. Your experience may have nothing to do with your sexual orientation or your gender identity (or it might), but it should be something you were afraid to tell others because you were afraid of being

judged for it. What did you worry about before telling other people? (This journal activity can also be a class discussion.)

7. Explore at least one of the definitions for people of various sexual orientations that have not been used in more formal or more medical language. Some of the words are more positive while some are negative. If you research the full etymology of the word, you may be surprised where it first came from and how it has evolved over time. Here is a list of words, some of which were covered in this chapter; feel free to come up with others: *AC/DC, ace, Bilitis, bulldagger, dyke, fag, fairy, fruit, joto/a, kathoey, kuchu, maricón, pansy, pouf, queen, Sapphist, stud*

Film and Television of Interest

Against the Law (2017, U.K., 84 minutes)
A biography, drama, and history all rolled into one. This film, written by Brian Fillis and Peter Wildeblood, examines a time in the 1950s when Wildeblood was imprisoned for being gay, since homosexuality was illegal in the U.K. at that time. The film includes interviews with elderly gay men in Britain who were arrested under the Criminal Amendment Act (an anti-homosexual law).

Apricot Groves (2016, Armenia, 78 minutes)
This complex and beautifully filmed drama focuses on an Iranian-Armenian young trans man who lives in the United States. He travels to Armenia to propose to his Armenian girlfriend he met in the United States.

(A)sexual (2011, U.S., 75 minutes)
This documentary explores people who are asexual and who face discrimination from other sexual minority communities. The film does an outstanding job of looking at stereotypes about asexual people.

Better Than Chocolate (1999, Canada, 101 minutes)
An entire community of friends composed of lesbians, gay men, heterosexuals, bisexuals, and trans people is the focus of this comedy romance. This Canadian feature film does an outstanding job of looking at a diverse LGBTQ+ community and a parent's acceptance of her daughter's diverse community.

Big Eden (2000, U.S., 118 minutes)
Winner of numerous film-festival awards, *Big Eden* looks at an idyllic world in a small Montana town where the entire community wants the gay protagonist, who has returned

home from New York, to be happy. Stereotypes about rural communities being homophobic are overturned in this heartwarming romance.

Boy Meets Girl (2014, U.S., 95 minutes)
Winner of multiple independent film awards, this romantic comedy takes place in rural Kentucky and focuses on a young trans woman who falls in love with a cisgender woman while she also does not realize that her cisgender male best friend is in love with her. The film beautifully navigates gender identities and sexual orientation from bisexual, lesbian, and heterosexual identities.

Cabaret (1972, U.S., 124 minutes)
This iconic film starring Liza Minnelli is a music-filled look at Weimar Berlin, which was a city open to diverse sexual orientations and gender identities before the Nazi Party came to power. *Cabaret* won eight Oscars and three Golden Globes.

Call Me Kuchu (2013, Canada, Uganda, 87 minutes)
This award-winning documentary follows the various iterations of the anti-homosexuality bill in Uganda. Featured in the film are scenes with the late LGBTQ+ activist David Kato and the tireless ally for the community Bishop Christopher Senyonjo. Also featured is John Abdallah Wambere (Longjones), who contributed to "Writings from the Community" in Chapter 7 of this book.

Chavela (2017, U.S., 90 minutes)
Chavela Vargas, a renowned singer, was the lover of the iconic Méxicana artist Frida Kahlo and collaborated with the famous Spanish film director Pedro Almodóvar. This documentary film, which premiered at the 2017 Berlin International Film Festival, looks at her life and her work as a sexual and gender outlaw.

Coming Out in the 1950s (2011, U.S., 15 minutes)
Phil Siegel's first documentary in a series of four explores the lives of people who came out as gay, lesbian, bisexual, and/or transgender in the 1950s. The sexual orientation and/or gender identity of most of the people interviewed in the film was illegal when they first came out of the closet.

Coming Out in the 1960s (2013, U.S., 26 minutes)
This second documentary by Phil Siegel explores the changing times from the 1950s into the 1960s as different people are interviewed about coming out of the closet during the decade of the Civil Rights movement, women's movement, the peace movement, the United Farmworkers' movement, and the beginning of the LGBTQ+ rights movement.

Coming Out in the 1970s (2014, U.S., 16 minutes)

Phil Siegel's third documentary includes him and others who came out of the closet right after the Stonewall Rebellion in New York ushered in the modern-day LGBTQ+ rights movement. The 1970s are seen as a time of fast-paced LGBTQ+ rights, activism, and partying.

Coming Out in the 1980s (2015, U.S., 17 minutes)

Siegel's final documentary in this series includes the author of this textbook. The 1980s were marked by the beginning of the AIDS pandemic and the lack of healthcare and governmental intervention to help those suffering.

Fire (1996, Canada, India, 104 minutes)

Deepa Mehta's groundbreaking lesbian feature film won numerous awards around the world. The film also brought about death threats. *Fire* changed the cinematic landscape for LGBTQ+ film.

Frida (2002, U.S., Canada, Mexico, 123 minutes)

Salma Hayek's Oscar-nominated depiction of the famous bisexual and gender-fluid Mexican artist Frida Kahlo is the subject of this feature-length film. Despite being in constant physical agony after a horrible accident, Frida Kahlo spent her adult life painting. The LGBTQ+ community has embraced her as an icon.

Gazon Maudit (French Twist) (1995, France, 104 minutes)

This French comedy is about a heterosexual couple who invite their neighbor, a lesbian, to move in with them. This film explores stereotypes about rigid definitions of sexual orientation.

God's Own Country (2017, U.K., 104 minutes)

The director Francis Lee delivers a raw and stunning film that takes place in rural England on a sheep farm. The film works on several complex levels as a look at socioeconomics and the struggles of the rural poor who work the land, as well as issues concerning Romanian immigrants. The gay men in the film do not have an urban social life. Rather, they are farmers trying to make ends meet.

Kinsey (2004, U.S., Germany, 118 minutes)

This Oscar-nominated biopic looks at the life of Alfred Kinsey, the sexologist who invented the Kinsey Scale.

Markova: Comfort Gay (2000, U.S., Philippines, 97 minutes)

This film is based on the true story of Walter Dempster Jr., a gay elder who grew up in the Philippines during World War II. This biopic follows Dempster as he grows up with a violent and homophobic brother. Dempster identifies as a gay man, yet he often embraces a female identity. This is a terrific film that looks at the fluidity of gender and sexual orientation.

La Mission (2009, U.S., 117 minutes)
This feature-length drama explores intersecting identities when a conservative Chicano father in a poor inner-city neighborhood finds out that his son is gay. This film was shot on location in San Francisco's Mission District.

Orange Is the New Black (2013–ongoing, television, U.S.)
This award-winning and popular television show about women in prison features Laverne Cox as an African American trans woman. Film and television often use cisgender actors to play the roles of trans people. *Orange Is the New Black* is important because Laverne Cox is a trans woman and a trans advocate.

Paris Is Burning (1990, U.S., 76 minutes)
Jennie Livingston's iconic and controversial documentary won numerous film awards, including Sundance's Grand Jury Prize and the National Society of Film Critics Award. It appears on most Top 10 LGBTQ+ film lists. The film documents the lives of African American and Latinx drag performers in New York City. Some of the people in the film identify as transgender; all the people in the film embody intersecting identities and identify outside a rigid gender binary. An outstanding film that considers race, class, sexual orientation, and gender identity in late twentieth-century America.

Pride (2014, U.K., 119 minutes)
Pride is an uplifting British film that focuses on the 1980s, when a group of gay men and lesbians in London decide to go to Wales and support the miners who are on strike there. At first, the Welsh mining community, which is far more conservative than London, wants nothing to do with the gay men and lesbians. As the film progresses, the connection between socioeconomic oppression and sexual-orientation oppression is made.

Purple Skies: Voices of Indian Lesbians, Bisexuals, and Transmen (2013, India, 67 minutes)
While there is a lot of information on Hijras in India (see Chapter 7 of this book), and a growing amount of information on trans women who do not identify as Hijras, there is very little on trans men. This documentary film focuses on the intersections among lesbians, bisexual women, and trans men in a country with laws that continually fluctuate over issues of LGBTQ+ rights.

Queer as Folk (1999–2000, television, U.K., 10 episodes)
This is an unflinching and groundbreaking queer television show. Before the debut of this show, there had never been a television show that depicted LGBTQ+ people with such raw honesty.

Queer as Folk (2000–2005, television, U.S., 83 episodes)

Because the British version of the series was such a huge success, U.S. television decided to create an American version. This series takes place in Pittsburgh and follows a group of LGBTQ+ friends. The U.S. series lasted for five seasons and won numerous awards.

Sense8 (2015–2018, television, U.S., 24 episodes)

Written and directed by J. Michael Straczynski, Lana Wachowski, and Lilly Wachowski, this Netflix original series beautifully links intersecting identities in a global science fiction drama. Eight people around the globe are part of one another in their thoughts and actions. The show depicts gender identities and sexual orientations in a full spectrum of diversity. A truly unique and stunning television series.

Shinjuku Boys (1995, U.K., Japan, 53 minutes)

This documentary film follows the lives of Shinjuku Boys—young trans men—who work in a nightclub in Tokyo. The Shinjuku Boys discuss the difficulties of dating the young women who come to the club.

States of Grace (2014, U.S., 74 minutes)

This multiple award–winning documentary follows Dr. Grace, an early AIDS activist, doctor, and Buddhist and her family as they struggle with her nearly debilitating car accident that has left her body broken and paralyzed. The film explores physical differences, race, spirituality, and chosen family.

Watermelon Woman (1996, U.S., 90 minutes)

The African American filmmaker Cheryl Dunye's award-winning drama explores contemporary interracial lesbian dating. Dunye also looks at the history of racism in Hollywood through the mammy figure in old films.

Welcome to My Queer Bookstore (2009, Taiwan, 19 minutes)

Larry Tung's short documentary is beautifully researched and filmed in Gin Gin's bookshop in Taipei, Taiwan. The bookstore serves as a gathering place for a very marginalized LGBTQ+ community. The film includes excellent interviews with the bookstore owner and academics who work to make Taiwan less conservative where LGBTQ+ issues are concerned.

NOTES

1. "The Anti-Homosexuality Act, 2014," Uganda, SCRIBD, https://www.scribd.com/document/208880087/Anti-Homosexuality-Act-2014 (accessed 9 July 2017).

2. "Uganda Court Annuls Anti-Homosexuality Law," BBC News, 1 August 2014, www.bbc.com/news/world-africa-28605400 (accessed 10 January 2018).

3. "Sexual Minorities Uganda: Justice and Equality," http://sexualminoritiesuganda.com/ (accessed 9 July 2017). Amnesty International, "Global Day of Action against Uganda's Anti-Homosexuality Bill," 10 February 2014, https://www.amnesty.org/en/press-releases/2014/02/global-day-action-against-uganda-s-anti-homosexuality-bill/ (accessed 9 July 2017).

4. Alan Blinder and Tamar Lewin, "Clerk in Kentucky Chooses Jail over Deal on Same-Sex Marriage," *New York Times,* 3 September 2015, https://www.nytimes.com/2015/09/04/us/kim-davis-same-sex-marriage.html (accessed 9 July 2017).

5. Alastair Jamieson, "Pope: Workers Have 'Human Right' to Refuse Same-Sex Marriage Licenses," *NBC News,* 28 September 2015, www.nbcnews.com/storyline/pope-francis-visits-america/pope-francis-i-understand-anger-catholic-church-sex-abuse-victims-n434681 (accessed 9 July 2017).

6. Pete Williams, "Supreme Court Allows Mississippi Anti-LGBT Law to Stand," *NBC News,* 8 January 2018, https://www.nbcnews.com/feature/nbc-out/supreme-court-allows-mississippi-anti-lgbt-law-stand-n835721 (accessed 10 January 2018).

7. Tanya Lokshina, "Anti-LGBT Violence in Chechnya," Human Rights Watch, 4 April 2017, https://www.hrw.org/news/2017/04/04/anti-lgbt-violence-chechnya (accessed 10 January 2018).

8. *Oxford English Dictionary* online, s.v. "Homosexual," www.oed.com/view/Entry/88110?redirectedFrom=homosexual#eid (accessed 15 October 2015).

9. *American Heritage Dictionary* online, s.v. "Homo," https://www.ahdictionary.com/word/search.html?q=homo (accessed 15 October 2015).

10. Neel Burton, "When Homosexuality Stopped Being a Mental Disorder," *Psychology Today* online, 18 September 2015, https://www.psychologytoday.com/blog/hide-and-seek/201509/when-homosexuality-stopped-being-mental-disorder (accessed 15 October 2015).

11. National Association for Research and Therapy of Homosexuality (NARTH), "Reparative Therapy," www.religioustolerance.org/hom_nart.htm (accessed 15 October 2015).

12. Movement Advancement Project, "Conversion Therapy Laws," www.lgbtmap.org/equality-maps/conversion_therapy (accessed 10 January 2018).

13. *Oxford English Dictionary* online, s.v. "Heterosexual," www.oed.com/view/Entry/86515?redirectedFrom=heterosexual#eid (accessed 15 October 2015).

14. *Oxford English Dictionary* online, s.v. "Hetero," www.oed.com/view/Entry/86423?rskey=0hGcFX&result=2#eid (accessed 15 October 2015).

15. "Heterosexism Fact Sheet," Scribd, https://www.scribd.com/document/349803848/heterosexism-fact-sheet (accessed 9 June 2018).

16. Lawrence et al. v. Texas, Cornell University Law School, Legal Information Institute, SCOTUS: https://www.law.cornell.edu/supct/html/02-102.ZS.html (accessed 9 July 2017).

17. "Where Is It Illegal to Be LGBT+?" http://stop-homophobia.com/where-is-being-gay-illegal (accessed 9 July 2017).

18. Kinsey Institute, "The Kinsey Scale," https://www.kinseyinstitute.org/research/publications/kinsey-scale.php (accessed 15 October 2015).

19. *Oxford English Dictionary* online, s.v. "Bisexual," www.oed.com/view/Entry/19448?redirectedFrom=bisexual#eid (accessed 15 October 2015).

20. *Oxford English Dictionary* online, s.v. "Pan," www.oed.com/view/Entry/136646#eid32124866 (accessed 17 October 2015).

21. Kim Ruehl, "Deck The Halls," *ThoughtCo.*, updated 6 March 2017, https://www.thoughtco.com/deck-the-halls-traditional-1322574 (accessed 9 July 2017).

22. *Oxford English Dictionary* online, s.v. "Gay," www.oed.com/view/Entry/77207?rskey=KJwM7R&result=1#eid (accessed 17 October 2015).

23. Gertrude Stein, "Miss Furr and Miss Skeene," in *Stein: Writings, 1903–1932* (New York: Library of America, 1998), 307–312.

24. R. B. Parkinson, *A Little Gay History: Desire and Diversity across the World* (London: British Museum Press, 2013).

25. Nic Holas, "Nic Holas on Why the Gay Community Reclaim Derogatory Words Like 'Poofter,'" news.com.au, 14 July 2014, www.news.com.au/lifestyle/real-life/nic-holas-on-why-the-gay-community-reclaim-derogatory-words-like-poofter/news-story/1462db05ae36d9c4add8976085875a83 (accessed 18 September 2015).

26. *Oxford English Dictionary* online, s.v. "Fairy," www.oed.com/view/Entry/67741?redirectedFrom=fairy#eid (accessed 25 September 2015).

27. "NYC Radical Faeries," http://vintage.radicalfaeries.net/ (accessed 9 July 2017).

28. "Dykes on Bikes," https://www.dykesonbikes.org/history (accessed 1 October 2015).

29. Valerie Mason-John, "What's in a Letter?" in *Queer African Reader,* ed. Sokari Ekine and Hakima Abbas (Dakar, Senegal: Pambazuka Press, 2013), 311.

30. Deepa Mehta, *Fire,* Trial by Fire Films, 1996.

31. Paola Antonelli, "MoMA Acquires the Rainbow Flag," *Inside/Out,* 17 June 2015, https://www.moma.org/explore/inside_out/2015/06/17/moma-acquires-the-rainbow-flag/?utm_campaign=062615a&utm_medium=instagram&utm_source=social (accessed 15 September 2015).

32. MenEngage Alliance, "Condemning David Kato's Murder," *Pambazuka News,* 23 February 2011, https://www.pambazuka.org/activism/condemning-david-katos-murder (accessed 9 July 2017). See also Malika Zouhali-Worrall and Katherine Fairfax Wright, *Call Me Kuchu,* Cinedigm, 2013.

33. Michael K. Lavers, "U.S. Grants Asylum to Prominent Ugandan LGBT Rights Activist," *Washington Blade,* 16 September 2014, www.washingtonblade.com/2014/09/16/u-s-grants-asylum-prominent-ugandan-lgbt-rights-advocate/ (accessed 10 October 2015). John Abdallah Wambere guest-lectured the Introduction to LGBT Studies class at City College of San Francisco in September 2014.

34. History World, "History of Uganda," www.historyworld.net/wrldhis/PlainTextHistories.asp?historyid=ad22 (accessed 27 November 2017).

35. SOGI is an acronym for Sexual Orientation and Gender Identity.

36. The twentieth-century novelist Jack Kerouac's *On the Road* features figures from the Beat movement, including a character based on the poet Allen Ginsberg, whose

1955 poem *Howl* was tried as obscene, in part for its frank depiction of gay sex.

37. Frank O'Hara was a twentieth-century poet and art critic.

38. Langston Hughes, a twentieth-century poet, columnist, and activist, was one of the major figures of the Harlem Renaissance.

39. Audre Lorde, a twentieth-century writer and activist, called herself a "Black Woman Poet Lesbian Mother Lover Teacher Friend Warrior."

BIBLIOGRAPHY

American Heritage Dictionary online. S.v. "Homo." https://www.ahdictionary.com/word/search.html?q=homo. Accessed 15 October 2015.

Amnesty International. "Global Day of Action against Uganda's Anti-Homosexuality Bill." 10 February 2014. https://www.amnesty.org/en/pressreleases/2014/02/global-day-action-against-uganda-s-anti-homosexuality-bill/. Accessed 9 July 2017.

"Anti-Homosexuality Act 2014." Uganda. SCRIBD. https://www.scribd.com/document/208880087/Anti-Homosexuality-Act-2014. Accessed 9 July 2017.

Antonelli, Paola. "MoMA Acquires the Rainbow Flag." *Inside/Out,* 17 June 2015. https://www.moma.org/explore/inside_out/2015/06/17/moma-acquires-the-rainbow-flag/?utm_campaign=062615a&utm_medium=instagram&utm_source=social. Accessed 15 September 2017.

Blinder, Alan, and Tamar Lewin. "Clerk in Kentucky Chooses Jail over Deal on Same-Sex Marriage." *New York Times,* 3 September 2015. https://www.nytimes.com/2015/09/04/us/kim-davis-same-sex-marriage.html. Accessed 9 July 2017.

Burton, Neel. "When Homosexuality Stopped Being a Mental Disorder." *Psychology Today* online, 18 September 2015. https://www.psychologytoday.com/blog/hide-and-seek/201509/when-homosexuality-stopped-being-mental-disorder. Accessed 15 October 2015.

"Dykes on Bikes." https://www.dykesonbikes.org/history. Accessed 1 October 2015.

"Heterosexism Fact Sheet," SCRIBD. https://www.scribd.com/document/349803848/heterosexism-fact-sheet. Accessed 9 June 2018.

History World. "History of Uganda." http://www.historyworld.net/wrldhis/PlainTextHistories.asp?historyid=ad22. Accessed 27 November 2017.

Holas, Nic. "Nic Holas on Why the Gay Community Reclaim Derogatory Words Like 'Poofter.'" news.com.au, 14 July 2014. http://www.news.com.au/lifestyle/real-life/nic-holas-on-why-the-gay-community-reclaim-derogatory-words-like-poofter/news-story/1462db05ae36d9c4add8976085875a83. Accessed 18 September 2015.

Jamieson, Alastair. "Pope: Workers Have 'Human Right' to Refuse Same-Sex Marriage Licenses." *NBC News.* www.nbcnews.com/storyline/pope-francis-visits-america/

pope-francis-i-understand-anger-catholic-church-sex-abuse-victims-n434681. Accessed 9 July 2017.

Kinsey Institute. "The Kinsey Scale." https://www.kinseyinstitute.org/research/publications/kinsey-scale.php. Accessed 15 October 2015.

Lavers, Michael K. "U.S. Grants Asylum to Prominent Ugandan LGBT Rights Activist." *Washington Blade,* 16 September 2014. www.washingtonblade.com/2014/09/16/us-grants-asylum-prominent-ugandan-lgbt-rights-advocate/. Accessed 10 October 2015.

Lawrence et al. v. Texas. Cornell University Law School, Legal Information Institute, SCOTUS. https://www.law.cornell.edu/supct/html/02-102.ZS.html. Accessed 9 July 2017.

Lokshina, Tanya. "Anti-LGBT Violence in Chechnya." Human Rights Watch, 4 April 2017. https://www.hrw.org/news/2017/04/04/anti-lgbt-violence-chechnya. Accessed 10 January 2018.

Mason-John, Valerie. "What's in a Letter?" In *Queer African Reader,* edited by Sokari Ekine and Hakima Abbas, 309–315. Dakar, Senegal: Pambazuka Press, 2013.

Mehta, Deepa. *Fire.* Trial by Fire Films, 1996.

MenEngage Alliance. "Condemning David Kato's Murder." *Pambazuka News,* 23 February 2011. https://www.pambazuka.org/activism/condemning-david-katos-murder. Accessed 9 July 2017.

Movement Advancement Project. "Conversion Therapy Laws." http://www.lgbtmap.org/equality-maps/conversion_therapy. Accessed 10 January 2018.

National Association for Research and Therapy of Homosexuality (NARTH). "Reparative Therapy." www.religioustolerance.org/hom_nart.htm. Accessed 15 October 2015.

"NYC Radical Faeries." http://vintage.radicalfaeries.net/. Accessed 9 July 2017.

Oxford English Dictionary online. www.oed.com/.

Parkinson, R. B. *A Little Gay History: Desire and Diversity across the World.* London: British Museum Press, 2013.

Ruehl, Kim. "Deck The Halls." *ThoughtCo.* Updated 6 March 2017. https://www.thoughtco.com/deck-the-halls-traditional-1322574. Accessed 9 July 2017.

Sexual Minorities Uganda. "Justice and Equality." http://sexualminoritiesuganda.com/. Accessed 9 July 2017.

Stein, Gertrude. "Miss Furr and Miss Skeene." In *Stein: Writings, 1903–1932.* New York: Library of America, 1998, 307–312.

"Uganda Court Annuls Anti-Homosexuality Law." *BBC News,* 1 August 2014. www.bbc.com/news/world-africa-28605400. Accessed 10 January 2018.

Wambere, John Abdallah. Guest lecture, Introduction to LGBT Studies class at City College of San Francisco. September 2015.

"Where Is It Illegal to Be LGBT+?" http://stop-homophobia.com/where-is-being-gay-illegal. Accessed 9 July 2017.

Williams, Pete. "Court Allows Mississippi Anti-LGBT Law to Stand." *NBC News*, 8 January 2018. https://www.nbcnews.com/feature/nbc-out/supreme-court-allows-misissippi-anti-lgbt-law-stand-n835721. Accessed 10 January 2018.

Zouhali-Worrall, Malika, and Katherine Fairfax Wright. *Call Me Kuchu*. Cinedigm, 2013.

CHAPTER 3

Modern Sexology: The Science of Objectification, or the Science of Empowerment?

What a curious thing to be so uptight about. Nature delights in diversity. Why don't human beings?
LOLA COLA*

Key Questions

1. The word normal means different things to different cultures. What does the word normal mean to you?

2. In what situations have you had to fill out a form that asked you to classify yourself in one way or another? What questions were asked? How did filling out this form make you feel?

3. Why is it important to create a scientific field that studies gender identity, gender expression, and sexual orientation?

4. Scientists are supposed to be unbiased; however, they often are not. To what extent do sexologists' own sets of identities matter when they are doing scientific work in the field of sexology?

Chapter Overview

This chapter begins with a look at the very public nineteenth-century (Victorian era, 1837–1901) obsession with people who were seen as different. During the

---

* Lola Cola, in Kate Davis's documentary film *Southern Comfort* (Docurama, 2001). Lola is a trans woman whose partner, Robert Eads, a trans man, died from ovarian cancer in large part because no medical clinic in rural Georgia wanted to provide medical care to a trans person. Robert Eads and his story will be explored in more detail in Chapter 6, which looks at medical access and healthcare for trans people.

Haefele-Thomas, Ardel, *Introduction to Transgender Studies*
dx.doi.org/10.17312/harringtonparkpress/2019.01.itts.003
© 2019 by Harrington Park Press

Victorian age, Italian, German, and British men of science measured bodies, observed actions, and attempted to classify all the differences they saw. Their goal was to create a *taxonomy* of humans around the world; they wanted to create a system to understand humans as diverse living organisms. They ran into trouble early on, however, because they used themselves as the *control group*—that is, the group that represented *normal*. Everything and everyone else was measured against these European men of science.

Part of the burgeoning field of taxonomy was **sexology,** the scientific study of human sexuality. Sexology quickly became controversial, partly because it created the equation that gender presentation equated to sexual orientation. Different groups of people whom the scientists deemed *abnormal* took public issue with the definitions these scientists set forth as absolutes.

This chapter introduces some of the individual sexologists whose ideas and theories about gender and sexual orientation have had a major influence on the ways that trans people are perceived and treated. The sexologists' theories offer insight into the reasons why, to this day, we still conflate gender identity, gender expression, and sexual orientation. The chapter ends with a look at trans people and trans allies in the twentieth and twenty-first centuries. Some of these people work in the field of sexology, but others do not. They have all worked tirelessly to reshape and broaden sexology as a more welcoming and inclusive field of study.

Introduction: Pathologies and Empowerment

Take a moment and think about your body. Can you remember a time when either you or someone else measured some part of your body? Height and weight are very common measurements. You might also have had your waist, chest, arms, and neck measured for a uniform. What if you went to a healthcare provider who measured *everything* on your body? Yes, everything. And what if, during the course of your conversation, you told the medical professional that you prefer lemonade to orange juice? After your doctor has taken all of your measurements, she tells you, quite seriously, that the size of your kneecap and the length of your thumb confirm that you are, in fact, a lemonade drinker. Does this pronouncement sound random and silly?

Now consider this situation instead. The doctor tells you that your sexual orientation and/or your gender identity were revealed by the measurement of your genitals. What would you think of that conclusion? When sexology first began, its practitioners drew these exact conclusions. In fact, the sexologists saw gender identity and gender expression as the signposts of normal and abnormal sexual behavior and sexual thoughts.

Even if you never heard about sexology before beginning this chapter, it is likely that the sexologists influenced the social and cultural ideas that you, your family, your friends, and your community have about gender and sexual orientation. In other words, today's social and cultural stereotypes about gender and sexuality began as perceived "truths from the experts." These stereotypes extend beyond gender and sexuality and often include other stereotypes about race, ethnicity, and class as well as physical, mental, and intellectual ability and differences.

As you read through this chapter, you will notice two different strands in sexological research:

1. Some sexologists write about some forms of sexual orientation, gender identity, and gender expression as **pathologies,** or diseases that affect individuals. These sexologists believe that these pathologies need to be labeled, studied, and cured. In short, these sexologists see any variation from the cisgender heteronormative model (including many sexual practices engaged in by cisgender heterosexuals) as a sickness.

2. Other sexologists write about sexual orientation and gender identity/gender expression as diverse variations in individuals. They believe that these variations need to be labeled, studied, and understood.

Many sexologists fall somewhere between these two groups. Notice, however, that both types of sexologists feel the need to label and study people in the context of sexual orientation and gender identity/gender expression. The two groups diverge in that the first group focuses on *curing* what they understand to be a pathology, whereas the second group sees a need for understanding that also paves the way toward acceptance.

The title of this chapter asks a question: Is sexology the science of *objectifying* people (that is, seeing people as objects or specimens to be studied), or is it the science of *empowerment* (which helps the oppressed achieve self-determination and self-definition)? Perhaps you rejected the binary and answered *both* or *neither*. If so, you are correct.

Let's Relabel That!

The *European Enlightenment,* which began in the eighteenth century, was an important intellectual and philosophical movement that remolded the structure of European society, culture, and thought. The Europeans (German, Dutch, French, English) did not just stay at home and observe themselves; they also traveled around the globe. Of course, the eighteenth-century Europeans were not the first Europeans to travel the world, but the ways they studied, wrote about, and discussed the people and the cultures they encountered were different from those of earlier generations. These global explorations led the eighteenth-century Europeans to encounter people from diverse geographic regions whose culture, religion, and social constructs (particularly with regard to gender identity, gender expression, and sexual orientation) were quite different from conventional European modes of behavior. Travelers often encountered cultures that permitted more fluid gender expressions, which the Europeans read as homosexual and thus abnormal. In other words, the Europeans studied the world through their own lens, which often involved Eurocentric ideas about bodies, sexual expression, laws, and religion.

As a result of their travels, European scientists and philosophers often reclassified and renamed the people, plants, and animals that they encountered, despite the fact that they already had their own names. On some of these voyages, the scientists found people, plants, and animals so different and so unusual that they brought them back to Europe and put them on display at various public events. Chapter 7 of this book focuses on Indigenous cultures around the globe and the devastating ways they were and continue to be ravaged by trips undertaken to gather "scientific information." For the purposes of this chapter, it is important to know that European sexology and its classification system became the dominant ways that sex and gender were measured and understood.

Step Right Up!

The Popularity of Sideshows: Race, Sex, and Gender on Display

How do you feel about speaking in public? Have you ever participated in a school play or sung in a choir? Maybe you've dabbled in karaoke at a party. In these cases, you chose to put yourself on display. Even if you had to present to a group of people as part of a class assignment, you still had some choice in the matter. But how would you feel if you were presented in public for the sole purpose of being on display? You are not singing. You are not acting. You are just sitting there so people can stare at you.

Consider the case of Julia Pastrana, an Indigenous woman born in Mexico in 1834. Pastrana was born with two rare genetic mutations that had no label at the time: "generalized hypertrichosis lanuginosa, which covered her face and body in thick hair, and gingival hyperplasia, which thickened her lips and gums."[1] She died during childbirth in 1860 in Russia. There a Russian scientist embalmed the bodies of Julia and her stillborn son so that Pastrana's husband could continue to display the mummies of his wife and child.[2]

Pastrana was famous throughout Europe, Canada, and the United States. She was paraded around by her husband, a customs administrator who had *purchased* her for the sole purpose of putting her on display as "The Bear Woman," "The Ape Woman," and/or "The Missing Link." Although slavery was outlawed in Mexico at the time, people involved in the circus, which was one of the few safe places for people who were different, were still bought and sold.[3] Scientists as well as the general public flocked to public spaces to see people like Pastrana put on display. After her husband's death, her body was still taken from place to place to be displayed until she wound up in a storage locker in Norway. In 2013, 153 years after Pastrana's death, the visual artist Laura Anderson Barbata, who had studied Pastrana's horrific story, took Pastrana's body back to Mexico for a proper burial.[4]

The tragic story of Julia Pastrana is not an unusual one from the nineteenth century. People flocked to London and the Great Exhibition of 1851, which offered *sideshows* that today would be called *freak shows*. Some of the biggest draws to these events were people who had medical conditions that made them look different from the average person. Popular displays included the thirty-two-year-old Chinese laborer known as Hoo Loo, afflicted with a scrotal tumor that weighed several pounds, and Mohammed Baux, "the Miniature Man of India." Scientists also crowded into these shows to take notes and add to their taxonomies.[5]

From the popularity and success of these sideshows, you can begin to see the ways that popular culture started to influence science and vice versa. You can also see the ways that ideas about *deformity* or *monstrosity* started to be imposed on people who exemplified sex or gendered differences on their bodies: Julia Pastrana had "too much" hair for a woman, Hoo Loo's scrotal tumor made his testicles "too" large, and Mohammed Baux's stature was "too short" for a man (you may recall Charlie Manzano's essay at the end of Chapter 1, "Five Foot Five," in which Charlie talks about societal notions about normal height for men). Underlying all these stories about people who are not European is an idea that they are evolutionary "throwbacks," "diseased," or otherwise inferior and less than fully human.

Degeneration and Criminal Anthropology

In 1857, when sideshows were popular throughout Europe, the French scientist Benedictin Augustin Morel published his work on *degeneration*. Morel believed that certain humans represented a biological "breakdown," a reversal of Darwin's ideas about evolution. According to Morel, this biological breakdown, which he called **devolution,** was genetic, and the people exhibiting devolution were *degenerating*. Morel called these people *degenerates* who carried a *hereditary taint*. Morel argued that morally repulsive individuals could pass their hereditary taint on to offspring and that the degeneration could be traced back through the family tree. Morel viewed abnormal bodies as a physical manifestation of degeneration.[6] In other words, Morel defined "normal" bodies and then considered deviations from the normal to be "abnormal."

Have you or someone you know ever said, "He looks like a serial killer"? Even if you were joking, there is someone who originally put forth the idea that you can tell criminal intent by someone's appearance. Nineteen years after Morel published his theories, the Italian anthropologist Cesare Lombroso tied Morel's ideas about degeneration to criminals. In his work *Criminal Man,* Lombroso wrote: "In general it may be said that in the distribution of hair, criminals of both sexes tend to exhibit characteristics of the opposite sex . . . the abdomen, pelvis, and reproductive organs sometimes show an inversion of sex-characteristics."[7] This inversion of the sex characteristics meant that men with a small stomach, pelvis, penis, and testicles (the opposite problem of Hoo Loo) looked feminine to Lombroso. This inversion also meant that women with a large vulva and clitoris looked too masculine to Lombroso. You may be asking yourself: Could it be that the people Lombroso was measuring were people with differences of sex development (DSD)? There is definitely that possibility, and it would not be the first time that people who had DSD had their bodies measured, put on display, and classified as abnormal. It is also likely that many of Lombroso's "specimens" were not people with DSD and that Lombroso had only one model of what he thought normal genitalia should look like.

The important thing to note here is that Morel's ideas of degeneration and Lombroso's ideas of the criminal can both be read on the body, and more specifically on the genitals. Even before the rise of sexology, stereotypes classified people with certain bodily characteristics as degenerates and criminals.

A decade later, Richard von Krafft-Ebing, the grandfather of sexology, who read and respected Lombroso, wrote the following in his book *Psychopathia Sexualis*: "Individuals of antipathic sexuality in whom not only the character and all the feelings are in accord with the abnormal sexual instinct, but also the frame, the features, voice, etc.; so that the individual approaches the opposite sex anthropologically. . . . This . . . represents a very high degree of degeneration."[8] In these two sentences, Krafft-Ebing marries degeneration, criminality, and sexology.

Sex Taxonomies: They Talked to a Stranger about *That*?

Have you ever heard it said that it is easier to talk to a complete stranger about your innermost secrets than it is to divulge that information to someone you know? As you begin to read excerpts from the life stories that patients shared with the sexologists, you may be wondering: Why did these people feel comfortable sharing the details of their bodies, emotions, fantasies, and sexual encounters? Perhaps they did not feel *completely* comfortable; however, they may have seen the sexologist as a professional man of medicine, one with whom they had no personal relationship. Although many people in the nineteenth century viewed science and medicine with a skeptical eye, scientists were also seen as powerful and magical. Those who were in favor of science believed it had the ability to unlock a deeper understanding of human behavior—which, in many ways, it certainly has. Those who felt different might have been more willing to talk to people who were willing to take *different* seriously and consider it scientifically.

Before the emergence of sexology, Western culture considered any sort of sexual practice that was not heterosexual and procreative (reproductive) as sinful. For example, masturbation was a sin. Heterosexual oral sex was a sin. Homosexuality of any kind was a sin. In European countries still influenced by the Roman Catholic Church, the confessional was the place where one confessed these sexual sins. When the Enlightenment swept across Europe, science and scientists began to move the discussion away from morality and sin and to focus, instead, on scientific explanations for sexual differences. It is important to remember, however, that many of the sexologists held religious beliefs. In other words, although they were attempting to classify and define human behavior in scientific terms, they still brought their own judgment—often influenced by ideas about sin—to the table.

FIGURE 3.1 Richard von Krafft-Ebing, by Cameron Rains. Richard von Krafft-Ebing was a German-Austrian sexologist whose work *Psychopathia Sexualis* set the tone for the ways that we still find cisnormative and heteronormative identities as the sole definitions of "normal."

Richard von Krafft-Ebing

The German-Austrian Richard von Krafft-Ebing (1840–1902) wrote the following at the beginning of his book on sexology: "The purpose of this treatise is a description of the pathological manifestations of the sexual life and an attempt to refer them to their underlying conditions."[9] With this proclamation in his preface to the first edition of *Psychopathia Sexualis*, Krafft-Ebing (figure 3.1) conveys the idea that his treatise will diagnose and explain pathologies, or abnormal sexual behavior. To this day, many of Krafft-Ebing's ideas help maintain stereotypes about sexual behavior and gender identity.

Psychopathia Sexualis: With Especial Reference to Antipathic Sexual Instinct: A Medico-Forensic Study was first published in Krafft-Ebing's native German in 1877 and then in English in 1886. Krafft-Ebing believed that his work would serve as a reference for scientists, doctors, lawyers, and judges. It is important to note that his work focused on the medical and legal professions. A doctor's responsibility is to diagnose and cure. Lawyers and judges ascertain criminal behavior, pass judgment, and incarcerate.

At the time of its publication, Krafft-Ebing's argument was a revelation in that, regardless of his own religious beliefs, he attempted to take the discussion of some forms of sexuality out of the realm of religion and sin. Within Krafft-Ebing's framework, people who masturbated, people who engaged in nonprocreative heterosexual sex, and people who engaged in homosexual sex were no longer doomed to hell. With this transformation, they were seen, instead, as diseased and in need of a cure. Because he was also still working within Lombroso's frame of criminology, disease and criminality became linked in sexology, whether that was Krafft-Ebing's intent or not.

Because Krafft-Ebing's intended audience was professional, the language he wrote in was accessible only to the highly educated. In both the original German version and the later English translations, whenever he discussed genital measurements and certain sexual behaviors, he switched to Latin. Why? Latin was the language used in the sciences and in legal systems. Writing in Latin, however, also ensured that laypeople could not read all the information. In other words, most of the people whom Krafft-Ebing studied and wrote about had no *agency* (control). They were merely *subjects*.

Thus, the *expertise* did not sit with the individual who embodied a particular identity or behavior. Rather, the expertise was left to the man of science. In what ways does the medical field still rely on the expertise of doctors rather than patients or individuals? In what ways has the medical field evolved? Many trans people still face an everyday struggle to have agency over their own bodies.

Krafft-Ebing began with a set of three controlling ideas:

1. His model for normal was *heterosexual* (he helped invent the term as it is still understood and used today).

2. Heterosexuality had to be focused on sex for procreation and not sex for pleasure.

3. Any sort of sexual desire, fantasy, or activity that was not heterosexual *and* procreative was considered not only abnormal but also a manifestation of a *disease*. Over half of Krafft-Ebing's book is dedicated to heterosexual sex practices that he labeled abnormal, including oral sex and men who eroticized women's feet.

These ideas about sexuality were new and fresh in that Krafft-Ebing studied them from a *scientific* and *medical* perspective. Krafft-Ebing's work brought a seriousness to the subject of sex and sexuality that made it a legitimate subject of study.

You may be wondering where trans identity fits into Krafft-Ebing's work. Before you read more excerpts from his work, it is important to remember that Krafft-Ebing read sexual orientation outside heteronormativity, and he read gender identity and gender expression outside strict ideas of the gender binary, as *symptoms* of one another. He did not differentiate between sexual orientation and gender identity/gender expression. In creating his classifications, Krafft-Ebing set up a scientific precedent, whether he meant to or not. He classified what we call a trans identity today as the absolute worst and most degenerate form of homosexuality (although the word *homosexuality* was not in use yet). Let's look at an example of his case studies to examine the ways that he often conflated gender identity and sexual orientation:

> Effemination (Case 122):
> I am convinced that the enigma of our existence can only be solved by the impartial scientist (or, at any rate, that light can be thrown upon it by him). For which reason I give this description of my life for the sole purpose of elucidating this cruel error of nature, and thus to benefit in all possible manner such fellow-beings as are afflicted in a similar way. Urnings there will be as long as the human race endures, for there were such ever since humanity began. But as science progresses, men will look upon the like of myself as subjects worthy rather of compassion than of disdain.[10]

Note that the person whose life becomes Case 122 is calling on the scientist to help him. He calls the scientist "impartial," although we know that Krafft-Ebing was partial in that he approached his subjects as people suffering from a disease. Krafft-Ebing also helped popularize certain labels. In the excerpt above, you see the word **urning,** which was one of the words Krafft-Ebing used for people whom today we would, generally speaking, understand to be gay men.

Case 122 continues his story: "At an early age I took a dislike to the manly sports practised by my companions; liked to play with little girls, who suited my character better than boys; was shy, and easily blushed."[11] When talking about men that he finds attractive, he says that their charms work on him "as if I were a real woman."[12] Here we see that Case 122's feelings of attraction to other men make him self-identify as though he were a woman. His self-description, however, does not necessarily mean that he is someone who would identify as transgender today. Case 122 helps illuminate the point that homosexuality was measured on a heterosexual scale. Although Case 122 is a man, the fact that he is attracted to men must mean he has an inner woman, which goes back to a heterosexual measurement scale. In Case 122 homosexuality and what we now call transgender identity are conflated.

This is how Krafft-Ebing conflated sexual orientation and gender identity: (1) the binary gender scheme is understood to be fixed, and (2) procreative heterosexuality is the only normal sexuality. We also need to remember that Richard von Krafft-Ebing saw everything through the lens of disease. After all, everyone who came to see him was a patient.

John Addington Symonds

John Addington Symonds (1840–1893) was not a sexologist. He was an English poet and philosopher. He was married to a woman who knew he was homosexual; this type of marriage was relatively common in nineteenth-century Britain. As long as you performed all the outward social actions that made you look heterosexual, you could lead your other life underground. Marriage was an economic and social arrangement, and homosexuality for men was still illegal.

Remember that Krafft-Ebing's case studies were written in scientific language, and the most explicit parts were in Latin. As a writer and a scholar who had come up through the best of the English school system, including his university work at Oxford, Symonds was also completely fluent in both Latin and Greek. Although *Psychopathia Sexualis* was written for scientists, educated people (usually men with financial means) often read intellectual works that were not in their specific areas of study. This is one of the reasons that Charles Darwin's work on natural selection and evolution was so popular.

After Symonds read *Psychopathia Sexualis,* he was so angry that he sat down and wrote a letter to Krafft-Ebing. In this letter he confronted Krafft-Ebing for the ways he categorized urnings. Symonds felt that Krafft-Ebing had missed a critical point. Krafft-Ebing said that urnings were neurotic and often had psychotic breakdowns *because* they were urnings. Symonds argued, instead, that urnings were more neurotic *because society and culture treated them as less than human.* The fact that great numbers of people had to hide who they really were is what made them mentally ill.[13] This argument is significant because Symonds offers an excellent example of someone outside the sciences who stood up to a scientific authority and said, "You did *not* get this right!" And, as you will see later in this chapter, trans people also stood up to modern sexologists and demanded to be heard as experts about their own bodies and identities.

Krafft-Ebing did read Symonds's letter. It is unclear if he wrote back to Symonds, but it is clear that he took Symonds's name off the letter and then included it as one of his case studies in a later edition of *Psychopathia Sexualis.* What if Krafft-Ebing had taken Symonds's point more seriously? What if Krafft-Ebing and other sexologists had heeded Symonds's advice and studied society's biases, homophobia, and heterosexism? How might such a perspective have increased society's understanding of people we now call LGBTQ+?

FIGURE 3.2 Magnus Hirschfeld, by Cameron Rains. Magnus Hirschfeld, a German sexologist who was also Jewish and gay, realized that his mentor, Krafft-Ebing, had been wrong to see gender identity and sexual orientation as one and the same. He is widely credited with coining the term *transvestite* to help protect people who were trans. He founded the Institut für Sexualwissen-schaft (Institute for Sexual Research), which the Nazis burned to the ground on May 10, 1933.

"The Einstein of Sex": Reclaiming Magnus Hirschfeld and the Institut für Sexualwissenschaft

I believe in Science, and I am convinced that Science and above all the Natural Sciences, must bring mankind, not only truth, but with truth, Justice, Liberty and Peace for all men.
MAGNUS HIRSCHFELD*

Like Richard von Krafft-Ebing and other scientists in the fields of psychology, anthropology, and sexology before him, Magnus Hirschfeld (1868–1935; figure 3.2) believed in science. Unlike the earlier sexologists, however, he believed that science done well and without judgment could become the great vehicle to make *all* people equal. Hirschfeld rejected the notion that any one race was superior to another. Hirschfeld also rejected the idea that any gender identity or sexual orientation should be held above another. For Hirschfeld, science was the key force for eliminating prejudice because science was supposed to be impartial. Imagine for a moment a meeting between Julia Pastrana and Magnus Hirschfeld. Rather than treating her as an oddity, he probably would have welcomed her into his residence.

---

* Magnus Hirschfeld, 1935, quoted in Elena Mancini, *Magnus Hirschfeld and the Quest for Sexual Freedom: A History of the First International Sexual Freedom Movement* (New York: Palgrave Macmillan, 2010), 31.

Dr. Magnus Hirschfeld was a visionary and a risk taker. Unfortunately, Hirschfeld was punished for his work to the extent that only now, in the twenty-first century, are we beginning to learn about his forward-thinking ideas and theories. For the first three decades of the twentieth century, he openly and tirelessly advocated for transgender and homosexual people in Germany and throughout Europe.[14] Hirschfeld was German and Jewish; in 1919 he established the Institut für Sexualwissenschaft (often translated into English as Institute for Sexual Research or Institute for Sexology) in Berlin, the first institution of its kind in the world. From 1919 to 1933 this institute attracted people from around the world who wanted to study and understand more about the growing science of sexology. Perhaps more important, Hirschfeld's institute became a safe place for people seeking advice and help for issues regarding sex, sexual orientation, and gender identity. The people who visited the well-respected clinic were highly diverse: heterosexual couples having difficulty getting pregnant, homosexual and bisexual men and women who were ridiculed for their sexual orientation, people who felt that their sex assigned at birth did not line up with their gender identity. All were welcome in Hirschfeld's clinic: "In treating his patients, Hirschfeld exhibited . . . a 'patient-centered' approach. He listened attentively and without judgment to his patients' accounts. . . . The emphasis of his treatment was placed on how the patients felt about and experienced their own conditions that society deemed pathological. . . . He encouraged his patients to understand and accept their natures and express them without remorse."[15]

Hirschfeld never made a secret of his own homosexuality. He was also very open about his disdain for the ways that many European scientists and men of letters depicted people of various races as inferior to European people. His two life partners were Karl Giese, a working-class German who was a Gentile, and Dr. Li Shiu Tong from Shanghai. When he died, Hirschfeld gave equally to each in his will.[16] When Hitler rose to power in Germany in the 1930s, the Nazi political agenda replaced the liberal Weimar Republic of Germany. In 1933, while Hirschfeld was on a global tour speaking about his various studies, he received news that the Nazis had burned down his institute.

Hirschfeld was one of the first sexologists to figure out that sexual orientation and gender identity were not fixed binary categories. He used the term *sexual intermediacy* to describe the nonbinary nature of sexual orientation; according to one historian, "Hirschfeld's thinking prefigures contemporary concepts of the continuum of sexual orientation, genderqueer expression, and sexual fluidity."[17] In early twentieth-century Berlin, Hirschfeld noted the difference between gay men who enjoyed dressing up as part of a burlesque and putting on a drag show and people assigned male at birth who dressed and acted like women because they felt like women. In a bold move, he worked with police authorities in Berlin to make sure that trans women, whom he called *transvestites* (Hirschfeld may have coined the term), had identification cards so that they would not be arrested for breaking Berlin's anti-cross-dressing laws. In other words, Hirschfeld was successful in making sure that trans women had legitimate identification to prevent them from being arrested.

In Chapter 6 you will be asked to consider governmental identification issues, so it will be good to remember Hirschfeld's pioneering work. Although he was not a surgeon, Hirschfeld was asked to be an anatomical authority for what may have been the first gender affirmation surgery in the West: Lili Elbe in Berlin in 1930. Elbe died a year later from infections and complications of the procedure. In 1935 Magnus Hirschfeld died in exile from his home. At the time of his death, it was thought that only a handful of his writings on gender and sexual orientation survived Hitler's mandated book burnings at the Institut für Sexualwissenschaft. Slowly, more of Hirschfeld's work is being found and is being cared for at various archives, such as the Wellcome Institute in London and the GLBT Historical Society in San Francisco. Where would trans rights and trans healthcare be now if we had not lost eighty years of access to Hirschfeld's studies?

Harry Benjamin

One of Magnus Hirschfeld's students from Berlin, Dr. Harry Benjamin (1885–1986; figure 3.3), is often considered *the* pioneer of transsexual studies. His 1966 book, *The Transsexual Phenomenon,* was a groundbreaking text that completely opened up the field of sexology to be inclusive of trans people. Benjamin is often credited with being the first person to argue that gender identity and sexual orientation were not the same, and that being transsexual and being homosexual were not the same. It is true that Benjamin did a lot of amazing and groundbreaking work in his lifetime (he lived to be 101 and did not stop practicing until he was in his nineties). As we now know, however, Magnus Hirschfeld had begun looking at and writing about the differences between gender identity and sexual orientation decades earlier.[18]

So why is Benjamin still credited as the first person to study transsexual or transgender people? Remember that Richard von Krafft-Ebing's work was written so that only scientists (usually men) and other highly educated people were able to read it. Also remember that sections of *Psychopathia Sexualis* (including those concerning body parts and sexual practices) were written in Latin so that

FIGURE 3.3 Harry Benjamin, by Cameron Rains. Harry Benjamin was born in Germany but is widely known as an American sexologist. He wrote the groundbreaking book *The Transsexual Phenomenon,* which was published in 1966. The book was accessible to audiences beyond the medical establishment, and it changed the lives of many trans people, especially trans women. To this day, the Standards of Care for trans people can be traced to Benjamin's work.

even if parts of the book did make it out "to the street," regular people would not understand what was written there. Also remember that the world is only now becoming aware of Magnus Hirschfeld's work, much of which was lost when his institute and library were burned to the ground in 1933. Most of Hirschfeld's surviving writings are in German and are slowly being translated.

In contrast, Harry Benjamin's book was available and accessible to *anyone who was able to go into a public library and read*. Think about how important Benjamin's book was for the trans people who wanted to read about other people like themselves—without a Latin translator! There are several accounts of trans women in San Francisco in Susan Stryker and Victor Silverman's groundbreaking documentary film, *Screaming Queens: The Riot at Compton's Cafeteria,* who recall the exact week in August 1966 when Benjamin's book came out and the ways that it changed their lives.[19] At that time, **sex-reassignment surgery (srs)** was almost unheard of; the exception was Christine Jorgensen, a G.I. who had had her surgery in Copenhagen in 1952. For many of these impoverished trans women in San Francisco's Tenderloin District, there had been no hope for medical intervention until Benjamin's book. *The Transsexual Phenomenon* made them realize that they could go to their doctors and begin discussing ways to move toward **gender affirmation** if they chose to have body modification. Of course, the influence of Benjamin's book extended far beyond the Tenderloin District and San Francisco.

Although Benjamin's book broke new ground by making gender-affirmation procedures seem accessible, the truth was that many trans people faced numerous barriers. As Joanne Meyerowitz writes, "In their interactions with doctors, transsexuals dreamed of the new possibilities created by medical science. But . . . they bumped up against the power of medical gatekeepers, the costs of commodified medical care, and the limits of technology."[20] Many trans people could not afford any type of body modification, whether access to hormones or surgery. There was also an inherent bias among many medical professionals, who often judged trans people on whether the *doctor* thought they could pass and whether the trans person was also clearly going to lead a heterosexual life.

(A quick note on terms here: Benjamin referred to gender-affirmation surgery as *sex-reassignment surgery*. If you look at medical documents, you may still see this term being used. Over the past few years, the terminology has been evolving. You may find reference to *gender-confirmation surgery* or, most recently, *gender-affirmation surgery*. Both words, *confirmation* and *affirmation,* move away from a strictly medical model of sex reassignment to one that is more positive and holistic. Also note that the word *gender* is more open and expansive than the word *sex*. For many trans people seeking surgical help to embody their full identity, *gender confirmation* is much more positive because it gives the trans person agency—they get to confirm their gender identity. Some advocates have begun using **gender-affirmation surgery** as an even more empowering and more positive term. The main thing to remember is that terms are always changing, and it is always best to use the term that each person feels is the most respectful. Throughout this book, you will find *gender-affirmation surgery* used because it is the most positive and empowering.)

Following the publication of Benjamin's "how to" book on gender-affirmation surgery (though he used the term *srs*), the field of surgery opened up, and with that came a need for a common code of ethics. The Harry Benjamin Standards of Care (SOC) are a set of healthcare standards for trans people. There are now several editions of the SOC because the issues have changed and evolved over time. The World Professional Association for Transgender Health (WPATH) is an international group that is composed of medical practitioners from around the world along with trans advocates, some of whom are also medical practitioners. The WPATH meets periodically to revise the Standards of Care and is working globally to declassify trans as a disease. An exercise at the end of this chapter asks you to conduct some online research on historic changes in the SOC and WPATH.

FIGURE 3.4. Sexology time line.

1886	Richard von Krafft-Ebing's *Psychopathia Sexualis* is published.
1919	Magnus Hirschfeld opens the Institut für Sexualwissenschaft.
1920	Havelock Ellis coins the term Eonism.
1948	Alfred Kinsey's Kinsey Scale is published in *Sexual Behavior in the Human Male*
1966	Harry Benjamin publishes *The Transsexual Phenomenon.*
2003	Dr. Marci Bowers takes over gender-affirmation surgeries at Mt. San Rafael Hospital in Trinidad, Colorado
2007	Dr. Christine McGinn opens the Papillon Gender Wellness Center.
2015	Dr. Li Yinhe gives a keynote speech at the Brookings Institution in Washington, D.C.

In the United States, **gender dysphoria** has been listed as a mental disorder in the *Diagnostic and Statistical Manual of Mental Disorders* (DSM). This classification has proven to be a double-edged sword for trans people seeking hormones and/ or surgery. On the one hand, when you have a diagnosis, you are able to get medical help. On the other hand, a diagnosis still carries the idea that you are sick. The most recent edition of the *DSM*, published in 2013, tried to counteract some of the negative connotation, but it did not go all the way. In some quarters it is expected that, within the next five years, the *DSM* might remove gender dysphoria completely.[21]

Figure 3.4 offers a time line of sexology. We will discuss the work of other pioneers of sexology, such as Dr. McGinn and Dr. Li Yinhe, a bit later in this chapter.

Taking Matters into Our Own Hands!

Although nobody argues that Harry Benjamin's work was not groundbreaking and game-changing, numerous trans people worked as sexologists before the publication of Benjamin's book. Even if they did not have degrees in sexology, by virtue of their lived experiences they were and are experts in the field. Of course, that is not to say that they all agree. For example, Virginia Prince, a strong advocate for trans women, argued in numerous articles that trans people could be only heterosexual. Later, Dallas Denny, another advocate for trans women and an activist, argued that sexual orientation and gender identity were not one and the same. If someone needed and/or wanted gender-affirmation surgery, hormones, and other procedures to feel more like a whole person, Denny argued, that desire for gender affirmation did not automatically mean that the person was heterosexual. For decades, however, many surgical centers working with trans people refused service if the person seeking help had not spent an appropriate amount of time under the care of a psychologist and if they had not fully embraced the most stereotypical attributes of the gender identity they were transitioning to. For example, trans women had to wear skirts and dresses, high heels, and makeup; they also had to act feminine according to the doctor's standards of femininity. The trans person also had to state that once they had transitioned, their sexual orientation would be heterosexual.

This is a good time to stop and reconsider Kinsey's scale from Chapter 2. Remember that the majority of people on that scale fall into the bisexual category. So what was going to happen to bisexual trans people under the early rules regarding gender-affirmation surgery? Were they left out in the cold? They probably were. Doctors performing gender-affirmation surgeries in the 1970s at

Stanford University Hospital blatantly said that they were not in the business of creating homosexuals.[22]

Along Comes Lou

Louis Graydon Sullivan (1951–1991) kept extensive diaries as he was growing up in a conservative Catholic family in Wisconsin.[23] When Sullivan was born, his family celebrated having a baby girl; however, from a very early age, he identified as a boy. In his diaries, he not only discussed the feeling of being misidentified as a girl, but also wrote about being a boy who was attracted to other boys. As the diaries reveal, Lou Sullivan was afraid that he was completely alone in the world because there was no word to describe him. He was transgender. He was gay. And during his childhood and adolescence in the 1960s, the general public may have been aware that trans women existed, but trans men—and particularly gay and bisexual trans men—were still largely invisible. In large part, thanks to Lou Sullivan and his work, gay, bisexual, and queer trans men now have a large international network.[24]

In 1975 Lou Sullivan moved to San Francisco and began applying to gender clinics so that he could have his gender-affirmation surgery. They all rejected him because he was open about being a gay man. At that time, the gender clinics still mandated that, postsurgery, a trans person would be heterosexual. (In some places gender-affirmation surgery still hinges on the understanding that the trans person will be heterosexual once the surgery is complete.[25]) One of the clinics that rejected Sullivan was Stanford University Hospital.

While Sullivan was trying to get accepted to various gender clinics, he wrote numerous articles focusing on female-to-male transsexuals (FTMs); worked tirelessly at a clearinghouse for people with gender dysphoria, making sure that trans men were included in the information; published the first information guide for trans men; and founded the world's first organization to work exclusively with trans men, FTM. In 1986, a decade after he began seeking gender-affirmation surgery, he was finally able to receive it. That same year, Lou Sullivan was also diagnosed with AIDS, which was devastating communities in San Francisco and across the world. Before he died from AIDS, he wrote the Stanford Dysphoria Clinic a letter, which now can be read at the GLBT Historical Society in San Francisco. In this letter he notes that Stanford said he could not live as a gay man, but the irony was that he was going to die as one.[26]

FIGURE 3.5 Li Yinhe, by Cameron Rains. Dr. Li Yinhe is a retired sexologist in the People's Republic of China. She has spent her entire professional life advocating for women's rights and LGBT rights in China.

Fighting the Tyranny of "Normal": Dr. Li Yinhe

One of the most progressive sexologists in the world is Dr. Li Yinhe (b. 1952; figure 3.5), an outspoken sexologist, feminist, and trans advocate throughout China and the world. Being an outspoken feminist in China is dangerous. As recently as 2015, five young feminist activists in China were jailed for thirty-seven days for attempting to distribute information about sexual harassment on public transportation on International Women's Day, March 8.[27] Gender equality is still seen as "too Western" a concept in China, and throughout the major cities, billboards everywhere tout traditional heterosexual nuclear families.[28] Despite political, cultural, and societal pressures that espouse very strict ideas of what constitutes *normal* in China, Dr. Li Yinhe has spent decades flying in the face of convention. In doing so, she has become an underground superhero sexologist for millions of Chinese queer and trans people.

Dr. Li Yinhe has been outspoken as a sexologist, but until 2014 she was private about her personal life. Then, in 2014, a news story accused her of being a lesbian. The article claimed that her identity as a lesbian informed her agenda as an open-minded and outspoken sexologist, and there was speculation that she and her partner had an adopted child who would never adjust socially because, according to the Chinese press, he was being raised by perverts. In response to this attack, Dr. Li Yinhe shocked the world when she did come out—not as a lesbian, but as a cisgender partner in a heterosexual relationship with a trans man.[29] Dr. Li Yinhe told her interviewer, "I am indeed a heterosexual, not a homosexual. . . . I have no interest at all in the female body."[30] Think for a moment about her advocacy and her language about her partner and her partner's body. She does not identify her partner's body as female; she sees him as male, which matches his identity.

A year later, Dr. Li Yinhe was a keynote speaker at the Brookings Institution in Washington, D.C., where she addressed her advocacy for lifting what she sees as outdated laws that criminalize sex work, pornography, and other sexual issues that the Chinese government still views as illegal and/or immoral.[31] Dr. Li Yinhe is now retired, but her legacy of pioneering work and advocacy continues to inspire people working on trans rights globally, and, more specifically, she has served as a model for a new generation of Chinese activists.

A Gender Wellness Clinic

Recall that Richard von Krafft-Ebing's ideas, interviews, and taxonomies made a crucial difference for people who today we would understand to be gay, lesbian, bisexual, and transgender. He viewed sex and sexuality through the lens of science, and his studies of gender identity/gender expression and sexual orientation moved away from the earlier religious models of sin and moral depravity, placing them in the realm of science and medicine (that is, as diseases rather than sins). In many places today, transgender people are still considered to be sick. In the twenty-first century, however, not yet 150 years after the initial publication of *Psychopathia Sexualis,* we finally can find some positive approaches toward transgender people in the field of sexology. Sometimes the improvement is merely a change in a word, or something small that can make a huge difference in trans people's lives.

Dr. Christine McGinn (figure 3.6) and her wife run the Papillon Gender Wellness Center in New Hope, Pennsylvania.[32] Dr. McGinn is a surgeon specializing in gender-affirmation surgery and hormone therapy. She is a trans woman, a lesbian, and the mother of twins. In her numerous interviews, Dr. McGinn recognizes the work of previous trans pioneers—people like Lou Sullivan—who paved the way for her to be fully comfortable with her trans and her lesbian identities.[33]

FIGURE 3.6 Christine McGinn, by Cameron Rains. Dr. Christine McGinn runs the Papillon Center in New Hope, Pennsylvania, which is pioneering in its approach to "gender wellness" rather than "gender dysphoria" or other diagnoses. Dr. McGinn is a trans woman who does not want other trans people to go through the same difficulties she had in accessing healthcare and gender affirmation.

The day before she retired from the navy as a surgeon, Christine McGinn had her commanding officer change her name to Christine, and she was able to leave the military with an honorable discharge, which was unusual.[34] During her own gender-affirmation surgery and the process leading up to it, she was appalled by the ways the medical system treated trans people. That is why she has devoted herself to making the Papillon Gender Wellness Center a safe place for people who identify anywhere on a gender spectrum to receive help and services. She performs all aspects of the center's gender-affirmation surgeries. With her privileges at various hospitals around the Philadelphia area, she and her team are educating doctors, nurses, and other healthcare providers on how to treat all people with dignity.

The filmmakers of the 2015 trans-themed film *The Danish Girl* (a drama that explores one of the first gender-affirmation surgeries, performed in 1931 on Lili Elbe), asked Dr. McGinn to be on the set as the medical expert.[35] In many ways, her participation in the film brings us full circle in the story of sexology and points to the *positive* results sexology can bring to trans people. Dr. McGinn was on set for the film reenactment of the historic event, but we should remember that Magnus Hirschfeld was in the operating room at the actual event helping out and giving advice so that Lili Elbe's true gender identity could be affirmed mentally, emotionally, and physically.

WRITINGS FROM THE COMMUNITY

BOBBI

The following story is from Jess T. Dugan and Vanessa Fabbre's collaborative project To Survive on This Shore: Photographs and Interviews with Transgender and Gender Non-Conforming Older Adults. *Jess T. Dugan's art explores "gender, sexuality, identity, and community."*[36] *Dugan received an MFA in photography from Columbia College Chicago and an MA in museum studies from Harvard University. Vanessa Fabbre is a professor in the Women, Gender, and Sexuality Studies Department at Washington University in St. Louis, Missouri. Her research focuses on gender identity and aging.*

Bobbi, 83, Detroit, MI, 2014
Photo by Jess T. Dugan.

I have traveled extensively, it started out when I was in the Air Force. I was the "grandfather," or whatever you'd call it—of the drone program. I mean, I played golf with presidents, with Jerry Ford and whatnot, and I certainly have met the older Bush and younger Bush and Reagan a couple of times. I've been in the White House. I've been up and down the Pentagon, all levels. And I've also worked extensively with the CIA.

Eleven years ago was my surgery, to this date almost. Eleven years ago, so I started hormones 12-plus years ago. And I really have been in the cross-dressing business or the transgender business since I was probably 4 or 5 years old. I mean, I've got that history. But I didn't know some of that history until I tracked back later in life, when I saw this more obviously in front of me. I said, "Oh, my god, this is what I was doing when I was 4 years old and 5 years old and 6," and of course, it all fits into a channel. But in that day—I'm talking about being born in 1930—that was the Great Depression.

There were no words for any of this. Except that I think my mother knew, because when I asked her to teach me to knit, she did, and she'd teach me some other things that I asked if I could do, like cross-stitch and whatnot. So all the basic clues were there all the way along.

I think people talk in either/or terms, right? Before transition and after. But to me it's really development. I'm proud of both lives. I'm proud of both me's, if you see what I'm saying. And I feel it's been a remarkable thing to have happened to a person. I'm grateful. You can't just become a woman with a knife or a pill or anything like that. It takes a whole combination in a sequence, in a formation. You've got this time span, it's a learning experience, it's a little bit of everything. It's what I call going through the internship phase, stumbling through the adolescent phase, then going through the maturity phase.

I have gone through the dating routine. That was my internship. I had to get through the Internet, go out and stumble on with it and flirt, and I got pretty good at it. I kinda worked at it. I'm not bad with words. And I could play peek-a-boo on Skype. Then I finally picked up Frank. I kidnapped him from the local bar up here one afternoon, an ex-Marine. And we dated for a long time. Finally one day, it was so nice that Sunday morning with our head on the pillows, I said, "Oh, I got something to tell you . . ." And after I told him he says, "You're better than any woman I've ever met. Now, come on, Bobbi, we can drop that." Didn't care a damn. Where I live now, I think some people know for sure who I am and don't really care. But I also don't have it written on my forehead. So there are those that don't. They just take me as another old lady, a nice old lady.

T. J. GUNDLING

The Trans Experience: A Biocultural Dialectic

Born and raised in the suburbs of northern New Jersey, T. J. Gundling is a recovering engineer who later earned a doctorate in anthropology at Yale University. Gundling, whose research interests include the history of human origins studies, and, more recently, transgender studies, is currently a tenured faculty member at a public university in the Garden State.

Gundling is a GNC Unitarian-Universalist with Buddhist leanings, a limited (but enthusiastic!) guitar player, and a big fan of 1970s glam rock. T.J. enjoys films involving ghosts, traveling, and preparing global cuisine.

In each person there is a different mixture of manly and womanly substances, and as we cannot find two leaves alike on a tree, then it is highly unlikely that we will find two humans whose manly and womanly characteristics exactly match in kind and number.
MAGNUS HIRSCHFELD*

---

* Magnus Hirschfeld, *Transvestites: The Erotic Drive to Cross-Dress* (1910). Translated by M. A. Lombardi-Nash (Buffalo: Prometheus Books, 1991).

Introduction

On April 24, 2015, the Olympic decathlon champion and reality TV star Bruce Jenner* appeared in a highly anticipated interview with the journalist Diane Sawyer in which he confirmed rumors that he was transgender and was planning to transition to life as a woman. In describing his experience, he asserted, "My brain is much more female than it is male; it's hard for people to understand that, but that's what my soul is . . . for all intents and purposes I am a woman." Less than two months later, in the wake of Caitlyn Jenner's debut on the cover of *Vanity Fair*, the feminist writer and filmmaker Elinor Burkett contributed an opinion piece to the *New York Times* in which she articulates the tension for feminists who support the freedom for trans-identified individuals to self-actualize, yet feel compelled to challenge certain specific contentions and demands made by some trans individuals. For Burkett, Jenner's assertion that she has the brain, and hence the mind, of a woman flies in the face of a central second-wave feminist trope that biology is not destiny. She implores the reader to reject the notion that women can be reduced to their female body parts, whether it be their brains, their breasts, or their genitals. Burkett instead argues that being a woman is more the result of a relentless process of gender socialization that a person who previously enjoyed male privilege couldn't possibly comprehend: "They [trans women] haven't traveled through the world as women and been shaped by all that entails. . . . The differences between male and female brains are caused by the 'drip, drip, drip' of the gendered environment."†

This debate exemplifies a long-standing pattern of explaining complex human behavior in terms of nature, on the one hand, and nurture, on the other.‡ This essay addresses the question of whether the charged dialogue between Jenner and Burkett signals a return to the bad old days of potential allies demonizing each other, or still has relevance in the early twenty-first century, as the trans community makes strides that would have seemed unimaginable even a genera-

---

* At the time of the interview, Jenner stated that the use of male pronouns and of "his" given name were appropriate. When I discuss Jenner post-transition, I will use female pronouns and her chosen name, Caitlyn. I am aware that the decision to adopt this approach contradicts some stylistic guidelines for writing about trans people that eschew the use of "dead" names and pronouns. Nonetheless, I am electing to honor the clearly stated wishes of the person under discussion.

† Elinor Burkett, "What Makes a Woman?" *New York Times*, 6 June 2015, Sunday Review, 6.

‡ With regard to trans issues, the Jenner-Burkett debate harks back to similar discourse of decades ago, most notably represented by Janice Raymond's now infamous polemic (Raymond, *The Transsexual Empire: The Making of the She-Male* [Boston: Beacon Press, 1979]) and Sandy Stone's belated, but nonetheless astute rejoinder (Stone, "The Empire Strikes Back: A Posttranssexual Manifesto," in *Body Guards: The Cultural Politics of Gender Ambiguity,* ed. Kristina Straub and Julia Epstein [New York: Routledge, 1991]).

tion ago. Before I offer a reply to this question, it is useful to provide a brief review of the historical roots of these two contrasting views of gender etiology, which are typically referred to as biological determinism and social constructionism.

Biological Determinism

During the nineteenth century, scientific study greatly expanded as a distinct, codified set of practices and procedures, often directly associated with the Modernist notion of inevitable *progress* toward a brighter future. Science positivists held that technological breakthroughs would dramatically improve the quality of human life, and thus the scientific method became highly authoritative as an epistemology, as did those who were engaged in such pursuits.* It was in this context that Charles Darwin developed his theories explaining the roots of biological diversity, and although he is best known for proposing the evolutionary mechanism of natural selection, he later introduced a related concept called sexual selection.† Sexual selection focused explicitly on traits directly related to attracting mates and thwarting competitors, and Darwin was interested in how such traits increased reproductive success and therefore became more common in subsequent generations.

Scientists have rightly asked why sexes even exist in the first place. After all, sex requires finding a mate and dilutes an individual's genetic contribution to their offspring, which is combined with their partner's. Still, biologists now hold that sexual reproduction is theoretically superior to asexual reproduction because it increases genetic diversity through combining two genomes and hence reduces susceptibility to infection and disease. It also provides natural and sexual selection with an increase in variation necessary for these evolutionary mechanisms to function. The differences between the sexes that evolve as a result of sexual selection are captured in the concept of sexual dimorphism. Primary sex differences aside (e.g., genitalia, gonads), sexual dimorphism is most easily discerned by examining secondary sex characteristics that become expressed upon reaching sexual maturity, such as differences in overall

---

* See John L. Heilbron, ed., *The Oxford Companion to the History of Modern Science* (New York: Oxford University Press, 2003), for one of many possible references on the history of science.

† Charles Darwin, *The Descent of Man and Selection in Relation to Sex* (London: John Murray, 1871). Like most scientific theories, sexual selection theory has elicited a fair amount of criticism. For example, see Joan Roughgarden, *Evolution's Rainbow: Diversity, Gender, and Sexuality in Nature and People* (Berkeley: University of California Press, 2004), for a relatively recent and accessible critique. Among other things, Roughgarden argues that Darwin overstated the competitive aspects of the theory and instead demonstrates clear examples of successful cooperative behaviors that increase evolutionary fitness.

size, in coloration, and the appearance of ornaments such as antlers. The intensity of sexual selection, and hence the level of sexual dimorphism, is often (but not always) correlated with how different the roles of females and males are in the reproductive process. Human dimorphism is considered relatively minor, there being only slight average differences in body size, fat distribution, and skeletal anatomy. Humans do have a few species-specific secondary sex traits, such as the appearance of breasts and broadening of the pelvis in females and the growth of facial hair and deepening of the voice in males.*

In sum, within this framework sexual reproduction leads to sexual selection, which in turn results in sexual dimorphism. Sexual selection theory therefore provides a scientific basis for the evolution of oppositional biological sexes, emphasizing fundamental differences between males and females of a species. For *Homo sapiens* this distinction is often uncritically extended to two distinct genders, whose erotic desire targets the opposite sex in the relentless quest to reproduce. The model therefore bolsters hetero- and cisnormative attitudes and practices, while disregarding less common sex/gender anatomy and behavior as pathological.

Social Constructionism

A determinist approach to understanding diversity in biological sex is attractive on several levels, not least in its use of a scientific epistemology to neatly carve species into two distinct types.† However, as this concept was historically applied to human beings, it is clear that many individuals were illegible within this narrative, most obviously members of sex and gender minorities. This exclusion eventually led to a concerted reaction by academics, activists, and allies that emphasized the role that societal norms play in privileging some identities while erasing others.

Challenges to the sex/gender binary developed as part of a broader set of social changes that emerged soon after the end of the Second World War and were characterized by a continual questioning of received wisdom, most pub-

---

*Tertiary sex characteristics are those that involve purported behavioral distinctions between the sexes. This is a highly controversial topic when discussing *Homo sapiens*, as it not only involves alleged temperamental and even cognitive differences between females and males, but also has been invoked to demonstrate the "naturalness" of the gender roles expected of individuals on the basis of their biological sex.

† See Roughgarden, Evolution's Rainbow, and Olivia Judson, *Dr. Tatiana's Sex Advice to All Creation: The Definitive Guide to the Evolutionary Biology of Sex* (New York: Henry Holt, 2002), for many exceptions!

‡ See, for example, Paula S. Rothenberg, ed., *Race, Class, and Gender in the United States: An Integrated Study*, 10th ed. (New York: Worth, 2016).

licly in the form of a variety of civil rights movements and the emergence of identity politics.‡ Within academia a new theoretical framework called post-modern social theory, or simply postmodernism, was gaining traction in the humanities and later the social sciences, which challenged the status quo in unprecedented ways. This framework serves as a reaction to the Modernist viewpoint that promotes the notion of unfettered progress toward human enlightenment and the understanding of alleged universal truths. Central to the postmodern perspective is the contention that human understanding is always contingent on cultural-historical particularities, so that there is no sin-gle knowledge, let alone universal truth.

One consequence of postmodernism is the refuting of the legitimacy of "nat-ural" categories reflecting such objective truths (e.g., woman vs. man) and an emphasis on the critical influence of social context on sculpting identity into culturally acceptable manifestations. The result is the limiting of expression and maintenance of bounded categories. The American gender theorist Judith Butler is perhaps the most well-known scholar to apply postmodernist thought to the concept of gender.* Her articulation of performativity refers to individu-als having no essential gender identity per se; rather, an identity emerges through repetition of linguistic actions, reproduction of social scripts, and relentless bound-ary policing. For example, males learn that expression of anger is considered appropriate and even rewarded, whereas females learn that such expression is negatively sanctioned and therefore should be repressed. In this sense, gender performativity is not unique to gender-nonconforming individuals, but is man-ifest among cisgender people as well.†

Hence, social constructionism undermines stable categorization and, there-fore, rejects the facile binary system used to pigeonhole every human being into one of only two sex or gender categories. In its most extreme form, construction-ism interprets gender differences as almost solely a consequence of an intense socialization process, while biological sex is trivialized beyond its obvious and necessary role in reproduction.

---

* See Jacques Derrida, *Of Grammatology*, trans. Gayatri Chakravorty Spivak (Baltimore: Johns Hopkins University Press, 1976), and Michel Foucault, *The History of Sexuality, Volume 1*, trans. Robert Hurley (1978; repr., New York: Vintage, 1990), for earlier foundational postmodern texts. Derrida focused on language and argued that words don't simply describe the "real" world that Modernism endeavors to reveal; they create that world. Along similar lines, Foucault deconstructed the term *homosexual,* which he claimed was transformed from a behavior into an identity in the nineteenth century, became a subject of scientific discourse, and was pathologized and subjected to medical intervention.

† Judith Butler, *Gender Trouble: Feminism and the Subversion of Identity* (New York: Routledge, 1990). Follow-ing Foucault, Butler's performativity conceptualizes gender expression as a collection of practices, rather than a stable, natural identity.

Does Etiology Matter?

With these two models of sex/gender etiology in mind, we can return to our original question: Is the Jenner-Burkett debate anachronistic, and therefore not worthy of consideration in the rapidly developing discourse addressing trans identity and inclusion? An argument might be made that etiology should not be particularly relevant. Given that so many individuals are disclosing their trans identities, and at progressively younger ages, why not simply accommodate greater sex/gender diversity? For one thing, how we imagine the *cause* of gender identity will undoubtedly influence social acceptance in a broad sense, and more specifically could affect medical and legal interventions in both positive and negative ways. Further, diversity *within* the transgender community, assuming such a community exists, is a critical factor. Jenner's transition and Burkett's reaction represent but one example of how a trans identity can be expressed and how it is received.

Biological factors, considered beyond our conscious control, are often privileged over lifestyle "choices" that we may elect to embrace or deny. Association studies targeting sexually dimorphic areas of the brain have yielded a few tantalizing results suggesting that trans people have brain anatomy comparable to that of their cisgender counterparts.[*] However, scientific evidence demonstrating that trans identities *are* biologically determined could be exploited by those who view transgender people negatively. If trans markers can be identified in utero, pregnancies can be terminated, and genetic sequences can potentially be "corrected" by future gene therapies.

The benefit of the constructionist model is that it undermines the imposition of narrowly prescribed gender roles, thereby permitting individuals greater freedom of expression that correlates more strongly with felt gender. If by extension trans identities are socially produced, however, they could be subject to reparative therapy.

Further, etiological concerns are not limited to second-wave feminists and baby-boomer transsexuals. Jazz Jennings is one of the most visible members of a burgeoning trans youth cohort, and in a recent interview she espoused a determinist position: "That's why I keep sharing my story with others—so that trans-

---

[*] See Francine Russo, "Is There Something Unique about the Transgender Brain?" *Scientific American Mind* (January/February 2016). Similarly, the upward shift in national polling numbers supporting civil rights for gay and lesbian people in the 1990s was at least in part facilitated by scientific studies that claimed to have located a "gay gene." Though the reduction of a complex human behavior to the action of a single genetic sequence is highly problematic, in the minds of the lay public it did suggest that homosexuals could no more change their target of desire than could heterosexuals.

[†] Jazz Jennings, "On Being Trans, Starting High School & More," *HRC Equality* (Summer 2015): 17.

gender kids and their parents can learn that it's okay to be transgender, that it's just another part of who a person is, no different than what color their hair is or how tall they are."[†] This could be interpreted as a twenty-first-century instantiation of the "born in the wrong body" trope that historically was so effective in conveying the trans experience to a skeptical cisgender audience.

But does acknowledging an innate basis for gender identity *necessarily* return us to a paradigm of biological determinism that relegates women, people of color, Indigenous peoples, and so on into subordinate categories? On the other hand, does the recognition of the profound effects of socialization automatically result in the wholesale elimination of sex/gender categories and an explosion of personalized, sui generis identities that in some cases transcend basic anatomy? After all, most people still seem reasonably comfortable with the sex binary, even if expected gender roles do commonly produce some degree of discomfort. Furthermore, association with a collective subaltern category can be a means of finding comfort and political empowerment.

A Framework for the Future?

Perhaps what we are witnessing is the emergence of a more nuanced and sophisticated understanding of sex/gender *systems* that adopts empirically sound and socially just elements of both the determinist and the constructionist models. Rather than viewing social attitudes toward sex/gender diversity as a historical pendulum inexorably oscillating between determinist and constructionist interpretive models, here I appropriate a dialectical framework that could potentially foment a more holistic perspective on variation in sex and gender.

Although dialectic methodology has complex historical roots, for our purposes it can be characterized as a means of resolving two contradictory ideas (the thesis and antithesis) by recourse to a third proposition called the synthesis, which reconciles the prior opposition and produces greater understanding. In our case the thesis is a paradigm of biological determinism that maintains that over the course of millions of years, *Homo sapiens* evolved as a sexually reproducing species in which males and females have become different from each other in fundamental ways not limited to their reproductive anatomy. The oppositional antithesis is a paradigm of social constructionism that focuses on lived experience within a conservative social system that tends to reproduce itself from generation to generation. Within this narrative, a relentless barrage of messages, embedded within customs, norms, and language, channel diversity into a manageable set of stable categories. Specifically, those assigned to one sex or another at birth, usually based on nothing more than a cursory visual inspection of external genital anatomy, are inflected over time into one of two hetero- and cisnormative gender roles that "naturally" juxtapose binary biological sex categories.

The synthesis lies in rejecting the interpretation of inherited biological makeup and learned sociocultural performance as oppositional poles on an explanatory continuum, and instead viewing them as components of an intricate dialectic, each influencing the other through a complex process of *bidirectional causality* and yielding widely diverse yet bounded sex and gender manifestations.* To return to our original protagonists, the dialectic model proposed here permits us to acknowledge that both Jenner and Burkett make valid points, which can be synthesized into a more complete understanding of what it means to be a gendered person in any given time and place. We can accept Jenner's childhood self-awareness of identifying with girls and women, while simultaneously approving Burkett's admonition of perpetuating a "hyper-feminine" presentation that many ciswomen reject.

Conclusion

Memoirs written across generations reveal stark contrasts in how individuals came to understand themselves as part of the diverse identity category we now call transgender.[†] Ethnographic studies of various nonbinary gender manifestations cross-culturally suggest that social environment is critically important. At the same time, it is worth considering that the vast majority of trans people articulate a narrative that includes a sense of discomfort with assigned sex and gender at an early age, which leads to dysphoria ranging from mild to acute.

We may never fully understand the underlying biocultural factors that lead a person to construe themselves as a woman, a man, or something else entirely, but to dismiss the lived experiences of so many gendered "others" across cultures and throughout time evinces a willful ignorance that has profound consequences. The application of the dialectic model offered here should not be cynically viewed as a perfunctory exercise in finding a tepid middle ground. Instead, it should be viewed as radical, in that it *anticipates* a diversity of human sexes and genders. Though it fundamentally disrupts both the determinist and

---

* Riki Lane, "Trans as Bodily Becoming: Rethinking the Biological as Diversity, Not Dichotomy," *Hypatia* 24.3 (2009): 136–157, makes the important observation that by relinquishing the study of the human material body to the natural sciences, scholars in the humanities and social sciences exacerbate the nature-nurture divide in the academy, which makes it difficult to engage in cross-disciplinary dialogue.

† In addition to the comparison of Jenner and Jennings discussed here, also see, for example, Jan Morris, *Conundrum* (New York: Harcourt Brace Jovanovich, 1974), versus Amy Ellis Nutt, *Becoming Nicole: The Transformation of an American Family* (New York: Random House, 2015).

the constructionist models, it nonetheless acknowledges both long- and short-term processes that have indelibly shaped us as a species, and as individuals.

Given the vagaries and contingencies of the evolutionary process as we understand it, broad variation in biological sex, sexuality, and gender identity should not come as any surprise. At the same time, from the point of conception onward, each of us follows a developmental path that is heavily influenced by external factors, from our mother's physiology to the language we acquire, from the attitudes and values we inculcate to the sensory stimuli that fill our days. The aspiration promoted here is that we begin to imagine our biologically evolving bodies and minds, growing and developing in a highly complex socio-cultural milieu, each feeding back on the other.* We don't emerge fully formed but are in a constant act of becoming.

Works Cited

Burkett, Elinor. "What Makes a Woman?" *New York Times,* 6 June 2015, Sunday Review, 1, 6–7.

Butler, Judith. *Gender Trouble: Feminism and the Subversion of Identity.* New York: Routledge, 1990.

Darwin, Charles R. *The Descent of Man and Selection in Relation to Sex.* London: John Murray, 1871.

Derrida, Jacques. *Of Grammatology.* Translated by Gayatri Chakravorty Spivak. Baltimore: Johns Hopkins University Press, 1976.

Foucault, Michel. *The History of Sexuality, Volume 1.* Translated by Robert Hurley. 1978. Reprint. New York: Vintage, 1990.

Heilbron, John L., ed. *The Oxford Companion to the History of Modern Science.* New York: Oxford University Press, 2003.

Hirschfeld, Magnus. *Transvestites: The Erotic Drive to Cross-Dress* (1910). Translated by M. A. Lombardi-Nash. Buffalo: Prometheus Books, 1991.

Jenner, Caitlyn. "Bruce Jenner, the Interview: A Diane Sawyer Special." ABC Television Network, broadcast 24 April 2015.

Jennings, Jazz. "On Being Trans, Starting High School & More." **HRC Equality** (Summer 2015): 17.

Judson, Olivia. *Dr. Tatiana's Sex Advice to All Creation: The Definitive Guide to the Evolutionary Biology of Sex.* New York: Henry Holt, 2002.

---

* Julie Nagoshi and Stephan/ie Brzuzy, "Transgender Theory: Embodying Research and Practice," *Journal of Women and Social Work* 25.4 (2010): 440, encourage trans people to create their "own transcendent narratives . . . derived from the mind and body dynamically working together to transcend social constructs of gender or any other social category."

Lane, Riki. "Trans as Bodily Becoming: Rethinking the Biological as Diversity, Not Dichotomy." *Hypatia* 24.3 (2009): 136–157.

Morris, Jan. *Conundrum*. New York: Harcourt Brace Jovanovich, 1974.

Nagoshi, Julie, and Stephan/ie Brzuzy. "Transgender Theory: Embodying Research and Practice." *Journal of Women and Social Work* 25.4 (2010): 431–443.

Nutt, Amy Ellis. *Becoming Nicole: The Transformation of an American Family*. New York: Random House, 2015.

Raymond, Janice G. *The Transsexual Empire: The Making of the She-Male*. Boston: Beacon Press, 1979.

Rothenberg, Paula S., ed. *Race, Class, and Gender in the United States: An Intergrated Study*. 10th ed. New York: Worth Publishers, 2016.

Roughgarden, Joan. *Evolution's Rainbow: Diversity, Gender, and Sexuality in Nature and People*. Berkeley: University of California Press, 2004.

Russo, Francine. "Is There Something Unique about the Transgender Brain?" *Scientific American Mind* (January/February 2016).

Stone, Sandy. "The Empire Strikes Back: A Posttranssexual Manifesto." In *Body Guards: The Cultural Politics of Gender Ambiguity*, edited by Kristina Straub and Julia Epstein. New York: Routledge, 1991.

Trevathan, Wenda R. *Human Birth: An Evolutionary Perspective*. 1987. Reprint. New Brunswick, N.J.: Transaction, 2011.

Key Concepts

devolution (p. 95)

gender affirmation (p. 104)

gender-affirmation surgery (p. 105)

gender dysphoria (p. 107)

pathologies (p. 92)

sexology (p. 91)

sex-reassignment surgery (srs) (p. 104)

urning (p. 99)

Activities, Discussion Questions, and Observations

1. In talking about her childhood, Bobbi discusses her mother's gladly teaching her to knit despite the fact that Bobbi was assigned male at birth. Bobbi looks to this family history as confirmation that her mother knew she was trans, although that terminology was not available to her at that time. What do Bobbi's mother's actions say about her? What would the various sexologists do with Bobbi's story? She was completely comfortable as a man for several years. She is completely comfortable as a woman now. What are your observations about Bobbi's story? How do Bobbi's story and Dr. McGinn's story reflect (or challenge) societal ideas about men in the military?

2. This activity focuses on T. J. Gundling's essay. Find a news article or one of the stories in this book that discusses coming out as trans. Is the language of the coming-out story centered on biological determinism and/or social constructionism? As you consider this question, also think of the ways that Gundling's dialectic, as you understand it, applies. How do you understand your own gender identity according to these models? (Note: Dialectic is the art of investigating or discussing the truth of opinions.)

3. This is a small-group discussion or a writing assignment. When we think of scientists and doctors in Western medicine and research, we tend to think of them as experts. Part of our perception is warranted because they have all spent years devoted to a particular field of study. In what ways are scientists and doctors experts? In what ways are the people they study and strive to help the experts? What does it mean to be "an expert"? As you consider these questions, you may want to think about yourself or someone you know who has been sick or injured, or who needs medical help. How much were you or the person you know able to participate in finding a way to feel better? In what ways did the medical practitioners listen? In what ways did they not listen? If you or someone you know has tried other forms of care, such as acupuncture, naturopathy, or chiropractic care, it might be useful to compare these patient-caregiver interactions with more traditional Western patient-doctor interactions. How much time did the practitioners spend with you or the person you know?

4. In this chapter you read about the evolution of various labels that sexologists have used for trans people. You could even argue that our culture is obsessed by labels. In what ways do you think labeling people can be helpful? In what ways do you think labeling people can be harmful? Explain your answers.

5. We are often taught that scientific research is completely objective and non-judgmental. Some areas of sexological study certainly have attempted to be unbiased; the Kinsey studies (see Chapter 2) are an excellent example. However, sexology is a scientific and medical field invented by humans to study what is most personal about other humans—specifically, their gender identity and sexual orientation. In what ways do you think sexologists bring their own ideas and their own biases into their research? How objective or subjective do you think they are? How did Krafft-Ebing's ideas of "normal" affect the ways he conducted research in the field of sexology? How do Dr. Christine McGinn's ideas of "normal" affect her work?

6. This is an in-class group discussion or writing project. This chapter provides several examples of people's history becoming silenced. For example, Krafft-Ebing removed Symonds's name on his letter and then included his story in his case study of urnings. Magnus Hirschfeld's work went up in smoke in 1933. These are histories and stories that we are just now discovering. But what about the countless other people whose ideas and lives we may never know anything about? Just within this chapter, whose story would you like to know more about? What group of people might you wonder about, and why? How do we go about recovering lost histories?

7. Look at the Standards of Care (SOC) put out by the World Professional Association for Transgender Health. Compare Version 6 to Version 7, and discuss the differences between the two versions. Also, note that up through Version 6, Gender Identity Disorder was the diagnosis. In Version 7, it is changed to Gender Dysphoria. How does changing the name affect the ways that you see the description? Specifically, discuss the ways that a "disorder" is different from a "dysphoria."

8. The Wellcome Centre in London is a great place to research the history of sexology and sexologists. As part of its special exhibit on sexology in 2015, it published a set of cartoons called *TransVengers*. This comic takes a group of contemporary trans teens and has them confront many of the sexologists that you read about in this chapter. Here is the link to the comic: https://next.wellcomecollec tion.org/articles/the-transvengers-webcomic/. What are your thoughts about the comic? What are some of the valid points that you think the teens have brought up? What are some other points you would like to see addressed?

Film and Television of Interest

The Danish Girl (2015, U.K., Germany, 119 minutes)
This film is loosely based on the life of Lili Elbe and her lover Gerda Wegener. Lili Elbe is possibly the first trans woman to undergo gender-affirmation surgery. Magnus Hirschfeld was famously the sexology consultant during the procedure. Sadly, Elbe died from complications following her surgeries.

The Devil Is in the Details (2016, France, 20 minutes)
Set in nineteenth-century France, this short film explores the experience of a young teacher-in-training who, after being in pain, is examined by a doctor who determines that she is male.

Different from the Others (1919, Germany, 50 minutes)
This is a silent film that has been brought out of obscurity. It is a fictional look at two gay men in Berlin who fall in love and battle the stereotypes of homosexuality. The film is a masterpiece in that it includes archival film sequences of Magnus Hirschfeld and explores his radical ideas that people of all sexual orientations and gender identities should be granted dignity and should have a chance at happiness.

The Einstein of Sex (1999, Germany, Netherlands, 100 minutes)
Magnus Hirschfeld was a Jewish, gay sexologist who was a pioneer in terms of LGBTQ+ rights. This film is a biopic about his life and his work.

Lili Longed to Feel Her Insides (2011, U.S., 5 minutes)
This short film is a fairy tale that pays tribute to Lili Elbe.

Li Yinhe: China's First Female Sexologist (www.makers.com/china/li-yinhe, 2017, Makers online film, 4 minutes and 29 seconds)
This very short interview subtitled in English gives the viewer an insight into Dr. Li Yinhe and her pioneering work in sexology in China. She is married to a trans man.

Lou Sullivan (2016, U.S., 30 minutes)
In this short documentary (part of the We've Been Around series of documentaries), the trans filmmaker and historian Rhys Ernst explore the life and legacy of Lou Sullivan, a gay trans man, AIDS activist, and founder of FTM International.

Paragraph 175 (2000, U.K., Germany, 81 minutes)
Rob Epstein and Jeffrey Friedman's award-winning documentary explores the ways gay men arrested by the Nazis were often used for sexological experimentation. The documentary follows the few remaining gay survivors from the concentration camps. This film also discusses Hirschfeld and the burning of his institue and library.

Southern Comfort (2001, U.S., 90 minutes)

Robert Eads was a trans man who was dying from ovarian cancer. He lived in rural Georgia and was a popular member of the trans community that comes together once a year for the Southern Comfort transgender convention. This documentary follows Robert and his group of friends, chosen family, and biological family during his last year. This is a beautiful film that shows the real consequences trans people face in an often hostile medical environment.

Trans (2012, U.S.,104 minutes)

At times this documentary film sensationalizes trans people. The strength of this film, however, lies in the stories of the trans people themselves. Several trans people are featured throughout this film, including a child whose parents are supportive. Most important, perhaps, is that this film's main focus is on Dr. Christine McGinn and her gender wellness center, the Papillon Center.

NOTES

1. Charles Wilson, "An Artist Finds a Dignified Ending for an Ugly Story," *New York Times,* 11 February 2013, www.nytimes.com/2013/02/12/arts/design/julia-pastrana-who-died-in-1860-to-be-buried-in-mexico.html (accessed 13 July 2017).

2. Jan Bondeson, *A Cabinet of Medical Curiosities* (Ithaca, N.Y.: Cornell University Press, 1997), 217.

3. Wilson, "An Artist Finds a Dignified Ending for an Ugly Story."

4. Ibid.

5. Meegan Kennedy, "'Poor Hoo Loo': Sentiment, Stoicism, and the Grotesque in British Imperial Medicine," in *Victorian Freaks: The Social Context of Freakery in Britain,* ed. by Marlene Tromp (Columbus: Ohio State University Press, 2008), 81. See also Marlene Tromp, "Empire and the Indian Freak: The 'Miniature Man' from Cawnpore and the 'Marvellous Indian Boy' on Tour in England," ibid., 165.

6. Kelly Hurley, "Hereditary Taint and Cultural Contagion: The Social Etiology of Fin-de-Siècle Degeneration Theory," *Nineteenth Century Contexts* 1.2 (1990): 193–195.

7. Gina Lombroso-Ferrero, *Criminal Man: According to the Classification of Cesare Lombroso, with an Introduction by Cesare Lombroso* (1911) (Montclair, N.J.: Patterson Smith, 1972), 17–19.

8. Richard von Krafft-Ebing, *Psychopathia Sexualis: With Especial Reference to Antipathic Sexual Instinct: A Medico-Forensic Study* (original first edition in German, 1877), 10th edition (London: Forgotten Books, 2012), 384.

9. Ibid., iv.

10. Ibid., Case 122, 375.

11. Ibid., 376.

12. Ibid., 377.

13. See Symonds's, *John Addington Symonds and Homosexuality: A Critical Edition of Sources,* ed. Sean Brady (Houndmills, Basingstoke: Palgrave Macmillan, 2012). This book contains Symonds's work on sexology and his collaborative writings with Havelock Ellis, even though, at the time, Symonds did not get any credit for working with Ellis.

14. Gerard Koskovich, "Through Knowledge to Justice: The Sexual World of Dr. Magnus Hirschfeld (1868–1935)," booklet for the GLBT Historical Museum, San Francisco, 2016, 1.

15. Mancini, *Magnus Hirschfeld and the Quest for Sexual Freedom,* 81.

16. Magnus-Hirschfeld-Gesellschaft, www.magnus-hirschfeld.de/start-en/; "The First Institute for Sexual Science (1919–1933)," www.magnus-hirschfeld.de/ausstellungen/institute/ (both accessed 27 June 2018).

17. Koskovich, "Through Knowledge to Justice," 1.

18. Harry Benjamin, *The Transsexual Phenomenon* (New York: Julian Press, 1966).

19. Several trans women were interviewed in Susan Stryker and Victor Silverman's film *Screaming Queens: The Riot at Compton's Cafeteria,* Frameline, 2005.

20. Joanne Meyerowitz, "A 'Fierce and Demanding' Drive," in *The Transgender Studies Reader,* ed. Susan Stryker and Stephen Whittle (New York: Routledge, 2006), 363.

21. Wynne Parry, "Gender Dysphoria: DSM-5 Reflects Shift in Perspective on Gender Identity," *HuffPost,* 4 August 2013, www.huffingtonpost.com/2013/06/04/gender-dysphoria-dsm-5_n_3385287.html (accessed 13 July 2017).

22. Dean Strauss, "Lou Sullivan," Making Queer History, https://www.makingqueerhistory.com/articles/2018/5/21/lou-sullivan (accessed 27 June 2018).

23. Online Archives of California, "Guide to the Louis Graydon Sullivan Papers, 1955–1991 (bulk 1961–1991)," http://pdf.oac.cdlib.org/pdf/glhs/sullivan.pdf (accessed 27 June 2018).

24. Lou Sullivan's diaries are in the holdings at the GLBT Historical Society archives in San Francisco. The public has access to them.

25. You can research trans rights in Iran as an excellent example here. Homosexuality is still punishable by imprisonment or death. The Iranian government will support gender-affirmation surgery, however, but only if the trans person will be heterosexual. There are also testimonies coming from LGBT asylum seekers who have left Iran that note the Iranian government will sometimes force gender surgeries on gay men in order to heterosexualize them. See Dan Littauer, "Iran Performed over 1,000 Gender Reassignment Operations in Four Years," *Gay Star News,* 4 December 2012, https://www.gaystarnews.com/article/iran-performed-over-1000-gender-reassignment-operations-four-years041212/#gs.u_yQtuI (accessed 15 July 2017).

26. Online Archive of California, "Guide to the Louis Graydon Sullivan Papers, 1961–1991," www.oac.cdlib.org/findaid/ark:/13030/tf9199n9v3/entire_text/ (accessed 15 July 2017).

27. Yuan Ren, "Chinese Feminist: 'If I Talk about Women's Rights in China, People Will Think I'm Sick,'" *Telegraph,* 15 April 2015, www.telegraph.co.uk/women/womens-life/11535311/Chinese-female-activist-Womens-rights-are-seen-as-a-sickness-here.html (accessed 14 July 2017).

28. Ibid.

29. Kenneth Tan, "Li Yinhe: My Partner Is a Transgender Man, and I Am Not a Lesbian," *Shanghaist,* 20 December 2014, http://shanghaiist.com/2014/12/20/li-yinhe-trans.php (accessed 15 July 2017).

30. Ibid.

31. Li Yinhe, keynote address, "Women, Sexuality, and Social Change in China" conference, Brookings Institution, Washington, D.C., 3 April 2015, https://www.brookings.edu/wp-content/uploads/2015/03/20150403_china_gender_sexuality_transcript.pdf (accessed 14 July 2017).

32.	Papillon Gender Wellness Center, www
.drchristinemcginn.com/ (accessed 15 July
2017).

33.	Interview with Dr. Christine McGinn in
Chris Arnold's documentary film, *Trans*,
RoseWorks/Sex Smart Films, 2012.

34.	Ibid.

35.	Papillon Gender Wellness Center, "Media
Appearances," www.drchristinemcginn
.com/drmcginn/media.php (accessed 15
July 2017).

36.	Jess Dugan, "Artist Statement," www
.jessdugan.com/statements/ (accessed 27
March 2018).

BIBLIOGRAPHY

Arnold, Chris. *Trans*. Film. RoseWorks/Sex Smart Films, 2012.

Bauer, J. Edgar. "Magnus Hirschfeld's Doctrine of Sexual Intermediaries and the Transgender Politics of (No-)Identity." www.iisg.nl/womhist/hirschfeld.doc. Accessed 15 November 2015.

Benjamin, Harry. *The Transsexual Phenomenon*. New York: Julian Press, 1966.

Bondeson, Jan. *A Cabinet of Medical Curiosities*. Ithaca, N.Y.: Cornell University Press, 1997.

Davis, Kate. *Southern Comfort*. Film. Docurama, 2001.

Hurley, Kelly. "Hereditary Taint and Cultural Contagion: The Social Etiology of Fin-de-Siècle Degeneration Theory." *Nineteenth Century Contexts* 1.2 (1990): 193–214.

Institute for Sexual Science. "The First Institute for Sexual Science (1919–1933)." www.magnus-hirschfeld.de/ausstellungen/institute/. Accessed 27 June 2018.

Kennedy, Meegan. "'Poor Hoo Loo': Sentiment, Stoicism, and the Grotesque in British Imperial Medicine." In *Victorian Freaks: The Social Context of Freakery in Britain*. Edited by Marlene Tromp, 70–113. Columbus: Ohio State University Press, 2008.

Koskovich, Gerard. "Through Knowledge to Justice: The Sexual World of Dr. Magnus Hirschfeld (1868–1935)." Booklet for the GLBT Historical Museum, San Francisco, 2016.

Krafft-Ebing, Richard von. *Psychopathia Sexualis: With Especial Reference to Antipathic Sexual Instinct: A Medico-Forensic Study* (1877). 10th edition. London: Forgotten Books, 2012.

Littauer, Dan. "Iran Performed Over 1,000 Gender Reassignment Operations in Four Years." *Gay Star News*, 4 December 2012. https://www.gaystarnews.com/article/iran-performed-over-1000-gender-reassignment-operations-four-years041212/#gs.u_yQtuI. Accessed 15 July 2017.

Lombroso-Ferrero, Gina. *Criminal Man: According to the Classification of Cesare Lombroso, with an Introduction by Cesare Lombroso*. Montclair, N.J.: Patterson Smith, 1972.

Magnus-Hirschfeld-Gesellschaft. www.magnus-hirschfeld.de/start-en/. Accessed 27 June 2018.

Online Archive of California. "Guide to the Louis Graydon Sullivan Papers, 1955–1991 (bulk 1961–1991)." http://pdf.oac.cdlib.org/pdf/glhs/sullivan.pdf. Accessed 27 June 2018.

Pace, Eric. "Harry Benjamin Dies at 101; Specialist in Transsexualism." *New York Times,* 27 August 1986. www.nytimes.com/1986/08/27/obituaries/harry-benjamin-dies-at -101-specialist-in-transsexualism.html. Accessed 17 December 2015.

Papillon Gender Wellness Center, www.drchristinemcginn.com/. Accessed 15 July 2017.

Parry, Wynne. "'Gender Dysphoria' DSM-5 Reflects Shift in Perspective on Gender Identity." *HuffPost,* 4 August 2013. www.huffingtonpost.com/2013/06/04/gender-dysphoria -dsm-5_n_3385287.html. Accessed 13 July 2017.

Ren, Yuan. "Chinese Feminist: 'If I Talk about Women's Rights in China, People Will Think I'm Sick.'" *Telegraph,* 15 April 2015. www.telegraph.co.uk/women/womens-life /11535311/Chinese-female-activist-Womens-rights-are-seen-as-a-sickness- here.html. Accessed 14 July 2017.

Stryker, Susan. "I Know Lou Sullivan Better Than Anybody I Never Met." *FTM Newsletter,* Summer 2007. https://www.ftmvariations.org/IMG/pdf/lousullivan.pdf. Accessed 11 July 2018.

———. *Screaming Queens: The Riot at Compton's Cafeteria.* Film. Frameline, 2005.

Sullivan, Louis Graydon. Diaries. GLBT Historical Society archives, San Francisco.

Symonds, John Addington. *John Addington Symonds and Homosexuality: A Critical Edition of Sources.* Edited by Sean Brady. Houndmills, Basingstoke: Palgrave Macmillan, 2012.

Tan, Kenneth. "Li Yinhe: My Partner Is a Transgender Man, and I Am Not a Lesbian." *Shanghaiist,* 20 December 2014. http://shanghaiist.com/2014/12/20/li-yinhe-trans.php. Accessed 15 July 2017.

TransVengers. The Wellcome Centre. https://next.wellcomecollection.org/articles/the-trans vengers-webcomic/. Accessed 15 July 2017.

Tromp, Marlene. "Empire and the Indian Freak: The 'Miniature Man' from Cawnpore and the 'Marvellous Indian Boy' on Tour in England." In *Victorian Freaks: The Social Context of Freakery in Britain,* edited by Marlene Tromp, 157–179. Columbus: Ohio State University Press, 2008.

Wilson, Charles. "An Artist Finds a Dignified Ending for an Ugly Story." *New York Times,* 11 February 2013. www.nytimes.com/2013/02/12/arts/design/julia-pastrana-who- died-in-1860-to-be-buried-in-mexico.html. Accessed 13 July 2017.

Yinhe, Li. Keynote address at "Women, Sexuality, and Social Change in China" conference at the Brookings Institution, Washington, D.C., 3 April 2015. https://www.brook ings.edu/wp-content/uploads/2015/03/20150403_china_gender_sexuality_tran script.pdf. Accessed 14 July 2017.

CHAPTER 4

Direct Action, Collective Histories, and Collective Activism: What a Riot!

All of us were working for so many movements at that time. Everyone was involved with the women's movement, the peace movement, the Civil Rights movement. We were all radicals. I believe that's what brought it around.

SYLVIA RIVERA*

Key Questions

1. Does rioting work?

2. Does protest work?

3. What kind of person would you expect to lead a political and social movement?

4. How do intersecting identities work in the context of riots and protests?

5. How did the split between L, G, B, and T come about?

6. How do we honor all histories of activism without privileging one group over another?

Chapter Overview

This chapter looks at political activism in the United States during the turbulent and politically charged 1950s and 1960s. The story of transgender activism, political movements, and coalition building is very much the story of intersecting identities and intersecting oppressions. In many cases, the beginnings of the legal reforms that support LGBTQ+ people in the United States today were brought about by trans people of color who lived at the poverty level or who were homeless. This convergence of being gender nonconforming or a gender outlaw, being

---

*Sylvia Rivera's interview, "I'm Glad I Was in the Stonewall Riot," in Leslie Feinberg, *Trans Liberation: Beyond Pink or Blue* (Boston: Beacon Press, 1998), 107.

Haefele-Thomas, Ardel, *Introduction to Transgender Studies*
dx.doi.org/10.17312/harringtonparkpress/2019.01.itts.004
© 2019 by Harrington Park Press

a person of color, and being someone who did not have financial security motivated and gave strength to these early activists. But this chapter does not solely focus on individuals who were part of historic activism; it also underscores the importance of collective histories and collective activism.

This chapter is not just about recovering lost heroes or arguing which exact person was responsible for a certain action. Rather, it is about the collective conditions and collective disruptions that helped shape activism. At the same time, it is also crucial to understand the ways that the LGBTQ+ community winds up becoming split, often in such a way that bisexual people are left out of conversations and transgender people are left out of important legislation, such as employment nondiscrimination protection. Infighting within the LGBTQ+ rights movement weakens us all; however, almost all civil rights and human rights movements have become divided. In minority histories, there is often an idea that there isn't enough pie to go around. This sort of thinking further silences marginalized people.

In looking at various forms of political action, from protests and riots to picket lines, you will also be examining how various groups of sexual and gender outlaws approached their need for recognition and rights. In many cases, another binary is set up: people who worked *within* existing political systems and people who fought for liberation *outside* existing political systems. Some questions to keep in mind as you read this chapter: Can a person be radical and still work within the system? Can those who work outside the system still bring about systemic change? These were critical questions not only for the LGBTQ+ rights movement of the 1950s and 1960s but also for other social and political movements like the Civil Rights movement, the women's rights movement, the United Farmworkers' movement, the American Indian Movement, and the peace movement.

Ultimately, this chapter asks you to think more expansively about history and to understand that there is room for multiple histories. History is a living thing. As such, it is ever-expansive and can be empowering if we truly let it be all-inclusive.

Introduction: A Need for Collective Histories

Have you read or heard former President Barack Obama's second inaugural address, which he gave on January 21, 2013? If not, here is a portion of what he said that evening: "We, the people, declare today that the most evident of truths —that all of us are created equal—is the star that guides us still; just as it guided our forebears through Seneca Falls, and Selma, and Stonewall."[1] With this reference to Stonewall, President Obama's speech marked a specific historic moment for the LGBTQ+ community. No sitting president in U.S. history had ever made a direct reference to the LGBTQ+ rights movement and struggle. Certainly, no sitting president before President Obama did so in a positive light and in the context of two other major historic moments in U.S. history.

Do you already know what happened at the three places President Obama mentioned in his speech: Seneca Falls, Selma, and Stonewall? Aside from the nice use of alliteration (each of the places begins with the same consonant, "s"), they also mark three specific sites, in order of occurrence, where major battles for social justice took place.

On July 19 and 20, 1848, over two hundred women and forty men gathered at a convention in **Seneca Falls,** New York, in support of *women's suffrage* (women's right to vote). The two women who organized the event, Elizabeth Cady Stanton and Lucretia Mott, were also abolitionists (people against slavery). One of the men in attendance was Frederick Douglass, a former slave, an activist, and a writer in the abolition movement. Like many others who attended the convention, Douglass understood the connections between the abolition movement and the women's suffrage movement. The result of the Seneca Falls Convention (figure 4.1) was "The Declaration of Sentiments and Grievances" modeled on the Declaration of Independence. The writing made the convention's purpose crystal clear: "We hold these truths to be self-evident: that all men *and women* are created equal."[2]

On March 7, 1965, a group of civil rights workers, which included people of many ethnicities and walks of life (including several religious leaders), were marching from **Selma** to Montgomery, Alabama, to secure voting rights for African Americans in the Jim Crow South (figure 4.2). A group of state troopers and other white county leaders physically attacked and beat them on the Edmund Pettus Bridge in Selma. Although many of the marchers were left bleeding and unconscious, on March 9 Dr. Martin Luther King Jr. led another group back to the bridge in protest.[3] By March 25, and bolstered by military police and thousands of supporters, the marchers made it to the Alabama state capitol, where they delivered their petition to Governor George Wallace, who did *not* support the movement. By August 6 of that year, however, President Lyndon Baines Johnson signed the Voting Rights Act into law.[4]

On June 28, 1969, in the very early hours of the morning, the police carried out a routine raid on the **Stonewall Inn,** a dive bar in Greenwich Village, New York City, that was often patronized by gay men, lesbians, bisexuals, and drag queens (the word *transgender* was not in common use yet).[5] This was not a wealthy neighborhood, and the clientele of the Stonewall Inn (figure 4.3) reflected the neighborhood's racial, ethnic, gender, and socioeconomic diversity. Because the Stonewall

FIGURE 4.1 "Seneca Falls," by Cameron Rains. The gathering at Seneca Falls, New York, in 1848 was the first women's rights convention in the United States. Although the former slave, abolitionist, activist, and prolific writer Frederick Douglass was an honored guest who underscored the similarities between women's suffrage and abolition, a group of African American women was banned from attending.

FIGURE 4.2 "Selma," by Cameron Rains. In March 1965 John Lewis and Hosea Williams organized a march from Selma, Alabama, to Montgomery, Alabama, as part of a Civil Rights protest. When the group of marchers reached the Edmund Pettus Bridge, they were met by white law enforcement officers, who beat them with clubs and attempted to drive them back with tear gas. This incident was one of many critical moments in the Civil Rights struggle.

FIGURE 4.3 "Stonewall," by Cameron Rains. Like Seneca Falls and Selma before it, the uprising at the Stonewall Inn in New York in 1969 is seen as the critical moment that sparked the "gay liberation" movement. If you look closely at the illustration, you can see that the other protests covered in this chapter are also depicted. What stories can be told by focusing on single historical moments like Stonewall? And what other stories get lost when we focus on just one event?

Inn had a reputation as a bar that would serve homosexuals, drag queens, and trans people (remember that these categories were not separated at the time and that the word *trans* was not a category for anyone yet), it was a relatively safe space for a variety of people who might not otherwise gather in the same social settings. The mere fact that the police and the public saw them as sexual and/or gender outlaws ensured that the inn's clientele, on any given night, was likely to be varied. The police raid itself was nothing new because in 1969 it was still illegal for any place, including bars, to allow more than three "known homosexuals" to gather together at one time. What was different was that in the early hours of this particular Sunday morning, the patrons of the Stonewall Inn refused to be bullied by the police. Their acts of resistance sparked a week of unrest in the streets of Greenwich Village. To this day, we mark the events of that night as the beginning of the LGBTQ+ rights movement in the United States.

President Obama was right to call out Seneca Falls, Selma, and Stonewall to help him exemplify moments in history when everyday people in the United States stood up to oppressive governmental and legal systems and said, "Enough is enough!" In specifying these three locations, however, President Obama inadvertently underscored the cultural myth that one exact historic moment defines a movement. But history is fluid; history is alive. The Seneca Falls Convention was an extremely important stop on the long road to women's suffrage in the United States; but how many other discussions, meetings, and acts of resistance among various women and men had already taken place before Seneca Falls? (Certainly, there were many.) The march from Selma to Montgomery for racial equality and voting rights was monumental. But how many other acts of resistance in the wake of beatings and lynchings had already taken place across the United States before Selma? (Again, there were many.) The Stonewall Rebellion may have broken open the closet doors to usher in the modern LGBTQ+ rights movement; however, on how many other days and nights did LGBTQ+ people stand up in both small and large ways against police brutality? Trans people of color were often at the forefront of these actions, but both mainstream culture *and* gay and lesbian culture often paint these momentous and courageous acts of defiance as white and cisgender. Doing so further marginalizes LGBTQ+ people of color, particularly trans people of color.

Go back to the beginning of this chapter and look at Sylvia Rivera's quote. Like so many other people, she was involved in numerous other political movements during the 1950s and 1960s. Rivera's point is that these movements, although given separate names, were related—especially for some of the most marginalized people in our society.

Would You Like a Protest with Your Coffee?

When you think of the "all-American" diner or the "always open" doughnut shop, the first things that come to your mind are probably not police raids, riots, and protests. Chances are, you have a favorite late-night place to study or meet up with friends. Why is it your favorite place? The answer could be as simple as "It's the only place open late" or "It's the cheapest place in town." Whether your favorite spot is a student-run café on your campus, a quirky little espresso bar around the corner, or the local diner, imagine yourself there with a group of friends unwinding after a long day.

Now, imagine police officers suddenly coming into the café. They have their batons in hand and demand that you all stand, go over to the corner, pull up your skirt or pull down your pants, and show them that you are wearing undergarments that are gender appropriate. You may wonder what the phrase "gender appropriate" even means. Let's say that the police decide your clothes are not gender appropriate. They have a van waiting outside. They arrest you and shove you into the van with a bunch of other people whom they deemed as not wearing "gender appropriate" clothing.

The three protests you will read about in this section have several things in common. First, they all happened in neighborhoods located in the impoverished part of an urban center. In the two West Coast cities, the neighborhoods had nicknames that exemplified the stereotype that they were poor and "dangerous." In Los Angeles, the neighborhood was Skid Row, which to this day in American slang denotes a dirty and unfavorable place. In San Francisco, the neighborhood was the Tenderloin; a tenderloin is a cut of beef. There is a lot of speculation about exactly how the neighborhood got this name. Many speculate that the Tenderloin was an area where vice cops took bribes to "not see" crimes (and because they got rich by doing this, they were able to afford tenderloin for dinner instead of ground beef). Another theory is that Tenderloin refers to a neighborhood known for sex work (prostitution) and that the "tender loin" referred to the flesh trade. In Philadelphia, the neighborhood was downtown at 13th and 17th Streets near Rittenhouse Square. In the case of Philadelphia, the neighborhood itself did not have a negative nickname, but the café on 13th Street in downtown Philadelphia was called "fag Dewey's" not only by people within the LGBTQ+ community who frequented the café but also by the police.

In each of these places, the café or shop where the protest or riot erupted was a twenty-four-hour spot that, *because* of its location, served a diverse group of people *especially* at night. For example, it was not at all uncommon for police officers, sex workers, and people leaving bars after closing time to all wind up in the same café at the same time.

These neighborhoods also shared socioeconomic characteristics. After World War II and the decade following (the 1950s), the middle class in the United States (more specifically, heterosexual, cisgender, white, middle-class people) no longer wanted to live in urban centers. Anyone who could afford to leave downtown areas for the suburbs did so, and the collective result is known as *white flight*. (Even blue-collar communities that were situated closer to downtown areas were still not located in the urban centers, and they were still recognized as what we would call "neighborhoods.") So, how did white flight affect the city centers?

By the late 1950s, the majority of people living in the downtown areas of major U.S. cities were some of the country's poorest people: specifically, people of color (particularly African American and *Latinx,* the gender-neutral form for Latino/a); recent immigrants; and white gay, lesbian, bisexual, and transgender people. Certainly, some LGBTQ+ people (particularly white but also some people of color) who were in the closet lived outside the urban centers, but if they wanted to find other people like themselves, they needed to go into the city, to the "wrong side of the tracks," to find the bars and clubs where they were at least marginally welcome. Police often raided these bars because it was illegal for two men or two women to dance together, and it was also illegal for someone to wear more than three pieces of "wrong gender" clothing.

The third, and possibly the most important, thing that these urban enclaves had in common was their population of people whose intersecting identities were part of the reason they were relegated to these areas. As noted earlier, these areas were extremely diverse. For example, a young and poor transgender African American person might have found a place like the Tenderloin or Skid Row to be the only relatively safe space to live. It might have been the only community where the person could find a landlord to rent to them. And it might very well have been the only place where that person could also find a community. Suburbs were the home of homogeneous, mostly white, populations. Even the more affluent neighborhoods or working-class neighborhoods with people of color were still focused on heterosexual nuclear families. Thus, people of color, the poor, the homeless, recent immigrants, *and* those who were either "out" as LGBTQ+ or who went out seeking other LGBTQ+ people wound up in the same places. Many of the poor people of color were also gay, lesbian, bisexual, and/or transgender and might even have been homeless *because* their families of origin had rejected them and kicked them out of the house—in many cases, when these people were teenagers.

It is also critical to remember that, at this time in the United States, several anti-cross-dressing or *anti-masquerading* laws were on the books. If you were not wearing the "correct" gender clothing, the police could arrest you. Note that the word *masquerade* carries the assumption that the person is being deceptive. In most states, being gay, lesbian, or bisexual was illegal. (These laws were known as **sodomy laws**, and definitions varied from state to state.)[6] As far as the police were concerned, there really was no differentiation between sexual orientation and gender identity. Often, people who would define themselves as trans today historically called themselves *queens*, *transvestites*, *cross-dressers*, or *butches*. This is not to say that all people who identify as queens or butches are trans, but it is important to remember that queens and butches were read not only as homo-sexual, but also as gender outlaws. We *can* make the argument that butches and queens trouble the gender binary.

Homosexual acts were a sex crime in the same way that being a sex worker was a sex crime. And many people who were LGBTQ+ also did sex work. These areas of urban neglect were home to rich and complex layers of diversity, and the people who inhabited and frequented these areas often did not have much to lose socially. Many of them, like the pioneer Sylvia Rivera, had been kicked out of their homes of origin at a young age. (Queer and trans youth still make up a disproportionate number of homeless youth in the United States today, and many of those youth are people of color.) The inhabitants of Skid Row, Rittenhouse Square, the Tenderloin, and Greenwich Village had little more than their dignity, which ultimately enabled and empowered them.

May 1959: *The Little Doughnut Shop That Could!*

Cooper's Donuts symbolized a sanctuary for not just the gay population of Los Angeles, but also for the overlooked transgender population. Their presence brought irrational prejudice, violence, and judgement, but Cooper's allowed them a space to take part in conversations and be who they were without the fear of scrutiny. The gathering and joint effort of LGBTQ+ people on the night of the riot is representative of the family that Cooper's created.*

Not long after it opened in Los Angeles's Skid Row (a poor, predominantly Latinx area), Cooper's Donuts became the site of one of the first-known LGBTQ+ upris-ings in the United States. During the day, the little downtown doughnut and coffee shop was popular with the Los Angeles Police Department. At night, not

* Cooper's Donuts, http://cdonuts1959.weebly.com/paper.html (accessed 2 March 2016).

only were the "graveyard shift" police officers customers at Cooper's, but from all historical accounts, it appears that this shop was also very welcoming to drag queens and other gender nonconforming customers.[7]

Interestingly, Cooper's sat between two gay bars: Harold's and the Waldorf, neither of which allowed **drags** (another name for queens, cross-dressers, and trans people) access because they were afraid that the LAPD would target and harass bar patrons even more than they already did if the bars allowed gender outlaws inside. There was an idea that if everyone came to the bar wearing gender-appropriate clothing, then the police might not raid as often. (At the time, Los Angeles had strict anti-cross-dressing and anti-masquerading laws.) So if trans people were denied access to the gay bars, then the bars might not fall under police scrutiny. In reality, the police merely waited outside the bars and then followed male couples and arrested them under the anti-sodomy laws.

Although there was some racial segregation at the gay bars, generally speaking, the lines of exclusion fell more on the "gender-appropriate" dress spectrum. In fact, in Los Angeles as early as 1951, a group known as Knights of the Clock was formed to help support interracial gay couples who faced racist and homophobic discrimination in housing and other services.[8]

By all accounts, though, Cooper's was a friendly place for many people who had nowhere else safe to go in the middle of the night: sex workers, hustlers, trans people, drag queens, butch lesbians—and most of the people in these categories were people of color. Then, one evening in May 1959, the police entered the shop and demanded that everyone show their identification. It should also be noted here that the LAPD in 1959 was white, presumed to be heterosexual, and cisgender male. If the sex on the customer's I.D. did not match their gender presentation, they were arrested. The group arrested that night were predominantly people of color, and all were wearing enough "wrong clothing" to be hauled out to the police cruiser.

One of those arrested was the now-famous Chicano author John Rechy, who wrote about the event in his classic 1963 novel, *City of Night*.[9] Once out at the patrol car, the group resisted. The other patrons of Cooper's, who had watched the arrests with anger and horror but resignation because they were used to such harassment, became empowered when the arrestees at the patrol car began to resist. Bolstered by the shift in energy, they ran out of Cooper's and started throwing doughnuts, cups of coffee, and garbage at the officers. The police dumped the people they had arrested onto the pavement and fled the scene, only to return with reinforcements.

The police went to get more help, but the people at Cooper's also wound up with reinforcements: people started streaming out of Harold's and the Waldorf, and they tried to overturn the police vehicle. According to one account, a couple of the drag queens enlivened everyone's mood as they danced around the police car. The riot ended when Main Street was closed to clean up the mess the next day.[10]

The incident at Cooper's Donuts may seem to be a small blip on the radar, but it is a representative moment in L.A.'s history of clashes between white, male, heteronormative uniformed authorities and minority groups violating the anti-masquerading laws, which the police enforced very broadly. The decade before the riot at Cooper's, over a ten-day period in June 1943, the Los Angeles neighborhoods of Chinatown, Chavez Ravine, East Los Angeles, and Watts (all neighborhoods and communities that were predominantly immigrant, Asian American, Mexican American, and/or African American) were swarmed by white military men who came from bases around Los Angeles, San Diego, and Las Vegas and were joined by other white civilians. These squads of servicemen and civilians broke into private homes, dragged people off public transit, and bombarded businesses to physically assault people because of their clothing. This ten-day period in L.A.'s history is now known as the *Zoot Suit Riots*.[11]

Zoot suits were a fashion in the 1940s. A zoot suit was basically a nice man's suit that was made overly large and baggy. Although young people of all ethnicities and races wore this style, Mexican Americans, in particular, were targeted by the white authorities because the clothes were seen as "un-American," not "gender normative" (because they exaggerated a gender "norm"), and a violation of anti-masquerading laws. During the Zoot Suit Riots, the servicemen hauled the youths out into the street, forced them onto the ground, shaved their heads, ripped their clothing off, and beat them up. The servicemen were making a violent statement that the "Zoot Suiters" were not wearing the "appropriate" clothing.

In one instance, the police arrested a group of three Mexican American women for what we could call a double anti-masquerading law violation: not only were the women wearing zoot suits, but instead of wearing the women's version of the suit that included a skirt, these women were wearing pants, which was viewed as masculine and as an act of cross-dressing rebellion.[12]

Although she was too young to have been a part of the Zoot Suit Riots, Nancy Valverde, a butch Chicanx barber in East Los Angeles, was repeatedly arrested throughout the 1950s by LAPD on these same anti-masquerading laws: "When I was about seventeen, I got picked up for masquerading . . . [by the police]. I said, 'What the heck is that?'" Nancy always wore trousers and loose button-down shirts. Although her outfit was not exactly the same as a zoot suit, the similarity was there. One of her arrests led to a three-month imprisonment.

April 1965: The Quaker City's Collaborative Sit-In

This Dewey's was near to the bars on 13th, Camac, and Chancellor Streets and it was open all night. It was the perfect hangout after the bars and the after hours clubs closed. Widely known as the "fag" Dewey's, it was noisily packed late into the night with a whole spectrum of drag queens, hustlers, dykes, leather men and Philly cops looking for a cup of coffee, a cross section of life on 13th Street.*

Like Cooper's Donuts on Skid Row in Los Angeles, the all-night counter service restaurant Dewey's Famous on 13th Street in Philadelphia was a bustling and welcoming place for people from all walks of life. Although the writer uses the derogatory term "fag," it is clear from the above quote that the term is being used by someone from within the LGBTQ+ community. "Fag" Dewey's was probably the nickname given to the coffee shop by people from that community. Note that the author describes this location as a "perfect hangout" and points out that a very diverse group of people felt comfortable there, including police officers.

Philadelphia has been deeply influenced by *Quaker* philosophy, which, in its broadest ideals, embraces pacifism and focuses on making decisions through discussion and consent rather than hierarchy. Along with the Quakers, Philadelphia, also known as "The City of Brotherly Love," was home to over half a million African Americans by 1965. It was also home to over 60,000 Puerto Ricans and a growing Jewish community. So it stands to reason that the clientele at Dewey's was ethnically diverse. Like L.A.'s Skid Row, inner-city Philadelphia was home to a predominantly poor population.[13]

According to various accounts, the managers of other Dewey's Famous locations all knew that the 13th Street Dewey's was welcoming to all people; however, they did not want their other lunch counters to be quite so accommodating. When the Dewey's Famous only a few blocks away on 17th Street near Rittenhouse Square also started to attract a large homosexual clientele (remember that *homosexual* was the general term used for all gender and sexual minorities), the management told the wait staff to refuse service to anyone who looked homosexual or who was wearing gender-nonconforming clothing—in other words, anyone who looked as though they were transgressing the gender binary.[14]

According to one newspaper account at that time, some of the people working at the 17th Street Dewey's got carried away with the management's request and began refusing service to all sorts of people. In this instance, instead of a

---

* Bob Skiba, "Dewey's Famous," Philadelphia Gayborhood Guru, https://thegayborhoodguru.wordpress.com/2013/01/28/deweys-famous/ (accessed 29 February 2016).

riot's erupting, the Janus Society (one of Philadelphia's early gay-rights groups) stood outside Dewey's handing out information about why a lunch counter sit-in was planned for the following week.

True to their word, the following week, 150 people from the various communities in that area of Philadelphia—people of different ethnicities, sexual orientations, and gender identities—came into Dewey's Famous cross-dressed, or wearing "gender inappropriate" clothing, and sat in until the police arrived. Almost everyone left peacefully, but a small number of people were arrested and then released. "The concept of a sit-in was really tied to the 1960s black civil-rights protests that were going on and with the era of civil disobedience," says Bob Skiba, archivist at the William Way LGBT Community Center in Philadelphia. "There were so many demonstrations around the city [Philadelphia], for racial equality and against the Vietnam War."[15]

The Dewey's sit-in was a success on two fronts. First, employees at Dewey's Famous locations throughout Philadelphia started serving everyone who came in regardless of their gender expression. Second, and perhaps more important, the sit-in at Dewey's underscores what happens when many parts of a community come together to make change. Imagine that: in 1965, 150 people regardless of their identity chose to wear "gender inappropriate" clothing and have a sit-in at a twenty-four-hour diner. They may not have been aware of it at the time, but their actions were the latest in a long line of historical social-justice-oriented protests carried out by everyday people against oppressive systems in the seventeenth, eighteenth, and nineteenth centuries.

The African American trans activist, scholar, and blogger Monica Roberts writes the following about the importance of the Dewey's protests: "As a person who has been involved for a decade in the struggle for transgender rights, it is deeply gratifying to know that African-American transgender activism isn't a new phenomenon. I'm estatic [sic] to discover another nugget of my African-American transgender history. I'm gratified to know that I'm a link in a chain that will eventually expand the 'We The People' in the constitution to include transgender ones as well."[16]

A little more than five years after Monica Roberts wrote this on her blog, *TransGriot,* in 2007, President Obama echoed her sentiment when he referred to Stonewall. In response to Monica Roberts's blog, however, some commenters claimed that it was specifically white cisgender gay men and lesbians who carried out the sit-in at Dewey's Famous in 1965, even though other historians, such as Mark Stein and Susan Stryker, have persuasively argued that the crowd was gender and racially diverse.[17]

There are some interesting questions that this disagreement over the history of the sit-in at Dewey's raises: Who gets to record history? Why are some parts of history saved while other parts fall to the wayside? What is at stake when people are denied a history? Why would people who are already marginalized want to silence other members of their community?

August 1966: The Compton's Cafeteria Riot—
"All the Sugar Shakers Went through the Windows!"[18]

Despite its relatively small size, San Francisco is a bustling international city. Its forty-seven square miles encompass immigrants from all over the world. By the 1960s, it had one of the largest Chinatowns in the West. As a port city, San Francisco had a reputation for being a little more "loose" than other major American cities. In 1967 San Francisco was home to the "Summer of Love" as over 100,000 hippies, flower children, and other people protesting against "the establishment" descended on the city. A year earlier, however, in 1966, San Francisco was the site of yet another riot involving gender transgression.

The summer after the peaceful sit-in at Dewey's Famous in Philadelphia, another uprising against police harassment occurred in the Tenderloin neighborhood in San Francisco, a neighborhood very similar to Skid Row in Los Angeles. Gene Compton's Cafeteria, a twenty-four-hour diner on the corner of Turk and Taylor Streets, was a safe space for many people in San Francisco, especially the large number of trans women and queer street youths, many of whom had been kicked out of their homes of origin because they were LGBTQ+. As Felicia Flame, a Vietnam navy combat veteran, AIDS activist and survivor, and trans resident in the Tenderloin in 1966 says: "It was just one of those ordinary nights when all of the girls would come to Compton's to drink coffee or just hang around to see what the night would bring. Every night at around two or three, we ["the girls," that is, trans women] would gather around to make sure we had made it through the night."[19]

For Felicia Flame, her trans sisters, and many LGBTQ+ street youths, Compton's was a beacon in the night. The café offered a bright, clean, and safe place for people who often had nowhere else to go to stay warm, dry, and protected. Here patrons could get a cup of coffee, some toast, and an egg for under two dollars.[20] Just as the night at Cooper's Donuts had seven years earlier, the night of the Compton's riot started like so many others. The police officers from the vice squad decided to enter the diner and require anyone who looked like they were violating the anti-masquerading laws to show identification. But on this night in August 1966, Compton's erupted in violence when the patrons fought back against the police. Grabbing cups of coffee, saucers, purses, shoes, and anything else they could get their hands on, they chased the police out of Compton's. Then the group from the café and other LGBTQ+ street youths outside Compton's turned over a police car and set it on fire.

Interestingly, the newspapers did not report on the incident in detail. In fact, as the historian and filmmaker Susan Stryker explains in the beginning of her documentary film about the riot, *Screaming Queens: The Riot at Compton's,* the incident would have remained hidden from history if Stryker had not come across an archived program for San Francisco's first Pride Parade in 1972 at the San Francisco GLBT Historical Society. Both the riots at Compton's and at Stonewall were commemorated in this program. Until Stryker's 2006 documentary, however, Compton's had been all but forgotten by the larger LGBTQ+ community.

The underlying history of Compton's offers another layer of complexity in that one of the police officers, Elliott Blackstone, supported the trans community that gathered at the coffee shop. Throughout his police career, he worked on a task force that tried to help unite the beat cops in the Tenderloin with the trans community they served. As Stryker notes in an interview, "He was a visionary . . . ahead of his time."[21] Although Blackstone often humbly claimed that he was just doing his job, it is clear that he took looking after the transgender community to heart. He conducted police sensitivity training, and he helped raise money for hormones for trans people through his church group. Many other police officers shunned Blackstone because of his openness to the LGBTQ+ community.

These three "coffee shop" protests—two violent and one peaceful—show a progression in the ways that protests were carried out. They also show a progression of support from other people in the community who had some power.

June 1969: One Police Raid Too Many at the Stonewall Inn

A heterogeneous street crowd started the resistance at Stonewall,
not a particular person.
SUSAN STRYKER*

Over-emphasis on that single event distorts our history and renders as lesser
other acts of equal—and even greater—courage, when circumstances of the time
of occurrence are considered.
JOHN RECHY[†]

* Susan Stryker, quoted in Ernesto Londoño, "Who Threw the First Brick at Stonewall?" *New York Times,* 26 August 2015, https://takingnote.blogs.nytimes.com/2015/08/26/who-threw-the-first-brick-at-stonewall/?_r=0 (accessed 15 July 2017).

† John Rechy, talk given at Adelante Gay Pride Gala, 24 June 2006, www.johnrechy.com/so_adel.htm (accessed 2 March 2016).

On June 28, 1969, the last Sunday of the month, the Stonewall Inn, a bar in Greenwich Village, was being patronized by the usual people: young gay male hustlers, drag queens, and other people from the neighborhood. It was an ethnically diverse crowd, as usual. The Stonewall was a grungy bar where people could get a drink, listen to music, and get off the street for a while. It was also probably a place where sex workers met their clients. On this particular Sunday evening, the New York police raided the bar. Such raids were not uncommon. The police entered with their clubs and demanded that all the people in drag begin to strip off their clothes so that the officers could count how many pieces of gender inappropriate clothing they were wearing. The police certainly did not expect the ensuing riot.

Nobody is sure who threw the first cocktail or the first shoe, but we do know that the fighting began in the bar and then erupted out on the streets of Greenwich Village. We also know that other people, many of whom were LGBTQ+, rushed out into the streets from surrounding bars in the neighborhood to help the rioters beat the police back. The Stonewall Rebellion differed from the L.A. and San Francisco riots in that the protest continued on and off for over a week and garnered attention across the United States and the world. As Miss Major Griffin-Gracy, a Stonewall veteran and African American trans woman and activist for incarcerated trans people, states, "There is no 'what it was and why it happened.' It was just the right time and the right place because when they came to get us out of there [the Stonewall Inn], *nobody* moved."[22]

Cooper's Donuts, Dewey's Famous, Compton's Cafeteria, and Stonewall all took place within the United States; however, the ramifications were global. To this day, most LGBTQ+ communities around the world from the most open and progressive to the most necessarily closeted and oppressed point to the Stonewall Rebellion, specifically, as the moment that the closet doors blew open. Ultimately, all these events were brought about by groups of marginalized people who had nothing to lose by standing up for their rights. Sylvia Rivera says:

> I'm glad I was in the Stonewall riot. I remember when someone threw a Molotov cocktail, I thought: "My god, the revolution is here. The revolution is finally here!" I always believed that we would have to fight back. I just knew that we would fight back. I just didn't know it would be that night. I am proud of myself as being there that night. If I had lost that moment, I would have been kind of hurt because that's when I saw the world change for me and my people. Of course, we still got a long way ahead of us.[23]

The Split between LGB and T in the United States

Think back to the Cooper's Donuts riot in 1959. What made Cooper's a special place? If you recall, the little doughnut shop was welcoming to everyone. Although Skid Row was a pretty rough area of Los Angeles, many of the establishments that were safe spaces for some people were not safe spaces for other people. Although Cooper's Donuts was located between two gay bars, even those bars discriminated against gender outlaws.

Does this discrimination mean that the gay people in those bars did not like drag queens, cross-dressers, or gender-nonconforming people? There are probably as many answers to this question as there were people in the bars. Ultimately, it was not the bars' patrons, but rather the bars' owners and hired bouncers, who decided who could enter.

Why would one marginalized group further marginalize another group within their own larger community? We need to remember that being gay in 1959 Los Angeles was illegal. We also need to remember that the LAPD was becoming more and more vigilant against "homosexuals" and other "deviants," and that one of the easiest ways to target gay people was to focus on those who did not wear "gender normative" clothing—that is, people violating the anti-masquerading laws. It is most likely that the clientele at Harold's and the Waldorf (people who were also vulnerable to being beaten and arrested by the police, having their names printed in the newspaper, and then finding themselves fired from their jobs and evicted from their apartments) were acting out of fear. The two bars wanted people to dress in "gender normative" clothing so they would not attract police attention. It is also important to remember, however, that when the ethnically and gender-diverse riot broke out at Cooper's, the gay people came running out of Harold's and the Waldorf to *help* with the riot.

Each of the three riots and the one sit-in that we've explored started with people being either arrested for or banned from a place becauseof their gender expression. And yet, many of the books and essays written about these protests have categorized them as "gay." Thankfully, many researchers and writers are attempting to paint a more detailed picture of the people who had the courage to stand up and say "No more!"

This is not to say that groups like the Mattachine Society and the Daughters of Bilitis, both **homophile** movement groups that took to the sidewalks in "gender appropriate" clothing to protest federal laws that discriminated against homosexuals, were not courageous and were not fighting oppression. (The word *homophile* was used by these earlier groups as a positive and politically forward-thinking term for homosexuals. After the Stonewall Rebellion, the word fell into disuse.) They *were* courageous in fighting oppression. Their methods were different, however, and their early ideas about *how* to carry out pickets and protests made their work inaccessible to many people who did not conform to rigid gender binary stereotypes of masculine and feminine. Gay and bisexual men who were seen as "too feminine" and lesbians and bisexual women who were seen as "too masculine" were often asked not to participate.[24]

Were there any rules about who could and could not participate in the Cooper's Donuts, Dewey's Famous, Compton's Cafeteria, and Stonewall events? The answer is no. One of the reasons that these protests were so inclusive was their spur-of-the-moment nature. It's a protest, and anyone and everyone is invited! Other types of protests, such as those by various homophile groups, not only were well planned-out in advance, but also had strict rules about who could participate. If you go online and study the photographs from these organized protests, you will see that the participants are wearing "gender appropriate" clothing, and the majority are white. Given the fact that these organized protests were conducted by people wearing either suits and ties or dresses, and that they were visible to everyone passing by, you can probably begin to make assumptions about their socioeconomic status. They wore nice clothes, and they had some kind of job or financial security that enabled them to be out in the middle of the day protesting. In other words, there was some kind of privilege at work.

One of the founders of Daughters of Bilitis, the lesbian activist Barbara Gittings, discusses the issue of "choosing visibility" in the film *Out of the Past*. She says that she always stopped to think about being so out. For her it was a calculated risk, but one she knew she had to take. Gittings understood her privileged financial situation and knew that she could be out without enduring the same consequences as many of her counterparts. Gittings was also aware that she represented hundreds of other people like herself who could not be out. (On another note, we can thank Barbara Gittings as a tireless advocate; she was one of the people who worked to get homosexuality removed from the *DSM*, which it was, in 1973. As you recall from Chapter 3, however, the *DSM* still considers some trans people to suffer from a psychological disorder.)

The LGBTQ+ rights movement has depended on *both* types of protest and advocacy: people working within the system and people working outside the system. Both forms of political activism are critical. The LGBTQ+ movement gets into trouble, and we begin to see damaging splits between LGB and T, when trans people are denigrated, ignored, and erased by people who are cisgender lesbian, gay, or bisexual. From all accounts, several of the people rioting at Stonewall were gender-nonconforming people of color like Sylvia Rivera, Marsha P. Johnson (both of whom are on the cover of this book), and Miss Major Griffin-Gracy. As we've seen, however, Stonewall has often been regarded as a "gay" rebellion. The historian Jessi Gan observes: "Though the iconography of Stonewall enabled middle-class white gays and lesbians to view themselves as resistant and transgressive, Stonewall narratives, in depicting agents of the riots as 'gay,' elided the central role of poor gender-variant people of color in that night's acts of resistance against New York City police."[25] Gan's comment underscores the split among cis gays, lesbians, bi people (although, arguably, cis and trans bisexuals are often left out of the conversations), and trans people of all sexual orientations.

Shortly after the Stonewall Rebellion, Sylvia Rivera and her soul mate, the African American trans revolutionary Marsha P. Johnson, and other trans people were often purposefully excluded from the newly forming gay political groups. By 1973, when New York City's Pride March included speeches from people in the community, Rivera was nearly forced off the stage by gay men and lesbians heckling her. The irony was painful: one of the revolutionaries whose actions on the night of the Stonewall Rebellion had made the 1973 Pride March possible was nearly dragged off the stage![26] In response to the heckling, Rivera commented: "I am not even in the back of the bus. My community is being pulled by a rope around our neck by the bumper of the damn bus. . . . Gay liberation but transgender nothing!"[27] Similarly, Miss Major noted: "I feel like we've been pushed to the outside and then prevented from looking in. It's the stares, the non-inclusion over decision-making, exclusion from events that would build this movement."[28]

Both Rivera and Johnson spent their adult lives working to help homeless LGBTQ+ youths in New York have a safe place to stay, even though Sylvia and Marsha were often homeless themselves. In many ways, the plight of people like Sylvia Rivera and Marsha P. Johnson highlights the devastation that the ruptures within the LGBTQ+ community can cause.

SONDA and ENDA: Everyone Needs a Seat on the Bus

These ruptures have been evident in various struggles at the city, state, and national levels as LGBTQ+ rights groups have attempted to codify nondiscrimination policies into law. Various local, state, and federal bills have been proposed to make sexual orientation, gender identity, and gender expression protected categories, like race and religion. Some cis gay and lesbian advocates have argued, however, that gender identity and gender expression should be *removed* from the bills so that they have a better chance of becoming law.

In the early 2000s, the Sexual Orientation Non-Discrimination Act (**SONDA**) was heading to the New York State capitol in Albany for a historic vote by the state senate. Many people within the LGBTQ+ community, however, felt that the bill did not go far enough because it left "gender identity" and "gender expression" out of the language. Thus, if the bill were to pass, it would not protect transgender people. To understand the irony of the situation, consider that Sylvia Rivera would be protected on the basis of her sexual orientation but *not* on the basis of her gender identity as a trans woman. The New York group trying to get the bill passed, Pride Agenda, refused to amend it to include gender identity and expression. In fact, Pride Agenda raised millions of dollars from within the LGBTQ+ community in an attempt to get the bill passed.

Quite literally on her deathbed in the hospital, Sylvia Rivera gathered local New York City politicians to plead with them to change the bill. Rivera was still struggling with an issue that she had faced within the LGBTQ+ community since 1969 (for thirty-three years).[29] One of the people who came to her hospital bed that day was the Reverend Elder Pat Bumgardner of the Metropolitan Community Church in New York City. Bumgardner is the founder of the Sylvia Rivera Memorial Food Pantry and Sylvia's Place, which is a safe house for LGBTQ+ street youths. In a discussion leading up to the vote for SONDA, Rev. Bumgardner discussed her support of a fully inclusive SONDA: "She [Sylvia Rivera] came to me one day and asked me if I understood what I was doing in terms of calling for an all-inclusive SONDA, if I knew what that meant. And I said that I did. It meant that I wouldn't leave her behind."[30] SONDA passed, but a trans-inclusive version of SONDA did not.

The Employment Non-Discrimination Act (**ENDA**) is a piece of proposed legislation that would prohibit discrimination in hiring or employment on the basis of sexual orientation. In 2007 Barney Frank, an out gay congressman from Massachusetts, originally proposed a fully inclusive ENDA, one that covered both sexual orientation and gender identity. The stakes for ENDA were high because this bill was at the federal level, much like the 1964 Civil Rights Act, which made discrimination in housing and employment based on race illegal in all fifty states, regardless of state laws that permitted discrimination on the basis of race. Fearing that the bill would not pass with transgender inclusion, the sponsors dropped gender identity from the bill. This was Barney Frank's argument that reflects his change of stance: "To take the position that if we are now able to enact legislation that will protect millions of Americans now and in the future from discrimination based on sexual orientation, we should decline to do so because we are not able to include transgender people as well is to fly in the face of every successful strategy ever used in expanding antidiscrimination laws. Even from the standpoint of ultimately including transgender people, it makes far more sense to go forward in a partial way if that is all we can do."[31]

With this controversial stand, Barney Frank and Elizabeth Birch (who was at that time executive director of the Human Rights Commission [HRC] and who was also against trans inclusion) faced immediate criticism not only from the trans community, but also from Tammy Baldwin, an out lesbian congresswoman, and many LGBTQ+ nonprofits like the National Center for Lesbian Rights (NCLR). It is critical to note here that the LGBTQ+ community in this case did not directly split along the lines of L, G, B, and T. Rather, several cis gay, lesbian, and bisexual allies denounced Frank and the HRC for their actions, pointing out that gender discrimination is ultimately at the root of discrimination that is based on sexual orientation, gender identity, and gender expression.

ENDA still has not passed; but after 2007 Barney Frank reintroduced all-inclusive ENDA bills.

New Zealand's Example: Georgina Beyer

Georgina Beyer, who is Maori and a trans woman, became the world's first-known trans person to be elected to a major government office. She was elected to the New Zealand Parliament in 1999.

How did Beyer make her way to Parliament? Having worked within the system in New Zealand—not an easy feat given the long and violent imperial silencing of Maori people in that country—Beyer became the Labour Party's candidate for the conservative Wairarapa electorate. Everyone was stunned when she won. On her first day on the Parliament floor, she said in her introductory speech: "I am the first transsexual in New Zealand to be standing in this House of Parliament. This is a first not only in New Zealand, ladies and gentlemen, but also in the world. This is an historic moment. We need to acknowledge that this country of ours leads the way in so many aspects. We have led the way for women getting the vote. We have led the way in the past, and I hope we will do so again in the future in social policy and certainly in human rights."[32] In this same speech, Beyer discussed the need for marginalized communities to stand up for one another and to work together.

During her eight-year tenure in New Zealand's Parliament, Beyer used her position to introduce and advocate for some of the most radical social justice laws in the world. She dedicated her time in Parliament to passing fully inclusive LGBTQ+ laws and progressive laws to help sex workers. As a former sex worker herself, she had an inside understanding of the legal protections that sex workers need. She received a surprising amount of respect and support from her fellow members of Parliament.

If you think about the saying "No one is free when others are oppressed," you will see that it applies to our discussion of the splits in the LGB and T communities. History is filled with examples of the ways that transgender people (especially transgender people of color) have been left out of human rights conversations. We must remember, however, the people who have refused to get on the bus if everyone could not ride: the Reverend Elder Pat Bumgardner, Congresswoman Tammy Baldwin, Parliamentarian Georgina Beyer, and the thousands of LGBTQ+ people who cried out against the noninclusive SONDA and the noninclusive ENDA.

Pioneers and activists like Miss Major Griffin-Gracy, Marsha P. Johnson, and Sylvia Rivera have all been a large part of why LGBTQ+ rights and LGBTQ+ issues have been in the news since 1969. Without a combination of Miss Major, Sylvia Rivera, Marsha P. Johnson, the trans women at Compton's, homeless trans street youths, our unidentified sit-in participants at Dewey's, and our fierce doughnut throwers at Cooper's, President Obama would not have had Stonewall to add to Seneca Falls and Selma.

WRITINGS FROM THE COMMUNITY

PAULINA ANGEL

Becoming an Activist

Paulina Angel is a trans woman of color from the Coachella Valley in Southern California. She is an LGBTQ+ rights activist and songwriter-musician. She serves as the executive director of Trans* Community Project, board member of Palm Springs Pride, and a volunteer member for both the Human Rights Campaign and Trans Student Educational Resources.

Coming Out in the Desert

I was born in a town called Indio, which is located within the Coachella Valley, about thirty minutes south of Palm Springs. When I was growing up, Palm Springs wasn't the gay mecca that we know today. Even as it became an LGBT destination, it was totally behind the times. Indio was also light years from being a progressive town; it was a city that was made up of a vast majority of Hispanics with old-fashioned ideals. In layman's terms: it wasn't the best place to live if you were different.

Coming out in the desert, you had little to no resources as an LGBTQ person. Our valley was stuck for the longest time to ideals from the mid-1980s. The "T" in LGBTQ barely existed, and the "Q" was basically a derogatory term that everyone—including myself—had an aversion to. Palm Springs is an area where people—including many wealthy, white gay men—came to retire. The city is removed from any activism, so I understand why the San Francisco activist Cleve Jones chose to live here for a moment.

When I originally came out as gay, I didn't know what transgender was, or if there was such a term. It wasn't until I started attending an LGBT youth drop-in center where I was told, "Oh, honey, you are not gay, you're transgender." I was always attracted to women and was never was really interested in guys (unless you include Darren Hayes of Savage Garden). When I came out as transgender, I thought I had to like men since I was becoming a woman, so I was stuck with this ideology until I made the journey to San Francisco. As I was starting to learn a lot about different parts of our community, especially as we got into the subdivisions of both trans and queer, I found that I actually identify as lesbian and as queer.

Activism

It was never my intention to become an activist or to be a leader. I always meant to be like Paul McCartney, not Harvey Milk. It was my ideology that activists and leaders were special people, and I never thought of myself as anybody extraordinary.

When you grow up in a place like the Coachella Valley, where dreams usually die, it doesn't give you much room to try to accomplish special things. A few people from Indio made their marks elsewhere, but never stuck around. For me, advocacy was something that happened by pure accident, and it began during my first year in college. I was attending College of the Desert in Palm Desert as a music major. I was recording my first album at the time, and I knew that I needed voice lessons because I couldn't sing that well. Shortly after being fired from Walmart, I enrolled in voice classes during the fall of 2006. My initial plans were to go for one semester, perfect my vocals, and then find a proper job. One day, I saw a couple of students making posters for Club Rush, the Gay-Straight Alliance (GSA) group. I asked them about their group and they encouraged me to join, so I figured, why not?

I decided to extend my time at the college to be more involved with the GSA. As the only transgender student, I felt it was my responsibility to be involved. It was around this time that I discovered certain flaws in my college when it came to transgender students. There was one incident when my professor divided the class by gender: girls on the left and boys on the right. I knew where I wanted to go, but I wasn't sure if I was allowed to. The girls called me to join them, so I did. My professor asked me what I was doing. Before I could say anything, some of the girls told him, "She can be with us." I hadn't transitioned yet, but the class had an understanding about me, so the professor allowed me to join the girls. The beautiful thing about the students is that they all got it—they all didn't need any explanation, they just knew. From that point on, I decided to help my college become more trans-friendly, so I stuck around and accepted the nomination to become the president of our GSA.

Within the next two years, I met with Board of Trustees members, the diversity campus group, and organized events that raised awareness about transgender issues and promoted LGBTQ visibility. At this time, I was given the name "the Harvey Milk of the College of the Desert." My work led me to become the first trans person elected to the student body organization of my college in an External Affairs position. I was then invited to participate in the Student Senate for California Community Colleges (SSCCC) in Sacramento.

While I was president of the GSA, I attended a student general assembly hosted by the SSCCC in Los Angeles in 2008. The event taught me how to have political power in education. I attended a few workshops, learned how to compose resolutions, and got a feel of how other campuses in California dealt with

LGBTQ student issues. After being elected External Affairs Officer in mid-2009, I attended the general assembly in San Francisco. I presented the first-ever student resolution dealing with gender identity equality. I spent the weekend lobbying for student leaders to support and vote on the resolution. I also hosted a special-interest meeting about my resolution and another resolution that got left over from the previous general assembly. Without serious opposition, both resolutions passed by a landslide.

After the general assembly, I became the first trans person elected to serve as a senator for the SSCCC. I served two terms; the first term I worked as a regional senator representing both Riverside and San Bernardino County. I was assigned an at-large position during my second term, which made me one of ten senators representing all 112 California community colleges in Sacramento. During my two terms, I worked feverishly on student bills as well as equity and diversity issues. I presented and facilitated workshops on how to advocate for LGBTQ equality on campus and passed a resolution for community colleges to recognize Harvey Milk Day. I've also co-authored a recommendation to Governor Jerry Brown to pass Senate Bill 48: FAIR Education Act.

One of my fellow senators called me an "activist" around this time. We were having a discussion about people who had overcome adversity and pursued opportunities that people in their situation wouldn't normally be able to. My friend Shawn said that there is one person who comes to mind that truly defines this term, and that person was me. It was true: I was a lower middle-class Hispanic trans woman and a survivor of child abuse. Somehow, despite every obstacle that was thrown at me, I found a way to do great work for the community and became an activist.

I briefly relocated to San Francisco to continue my studies in 2012. Sadly, because of personal hardship, I had to drop out of college and take a semiretirement from my work. When I returned to the desert, I thought my work as an activist was done. I went back to my music, completed two albums, and continued to write songs.

In 2014 I met a dynamic trans woman activist. She had recently moved to the desert after living in Seattle for years. I had no intention of becoming an activist again. I thought activism was behind me, and I was focused on finding a way to get back to San Francisco to continue my education. The trans woman activist told me that I could make a difference for our community in the desert. I had never been involved in the Palm Springs community before and was terrified of the idea. I've always said that the Palm Springs LGBTQ community was behind the times and was basically stuck in 1985. I wasn't sure if I was the person to bring it up to speed, but we did it.

I'm currently executive director of the Trans* Community Project, which has allowed me to help bring visibility to trans and queer issues by putting to the test everything I've learned as a student leader and a brief resident of San Francisco. I'm also a member of the Palm Springs Steering Committee for the Human Rights Campaign, which allowed me to really help the organization do more work for the trans community alongside members of other steering committees across America. I'm the first-ever trans person to join the Greater Palm Springs Pride Board of Directors, and possibly the youngest person as well. Since 2014 I've helped our community become more progressive and current on LGBT issues through educational events and town hall rallies. My work led me to be awarded the Spirit of Stonewall Emerging Leaders award at last year's Pride celebration. I'm also a volunteer member for both Equality California and Trans Students Educational Resources. I love the work I do.

Intersectionalities

As a woman of color, it had taken me years to fully embrace my Hispanic heritage. When you live in a town like Indio, you didn't really feel that out of place. It wasn't till I started to get involved in things in Palm Springs and Sacramento that I started to realize the difference. In Palm Springs, the majority of the trans community is white, and many have privilege because a lot have either had the surgeries or have money that has allowed them to pass. I don't have such privileges, so when I'm around them I feel out of place, although a few of them have accepted me into their circle of friends. However, most of the time I feel I have to work harder to prove that I belong in their community.

JESUS CORONADO

Coming Out as a Trans Man

I am a Mexican trans man, going to school for the first time since the third grade in my thirties, finishing community college, and getting ready to transfer to UC Berkeley. I have overcome many challenges thanks to my resourcefulness, strong work ethic, and will to fight and live. Making a difference is important to me. I want to work against the oppression that I have lived through as a trans person of color and an immigrant. In my journey I hope to inspire trans youth and find a way to support them in their journey.

When I first arrived in the U.S. from Guadalajara, Mexico, I learned that there were many parts of the LGBT community. For example: butch, stud, femme, gay, and transgender. When I was in Mexico, the only thing I knew was that I liked girls. My best friend and his partner introduced me and my girlfriend to the queer community and everything it had to offer. It was the first time someone gave me a label: they told me I was a "stud." The only thing I knew about being a "stud" was that they look and act like guys, so I agreed.

As time went on, I became depressed. My depression just kept getting worse, my seven-year relationship ended, and I was a mess. No doctor, medicine, girlfriend, or friend could have helped me at the time.

Then one of my best friends told us that he was transitioning. I was confused because I had seen what happens to other folks who transition. Many people in the queer community no longer saw those who transitioned as a part of the community—they became "straight."

After my friend's announcement, I decided to speak with my doctor and counselor and tell them what I had been experiencing throughout my life—I am a trans man. My doctor and I began to consider options, and, after three years, she finally agreed to help me transition. She wanted to help sooner, but we had to get my depression under control, just enough to deal with the testosterone.

The next step was coming out to my friends and family. I didn't have to come out when I had been perceived as a "stud." My family and friends knew that I was "gay" before I knew myself. I knew the coming-out process would take time, but I just didn't expect the consequences. I never realized that giving myself permission to be me would bring with it so much loss.

I had something important to tell my friends, and my heart raced every time I got ready to speak. Each time, I would hear again all the bad things they had to say about trans people, and so I waited. The longer I waited to speak, the angrier and more resentful I became. When I finally told them that I am a trans man and I wanted to transition, there was a weird silence in the room. Somehow, after I saw their faces, I allowed myself to be convinced to go back into the closet. We talked about how bad being transgender was and how it supposedly had ruined our other friend's life. I admitted to them that maybe I was wrong. Maybe because I feared what was about to happen.

My anger built and built, until it finally exploded on my "best friend's" birthday. Our friendship ended. After that I moved out of his house.

My friends were the people who had promised to love me and be there for me no matter what. But after I decided to come out as a trans man, I received no support from them, including many friends in the queer community. For trans folks, it can be difficult because we have often felt rejected by both the queer and straight community—at least until recently. When I came out, I lost almost every friend around me. Not only because of my transition, but also because of the depression and anger that had built up in me.

Not long after I moved out, I finally began my transition, which I had planned with my doctor a year before. For me, the transition was the greatest thing that's ever happened. I'm finally happy and present in the world that I tried to leave so many times. I don't regret my coming out as trans and losing friends, but I regret not realizing who my true friends were sooner.

Key Concepts

drags (p. 140)
ENDA (p. 150)
homophile (p. 147)
Selma (p. 132)
Seneca Falls (p. 132)
sodomy laws (p. 139)
SONDA (p. 150)
Stonewall Inn (p. 132)

Activities, Discussion Questions, and Observations

1. Both Paulina and Jesus discuss various ways that they have struggled as outsiders within different communities. Look at both their stories and discuss the ways that they have dealt with being outsiders. If you could ask either of them a question, what would that question be?

2. Like many political and social movements in the United States in the 1960s, the modern LGBTQ+ movement and, more specifically, early involvement by transgender activists came about through riots. Think of other riots in the United States in the twentieth and twenty-first centuries. Who was rioting and why? What are some of the advantages to rioting? What are some of the disadvantages?

3. For this assignment, you will need to view two different Stonewall films: the 1995 film entitled *Stonewall* and the 2015 film also entitled. Both films are docudramas, which means that they are fictional documentaries. Conduct a bit of background research on the directors of the two films and then, after you have viewed them both, compare the films. How did they choose to tell the story of the Stonewall Rebellion in New York City in the summer of 1969?

4. Research the history of anti-masquerading or anti-cross-dressing laws in two states of your choice. When did the laws go into effect? Why? When were the laws abolished?

5. Think of everything you know about the Civil Rights movement in the United States. At what moment do you think the movement started? Was it when people like Harriet Tubman ferried enslaved people to safety via the Underground Railroad? Was it when the former slave and abolitionist Frederick

Douglass was invited to speak at the Seneca Falls women's rights convention, where he drew parallels between the plight of slaves and the plight of white women? Did you choose that moment in 1955 when Rosa Parks refused to give up her bus seat? Or did you choose Dr. Martin Luther King Jr.'s famous "I Have a Dream" speech given at the 1963 March on Washington? If you chose any of these moments (or others not mentioned here), you are correct. The important point is that when we think about history, it is often easier to put it into the context of *one* exact historic moment. Pick another human rights movement or social justice movement in the United States or in another country. When do you think the movement began? Then research and trace the history of that movement.

6. What is at stake in trying to claim any one place or any one moment as a starting point for a history? How can we help these histories all work together rather than continue fighting over who started what? Isn't the end result, or where we are now and where we are going, equally important?

7. In social and political movements, there is often tension between people who want to work within the existing power structures and systems, and people who want nothing to do with that system and would rather start over. What are the advantages and disadvantages of each approach? Which are you more comfortable with and why?

8. In the following section, "Film and Television of Interest," three items in the list focus on the life of the trans activist Marsha P. Johnson: one film from 2012 entitled *Pay It No Mind*, one film from 2016 entitled *The Death and Life of Marsha P. Johnson*, and one film from 2018 entitled *Happy Birthday, Marsha!* Watch two or three of these films and focus on comparisons between them. If you conduct some research, you will find that there has been controversy, in particular between the filmmakers of the 2016 and 2017 films. The controversy centers on the idea that trans people should be at the forefront of telling trans stories and on accusations of a trans filmmaker's long, hard work in the archives being usurped by a cis filmmaker. How does each film approach the subject matter of Marsha P. Johnson, her life, and her love for and work with Sylvia Rivera? What are the differences in the ways that their stories are told? Can you tell what is at stake for each filmmaker? Which film is your favorite? Why? And why might it be important to have several different explorations of the same topic?

Film and Television of Interest

After Stonewall (1999, U.S., 88 minutes)
This documentary looks at the LGBTQ+ rights movement in the thirty years between 1969 and 1999. Several leaders in the LGBTQ+ community are interviewed.

Before Stonewall (1984, U.S., 87 minutes)
This documentary looks at early LGBTQ+ rights leaders in the years leading up to the Stonewall Rebellion. Of particular note, the film interviews Barbara Gittings from the Daughters of Bilitis and Harry Hay from the Mattachine Society. The main focus of the film is on the early homophile movement. Transgender people are, more or less, left out of the film.

Brother Outsider: The Life of Bayard Rustin (2003, U.S., 83 minutes)
This documentary film explores the lifelong activism of Bayard Rustin, an African American, Quaker, pacifist, and gay activist. Rustin is one of the unsung heroes of the 1960s Civil Rights movement. He almost singlehandedly organized the historic 1963 March on Washington at which Dr. Martin Luther King Jr. gave his famous "I Have a Dream" speech.

Coming Out in the 1950s (2011, U.S., 15 minutes)
Phil Siegel's first documentary in a series of four explores the lives of people who came out as gay, lesbian, bisexual, and/or transgender in the 1950s. The sexual orientation and/or gender identity of most of the people interviewed in the film was illegal when they first came out of the closet.

Coming Out in the 1960s (2013, U.S., 26 minutes)
This second documentary by Phil Siegel explores the changing times from the 1950s into the 1960s as different people are interviewed about coming out of the closet during the decade of the Civil Rights movement, women's movement, the peace movement, the United Farmworkers' movement, and the beginning of the LGBTQ+ rights movement.

The Death and Life of Marsha P. Johnson (2016, U.S., 105 minutes)
David France's documentary film uses rare archival footage and interviews to explore the tragic death of Marsha P. Johnson and the ways that the New York City police quickly ruled her death a suicide. People within the trans community, in particular, know that the police viewed Marsha P. Johnson as just another trans woman of color. This documentary follows Victoria Cruz, a social justice advocate and trans woman, as she goes all over the city trying to seek justice for Marsha's murder.

Envisioning Justice (2013, U.S., 32 minutes)
Pauline Park is a Korean-born trans woman who was adopted by white parents in the United States. This short documentary features Park talking about coming out as trans

and her activist work in New York. Pauline Park has worked on the same issues of trans equality that Sylvia Rivera worked on. Pauline Park continues the fight for trans rights.

Georgie Girl (2001, New Zealand, 69 minutes)
Georgina Beyer, who is Maori and lives in New Zealand, became the first openly transgender elected member of Parliament in the world. This award-winning documentary follows her life and her groundbreaking work in politics as an advocate for equity and access for all people.

Happy Birthday, Marsha! (2018, U.S., 14 minutes)
This film was researched, written, and directed by queer and trans artists and historians Reina Gossett and Sasha Wortzel. This short drama uses archival footage as well as dramatization to explore the lives of and love between Marsha P. Johnson and Sylvia Rivera.

Hope along the Wind: The Life of Harry Hay (2002, U.S., 57 minutes)
This biopic and documentary focuses on the life of Harry Hay, the founder of the Mattachine Society, a gay men's group that promoted gay rights beginning in the 1950s.

The Lavender Scare (2016, U.S., 88 minutes)
In 1953 President Eisenhower signed an executive order that banned gay and lesbian people from working in the federal government. This documentary looks at the time in the 1950s when being gay or lesbian was equated with being communist; not only was there a red scare in the United States, but there was also a lavender scare. This film also helps show the ways that early movements working within the system, such as the Daughters of Bilitis and the Mattachine Society, first started to form in response to these federal mandates.

Major! (2015, U.S., 95 minutes)
This multiple award–winning documentary focuses on the life and continued pioneering work of Miss Major Griffin-Gracy. The film includes outstanding archival footage and interviews with Miss Major and her support network. Of particular note is her work with TGI Justice, a nonprofit organization that advocates for trans people in prison.

No Secret Anymore: The Times of Del Martin and Phyllis Lyon (2003, U.S., 57 minutes)
Del Martin and Phyllis Lyon, lifetime partners, were also two of the founding members of the Daughters of Bilitis. They worked both within and outside systems of power and focused on lesbian rights.

On These Shoulders We Stand (2010, U.S., 75 minutes)

Glenne McElhinney's documentary looks at LGBTQ+ elders in Los Angeles. Of special note is the interview with Nancy Valverde, which examines the intersections of racial, gender, and sexual orientation oppression in Los Angeles in the 1950s.

Pay It No Mind—The Life and Times of Marsha P. Johnson (2012, U.S., 54 minutes)

This documentary looks at the life of Marsha P. Johnson and the joy she brought to the community in Greenwich Village—especially the LGBTQ+ community—in New York City. The film discusses her love relationship with Sylvia Rivera, who was also one of the pioneers of the LGBTQ+ rights movement and a Stonewall Rebellion veteran.

Screaming Queens: The Riot at Compton's (2005, U.S., 57 minutes)

Victor Silverman and Susan Stryker directed this documentary, which brought the 1966 Compton's Cafeteria riots out of silence. Using archival footage and oral histories from trans women who lived in the Tenderloin during the 1960s, the film gives the viewer a full picture of the events that led up to the night of the riots.

S.T.A.R. (2016, U.S., 30 minutes)

The trans filmmaker Rhys Ernst has a series of short film documentaries entitled We've Been Around that explore historic trans figures who are mostly unknown. In this documentary, Ernst explores Marsha P. Johnson and Sylvia Rivera and the founding of Street Transvestite Action Revolutionaries (S.T.A.R.).

Stonewall (1995, U.S., 99 minutes)

The Stonewall Rebellion is reimagined in this fictionalization of the events leading up to and taking place at the Stonewall Inn on the last Sunday in June 1969. The film looks at a diverse group of characters and includes people across the LGBTQ+ spectrum, including LGBTQ+ people of color. Part drama and part musical, the film also includes a group of African American and Latinx drag queens who serve as the Greek chorus in the background of the film.

Stonewall (2015, U.K., 129 minutes)

In this fictionalization of the night of the Stonewall Rebellion, the filmmaker Roland Emmerich envisions Stonewall as a predominantly white and cisgender gay riot. This film faced controversy and a picket in the United States.

Stonewall Uprising (2011, television, U.S., 80 minutes)

This documentary made for public television in the United States uses archival footage to examine the Stonewall Rebellion. The film has interesting interviews with veterans of the riots as well as an interview with a police officer who was on duty the night the riots broke out.

Sylvia Rivera Trans Movement Founder (**https://www.youtube.com/watch?v=ybnH0H B0lqc, 2011, U.S., 25 minutes**)
This YouTube video has some stunning interviews with Sylvia Rivera. From her being booed off the stage at the liberation march in the 1970s to her discussing the death of her beloved Marsha P. Johnson, this video is full of raw footage. Most notably, Rivera takes the filmmaker into her cardboard house in an abandoned and garbage-strewn area near the Hudson River. Rivera discusses her struggle with addiction and her desire and work to help other homeless people.

Umbrella (**2017, U.S., 15 minutes**)
From the trans director Rhys Ernst comes this powerful documentary that focuses on trans political activism and the desire to create change at the beginning of the Trump administration.

NOTES

1. White House, Office of the Press Secretary, "Inaugural Address by President Barack Obama," 21 January 2013, https://obama whitehouse.archives.gov/the-press-office /2013/01/21/inaugural-address-president -barack-obama (accessed 14 July 2017).

2. Declaration of Independence, 4 July 1776, www.ushistory.org/Declaration/document /(accessed 14 July 2017).

3. John Lewis and Andrew Aydin, with illus- trations by Nate Powell, *March: Book One* (Marietta, Ga.: Top Shelf Productions, 2013). This is the first in a trilogy on the Civil Rights movement by Senator John Lewis.

4. Voting Rights Act, https://www.ourdocu ments.gov/doc.php?flash=true&doc=100& page=transcript (accessed 19 June 2018).

5. David Carter, *Stonewall* (New York: St. Martin's Press, 2004), 290.

6. In 2003 the U.S. Supreme Court ruled in the case of Lawrence et al. v. Texas. The ruling overturned all the remaining sodomy laws in the United States. Before this ruling, in 1986, in the case of Bowers v. Hardwick, the U.S. Supreme Court upheld the Georgia sodomy laws by a 5–4 vote. It took seven- teen years for these laws to finally fall in 2003. Bowers v. Hardwick 478 U.S. 186 (1986), https://supreme.justia.com/cases/ federal /us/478/186/case.html; Lawrence v. Texas (2003), https://www.supreme court.gov/oral_arguments/argument_ transcripts /2002/02-102.pdf (both accessed 15 July 2017).

7. Cooper's Donuts, http://cdonuts1959 .weebly.com/paper.html (accessed 2 March 2016).

8. Tom De Simone, Teresa Wang, Melissa Lopez, Diem Tran, Andy Sacher, Kersu Dalal, and Justin Emerick, *Lavender Los Angeles: Roots of Equality* (Charleston, S.C.: Arcadia Publishing, 2011), 86.

9. John Rechy identifies specifically as Chi- cano. Because this term refers to a specific person, it is respectful to use the term he uses. When speaking in a general sense, though, Chicanx works like Latinx to be inclusive of all gender identities of people who identify as Chicanx and/or Latinx.

10. De Simone et al., *Lavender Los Angeles,* 99. See also Susan Stryker, *Transgender History: The Roots of Today's Revolution,* rev. ed.(Berkeley: Seal Press, 2017), 80–84; "Cooper's Donuts," http://cdonuts1959 .weebly.com/paper.html; and Eric Brightwell, "The Cooper Do-nuts Uprising," Amoeblog, 17 June 2013, www.amoeba .com/blog/2013/06/eric-s-blog/the-cooper-do-nuts-uprising-lgbt-heritage-month .html (accessed 3 February 2016).

11. Catherine S. Ramírez, *The Woman in the Zoot Suit: Gender, Nationalism, and the Cultural Politics of Memory* (Durham: Duke University Press, 2009), ix–x.

12. Ibid., 75–76.

13. James Wolfinger, "African American Migration," *Encyclopedia of Greater Philadelphia,* philadelphiaencyclopedia.org/archive/ african-american-migration/; "Virtual Jewish World, Philadelphia, Pennsylvania," www.jewishvirtuallibrary.org/jsource/vjw /philadelphia.html#7; "Latino Philadelphia at a Glance," Historical Society of Pennsylvania, hsp.org/sites/default/files/leg acy_files/migrated/latinophiladelphiaata glance.pdf (all accessed 4 April 2016).

14. Bob Skiba, "Dewey's Famous," Philadelphia Gayborhood Guru, https://thegayborhood guru.wordpress.com/2013/01/28/deweys -famous/ (accessed 29 February 2016).

15. Bob Skiba, quoted in Jen Colletta, "Fifty Years Pass since Seminal Dewey's Sit-Ins," *Philadelphia Gay News,* 23 April 2015, www .epgn.com/news/local/8754-fifty-years-pass-since-seminal-dewey-s-sit-ins (accessed March 2016).

16. Monica Roberts, "The 1965 Dewey's Lunch Counter Sit-In," *TransGriot,*18 October 2007, http://transgriot.blogspot. com/2007/10/1965-deweys-lunch-counter-sit-it.html (accessed 21 February 2016).

17. Marc Stein, *City of Sisterly and Brotherly Loves: Lesbian and Gay Philadelphia, 1945–1972* (Chicago: University of Chicago Press, 2000); Stryker, *Transgender History.*

18. Susan Stryker and Victor Silverman, *Screaming Queens: The Riot at Compton's* (film), Frameline, 2005.

19. Ibid.

20. Ibid.

21. Stryker is quoted in Wyatt Buchanan, "Pride Parade Salute for an Unlikely Ally/Police Officer Who Reached Out in 1960s to Be Grand Marshal," *SFGate,* 23 June 2006, www.sfgate .com/bayarea/article/SAN-FRANCISCO-Pride-parade-salute-for -an-2532708.php (accessed 18 April 2016).

22. Miss Major Griffin-Gracy, interview by Andrea Jenkins for the Transgender Oral History Project, Tretter Collection, University of Minnesota, https://www.youtube .com/watch?v=O8gKdAOQyyI (accessed 16 March 2016).

23. "I'm Glad I Was in the Stonewall Riot," interview with Sylvia Rivera, in *Street Transvestite Action Revolutionaries: Survival, Revolt, and Queer Antagonist Struggle* (N.p.: Untorelli Press, n.d.), 14, https://untorelli press.noblogs.org/files/2011/12/STAR.pdf (accessed 16 April 2016).

24. Teresa Theophano, "Daughters of Bilitis," *glbtq encyclopedia,* www.glbtqarchive.com/ ssh/daughters_bilitis_S.pdf; and Craig Kaczorowski, "The Mattachine Society," *glbtq encyclopedia,* www.glbtqarchive.com/ ssh/mattachine_society_S.pdf (both accessed 15 July 2017).

25. Jessi Gan, "'Still at the Back of the Bus': Sylvia Rivera's Struggle," in *The Transgender Studies Reader 2,* ed. Susan Stryker and Aren Z. Aizura (New York: Routledge, 2013), 292.

26. Randolfe Wicker, *Sylvia Rivera Trans Movement Founder*, https://www.youtube.com/watch?v=ybnH0HB0lqc (accessed 15 July 2017). This information is also available in David France's *The Death and Life of Marsha P. Johnson* (film), Frameline, 2017.

27. Sylvia Rivera, Speech to the Latino Gay Men of New York, June 2001, *Centro Journal* 19.1 (2007): 120.

28. Jessica Stern, "This Is What Pride Looks Like: Miss Major and the Violence, Poverty, and Incarceration of Low-Income Transgender Women," *S&F Online* 10.1–2 (2011–2012), http://sfonline.barnard.edu/a-new-queer-agenda /this-is-what-pride-looks-like-miss-major -and-the-violence-poverty-and-incarcera- tion-of-low-income-transgender-women /2/ (accessed 3 February 2016).

29. Wicker, *Sylvia Rivera Trans Movement Founder*.

30. Rev. Elder Pat Bumgardner, interview on Sylvia Rivera and SONDA, ibid.

31. John Aravosis, "Barney on ENDA Transgender Controversy. And, He's Right," *Americablog,* 28 September 2007, http://america blog.com/2007/09/barney-on-enda-trans gender-controversy-and-hes-right.html (accessed 16 April 2016).

32. Georgina Beyer speaking to the New Zealand Parliament on her first day. Annie Goldson and Peter Wells, *Georgie Girl* (film), Women Make Movies, 2001.

BIBLIOGRAPHY

Aravosis, John. "Barney on ENDA Transgender Controversy. And, He's Right." Americablog, 28 September 2007. http://americablog.com/2007/09/barney-on-enda-transgender -controversy-and-hes-right.html. Accessed 16 April 2016

Avery, Dan. "5 Pre-Stonewall Moments That Changed the Course of LGBT History." Logo, 1 June 2014. www.newnownext.com/5-pre-stonewall-events-that-shaped-the- lgbt-community-trailblazers/06/2014/. Accessed 4 March 2016.

Beyer, Georgina. "Assume Nothing—Georgina Beyer." https://www.youtube.com/watch ?v=fdC5F1EFLQo. Accessed 4 April 2018.

Bigelow, Bill. "Seneca Falls, 1848: Women Organize for Equality." Zinn Education Project. http://zinnedproject.org/materials/seneca-falls/. Accessed 2 March 2016.

Bowers v. Hardwick, 478 U.S. 186 (1986). https://supreme.justia.com/cases/federal/us/478 /186/case.html. Accessed 15 July 2017.

Brightwell, Eric. "The Cooper's Do-nuts Uprising—LGBT Heritage Month." Amoeblog, 17 June 2013. www.amoeba.com/blog/2013/06/eric-s-blog/the-cooper-do-nuts-up- rising-lgbt-heritage-month.html. Accessed 3 February 2016.

Buchanan, Wyatt. "Pride Parade Salute for an Unlikely Ally/Police Officer Who Reached Out in 1960s to Be Grand Marshal." *SFGate,* 23 June 2006. www.sfgate.com/ bayarea/article/SAN-FRANCISCO-Pride-parade-salute-for-an-2532708.php. Accessed 18 April 2016.

Bumgardner, Rev. Elder Pat. Interview on Sylvia Rivera and SONDA. In Randolfe Wicker, *Sylvia Rivera Trans Movement Founder.* https://www.youtube.com/watch?v=ybn-H0HB0lqc. Accessed 15 July 2017.

Carter, David. *Stonewall.* New York: St. Martin's Press, 2004.

Casey, Forest. "How Los Angeles Created Skid Row." *Daily Beast,* 8 March 2015. https://www.thedailybeast.com/how-los-angeles-created-skid-row. Accessed 5 April 2018.

Colletta, Jen. "Fifty Years Pass since Seminal Dewey's Sit-Ins." *Philadelphia Gay News*, 23 April 2015. www.epgn.com/news/local/8754-fifty-years-pass-since-seminal-dewey-s-sit-ins. Accessed March 2016.

Cooper's Donuts. http://cdonuts1959.weebly.com/paper.html. Accessed 2 March 2016.

Declaration of Independence. www.ushistory.org/Declaration/document/. Accessed 14 July 2017.

De Simone, Tom, Teresa Wang, Melissa Lopez, Diem Tran, Andy Sacher, Kersu Dalal, and Justin Emerick. *Lavender Los Angeles: Roots of Equality.* Charleston, S.C.: Arcadia Publishing, 2011.

Dewan, Shaila K. "On Eve of Vote, Gay Rights Bill Is Besieged from Within." *New York Times,* 16 December 2002. www.nytimes.com/2002/12/16/nyregion/on-eve-of-vote-gay-rights-bill-is-besieged-from-within.html?pagewanted=all. Accessed 16 April 2016.

Faderman, Lillian, and Stuart Timmons. *Gay L.A.: A History of Sexual Outlaws, Power Politics, and Lipstick Lesbians.* New York: Basic Books, 2006.

Feinberg, Leslie. *Trans Liberation: Beyond Pink or Blue.* Boston: Beacon Press, 1998.

France, David. *The Death and Life of Marsha P. Johnson.* Film. Frameline, 2017.

Gan, Jessi. "'Still at the Back of the Bus': Sylvia Rivera's Struggle." In *Transgender Studies Reader 2,* edited by Susan Stryker and Aren Z. Aizura, 291–301. New York: Routledge, 2013.

Goldson, Annie, and Peter Wells. *Georgie Girl.* Film. Women Make Movies, 2001.

Kaczorowski, Craig. "The Mattachine Society." *glbtq encyclopedia.* www.glbtqarchive.com/ssh/mattachine_society_S.pdf. Accessed 15 July 2017.

"Latino Philadelphia at a Glance." Historical Society of Pennsylvania. http://hsp.org/sites/default/files/legacy_files/migrated/latinophiladelphiaataglance.pdf. Accessed 4 April 2016.

Lawrence et al. v. Texas. United States Supreme Court. https://www.supremecourt.gov/oral_arguments/argument_transcripts/2002/02-102.pdf. Accessed 15 July 2017.

Learning English. "Words and Their Stories: Nicknames for Philadelphia and Boston." http://learningenglish.voanews.com/content/nicknames-for-philadelphia-and-boston-89834907/112420.html. Accessed 9 April 2016.

Lewis, John, and Andrew Aydin, with illustrations by Nate Powell. *March: Book One.* Marietta, Ga.: Top Shelf Productions, 2013.

Londoño, Ernesto. "Who Threw the First Brick at Stonewall?" *New York Times,* 26 August 2015. https://takingnote.blogs.nytimes.com/2015/08/26/who-threw-the-first-brick-at-stonewall/?_r=0. Accessed 15 July 2017.

Major Griffin-Gracy, Miss. Interview by Andrea Jenkins for the Transgender Oral History Project, Tretter Collection, University of Minnesota. https://www.youtube.com/watch?v=O8gKdAOQyyI. Accessed 16 March 2016.

McElhinney, Glenne. *On These Shoulders We Stand.* Part of Impact Stories: An Oral History Project Gathering Stories from the California LGBT Community. Film. 2010.

Moffitt, Evan. "10 Years before Stonewall, There Was the Cooper's Donuts Riot." *Out Magazine,* 31 May 2015. https://www.out.com/today-gay-history/2015/5/31/today-gay-history-10-years-stonewall-there-was-coopers-donuts-riot. Accessed 3 February 2016.

Ramírez, Catherine S. *The Woman in the Zoot Suit: Gender, Nationalism, and the Cultural Politics of Memory.* Durham: Duke University Press, 2009.

Rechy, John. Talk given at Adelante Gay Pride Gala, 24 June 2006. www.johnrechy.com/so_adel.htm. Accessed 2 March 2016.

Rivera, Sylvia. Speech to the Latino Gay Men of New York, June 2001. *Centro Journal* 19.1 (2007): 116–123.

Roberts, Monica. "Georgina Beyer Election to NZ Parliament Tenth Anniversary." *TransGriot,* 27 November 2009. http://transgriot.blogspot.com/2009/11/georgina-beyer-election-to-nz.html. Accessed 16 March 2016.

———. "Miss Major Talks Stonewall." *TransGriot,* 11 July 2015. http://transgriot.blogspot.com/2015/07/miss-major-talks-stonewall.html. Accessed 16 March 2016.

———. "The 1965 Dewey's Lunch Counter Sit-In." *TransGriot.* 18 October 2007. http://transgriot.blogspot.com/2007/10/1965-deweys-lunch-counter-sit-it.html. Accessed 21 February 2016.

Skiba, Bob. "Dewey's Famous." Philadelphia Gayborhood Guru. https://thegayborhoodguru.wordpress.com/2013/01/28/deweys-famous/. Accessed 29 February 2016.

Steen, Jeff. "Liberation vs. Assimilation: Can the LGBT Community Achieve Both Equality and Cultural Identity?" *OutFront,* 6 August 2013. https://www.outfrontmagazine.com/trending/liberation-vs-assimilation-can-the-lgbt-community-achieve-both-equality-and-cultural-identity/. Accessed 5 April 2018.

Stein, Marc. *City of Sisterly and Brotherly Loves: Lesbian and Gay Philadelphia, 1945–1972.* Chicago: University of Chicago Press, 2000.

Stern, Jessica. "This Is What Pride Looks Like: Miss Major and the Violence, Poverty, and Incarceration of Low-Income Transgender Women." *S&F Online* 10.1–2 (2011–2012). http://sfonline.barnard.edu/a-new-queer-agenda/this-is-what-pride-looks-like-miss-major-and-the-violence-poverty-and-incarceration-of-low-income-transgender-women/2/. Accessed 3 February 2016.

Street Transvestite Action Revolutionaries: Survival, Revolt, and Queer Antagonist Struggle. N.p.: Untorelli Press, n.d. https://untorellipress.noblogs.org/files/2011/12/STAR.pdf. Accessed 16 April 2016.

Stryker, Susan. *Transgender History: The Roots of Today's Revolution.* Revised edition. Berkeley: Seal Press, 2017.

Stryker, Susan, and Victor Silverman. *Screaming Queens: The Riot at Compton's*. Film. Frameline, 2005.

"The Tenderloin: What's in a Name?" *Hoodline,* 6 July 2015. http://hoodline.com/2015/07/the-tenderloin-what-s-in-a-name. Accessed 7 March 2016.

TGI Justice. http://www.tgijp.org/mission-and-staff.html. Accessed 15 October 2015.

Theophano, Teresa. "Daughters of Bilitis." *glbtq encyclopedia*. www.glbtqarchive.com/ssh/daughters_bilitis_S.pdf. Accessed 15 July 2017.

This Day in History. "1848: Seneca Falls Convention Begins." History Channel. www.history.com/this-day-in-history/seneca-falls-convention-begins. Accessed 4 March 2016.

"Virtual Jewish World, Philadelphia, Pennsylvania." www.jewishvirtuallibrary.org/jsource/vjw/philadelphia.html#7. Accessed 4 April 2016.

Voting Rights Act. https://www.ourdocuments.gov/doc.php?flash=true&doc=100&page=transcript (accessed 19 June 2018).

White House. "Selma to Montgomery: 50 Years Later." https://obamawhitehouse.archives.gov/node/324821. Accessed 19 June 2018.

White House, Office of the Press Secretary. "Inaugural Address by President Barack Obama." 21 January 2013. https://obamawhitehouse.archives.gov/the-press-office/2013/01/21/inaugural-address-president-barack-obama. Accessed 14 July 2017.

Wicker, Randolfe. *Sylvia Rivera Trans Movement Founder*. https://www.youtube.com/watch?v=ybnH0HB0lqc. Accessed 15 July 2017.

Wolfinger, James. "African American Migration." *The Encyclopedia of Greater Philadelphia*. http://philadelphiaencyclopedia.org/archive/african-american-migration/. Accessed 4 April 2016.

CHAPTER 5

Navigating Binary Spaces
Bathrooms, Schools, Sports

Key Questions

1. When you are moving through your day-to-day life and you are out in public, how much do you have to plan ahead to find a bathroom? Do you have fears about finding a bathroom?

2. Were there unisex bathroom options at your elementary, middle, or high school?

3. How was gender discussed in your elementary school, your middle school, and your high school? How was gender presented in the books in your school library? Did your school library have books with trans characters?

4. Were there any sports teams at your school that were not separated by gender? Were there any trans athletes at your school?

5. Do you participate in sports? How much have you thought about gender issues in your sport?

Chapter Overview

This chapter focuses on issues relating to trans accessibility in three interconnected areas: bathrooms, schools, and sports. Public restrooms are everywhere you go. And in schools, restrooms are often strictly monitored gendered spaces. Sports participation often begins through school. Whether sports are tied to student athletics or move onto the international stage like the Olympics, bathrooms are also often at the center of gender policing and monitoring in terms of locker rooms and who can and cannot use them. Historically, many of these public arenas have been challenging for numerous groups of people with respect to full and equal access: women, people of color, people from a culture's nondominant religion, and people who are differently abled, to name just a few. It is important to keep these other groups in mind as you read about the ways that trans people face and overcome challenges to full and equal access. You will also see that advocacy over bathroom access can sometimes help change

Haefele-Thomas, Ardel, *Introduction to Transgender Studies*
dx.doi.org/10.17312/harringtonparkpress/2019.01.itts.005
© 2019 by Harrington Park Press

public policy that affects schools and larger educational concerns. And in sports, the debate about binary gendered locker rooms moves us to much broader questions about overall gender equality in athletics. What would a sport without gender designations look like? As you read through this chapter and Chapter 6, be sure to note the ways that familial relationships are interwoven throughout all these public access issues.

Introduction: Do You Think about Where You're Going?

Take a moment and think about all of the places you go in your day-to-day life. You probably went to class this week. Maybe you went shopping for groceries or other supplies. Did you either participate in or go to any sporting events? Perhaps you had some down time when you went to a movie or concert. How much did you have to plan ahead as you went about your life? You may have had to get to the movie or sporting event on time, but other than that, were you "good to go"?

Some of you may have put extra thought into where you were going, how you would get there, and how people at these destinations would treat you. Is it safe to be fully *you* wherever you go? This chapter explores the obvious and the subtle accessibility issues and barriers that trans people, as well as gender-non-conforming cis people, often face when trying to get on with daily life. As you will see, sometimes being trans is only a part of the issue. What if someone is a trans person of color? Or what if someone is a trans person who is differently abled? Intersecting identities can certainly compound accessibility issues. As you consider the various problems and situations in this chapter, also think about your own opportunities for advocacy and activism where full access is concerned.

Everyone's Gotta Do It!

Chances are, while you were out and about in your daily life this past week, you used a public bathroom. Whatever you call it—the toilet, *baño,* restroom, *toire,* can, loo, facilities, powder room, restroom—we all have to use that room at some point.

As you were moving through your daily activities, did you need to think about and plan which bathroom you were going to use? If you answered "yes" to this question, then also think about the reason(s) you needed to plan ahead. There can be many reasons. If you answered "no," then you have a bit of privilege even if you have never thought of it in those terms. As you learned in earlier chapters, privilege is often something you don't have to think about. It is a privilege to say, "Hey, I gotta go!" And then you go.

Here is a historical U.S. bathroom question for you: What do the legendary jazz artist Billie Holiday, four-term U.S. President Franklin Delano Roosevelt, West Point graduate Marene (Nyberg) Allison, and 2005 Hurricane Katrina survivor Sharlie Vicks all have in common? At various points in their lives, they all had to carefully calculate where they could access a public bathroom and then safely use that bathroom. Today there are various bathroom apps available.

Racial Segregation and Restrooms

In the 1930s Billie Holiday (figure 5.1), an African American jazz vocalist, joined the Artie Shaw band (a group of white jazz musicians) to tour the United States. Artie Shaw wanted a unique jazz vocalist, and at that time, "Lady Day" (as Holiday was called) and her sultry voice were perfect. This was the 1930s, however, and the tour included states in the American South, which had strict **Jim Crow laws** enforcing racial segregation in both public and private. (Jim Crow laws were more obvious and strict in the South, but segregation in public facilities was often the norm in the North as well.) Here is what Billie Holiday said about traveling in the Jim Crow South: "Eating was a mess, sleeping was a problem, but the biggest drag of all was the simple little thing like finding a place to go to the bathroom."[1]

Time and again the entire band attempted to stop the tour bus in various towns to eat, sleep, and go to the bathroom (think about your own road trips and how many "pit stops" you have to make). In some towns the band would find "colored only" toilets and water fountains in the same vicinity as the "whites only" toilets and water fountains. More often than not, though, finding a public restroom for white people did not automatically mean that African Americans and other people of color could also find a facility nearby. If you have seen the 2016 Oscar-nominated film *Hidden Figures,* which focuses on African American women working at NASA, you may recall scenes where one of the characters had to walk a long distance from the building where she worked to get to the "colored only" bathroom located in a far-off basement. Although the film approaches the topic with humor, it does not exaggerate the situation. Even if there was a "colored" restroom, there was no guarantee that it would be open or even marginally clean or equipped with toilets with seats, urinals, or even toilet paper. Billie Holiday could have gone to any public women's restroom in the United States after passage of the 1964 Civil Rights Act, more than thirty years after her touring with the Artie Shaw band. That is a long time to wait to pee.

FIGURE 5.1 "Tonight: Billie Holiday," by Cameron Rains. The jazz singer Billie Holiday played to sold-out, mixed-race crowds at venues from New York City to Atlanta. But when she traveled in the American South, even her star power could not open bathroom doors for her—and she had to wait to relieve herself in a "Colored" restroom.

Restrooms before the Americans with Disabilities Act

Franklin Delano Roosevelt (FDR, figure 5.2) was the thirty-second president of the United States. He served the longest term of any U.S. president, from 1933 to 1945. In fact, term limits for presidents were put in place upon his death. Many of us do not know that FDR was paralyzed from the waist down after contracting polio when he was thirty-nine years old. On a few occasions, FDR wore constricting leg braces in order to stand up and give a speech, but he always had to hold on to either a crutch or another person. In his day-to-day life, FDR traveled by wheelchair, although very few photographs showing him in a wheelchair exist because White House aides and the president worried that people would not see him as "manly" or "powerful" enough if they saw him struggle physically.

As president of the United States, Roosevelt was arguably one of the most powerful people in the world, and yet, when he was away from the White House, he had to worry about finding accessible restrooms. Imagine a time before the handicapped stalls in public bathrooms. How did FDR navigate these situations? Because he was the president, he had help. There were always personal aides available to help him get to the bathroom.[2] But what if someone else had the exact same paralysis from polio but was not the president? You guessed it: they had to limit their time in public, and they had to time their travel very carefully.

FIGURE 5.2 President Roosevelt, by Cameron Rains. During Franklin Delano Roosevelt's unprecedented four terms as president, from 1933 to 1945, he usually chose to disguise his disability from the public. Because he was a wheelchair user, public buildings with stairs and many public restrooms were difficult and often impossible for him to navigate.

Forty-five years after FDR died, in 1990, the **Americans with Disabilities Act (ADA)** passed. The ADA is a large document, but one part of the act states that public accommodations must be made for people who are differently abled. The ADA covers bathrooms in public places.[3]

Men-Only Spaces and Restrooms

In 1976 Marene Nyberg was one of 119 women accepted to West Point, the United States Military Academy. Until a 1975 congressional bill that demanded U.S. service academies open their doors to women, West Point had, for nearly 175 years, been exclusively male. The administration at West Point did not plan very well for the new students. Nyberg says: "From a change management perspective, [West Point] took the absolute worst way. You can do it the right way, the wrong way or the worst way. West Point decided to take the worst way. . . . It was very evident they had not prepared. Simple things like the bathrooms were not done."[4]

West Point is not the only academic institution that did not expect women. In fact, the majority of colleges and universities built before the twentieth century in the United States (and many other countries) presumed that education was for men only. For example, the University of Florida began to admit women in 1947, the University of San Francisco in 1964, and Columbia University in 1983 (though Barnard College, a women's school, has been affiliated with Columbia and remained so even after Columbia became coeducational). But the bathroom facilities in the buildings were not so quick to catch up. To this day, in some of the oldest buildings on these campuses, and most college and university campuses built in the eighteenth, nineteenth, and early twentieth centuries, you can still find women's restrooms that have urinals. Sometimes the schools kept the bathrooms "as is" because of the building codes, which are regulations that must be followed for a building to pass a state, county, or city inspection. Instead of replumbing the bathrooms, the institutions left the urinals intact and hung a "women's" sign on the door.

In the United States, the 1970s were also marked by the fight for the Equal Rights Amendment (ERA), which stated that nobody could be denied equality of rights "by any state on account of sex."[5] Part of the major argument against the ERA was that if it did pass, men and women would have to share bathrooms.[6] Not enough states ratified the amendment, so it did not pass; a major reason for its failing was the bathroom issue. In other words, the ERA went down the toilet!

Cisgender Men or Cisgender Women Only in Public Restrooms

When Billie Holiday encountered whites-only and colored-only public bathrooms in the American South, she completely understood what those signs meant and where she, as an African American woman, was supposed to go. What about today, though, in public places that have restrooms marked Men and Women? Do these signs mean that anyone who identifies on one end of the binary as either a man or as a woman can go into the appropriate restroom? In the ideal scenario, the answer is yes; however, this was not the situation that Sharlie Vicks encountered.

At the end of August 2005, the Gulf Coast towns in Louisiana and Mississippi braced themselves for Katrina, a Category 5 hurricane. Although an evacuation order had been issued, people in the impoverished parts of New Orleans were unable to leave before the storm hit, in large part because the city did not supply buses or any other mass transit as a means of escape. That being said, people living along the Gulf Coast had certainly weathered numerous hurricanes before, so those left behind readied themselves.

Of course, you are probably aware of the mass devastation and tragedy that Hurricane Katrina caused. For people caught in the hardest-hit areas, survival was nothing short of miraculous. Sharlie Vicks and her two nieces were three of the survivors. When Katrina surged into New Orleans and the levees broke, they literally had to swim for their lives. Once they reached solid ground, they were

FIGURE 5.3 "Cis Women Only," by Cameron Rains. The contemporary debates about transgender people being able to use the bathroom that aligns with their gender identity as well as debates about all-gender bathrooms suggest that we have not come as far as we would like from the days of bathrooms labeled "Whites Only."

out on the road for several days without food or water. Obviously, they did not have access to clean clothes, medical supplies, or even a toothbrush.

Once Sharlie and her nieces were found and taken to a safe refuge sponsored by Texas A&M University, one of the first things on their minds after they ate and drank was finding a place to go to the bathroom and clean up. It was there, in the women's restroom, that Sharlie was arrested and taken to jail for being in the "wrong" bathroom. After surviving the hurricane and helping her nieces to safety, Sharlie was locked up for wanting to use a bathroom.[7]

Although Sharlie Vicks identifies as a woman, her story exemplifies the ways that "Men's" and "Women's" restrooms quite often mean "Cisgender Only" restrooms (figure 5.3). In 2005, as a transgender woman, Sharlie Vicks had no legal protections in the state of Texas because its laws did not cover or protect her in public accommodations. As an African American, four decades earlier, she would have had to use a colored-only bathroom, which, ironically, might not have been policed as much as the women's room she attempted to use in 2005 because authorities cared little about policing the colored-only bathrooms as vigilantly as they guarded the whites-only public facilities.

Clearly, the state of Texas did not have any protections where public facilities and trans people were concerned; however, this problem is not unique to Texas. In 2015 San Francisco, which is often viewed as the most liberal place in the United

States, made headlines with another "Cisgender Only" public restroom story.

Lilith is a differently abled trans woman living in the San Francisco Bay Area. Within the span of two weeks in the spring of 2015, she encountered two very different incidents when she went to use the "powder room."

In the first incident, Lilith was shopping in a downtown San Francisco mall where she went to the ladies' room. As she came out of the stall to wash her hands, another customer looked at her and asked if she was in the wrong bathroom. Lilith told her that she was a woman and then pulled her California state identification (she does not have a driver's license) out of her purse. Once the other customer saw the "F" for female on the I.D., she became very embarrassed and apologetic. Lilith took it in stride. In this case, Lilith encountered another citizen, much the same way Sharlie Vicks had encountered another citizen, in a public women's restroom. The laws in Texas allowed the woman encountering Sharlie to call in the police. The laws in California did not allow the woman to call in the police. Once Lilith proved by way of her I.D. card that she did, in fact, belong in that restroom, the woman apologized. Sharlie Vicks had no I.D. to "prove" anything because she was lucky to have escaped the ravages of Hurricane Katrina alive.

Though laws and protection ordinances are crucial in helping trans and gender-nonconforming people navigate public places, there is still no guarantee that people, including law enforcement authorities, will be educated about or adhere to these laws. As an analogy, the Civil Rights Act was passed in 1964, but that does not mean that we no longer have issues with racism in our society. Two weeks after the incident in the bathroom at the mall, Lilith had another negative encounter in the women's restroom at her public university, which is governed by the laws of the State of California.

LILITH: As I walked to the restroom, the officer of the campus followed me and gave me a VERY STERN look. At first I thought it was coincidence that he followed me, but that changed when he entered the women's restroom with me. As a woman and him as a person of authority and a male, I began to feel unsafe when he came in with me. I asked him immediately, "Why are you following me into the bathroom?" He replied, "I followed you in here because I have to ask you to leave."

I asked, "Why? I need to go to the bathroom, this is the bathroom, what is the issue?" He said, "You're not allowed in here and you know better." I became more confused and replied, "Excuse me?" He replied, "You are a male, you know it, and if you don't leave this restroom I will need to escort you out." I showed him my CA I.D. that clearly states an F designating my gender as female legally. He replied, "I don't care." He then escorted me out of the women's restroom and into the men's restroom and said, "I will wait by the door to ensure you finish your business in here, and if I catch you trying to go back, you will not be welcomed back on this campus anymore."

Imagine Lilith's fear as the armed campus police officer followed her into the restroom. What was he going to do to her? Was he going to beat her up? Was he going to rape her? Lilith was legally covered by two separate pieces of legislation: ADA compliance laws (because she is differently abled) and equal-protection laws that include gender identity and gender expression. How much did the actual laws matter in that moment of harassment? What would you have done if you were Lilith?

The biggest difference between Sharlie's and Lilith's cases is the legal recourse each had after her incident. For Sharlie, just being released from jail was a minor miracle; she had no other legal recourse. Once Lilith was out of the harmful situation, she was able to file legal complaints against the officer with the university and with the city and county. But in the moment of the incidents in the public bathrooms, both women received the same message: "Women's restroom means cisgender *as well as* gender-conforming cisgender women's restroom." Just because someone identifies as a cisgender woman, that does not automatically mean she is not going to be bullied in the bathroom if she is, for some reason, seen as gender nonconforming. There are plenty of cisgender women all across the sexual orientation spectrum who are gender nonconforming and who also get harassed in the bathroom either by someone else using the bathroom or by an authority figure outside the bathroom. In another incident at the same public school where Lilith had the terrifying experience with the police officer, a cisgender woman who is on active military duty but takes night and weekend classes was thrown out of the women's restroom by the custodian.

Unisex/Gender-Neutral/All-Genders Public Restrooms

One of the ways around the gender binary divide and the assumption that the "men's" restroom and the "women's" restroom are for cisgender people (and cisgender gender-conforming people, more precisely) only is to have all public restrooms designated as unisex, gender neutral, or all genders. This proposal has met with huge public controversy and debate. Another problem-solving approach to the public bathroom issue has been for public places to have a men's, women's, *and* unisex or all-gender bathroom available. Currently, there is legislation being worked on in several U.S. cities and towns that will also guarantee that any restroom that is a "one holer" (that is, is one room with a lock on the door) automatically needs to be an all-gender bathroom. There should be safe spaces in public for all people to use the bathroom. It is that simple.

In the various historical accounts we've discussed, at least three of the bathroom incidents took place on college campuses: West Point, Texas A&M, and a public university in northern California. What do you think the debates might be, though, if we shift our focus from these university examples to preschool through high school settings?

Full Access in Educational Settings

What does it mean for students from preschool through high school to have full access in their educational settings and their educational curricula? Much like bathrooms, full access in educational settings, particularly in the United States, can, historically, be looked at in terms of race, ability, and gender. From racially segregated educational systems that argued separate was equal to entire schools or classrooms set aside for children with learning differences and/or who are differently abled, to schools that segregate on the basis of gender, the question we need to ask is: Does each student have full and equal access to the curriculum?

In some situations, schools that are segregated by race, ability, and gender can be empowering. For example, historically black colleges and universities (HBCs), schools that are equipped to work in a supportive and caring environment with children who are differently abled and/or who have learning differences, and girls' schools and women's colleges where the focus is on giving girls and women a voice are all examples of the ways that historically marginalized people can have a safe space for learning.[8]

When segregation is something that is imposed rather than chosen, however, it becomes disempowering. For example, in 1896 the U.S. Supreme Court ruled that public schools in the United States could be racially segregated. This decision, known as *Plessy v. Ferguson*, ruled in support of "separate but equal." For the next fifty-eight years, segregation in public educational settings was completely legal, although separate was certainly *not* equal. The educational materials such as books and the school buildings for white children were much newer and better than the materials and buildings for children of color, specifically African American children. In 1954 the famous Supreme Court case *Brown v. Board of Education of Topeka* overturned *Plessy v. Ferguson* and stated that racial segregation in public schools was unconstitutional.[9]

Think about your own time in school, from preschool to high school. How often were you and your classmates asked to separate out along a binary gender line? For children who are trans and identify solidly as either a boy or a girl and for children who identify as nonbinary, school can become a stressful place, and stress does not help make the curriculum fully accessible.

Gender in the Schools

It's really basic daily things. . . . Knowing that when you have to go to the bathroom that you can find a bathroom and you can use it and that's the end of it.
ANN TRAVERS, PROFESSOR OF SOCIOLOGY, SIMON FRASER UNIVERSITY*

Think back to the stories you read and listened to in preschool and grammar school. Did they support gender stereotypes?

A Preschool without Gender

Egalia is a preschool in Stockholm, Sweden. If you visit during school hours, you will see what you would expect to see at a preschool: small children running around, playing in sandboxes, sitting at tables doing art projects, and listening to their teacher read a story before snack time. But what kinds of stories do the teachers read? Not the usual story of a knight in shining armor rescuing a princess from the clutches of an evil stepmother. Egalia has a very strict process for making sure that all the age-appropriate board books on the shelves for the students, as well as all the "read-aloud" books that the teachers use during story time, do not depict gender stereotypes. Stories that support a strict gender binary? Gone. Stories that socialize girls to be girls and boys to be boys? Gone. What can happen on a larger social and cultural level if other preschools follow Egalia's example?

Preschool is the gateway to education and school systems that, more often than not, underscore the gender binary and continue to ingrain gender inequality deeply within society and culture. Back in Chapter 1, you were presented

---

* Travers is quoted in Amy Judd, "Motion Passes for Genderless Bathrooms in Vancouver Schools," *Global News*, 17 June 2014, http://globalnews.ca/news/1398131/motion-passes-for-genderless-bathrooms-in-vancouver-schools/ (accessed 21 June 2016).

with a hypothetical scene in a preschool, in which a little boy wanted to wear a princess dress. In that situation, all the kids are paying attention to the teacher's reaction. If the teacher or another authority figure tells the boy that boys cannot wear princess dresses, then that is the lesson the children will learn. If, however, the authority figure does not make comments about "gender-appropriate" costumes and toys, then the message is that kids are kids and all the costumes for dress-up are just that: costumes for fun.

As a preschool, Egalia has effected huge change at the national level in Sweden. What started out as nongendered best practices for the school has turned into national policy. Not only has Sweden followed the preschool's example with **gender advisers** in most schools, but at a national level Sweden now includes the gender-neutral pronoun *hen* in dictionaries and on state documents.[10]

Middle School Student Takes on Catholic School

In 2015, at the age of twelve, Tru Wilson appeared as number 20 in *Vancouver Magazine*'s "50 most powerful people."[11] The middle schooler won this award for, at the age of ten, having taken on her Vancouver Catholic school, Sacred Heart in Delta, for not allowing her to attend as a girl. Starting in kindergarten, the child clearly identified as a girl. In early elementary school, Tru's mother, Michelle, recalls that the principal told Tru to "tone that stuff down" after Tru told her teacher that she was a "girly-boy."[12] When Tru's parents lobbied the school to let her attend as a girl, the school asked for referrals from doctors who would uphold Tru's gender identity as a girl. When the Wilsons provided these materials, the school insisted on choosing the doctor—one who would support the Catholic faith. The school argued that allowing a trans child would go against religious teachings. Tru "was living as a girl at home, at her dance class, on her basketball team," but at school she had to "pretend to be a boy."[13]

The fight with the school became so uncomfortable for Tru and her family that they moved her to a public school in the Vancouver system, which had already started working on full gender inclusion. The family filed a human rights complaint against the individual school *and* the Catholic Independent Schools of the Vancouver Archdiocese.[14] In 2014 the Catholic School Board in Canada became "one of the first in North America to develop a policy to support gender expression."[15]

Tru Wilson, now in high school, continues to speak out and advocate for trans youths with the love and support of her family and her community. Although she has had difficult moments, including losing her best friend because the friend's parents do not want their child hanging out with a trans person, Tru has perse-vered and made an entire school system a safer place for trans and gender-non-conforming students.[16]

Take a moment and think about your time in middle school and high school. Were you in school clubs? Did you participate in sports? And, of course, you probably had homework to navigate. For students, school takes a lot of time and work, regardless of their academic achievements or extracurricular activities. For a student activist like Tru, imagine how much extra time and effort it took for her and her family to fight an entire school system for full access to the curriculum in a safe environment. For some of you, this story will resonate because you also had to fight for full access to a school curriculum, whether on the grounds of gender identity and/or expression, physical and/or learning ability, socioeconomic status, language, racial, ethnic or immigration barriers, religious barriers, or any combination of these or other intersecting identities.

Texas High School Wrestler

Mack Beggs, a Trinity High School student in Euless, Texas (a suburb of Dallas–Fort Worth), is a young trans man. Although he lives in the Bible Belt, his family is supportive of his transition, which he started in 2011. His teachers and the school administration are supportive. He has supportive friends. He competes on the high school wrestling team. In February 2016 he won the state wrestling title. So what is the problem? Texas state law forced him to compete in the girls' division.[17]

Although questions about which locker room Mack should use have certainly come up in the discussions about his competing on *either* the girls' or the boys' wrestling team at Trinity High, these questions have not been the main focus of discussion. Rather, some of the parents of the girls on the Trinity girls' team, as well as parents of girls at other schools in Mack's weight division, argue that Mack has an unfair advantage because he is on testosterone. They have also had their daughters forfeit matches with him because they were afraid that he would hurt the girls.[18] Wrestling categories are organized by weight, so Mack would be competing against girls in the 110-pound weight category. In other words, Mack and the girls he would wrestle against weigh the same. So what were the parents who made their daughters forfeit worried about? The state of Texas and the school system will not let him compete as a boy. In this case, his own school, friends, and coach are all ready for him to compete as a boy, but larger governing bodies have prohibited him from doing so.

This is not to say that everything has been easy for Mack at his school in Euless, but the fact that so many people have supported him has made a huge difference. Mack has a family who loves and supports him as he is. With this support, as well as the support of the school administration, he has been empowered to be himself. Support from people in power is extremely important at a time when bullying in schools is on the rise. In a 2017 interview with *One Love, All Equal*, Mack discussed his worry about larger U.S. federal policies and the rise in bullying:

> "Four years ago, I was in a really bad place because I wasn't myself. . . . I told myself I don't ever want to feel that way again and then started to transition (to male). So when I hear people who don't understand, who have hatred, I don't let it get to me because you can't give up when people say you can't do something or be who you want to be. If you let it control you, you'll never go anywhere in life. Other people can't feel what you feel. My message to transgender kids, to anyone who is struggling, is to 'do you.'"
>
> Beggs' story comes at a crucial time for transgender rights. . . . The Trump administration announced an end to federal protections that allowed transgender students to use facilities based on their gender identity, thus leaving states and school districts to determine their policies.
>
> "It's ridiculous and dangerous," Beggs says, adding that he fears the change will lead to bullying. "Trump is leaving so many variables out. Who is going to protect these kids in school who have to watch their back every single day?"[19]

Mack has focused on his wrestling and the fight for his right to compete as a boy; however, he has also become an advocate for trans youth in schools in his home state of Texas and beyond.

Going for the Gold: Trans Athletes

When you think about transgender issues and sports, the first person who may come to mind is Caitlyn Jenner, who won the gold medal in the decathlon in the 1976 Olympics. It is important to remember, however, that Jenner's coming out as a trans woman happened well after she stopped competing. This section looks specifically at trans people who are or were out when actively competing. Whether on the world stage at the Olympics or on a small-town school sports team, all these athletes came out as trans, with the exception of one athlete who has differences of sex development (DSD). Together they have kept the conversation about gender in sports in the spotlight.

The issues of trans people in sports is much broader than trans people. Instead, it goes to the heart of gender stereotypes in the world of sports. Sports can be the lens through which we see the effects of sexism before we even get to cissexism.

Victory Lap?

It is more powerful than governments breaking down barriers. It laughs in the face of all types of discrimination.

NELSON MANDELA*

Caster Semenya, a South African track star, won the eight-hundred-meter run at the 2009 World Championships. She should have been ready to do her victory lap; however, the win came at a great cost to Semenya, who has differences of sex development (also known as intersex).[20] Before the event, she was "subjected to genetic, gynecological, psychological, and endocrine 'gender verification' testing to determine her eligibility to compete as a woman."[21] She was eighteen years old when she was subjected to all these tests. Another important point is that Caster Semenya is a black South African in a country with a long history of colonial violence and apartheid laws.

Two South African groups that focus on intersex/DSD and transgender rights are Intersex South Africa and Gender DynamiX, and both were quick to point out the intersecting oppressions that Semenya faced as her body and her genetics were scrutinized because some of her white South African competitors, as well as competitors from other countries, complained that she was "too masculine." Although South Africa has one of the broadest sets of human rights laws in the world, gender is still expected to fall within a binary. Semenya identifies as a woman; however, the fact that she has differences of sex development has highlighted the problem of the gender binary as an inherent basis of athletics. In this way, sports are automatically closed to intersex/DSD people. Although intersex/DSD and transgender are not the same, some of the issues about sex binaries and gender binaries need to be addressed. How can sports authorities level the playing fields?

Game, Set, Match!

I was a reluctant pioneer, so I can't take that much credit for it.

RENÉE RICHARDS†

In the five-year span between 1976 and 1981, the international tennis world was rocked by two separate events that involved gender identity and sexual orienta-

---

* Nelson Mandela, speaking about sport at the Laureus World Sports Awards, 2000, quoted in Jeff Sheng, *Fearless: Portraits of LGBT Student Athletes* (Los Angeles: Somebody Books, 2015), n.p.

† Richards quoted in Michael Hainey, "The Woman Who Paved the Way for Men to Become Women," *GQ*, 26 May 2015, www.gq.com/story/renee-richards-interview (accessed 18 July 2017).

tion. In 1976 Renée Richards, a trans woman and professional tennis player, was barred from playing in Wimbledon, the Italian Open, and the U.S. Open.[22] She took the United States Tennis Association to court and won when a New York Supreme Court judge ruled that Richards had been discriminated against because of her gender.[23] When she played in the U.S. Open in 1977, she made it to the finals in women's doubles.

In 1981 Billie Jean King, the tennis superstar who forever changed the face of women's tennis (and, it can be argued, women's sports in general) was outed as a lesbian.[24] Within twenty-four hours, she had lost all of her sponsorship, which amounted to $2 million (a huge amount at that time). In 2009, though, Billie Jean King received the Presidential Medal of Freedom from President Obama.[25]

Richards and King have several things in common, aside from being professional tennis players who appeared on the world stage. They both coached Martina Navratilova, and they were both reluctant pioneers. Initially, though, Renée Richards did not hit the same roadblocks that Billie Jean King did. Does this mean that in the 1970s and 1980s the public was more open to trans people than it was to gay people? Probably not. Both women were embroiled in controversy. The big difference was that Renée Richards *made her own choice* to come out as trans locally and publicly, first in La Jolla, California (where she had moved to begin her new life as a woman), and then internationally by suing the United States Tennis Association so that she could play in the U.S. Open. Renée Richards had *agency* in her actions, whereas Billie Jean King did not—at least not in 1981. Now Richards lives a quiet life in upstate New York, and King, who is completely out as a lesbian, continues to be an international advocate for LGBTQ+ athletes. King was part of the LGBTQ+ task-force delegation that went to Russia during the 2014 Winter Olympics in Sochi to be a mentor, witness, and monitor for the safety of LGBTQ+ athletes in the face of Russia's anti-LGBTQ+ stance—the so-called "LGBT Propaganda Laws."[26]

You may be wondering what gave Renée Richards the strength, as a trans woman in the 1970s, when there was not much public information available concerning trans issues, to take on an institution as big as the U.S. Tennis Association. Part of her motivation, shared by so many women in sports, came from being told she could not participate. She was facing gender discrimination. In the years since, however, in every interview she has given, Richards tells a story about her intersecting identities and her recognition that her fight was not *just* for the rights of a trans woman but also for other groups who have been told "You cannot do this." Here is her story:

And the other reason was because I was getting a lot of calls from people who were downtrodden, who were part of sexual minorities, who were part of ethnic minorities. And they said, Renée, you've got to go and do this. You've got to take up this fight. You can't just take what they say and go back and lead a private life. And I remember one in particular. It was a woman who had been one of the umpires in the tournament out there in La Jolla who had known me in my former life in New York.

And she said you've got to do this, because, you know, I'm part Filipino and my husband is black and the two sons I have that are tennis players are black, and we're always fighting to be accepted. And you've got to show that if it's your right to be accepted, to do what you are entitled to do, you've got to do it. So it was remarks from people like her—Virginia Glass, . . . I'll never forget her—in La Jolla at that time that spurred me on to do it.[27]

Renée Richards recognized that being out as a trans woman in the world of tennis specifically, and the world of sports generally, meant that the fight was not just about *her* right to compete as a trans woman. Instead, her fight became a fight for all marginalized people in athletics. Her legal win in 1976, the same year that Jenner won her gold medal, opened the door for countless athletes. She set a world precedent. Remember, though, that between Renée Richards's and Caster Semenya's cases, three decades apart, advocacy efforts by other individuals and groups surely had an influence. Because of the issues that *both* Richards and Semenya raised about sex, gender identity, and gender binaries in sports, in 2016 the governing body of the Olympics finally ruled that trans athletes can participate in Olympic sports according to their gender identity regardless of medical interventions.[28]

LGBTQ+ Powerlifters: A Solution?

Imagine this: an old-school weight-lifting gym in Bethnal Green, one of London's historic and vibrant working-class and immigrant neighborhoods. It is the end of July, and the gym is hot and humid. Only a couple of dusty fans circulate the air. Members of an international delegation of LGBTQ+ powerlifting competitors are convening to discuss international powerlifting policies and gender identity. This old-school gym may not seem like a place where revolutionary decisions about gender and sports could come about; however, that is exactly what happened there.

Like most sports, powerlifting requires that participants register as either male or female. For binary trans people, this requirement may sound easy because they do identify as male or female. Internationally sanctioned powerlifting tournaments, however, have mandatory drug testing for steroids and hormones. What, then, happens to trans people who take hormones for their health and well-being? At the same time, nonbinary trans powerlifters, regardless of whether they are on hormone therapy, ask why powerlifting has to be a gendered sport at all. Why can't competitors simply register under their weight? And why can't the weight classes be the competition grouping?

Some competitors concerned about fairness issues bring up the idea of men's greater "natural" strength. The implicit argument is that cis women should not even show up at competitions. Others argue that trans men have a disadvantage going into the men's categories. Again, the underlying argument is that sex determines strength. What really determines strength is training, diet, and health. If this group of powerlifters can get the policies changed at the level of the International Powerlifting Federation, what statement would that send to the world of powerlifting—and beyond, into the larger world of sports?[29]

In 2018 the LGBT International Powerlifting Competition became the first international powerlifting competition in the world to offer an MX category for people who do not identify along the gender binary. This category includes nonbinary trans people and people who have differences in sex development (DSD) who do not identify as male or female. The powerlifting federation already recognized the right of trans people and people with DSD who do identify on the gender binary to compete in their binary gender category. This global policy change in powerlifting did not take place in a governmental office or a court of law. A small and determined group of powerlifters worked together for an afternoon in the old dusty gym to create global change in the sport.[30]

WRITINGS FROM THE COMMUNITY

LUKE

Life as a Trans Teenager

Luke is a fifteen-year-old trans man living in San Francisco and attending a public high school. His transition is ongoing, and he's one of the lucky people to have a large number of friends and family supporting him. He hopes to teach his peers and other kids in the city about gender issues and pursue a career fighting for LGBT rights.

They say the hardest people to come out to are your parents. Some even say that this one moment—whether they offer support or revulsion—is a life changer. I remember that day perfectly. I owe it all to my sister, really, for arranging it in the first place. She alleviated my mom's growing suspicions and asked her to put aside some time on a Tuesday night to have a "family meeting." I'm not sure what I expected. I don't even know what I wanted them to say.

But when I finally said the unspoken words that had been lingering in my mind for months, "I'm trans," there were no bursts of light or music. Instead, there was an awkward silence as we all tried to figure out what to say next. That was not my life-changing moment. My moment had happened a few months earlier and was not a sudden burst of revelation—but, rather, the inescapable outcome of several months of speculation.

I can't say when I first noticed that something was off. I know I was never quite comfortable after puberty started to take effect. I know at one point I started dreaming about what it would be like to have short hair. But the rest of the details have drifted off and gotten lost in the invasion of new thoughts and memories. I remember, after I started having suspicions, my family stumbled upon a documentary called *Growing Up Trans* on PBS's *Frontline*. It was at the same time reassuring and very, very disheartening. Surely, we wouldn't be able to afford all those treatments? All those surgeries? Therapy sessions? Hormones? Treatments that suddenly sounded *very* necessary to me. So, I put my feelings in a box and shelved them for a while. I didn't ignore them completely. Yet every time I took those thoughts down to sift through them—they sounded more and more believable. One day, after doing a bit more research, I came to the conclusion: *Why should I put it off? This makes sense. I am trans.*

So, I was tense as I sat and waited for my mom's verdict several months later. I began to panic as the silence stretched on and the idea that I might have to live with what I was given started to invade my thoughts. But I need not have worried. I remember she first asked for clarification as to what being transgender actually meant. The rest of the evening is a bit blurry, though the general feeling of relief hangs over it all. It turned out her biggest concern was what wearing four sports bras would do to my chest. We ordered my first binder that night.

Since then, things have moved at a rate I could've never imagined in my wildest dreams. Here I am writing this now, almost exactly a year since I came out to my parents: my name is changed in the school system, I'm five months on testosterone, and I'm anticipating top surgery in three months. At times like these when I reflect on how relatively easy and smooth my process has been—and how supportive everyone is—I forget that some parts were hard. But they were, not only before my transition, but because of it too.

I now carry with me a caution I never had before. I'm more aware of how I look and act, how I walk and talk. I'm always on the lookout for anything that could give me away. I've become aware of the subtle differences between girls and boys—stuff no one really thinks about. For example: boys throw their shoulders forward and lean back a little when they walk. I've had to find the right balance between what comes naturally to me and what the world expects me to do. In a way, finding the balance is the hardest part.

There is of course dysphoria, which strikes at the most inopportune times. The fear I feel whenever another guy walks into the public bathroom. But having to hold an awareness of what I look like, and what I can do to improve it, is just exhausting—a challenge I never anticipated. There are so many difficult things about being trans. While some of the difficult things are more obvious than others, we still hear about them quite a lot. But one rarely hears about the good parts, the funny parts, and the weird parts. The way my sister defends me and explains my dysphoria by asking skeptical women how they would feel if they had a penis. The way I use my "Misgender Corrector"—a spray bottle I squirt my family with when they slip up with my pronouns. My internal laughter when someone says, "He has more balls than you." Not to mention the entire misadventure when it comes to ordering my packer. (Let's just say that they ran out of ones with my skin tone, and I'm very impressed with the way cis guys keep it all tucked in there.)

On a more serious note, discovering your transgender identity at a young age forces you to mature faster. It forces you to think about the greater world and the future in ways some other people your age couldn't even imagine. It forces you to find security in your own independence and constantly make adult decisions. While this may seem like a bad thing, I actually find myself enjoying this aspect of the trans experience. Not only am I secure in my now strongly rooted ideas and identities, but I feel more prepared for the world after I leave the comfort of my home. There's discrimination and struggle that come with all trans experiences, but I've also found this privilege in mine: having lived with two different gender identities and having seen and been seen by the world in two different ways made me aware of functions of society that we take for granted. For example, people didn't bat an eye when I mentioned I was a tap dancer before I transitioned, but they ask if I plan to continue whenever it's brought up now. I'm the same person I always was, but people just expect me to behave differently now.

There's no way to describe gender dysphoria that would make cis people understand. Just like there are no words women could use on me that would convince me breasts are desirable. There are no words I could use to describe my transition or life as a trans teenager that I feel would do it justice. Like every life, it's complex and multilayered and full of contradictions.

HANNE

When My Daughter Became My Son

Hanne moved to San Francisco from Germany in her mid-twenties as an international hotel business student to gain work experience and improve her English. Fast-forward twenty years of being happily married, she is now a part-time small business assistant, a part-time student at City College of San Francisco, a part-time volunteer at her kids' public high school, and a full-time mom. She is the proud mother of two wonderful children, who have enriched her life in so many ways and who have both been supportive and patient teachers to her on this transitional journey. (Luke, whose story appears above, is her son.)

At the end of an emotional day when my teen daughter told my husband and me that she has known for a while that she was transgender, I scribbled down these thoughts in a new notebook, which became my "trans journal":

> —*So proud of my younger daughter!*
> —*So impressed by her maturity level to know how she feels and who she is!*
> —*Thankful that her older sister is her "go-to person" and has been so supportive since her sister had told her about her true gender identity five months earlier!*
> —*Love them both so much!*
> —*Still very sad . . .*

With this astonishing revelation and the thoughts and worries swirling in my head, it took me a couple of days to be able to understand and express why I was so sad. I was saddened and afraid that I would be "losing" my daughter. It's not that I didn't like boys or that I didn't want to have a son, but I loved having two girls! It was familiar. It had been a magical time seeing those two grow up, and I had hoped they would carry that close sisterhood bond into adulthood. I also felt so guilty and heavyhearted that I, as her mom, did not realize earlier that my daughter was in such distress, and that she had to figure out her true gender identity all by herself.

There had been signs that something was off: her extreme moodiness, isolating herself in her room, and being quieter and less social overall. I reassured myself these were all normal signs of a brooding teenager. Her decision to cut off her long hair, her request to buy boys' shorts, and her overall repulsion toward the revealing dance costume assigned for an annual performance didn't make me that suspicious, since she had always been rather a tomboy. So when my daughter came out as trans, I felt instant relief because I finally knew the reason *why* she had acted so differently and had been depressed at times. The feeling of relief was followed by worry and sadness—I became scared for her safety. Even though we live in San Francisco—a progressive city—I knew that my daughter's life would become more challenging and difficult as a transgender person. She might be bullied or discriminated against as soon as she started her social transition.

My daughter was close to graduating middle school when she told us. After a lot of research and conversations with gender specialists, we decided as a family it would be easier and less confusing to start the social transition over the summer. We would have time to inform all of our friends and family and get used to his chosen name, Luke, and his male pronouns. It also gave the school district enough time to change his name and gender in their systems and inform Luke's new school about the transition so he could start high school in the fall as a boy. Once we had adjusted to his social transition, we would tackle the medical process of getting authorization to start hormone treatment.

I felt relieved and thankful that Luke agreed to the proposed time line for his social and physical transition, since I realized that I also needed to adapt to this new situation. Perhaps I was selfish, but I needed more time over the summer to say "good-bye" to my daughter, the child I knew, before I could make the transition and welcome my son. In hindsight, I think I was scared of not being able to recognize Luke as my child anymore. Even thought he emphasized, "Mom, it's still the same me inside," I was terrified that my son would not anymore be the compassionate, loyal, smart, witty, and fiercely independent person whom I loved so much.

It's been a little over a year since my son came out. The social transition has gone quite well. Our family and friends have been very supportive and accepting of him as a boy. They each try very hard to remember to use Luke's name and male pronouns. Some of the people who have known Luke the longest have had the most difficult time adjusting and switching to his new name, including me—his mother! "Because I birthed you!" became my humorous excuse for my unintentional forgetfulness. Meanwhile, he sprayed his friends and cousins with the "Misgender Corrector" water bottle whenever they used the wrong name over the summer. (Luke and his sister thought it is easier to use a fun approach to break old habits.) Even now when we talk about events in the past, especially about when Luke was a baby, I sometimes catch myself thinking of him as my daughter and saying the wrong name. This irritates Luke since it makes him feel that I still see him as a girl. One day, when Luke is older and fully established in his male identity, I hope that he can embrace the female influence on his childhood years. I hope that he will realize that experiencing both genders has enriched his life and helps make him truly a well-rounded person who can relate to both male and female issues.

The last year has been quite an emotional roller coaster for Luke and the whole family, but we have accomplished so much together as a family. We feel stronger and more closely connected. Luke has adjusted to high school pretty well, his new classmates accept him as a boy, and he is using the boys' bathroom and locker room without anyone asking questions or complaining. With the help and support of our insightful therapist, Luke started hormone blockers and testosterone injections four months ago to begin his physical transition. We are all very excited that his voice is starting to crack, and I'm relieved to realize that I am no longer sad or afraid of the other physical changes that lie ahead. I am able to embrace the physical changes much more easily because I see how much happier and hopeful Luke is about living as his authentic self in the future.

I have become Luke's most outspoken advocate, fighting (and yelling) for his rights when our insurance company and drugstores deny him services. He and his sister have been my most knowledgeable teachers with anything transgender-related over the last year, and I want to thank them for their wisdom and patience. Through Luke's transition, I also have become aware that one cannot take anything for granted, not the health of your children or their gender. Once one comes to terms with that realization that anything could change, it is quite a humbling and liberating experience! The day that my child came out to us as transgender, I titled my journal entry "The Day My Daughter Became My Son"! I guess my heart had already embraced the change that day—it just took my brain a little longer to catch up!

CHRIS

The following story is from Jess T. Dugan and Vanessa Fabbre's collaborative project To Survive on This Shore: Photographs and Interviews with Transgender and Gender Non-Conforming Older Adults. *Jess T. Dugan's art explores "gender, sexuality, identity, and community."*[31] *Dugan received an MFA in photography from Columbia College Chicago and an MA in museum studies from Harvard University. Vanessa Fabbre is a professor in the Women, Gender, and Sexuality Studies Department at Washington University in St. Louis, Missouri. Her focus is on gender identity and aging.*

Chris, 52, Boston, MA, 2013.
Photo by Jess T. Dugan.

I feel like I was always punished for my masculinity when I was female-designated by both straight people and lesbians. I was not the kind of woman that either women or men wanted to be around. I was way too scary, and people didn't know what to do with me. I was always a fish out of water in terms of my gender presentation. In a huge way, my transition has been like nirvana for it to get all aligned with me, and then have the world treat me well while I'm aligned has been amazing. I mean just really amazing for me. So I lived in that lesbian world even as it was difficult to do.

I actually gave birth to both of our children, which was never inconsistent with my sense of still being a man and being pregnant, and I know that many people can't understand that, or they might have some understanding. But it was not inconsistent for me to be with my male identity and want to have children.

Integrating all of our identities as a family has been a journey. So my spouse and former spouse identify as lesbians, my kids identified as part of a lesbian family, so applying to colleges, how do you explain on the FAFSA forms for the federal government that somebody's a biological mother and at the same time they're legally a man and what's their legal relationship, and how do you explain that I am legally a man that was never married to my former spouse who is legally their mother because we were a lesbian couple?

So there's layer upon layer upon layer of complication when interfacing in the world, even as it was not very much of a blip in terms of my family's experience of me and didn't change a whole lot the way our family life ran, was not really that big of a deal. And yet, this interface out in the world became a pretty big deal.

Key Concepts

Americans with Disabilities Act (ADA) (p. 174)
gender adviser (p. 181)
Jim Crow laws (p. 172)

Activities, Discussion Questions, and Observations

1. Like Mack, Luke has benefited from family support. As you have now read Luke's piece in "Writings from the Community," what similarities do you see in Luke's and Mack's stories? How does Luke's writing bring together the aspects of access that are discussed in this chapter?

2. Hanne is Luke's mother, and she has shared a very personal essay about learning that she has a trans child. What are some of the issues that Hanne talks about? How is Hanne's view of trans issues different from Luke's? In what ways are they the same?

3. Chris is a trans man who lived in the lesbian community and gave birth to his and his partner's two children. In his story, he discusses various issues with access. Chris is a trans parent. Hanne is a cis parent. For this exercise, imagine Chris and Hanne in a dialogue with each other. You could also imagine Chris in a dialogue with Luke. How might the conversation go? What advice might Chris give Hanne? And what advice might Hanne give Chris?

4. In 2015 Tru Wilson was recognized in *Vancouver Magazine* as one of the fifty most influential people in British Columbia. She was twelve years old at the time. Research Tru's story as she and her family filed a complaint against her Catholic school that resulted in a first-ever policy that supported a child's right to transition in school. Here is a short video about Tru Wilson: https://canadainaday.ca/ambassadors/tru-wilson. Discuss some of the points Tru makes in this film. And think about your own middle or high school. What was your school's policy regarding trans students? Did it *have* a policy regarding trans students? What does it mean for a school district to have something like a "Welcoming Schools" policy?

5. The first section of this chapter explored various issues concerning bathroom accessibility. As you learned, public restrooms have historically been a hotly

debated topic, from Jim Crow laws and ADA compliance to gender-neutral/all-genders/unisex facilities. The purpose of this exercise is to determine how accessible public restrooms are in your surroundings, which include buildings on your school's campus; buildings in the local government agencies, such as courthouses and city hall; shopping malls; hospitals; and public sports facilities. To make this assignment more fun, it is good to work in pairs.

The extent of this assignment will vary widely depending on where you are located and your means of transportation. No matter where you are, though, you can carry out the experiment. If you are in a remote location at a small college that sits outside a town, then you will probably want to focus exclusively on your school's campus unless there is an easy way for you to get into town. If you are in an urban area with good public transit options, you might want to look at more than one type of venue.

As an entire group, your class will first come up with the criteria for evaluating public restrooms. As a group, come up with a reasonable number of requirements for safe and easy-to-find bathrooms that are accessible to *all* people in the community. You should have no more than eight to ten criteria. This set of criteria will then become your basis for grading each of the facilities.

Each pair will do the following:

a. Choose a public venue. If you are on a more remote campus, split the campus up by buildings. Each pair can take one or two buildings, depending on campus size. If you are in a more populated area, then each pair can decide what type of public venue they would like to explore. Make sure that both members are able to find a time to go there together, which will take some planning ahead.

b. Record your findings in the categories that your class has chosen and then grade the public venue on a regular grading scale: A+ to F.

Two components to this assignment can be used together or independently.

a. In-class presentation of your findings: have some fun with the assignment. For example, you might want to take a selfie at a particularly good or a particularly horrific bathroom site. (Make sure nobody else is in the bathroom.) For a five-minute in-class presentation, you might want to share the images that you snapped, or you might choose to describe the facilities. Tell your classmates why you chose the venue, what you expected to find, and then what you found.

b. Written report to be turned in: along with your grade sheet as a cover page—it will evaluate each of the criteria—describe your experience of going to the public venue. What did you expect to find? What did you find? Were the accessible restrooms in a remote place? Was there open access to them, or did you have to ask someone for a key? And most important, how can the venue improve? If it is perfect, then make a note of that and explain why it is perfect.

6. Places of worship (churches, mosques, synagogues, temples) are interesting in that they are open to the public and yet they can also feel familial and private. In the United States, there is a separation of church and state, so places of worship do not have to follow federal government mandates about accessibility. In "good faith," however, most places of worship do try to achieve a level of accessibility. For this assignment, use the Internet to find three or four religious places that are positive and affirming toward trans people. What are the different religions that you researched? How do you know that it is positive and affirming for trans people? Is the religious leader of the community (such as a rabbi or preacher) trans? Does the house of worship offer a group for LGBTQ+ community members? Here is a website that might help your research: www.welcomingresources.org/.

7. Colleges and universities fall into several categories. In the United States, many colleges and universities are public institutions that must adhere to federal and state laws. Others are private liberal arts colleges and private universities (some of them affiliated with a religion) that do not necessarily have to follow the federal and state laws. For this assignment, pick two colleges or universities other than the one you are currently attending and research the following questions about gender identity and/or gender expression:

- Does the school have a nondiscrimination policy? If it does, whom does the policy include? For example, does the policy specifically state that the school will not discriminate based on race, religion, gender, sexual orientation, gender identity, or gender expression? Remember that if *gender* is included but not *gender identity* and *gender expression,* that usually means that the school is open to men *or* women (there is both a cisgender and a binary assumption here).

- Does the school have a student support group, resource center, social club, or any other group that clearly signals that people of all genders are welcome?

- If you are able to look at some of the college forms that ask about gender, do they have only two choices? Do they have a "fill in the blank"? Do they use the word *sex* or *gender*?

- If you have chosen to research either a women's college or a men's college, check on the school's policy regarding trans men and trans women. When they say "men" and "women," are they making a cisgender assumption? Do they still hold to a binary even if they are welcoming to transgender people? In other words, are they happy to include people who have crossed the binary but perhaps not people who are nonbinary trans?

- If you have chosen a public state university or a public state college, such as a community college, how do the state laws govern the university's or college's policies?

8. This assignment could be conducted as a class discussion in which students make arguments on different sides of the gender and sports debate. Mack Beggs won the Texas state wrestling championship in the girls' category, and numerous parents and student athletes claimed that his victory was unfair. Mack thinks it is unfair, too. He wants to compete on the boys' wrestling team because he identifies as a boy, and he has already been on hormone treatment. The argument is that his testosterone gives him an unfair advantage against the cisgender girls he wrestles against. Another argument arises with trans women athletes. It goes like this: even if they are on hormone blockers to block testosterone and are on estrogen and progesterone, or if they have been through full gender-affirmation surgical procedures, they may have an unfair advantage because they are stronger and bigger than cisgender women. The same argument is not often heard when trans men compete on men's teams. Have we been socially and culturally convinced that women and men, and girls and boys, cannot compete against one another? What happens to nonbinary trans athletes who want to participate but who also do not want to have to choose a women's *or* a men's category? What would happen if the world of sports used age and weight classifications instead of gender classifications? In what ways would this change affect sports? How would such a policy level the playing field for all genders? In what ways might this policy create more discrimination, again based on sex and gender?

Film and Television of Interest

Butterfly (2014, Ireland, 13 minutes)

This short documentary focuses on a trans couple who both live with Asperger's syndrome. It is a warm film that shows the ways that they support each other and the ways that their small community supports them. It is also an excellent look at people who are on the autism spectrum.

Canada in a Day (https://canadainaday.ca/ambassadors/tru-wilson, 2016, Canada, 2 minutes)

This very short video gives the viewer a chance to meet Tru Wilson, the Canadian teen trans advocate.

Creating Gender Inclusive Schools (2016, U.S., 21 minutes)

Peralta Elementary School in Oakland, California, is the site of an inclusive teaching method, Gender Spectrum. This short documentary demonstrates the ways that teachers and students can have safe and empowering conversations about gender diversity in school settings.

Deep Run (2015, U.S., 75 minutes)

Cole is a young trans man living in North Carolina, one of the worst states in which to live if you are transgender. This documentary film follows Cole and his girlfriend, Ashley, as they face a community of conservative Christians who see them as damned. This movie does a beautiful job of looking at the diversity within Christianity as it explores the ways religion can shame or empower.

Dorcas and Caster Semenya (2012, South Africa, 3 minutes)

This is a poignant and powerful short documentary featuring Caster Semenya and her mother, who always tells her that she is beautiful the way God made her. There is a discussion about the intense chromosomal and drug testing Semenya was forced to undergo to be able to run track on the world stage when her womanhood was called into question.

52 Tuesdays (2013, Australia, 109 minutes)

Winner of the Best Dramatic Directing Award at Sundance and Best Film at the Berlin Film Festival, 52 Tuesdays focuses on the relationship between a sixteen-year-old girl and her mother, who is coming out as a trans man. The film is a beautiful and artistic piece in and of itself because the actors were not professional and were given the script only one week at a time, and the film was filmed only on Tuesdays.

Girl Unbound: The War to Be Her (2016, Pakistan, Canada, 80 minutes)
Maria Toorpakai, an outstanding squash player, was assigned female at birth but as a youth passed as a boy in order to play squash in a region of Pakistan controlled by the Taliban, who do not allow girls to go to school, never mind play sports. This is a beautiful documentary about a gender-fluid squash player on the international stage whose biggest support comes from family in a region controlled by conservative religious ideals and laws.

Growing Up Coy (2016, U.S., 83 minutes)
A Colorado family's struggle to support their transgender six-year-old is the focus of this documentary. Their legal fight became a landmark civil rights case. An excellent look at the rights of parents and the rights of trans children.

Hidden Figures (2016, U.S., 127 minutes)
This dramatization looks at the lives of the nearly forgotten brilliant African American women who worked at NASA and were crucial to the U.S. effort to send astronauts into space. Of particular note are the scenes where the women have to run across the NASA campus to find a bathroom they were allowed to use because the bathrooms in the buildings where they worked were for "whites only."

Lady Sings the Blues (1972, U.S., 144 minutes)
Diana Ross, Billy Dee Williams, and Richard Pryor star in this dramatization of the life of Billie Holiday.

The Legend of Billie Jean King: The Battle of the Sexes (2013, U.K., 60 minutes)
This British television documentary from BBC4 explores Billie Jean King and the famous Battle of the Sexes—the tennis match between her and Bobby Riggs.

Lives Worth Living (2011, U.S., 53 minutes)
This documentary takes a look at the positive effect of the passage of ADA laws for people with disabilities. An excellent look at the history of disability laws in the United States.

Ma Vie en Rose (1997, Belgium, 88 minutes)
Although there are many more choices now if you want to watch a film that looks at the lives and experiences that trans and gender-nonconforming children often have, this film remains a classic. This Belgian drama follows a young trans girl as her family and her community continually try to force her to be the boy she was identified as at birth.

Raising Zoey (2016, U.S., 54 minutes)
With the help of her mother and the ACLU, Zoey is able to sue her school and put an end to students and teachers bullying her because she is transgender. This is an outstanding documentary that shows how painful and cruel an unsupportive school environment can be. It also shows how strong family and allies can be.

Renée (2011, U.S., 79 minutes)

This documentary focuses on the life of Renée Richards, who made international news when she came out as a trans woman on the international tennis circuit. The film includes interviews with Richards and has excellent clips from her tennis matches.

A Self-Made Man (2013, U.S., 57 minutes)

The focus of this documentary is on the work that a trans man, Tony, does with gender-nonconforming youth and their parents to create a safe space for the entire family.

Songs for Alexis (2014, Denmark, 75 minutes)

This documentary explores the relationship between a trans teenager and his girlfriend. The young trans man, Ryan, has a supportive mother, but his girlfriend, Alexis, has a father who is hostile and transphobic. An excellent look at family dynamics and trans issues.

Swim Suit (2006, U.S., 14 minutes)

This is a short meditation on a young trans man who wants to transition, but who also desperately wants to continue swimming on his college swim team, which, however, is a women's team.

Too Fast to Be a Woman? The Story of Caster Semenya (2011, U.K., South Africa, 49 minutes)

This is an outstanding documentary that chronicles the struggles of Caster Semenya, an international track star who was forced to undergo chromosomal testing. Semenya has differences in sex development (DSD, also known as intersex). The film looks at underlying misogyny regarding women in sports. There is also an exploration of the racist attitudes that many of Semenya's opponents displayed throughout the controversy, before she was allowed to run in international meets after her forced testing.

Transparent (2005, U.S., 61 minutes)

First-person stories throughout this documentary focus on trans men who have given birth to their children. The film also focuses on diverse gender dynamics within families.

Valentine Road (2013, U.S., 89 minutes)

An award-winning film that examines the murder of Larry King, a gender-nonconforming youth of color, who was shot and killed by a classmate. This documentary looks at school bullying and the ways that violence in schools against gender-nonconforming children can be deadly.

The Women's Bathroom Project (2016, U.S., 6 minutes)

Here it is in a short film: the topic of a trans woman talking with a young child in a women's bathroom. The video is sensitively and beautifully done.

NOTES

1. Bud Kliment, *Billie Holiday: Singer* (Los Angeles: Melrose Square Publishing, 1990), 86.

2. Amy Berish, "FDR and Polio," FDR Presidential Library and Museum, https://fdrlibrary.org/polio (accessed 18 July 2017).

3. U.S. Department of Labor, Americans with Disabilities Act, https://www.dol.gov/general/topic/disability/ada (accessed 18 July 2017).

4. Marcy Reborchick, "At the Gates of West Point," Women's Memorial, January 2007, https://www.womensmemorial.org/oral-history/detail/?s=at-the-gates-of-west-point (accessed 5 April 2018).

5. "The Equal Rights Amendment: Unfinished Business for the Constitution," www.equalrightsamendment.org/ (accessed 16 February 2018).

6. Amanda Terkel, "Bathroom Panic Has Long Stood in the Way of Equal Rights," *HuffPost: Politics,* 24 March 2016, https://www.huffingtonpost.com/entry/bathroom-panic_us_56f40300e4b0c3ef521820e3 (accessed 12 February 2018).

7. Mandy Carter, "Southerners on New Ground: Our Lesbian, Gay, Bisexual, and Transgender Community," in *What Lies Beneath: Katrina, Race, and the State of the Nation,* ed. South End Press Collective (Boston: South End Press, 2007), 54–64.

8. Some women's colleges are now fully embracing cisgender *and* transgender women. This has not been an easy battle, but more and more, women's colleges have begun to change their policies to include trans women. Interestingly, most U.S. women's colleges have been much more open to trans men who identified as women at the time of their acceptance to college.

9. "Brown v. Board of Education," History Channel, http://www.history.com/topics/black-history/brown-v-board-of-education-of-topeka (accessed 12 February 2018).

10. Cordelia Hebblethwaite, "Sweden's 'Gender-Neutral' Pre-School," *BBC News,* 8 July 2011, www.bbc.com/news/world-europe-14038419 (accessed 18 July 2017); Anthony Faiola, "In Europe, Creating a Post-Gender World One Small Rule at a Time," *Washington Post,* 12 June 2015, https://www.washingtonpost.com/world/europe/the-remarkable-ways-europe-is-changing-how-people-talk-about-gender/2015/06/12/af435d48-0df0-11e5-a0fe-dccfea4653ee_story.html?utm_term=.41d733b1cb7b (accessed 18 July 2017).

11. Frances Bula, Chris Koentges, Gary Mason, Gary Stephen Ross, and the editors, "The 50 Most Powerful People in Vancouver (2015)," *Vancouver Magazine,* 17 November 2015, http://vanmag.com/best-of-the-city/the-50-most-powerful-people-in-vancouver-2015/ (accessed 19 February 2018).

12. Ibid.

13. Ibid..

14. Craig Takeuchi, "Trans Activist Tru Wilson Named 2017 Sexual Health Champion by Vancouver's Options for Sexual Health," *Georgia Straight,* 15 February 2017, https://www.straight.com/blogra/869576/trans-activist-tru-wilson-named-2017-sexual-health-champion-vancouvers-options-sexual (accessed 19 February 2018).

15. Ibid.

16. See ibid. for Tru's discussion of losing her best friend.

17. Faith Haleh Robinson and Nadeem Muaddi, "Transgender Boy Wins Girls' Wrestling Championship in Texas," CNN, 27 February 2017, www.cnn.com/2017/02/27/us

/texas-transgender-wrestler-trnd-hold /index.html (accessed 10 July 2017).

18. One Love, All Equal, "Mack Beggs, a Trans Wrestler, Shares Advice with Trans Community," 6 March 2017, https://onelove allequal.org/2017/03/06/mack-beggs -trans-wrestler-shares-advice-trans -community/ (accessed 18 July 2017).

19. Ibid.

20. Semenya uses the term *intersex* for herself and not *differences in sex development*. For this discussion of Semenya, I will use *DSD* out of respect.

21. Amanda Lock Swarr with Sally Gross and Liesl Theron, "South African Intersex Activism: Caster Semenya's Impact and Import," *Feminist Studies* 35.3 (2009): 657–662.

22. Lauren Holter, "Renee Richards Is a Transgender Sports Icon Who Paved the Way for Caitlyn Jenner with a Game-Changing Lawsuit Back in 1975," *Bustle*, 4 June 2015, https://www.bustle.com/articles/88119 -renee-richards-is-a-transgender-sports -icon-who-paved-the-way-for-caitlyn -jenner-with-a (accessed 18 July 2017).

23. Ibid.

24. Jim Buzinski, "Moment #3: Tennis Great Billie Jean King Outed," *Outsports: A Voice for LGBT Athletes,* 2 October 2011, https:// www.outsports.com/2011/10/2/4051938 /moment-3-tennis-great-billie-jean-king -outed. Accessed on 18 July 2017.

25. Ibid.

26. Russia's anti-LGBT policies are well known. Billie Jean King joined a group of out U.S. athletes who went to Russia to educate and advocate for LGBT athletes.

27. Renée Richards, "The Second Half of My Life," interview by Neal Conan on *Talk of the Nation,* National Public Radio, 8 February 2007, www.npr.org/templates/story/ story.php?storyId=7277665 (accessed 18 July 2017).

28. Associated Press, "IOC Rules Transgender Athletes Can Take Part in Olympics without Surgery," *Guardian*, 24 January 2016, https://www.theguardian.com/sport /2016/jan/25/ioc-rules-transgender- athletes-can-take-part-in-olympics -without-surgery (accessed 18 July 2017).

29. The National Center for Lesbian Rights (NCLR) has a long-standing Sports Project that provides training, technical assistance, and, when needed, legal solutions to LGBTQ+ athletes, teams, coaches, and sports federations. They, alongside other LGBTQ+ advocacy groups, continue to strive for more equitable access and fair treatment for trans and intersex/DSD athletes and for sex and gender equality in sports. They closely followed the story of Caster Semenya, and Billie Jean King partnered with them as part of the delegation that went to the Winter Olympics in Sochi, Russia.

30. Chris Morgan, "Grace, Grit, and Glory," *Transliving Magazine*, March 2018, http:// lgbtpowerlifting.org/?page_id=286 (accessed 25 March 2018).

31. Jess Dugan, "Artist Statement," www .jessdugan.com/statements/ (accessed 27 March 2018).

BIBLIOGRAPHY

ADA Standards. www.ada.gov/regs2010/2010ADAStandards/2010ADAStandards_prt.pdf. Accessed 15 March 2016.

Associated Press. "IOC Rules Transgender Athletes Can Take Part in Olympics without Surgery." *Guardian,* 24 January 2016. https://www.theguardian.com/sport/2016/jan/25/ioc-rules-transgender-athletes-can-take-part-in-olympics-without-surgery. Accessed 18 July 2017.

Berish, Amy. "FDR and Polio." FDR Presidential Library and Museum. https://fdrlibrary.org/polio. Accessed 18 July 2017.

Brown v. Board of Education. History Channel. www.history.com/topics/black-history/brown-v-board-of-education-of-topeka. Accessed 12 February 2018.

Bula, Frances, Chris Koentges, Gary Mason, Gary Stephen Ross, and the editors. "The 50 Most Powerful People in Vancouver (2015)." *Vancouver Magazine,* 17 November 2015. http://vanmag.com/best-of-the-city/the-50-most-powerful-people-in-vancouver-2015/. Accessed 19 February 2018.

Carter, Mandy. "Southerners on New Ground: Our Lesbian, Gay, Bisexual, and Transgender Community." In *What Lies Beneath: Katrina, Race, and the State of the Nation,* edited by South End Press Collective, 54–64. Boston: South End Press, 2007.

Faiola, Anthony. "In Europe, Creating a Post-Gender World One Small Rule at a Time." *Washington Post,* 12 June 2015. https://www.washingtonpost.com/world/europe/the-remarkable-ways-europe-is-changing-how-people-talk-about-gender/2015/06/12/af435d48-0df0-11e5-a0fe-dccfea4653ee_story.html?utm_term=.41d733b1cb7b. Accessed 18 July 2017.

Hainey, Michael. "The Woman Who Paved the Way for Men to Become Women." *GQ,* 26 May 2015. www.gq.com/story/renee-richards-interview. Accessed 18 July 2017.

Hebblethwaite, Cordelia. "Sweden's 'Gender-Neutral' Pre-School." *BBC News,* 8 July 2011. www.bbc.com/news/world-europe-14038419. Accessed 18 July 2017.

Holter, Lauren. "Renee Richards Is a Transgender Sports Icon Who Paved the Way for Caitlyn Jenner with a Game-Changing Lawsuit Back in 1975." *Bustle,* 4 June 2015. https://www.bustle.com/articles/88119-renee-richards-is-a-transgender-sports-icon-who-paved-the-way-for-caitlyn-jenner-with-a. Accessed 18 July 2017.

Judd, Amy. "Motion Passes for Genderless Bathrooms in Vancouver Schools." Interview of Dr. Ann Travers, professor of sociology at Simon Fraser University, Vancouver. *Global News,* 17 June 2014. http://globalnews.ca/news/1398131/motion-passes-for-genderless-bathrooms-in-vancouver-schools/. Accessed 21 June 2016.

Kliment, Bud. *Billie Holiday: Singer.* Los Angeles: Melrose Square Publishing, 1990.

One Love, All Equal. "Mack Beggs, a Trans Wrestler, Shares Advice with Trans Community." 6 March 2017. https://oneloveallequal.org/2017/03/06/mack-beggs-trans-wrestler-shares-advice-trans-community/. Accessed 18 July 2017.

Reborchick, Marcy. "At the Gates of West Point." Women's Memorial, January 2007. https://www.womensmemorial.org/oral-history/detail/?s=at-the-gates-of-west-point. Accessed 5 April 2018.

Renée Richards. "The Second Half of My Life." Interview by Neal Conan on *Talk of the Nation*, National Public Radio, 8 February 2007. www.npr.org/templates/story/story.php?storyId=7277665. Accessed 18 July 2017.

Robinson, Faith Haleh, and Nadeem Muaddi. "Transgender Boy Wins Girls' Wrestling Championship in Texas." CNN, 27 February 2017. www.cnn.com/2017/02/27/us/texas-transgender-wrestler-trnd-hold/index.html. Accessed 10 July 2017.

Sheng, Jeff. *Fearless: Portraits of LGBT Student Athletes*. Los Angeles: Somebody Books, 2015.

Swarr, Amanda Lock, with Sally Gross and Liesl Theron. "South African Intersex Activism: Caster Semenya's Impact and Import." *Feminist Studies* 35.3. (2009): 657–662.

Takeuchi, Craig. "Trans Activist Tru Wilson Named 2017 Sexual Health Champion by Vancouver's Options for Sexual Health." *Georgia Straight,* 15 February 2017. https://www.straight.com/blogra/869576/trans-activist-tru-wilson-named-2017-sexual-health-champion-vancouvers-options-sexual. Accessed 19 February 2018.

Terkel, Amanda. "Bathroom Panic Has Long Stood in the Way of Equal Rights." *HuffPost: Politics,* 24 March 2016. https://www.huffingtonpost.com/entry/bathroompanic_us_56f40300e4b0c3ef521820e3. Accessed 12 February 2018.

U.S. Department of Labor. Americans with Disabilities Act. https://www.dol.gov/general/topic/disability/ada. Accessed 18 July 2017.

CHAPTER 6

Navigating Government Documents, Work, and Healthcare: I'll Need to See Some I.D. with That

Key Questions

1. Why might trans people, whether they have crossed the gender binary or identify as nonbinary, find government offices like the Department of Motor Vehicles or the passport office more stressful than someone who is not trans?

2. What are some of the "access to success" issues that trans people face in the workplace?

3. Does the type of work trans people are engaged in matter when it comes to issues of accessibility?

4. What approaches to healthcare could be welcoming to trans people?

5. What are some of the specific issues concerning violence against trans people in general and trans women of color in particular?

Chapter Overview

In Chapter 5 you considered issues of access for trans people in public places such as bathrooms and schools and in sports. When a trans athlete has trained for months or years and is ready to go to an international competition, how do they get there? Usually the journey involves a trip to the airport with a passport in hand. You may already know that, for some trans people, getting a passport can be difficult, perhaps even impossible, especially if the trans person is also nonbinary.

This chapter begins by looking at trans access to government documents. As the chapter unfolds, it also explores broader issues concerning work access, workplace environment, and the kinds of work open to trans people. Often,

Haefele-Thomas, Ardel, *Introduction to Transgender Studies*
dx.doi.org/10.17312/harringtonparkpress/2019.01.itts.006
© 2019 by Harrington Park Pressw

getting credit, opening a bank account, applying to colleges, accessing financial aid, and applying for health benefits become almost insurmountable obstacles for trans people. The chapter concludes by examining healthcare access for trans people, with a special focus on access for trans youths and trans elders. Government policies, workplace laws and rules, and healthcare codes of conduct vary from country to country, and even state to state, so this chapter is not meant to be exhaustive. Rather, it examines some problems and considers some possible solutions.

Introduction: Government Documents—Red Tape, Existential Crises

As you begin this chapter, continue to think about the various places you have gone over the past week. Did you go to work? Did you have an appointment with your doctor or need the urgent-care clinic? Maybe you had to run one of those errands that we all dread, like going to the passport office or the Department of Motor Vehicles (DMV). Errands to obtain government documents are often tiring and tedious. If you also happen to be trans, these places—the workplace, the passport office, and the health clinic—often present areas of danger.

Legal Identification

 KELLY KELLY "We have to adapt to constantly changing dynamics of having our bodies regulated (by law enforcement and the medical-industrial complex) and by the state, which perpetuates endless administrative violences against trans people by making us select only one of two possible genders. Why is our gender even necessary on college applications, work applications, medical applications? What if our legal documents just stated 'human being'? Why is everything gendered?"

Do you remember Kelly Kelly from Chapters 1 and 2? In her comment above, she makes several important points about the ways that we all have to indicate our gender on numerous forms. For some people, these forms create what can feel like an existential crisis every time they have to mark a box; for others, the questions are just red tape. What does Kelly Kelly mean by the "administrative violences" that are committed against trans people? What other groups of people might also feel these violences? Now think about various forms of government in historic contexts. Who, in the past, might have also experienced a sense of violence?

Your Very First I.D.

Do you remember the babies from Chapters 1 and 2 who were in their strollers at the park? Before they were out and about, they had already been stamped and approved with an official government identification: the birth certificate. Do you have your birth certificate? Do you know everything that is listed on it? Think about what birth certificates can list: sex, date of birth, parents, race, ethnicity, geographic location. In the United States, birth certificates vary from state to state. Some list race, and others do not. Some list birth weight and length, and others do not. *Sex is always on the birth certificate.* Date of birth is always on the birth certificate. If, for any reason, someone needs to change their birth certificate, it becomes a very serious, anxiety-producing endeavor for the person trying to change the information and often causes a bureaucratic headache for the government being petitioned to grant the change.[1]

Why might a birth certificate need to be changed? If a baby was born with differences in sex development (also known as intersex), and if a surgical procedure is performed, then the baby's sex might need to be changed. In the United States, when a child goes through a legal adoption, the birth certificate is changed to reflect the adoptive parents as the birth parents.

Your birth certificate is often revered as your original moment: your origin story according to the government. At least in the United States, there are many ways that a birth certificate can show cultural erasures and discriminatory practices. For example, African American children born into slavery did not have identity documents because they were seen as property rather than people. Although slavery was abolished in 1865, discrimination against African American people continues, as in the struggle for voting rights in predominantly African American precincts not only in the South but all over the United States.

For trans people of all ethnicities in the United States, the Williams Institute at the UCLA School of Law found that in the 2016 presidential election, more than 34,000 transgender voters could have been disenfranchised in states that had strict voter I.D. laws.[2] Here are the key findings of this study:

- Thirty percent of the voting-eligible transgender population in eight states (Alabama, Georgia, Indiana, Kansas, Mississippi, Tennessee, Virginia, and Wisconsin) have no identification or records that accurately reflect their gender.

- It is likely that transgender people of color, youths, students, people with low income, and people with disabilities are overrepresented among those who do not have an accurate I.D. for voting.

- For these 34,000 voting-eligible transgender people to obtain accurate I.D.s for voting, they must comply with the state and federal requirements for updating I.D.s. These requirements vary widely by state or federal agency and can be difficult and costly to meet.[3]

Note here, too, the ways that intersecting identities add another layer of complexity to whether people have access to their right to vote.

For trans people in the United States who need to change their sex on a birth certificate, the policies vary from state to state. For example, Alabama will not change an original birth certificate for someone who changes gender identity; the state will, however, issue an amended birth certificate. In contrast, Colorado will change both name and sex, and it will issue a new birth certificate rather than amending the old one. In Mississippi, the revised name and gender identity can go on the birth certificate, but only in the margins next to the original name and sex designation.[4]

Take a moment to think about these different policies. What is the difference between an original birth certificate that has been changed and an amended birth certificate? The amended certificate in Alabama is a separate document from the original. In Mississippi the original birth certificate has the name change in the margins so that both names and both sex designations wind up on the same piece of paper. Meanwhile, in Colorado you can get a completely new birth certificate. For trans people in Mississippi, think about how it would feel to show your birth certificate to a person in a position of authority. What could happen if you have a birth certificate with two names and two sexes on it?

In the autumn of 2017, California became the first U.S. state to allow nonbinary as a gender designation on birth certificates when Governor Jerry Brown signed Senate Bill 179 (the Gender Recognition Act) into law. California became the second state to allow a nonbinary or third gender marker on driver's licenses.[5]

In Canada the birth certificate law varies from province to province. In Alberta a person used to need the signatures of two physicians and proof of gender-affirmation surgery to get a new birth certificate; this practice was found to be unconstitutional.[6] In British Columbia in 2017, upon parental request, a baby was issued a health card without any gender identity. The government, however, still wants to put the baby's sex on the birth certificate. The baby's parent, Kory Doti, who is a transgender activist, argues that the baby should not be put into a gendered box. Indeed, growing numbers of advocates in Canada make the argument that gender does not need to be on any government documents.[7]

Another example: England and Wales will not draw up a new birth certificate or amend the old one. The argument is that the birth certificate is a historical record and should remain intact as such. This does not mean, though, that you cannot change your name. The most common way to start using the name with which you identify is to begin using your name in day-to-day life. If you are under the age of sixteen, you will need parental consent.[8] Although it is easy to change your name, many organizations will still ask for legal documentation even though you could, technically, argue that the request goes against the law.[9] Some groups in England and Wales are struggling with these issues because they are receiving mixed messages about needing a document called a Deed Poll to change a name. If you need your birth certificate for another type of government document (such as a passport), you must include your birth certificate and the Deed Poll.[10]

The policies regarding birth certificate changes in Canada, England, and Wales bring up several questions. Why do you think that Alberta's old law, which made the trans person prove that they had been under a doctor's care and had undergone gender-affirmation surgery, was declared unconstitutional? What do you think about the ongoing discussion in British Columbia to remove gender markers from all government documents? Why do we need gender on government documents? What would happen if gender is removed? Finally, imagine a trans person in England or Wales who needs to get a passport. It appears that they have to include their original, unchanged birth certificate with the Deed Poll, at least if they want to get through the process smoothly. Is this policy any different from Mississippi's writing in the margins of the original birth certificate? If so, what are the differences?

Going Global

Are you feeling tied up in all that birth certificate red tape? Maybe a trip to another country could ease the stress. If you do not have a passport, though, you will encounter even more red tape. Passports are not only a form of identification, they are also the means by which people have the freedom to travel from one country to another. If you live in the United States and you do not have a passport, you can visit only other U.S. states or U.S. territories. What if you are planning an epic road trip to Alaska? If you don't have a passport, you will not be able to drive there because a large part of the journey will take you across Canada, which no longer accepts a driver's license for entry into the country.

If you are a U.S. citizen and have transitioned across the gender binary, guess where you need to go first to get a new passport that reflects your proper gender identity. Did you guess the passport office? If so, you are wrong. Your first stop has to be your doctor's office. The National Center for Transgender Equality has some helpful online information for trans people who need a new passport with the appropriate gender markers. According to the information, you can get a new passport "if you have had clinical treatment determined by your doctor to be appropriate in your case to facilitate gender transition."[11] Note that your doctor determines if the treatment has been appropriate for *you*.

Under the Obama administration, advocacy work in the United States was moving toward a person's being able to have a proper gender marker regardless of any type of body modification; however, under the Trump administration, the policies may not be as broad. The important thing to remember is that, like bathroom policies and those governing military service, the laws surrounding trans issues are often in flux. Think back to Alberta's law about changing a birth certificate. The original law required the person to have undergone gender-affirmation surgery; later that law was deemed unconstitutional. The current U.S. passport law leaves some room for flexibility by requiring the trans person's doctor to determine if the treatment was appropriate. But what does *appropriate* mean? Do the criteria vary from doctor to doctor, patient to patient, and state to state? The answer is probably "yes" to all, but think about issues of expertise and agency. Who is the expert about a person's body: the person or the doctor? On the basis of current law, the doctor is the expert, because a gender change on a passport must be medically sanctioned.

In the United States, gender can be changed on the passport from *either* male to female *or* female to male. What if the person getting ready to travel internationally is Two Spirit? What happens to nonbinary trans people and to people who do not identify as solely male or solely female? What happens to someone who identifies as both? Currently in the United States, nonbinary trans people must pick *one* side of the binary, but not all countries have this requirement.

Countries that allow a third gender category, usually marked as "x," include Nepal, Germany, India, and Argentina. In the case of India, the third gender category makes passports accessible to **Hijras,** who identify as neither women nor men. *Hijras* have lived in India for thousands of years. (You will learn more about *Hijras* and Indian culture in Chapter 7.) Another group of people who might be interested in the third gender option are people with differences in sex development (DSD). Germany has chosen to have a third gender option so that parents of infants with DSD can leave the sex designation blank on the birth certificate. In addition, adults with DSD in Germany can opt for a third gender option on passports.[12] In 2015 Dana Zzyym, a Colorado resident, navy veteran, and activist with Organisation Intersex International, began work with Lambda

Legal to sue the U.S. government to allow a third gender option on passports. As a person who has differences in sex development and does not identify as either male or female, Zzyym was unable to participate in an international DSD/intersex conference in Mexico City because of the lack of the third gender option on the U.S. passport. Interestingly, citizens who identify as a third gender from countries that allow the "x" on the passport can enter the United States; however, without a passport, Zzyym cannot travel outside the United States at this time.[13] Some nonbinary people decide to choose either male or female for their passports because they will then encounter less trouble when traveling internationally.

In June 2017 Oregon became the first U.S. state to add a third gender option to driver's licenses.[14] The law went into effect on 3 July 2017. Governor Kate Brown said this about the new law: "We must proactively break down the barriers of institutional bias," adding that it could help Oregon foster "a society that upholds the rights, liberties and dignity of each of its people."[15] It will be interesting to see which other states follow Oregon's example. How much time will elapse between the availability of a third gender category for driver's licenses and the availability of a third gender category for passports?

The Workplace: "You Better Work!"

Here is a question for you: What year did the Equal Rights Amendment (ERA) pass in the United States? This amendment to the U.S. Constitution would guarantee that nobody could be denied equality of rights "by any state on account of sex."[16] There was also an underlying assumption that the ERA would also, ultimately, guarantee equal pay for equal work. The answer, however, is that the ERA never passed. During his first one hundred days in office, President Obama signed the Lilly Ledbetter Fair Pay Act.[17] This does not mean that women now receive equal pay for equal work, but at least a federal law on the books says they should. Note, though, that equality of rights on the basis of sex is still not written into constitutional law.

When you think about gender equality in the workplace, do you also think about transgender equality in the workplace? What are the first steps you must take to get a job? You fill out an application, and somewhere in the application and hiring process, you have to show some form of government identification.

Like the passport situation, full access for trans people in the workplace depends on location. In 2012 Argentina became possibly the most trans-friendly country in the world. The gender identity bill, which went through Argentina's federal government in 2012, includes policies intended to prevent discrimination against trans people in healthcare, housing, and employment. Mauro Cabral, the executive director of Global Action for Trans Equality (GATE), said: "This legal change in Argentina is also a message going beyond borders. It is a message for countries in the region to advance their commitments on gender identity and human rights issues. A message for all those countries that even today consecrate human rights violations such as forced sterilization in their gender identity laws. This law sends a clear message against transphobic violence, and affirms the full status as humans of trans* people and their right to all rights."[18] Cabral's statement makes it clear that other countries around the world need to follow Argentina's actions where trans rights are concerned; however, global change has been slow and often fluctuating. For example, in the United States in July 2015 the Pentagon began serious discussion about removing the ban on transgender people serving in the military. Part of the argument was that trans people were already serving honorably in all branches of the U.S. armed services. By June 2016 the ban was officially removed. Eleven months later, in July 2017, however, after the administration change from President Obama to President Trump, the ban was reinstated.[19]

In the United States, trans people have had diverse experiences in workplace situations, from abusive and dangerous to safe and supportive. For anyone, regardless of gender identity, being treated well in workplace situations depends on the kind of power structure within the job. Power structures vary from company to company or, for academic settings, from college or university to college or university. Some companies include full protections for their employees that include gender identity and/or gender expression, while others do not. The same is true of colleges and universities; some prohibit discrimination on the basis of gender identity and/or gender expression, while others do not. Just because a place of employment has policies that prohibit discrimination on the basis of *gender* and/or *sexual orientation,* however, does not automatically mean that trans people are protected. "Gender" on these policies usually signals that the employer does not discriminate against women. And just because a workplace may be open to gay, lesbian, and bisexual people does not automatically mean that it is open to trans people. The U.S. military can serve as an example here. As of January 2018, gay, lesbian, and bisexual people could serve openly in the U.S. military; however, trans people could not.

Other factors in considering whether an employer offers a safe space for trans people could include the worker's socioeconomic status, age, ability, race, and union protections. Throughout the United States, unions have become more proactive about trans rights in the workplace in much the same way that unions have fought against women's gender oppression in the workplace over the past few decades. For many unions, the language has moved toward gender equality for all genders, which includes trans people.

Another major factor in the workplace is whether the trans person can and/or chooses to **pass.** Of course, passing assumes that the trans employee has crossed the gender binary. For many nonbinary trans people who do not embody a clearly male or female expression, for many nonbinary trans people who do look specifically male or specifically female on any given day, and for trans people who have crossed the gender binary but who still may not pass, the work world can be a cruel place. Imagine a nonbinary trans person who uses a neutral pronoun like "they" who, every day at work, is referred to as "she" *even if* they have let their coworkers and their boss know they use neutral pronouns. Or imagine a trans woman who has to deal with everyone at her job continuing to refer to her as "he." How might this day-to-day level of denigration of a person's identity—known as **microaggression**—make them feel? How might these situations at work affect an employee's work production, not to mention their self-esteem and overall well-being?

Miss Major Griffin-Gracy, Prison Systems, and Work

You may remember Miss Major Griffin-Gracy from Chapter 4 (figure 6.1). She was one of the people arrested at the Stonewall Inn on the night the riots broke out in June 1969. She is now in her seventies and is one of the few Stonewall veterans still alive. For decades, Miss Major has worked with social justice movements aiming to improve the lives of incarcerated trans people.

Miss Major is no stranger to prison. As a former sex worker, she spent time in both Attica and Sing Sing, where she met other prisoners who had worked within the Black Panther Movement and other political organizations striving for social justice. At Sing Sing, she became even more politicized when she saw how the wardens and other prisoners treated the trans women of color. In most U.S. jails and prisons, trans women are still housed with men. The penal system does not recognize gender identity outside cisnormativity. In prison trans women are often raped and brutalized. One of the safest places for trans women in prison is solitary confinement. Solitary confinement may be a safer place for a trans woman; however, being put in solitary is also a brutal form of punishment. Placement in solitary stays on your permanent record and signals that you have been a difficult prisoner. This stigma can have further negative ramifications after release from prison because people placed in solitary do not have oppor-

FIGURE 6.1 Miss Major Griffin-Gracy, by Cameron Rains. Miss Major Griffin-Gracy has been a leading trans activist for almost fifty years, linking the movement to other civil rights groups, including the Black Panthers. She founded TGI Justice, a prison-reform organization that advocates for gender-appropriate and just treatment of transgender prisoners. Now in her seventies, she is still a force to be reckoned with.

tunities for job-training programs and other benefits that the prison might offer to help improve outcomes upon prisoners' release.

In 2005 Miss Major became the first staff organizer for TGI Justice, which is "a group of transgender, gender variant and intersex people—inside and outside of prisons, jails and detention centers—creating a united family in the struggle for survival and freedom."[20]

In addition to working with transgender, genderqueer, and people with differences in sex development coming out of jails and prisons across the United States, TGI Justice has been working toward recognizing the layers of systemic violence that affect trans women of color. When Marsha P. Johnson was brutally murdered and thrown into the Hudson River, the NYPD was quick to claim it was a suicide; however, her loved ones in the community knew that she had been killed, and now the FBI is finally revisiting the evidence because of the dogged determination of members of Marsha's community, who are demanding justice. The murder rates for all trans people, and trans women of color specifically, are on the rise in the United States. As part of its work, TGI Justice has written an open letter to the community:

> Transphobia is as deeply rooted in our society as it is dangerous. It exists in all of us, because in America that is how we are socialized—to adhere to a prescriptive set of traditional gender identities and conservative values that leave little room for freedom of choice or individuality. Eliminating transphobia, and stopping the violence perpetuated against Black trans women in particular, requires each of us to be daring enough to reflect on how we have all contributed to it, and to be mindful of how we have, whether we are aware of it or not, given rise to an environment in which transgender

people are in danger doing everyday activities like walking down the street, going to work, or having a cup of coffee. It requires educators to begin teaching lessons on the history of transgender people, for legislators to take seriously their job to protect every single person they claim to represent, and for everyday people to intervene when witnessing violence against trans people.[21]

This letter asks us all to remember that we need to take care of one another and stand up for people in our communities. It is important to understand that some of the violence experienced by trans people is caused by our various systems that do not allow full access for trans people. The murders referred to in TGI Justice's letter did not happen in a vacuum. Rather, they go back to the idea of administrative violence that Kelly Kelly talks about at the start of this chapter. When marginalized communities are denied basic access, they receive a message that they are not legitimate, not real. After all, if you don't have a birth certificate, how can you be a real person?

When Miss Major turned seventy and went to claim her Social Security, her agent at the Social Security Office told her that she had worked only five years, so she would receive only five years' worth of retirement benefits. Of course, Miss Major had worked since she was in her teens: sex work, prison reform, and other jobs that were open to her as an African American trans woman. Her only *legitimate* work had been with TGI Justice. Even though she has problems with her health, Miss Major moved to Little Rock, Arkansas, to help incarcerated trans people there. She is a Stonewall veteran, an LGBTQ icon, a national treasure, and a spokesperson who has addressed the United Nations in Geneva, yet the U.S. government's paperwork says she has worked only five years.[22]

Conversely, in 2015 in Argentina, a judge in Buenos Aires made international headlines when he ruled that Ms. G., a trans woman who had been horribly abused at the hands of police and judicial systems, was to receive a public pension for the rest of her life. Judge Victor Trionfetti stated that "as a result of the discrimination and the institutional violence—of a general, constant, and direct nature permitted by an absent State and promoted by police officers," she would be given a monthly living wage.[23] Ms. G. had worked as a sex worker and then later a seamstress. She was raped and brutalized by the police. Although Judge Trionfetti made it clear that he was ruling on Ms. G. as a single case, human rights advocates are working to expand this case as setting a legal precedent that can help other people in Ms. G.'s situation.[24]

The Healthcare System: Dying for Care

The documentary film *Southern Comfort* opens with the sights and sounds of rural Georgia at sunrise on a spring morning. The camera pans a rural scene, including a dogwood tree with its fragile white flowers, and the viewer hears roosters crowing. It eventually focuses on a solitary figure sitting in a chair looking into the distance. Without turning to look at the camera, he begins to speak: "It's Easter morning and it's sunrise. And I wish I could understand why they did what they did. Why they had to feel that way. And I know in a way that they have contributed to my dying here. But I can't hate them. . . . I can't say I actually forgive them for what they've done. I think that's more between them and God. . . . I guess what makes me most sad is that they probably feel like they did the right thing."[25]

Robert Eads (1945–1999), a trans man, alludes to the fact that he is dying from ovarian cancer. After being turned away by twenty hospitals and clinics where staff were too embarrassed, felt too awkward, or were worried about their reputations, he was finally given treatment, but by then it was too late.

Robert Eads was not wealthy. He lived in a trailer on some land in Toccoa, Georgia. Before he returned home to Georgia, doctors in Florida (where he had undergone top surgery) advised him that he did not need to have a full hysterectomy because he was already in his forties and starting menopause. At one point in the film, he notes the irony that the only female thing left on him was killing him.[26]

Robert sought medical help as soon as he knew something was horribly wrong, only to be turned away by numerous doctors and clinics. Robert's story is not unusual; in fact, many trans men have stories similar to Robert's. His experience exemplifies why so many trans people do not want to seek medical help: they are afraid of being judged and rejected. It is not an exaggeration to say that a trans person can walk into a clinic with a broken arm, but the moment the person is out about being trans, the nurses and doctors suddenly want to look at the genitals. Pretty soon, the broken arm gets forgotten.

Imagine hanging out with friends in a study group. You are all preparing class presentations. As one of your friends gets up to go get some water, they suddenly collapse on the floor and begin having a seizure. Once you've made sure they are not going to hurt themselves while they are having convulsions, you call the paramedics, who arrive quickly. Now, imagine this: your friend is nonbinary trans. When the paramedics arrive, they ask, "What is her name? And have you been timing her seizures?" You explain that your friend uses *they*

FIGURE. 6.2 "Select One," by Cameron Rains. Today in the United States and in many other parts of the world, routine medical forms and government documents insist that people select either "male" or "female" before they can access basic medical care or government services. For many people who do not identify within the gender binary, these forms can block much-needed medical care.

UNFORTUNATELY WE CANNOT BEGIN YOUR LIFE-SAVING SURGERY UNTIL YOU SELECT ONE OF THESE TWO GENDER OPTIONS!

pronouns, not *she* pronouns. The paramedics look at you as if you're suddenly speaking Greek. They continue to ignore you as your friend is finally able to sit up on their own, but your friend is confused and groggy. The paramedics say, "Ma'am, do you have a known seizure disorder? We don't see a medic alert tag." Your friend, who is already feeling awful, is now upset and says, "I am not a woman. Please don't call me ma'am." The paramedics look at each other in disgust and walk away. What does your friend's gender have to do with the seizure? Nothing. Yet incidents like this one happen often. (See figure 6.2.)

Fortunately, not all trans people have negative experiences at the doctor's office, in the emergency room, and at the hospital. In the United States, things are slowly changing, and more doctors and nurses receive training on the ways that working with trans people requires education about gender identities and models of cultural competence that allow them to provide better and more supportive care to marginalized communities. In 2014 Oxford University Press published a groundbreaking book entitled *Trans Bodies, Trans Selves: A Resource for the Transgender Community*. It discusses numerous medical and health access issues for trans people and includes voices from the trans community. More and more medical practices and medical schools now include this text as a resource guide.[27]

In the "Writings from the Community" section at the end of this chapter, you will hear from two young doctors in New York who discuss the ways that trans issues are addressed (or not addressed) as part of their medical school training. You will also find an essay from a woman who fought to make the medical forms at the Veteran's Affairs Commission more inclusive.

Righting the Wrongs of Others

As you read in Chapter 3, Dr. Christine McGinn, a surgeon who is also a trans woman, has created the Papillon Gender Wellness Center in Pennsylvania. One of the pioneering transgender surgeons in the United States who served as a role model for Dr. McGinn is Dr. Marci Bowers, who is also a trans woman who worked for years in Trinidad, Colorado. Interestingly, Trinidad, Colorado, a small town on the Colorado–New Mexico border, was one of the premier places in the United States to go for gender-affirmation surgery as early as the 1970s.[28] A growing number of clinics throughout the world are headed by trans doctors and their allies who are there to perform gender-affirmation surgery, prescribe hormones, and/or to make sure that their clinic is a safe space for people of all gender identities. For example, there is the Sherbourne Health Centre in Toronto, Canada, the Tavistock and Portman Clinic in London, England, and the Transgender Clinic at Groote Schuur Hospital in Cape Town, South Africa. Just as it is crucial that more and more trans people are becoming healthcare providers, it is also important to acknowledge allies who have worked tirelessly in the field of access to healthcare for trans people, including gender-affirmation surgery.

One internationally renowned ally in the field of gender-affirmation surgery is Dr. Preecha Tiewtranon (figure 6.3), who has been doing gender-affirmation surgeries for over thirty years in Bangkok, Thailand. For many people in the United States, clinics like the one in Trinidad, Colorado, and other domestic hospitals that perform gender-affirmation procedures are very expensive because many employers and insurance companies still view these procedures as elective surgery. If a trans person is able to get a passport and is able to schedule a trip to Thailand, however, Dr. Preecha's clinic has proven to be more affordable, even with the travel and lodging costs included. By training his colleagues and students, Dr. Preecha has set an example of being an outstanding ally.

Dr. Preecha's work in the trans community began in 1978, when he became an international pioneer in fixing botched sex-reassignment surgeries (srs) performed by other surgeons who were not qualified to carry out gender-affirmation surgery.[29] Dr. Preecha is now in semiretirement, but he has trained a

FIGURE 6.3 Dr. Preecha Tiewtranon, by Cameron Rains. One internationally renowned ally in the field of gender-affirmation surgery is Dr. Preecha Tiewtranon, who has been doing gender-affirmation surgeries for over thirty years in Bangkok, Thailand. Now semiretired, Dr. Tiewtranon is training a new generation of surgeons.

new generation of Thai surgeons to perform gender-affirmation surgeries. He is an outstanding ally because he has been at the forefront of educating the world about gender identity and many people's need for gender-affirmation procedures. He has also done outreach in the communities surrounding the facilities so that hotels and restaurants are welcoming to the people who have arrived from many different parts of the globe to have their gender-affirmation procedures performed by some of the world's best practitioners.

WRITINGS FROM THE COMMUNITY

INTERVIEW WITH DR. JULES CHYTEN-BRENNAN AND DR. MAT KLADNEY

Jules Chyten-Brennan, D.O., is currently a general internal medicine fellow at Montefiore Medical Center, doing research on community-driven integration of trans healthcare throughout large mainstream medical institutions. Jules graduated from Rowan University School of Osteopathic Medicine and completed an internal medicine residency in Montefiore's Primary Care and Social Medicine program in the Bronx, New York, and is working to integrate transgender healthcare throughout the Montefiore system. He has a particular interest in providing healthcare for trans people at the intersections of other medically underserved populations, including a focus on substance use treatment, healthcare for incarcerated and recently incarcerated people, and HIV care.

Mat Kladney, M.D., is currently the chief resident for the social internal medicine residency at Montefiore Medical Center in the Bronx, New York; he earned his M.D. at the University of California at San Francisco. His research interests include medication-assisted treatment for substance use and medical education. He is currently rewriting the LGBT curriculum at Albert Einstein College of Medicine. Before his career in medicine, he worked as an Americorps volunteer, an overdose prevention educator, and a bartender.

Q: What type of training focused on trans people did you have in medical school?

JULES: We had one lecture focused on trans health during our "professionalism" curriculum. It touched on a bit of trans etiquette and mentioned the WPATH [World Professional Association for Transgender Health] guidelines (though they were outdated—the most recent had just come out). There was no mention of nonbinary or genderqueer people. All in all (with expectations set low) I thought it was actually pretty decent. We also had a clip from the documentary *Southern Comfort* playing during our ethics curriculum. The documentary seemed a bit sensationalist, but got people talking.

MAT: As a medical student, we had one lecture about gender identity and transgender issues. This was focused primarily on using appropriate terminology and pronouns.

Q: How was your medical school's training in LGBT healthcare in general?

JULES: It was pretty nonexistent. The dean of the school was pretty conservatively Catholic, and I was told he squashed a few efforts here and there. I supplemented on my own by shadowing at the closest LGBT clinic.

MAT: UCSF's curriculum prides itself on having more LGBT curriculum than most medical schools. We primarily covered the health disparities faced by the LGBT community. Notably, the transgender portions of these sessions were the least informative, usually with the caveat that there is little research on the transgender community, so no data can be presented.

Q: You are both now residents at a major urban hospital that focuses on people who are at poverty level, below poverty level, and homeless. How many patients who were out as trans have you encountered so far?

JULES: Sadly, I have only come across one trans patient at our outpatient clinic. She is generally treated respectfully by staff, though there have been incidents of maltreatment. One day, she was upset with the front desk staff and raised her voice. One of the front desk supervisors who had been using the patient's correct pronoun, switched and began heatedly calling her "him."

MAT: I have worked with two transgender patients thus far. One patient was out and had already transitioned through hormone therapy. The other patient came to me for normal primary care and he eventually came out to me as a trans man. I have not encountered any patients who identify as nonbinary or genderqueer thus far.

Q: In what ways do you make it clear to your trans patients that you are an ally and that it is safe for them to be out with you?

JULES: This is a complicated question. I am trans, but also a trans man and a doctor. So I fall on both sides of this relationship. I'm not usually out with patients, although I am out in public space and at events where I might draw in trans and queer patients from the community. I've been considering more visual signs like wearing a pin or hanging a sign at our clinic.

MAT: I wear a rainbow triangle pin on my white coat, but when I don't wear my white coat I have fewer visual cues illustrating my ally status. I am sure to ask all patients about sexual orientation, and I ask them what name they prefer to be called. To be honest, our clinic isn't a particularly LGBT friendly (or unfriendly) place despite being staffed by many LGBT physicians.

Q: What policies does your hospital have about gender identity and gender expression? In other words, does your hospital offer more than two gender options on forms and in practice?

JULES: Our patient and employee nondiscrimination policies include gender identity. The gender options vary by form.

MAT: The only gender policies that exist at my current hospital relate to room assignments. People are assigned to male or female rooms; however, I believe that if a patient is trans, they are assigned to a private room. We are using a medical records system for the forms that only allows "male" or "female"; however, there is a trans working group that is training the medical records department on other options.

Q: How many of the trans patients embody intersecting identities?

JULES: All of them.

MAT: All of them. My patient population is primarily composed of people of color who are below the poverty line.

Q: Please share any positive or negative stories and any last things you would like to say about yourself as a doctor.

JULES: When the Caitlyn Jenner story broke, I got a lot of insight into people's opinions about trans issues. I was pleasantly surprised to hear one of my critical care fellows speaking up for trans people among the staff and talking about letting her son experiment with nail polish. I was less happy to hear several nurses using words like "freak" and "unnatural." I have been working with a group of providers to make my institution more trans friendly and on expanding trans health resources. People have been coming out from all over expressing support and interest and asking for training. It is nice to see so much support.

MAT: I am very fortunate to be working at a clinic that has physicians who are all shades of the LGBT rainbow. We have also done a really good job of recruiting physicians who are allies, and I have no fear of referring trans patients to my colleagues. Unfortunately, the same is not true for other staff at my clinic. Our medical records system, which is getting updated, still does not have a trans option per se, but we have changed the forms enough so that it does allow me to prepare my staff with appropriate pronouns and how to address my patients.

VERONIKA FIMBRES

My "Tea"!

Veronika Fimbres is a transgender and HIV activist who has lived in San Francisco for more than two decades. After serving in the navy and marines, then working as a sex worker and a model, she became a licensed vocational nurse. She is currently working as a hospice nurse. When she was appointed by the Board of Supervisors to the San Francisco Veterans' Affairs Commission—a post she held for fourteen years—she became the first transgender person to serve on a city board or commission. In recognition of her outspoken efforts to remove barriers for those living with HIV/AIDS, especially transgender people, she received the Fred Skau Outstanding Volunteer of the Year Award from the AIDS Emergency Fund and the Bobby Campbell AIDS Hero Award from the Sisters of Perpetual Indulgence. In 2013 she was honored as a community grand marshal of the San Francisco LGBT Pride Parade. In 2018 she also threw her hat into the governor's race in California

Surviving

My name is Veronika Fimbres. It wasn't always that. I identify as a trans woman, though I am a woman who happens to be trans. I am turning sixty-five this year. I am black, and like most trans women in my era—Queens or Shemales—I had to work the streets. I prostituted in San Diego, New York City, and here and there or wherever it was convenient. It was necessary for my survival.

A Vietnam-era veteran of the United States Navy, I served honorably with the navy and later the marines, in Field Medical Service School, at Camp Pendleton. I operated the surgical tent in the "MASH" unit. I am in therapy because of the sexual abuses I suffered in the military—I have PTSD.

I was, and remain, a smart woman. I have been beaten, stabbed, had a gun pulled on me, been raped quite a few times, and been a proactive victim of domestic violence—I fought back! I have been jailed before. I will say that the older you get, the worse jail seems.

Evansville Will Never Be the Same

I was a free-base crack addict while living in New York. I went—as I call it— "down the toilet" during that time. I was homeless on the streets and lost everything. I had a friend who would feed me food that was thrown away in the Dumpster because he didn't want me to dig for it. I slept in a step van off the Hudson River with thirteen other crack addicts.

I got sick and my mother asked me to come home, so I went to Indiana, where she lived. I had a month of relapse and wrote bad checks on my own account. I was caught. The incident was published in the local newspaper. I read an article about a "man in a dress" with my name attached below. I was horrified and called my attorney. Evansville, Indiana, will never be the same. As a result, three guys I was dating broke it off, and the Strip Club on Main Street posted a banner that said, "Real Women Only!"

Serving San Francisco: Making Access Easier

I am a longtime AIDS survivor, having made it since 1987, when I was told I needed to say my "good-byes." I'm still here thirty years later, but I've lost many loved ones. My youngest brother died of AIDS a few days before my birthday in 1992. My fiancé died of AIDS the following month. I was devastated. I came to San Francisco to save my life. I got to the city, a place for new beginnings, in 1996. I have called it home ever since.

I have been a licensed vocational nurse for over thirty-four years. I've worked as a staff nurse at Hospice by the Bay and safety nurse at San Quentin State Prison. I am the first trans person to ever work at San Quentin as a safety nurse. I introduced the San Francisco County Jail to programs for trans inmates who were omitted and ostracized.

My claim to San Francisco history is that I am the first trans officer in the history of the City and County of San Francisco's boards and commissions—serving nearly fifteen years as a commissioner of Veteran's Affairs. My work on the commission provided veterans better access to the Veterans' Affairs Hospital by having the No. 38 Geary–Muni bus change its marquee to read, "VA Hospital"!

In addition, I have won and received numerous awards from the governor, the city and county, and many AIDS service organizations, where I have volunteered and given it my all. I was open and out while serving on the Ryan White Care Council, where I was responsible for there being another box for gender instead of only providing binary options on health department documents and applications. The epidemiology and surveillance unit of the health department's AIDS offices were lumping transgender people with men for their serology and epidemiology studies and statistics on HIV/AIDS. I was outraged! I told them that I was not a man and that no trans person should be mislabeled and lumped together with other identified groups. That was all it took. They included a box for the identity of trans individuals and further broke down the M2F and F2M categories soon after. I didn't stop there. Providers needed training on how to work with trans HIV patients, so I helped the council allocate $80,000 for the first educational symposium that helped train providers on trans HIV issues.

The GLBT Historical Society has called me a "living legend," and, according to them, I am famous. Famous is not far from infamous, so it depends on how you look at it.

DALLAS DENNY

I Don't Fear the Reaper

Dallas Denny is a leader in the transgender rights movement. Her work as a writer, editor, speaker, and community builder has played a significant role in the advancement of rights for transsexual and transgender people in North America and around the world. The entirety of Dallas's work is available at her website: www.dallasdenny.com.

When I was a child I didn't want to even think about growing old. Old people were cranky. Wrinkled. Feeble. Slow. Sick. Out of touch. They seemed used up, collapsed in upon themselves, or else bloated—and yet I knew that if I survived, I would, inevitably, become like them.

But that would be a long time coming, and there was no need to think about it, and so I didn't, much. I would probably die young anyway, in a fiery car crash or of some obscure disease.

When I became a young adult I knew the day I would become old had grown closer, but it still seemed impossibly far off, and there was always that car crash in my future. I tried not to think about aging, but that was becoming increasingly difficult.

And then I met Miss Dee and I lost my fear of growing old.

Miss Dee was my supervisor. She was smart and witty and kind and we were not dissimilar in our outlooks on life—and when I played table tennis with her she cleaned my clock, and not just once, but three times in a row. I was impressed; she was, after all, sixty years my senior.

Ms. Dee was not, of course, like most people in their eighties, but the mere fact of her existence was proof I need not age into a curmudgeon or vote Republican or fill my house with bric-a-brac. My twenty-four-year-old self took away from that Ping-Pong massacre the realization that it was possible to be mentally and physically fit and up-to-date and old, all at the same time.

My eighty-fourth birthday is still sixteen years away, and, should I live to see it, my most fervent hope is to be as much like Miss Dee as possible. I know I won't magically acquire her athletic skills, but in other respects I seem to be on the right road.

As I write this (at age sixty-eight), I'm pretty much the same person I was at twenty-four. I have learned much and I have acquired new skills along the way and refined the skills I already had. I've gained experience and have more tales to tell, but my interests, my political sensibilities, my tastes in music and literature and art, and my sense of humor are all much the same. The same things please me and the same things offend me.

I still love the wilderness. I still like open cars and motorcycles. I still like to sing and play guitar. I am still a geek, loving computers and science and all things technical. I'm still an omnivorous reader, and I still love movies, old and new. I still rail against mean people in politics.

I look much the same as ever, or, rather, like a logical timeworn extension of my earlier self. My hair is still mostly its original color and I have few wrinkles. My hearing is still good and so are my reflexes.

Of course I have changed in many ways. My body has stiffened and I have acquired a variety of medical diagnoses that require me to take oral medications and may well one day kill me. I use a CPAP machine [for sleep apnea] when sleeping. The skin on my forearms and lower legs has become thin and is easily damaged. My eyesight has deteriorated; my distance and night vision are still good, but I can no longer read small print without glasses. I require more sleep. I can't lift as much weight as I once could, and I tire more easily. I take more naps—but then I have always loved naps and now, being retired, I have time to take them, so perhaps that's a good thing.

I have to think twice before climbing ladders or jumping down from walls, and my days of leaping out of airplanes are behind me, but I'm still able to do most of the things I did when I was younger. I hike long distances, I ride my motorcycle, I put the top of my Miata down in freezing weather, and I never pass up an opportunity to embark upon an adventure.

I regret my assorted infirmities and know I will grow more infirm as I age, but thanks to Miss Dee I don't dread my future. In the end, I think, it's more about attitude than time.

Ordinarily I would at this point say, "Good job, Dallas, now let's move on to that other chapter you promised to write," but there's the fact of my transsexualism, which has allowed me to experience life both as a boy and young man and as a young, middle-aged, and older woman.

I had a full-time boyhood, but I also had a girlhood of sorts. It was episodic and temporary, but a girlhood nonetheless.

By the time I was in my mid-teens I was going out in public dressed as a girl. I was frightened half to death most of the time, and with reason, for those were dangerous days for people like me. Discovery could result in harassment, arrest, beating, rape, death, or commitment to a mental hospital. None of those things happened to me because I told no one and because by some miracle of biology I passed easily and in all sorts of circumstances as a young woman, and a pretty one at that.

Like most young women, I was sexualized by men, who, upon one look at me, would attempt to coerce, romance, and seduce me. Some just wanted a quick sex fix, and some professed to want me as a girlfriend. I sometimes wanted to respond to their advances, but I considered it too dangerous to meet them more than once. I became adept at keeping men at a distance. I learned, by working temp jobs as a woman, that I was expected to be subservient and obedient and deferential toward men. Because I was afraid of being found out, I complied, but it chafed me and intensified my feminism.

By my mid-twenties my facial hair had come in and my hair had begun to thin, and for the first time it required some artifice to be able to pass as a woman. I hated the heavy wigs and thick makeup that were required. I still went out in public, but now I was on occasion found out. Luckily, nothing happened to me.

Just shy of my thirtieth birthday I began taking estrogen, and testosterone stopped affecting my body. My body began to soften and my hair grew thicker. After a few years people began to read me as female even when I was presenting as male. I began electrolysis when I was thirty-eight, and, thanks to electrolysis, my thick facial hair was gone, replaced by the fine, nearly invisible vellus hairs that characterize women's faces.

At age forty I transitioned and moved to Atlanta. In those days transsexuals were instructed to blend into society, not telling anyone of their status, and I believed that was what I was supposed to do. I was lucky enough to immediately find a professional position much like the one I had just left. Thanks to my appearance, my androgynous name, and cooperation from my previous employer, no one knew or suspected I had not always been female.

Society had changed since my public appearances as a young woman. Women were well-integrated in the agency at which I worked, and I was respected and taken seriously. Men would occasionally flirt with me, talk over me, or claim my ideas as their own, but much had changed. That was due partly to changing times, and partly to my age. The days of not being able to walk down the street without getting whistles were behind me.

As my fiftieth birthday approached I entered what I call my invisible phase. Now that I was aging, I was no longer being seen as a sex object. People —especially men, but sometimes women—would seem to just not notice me. It was as if I weren't there. All my life, even when I was presenting as male, people have held doors open for me. Now they would let doors slam in my face—not to be mean, but because I just didn't register to them. In department stores, salespeople would ignore me and wait on customers newly arrived. In line at fast-food restaurants, I would often have to ask for my order to be taken. I could somewhat alleviate this invisibility by speaking more loudly and approaching others more closely.

In my sixties I somehow became less invisible. I still get ignored on occasion, but not nearly as much as I did during my middle age. I think it's because I'm now given the respect accorded to the elderly.

I take all this with a grain of salt. To be truthful, I was never comfortable being viewed as a sexual object. Sexual attention was flattering when I was a teenager, but in a way it was anything but, as it was based entirely on my appearance and not my mind or my personality. It always made me uncomfortable and sometimes it was just beyond inappropriate. I don't regret getting that sort of attention when I was younger, but I'm happy it's behind me, even if it has been replaced by my current semi-invisibility.

I was lucky enough to find, at age fifty-seven, the woman I would marry. She's twenty years my junior and helps me stay young. Our tastes in music and film are different, but our geekiness and shared sense of humor keep our lives interesting.

I understand that one day I might no longer be able to ride my motorcycle or drive my car. The future is opaque for all of us, and I'm no exception—but it's been a great ride so far and I go into that future undaunted. I don't fear the reaper.

Key Concepts

Hijras (p. 211)
microaggression (p. 214)
pass (p. 214)

Activities, Discussion Questions, and Observations

1. Jules and Mat are both doctors who have just finished their medical school training and are now practicing at an urban hospital. Look through their answers to the questions and list five other questions you would like to ask them. Now that they are doctors, what can they do to help make medical care more accessible for *all* people?

2. Veronika discusses several parts of her life both as a patient and as someone who has been able to make positive changes for trans people in medical settings. What about her story is most compelling to you? What questions would you like to ask her?

3. Dallas Denny is one of the pioneers of the trans movement. Her story chronicles growing up trans and needing to be in the closet about it, but her story also makes the argument that she always has been the Dallas she is now. How does Dallas view the aging process? What is the overall tone of her story? Who do you think her main audience is?

4. For this exercise, you can choose to research either two countries that are culturally and/or geographically close to each other or two states that are geographically close to each other. Examples would be Uruguay and Paraguay (they are geographically close to each other) or Illinois and Oklahoma (they both have urban centers but also rely heavily on a farming economy). But feel free to choose others. Conduct some online research to determine the rights that trans people are afforded in the two countries or the two states. What ideas did you have before you started your research? What did you find out about each place? If their laws and protections regarding trans people are vastly different, what do you think are the reasons? Would it be safe for trans people to live in these places?

5. For this exercise, research the origins of the International Transgender Day of Remembrance, which is November 20, as well as the International Transgender Day of Visibility, which is March 31. Both days are meant to help raise awareness about trans issues. What are the differences between the two international days? Why is it important to have two separate special days like these?

6. View the 2000 documentary film *Southern Comfort,* directed by Kate Davis. After watching the film, discuss it in terms of the Standards of Care (SOC). Also discuss the film in terms of sexology. For example, Robert Eads encounters resistance to treating him at several medical clinics. What models of sexology are these doctors and nurses using?

7. This assignment focuses on trans people navigating various issues in rural locations in the United States and Canada. Healthcare is one of their main concerns. If you are able to view both Kate Davis's documentary *Southern Comfort* and Christopher Moore's documentary *Rural Transcapes,* they will both be useful for this assignment.
   a. If you are able to view the films: How do the doctors treat the trans people in the films? What different stories do trans people tell about their encounters in the healthcare systems? What are the strengths and benefits that the community gives to the people portrayed in the films? What are the advantages of being in a rural community? What are the disadvantages of being in a rural community?
   b. If you do not have access to either film, then you can still research trans care in rural settings. Be sure to pick a couple of different places that are geographically diverse, and see if you can find out anything about healthcare policies for trans people in those settings.

8. This is an in-class activity. You and a small group (three or four or more) of your peers are going to open up a new medical practice in town. It is a general medical practice where everyone is welcome. What are some basic

rules that will make your practice a welcoming space for all people in the town? Come up with a list of ways you can make your medical practice a safe space for everyone.

9. Some countries, including Canada, are considering removing gender from all forms of identification. Part of the argument is that gender is not necessary for government documents. What are some of the positive outcomes if gender is removed entirely from government documents? Why might it be important to track gender? How does tracking gender help public policy?

10. For an in-class debate and discussion, first choose a country that does not currently allow for a third gender possibility on its passports. Then divide students up into three groups: (1) government officials who have the power to change laws and policy and who can implement a new passport law, (2) an advocacy group for trans and nonbinary people, and (3) an advocacy group for people who want to keep the gender binary in place. All three groups are composed of a very diverse group of people; some of them may surprise you. (Students can choose their own persona and profile, or the instructor can come up with some profiles of people in each group.) The government officials will listen to arguments for and against a third gender category on passports from the two advocacy groups. People in the advocacy groups need to come up with a plan for how they are going to make their argument. What personal issues will these advocates bring to the argument? What historical facts will the advocates present? Which other countries and cultures will each group bring in to strengthen the argument? The government officials will be able to ask questions of each group, and then they will make the final decision. Will your country offer a third gender option on passports? Or will your country stick with male and female for the passports?

    What questions were raised during the debate? Because one of the main functions of a passport is to allow a person to travel across international borders, what might be some of the issues with changing to a third gender category?

11. The list of countries allowing a third gender option on passports and other government documents is slowly growing. For this assignment, pick one of the following countries to research:

- Australia
- Bangladesh

- Denmark

- Germany

- India

- Nepal

- New Zealand

- Pakistan

When did the country begin to allow a third gender category on the passport? Perhaps more important, *why* did that country's government make this decision? Were the arguments based in pre- or postcolonial history? Were the arguments based on science? Were the arguments based on a concern for human rights? The answer may be a combination of all of these. Finally, how is that third gender identity listed on the passport? As you were researching, did you come across any other countries that are considering using a third gender on their passports? If so, which ones?

Film and Television of Interest

Black Is Blue **(2014, U.S., 21 minutes)**
The award-winning queer African American filmmaker Cheryl Dunye explores an African American trans man's journey as a security guard as he navigates passing as a man and keeping his job. Dunye's short film looks at the intersections of race and gender and the issues of job security for trans people.

Boys Don't Cry **(1999, U.S., 118 minutes)**
Hilary Swank won an Oscar for this dramatization of the story of Brandon Teena, a young trans man who was brutally murdered in Nebraska by men who were furious that he was dating a local cis woman. This dramatization is more violent than the documentary *The Brandon Teena Story*.

The Brandon Teena Story **(1998, U.S., 88 minutes)**
Brandon Teena, a young trans man in Nebraska, was brutally murdered for being transgender. The film *Boys Don't Cry*, which garnered two Academy Awards, is the dramatization of Teena's story. This film is the documentary that explores Brandon Teena's short life.

Draft Day **(2015, Thailand, 9 minutes)**
In this short documentary, the viewer sees the process that trans women in Thailand go through as they wait to find out if they are going to be drafted into military service.

A Girl Like Me: The Gwen Araujo Story (2006, U.S., 88 minutes)
This made-for-television film is based on the true story of Gwen Araujo, a young trans woman of color who was murdered by four men because she was transgender.

Just Charlie (2017, U.K., 100 minutes)
This British drama focuses on a fourteen-year-old soccer star who everyone assumes is the boy and sporting hero they always wanted him to be. In reality, she is a young trans woman who just wants to be herself outside everyone's expectations. This is a stunning film that looks at the ways friends and family can sometimes be divided between being resilient allies and antagonists who cause pain.

Major! (2015, U.S., 95 minutes)
This multiple award–winning documentary focuses on the life and continued pioneering work of Miss Major Griffin-Gracy. The film includes outstanding archival footage and interviews with Miss Major and her support network. Of particular note, her work with TGI Justice, a nonprofit organization that advocates for trans people in prison, is featured.

Quick Change (2013, Philippines, 98 minutes)
The topic of this film from the Philippines is the clandestine collagen injections that Dorina gives under the table from her home in Manila to trans clients focused on beauty pageants. The film has moments of humor, but within that, the dangerous side of getting illegal collagen and hormones is brought to light. For the trans women, though, there are not many other choices. This film underscores the need for broad-reaching trans health initiatives globally.

Remember Me in Red (2010, U.S., Mexico, 16 minutes)
This haunting and empowering short film focuses on the death of a young trans woman, Alma, whose friends are gathering together to bury her in the most respectful way, which includes laying her to rest in her favorite red dress. Alma's parents arrive and insist that she be buried as their son.

Rural Transcapes (2014, Canada, 30 minutes)
Chris Moore, the founder of Trans Connect (a rural trans outreach program in the interior of British Columbia), filmed this insightful documentary about trans people who have chosen to live in a rural setting as opposed to an urban one that has more healthcare and other support services for trans people. *Rural Transcapes* contains interviews with trans people and healthcare providers in Nelson, British Columbia. The film offers an excellent contrast with Kate Davis's *Southern Comfort*.

Sex Change Hospital (2006, U.S., 47 minutes)

Dr. Marci Bowers is a trans woman and surgeon for people seeking gender-affirmation surgeries. This documentary follows Dr. Bowers as she works with her patients. It is unique because Dr. Bowers brings her own personal journey as a trans woman with her as she works with her patients.

Simply Love (2006, Netherlands, 50 minutes)

Elders are hardly ever the focus of film projects. In *Simply Love,* we are treated to Marcella and Marijke's love story when they find each other again after forty years. When the couple originally dated in 1964, Marcella was Marcel. This is a gorgeous documentary that shows that love knows no gender boundaries.

Soldier's Girl (2003, U.S., 112 minutes)

This film's director, Frank Pierson, was nominated for an Emmy for Best Director; the film is based on the true story of a soldier in the U.S. Army who falls for a trans woman. The film is brutal and tragic, but it does an outstanding job of looking at misconceptions about couples who are composed of a trans person and a cis person.

Southern Comfort (2001, U.S., 90 minutes)

Robert Eads was a trans man who was dying of ovarian cancer. He lived in rural Georgia and was an important part of the trans community that comes together once a year for the Southern Comfort transgender convention. This documentary follows Robert and his group of friends, chosen family, and biological family during his last year. This is a beautiful film that shows the real consequences trans people face in an often hostile medical environment.

Trained in the Ways of Men (2007, U.S., 102 minutes)

Gwen Araujo, a trans teen from the San Francisco Bay Area, was beaten and strangled by four young men after they found out she was transgender. This documentary film contains interviews with Gwen's family (who were supportive of their trans teenager) as well as footage of the two trials at which Gwen's murderers used the defense of "trans panic" to argue for lighter sentencing.

Transforming Family (2013, Canada, 11 minutes)

This short Canadian film looks at families with trans and gender-nonconforming parents. The film captures various family issues that come up within the home as well as in the broader culture.

Transgender Tuesdays (2012, U.S., 60 minutes)

Winner of several film awards, *Transgender Tuesdays* is a documentary that focuses on a healthcare clinic in San Francisco. Doctors at the free Tom Waddell Urban Health Clinic began to notice that when trans people did visit the clinic, they were often already very sick with cancer, HIV/AIDS, or other diseases because they were too afraid, as trans people, to seek medical help early on. The clinic started a policy that Tuesdays were devoted specifically to the trans community (trans people are welcome in the clinic all days of the week) as a way of making a statement about the necessity of safe healthcare spaces for trans people.

Transit Havana (2016, Germany, Netherlands, and Cuba, 88 minutes)

Mariela Castro, who is director of the Cuban National Center for Sex Education, is striving to make sure that trans Cubans are completely accepted within the fabric of Cuban society. This film documents the people who are waiting to be one of five chosen each year for gender-affirmation surgery. The film provides an excellent look at the complex governmental systems that attempt to help people while these same systems also regulate people.

TransMilitary (2018, U.S., 93 minutes)

The largest employer of transgender people in the United States is the military. The filmmakers Fiona Dawson and Gabriel Silverman's feature-length documentary focuses on four trans people who are out as trans and who proudly serve in the U.S. military. In 2016 the transgender ban in the U.S. military was lifted; however, beginning in 2017, the Trump administration has been working to put the ban back in place. This film offers viewers an outstanding look at the ways fluctuating policies have very personal effects on people attempting to serve their country with honor and dignity.

Woman on Fire (2016, U.S., 85 minutes)

This documentary film follows Brooke Guinan, an FDNY firefighter. New York City still has a very low percentage of cisgender women firefighters, and Brooke is the first trans woman firefighter on the force. Through interviews with Brooke, her family of origin, and her firehouse family, this documentary examines the day-to-day realities of being out as a trans person on the job as a first responder.

NOTES

1. Laws are changing rapidly around the world where trans legal documents are concerned. The information in this chapter is up-to-date as of spring 2018.

2. Jody L. Herman, "Strict Voter ID Laws May Disenfranchise More Than 34,000 Transgender Voters in the 2016 November Election," Williams Institute—UCLA School of Law, September 2016, https://williams institute.law.ucla.edu/research/strict-voter-id-laws-may-disenfranchise-more-than-34000-transgender-voters-in-the-2016-november-election/ (accessed 19 February 2018).

3. Ibid.

4. "U.S. States and Canadian Provinces: Instructions for Changing Name and Sex on Birth Certificate," http://drbecky.com/birthcert.html (accessed 12 July 2017).

5. John Paul Brammer, "California Paves Way for 'Nonbinary' Birth Certificates," *NBC News*, 23 October 2017, https://www.nbcnews.com/feature/nbc-out/california-paves-way-nonbinary-birth-certificates-n813436 (accessed 19 February 2018).

6. Chris Purdy, "Judge Says Law Violates Transgender Rights," *Global News*, 23 April 2014, http://globalnews.ca/news/1287396/judge-says-law-violates-transgender-rights/ (accessed 12 July 2017).

7. Ashifa Kassam, "'The Systems Violating Everyone': The Canadian Trans Parent Fighting to Keep Gender Markers off Cards," *Guardian*, 5 July 2017, https://www.the guardian.com/world/2017/jul/06/the systems-violating-everyone-the-canadi an-trans-parent-fighting-to-keep-gender-off-cards (accessed 12 July 2017).

8. See "Changing My Name and Title," *UK Trans Info*, http://uktrans.info/namechange (accessed 19 February 2018).

9. Jane Fae, "Name Change: The Issues," Word Press, https://changeofidentity.wordpress .com/2015/06/23/name-change-the-issues/ (accessed 19 February 2018; the site requires registration).

10. UK Deed Poll, "Changing a Name on a Birth Certificate in England and Wales," www.ukdp.co.uk/name-change-birth-cer tificate-england-and-wales/ (accessed 12 July 2017).

11. "Know Your Rights: Passports," National Center for Transgender Equality, www .transequality.org/know-your-rights/pass ports (accessed 11 July 2017).

12. Aron Macarow, "These Eleven Countries Are Way Ahead of the US on Trans Issues," *attn:*, https://www.attn.com/stories/868/transgender-passport-status (accessed 17 July 2017).

13. "Colorado Resident Sues US Government to Put Third Gender Option on Passports," *Guardian*, 26 October 2015, https://www .theguardian.com/world/2015/oct/26/passports-third-gender-option-lawsuit -colorado-resident (accessed 17 July 2017).

14. Mary Emily O'Hara, "Oregon Becomes First State to Add Third Gender to Driver's Licenses," *NBC News*, 15 June 2017, www .nbcnews.com/feature/nbc-out/oregon-becomes-first-state-add-third-gender-driver-s-licenses-n772891 (accessed 17 July 2017).

15. Ibid.

16. "The Equal Rights Amendment: Unfinished Business for the Constitution," www .equalrightsamendment.org/ (accessed 16 February 2018).

17. "Lilly Ledbetter Fair Pay Act," http://lillyledbetter.com/ (accessed 17 July 2017).

18. Mauro Cabral, executive director of GATE, quoted in OutRight Action International, 8 June 2012, "Argentina Adopts Landmark Legislation in Recognition of Gender Identity," https://www.outrightinternational.org/content/argentina-adopts-landmark-legislation-recognition-gender-identity-it%E2%80%99s-%E2%80%98talk-town%E2%80%99-south (accessed 16 February 2018).

19. Jonah Engel Bromwich, "How U.S. Military Policy on Transgender Personnel Changed under Obama," *New York Times,* 26 July 2017, https://www.nytimes.com/2017/07/26/us/politics/trans-military-trump-timeline.html (accessed 16 February 2018).

20. "TGI Justice Mission," www.tgijp.org/mission-and-staff.html (accessed 17 July 2017).

21. "Expanding Black Trans Safety: An Open Letter to Our Beloved Community," TGI Justice, www.tgijp.org/ (accessed 17 July 2017).

22. Miss Major Griffin-Gracy, talk given at California Institute of Integral Science, San Francisco, 14 October 2015.

23. Francisco Berreta, "G.N.B. v. the Government of the City of Buenos Aires, 2015," *Transgender Studies Quarterly* 51.4 (Fall 2018); courtesy of Paisley Currah and Susan Stryker, series editors.

24. Ibid.

25. Kate Davis, *Southern Comfort* (film), Docurama, 2000.

26. Ibid.

27. Laura Erickson-Schroth, ed., *Trans Bodies, Trans Selves: A Resource for the Transgender Community.* Oxford: Oxford University Press, 2014.

28. Seth Doane, "The Sex Change Capital of the U.S.," *CBS News,* 7 September 2008, https://www.cbsnews.com/news/the-sex-change-capital-of-the-us/ (accessed 17 February 2018).

29. "He's the King of Sex Change Ops," *Electric New Paper,* Singapore, 26 December 2004, http://ai.eecs.umich.edu/people/conway/TS/SRS/Dr.Preecha.html (accessed 12 July 2017).

BIBLIOGRAPHY

Berreta, Francisco. "G.N.B. v. the Government of the City of Buenos Aires, 2015." *Transgender Studies Quarterly* 51.4 (Fall 2018).

Brammer, John Paul. "California Paves Way for 'Nonbinary' Birth Certificates." *NBC News,* 23 October 2017. https://www.nbcnews.com/feature/nbc-out/california-paves-way-nonbinary-birth-certificates-n813436. Accessed 19 February 2018.

Bromwich, Jonah Engel. "How U.S. Military Policy on Transgender Personnel Changed under Obama." *New York Times,* 26 July 2017. https://www.nytimes.com/2017/07/26/us/politics/trans-military-trump-timeline.html. Accessed 16 February 2018.

"Changing My Name and Title." UK Trans Info. http://uktrans.info/namechange. Accessed 19 February 2018.

"Colorado Resident Sues US Government to Put Third Gender Option on Passports." *Guardian,* 26 October 2015. https://www.theguardian.com/world/2015/oct/26/passports-third-gender-option-lawsuit-colorado-resident. Accessed 17 July 2017.

Davis, Kate. *Southern Comfort.* Film. Docurama, 2000.

Doane, Seth. "The Sex Change Capital of the U.S." *CBS News,* 7 September 2008. https://www.cbsnews.com/news/the-sex-change-capital-of-the-us/. Accessed 17 February 2018.

"The Equal Rights Amendment: Unfinished Business for the Constitution." www.equalrightsamendment.org/. Accessed 16 February 2018.

Erickson-Schroth, Laura, ed. *Trans Bodies, Trans Selves: A Resource for the Transgender Community.* Oxford: Oxford University Press, 2014.

"Expanding Black Trans Safety: An Open Letter to Our Beloved Community." TGI Justice. www.tgijp.org/. Accessed 17 July 2017.

Fae, Jane. "Name Change: The Issues." Word Press. https://changeofidentity.wordpress.com/2015/06/23/name-change-the-issues/. Accessed 19 February 2018; the site requires registration.

Harrison, Jack. "Argentina Becomes the World's Most Transgender Friendly Country." National LGBTQ Task Force, 24 May 2012. https://thetaskforceblog.org /2012/05/24/argentina-becomes-the-worlds-most-transgender-friendly-country/. Accessed 17 July 2017.

Herman, Jody L. "Strict Voter ID Laws May Disenfranchise More Than 34,000 Transgender Voters in the 2016 November Election." Williams Institute UCLA School of Law, September 2016. https://williamsinstitute.law.ucla.edu/research/strict-voter-id-laws-may-disenfranchise-more-than-34000-transgender-voters-in-the-2016-november-election/. Accessed 19 February 2018.

"He's the King of Sex Change Ops." Electric New Paper, Singapore, December 26, 2004, http://ai.eecs.umich.edu/people/conway/TS/SRS/Dr.Preecha.html. Accessed on 12 July 2017.

Kassam, Ashifa. "'The Systems Violating Everyone': The Canadian Trans Parent Fighting to Keep Gender Markers Off Cards." *Guardian,* 5 July 2017. https://www.theguardian.com/world/2017/jul/06/the-systems-violating-everyone-the-canadian-trans-parent-fighting-to-keep-gender-off-cards. Accessed 12 July 2017.

"Know Your Rights: Passports." National Center for Transgender Equality. www.transequality.org/know-your-rights/passports. Accessed 11 July 2017.

"Lilly Ledbetter Fair Pay Act." http://lillyledbetter.com/. Accessed on 17 July 2017.

Macarow, Aron. "These Eleven Countries Are Way Ahead of the US on Trans Issues." *attn:* https://www.attn.com/stories/868/transgender-passport-status. Accessed 17 July 2017.

Major Griffin-Gracy, Miss. Talk given at California Institute of Integral Science, San Francisco, 14 October 2015.

O'Hara, Mary Emily. "Oregon Becomes First State to Add Third Gender to Driver's Licenses." *NBC News,* 15 June 2017. www.nbcnews.com/feature/nbc-out/oregon-becomes-first-state-add-third-gender-driver-s-licenses-n772891. Accessed 17 July 2017.

OutRight Action International. "Argentina Adopts Landmark Legislation in Recognition of Gender Identity." 8 June 2012. https://www.outrightinternational.org/content/argentina-adopts-landmark-legislation-recognition-gender-identity-it%E2%80%99s-%E2%80%98talk-town%E2%80%99-south. Accessed 16 February 2018.

Purdy, Chris. "Judge Says Law Violates Transgender Rights." *Global News*, 23 April 2014. http://globalnews.ca/news/1287396/judge-says-law-violates-transgender-rights/. Accessed 12 July 2017.

TGI Justice Mission. http://www.tgijp.org/mission-and-staff.html. Accessed 17 July 2017.

UK Deed Poll. "Changing a Name on a Birth Certificate in England and Wales." www.ukdp.co.uk/name-change-birth-certificate-england-and-wales/. Accessed 12 July 2017.

"U.S. States and Canadian Provinces: Instructions for Changing Name and Sex on Birth Certificate." http://drbecky.com/birthcert.html. Accessed 12 July 2017.

CHAPTER 7

Global Gender Diversity throughout the Ages
We Have Always Been with You

Key Questions

1. Much of the historic record we have about some ancient cultures comes from Western European explorers who wrote extensive diaries as they sailed around the world. In some cases, the explorers wrote precise accounts of the places and people they encountered, but some of their content was censored "back home," in Europe. What problems might we encounter in trying to understand these ancient cultures through the lens of the explorers? Who gets to record history, and what gets recorded?

2. We often understand history in terms of specific people and their life stories—the "great individuals." Individual people are certainly important to history, but individual and community histories are often lost in ancient cultures that have suffered the violence of colonialism. Now, as previously silenced histories are brought to light, what can we learn about gender diversity in ancient cultures? What are the dangers of romanticizing some of these histories? What is at stake for the communities concerned as their histories are given voice again?

3. Is there any way "back to the past" that frees us from the colonial history? How difficult is it to discover a history that has been hidden for hundreds or thousands of years?

4. Have you ever heard of a third gender identity or of multiple gender identities in any ancient culture? If so, which culture, and where did you learn about it?

Haefele-Thomas, Ardel, *Introduction to Transgender Studies*
dx.doi.org/10.17312/harringtonparkpress/2019.01.itts.007
© 2019 by Harrington Park Press

Chapter Overview

In this chapter, you will read about India, Africa, the Pacific Rim, and continental North America from ancient times to the present day. Traditionally, cultures in these areas included gender identities beyond the man-woman binary. Their languages reflected these multiple gender categories: *Māhū, Nádleeh, Hijra, Fa'afafine,* and *Winkte,* to name just a few.[1] In many cases, the gender-fluid figures were revered and given a special place in society. They served as healers, bearers of good luck, and spiritual guides in the precolonial era. In some cases, these gender variations existed for thousands of years before **first contact,** the term used to denote the point when Indigenous communities first encountered various explorers (mostly European). You may have heard these encounters described as explorers "discovering" the peoples around the globe. For example, it is common to hear that Columbus "discovered" the Americas. The Indigenous people on the North and South American continents did not need anyone to "find" them or to "discover" them; they knew exactly where they were.

As you read this chapter, it is important to remember that it is almost impossible to understand the cultures discussed in any "pure" sense removed from the ramifications of imperialism and colonialism. **Imperialism** is "the extension and maintenance of a country's power or influence through trade, diplomacy, military, or cultural dominance."[2] **Colonialism,** which goes hand in hand with imperialism, is "the policy or practice of acquiring full or partial control over another country, occupying it with settlers, and exploiting it economically."[3] As the chapter unfolds, you will see how the new imperial rulers misunderstood and criminalized the community members who embraced and honored gender diversity. A rigid gender binary was instituted as part of the violence of colonialism; this binary was an attempt to eradicate the more open gender possibilities. The near decimation of Indigenous histories means that millions of voices from the past have been lost to us.

Colonialism is not a thing of the past; it is ongoing. Even in governments and nations that have thrown off the imperial power that once dominated them, the colonial laws are often still in place, particularly laws regarding gender identity, gender expression, and sexual orientation. The stereotypes and cultural misreadings found in the explorers' accounts often informed the historic perception. Many of these accounts helped fuel the momentum of imperial and colonial laws that criminalized Indigenous traditions.

The last part of this chapter examines the ways that many cultures have begun to reclaim their ancient identities, religions, and laws. Given the silenced histories, the imposition of non-Indigenous languages, and the colonial attempts to obliterate tradition, these efforts at recovery and empowerment can be very difficult.

Introduction: The Trouble with History

I imagine someone walking through the ruins of my house, years later when I am gone and anyone who knew me and my family and nation is gone and there are only stories as to what happened to us. Did we flee from an enemy, or die of famine or floods? The story depends on who is telling it.
JOY HARJO*

Joy Harjo, the first Indigenous person to win the prestigious Wallace Stevens Award from the Academy of American Poets (in 2015), was born in Tulsa, Oklahoma, and is a member of the Mvskoke Nation.[4] In the above excerpt from one of her poems, Harjo contemplates what would happen if someone who never knew her, her family, her community, or her nation walked through her abandoned house long after she and everyone who knew her had died. She writes that "there are only stories" about what *might* have happened. There will be stories, but no facts. There will be no answers. The truth about what happened depends on who tells the story.

Harjo's poem contemplates history as something not necessarily rooted solely in fact, but rather in history as a story. Indeed, history is not only the story of people's lives; it is also the story of global events. This is not to say that history does not deal in facts. Dates of events are usually facts. The ways of seeing and understanding the events on a given date, however, may be as varied as the number of people who witnessed the event. And if the event involved death, those who were killed cannot tell their story, so we rely on others to tell it for them.

Harjo's poem focuses specifically on the difficulty of uncovering Indigenous histories that have been erased for centuries. By writing that the story depends on the teller, she points to the fact that the history of North America's Indigenous people completely depends on *who* is recovering the story of the past, *how* they are recovering that story, and *why* they are recovering that story. Often, in fact, there is no written history before the first phases of colonial contact. Thus, many histories of cultures that honored and accepted gender diversity are writ-

---

* Joy Harjo, "There Is No Such Thing as a One-Way Land Bridge," in *A Map to the Next World: Poetry and Tales* (New York: W. W. Norton, 2000), 38.

ten by observers who understood only their own culture's gender binary. These storytellers often described this gender diversity as "disgusting" and "sinful." We are left to wonder what story the ancient Indigenous people would have told.

Chapter 4 explored various riots and protests in the United States in the second half of the twentieth century. Recall that some of these histories of uprisings by early trans and gender-nonconforming people are just now being discovered. Fortunately, some of the people who took part in these early movements are still alive; they are coming forward with their stories. For those who are no longer with us, like Marsha P. Johnson and Sylvia Rivera, we have to rely on the materials they left behind in their writings, in their interviews, and in documentary films. The accounts of their friends and loved ones can also help us build a more complete historic picture. But even among the people who were at these riots and protests in the second half of the twentieth century, when almost everyone was able to write, record, or be interviewed about *their* history and *their* reality, we still have numerous and sometimes conflicting accounts. If these stories and histories from the twentieth century prove difficult to find and reconstruct, imagine what happens when we try to explore trans identities and expressions in cultures and societies much further in the past—hundreds and even thousands of years ago.

PBS, a U.S. media-based outlet, has posted an online interactive map of ancient and Indigenous gender diversity around the globe: "A Map of Gender-Diverse Cultures" (www.pbs.org/independentlens/content/two-spirits_map-html). As the map shows, diverse gender identities and expressions were common in numerous cultures around the world for centuries. This map discusses the gender binary in Western terms. In other words, the claim is that Western culture tends to see only within various dichotomies: gay/straight, male/female, and man/woman. There are, however, some examples of nonbinary gender in ancient Western cultures as well, particularly in Greek and Roman culture.

Through the violence of imperialism and continued colonization, myriad gender identities, behaviors, and possibilities were demonized and nearly obliterated. Nonbinary gender was often associated with the sacred, so when a rigid gender binary system was forced on these cultures, many ancient spiritual practices nearly died.

As you read this chapter, remember that imperialism and colonialism might look very different from place to place. A knowledge of the subtle nuances in the different colonizers' cultures is critical if we are to gain a deeper understanding of how and why various cultures are having very different conversations about gender identity today. Also remember that precolonial cultures did not necessarily offer a gender-diverse utopia—the situation is always more complicated than that. Nonetheless, this chapter shows the rich and nuanced path that leads back to ancient cultures that revered, honored, and even worshipped their community members who embodied nonbinary gender identities and gender expressions. And the path leading back also leads us forward.

Thanks, but We Already Had a Name: Misunderstanding, Misrecognition, Imperial Violence, and Colonial Laws

You call someplace paradise—kissing it good-bye.
DON HENLEY AND GLENN FREY, "THE LAST RESORT"*

The ramifications of imperialism and colonialism are many, from Indigenous populations being wiped out through contagions like smallpox and Hansen's disease (leprosy) to the obliteration of original languages and spiritual practices. All aspects of a culture and society are deeply affected through imperial takeover and subsequent colonization.

Mislabeling

Many aspects of gender identities, behaviors, and practices suffered as a result of first contact. Typically, colonizers viewed Indigenous people through their own gender-biased lens, keeping extensive notes in their journals that would eventually be published back home in Europe, where the general reading public would devour stories of "exotic" adventure. Nonbinary gender behavior, practice, and identity both intrigued and disgusted the explorers, who imposed their own social and cultural biases on nonbinary people. Their obsessive need to classify and label people whom today we would call nonbinary or trans is similar to the sexologists' attempts to create taxonomies (see Chapter 3). The colonizers brought labels like *hermaphrodite, eunuch,* and *sodomite* with them as they tried to label people and behaviors. The Indigenous people already had names for themselves: *Māhū, Fa'afafine, Hijra,* and *Nádleeh,* to name just a few.

In the 1590s Andrew Battell, an English sailor, wrote the following about the Imbangala (or Mbangala) in the region we know as Angola in southwestern Africa: "They are beastly in their living, for they have men in women's apparel, whom they keepe among their wives."[5] As the scholar Marc Epprecht has noted,

* Don Henley and Glenn Frey, "The Last Resort," *Hotel California* (Asylum Records, 1976).

various explorers over a three-hundred-year span described a category of people in this region as men wearing women's clothing and taking part in day-to-day activities and cultural ceremonies. Jean-Baptiste Labat, a French clergyman and explorer in the same region who lived a century after Battell, described the leader of a group whom he defined as cross-dressed male diviners (people with supernatural powers) as "a shameless, impudent, lewd man . . . deceitful to the last, without honor. He dresses ordinarily as a woman and makes an honor of being called Grandmother."[6] How would you describe the tone used by Battell and Labat? How did they feel about the people they described? What words are predominant in their descriptions? And how would you feel if a stranger from another land came to observe you and described you in this way?

These two examples of explorers in Angola speak volumes about the ways that Europeans used their own value systems to judge and misread people in other parts of the world. Both Battell and Labat viewed the "cross-dressed" men as homosexual. From all accounts, they did *not* read the people described as third gender or nonbinary. *Yet again, gender and sexual orientation get mistaken for each other.* These nonbinary people may have been what we understand today as bisexual. They could have been homosexual, heterosexual, or asexual. The important point here is that, regardless of sexual orientation, their gender display appears to have embraced a certain fluidity.

Africa and India were colonized in vastly different ways. For example, many parts of Africa were colonized (and still are being colonized; Uganda is an example) as part of the Christian missionary crusade. But, historically, there has also always been a socioeconomic underpinning of colonialism—particularly in places like South Africa and Sierra Leone, where imperial powers continue to accrue wealth through the diamond mines by exploiting the local workers. Like Africa, India became very interesting to the British as a place to expand its wealth. The British established the East India Company in 1600. Until 1857 the consensus in Britain was to "let" the people of India keep their religions and customs as long as the British could continue to trade in spices and gunpowder. Over a 335-year span, the British slowly took over India as their company became a monopoly that dominated India until Indian Independence in 1947.

Although the imperial and colonial histories of India and Africa are quite different, the misreadings of people within those cultures who defied the gender binary were quite similar. The following is an excerpt from the travel diaries of James Forbes, a writer for the East India Company who traveled extensively throughout India in the late 1700s. He wrote about his encounters with people, animals, and plants:

Among the followers of an oriental [sic] camp, at least of the Mahratta camp to which we were attached, I must not omit the hermaphrodites; there were a great number of them in the different bazaars, and I believe all in the capacity of cooks. In mentioning these singular people, I am aware I tread on tender ground. . . . There were a considerable number of human beings called hermaphrodites in the camp, who were compelled, by way of distinguishing them from other castes, to wear the habit of a female, and the turban of a man. I was called into a private tent, to a meeting between the surgeon-major and several medical gentlemen of the army, to examine some of these people: my visit was short and the objects disgusting.[7]

Like Battell and Labat, Forbes writes in a tone of both fascination and disgust. And like Battell and Labat, he misreads and misunderstands the people he describes. Whereas Battell and Labat both associated "cross-dressing" with sin and homosexuality, Forbes read the people, instead, as "hermaphrodites," which is the old term for people who have differences of sex development (DSD). Also note that Forbes describes going into a tent to look at the people; presumably he went into the tent to examine their genitals, which would have violated their personal space. What is most telling about Forbes's account is his note that there were "a great number of them." Forbes makes it clear that people of multiple genders were not an anomaly. Rather, many communities and cultures around the world had members who embodied nonbinary gender expression.

The people whom Forbes refers to as "hermaphrodites" were, in fact, **Hijras.** The term *Hijra* comes from Urdu, but "no English term is adequate to capture the complexity of *Hijra* identity, which cannot be understood solely in terms of sexuality or gender."[8] *Hijras*, who have existed in written record for over four thousand years, are complex figures. We know that *Hijras* did have their spiritual place in society. They were often at the bottom of the caste system, even though it was believed that they had special powers. Even today, it is bad luck to turn a *Hijra* away from one's wedding or from one's newborn baby because they are seen as people who can bless *or* curse others. Not only do *Hijras* embrace a gender identity and expression outside a male-female binary, but they also often embrace Hinduism, Islam, and sometimes other religions. Some *Hijras* choose to have a **penectomy** (the removal of the penis); this procedure is often done in the temple of a goddess known as the *Hijra* deity, Bahuchara Mata.[9]

Before and during British rule in India, *Hijras* were the money collectors for their communities. They made their living by collecting taxes for townships, and they got to keep a bit of the money to live on. The British government did not want to let go of any of "its" money, so it demonized the *Hijras*. Forbes used the term *hermaphrodite* to describe *Hijras* (when they already had a very old name within their own culture), but he was using an English term that at least did not mix gender identity or gender expression with sexual orientation. He superimposed an English word on the *Hijras,* and a long line of other British writers would do the same when they used the term *eunuch* for the *Hijras.* (A **eunuch** is someone who has had their testicles, but not their penis, removed.) Over the course of British imperial rule in India, the *Hijras* were ultimately criminalized under the British Penal Code, which made sodomy (defined specifically as men having sex with men) illegal.[10] So, although Forbes and other early British observers of *Hijras* did not confuse gender with sexual orientation, the nineteenth-century British laws under the rule of Queen Victoria certainly classified *Hijras* as "sodomites" (homosexuals). Gender identity and gender expression merged with sexual orientation.

Eurocentric Gender Stereotypes and the Negation of Women

By now, you have probably noticed many similarities in the stories of European explorers and writers and their encounters with gender-diverse people around the world. A major similarity from place to place is the disgust exhibited by the men writing the historical accounts. You may also have noticed that, in almost all the examples, these writers and observers discuss people whom they have identified as "male" or "men" acting like "females" or "women." True, the gender binary is certainly imposed throughout the accounts. But the writers are concerned with people assigned male at birth. And part of what they find so awful is that the "men" are acting like "women." You may be wondering if there were people assigned female at birth who embraced "male" identities. The answer is most surely yes; however, that history is even more difficult to extract from the silent past.

Even as Europeans imposed words like *eunuch, sodomite,* and *hermaphrodite* on local peoples, they also imposed ideas about "masculine" and "feminine" spheres in which the importance of women and women's work was undermined or ignored.

When Captain Cook, a British explorer and cartographer in the Royal Navy, first landed on the beach in Hawai'i in 1778, he and his men were dumbfounded by people whom they identified as men wearing what they assumed to be women's clothing. Cook and his men inferred that the people whom they read as cross-dressing were homosexuals, or **sodomites** (the word that would have been used at the time). The people they encountered were highly regarded within Hawai'ian culture: the **Māhū**, who are third-gender people, were often seen as powerful healers.[11] The historian Kathleen Wilson writes the following about

Cook's misrecognition: "Within the gender complimentarity [sic] of eastern Polynesian culture, the *mahu* were seen possibly as a third gender, or as women; men having sexual relations with them did not think of themselves as 'sodomites' nor did *mahu* have sex with each other. . . . The social acceptance of the *mahu* in eastern Polynesian societies may have actually expressed the associations of women's reproductive functions with the divine—and hence the identification of the feminine with positive, rather than negative, hierarchies and characteristics."[12]

Captain Cook probably felt quite a bit of confusion because women were not honored "back home." In other words, a person perceived to be a man who appeared to be feminine or effeminate was read as "homosexual." Cook's Western cultural norms included a binary mind-set. From our twenty-first-century perspective, we can see that one of the problems was the explorers' inability to translate terms like *Māhū, Hijra,* and *Nádleeh* into Western words (English in this case) that accurately described these people's identities (see figure 7.1).

There is also the problem of not honoring cultures that existed for thousands of years before contact. As one scholar has noted, "*Māhū* have been visible as family and community members since the pre-contact period. Early European voyagers' logs and early ethnographic accounts introduced Tahitian *māhū* into the Western colonial imagination."[13] This "colonial imagination" began the process of consistently erasing the traditional respect for gender-diverse people within these various cultures. It is only now, in the twenty-first century, that more extensive recovery efforts have begun to question the terms that the "experts" (that is, the historians and anthropologists) have put forth. Often these modern recovery efforts are being carried out by people whose cultures have been misrepresented.

The contemporary **Fa'afafine** (the Samoan term for gender diverse) author Dan Taulapapa McMullin writes:

> There was an anthropology tale that I often see told as though it were a matter of fact or research, that Samoan families without daughters choose one of their boy children to become fa'afafine for the expected duties. I have sisters and I wasn't aware of being chosen to fulfill a role. I wanted to hang out with my great-grandmother and make siapo paintings, and iron clothes smooth with the flat iron. . . . That was my desire and choice, and she and my family in Samoa supported my will to be. The naming of fa'afafine accompanies the event of the person.[14]

Note that McMullin was not chosen by family to be a *Fa'afafine* because of any lack of daughters; rather, the choice was McMullin's, with the blessing of family.

FIGURE 7.1 "First Contact," by Cameron Rains. European explorers often encountered Indigenous people who honored gender diversity. Rather than take the time to learn the rich heritage and customs surrounding gender diversity, they mislabeled gender-diverse people with incorrect terminology such as *sodomite*.

"OH, DON'T WORRY ABOUT EXPLAINING YOUR CUSTOMS— I'M JUST GONNA GO AHEAD AND FILE YOU UNDER 'SODOMITE' IN THE OL' LOG."

The myth that McMullin points out appears throughout many historical records that discuss gender diversity in the Pacific Islands. Again we see the underlying idea of multiple genders needing to be reduced to a male-female binary within heteronormative, Eurocentric ideas of who does what kind of work and tasks. The gender definitions and stereotypes about what is "women's work" and what is "men's work" (which we examined in detail in Chapter 1) are clearly at play here.

As one last example (among many), we will focus on Navajo culture in North America. As Wesley Thomas has written: "Multiple genders were part of the norm in the Navajo culture before the 1890s. From the 1890s until the 1930s, dramatic changes took place in the lives of Navajos because of exposure to, and constant pressures from, Western culture—not the least of which was the imposition of Christianity."[15] Thomas discusses the ways that spiritual leaders and healers during this round of colonization in the late 1800s began to go more "underground" and not share their vocation. Thomas also argues that Western culture and Christianity do not look kindly on gender diversity, so there is still pressure for gender-diverse folks to be quiet. Although Thomas wrote in the late 1990s, there is still a reluctance among gender-diverse people to be open about their identities.

Thomas, who is Navajo, believes it is important to focus on **Nádleeh** (gender-fluid and spiritually powerful) people who are Navajo. According to Thomas, gender terminology in Navajo language and culture is very complex. There are different words for people depending on their age, not necessarily what we would call their biological sex.[16] Thomas discusses what we would today see as binary gender roles in labor: for example, women in the domestic sphere and men building homes, hunting, and harvesting. Thomas writes, however: "A *nádleeh* mixes various aspects of the behaviors, activities, and occupations of both females and males. The older Navajo people recognize five traditional gender categories."[17] These five categories do not match what we understand as gender in the West. Rather, they denote different genders in each person's life according to what phase of life that person is in. In other words, gender is about age.

Back to the Past to Pave the Way for the Future: Postcolonial Progress

In Navajo tradition, there is no concept of gender dysphoria; rather, there is a concept of gender diversity.
WESLEY THOMAS[†]

Raid archeologists' camps
and steal shovels
to rebury the dead

Gather stories like harvest
and sing honor songs
QWO-LI DRISKILL[†]

Wesley Thomas (who is Navajo) and Qwo-Li Driskill (who is Cherokee) offer suggestions for the ways we can move forward from imperial and colonial hangover. Thomas underscores Navajo tradition (or the old ways) to make the point that gender diversity is normal, as opposed to "gender dysphoria," a Western label that denotes any gender diversity outside the binary as sick. Qwo-Li Driskill suggests that we combine direct action (to raid the archaeologist camps and gather the ancestral bones back to where they belong) and a return to tradition with the goal of reclaiming memory, telling stories, and singing the ancient honor songs. Both Thomas and Driskill believe that Indigenous people need to make their own definitions and tell their own stories.

For Indigenous people in North America, there has been a late twentieth- and early twenty-first-century movement to create a unifying community response in the face of continued oppression. The term **Two-Spirit** (which you

---

[*] Wesley Thomas, "Navajo Cultural Constructions of Gender and Sexuality," in *Two-Spirit People: Native American Gender Identity, Sexuality, and Spirituality*, ed. Sue-Ellen Jacobs, Wesley Thomas, and Sabine Lang (Chicago: University of Chicago Press, 1997), 160.

[†] Qwo-Li Driskill, *Walking with Ghosts* (Cambridge, U.K.: Salt, 2005), 5.

learned in Chapter 1) was born in 1990 at an Indigenous LGBTQ+ convention as an alternative, self-named, and empowering term in the face of the French term *berdache,* which had been used to describe various gender diversities and sexual orientations outside heterosexual parameters in Indigenous cultures. This is not to say that all the tribal nations throughout North America are the same. Many still hold on to their own precise words and terminologies, including *Winkte* (Lakota), *Nádleeh* (Navajo), and *Asegi udanto* (Cherokee). There is also an understanding, however, that there is strength in numbers:

> For some of us, this history was still close. Some of us knew words for people like us, had grandparents who whispered to us that we once were honored. For others, even deep research could not unearth the songs we once sang. Scholars had their own word for our queer ancestors: berdache. A French word derived, ultimately, from a word for a "kept boy," it rang harsh in our ears. It came of misunderstandings, beliefs that our only purpose was for the illicit sexual pleasure of our more masculine brothers. So we gave ourselves a new name. Two-spirit was never intended to be defined only literally, as non-Natives so often describe it, as a person with a male and female spirit. It was always meant to be much more than that. It was meant to be a home for queer and trans Native people in the English language, in a time when that is the language most of us know best. It was meant to encompass all of the things we experience that cannot be summed up in any other way.[18]

The birth of the term *Two-Spirit* is an excellent example of diverse groups of people from different tribal affiliations across North America coming together to create new terminology and to reclaim the power to name themselves. In the "Writings from the Community" at the end of this chapter, you will find a piece by Eileen Chester, who is Two-Spirit and lives in Canada. In her piece she talks about the clash between Western terms and the Indigenous term.

In the postcolonial world, empowerment for Two-Spirit people is not limited to joining forces across tribal affiliation. Two-Spirit people from multiple tribes have worked together to battle numerous forms of oppression. The following statement was issued by the group Bay Area American Indian Two-Spirits (BAAITS) on 16 June 2016 following the 12 June massacre of forty-nine people and the wounding of fifty-three others in the Pulse LGBTQ+ nightclub in Orlando, Florida:

> With Orlando on our minds and in our hearts we mourn these deaths. Crossing over affects all who love deeply, from those who walk into the spirit world, to those who remain rooted to our planet. As Native people we are no stranger to the lasting effects of massacres and loss, but now is not the time to speak of our pain. Now is the time to stand in solidarity with our LGBTQ black and brown community, and with all of our relations. Let

Wounded Knee and Orlando stand hand in hand as evidence that our bodies are still being shot down while dancing.

In many tribes across our First Nations, our two-spirit people fulfilled specific roles in our cultures. In the world there is a place for all genders and sexualities. Killing like this lays especially heavy in our hearts as we are reminded by the families' and loved ones' testimonials; how each of the victims walked through their lives as individuals. Each carried with them sacred medicine meant for this world, and now the world must live without this healing. We as Bay Area American Indian Two-Spirits want to remind the world that there is hope in love, and we do not tolerate pitting one group or its pain against another. We must recognize where the sickness sits. And turn towards loving and valuing all of our siblings.[19]

In this statement, BAAITS exemplifies community building across cultures; all those who perished in the massacre were LGBTQ+ people and their allies and loved ones. The statement draws parallels between the Pulse shootings (a twenty-first-century hate crime against LGBTQ+ people of color) and one of the worst massacres of Native North Americans perpetrated by colonial and governmental powers: the land grab (Wounded Knee). BAAITS's statement also shows the existence of strong intersecting support systems, and it harkens back to a past that valued gender-diverse people. The term *Two-Spirit* draws together those marginalized by their gender identity, gender expression, and/or sexual orientation, reminding them that they were considered sacred before first contact with European cultures.

There are other examples of gender-diverse people moving toward a renewed sense of identity that harkens back to precolonial times. Despite centuries of criminalization under British colonial rule, the *Hijras* in India are still there. In fact, because of the *Hijras'* legal efforts as well as their cultural and spiritual significance, India became one of the first countries to add a third gender category to its passports.

In South Africa the human rights protection laws are all-encompassing; however, laws do not eliminate discrimination overnight. Though laws can change rapidly, cultural attitudes often take generations to come around. South Africa is one of the few places in Africa that is at all safe for LGBTQ+ people. In other parts of Africa (particularly Uganda, Kenya, and Nigeria), being LGBTQ+ can be a death sentence. As you learned in Chapter 2, several LGBTQ+ people from these countries have had to seek asylum abroad in order to stay alive. The irony is that the countries where they seek asylum are often the same nations that originally colonized their home countries. In the second selection in "Writings from the Community" at the end of this chapter, you will read John (Longjones) Abdallah Wambere's story about needing to seek immediate asylum in

FIGURE 7.2 *Kumu Hina, by Cameron Rains.* Hina Wong-Kalu, who is *Māhū*, is a teacher working to bring Hawai'ian traditions back to the Indigenous people of the islands. She has been featured in three films that focus on the intersections of colonial violence and cultural misunderstanding. Kumu (meaning "teacher") Hina strives to empower her Indigenous community.

the United States during a visit from Uganda. At this time, the Ugandan LGBTQ+ community is attempting to recover ancient stories of gender diversity, but these stories have been all but obliterated by centuries of imperial violence.

Hope in Hawai'i

Many cultural recovery projects are working to bring back precolonial memory. In Hawai'i, for example, Kumu Hina, who is *Māhū*, has worked tirelessly with others in the Indigenous Hawai'ian community to bring nearly lost cultural practices back to the islands (see figure 7.2). As a result of decades of work by the community, many of the public schools in Hawai'i now teach the original language along with the ancient hula. And within the ancient hula, there is a place for people who are *Māhū*. There are also many organized antibullying efforts in the public school system in Hawai'i. These programs and teachings go back to ancient Hawai'ian ideas of *Aloha* and the sacred welcoming of all people that this word conveys. Here is the "Pledge of Aloha":

> I believe that every person has a role in society, and deserves to be included and treated with respect in their family, school, and community.
>
> I believe that every person should be free to express what is truly in their heart and mind, whether male, female, or in the middle.
>
> I believe that every person should be able to practice their cultural traditions, and to know and perpetuate the wisdom of their ancestors for future generations.
>
> I believe these values are embodied in aloha: love, honor and respect for all.
>
> Therefore, I pledge to live aloha in everything I do, and to inspire people of all ages to do the same.[20]

EILEEN CHESTER

Healing

Eileen Chester is a Two-Spirit First Nations person from the Nuu-chah-nulth Territory on the west coast of Vancouver Island in British Columbia, Canada, where she attends Camosun College, works at the Victoria Disability Resource Centre, volunteers for several other nonprofit organizations, and has a paper route. Eileen's essay explores the harassment and discrimination she suffered as a Two-Spirit person while seeking help with addiction at several rehabilitation centers that serve First Nations people.

I really need to start from this point in my life, simply because it is so painful to face my past. I did not expect old wounds from the past to reopen. I thought I buried those years ago. I cried the hurt this morning with a supportive worker. I needed to heal this fearful pain, rather than procrastinate and try to forget it.

More than once, I have been harassed and discriminated against for simply being myself, even in exclusively First Nations treatment centers. Discrimination has reared its ugly face at me again, even mindful as I am right now. It never really occurred to me that it would happen once more and reopen an old wound.

My older wound occurred at the original First Nations treatment center in the mid-2000s. I was harassed and discriminated against for being transgender or a cross-dresser, although I identify myself as a Two-Spirited person of the First Nations. The treatment center was facing legal challenges; eventually, I brought my case before the British Columbia Human Rights Tribunal. As painful as these experiences were, I was clean and sober for eighteen months during this time. I was originally there for my addictions to substances and, sadly, I relapsed. I was in and out of jails, hospitals, and even became homeless again due to the memory and emotional impact of what happened to me there.

These wounds were reopened again at the second First Nations Clinic, where I went for my alcohol and drug program in the spring of 2014. This time, despite traumatic harassment and discrimination, I was clean for six months. I inevitably started using again, due to the trauma and harassment I experienced at both organizations, which had been supposed to be safe places for me as a First Nations person.

Revisiting my old, painful scars is scary. I didn't want to think about them and began to isolate myself in my room earlier today as I thought of sharing these experiences—I did not want to touch the pain again. Reopening old scars is twice as painful as the original hurt, hurt that I thought I had left behind over seven years ago at the first treatment center. I feel discouraged and am even sighing as I type this. I did not ask for this pain; it is not mine, but it happened to me. Here I sit, and, God, you know where I am with these past and recent scars caused by other people's hurtful judgment and their unfair persecution of me for being true to myself. The First Nations treatment centers were supposed to heal and help, not hurt.

That was then, this is now. I look at my past and see just how far I have come. I have kids who do not really know me. They are aware of my change and were the first ones on my mind before I came out. Then I decided to proceed to be me. They would have a choice like everyone else: accept me or not. What's important is that I made a decision to be me and—all of me—no matter what they think. My own family's thoughts of me, like everyone else's, are of no concern to me anymore. This sentiment extends to organizations and society at large, simply because I no longer care what anyone thinks of my life and what they see.

I made this very sacrifice for my female spirit, not the male/man essence of who I am. I want my female spirit to be freed. And she is! I hid in a million bedrooms. A hundred thousand bathrooms, a few dark places where no one would see me. I hid under $e = mc^2$ pairs of jeans (with pantyhose underneath). I was warned by others not to do this alone. I have and did and done. It was, and is, painful from time to time, but it is worth being true to myself. It is not about the clothes or gender or the names that I bear—it is about being true to myself and about being free to be who I am today.

I sit here, dressed as I am every day, and I get stoked—like wow. I have a male body in essence, but my body houses a female spirit, hence I identify as Two-Spirited. It took me a while to actually really understand the message from our spirit world. I was affirmed by our spirit world not to change, not to undergo a sex-change surgery.

When I first came out, I really wanted to seek out different ways that people express themselves: Transgender, Transsexual, Cross-dresser, Drag Queen, Transvestite, Female Impersonator. Before I came to be myself, a very sweet man came right up to my face in a very kind way. He stated out loud that I am Two-Spirited. Back then I was not even out as Eileen.

It all started by asking and confiding about myself to my big sister. Then to a power greater than I. I checked out several different support groups. I first went to a very small organization called Transcend, where a meeting was held once a month if we were lucky. There I met wonderful transgendered women who were just beginning their lives from male to female. I learned about hormones and other insights from a few who identified as Drag Queens. That was such a lesson for my own discovery of where I might fit in. I made a decision to keep my body the way my body came into our world we share. No hormones, no breast implants. Not to have my penis removed. This is "as is," the way God made me, and I am happy with myself—a Two-Spirited and proud feminine cross-dresser. I dream that your dream be as real as you can be and know that you are not as alone as you think you are. My name is Eileen Amber Lynn-Ernest Ronald Chester Jr.

JOHN (LONGJONES) ABDALLAH WAMBERE

LGBTI Identities and Rights in Uganda

John (Longjones) Abdallah Wambere is one of the activists featured in the film Call Me Kuchu, *which looks at the criminalization of LGBTQ+ people in Uganda. In Uganda he worked with HIV and AIDS education and outreach as well as with the political advocacy group Sexual Minorities of Uganda (SMUG). His friend David Kato, who was internationally known as an LGBTQ+ human rights advocate, was murdered for his work. A few years after Kato's murder, Wambere, on a trip to the United States, had to seek asylum because friends warned him that if he returned home, he, too, would be killed. John Abdallah Wambere has now been in the United States for a few years, and his asylum case was successful. Though he is thankful to be in the United States, he is still heartsick over not being able to see his beloved home or his family in Uganda. He continues to fight for human rights in Uganda.*

I was born in Mbale, a town in Eastern Uganda located by the slopes of Mt. Elgon and about 225 miles from the capital city, Kampala. When I was about twelve years old, I heard rumors and stories from friends and neighbors questioning certain persons' sexualities in the community. It was rare to hear conversations about any LGBTI individuals or "homosexuals." Sexuality wasn't something discussed often in my culture, let alone studied in school, which left many people ignorant and generally uninformed about sexuality, gender identities, and orientation.

The border towns of Uganda and Kenya—Lwakhakha, Malaba, and Busia—were about an hour-and-a-half drive from Mbale. There were many stories about homosexuals existing in Kenya. I understood the meaning of the term *homosexuality*, although the term *heterosexual* was used less often. I don't remember my parents talking to me at any point about sex. In my teenage years, I heard more talk of heterosexual stories. Stories about homosexuals only came up when something particular happened or someone was discussing a specific character, music video, or movie that raised concerns for them.

My sexual orientation was eventually questioned by some of my relatives and friends. My sexual identity came up when they described someone who acted "macho" or "feminine" and who had slept with or been seen with girls. Even though I was around girls most of the time, I was more into playing their role than being the masculine figure among them. I recall when some of my brother's friends referred to me as *Mudiga* in my mother tongue—a homosexual. At the mention of such a word, I would freeze, feel scared, and worry that they would beat me up. I tried to avoid conversations about homosexuality as much as possible because I felt like the discussion was always indirectly pointed at me. When some friends and I watched TV musicians like Boy George, the late Prince, or George Michael and his one dangling earring, the conversation quickly led to questioning each musician's sexual identity. We debated each time Boy George's song "Karma Chameleon" came on the radio. After many arguments, we concluded that he was a hermaphrodite. Young adult men like my friends drew false conclusions that if someone was dressed in feminine clothing as a teenager, they were homosexual or trying to lure men. We weren't familiar with the concept of cross-dressing. There was no differentiation between homosexuals and transgender people. The terms *transgender* and *intersex* were not used anywhere.

There were homosexual people in my community who were struggling. Some thought that they were the only ones in the world who felt attracted to the same sex. Some even lived in isolation to avoid embarrassment and name-calling. If a transgender person walked through town during the day, you would hear deafening noise in the streets. Men, women, and children would run and follow the person, scream insults at them, and even push them. They felt powerless. Work along the street would come to a standstill. Some people would be sympathetic to the transgender person being attacked. Some would shout, "Go to Mombasa!"—referring to the Kenyan city where, word was, homosexuality was common. I was struggling myself, and hearing a word like "Mombasa" made me excited and wish I could be there. I began to take note of the places mentioned in such insults.

In my time growing up, a lack of knowledge about diversity, sexual education, and the mysteries surrounding gender identity, expression, and orientation were all part of my culture. Sexuality was never debated or discussed, and, even if it was questioned, it was not a topic spoken about openly. Teenage girls were to be lectured by their aunties on sexual matters and not directly by their parents. Sexual education was often learned through peers, literature, or, especially in rural settings, even the act of sex itself. There is a lot of ignorance around sexual and gender identities, especially transgender people, and for a time they all fell under the umbrella term of *homosexual*. There was less knowledge about same-sex behavior because people saw it as a curse or a sign that a person was mentally ill or bewitched. Others considered homosexuality a blessing or associated it with healing powers or causing misery in others. Some believed that homosexuals were HIV-free, especially because, in Africa, HIV is considered a heterosexual disease.

Unfortunately, Uganda has never been safe for LGBTI people, despite all the struggles and fights for equality. To put it straight, it has become more dangerous to identify as homosexual or transgender than before because of the increasing awareness of who we are, our public visibility, our demand for equality and protection from the state. Religious influences encourage hate and homophobia, not to mention the current colonial laws and those that are being amended and introduced—the Marriage and Divorce Bill, Equal Opportunities Act, Public Management Act, Anti-Gay Bill/Act of 2009, and Non-Governmental Organizations Act—which make it even worse to live as or even offer services to transgender or gay people. Although the term LGBTI exists, the major letters that have stood out have been the "L" and "G." The "T" was never discussed and little was known about it. The letters didn't seem to have meaning, but were associated at the time with sexual acts.

Some of the challenges that transgender people face in my country today, and perhaps in many parts of the world, center on visibility. *Transgender* wasn't a well-known term until the late twentieth century, when more information and training on sexuality became available to activists and community leaders. I later started to see more friends identify as transgender. Now, the letter "T" represents how one feels inside, regardless of the body one was born into. This concept was confusing to me, and understanding it is still a challenge. I remember friends telling me that I am, or should be, transgender; I told them, "If you judge people by their actions, you are wrong." I have never felt I was in a wrong body, let alone thought about the procedures that come with transitioning; I have always felt happy as a gay man. I recall clearly two of my close friends who wore wigs, dresses, makeup, high-heeled shoes, carried handbags, and had artificial boobs. I always thought they were expressing their identity as gay men, but now I realize they are transgender.

Uganda was a British colony, and when the missionaries came to Uganda way back in the 1800s, the inhabitants were already practicing traditional religion; they worshipped lakes, mountains, and rivers. There was a god of rain, riches, fertility and one for blessings, and so on. A person needed to call upon the ancestral spirits to protect them. When the missionaries arrived, things started to take a new twist, and there was only a little resistance, perhaps because they had powerful weapons that could kill from a distance—guns. They taught the Bible and started converting the Indigenous people; they set up schools and hospitals and made the locals believe in them. These resources came with strings; they offered protection to the kings and provided powerful rifles to help them protect their kingdoms. Religion and politics clearly worked hand in hand. Most health and educational institutions in Uganda were founded under Christian-operated institutions or churches. The idea was to teach religion to families in their congregations and to win new converts. Christianity has remained significant in the lives of many Ugandans; today the country is predominantly Christian. Over the years, religion has played a significant role in Uganda's politics. The Democratic Party is dominated mainly by Catholics and some Muslims. Today, perhaps more than ever, the ruling party is dominated by the Anglicans and Born-Again Christians (Pentecostals).

In 1986 I remember the National Resistance Movement (NRM), the current ruling party, took over Uganda through guerrilla warfare. At that time, I learned of a new local disease called "slim"— HIV/AIDS. Rumor had it that the NRM soldiers brought slim, and it was said that they were sexually involved with the apes while in the bush and had contracted the disease as a result. Nothing was known about HIV/AIDS. One thing I recall is that Uganda was badly hit by the AIDS epidemic. Philly Bongoley Lutaaya, a Uganda-born musician, was living in Sweden when he came out as HIV-positive. Many believed he was paid to claim so. Others believed he was avoiding women who may have been targeting him for his wealth. Uganda's president Yoweri Museveni took the lead to advocate and fight HIV/AIDS, which led to some progress.

Missionaries have continued to flood Uganda with the message of converting the locals. This has led to division and hate among people, judging others instead of loving them and forgiving each other. The most successful churches, especially the Pentecostal, are founded on money from white missionaries. Any church that hasn't embraced a white missionary has lagged behind. We have very powerful church leaders, very powerful indeed. During the time that HIV was at its height in Uganda, churches supported and cared for the families and the individuals suffering from the epidemic. This was another factor that made Ugandans believe more and more in the religious institutions. The churches have remained key, and because it's believed that their duty is to teach morality, they have increasingly condemned homosexuals and even called for their killing. It's a shame that in the twenty-first century we still see white missionaries in Africa, particularly Uganda, claiming to bring the gospel and teach people the values of families and morals.

Key Concepts

colonialism (p. 241)

eunuch (p. 247)

Fa'afafine (p. 248)

first contact (p. 241)

Hijra (p. 247)

imperialism (p. 241)

Māhū (p. 247)

Nádleeh (p. 249)

penectomy (p. 247)

sodomite (p. 247)

Two-Spirit (p. 250)

Activities, Discussion Questions, and Observations

1. What are some of the main points you took away from the writings of Eileen Chester and John Abdallah Wambere? How do their essays discuss the ramifications of colonialism? How do they understand the ways that colonialism affected their own lives? If you could ask each of them a question, what would it be?

2. When Eileen Chester refers to her original wound, what do you think she might be referring to? In what ways do Eileen's intersecting identities complicate her efforts at recovery?

3. Ancient Greece and ancient Rome are often seen as the birthplaces of Western culture as we know it. In many of this chapter's examples, the focus has been on the violent imperialism carried out by many Western nations. But many Western cultures also historically honored nonbinary gender identities and expressions.

   For this activity, focus on ancient Greece, Rome, Scandinavia (the Vikings), the British Isles (Celtic culture), or early modern Spain or Portugal. Research how nonbinary gender identities and expressions were perceived in one of these cultures. Over time, what happened to the gender system in that culture, and what made it move toward a stricter binary? How difficult was it for you to find information about the culture?

4. What do you know about your own ancestry? Where did your ancestors originate? Are you able to trace a family tree back more than two hundred years?

If you cannot, think about the reasons why you cannot. These reasons may be various and multiple. Write a paragraph explaining how far back you can trace your ancestry. If you cannot trace it at all beyond yourself, this would be a great time to write about what your lack of family history means to you. For some, it means a sense of freedom and the ability to invent oneself completely. For others, it is sad or frustrating. But remember that sometimes the silences and the lack of information can still tell you a lot.

If you can trace your ancestors back more than two hundred years, think about the reasons why you can do so. Where did you go to begin your search for your ancestry? Are you living in the same geographic place where your ancestors lived? What was the geographic trajectory of your ancestral history?

5. Throughout this chapter, you read quotes and excerpts from anthropologists who have studied gender diversity in various cultures. Look back to the excerpt from Qwo-Li Driskill's poem. Driskill notes that becoming empowered as Two-Spirit people requires them to kick the archaeologists and anthropologists out. Is there a way to study other cultures in a respectful manner? How would you approach your own culture to study it? Is there some difference in the way you would approach a culture that you may know because it is part of you as opposed to a culture that is not part of you?

Film and Television of Interest

Aboriginal People's Television Network Investigates: Two-Spirit, Part 1 (2014, Aboriginal Canada, 60 minutes)
This is an episode on Two-Spirit people in Canada. It is an in-depth news series.

Bro'Town (2004, Maori New Zealand, Samoan Fa'afafine, approximately 30 minutes per episode)
This animated television series from New Zealand follows a group of boys in a Catholic boys' school. The principal of the school is a *Fa'afafine* and is depicted in a positive light. One episode in particular, in which the principal is nearly lynched by an angry and ignorant mob, shows that transphobic stereotypes can be devastating. Despite the emotionally heavy material, the show manages to be humorous.

Call Her Ganda (2018, U.S., Philippines, 93 minutes)
This painful and beautiful documentary film looks at the life of Jennifer, a young trans woman in the Philippines, who was murdered by a U.S. Marine in a transphobic rage. Through interviews with Jennifer's family and friends seeking justice for the murder of their loved one, this film explores the complexity of the United States' relationship as a colonial power in the Philippines.

Call Me Kuchu (2012, U.K., Uganda, 90 minutes)

This award-winning documentary follows a group of LGBTQ+ advocates in Uganda as they fight against the "kill the gays" bill. The film looks at the ways that decades of violent imperialism and the continued colonization of the country by Christian missionaries have created a hostile place for gender and sexual minorities. John (Longjones) Abdallah Wambere is one of the people featured in the film.

Fa'afafine Documentary (2017, Samoa, New Zealand, 46 minutes)

This documentary interviews several people who identify as third gender or *Fa'afafine* in Samoa and New Zealand. The interviewees discuss colonialism and its influence on their traditional third-gender identity. This is an empowering documentary that gives voice to *Fa'afafine*.

Georgie Girl (2001, New Zealand, 69 minutes)

Georgina Beyer, who is Maori and lives in New Zealand, became the first openly transgender elected member of Parliament in the world. This award-winning documentary film follows her life and her groundbreaking work in politics as an advocate for equity and access for all people.

Harsh Beauty (2005, India, 53 minutes)

This documentary film focuses on *Hijras* in India. Through interviews, the audience meets numerous *Hijras* and learns about their spiritual practice as well as the hardships of living on the streets in urban centers in India.

The Hidden Gem (2013, Australia, 26 minutes)

Jemma is an Aboriginal trans woman born in Queensland who lives in Sydney, Australia. In this documentary, she discusses her struggles with addiction and with rejection from her biological family.

Ke Kūlana He Māhū: Remembering a Sense of Place (2001, U.S., 67 minutes)

One of the people interviewed in this outstanding documentary says that the West imposed "the tyranny of the binary frame." *Ke Kūlana He Māhū* was the first film of its kind to look at gender diversity and sexual orientation in Indigenous Hawai'ian culture. As a history lesson on both third-gender people and the colonial violence that nearly eradicated traditional Hawai'ian culture, the film focuses on multiple levels of intersecting identities.

Kumu Hina (2015, U.S., 77 minutes)

Hinaleimoana Wong Kalu (Hina) is a cultural icon and teacher (*kumu*) in Hawai'i. She is *Māhū* and has spent her life striving to battle against the leftovers of colonial transphobia and homophobia. Kumu Hina teaches Indigenous Hawai'ian values at a public school. This film is a longer, in-depth documentary that delves into her life.

Lady Eva (2017, U.S., 11 minutes)
The directors of *Kumu Hina* explore the life of Lady Eva, a *Leiti* (third gender in Tonga) navigating Tongan culture that is often heavily Evangelical Christian and conservative—continuing legacies from colonization.

Leitis in Waiting (2018, Tonga, 72 minutes)
Tonga is the only South Pacific island to escape colonization; the effects of Western ideas about binary gender and racist attitudes have nevertheless influenced the island kingdom. This documentary film focuses on *leitis,* trans women whose job has been, for centuries, to serve the royal family of the island nation. This film explores the ways that Tonga is attempting to keep alive these ancient traditions that welcome gender diversity in the face of the onslaught of white, U.S. Christian missionaries who have been arriving there and who are trying to convert the Indigenous people.

Muxes (2016, Mexico, 10 minutes)
This short documentary looks at a community of *Muxes* (third gender) people in the Indigenous community in Juchitán, Mexico.

My Inner Turmoil (2012, U.S., 9 minutes)
This short film explores an Indian woman's struggle as she lives life in two genders. It is important to note that here the focus is on a transgender woman, not a *Hijra.*

A Place in the Middle: A Strength-Based Approach to Gender Diversity and Inclusion (2015, U.S., 25 minutes)
This short film is easily accessible and aired on PBS in 2015. Taking the part of the documentary *Kumu Hina* that focuses on a middle school youth who identifies outside the gender binary, this award-winning film looks at intersecting identities and ways to combat bullying and bring about inclusion.

Purple Skies: Voices of Indian Lesbians, Bisexuals, and Transmen (2013, India, 67 minutes)
Though there is a lot of information on *Hijras* in India, and a growing amount of information on trans women who do not identify as *Hijras,* there is very little on trans men. This documentary focuses on the intersections among lesbians, bisexual women, and trans men in a country with laws that continually fluctuate over issues of LGBTQ+ rights.

The Queendom of Tonga (2017, U.S., 50 minutes)

When Brian Favorite joined the Peace Corps and traveled to Tonga, he was warned that, as a gay man, he was going to have to be in the closet during his time there. Instead, he found an amazing community of third-gender Tongans who were more than happy to take him in and become part of this documentary.

Shabnam Mousi (2005, India, 150 minutes)

For fans of Bollywood film, this musical will not disappoint. Although the film is a fiction-alized musical, it is based on the life of a *Hijra* who became a successful politician in India.

Two-Spirit People (1992, U.S., 20 minutes)

This was one of the first films to explore Indigenous cultures in the Americas and the gender diversity embraced in many of those cultures before colonization.

Two Spirits (2009, U.S., 65 minutes)

At the age of sixteen, Fred Martinez, who was Navajo, was murdered by someone who bragged that he had killed a gay youth. Fred was revered in his Navajo community as a *Nádleeh* (Two-Spirit) person. This documentary explores the ways that Indigenous gender identities outside the binary are still misunderstood.

NOTES

1. Many of these terms have more than one spelling because the word itself is not English in origin, so if you are doing research on them, you will find different spellings. In the Americas, many tribes had specific names for people who would, at this time, identify under the Two-Spirit umbrella. *Nádleeh* is the Navajo term, *Winkte* is a Lakota term, and *Asegi udanto* is the Cherokee term, for example.

2. *Oxford English Dictionary*, s.v. "Imperialism," www.oed.com/view/Entry/92285?redi rectedFrom=Imperialism#eid (accessed 15 July 2016).

3. *Oxford Dictionaries*, s.v. "Colonialism," www .oxforddictionaries.com/us/definition/ american_english/colonialism (accessed 15 July 2016).

4. Joy Harjo, http://joyharjo.com/ (accessed 9 August 2016). Harjo is reclaiming the Indigenous spelling of the term "Mvskoke" which was Anglicized as "Muskogee" (as in the Oklahoma town) or "Muscogee." Her nation has also been known as "Muscogee/ Creek," one of the Indigenous nations forced to march hundreds of miles away from their homeland in the area that we refer to as the southeastern United States. This march is known as the Trail of Tears, on which thousands of Cherokee, Creek, Choctaw, Chickasaw, and Seminole persons died in horrific weather conditions. They were forced to move to the area we know today as Oklahoma. See also Alex Jacobs, "Exclusive: Joy Harjo Speaks on Winning Poetry's Most Prestigious Award," *Indian Country Today*, 11 September 2015, https://indiancountrymedianetwork.com /culture/arts-entertainment/exclusive- joy-harjo-speaks-on-winning-poetrys- most-prestigious-award/ (accessed 11 February 2018).

5. Marc Epprecht, "'Bisexuality' and the Politics of Normal African Ethnography," *Anthropologica* 48 (2006): 189.

6. Ibid.

7. James Forbes, *Oriental Memoirs: Selected and Abridged from a Series of Familiar Letters Written during Seventeen Years Residence in India: Including Observations on Parts of Africa and South America, and a Narrative of Occurrences in Four India Voyages*, 4 vols. (London: White, Cochrane, and Co., 1813), 2:62. Available at Stanford University Special Collections.

8. Bret Boyce, "Sexuality and Gender Identity under the Constitution of India," *Journal of Gender, Race & Justice* 18.1 (2015): 21.

9. Homa Khaleeli, "Hijra: India's Third Gender Claims Its Place in Law," *Guardian,* 16 April 2014, https://www.theguardian.com/ society/2014/apr/16/india-third-gender- claims-place-in-law (accessed 18 July 2017).

10. Interestingly, British laws did not criminalize lesbians. It was believed that two women could not have sex with each other, so there was no reason to have a law banning sex between two women. Paragraph 175 of the German Penal Code, which was especially enforced throughout Nazi Germany, also chose not to criminalize sex between women for much the same reason.

11. Brent Anbe and Kathryn Xian, *Ke Kūlana He Māhū: Remembering a Sense of Place* (film), Zang Pictures, 2001.

12. Kathleen Wilson, "Thinking Back: Gender Misrecognition and Polynesian Subversions aboard the Cook Voyages," in *A New Imperial History: Culture, Identity, and Modernity in Britain and the Empire, 1660–1840*, ed. Kathleen Wilson (Cambridge: Cambridge University Press, 2004), 358–359.

13. Makiko Kuwahara, "Living as and Living with Māhū and Raerae: Geopolitics, Sex, and Gender in the Society Islands," in *Gender on the Edge: Transgender, Gay, and Other Pacific Islanders,* ed. Niko Besnier and Kalissa Alexeyeff (Honolulu: University of Hawai'i Press, 2014), 94.

14. Dan Taulapapa McMullin, "*Fa'afafine* Notes: On Tagaloa, Jesus, and Nafanua," in *Queer Indigenous Studies: Critical Interventions in Theory, Politics, and Literature,* ed. Qwo-Li Driskill, Chris Finley, Brian Joseph Gilley, and Scott Lauria Morgensen (Tucson: University of Arizona Press, 2011), 81.

15. Wesley Thomas, "Navajo Cultural Constructions of Gender and Sexuality," in *Two- Spirit People: Native American Gender Identity, Sexuality, and Spirituality,* ed. Sue-Ellen Jacobs, Wesley Thomas, and Sabine Lang (Chicago: University of Chicago Press, 1997), 156.

16. Ibid., 157.

17. Ibid., 158.

18. Kai Minosh, "Why Non-Natives Appropriating 'Two-Spirit' Hurts," BGD, 21 July 2016, www.blackgirldangerous.org/2016/07/appropriating-two-spirit/ (accessed 4 August 2016).

19. Bay Area American Indian Two-Spirits, "Statement about the Massacre in Orlando," www.baaits.org, accessed 16 June 2016 (students needing access to this quote may need to e-mail the agency).

20. "Pledge of Aloha," A Place in the Middle: A Strength-Based Approach to Gender Diversity & Inclusion, www.APlaceinthe Middle.org/pledge-of-aloha (accessed 10 April 2018).

BIBLIOGRAPHY

Anbe, Brent, and Kathryn Xian. *Ke Kūlana He Māhū: Remembering a Sense of Place.* Film. Zang Pictures, 2001.

Anguksuar [Richard LaFortune]. "A Postcolonial Colonial Perspective on Western [Mis] Conceptions of the Cosmos and the Restoration of Indigenous Taxonomies." In *Two-Spirit People: Native American Gender Identity, Sexuality, and Spirituality,* edited by Sue-Ellen Jacobs, Wesley Thomas, and Sabine Lang, 217–222. Chicago: University of Chicago Press, 1997.

Bay Area American Indian Two-Spirits. "Statement about the Massacre in Orlando." www.baaits.org. Accessed 16 June 2016; students needing access to this quote may need to e-mail the agency.

Boyce, Bret. "Sexuality and Gender Identity under the Constitution of India." *Journal of Gender, Race, and Justice* 18.1 (2015): 1–64.

Driskill, Qwo-Li. *Walking with Ghosts.* Cambridge, U.K.: Salt, 2005.

Epprecht, Marc. "'Bisexuality' and the Politics of Normal in Africa Ethnography." *Anthropologica* 48 (2006): 187–201.

Frey, Glenn, and Don Henley. "The Last Resort." *Hotel California.* Asylum Records, 1976.

Harjo, Joy. *A Map to the Next World: Poetry and Tales.* New York: W. W. Norton, 2000.

Isanna, Kaiila. "Stories from Unci" (blog). http://kaiilaisanna.weebly.com/stories-from-unci.html. Accessed 17 June 17 2016.

Jacobs, Alex. "Exclusive: Joy Harjo Speaks on Winning Poetry's Most Prestigious Award. *Indian Country Today*, 11 September 2015. https://indiancountrymedianetwork.com/culture/arts-entertainment/exclusive-joy-harjo-speaks-on-winning-poetrys-most-prestigious-award/. Accessed 11 February 2018.

Khaleeli, Homa. "Hijra: India's Third Gender Claims Its Place in Law." *Guardian*, 16 April 2014. https://www.theguardian.com/society/2014/apr/16/india-third-gender-claims-place-in-law. Accessed 18 July 2017.

Kuwahara, Makiko. "Living as and Living with Māhū and Raerae: Geopolitics, Sex, and Gender in the Society Islands." In *Gender on the Edge: Transgender, Gay, and Other Pacific Islanders,* edited by Niko Besnier and Kalissa Alexeyeff, 93–114. Honolulu: University of Hawai'i Press, 2014.

Lang, Sabine. *Men as Women, Women as Men: Changing Gender in Native American Cultures.* Austin: University of Texas Press, 1998.

"A Map of Gender-Diverse Cultures." *Independent Lens.* www.pbs.org/independentlens/content/two-spirits_map-html. Accessed 15 August 2016.

McMullin, Dan Taulapapa. "*Fa'afafine* Notes: On Tagaloa, Jesus, and Nafanua." In *Queer Indigenous Studies: Critical Interventions in Theory, Politics, and Literature,* edited by Qwo-Li Driskill, Chris Finley, Brian Joseph Gilley, and Scott Lauria Morgensen, 80–94. Tucson: University of Arizona Press, 2011.

Minosh, Kai. "Why Non-Natives Appropriating 'Two-Spirit' Hurts," *BGD*, 21 July 2016. www.blackgirldangerous.org/2016/07/appropriating-twspirit/. Accessed 4 August 2016.

"Pledge of Aloha." A Place in the Middle: A Hawaiian Approach to Bullying Prevention. www.APlaceintheMiddle.org/pledge-of-aloha. Accessed 10 April 2018.

Thomas, Wesley. "Navajo Cultural Constructions of Gender and Sexuality." In *Two-Spirit People: Native American Gender Identity, Sexuality, and Spirituality,* edited by Sue-Ellen Jacobs, Wesley Thomas, and Sabine Lang, 156–173. Chicago: University of Chicago Press, 1997.

Wilson, Kathleen. "Thinking Back: Gender Misrecognition and Polynesian Subversions aboard the Cook Voyages." In *A New Imperial History: Culture, Identity and Modernity in Britain and the Empire, 1660–1840,* edited by Kathleen Wilson, 345–362. Cambridge: Cambridge University Press, 2004.

CHAPTER 8

Four Historical Figures Who Cross-Dressed
The Adventurer, the Ambassador, the Surgeon, and the Seamstres

Key Questions

1. Why did people in the past cross-dress? How is cross-dressing different now? How is it the same?

2. Can the words transgender or trans be correctly used when discussing people in the past, before these words were invented? What are some complexities of ascribing a trans identity to people from the past?

3. What are some of the differences between a person writing their own life story (an autobiography) and a scholar writing that same life story (a biography)? What are some of the similarities?

4. How were the individuals who cross-dressed written and talked about during their lifetimes? Historically, were they written about with respect? How are they written about today?

5. As you read through this chapter, consider the individuals discussed. Where did they live? What century did they live in? What were the conditions of their lives? What can we surmise about the cultures and societies that they were part of?

6. How did intersecting identities affect each of the individuals whose stories are told in this chapter? What parallels can you draw between these individuals and other examples of intersecting identities throughout this book?

Haefele-Thomas, Ardel, *Introduction to Transgender Studies*
dx.doi.org/10.17312/harringtonparkpress/2019.01.itts.008
© 2019 by Harrington Park Press

Chapter Overview

How does what you wear define who you are? Keep this question in mind as you read this chapter, which explores individuals who cross-dressed in the seventeenth, eighteenth, and nineteenth centuries. Chapter 7 focused on various cultures that, historically, honored the possibility of diverse gender identities beyond a male-female binary. Generally speaking, this chapter returns to the gender binary by exploring three individuals who traversed this binary: Catalina/Don Antonio de Erauso, Dr. James Miranda Barry, and Frances Thompson. A fourth person, the Chevalier/Chevalière d'Éon, poses an interesting case study because they never fully embraced either side of the gender binary.

Learning about these individuals requires an understanding of the time periods in which they lived, their geographic locations, their social and cultural backgrounds, and their family structures or lack of family structures. Their choice of clothing became a powerful way for them to present themselves to the world. The change in clothing was their first step in projecting their gender identities to the outside world. Though the four people explored in this chapter may have started to cross-dress because of a specific situation, it is clear that the new gender they embodied by way of their clothing was complex and, in most cases, permanent.

Introduction

Clothing and Gender

Think about the different ways you feel and act depending on your clothing choices. How do you feel if you have to dress for a fancy dinner, a party, or a wedding? What clothes do you choose for the occasion? Do you wear a tie and jacket? A dress and high heels? And how do you act in these clothes? Later, when you are able to put on your sneakers and sweats, how do you feel? How do you act? Even if you don't give much thought to your manner of dress, your clothes not only present you to the world in a very specific way, but also influence how you feel and the ways you carry yourself. How much does your clothing represent who you are in your everyday life? How does your clothing express your gender identity? Do your clothes represent your religion, your culture, your social status? When you are out in public, does your clothing mark you as "different" from those around you? Or does your outfit mark you as "the same" as those around you?

Clothing can be political. From reading about the anti-masquerading or anti-cross-dressing laws in the United States in Chapter 4, you know that clothing has been at the heart of many laws and legal cases. For modern examples, think about laws in various K–12 schools in the United States that forbid students to wear hoodies and specific colors. A sweatshirt with a hood, in and of itself, is not illegal; it is a piece of clothing that cannot do anything except be worn, sit in a drawer, or lie in the middle of the floor until you toss it into the hamper. Rather, the public is told that the anti-hoodie school rules exist to decrease gang activity or disruptive behaviors. In France there is ongoing controversy over laws that prevent Muslim women from wearing their hijab (headscarf) in public. Women in France are perfectly free to wear hats, just as women who are nuns are able to move about in their habits. The laws forbidding the hijab make it illegal for a Muslim woman to clearly mark herself in public as Muslim.[1]

Historically, from the 1300s through the 1600s, England and other European countries passed laws that dictated proper clothing and social behavior (which was seen as inherently tied to clothing). These rigorous laws were known as **sumptuary laws.** Generally speaking, these laws were put into place by the aristocracy or religious leaders—the people in power—to prevent those lower on the socioeconomic scale from pretending to have greater social status by way of their clothing.[2] In other words, the laws were intended to force people without wealth or power to *appear* poor and disempowered in public. As soon as these laws were put into place, protesters and rebels began making clothes that mimicked the garb of the rich and powerful.

These laws suggest an underlying argument that clothing is not just something to cover nakedness. Rather, clothing makes the person, or at least the public persona. That is, you are what you wear. In fact, for hundreds of years, generally speaking, the only way a person could cross the gender binary and live a life that felt more authentic was to wear the clothes of the "opposite sex." The four individuals on whom we focus in this chapter donned the clothing that was deemed "inappropriate" for the sex assigned to them at birth. As they did so, each of them **passed** in their day-to-day lives as the gender their clothes expressed. Of course, along with their clothing, each of these individuals also carefully adopted tones of voice, behaviors, and ways of being in the world that supported their gender presentation.

The individuals whose stories you will explore in this chapter pose an interesting contrast to ways of being trans in modern society, where we understand the term *transgender* not only in a broad sense as an umbrella term for people who identify as a gender that is different from the one that society has assigned to them, but also in the context of individuals having the possibility of access to hormones, gender-affirmation surgeries, and other aspects of crossing the gender binary. Before the twentieth century, the only way to cross the gender binary was to cross-dress and to fully embody the "other" gender.

History and Gender

This chapter is not only about various people who cross-dressed. In some ways, it is also about the ways that historians have interpreted and defined the people who cross-dressed. In a few cases, scholars have honored an individual's gender expression and gender identity. In most cases, however, scholars have used the pronoun associated with the person's sex assigned at birth as well as descriptions of their genitalia. You may be wondering how a twenty-first-century writer would know anything about a seventeenth-century person's genitals! That is a good thing to wonder about because we usually do not think about historical figures and their genitals. Time after time, however, the "evidence" of a person's genitals is given more weight than the person's own accounts of their actions over a lifetime.

All the people discussed in this chapter had specific reasons for cross-dressing, most of which we may never know because their histories are incomplete at best and, at worst, presented as scandalous and sensationalistic. In other words, popular accounts during their lifetimes presented them as freaks, much as Julia Pastrana was presented and discussed during her lifetime (see Chapter 3). Today, in the twenty-first century, we can begin to explore the conditions and circumstances of their lives and how they reflected the society and culture of their times.

The Power Ladder

In Western culture, gender transgressions have almost always been viewed much more kindly if an individual traded up a rung on the social ladder. For example, when a person assigned female at birth cross-dressed and passed as a man, generally speaking, people in that individual's culture understood that decision. As you will see in this chapter, women have rarely had much power, and their life choices have often been very limited. So for a person assigned female at birth to cross-dress and go about life as a man, even if doing so meant violating anti-masquerading laws, that person's contemporaries at least *understood* the desire to have more freedom or power. An outstanding historical example of women trading up the social ladder are the women who have, for centuries, cross-dressed as teenage boys or young men to join military service and fight wars. In Chapter 10 you will read about China's legendary General Mulan.

Cross-dressing to serve in the military is often viewed as heroic, patriotic, and completely temporary and situational. In this case, does the person assigned female at birth who has cross-dressed and passed as a man identify as a man? Does this person identify as a woman who is cross-dressed? Does the individual identify as a woman *and* as a man while in the military? There is no one answer. But we can make one generalization: history often paints people assigned female at birth who cross-dress as doing so in order to take part in an event or a profession from which they otherwise would be barred. Once the event has passed or the service is complete, then (historically) she was expected to resume life as a woman, which usually meant returning to the domestic sphere as a wife and mother.

Though society has tended to be kinder to people assigned female at birth who dressed as men, the opposite can be said of people assigned male at birth who went about in public dressed as women. Unless men were cross-dressing for comedic purposes in the theater or other public venues, cross-dressing as a woman was much more scandalous: Why would a man want to fall down a rung on the social ladder? Underlying society's understanding and tolerance of people assigned female at birth who cross-dressed and the ridicule and shaming of people assigned male at birth who cross-dressed is the idea that to be womanly—to be feminine—is inferior. Misogyny lies at the core of this age-old patriarchal construction of the gender hierarchy.

In Their Own Words: The Memoirs of Catalina/Don Antonio de Erauso and the Chevalier/Chevalière d'Éon

Catalina de Erauso (1585–1650? Spain, Peru, and Mexico) and the Chevalier/ Chevalière d'Éon (1728–1810, France and England) both wrote memoirs in which they discuss cross-dressing as an integral part of their lives.[3] De Erauso and d'Éon write about their feelings and identification with the gender that their clothing and their attitude displayed, *not only in their public appearances, but also to themselves privately*. Thus, we have a unique glimpse into their feelings about what, today, we would understand as a trans identity. Such intimate memoirs from this period are very rare.

De Erauso and d'Éon had different reasons for writing their life stories, so what they wrote and their approach to the writing varied. Think about the ways you write in different circumstances. We write differently depending on what, why, and for whom we are writing. Think of the contrast between a paper you write for school and the text message you send to a friend. What if you had to write your life story to avoid being executed? That is the exact situation that de Erauso faced. What if you were writing your life story because your gender identity had become so sensationalized in the public eye that bets had been taken, and you feared being pinned down in public and stripped of your clothing? That was the situation that d'Éon faced.

Throughout de Erauso's and d'Éon's writings, you can see the ways that gender expression can be contextual. Each had complex gender identities whose nuances changed over time. De Erauso's and d'Éon's memoirs functioned as a way to invent themselves in the face of intense public scrutiny. You may be asking: Were de Erauso and d'Éon reliable narrators of their own life stories? They both were facing intense public scrutiny; how might that scrutiny have affected the ways that they wrote about themselves? De Erauso's writing reads like an adventure story, which makes sense because de Erauso knew that the writing had to be compelling enough to stave off execution. The stakes may not have been life or death for d'Éon, but they clearly knew that their memoirs would be read. Interestingly, contemporary accounts of d'Éon's life story vary in the ways that d'Éon discusses living as a man, living as a woman, and, ultimately, living in the middle ground between the poles of male and female.

Basque Adventurer: Catalina de Erauso/Don Antonio de Erauso

There, I holed up for three days, planning and re-planning and cutting myself out a suit of clothes. With the blue woolen bodice I had made a pair of breeches, and with the green petticoat I wore underneath, a doublet and hose—my nun's habit was useless and I threw it away, I cut my hair and threw it away.
CATALINA DE ERAUSO[4]

Catalina de Erauso (figure 8.1), also known as the Lieutenant Nun, was born in 1585 into a relatively large Basque family (an ancient culture inhabiting the north of Spain and the south of France in the Pyrenees). In 1589 de Erauso's parents placed the four-year-old in a Dominican convent in San Sebastián. Aunts and sisters were already living in the convent. Large Spanish families often saw girls as both needing to be protected and needing to be occupied, because they were not allowed to work in the family business or on the family farm the ways boys could.

FIGURE 8.1 Catalina de Erauso, by Cameron Rains. Like many famous historical people assigned female at birth who cross-dressed and passed as men to join institutions such as the military or the church, Catalina/Don Antonio de Erauso escaped a convent in Spain and reimagined himself as a man. De Erauso's story, however, is unique because the pope gave him a choice of living as a man or as a woman; he chose to live as a man. His memoir recounts his transition and his adventures around the world.

According to de Erauso's memoirs, at the age of fifteen, just before taking final vows, de Erauso was caught up in an argument with an older nun who was physically violent. To flee from the beating, de Erauso borrowed an aunt's keys, using them to break out of the convent and run away into a nearby forest. There Catalina de Erauso transformed the nun's clothing into an outfit that would be suitable for a young man. With dramatic flair, de Erauso tells readers that the nun's habit and the long hair were both worthless, and both were thrown away.

You may be wondering how de Erauso managed to cut and sew while hiding in a forest. It is possible that the teenage de Erauso managed to lay hands on needle and thread before escaping the convent, but remember that de Erauso wrote the memoir to be sensationalistic; de Erauso was writing under the threat of death. In fact, details like the transformation of the nun's clothing in the forest help the story of Catalina de Erauso, the cross-dressed adventurer, take on a legendary tone. But the fact that someone's story becomes a legend does not necessarily mean the story does not hold truth. A journal or a diary might well have captured more of de Erauso's feelings closer to the moments when the narrated events took place. The goal of a memoir, however, is to recall one's life, and it is tempting to recast events in more exciting ways.

In reality, the young runaway must have been scared and hungry hiding out in a forest with no possibility of a future outside the convent walls as a young woman. At the age of fifteen, de Erauso understood that to escape and move about in the world, the best thing to do was to appear publicly as a young man. A young woman wandering around the Spanish countryside would be both suspicious and in danger. In sixteenth-century Spain, there were only two respectable things for a young woman to do: get married and start a family, or go into a convent. Clearly, de Erauso was unwilling to do either. It was not safe for de Erauso to be out and about in public as a young woman who was neither married nor a nun. De Erauso knew that freedom and mobility in the world were equated with being male.

Within de Erauso's first year of being in public as a young man, he encountered both his parents. Neither recognized him. De Erauso writes, "One day, I went to hear mass at my old convent, the same mass my mother attended, and I saw that when she looked at me she did not recognize me."[5] The near encounter with his father sends de Erauso fleeing from the village: "When I heard the anguish in my father's voice, I backed off slowly and slipped away to my room. I got my clothes and some eight doubloons I had squirreled away and made my way to an inn, where I slept that night, and caught wind of a driver leaving the next morning for Bilbao. I . . . left the next day, with no better idea of where to go, or what to do, than let myself be carried off like a feather in the wind."[6]

This passage is important for two reasons. First, it exonerates his parents and others he encountered because it is clear that they are not part of de Erauso's escape from the convent. It was not necessarily illegal for females to cross-dress, but it could possibly have brought shame on the family. Second, it creates a heroic sense of complete passing as male. De Erauso tells a great adventure story; however, when he writes about the loss of his family, his tone is often sad. Although de Erauso lived in a time long before we had labels like "transgender" and "transvestite," his story conveys the timeless truth that trans people are often completely cut off from their families. The sense of isolation that haunts de Erauso's story reaches out to us four centuries later.

Adulthood in Peru

Perhaps staying in Spain felt too physically and emotionally dangerous and depressing for the young de Erauso. So in 1603 the eighteen-year-old took a job on a ship that was sailing to Peru as part of Spain's colonial mission to the Americas. Even away from Spain, though, it appears that de Erauso still sought out family, as he became his uncle's cabin boy. After quitting service to his uncle on the ship, he again sought out family after landing in Peru, when "I stayed behind as my brother's soldier, and dined at his table for three years, all the while never letting on to my secret."[7] It may seem strange that none of de Erauso's family recognized him, but remember that the family had sent the young Catalina into a convent at the age of four. And people's gender was truly identified by clothing at this time; a male soldier would have worn heavy shirts and armor.

De Erauso's Arrest and Return to a Convent

In Guamanga, Peru, de Erauso encountered bad luck at a gambling house. The sheriff attempted to arrest him, and they got into a duel with their swords. De Erauso killed the sheriff (not the first person he had killed in a sword duel, but the first time he was caught in the act). A senior bishop on his way to church intervened just as the sheriff's men were ready to arrest or kill de Erauso. The bishop took the wounded de Erauso into the safety of the church, which is a place where people can seek asylum. When the bishop asked de Erauso to recount his story, he began with his usual tales of ocean crossings and adventure, but as he talked, something spiritual happened: "All the while I was speaking, I felt a calm sweeping over me, I felt as if I were humbled before God. . . . I revealed myself to the bishop and told him, "I am a woman. . . . I left the convent . . . undressed myself and dressed myself up again . . . traveled here and there, embarked, disembarked, hustled, killed, maimed, wreaked havoc, and roamed about, until coming to a stop in this very instant, at the feet of Your Eminence."[8]

The bishop did not believe de Erauso's confession, but de Erauso made a deal with him, saying, "Let other women examine me—I will submit to such a test."[9] The bishop sent two elderly women to examine de Erauso, who wrote that they "found me to be a woman, and were ready to swear it under oath . . . they found me to be an intact virgin."[10] Interestingly, the bishop saw de Erauso's life and adventures as honorable *because* the adventurer remained a virgin. Within a week, the bishop had helped de Erauso enter into the Santa Clara convent in Guamanga to save him from imprisonment and execution for the killing of the sheriff. For de Erauso, though, the convent proved to be another sort of prison.

Why would de Erauso so willingly give up male privilege to go back into a nunnery? Could part of the appeal have been de Erauso's almost immediate celebrity status among the citizens who heard the story? Or did de Erauso, knowing that his memoir was going to be read by the bishop and others in the church, feel it was necessary to write positively about going into the convent? Remember that de Erauso was writing for his life—to avoid execution. Did de Erauso feel the need to make the memoir sympathetic and repentant? What would you have done in the same situation? After all, the bishop saved de Erauso from the authorities and from certain death.

What Was de Erauso's Gender Identity?

If de Erauso's story ended in the convent, we could make a good argument that the "Lieutenant Nun's" life followed the trajectory of so many women who, for various reasons, made a choice or found it necessary to cross-dress as a man. After all, de Erauso joined the military as a man because women were barred from this type of service. De Erauso's story, however, does not end in the convent in 1620. Rather, six years later, after telling Pope Urban VIII stories of a childhood spent in a convent, teenage years and young adulthood spent as a military man in Peru, and then the recent time back in a convent, de Erauso tells readers, "His Holiness seemed amazed to hear such things, and graciously gave me leave to pursue my life in men's clothing."[11] The pope gave de Erauso a *choice,* and he chose to embrace manhood. One of the last accounts we have of de Erauso has him living in Mexico in 1630 as Don Antonio de Erauso, a merchant and mule driver. Accounts of him from the 1640s present him as a person of courage who everyone knew was assigned female at birth, but who dressed as a man and wore a sword and dagger.

From the time of his death, historians and biographers have grappled with de Erauso's gender identity. As one historian notes: "Catalina could not escape her reputation, even in New Spain where she might have hoped to pass herself off as somebody other than a woman in male clothing. During her earlier career, she had to keep moving in order to guard her secret. Once her secret was out, she became a freak, neither man nor woman, and no amount of moving from place to place could have helped that."[12] Though contemporary accounts of de Erauso indicate that people in Europe, as well as Mexico and Peru, were interested in the legendary figure of the Lieutenant Nun, it is not clear that people in the seventeenth century viewed de Erauso as a "freak." Rather, this is the word that the historian used to describe him. In what ways, then, do biographers and historians influence the ways that future scholars view historical figures?

Almost all historians who have researched de Erauso as a seventeenth-century transgender person use feminine pronouns when writing about the Basque adventurer. At least one historian, Eva Mendieta, argues that de Erauso had "gender dysphoria"—in other words, a transgender identity. She writes, "In Erauso, her profanity, her fights, her ability to perform physically demanding tasks—the entire repertoire of male behavior—had to turn into a second skin for her, becoming a natural part of her appearance and personality." The historian continues, "What is extraordinary, however, is that even when her true sexual identity was known in Spain and the Americas, she continued to be treated and referred to as a man, thus making her male status a public and official matter."[13]

Pedro de la Valle, one of de Erauso's contemporaries, described de Erauso in the following way: "Tall and powerfully built, and with a masculine air, she has no more breasts than a girl. She told me she had used some sort of remedy to make them disappear. I believe it was a poultice given her by an Italian it hurt a great deal, but since it neither harmed nor deformed her, the effect was very much to her liking."[14] Mendieta states, "Submitting her body to this invasive procedure implies that she early on chose a path of no return with respect to male identity."[15] How are we supposed to understand Mendieta's use of feminine pronouns for de Erauso, even when this same historian has argued that de Erauso was male—to himself, his church, and his communities in Europe and the Americas? Note also the ways that misogyny plays out in de Erauso's case: there is an assumption that a woman cannot be strong and does not have the capacity to duel. Why does the female pronoun, the pronoun corresponding to female genitals, continue to be used for de Erauso when it is clear that de Erauso identified as a man?

Embracing the Middle Ground: The Chevalier/Chevalière d'Éon

The trailblazing story of the Chevalier d'Eon is an astonishing example of the level of tolerance and acceptance that was possible long before transgender issues were acknowledged or discussed.

NICHOLAS CULLINAN[16]

Charles-Geneviève-Louise-Auguste-André-Thimothée d'Éon de Beaumont (imagine this name being called out at graduation) is one of the most famous trans historical figures. The quotation above comes from the London's National Portrait Gallery's *Director's Trail,* a self-guided tour brochure that proudly displays a painting of d'Éon. D'Éon inspired one of the first-known underground transgender societies in the world (the Beaumont Society) and a magazine. Both are still in existence. The Beaumont Society, located in London, enjoys an international membership, and its magazine has worldwide readership. Havelock Ellis, one of the early sexologists, named an entire type of "transvestism" as "Eonism" after the Chevalier/Chevalière d'Éon.[17]

The Life and Work of the Chevalier/Chevalière d'Éon

The Chevalier/Chevalière d'Éon (figure 8.2) was born on 5 October 1728 in Tonnerre, France, into a family with a moderate amount of money and connections to the French court. D'Éon died on 21 May 1810 in exile and in relative poverty in London, England.[18]

FIGURE 8.2 The Chevalier/Chevalière d'Éon, by Cameron Rains. The bones of the Chevalier/Chevalière d'Éon lie in a community paupers' grave in London at St. Pancras Old Church Churchyard because d'Éon died in poverty in 1810. For half of their life, d'Éon lived as a man and was a high-level French spy. For the second half, d'Éon lived as a woman in London. D'Éon's memoirs offer insight into a rich history of a community of gender outlaws.

D'Éon's declining socioeconomic situation from 1777 onward was directly affected by d'Éon's gender expression. Starting at the age of twenty-five, d'Éon held numerous important positions in French public service, including a period as an economics and taxation expert. In 1753 d'Éon published the first of several books that focused on the French economy and taxation. In 1756 King Louis XV asked d'Éon to become France's ambassador to Russia. Four years later, d'Éon went into the military and became a captain of the dragoons and an expert with the sword.[19] D'Éon was so well respected in the military that, in 1762, at the age of thirty-four, d'Éon was chosen to be on the negotiating team between France and England at the end of the Seven Years' War. The Treaty of Paris, which was a peace treaty between England and France, was "personally carried from London to Paris by d'Éon in February 1763."[20] For d'Éon's honorable and patriotic work, King Louis XV awarded d'Éon the Cross of Saint Louis and gave the ambassador the title "Chevalier."[21] King Louis XV trusted d'Éon with national security to the point that the Chevalier/Chevalière then became one of a very small group of the king's secret spies in England.

Not Much Has Changed: Trans Harassment in 1771

Nobody knows why, but in 1771 the London newspapers were on fire with stories that the Chevalier d'Éon was, in fact, the *Chevalière* d'Éon—in other words, a woman cross-dressed as a man. Why might newspapers perpetuate such a story? Can you think of examples in today's media in which something similar happened?

Interestingly, d'Éon did not deny the stories in the press and refused a physical exam by doctors. For some time in England, people had assumed that d'Éon was a woman who cross-dressed in order to serve in the military and work in public service, both occupations reserved solely for men. In fact, the famous early feminist Mary Wollstonecraft (1759–1797) praised the Chevalière d'Éon for proving that women truly could do any task that they set their minds and hearts to. Wollstonecraft was not alone in thinking that all the treaty work, dragoon work, and writing about economics had been done by a woman cross-dressed as a man, and that d'Éon's purpose in cross-dressing was to take on these duties forbidden to women. Indeed, famous public figures like Wollstonecraft encouraged d'Éon to finally "come out of the closet" and embrace being out as a woman. In other words, they believed it was safe for d'Éon to stop cross-dressing because everyone knew d'Éon was a woman anyway.

The English press continually published articles claiming that d'Éon was a woman cross-dressed as a man, and finally the sensationalism of the story reached such a fevered pitch that numerous people placed underground bets on d'Éon's sex. Many were tried in a court of law and charged with illegal gambling. It is one thing to place bets on your favorite sports team, but can you imagine how d'Éon must have felt about the public placing bets on their sex or gender identity (at that time, sex and gender would have been understood to be the same)? D'Éon wrote the following in two separate letters (in March and May 1771) to Charles-François, le comte de Broglie, who was one of the king of France's secret deputies:

> I have the vexation of hearing, and even reading in the English papers, all the extraordinary reports coming from Paris, London and even St. Petersburg about the uncertainty of my sex. In this country of gamblers they have caused such excitement that they are issuing insurance policies for considerable sums at the Court and in the City on so indecent a subject. . . . I am warned on all sides that several rich people have conceived the project of having me seized, by force or cunning, in order to examine me against my will. This I would not tolerate and it might put me under the necessity of killing someone. . . . I pray God daily to deliver me from this life and from wicked men.[22]

D'Éon's plea to a fellow French official over two hundred years ago may seem like a historical artifact, but d'Éon's situation could happen today. As you saw in earlier chapters, people whose gender identity or sex is perceived as ambiguous are still physically violated by people who want to know if the person is a man or a woman, a boy *or* a girl. In the last line of the quotation above, you can see the Chevalier/Chevalière's desperation to escape from the unwanted attention, even if doing so means dying. Note that three of the issues that d'Éon brings up still affect trans people today: (1) the idea that a group of people can seize someone and molest them by stripping their clothes off; (2) the strength that d'Éon displays in writing about the possible "necessity of killing someone" in self-defense; and (3) the desperation to put a permanent stop to the bullying.

The Chevalier/Chevalière d'Éon felt so harassed that they took an impromptu trip to Germany shortly after sending the letters in May 1771. A month later, in the 24 June edition of the *Reading Mercury and Oxford Gazette,* the newspaper editors translated the following letter, written in French by d'Éon to a loyal friend in England: "I arrive this moment from Germany . . . very much fatigued. . . . I have seen at Hamburg, in one of the English papers, what your heart has done for me during my absence. I was so affected by it as to shed tears. This has determined me to return to England sooner than I had hoped, to thank my real friends, like you."[23] D'Éon's sad and kind note to a friend underscores the importance of friends and allies in the face of harassment.

King Louis XVI Orders Women's Wear

D'Éon's plea to the French official and the amount of publicity in England finally reached King Louis XV's attention, and he, too, began to wonder about d'Éon's sex. He sent a spy undercover to report back on one of his own secret spies, and in 1772, the story brought back to the palace of Versailles was that d'Éon was a woman. When Louis XVI, the next king, took the French throne, he also assumed that d'Éon was a woman. From 1777 to 1785, when d'Éon returned to their childhood home in France, the new king *ordered* d'Éon to wear women's clothes.[24]

Think about this order for a moment. The pope gave de Erauso permission to choose the clothing and the gender presentation that were most comfortable for him. Cross-dressing enabled de Erauso to be the man he wanted to be. In contrast, for d'Éon, the king ordered women's wear. D'Éon's case may be more complex than de Erauso's in that, publicly, d'Éon did not claim one side of the gender binary or the other. Rather, d'Éon embraced more of a middle ground. You could ask: What constituted cross-dressing for d'Éon? Was it the captain of the dragoons uniform? The dresses made by the queen's wardrobe director, Rose Bertin? Neither? Both? If you look at various portraits of the Chevalier/Chevalière d'Éon—and most of them are portraits of d'Éon in women's clothing—you will see that d'Éon *always* wears the beautiful Cross of Saint Louis. Women were not allowed into the French military in the eighteenth century, nor were they given this badge of honor. So d'Éon's clothing and presentation are always a combination of masculine and feminine.

Writing for a Curious Public: D'Éon's Memoirs

Unlike de Erauso, who wrote his memoirs to avoid execution, d'Éon wrote their memoirs in private over the course of three decades. (If you would like to study the Chevalier/Chevalière d'Éon's original memoirs, which are written in French, they are available in England at the Leeds University Library. They have been translated into English.) D'Éon wrote their life story with the intention that the public of the early nineteenth century would be reading it. D'Éon died in 1810, however, before the memoirs were published. In 1836 d'Éon's writing was edited by a French historian, Frédéric Gaillardet, but an English translation of selections from d'Éon's diaries was not published until 1970. Because it came first, Gaillardet's book set the tone for future scholars interested in the legendary d'Éon. The following excerpt comes from Gaillardet's introduction to his translation of d'Éon's memoirs: "Which of these two persons was the true one? Which of these two sexes, the masculine or the feminine, was the simulated one? Did the individual who assumed them each in turn, unite both? Was he single or double; a normal human being or a freak? In short, was he man, woman or hermaphrodite?"[25]

This excerpt from 1836, well before sexology became a field of study, still resonates in the questions it asks about transgender, nonbinary, and other gender-diverse people. How might these questions have influenced the ways that future sexologists would approach not only d'Éon but also other people who cross-dressed, crossed the gender binary, or remained in the middle ground? How would history have been changed (if at all) if Gaillardet and other historians had kept their language and opinions neutral? Just the removal of the word "freak" would have changed the tone of Gaillardet's description. What if Gaillardet had simply let d'Éon's memoirs speak for themselves? What other biases do you detect in Gaillardet's introduction to d'Éon's life story?

Those who study d'Éon can find themselves in a complex position. For example, even if you find Gaillardet's tone and approach offensive, his book was, and is, the first publication regarding d'Éon following their death, which makes it a unique part of the historical record. More to the point, Gaillardet's book is full of examples of d'Éon's own writing; this was the first time d'Éon's writing was made accessible to a larger audience. Perhaps Gaillardet's language and judgment are offensive; yet, for decades, his book was the *only* place in which to read the Chevalier/Chevalière d'Éon's memoirs unless you could go to Leeds, England,

and read the original manuscripts in French. In addition, Gaillardet wrote his book while some of d'Éon's contemporaries were still alive, so his book includes their views on d'Éon.

The Chevalier/Chevalière d'Éon seems to be having a last laugh in that their memoirs raise more questions than provide answers. D'Éon changed information about their sex and gender identity in their memoirs. Specifically, in the first memoir, d'Éon writes that they were born with genitalia that were not specifically male or female; today we would use the term *differences of sex development (DSD)* or *intersex* (which may be part of the reason for Gaillardet's use of the term *hermaphrodite*). D'Éon goes on to say that their family had suffered the death of a son, so they raised d'Éon as a boy. D'Éon writes, "My father had me baptized with the names of both male and female saints in order to avoid any error," and "My grandmother and my mother, both extremely pious women, hesitated and meditated a long time about whether I was to be treated as a girl or a boy."[26] D'Éon was raised as a boy, but the autobiography implies that d'Éon was assigned female at birth.

Over the course of the nearly thirty years that d'Éon lived as a woman, d'Éon constantly revised their autobiography to such an extent that it is not clear what d'Éon's sex assignment was at birth, though we should not get stuck on that question. Rather, we should remember that the Chevalier/Chevalière d'Éon was a French public servant who spent 1728–1777 (forty-nine years) outwardly dressed as a man and then 1777–1810 (thirty-three years) outwardly dressed as a woman. Remember that many people wanted d'Éon to stop cross-dressing as a man and get on with the business of being a successful woman who proved that women could do anything a man could do. So, when in 1777 the king ordered d'Éon to dress as a woman (and later when the monarchy no longer cared, but d'Éon continued to dress as a woman), many assumed that d'Éon had finally embraced "true" womanhood.

As d'Éon's twenty-first-century biographers and translators note, "D'Éon lived nearly half his life as a woman by writing his way across the gender barrier."[27] But does our obsession with putting the Chevalier/Chevalière d'Éon into a gendered box of either "man" *or* "woman" keep us from fully understanding this person's rich history? Through clothing, as noted above, d'Éon always appeared dressed in that middle ground, having portraits painted while wearing a dress and proudly displaying the military cross.

By the end of the nineteenth century, the Chevalier/Chevalière d'Éon had become almost legendary. Consider the following excerpt from an article entitled "Duellists in Petticoats," published in 1895 in the *Leeds Times*:

> As dauntless a fighter as ever buckled a sword during the years when Louis XV was King . . . was the Chevaliere d'Eon. Whether this strange being was a man or woman—improbable as it may seem—is not positively known to this day. For nearly two centuries historians have disputed over this vexed question, and romancers have spun countless tales based upon the incidents in the Chevaliere's adventurous career. . . . For many years he (or she) was one of Louis XV's secret agents, and among the best diplomatists in Europe, wearing with equal grace the habiliments of either sex. In woman's garb D'Eon was ambassadress to the court of the Empress Elizabeth of Russia from 1755 to 1760, and later, as a man, was Ambassador to England. The Chevaliere's face was beardless and the voice high pitched. When dressed in feminine attire D'Eon was as handsome a woman as any in the Courts of Europe, and as a man, in the silk and satin bravery of those picturesque times, there was not a noble among all the courtiers who could drink deeper or throw dice for higher stakes than the Chevaliere. No man's hand more readily sought the hilt of his sword than did D'Eon's. The Chevaliere was one of the best swordsmen of the epoch, and was a noted and much-feared duellist. She (for on this occasion the Chevaliere wore the costume of the gentler sex) had a notable encounter with the Chevalier de St. Georges one bright summer's day in the Palace Royale . . . and was wounded in her sword-arm. As soon as she recovered from her hurt she again picked a quarrel with her former adversary and ran him through the body.[28]

Whether this article was meant to be funny or not, you can see that the writer conveys a sense of d'Éon's existing in the middle of the gender binary. Note that the writer uses the feminine "Chevalière" and "she" pronouns throughout the article. The clothing did, indeed, make the woman. Yet, if you reread the description, you will also find that the author makes it clear that this swordsperson was gender fluid. It is interesting to note that a newspaper account at the end of the Victorian era was seemingly comfortable with the gender and sex ambiguity of the Chevalier/Chevalière d'Éon. We do not usually equate the late nineteenth century with having a kind view of people who sat outside gender norms. It is always important to remember, however, that, within any time period, people who respected gender diversity did exist.

Poverty and Death

France refused to grant the Chevalier/Chevalière d'Éon any monthly allowance. One explanation is the uproar and confusion following the French Revolution, but another part of it was d'Éon's recognition as a woman in France. Women could not collect a pension from the state, and, therefore, d'Éon was unable to collect any veteran's pay for all the years of service in the dragoons and as one of the king's spies. Queen Charlotte of England, though, provided a small allowance to d'Éon each month, although it was barely enough to pay for food and lodging.

D'Éon attempted to make a living through public sword duels that sensationalized a woman French military veteran. What distinguishes the sensationalism in these shows from sideshows and freak shows (discussed in Chapter 3) is the fact that the Chevalier/Chevalière d'Éon consented to the duels and agreed to be on display. It was not uncommon to see an announcement like this one:

> For One Night Only
> At a Great Room, The HOTEL, CHESTER.
> This present Friday, March 27, 1795,
> The Celebrated
> *CHEVALIERE D'EON,*
> Will Make
> An Assault d'Armes,
> With an English Gentleman,
> A Professor in the Art of Fencing
> The Chevaliere will appear in the same UNIFORM
> which she wore at the time when she served as
> CAPTAIN of DRAGOONS in the army.[29]

On this occasion, d'Éon and the professor were the centerpiece amusement; however, d'Éon often performed at the intermission during stage plays. In 1796 the Chevalier/Chevalière was seriously injured, which ended this source of income. In 1804 d'Éon was incarcerated in debtor's prison in London, unable to pay basic lodging fees and daily maintenance. After several months, d'Éon was released when Mrs. Cole, a friend, raised enough money to free d'Éon from debtors' prison. They lived together as roommates until d'Éon's death in 1810.[30]

Below are excerpts from two different newspaper reports in late May 1810 about the Chevalier/Chevalière d'Éon's death. Note the different ways they discuss the revelation about d'Éon's genitals.

The Chevalier D'Eon . . . died at his lodgings in New Milman Street, Guilford Street, on Tuesday last. . . . It will be remembered that a great doubt at one time existed to which gender he belonged, which, however, was set at rest by the verdict of 12 matrons who decided in favour of the female; and from that time to the present he wore the costume of that sex. But on his decease taking place it was unexpectedly discovered that the Chevalier was a perfect male![31]

The companion and friend of the Chevalier, Madame Cole . . . deemed it right to send for a surgeon. . . . The following is a certificate of the professional gentleman who operated: "I hereby certify, that I have inspected and dissected the body of the Chevalier D'Eon, in the presence of Mr. Adair, Mr. Wilson, and Le Pere Elizee, and have found the male organs in every respect perfectly formed. T. Copeland, Surgeon, Golden Square."[32]

What are some of the differences in the ways that d'Éon's body was looked at? How does the tone of the first newspaper account, which says that d'Éon was discovered to be a "perfect male," contrast with the account from the doctor who acted as the coroner and wrote about inspecting and dissecting? Also note the ways that d'Éon's *genital configuration* and not d'Éon's *gender expression* dictated how the newspapers covered the story.

"The Philosopher of Gender":[33] Identifying a Trans Community

In the archival boxes that house d'Éon's memoirs, scholars have discovered an entire book of d'Éon's philosophical and spiritual writings. The book's title, translated into English, is *The Pious Metamorphoses; or, The History of Women Who Disguised Their Sex in Order to Consecrate Themselves to God and to Adopt the Monastic Life and Who Have Been Recognized as Saintly by the Greek and Latin Church*.[34] In *The Pious Metamorphoses* d'Éon explores numerous saints who were assigned female at birth and who cross-dressed as men to participate more actively in the Catholic Church. For various reasons, they did not wish to become nuns. Rather, they sought the duties and intellectual community that were reserved for men. The saints discussed in d'Éon's writing had a very specific purpose for cross-dressing; the Catholic Church, much like the military and the medical profession, did not allow women to hold the most visible and respected positions, which were for men only. As the authors of one of d'Éon's translated memoirs argue, "D'Eon used these examples not only to create a social context and historic tradition for his transgender life but also to give it legitimacy and spiritual meaning."[35]

D'Éon's writing focuses on the intersections of gender identity and religious devotion. De Erauso clearly moved *away* from religion once he embraced being a man; in contrast, d'Éon, as the Chevalière, moved *toward* religion for comfort and empowerment. D'Éon writes: "I was struck, while secretly disguised myself, by the example of the extraordinary women who, like me, lied by wearing the costume of a sex that was not theirs in order to follow a courageous instinct that led them to march to a different drummer, which they could not have done wearing the costume of their own sex. That I was . . . struck by the phenomenon is easy to understand: these were like so many mirrors *reflecting my own image.*"[36]

D'Éon needed to use words such as *disguised, lied,* and *costume* because those were the only terms available in the eighteenth century. Today, of course, these words are offensive when used to describe trans people. But well before words like *transvestite, transsexual,* and *transgender* were invented, the Chevalier/Chevalière d'Éon managed to capture a sense of belonging with others who found it necessary to cross-dress in order to realize their full potential as spiritual human beings. Also, today we would recognize that sex and gender identity are different.

Actions Speak Louder: Social Justice Advocates Dr. James Miranda Barry and Frances Thompson

At first glance, James Barry (1795?–1865; Scotland, England, South Africa, Jamaica, Corfu, and Canada) and Frances Thompson (1840?–1876; United States) might appear to have only superficial things in common. Both lived in the nineteenth century, and their birth dates are unknown. James Barry was a British army surgeon who lived in such diverse places as England, South Africa, Jamaica, and Canada; he was highly educated and spent the majority of his life as the inspector of various hospitals in the British colonies. Frances Thompson was a freed slave who, possibly as young as age nine, made her way from a Maryland plantation to live in South Memphis, Tennessee, where she lived with another freedwoman, Lucy Smith. They took in sewing and laundry to make a living. Barry and Thompson lived vastly different lives, yet the doctor and the seamstress both spoke out against social injustice. They also became infamous when their cross-dressing became public knowledge.

Unlike de Erauso and d'Éon, who both wrote about their gender identities for public audiences, neither Barry nor Thompson left us any writing on the subject (at least to our knowledge at this time). Although Barry and Thompson did not write specifically about their reasons for cross-dressing, other sources offer rich details about their lives, their actions, and their words.

For example, what can we learn from Barry's writing about his work as an inspector of hospitals, prisons, and military outposts? What can we learn from Thompson's testimony at a congressional hearing as she spoke up for herself and her African American community shortly after violent attacks against them? Because neither Barry nor Thompson was speaking or writing for an audience *about* their gender identity or expression, they may have been more free to be in the world as themselves until their cross-dressing became public knowledge.

Speaking Up for the Silenced: Dr. James Miranda Barry

Dr. James Barry was one of the most outstanding medical practitioners ever to have practised in South Africa. It must be contended that he was also one of the foremost social reformers in South Africa.

PERCY LAIDLER AND MICHAEL GELFAND[37]

Dr. James Miranda Barry's biography does not start at the usual place—with a birth. James Miranda Barry (figure 8.3) may have been born in 1789 in Cork, Ireland, and given the name Margaret Bulkley.[38] He may have been born in 1795. At one time, Barry said he was born "about 1799."[39] After his death in 1865, no family member or friend came to claim his body or the items he left behind.[40]

Although recent biographies have engaged in speculation regarding the year of Barry's birth, the mystery remains: Where, when, and to whom was the person who would become Dr. James Miranda Barry born? There are many theories, but no facts. We do not know when the child assigned female at birth began wearing boys' clothes. We *do* know that in December 1809, a youth named James Miranda Barry signed the matriculation roster at the University of Edinburgh as a literary and medical student.[41] We also know that he had to gain special permission to attend certain classes that were considered morally improper for a boy as young as eleven or twelve. Barry gained admission to these classes (usually limited to men at least eighteen years old) and became possibly the youngest student ever admitted to the outstanding medical school. He also took courses above and beyond the requirements and excelled in all of them. For example, Barry studied practical anatomy (few students studied this topic), as well as midwifery and dissection, neither of which was required for medical students.[42] Barry wrote a thesis on groin hernias and passed the medical board exams (entirely in Latin) with flying colors. Girls and women were *not* allowed to attend medical school anywhere in Britain at this time.

FIGURE 8.3 Dr. James Miranda Barry, by Cameron Rains. Historians often argue that Dr. James Miranda Barry was the first woman surgeon in Britain; however, it is clear that Dr. Barry lived his entire adult life as a man, which helps us make the argument that he may have been the first trans surgeon in Britain. Dr. Barry's medical reforms for marginalized communities in South Africa illustrate his social justice work even as he was tethered by "proper" British laws.

London Apprenticeship

After medical school, Barry left Edinburgh for London and became a pupil dresser (an apprentice) to one of London's top surgeons, Sir Astley Cooper.[43] Barry worked with his mentor at two hospitals: Guy's Hospital, a "voluntary hospital" that specialized in treating people who were seen as incurable, insane, or both, and St. Thomas's Royal Hospital, which treated people with fevers and sexually transmitted diseases (STDs). Many hospitals at the time refused to treat STDs because they viewed patients who had them as morally tainted, but St. Thomas's did not turn anyone away.[44] The "royal" in St. Thomas's name meant that the hospital was under a royal governmental charter; all members of the royal family had their own doctors who attended them at the palace or other private chambers.

Both hospitals were located in London's Southwark neighborhood, which is today an eclectic and hip neighborhood where you can shop at the historic Borough Market, a bustling outdoor farmer's market with cafés, bakeries, flower shops, and international food stalls. Back in Barry's time, and for centuries before, the area was an outpost for outlaws: a dank and dangerous location that was home to prisons, bars, gambling houses, and brothels. (The area was drained swampland from the Thames River, which was full of garbage, sewage, and dead bodies.)

Imagine the young Dr. Barry in his **surtout** (a long coat that he always wore, possibly to hide his breasts) walking along the streets of Southwark late at night, after hours of watching the dead bodies of criminals from nearby jails or drowning victims floating in the Thames being dissected at Guy's or St. Thomas's. Think of his aching feet from hours standing near the operating table as Cooper operated as quickly as he could on bleeding patients who were screaming and only partly unconscious because anesthesia was imperfect at best, and usually not effective at all.[45] No fresh air circulated in the operating theater. Blood oozed off the operating tables and pooled on the straw covering the floor. Most apprentices did not make it through the day without vomiting, fainting, or both. From all accounts, the steady and strong Dr. James Barry was always at the ready to assist his mentor.

Barry certainly learned efficient and precise surgical skills during his apprenticeship, but he could have learned something beyond the surgical methods to help treat sick bodies. At the two hospitals he could have learned to understand the empathy and human kindness needed *especially* when working with society's poorest, sickest, and most outcast. Barry saw, firsthand, that all people felt pain and bled equally, regardless of their social status. In the 1800s the poverty-stricken people of Southwark were often considered as "foreign" and "different" as the people who fell under Dutch and then British colonial rule in South Africa. In many ways, working in this marginalized London neighborhood prepared Barry for the conditions awaiting him in the army when he voyaged to South Africa. Barry took not only his surgical skills but also a deep sense of empathy with him when he enlisted in the English army as a surgeon in 1813.

Arrival in South Africa

A champion of the socially marginalized and economically dispossessed, Barry prioritized the treatment of women, prostitutes, slaves, the insane, lepers and children.

RACHEL HOLMES[46]

This quotation comes from a twentieth-century historian who clearly respected Barry and his tireless work as a surgeon in South Africa. During Barry's lifetime, though, the doctor struggled constantly with the British military and governmental authority figures because he valued and treated his patients, regardless of their ethnicity, gender, or social standing, with disregard for the class- and gender-based rules of British society. From the moment he stepped off the ship in a South African port in August 1816, Barry treated all his patients as human beings who needed his help and care.

At that time, slavery was still legal. In fact, it was not until two years after Barry's arrival, in 1818, that the government passed a resolution that children born of slaves would be free.[47] In attending to his patients, however, Barry chose not to act like the majority of other English army physicians. For example, a slave was killed by a "domestic correction with the birch."[48] The surgeon who was originally in charge of examining the body, and who was clearly interested in defending the slave owner, wrote on the official report that the slave had eaten too much and died from overindulgence. As one of the army inspectors, "Barry studied the report and regretted deeply that he was obliged to declare the certificate most incorrect and unprofessional." Barry concluded that the slave had died from the beating.[49] Not only did Barry contradict the older surgeon, but he also made an official statement that blew the whistle on both the surgeon and the slave owner who committed the murder. As you can imagine, Barry's actions greatly upset the established British hierarchy of Cape Town (today one of South Africa's three capital cities).

How did Barry get away with such insubordination? While he upset the centuries-old English hierarchy, he also impressed many important people with his skill. For example, in 1826 he answered an urgent call to the home of a wealthy British family. There he found the lady of the house in labor and near death. At this time, many women and infants died during childbirth, regardless of social standing or financial means. Barry's work in midwifery (remember that the course had not been a requirement at Edinburgh) came in handy, and he successfully delivered the baby by way of cesarean section (C-section). He became the fourth doctor in the world and the first British doctor to accomplish a C-section without losing either the mother or the child.[50] Because he helped save the lives of two members of an established British family, he was given some leeway when he took a stand against the human rights violations he saw in South Africa.

Drug Distribution and Drug Quality

What do you expect when you go to the pharmacy to pick up a prescription? Other than a long line, you probably expect that your drugs have undergone a quality-control screening. You probably also assume that the pharmacist has filled the prescription according to the doctor's orders. In the nineteenth century, though, these assumptions were sometimes false, particularly in colonial outposts like South Africa.

It came to Barry's attention that the proprietor of one chemist's shop (pharmacy) was dispensing medicine "without a licence." In fact, the proprietor was practicing medicine to the detriment of the patients; he had unskillfully treated a poor man, causing the man's death. Barry evidently lost no time in bringing the proprietor's negligent actions and identity to "the attention of the townspeople."[51] Barry not only called out the chemists (pharmacists) who were using wrong ingredients (most of them cheap materials for which they could overcharge), but also went public, ensuring that the local people knew about the crooked pharmacists. He helped reform the entire pharmaceutical industry in Cape Town by insisting that "all apothecaries and vendors of medicines were answerable that their laudanum, opium, arsenic and other powerful medicines, commonly denominated poisons, were kept in secure places and not sold in great or dangerous quantities without a written permission or prescription from a regular physician or surgeon."[52] In other words, Barry made certain that physicians and surgeons were in charge of the prescriptions, not the pharmacists. Most people who benefited from Barry's activism were poor: the wealthy did not get their medicine in so lowly a place as a chemist's shop.

Sickness and Social Justice

A brilliant diagnostician, firm and kind in the sickroom.
JUNE ROSE[53]

It would have been easy for Barry to work with the army hospitals in Cape Town and to remain there in relative comfort, like so many of his colleagues who lived in their fine old homes with plenty of space, while "the Hottentots, Malays and Negroes lived in squalor and misery; those who were sick were sent to prison."[54] But that was not the path he chose. According to two prominent South African medical historians, Barry "asked that the Inspectorate of Lepers, The Tronk, Somerset Hospital and Robben Island be added to his duties, because these places were in a lamentable state and his predecessors in office had never professionally supervised them."[55] In other words, Barry *asked* to be put in charge of the two prisons, the "Tronk" and Robben Island, and two hospitals populated by people with leprosy, sexually transmitted diseases (STDs), and other illnesses that branded them as social outcasts. At the time, it was not unusual to put sick people in prisons as a way to remove them from public spaces. It is also important to remember that the majority of people in these hospitals and prisons were poor people of color suffering from horrible conditions.

Today leprosy is known by a less distressing name, Hansen's disease, and it can be cured when treated early; however, it has not been eradicated. In the nineteenth century, leprosy was one of the most dreaded illnesses, and people who had the disease were stigmatized. To this day, we use the word *leper* metaphorically to mean someone who is a societal outcast.

Within a year of Barry's arrival in Cape Town, a special hospital for people with leprosy was established. The hospital was named Hemel and Aarde (Heaven and Earth in Dutch). When Barry first arrived at Hemel and Aarde, he was appalled by the treatment and condition of the patients. The doctor found the patients weak and lying on the ground unable to move out of their own urine, feces, and vomit. They had no water and no food. Barry wrote, "It is cruel to the unfortunate Lepers if means be not taken for their benefit, and comfort, as well as to prevent the spreading of a Disease."[56] Note that Barry's first concern is the patients' benefit and comfort.

Barry was also angry over the societal injustice and the inherent racism that played out on the sick wards. Here is an excerpt of a letter he wrote to the administrator in charge of all of the army hospitals: "I beg leave to call your Lordship's attention to a circumstance which forcibly shocks me . . . the subjects sent to the Institution are all in advanced stage of the Disease:—it also appears that the generality of lepers are prize-negroes, or Hottentots, under Indenture, thus; not being actual (or valuable) property, their services are used as long as possible; and when they become useless in point of labour, and disgusting to the sight, they are sent to the Institution. . . . In the early stage of Leprosy much can be done."[57]

Barry notes that the patients were predominantly indentured servants, which meant that they were not slaves and therefore were not as valuable to the white landowners because they were technically not property. Just because they were not owned, though, does not mean that they were in a good situation. They were still forced to work for the white households throughout Cape Town *even while they were sick*. Barry called out his British peers on their inhumanity as they used up the laborers and then discarded them when they became too sick to work.

The Broad Scope of Barry's Reforms

Barry's ideas about hospital reform reached beyond the relatively narrow scope of Western medicine. Barry also advocated for what we would call today **holistic medicine,** the idea that the entire person and not just the disease should be considered and cared for. Beyond medicine, Barry's reforms had a much larger social justice agenda. As scholars have noted, "Barry's reforms were met with great opposition. There was no easy victory for him and more and more opposition was built up against him. But nothing daunted his determination to see a better and more humane medical service for *all* people of the Cape. His greatness became evident years after his demise."[58]

Barry's commitment to the humane treatment of patients extended to blowing the whistle on male hospital attendants who had been sexually assaulting and raping the women patients. As members of the hospital staff, the men presumed that nobody would believe the sick women, who were already stigmatized for being poor, for being women of color, and for being sick. In a letter to his superior officer, Barry wrote that he found the circumstances "disgusting" and "immediately hired a respectable woman of colour as Matron."[59] In effect, Barry fired the male attendants and hired a local woman of color, which was extraordinary in South Africa at the time. As one of Barry's biographers notes, "A clear sense of his disgust at the sexual economy of the civil hospital emerges. . . . Barry's righteous anger at the 'greatest irregularities' to which the female patients were subjected signifies a keen understanding of their extreme economic and social vulnerability, a vulnerability he was determined to correct."[60]

Barry's reforms in South Africa were just the beginning of his crusade for social justice. Wherever Dr. James Miranda Barry's military orders took him, he always fought the system to improve the conditions of people who had no social or political voice. He fought against the ways that Indigenous people in Jamaica were treated and worked to reverse the governmental neglect of the poorest Canadian foot soldiers. As Rachel Holmes, one of his South African biographers writes, "Millions of people . . . are still rocked by the legacy of colonialism, the effects of which Barry strove so ardently to ameliorate. Barry never truly belonged anywhere, but it was in his progressive desire to struggle against injustice and inequality that Barry finally can claim his belonging."[61]

The Good Doctor's Death

In 1865 Barry's own body passed into history as one of the most disputed corpses of the modern age.
RACHEL HOLMES [62]

On his last tour of duty, in Canada, Barry became very sick, and he was forced to return home to London. In 1865 he battled weight loss and dysentery, both worsened by the unexpected heat wave that hit London in July. There was no air conditioning in the nineteenth century, and Barry's income was so small that he might not have had a ceiling fan or even any windows to open. On 25 July 1865 Dr. James Miranda Barry died. He had specifically asked that his body not be stripped of clothing in preparation for burial, and, in fact, the only two beings who were allowed into his private quarters were his dog, Psyche, and his black man-servant, who in all the historic records is named only as "Black John." Nobody seems to know what happened to either the servant or the dog immediately following Barry's death.

Sophia Bishop, a charwoman (a menial housekeeper), did not get Barry's message. Out of respect for him and because of the terrible heat wave, she immediately stripped his body to wash and prepare him for burial. Bishop found what she identified as female genitalia; however, she apparently waited until after he was safely buried in Kensal Green Cemetery (where his bones still rest) before she went to the main military post at Horse Guards in London to relate her discovery.

The military tried to minimize the rumors about Barry's being "female," but the story swept through local, national, and international newspapers. Since then, many books, plays, television episodes, and films have sensationalized Barry's life. Interestingly, even while Barry was still alive, several people noted the possibility that he was cross-dressed. For example, in an 1829 diary entry, Mrs. Fenton, the wife of a British military man stationed on the island of Mauritius, talks about going for a walk around the island with her sickly newborn baby and her friend Dr. Barry. Mrs. Fenton writes, "There is certainly something extraordinary about . . . Dr. Barry."[63] She then recounts a story told to her by a friend who was a nurse in India who had a patient in desperate need of a doctor. In the middle of the night, the nurse ran in to Barry's room for help: "She ran . . . and made an unceremonious entrance into his room. Thereon he flew into a most violent passion. She declares, and steadily maintains, that . . . Dr. Barry *was* and *is a woman*."[64]

The First Woman Doctor in Great Britain?

Although Dr. James Miranda Barry lived every day of his very public life as a man, immediately following Sophia Bishop's revelation, numerous historians and advocates for women's rights rushed in to claim his womanhood. We need to consider why claiming Barry as a woman might be important for scholars interested in women's history.

The year that Barry died, a woman named Elizabeth Garrett Anderson fought against the British rules banning women from medical school. The male medical establishment was up in arms that a woman might enter their halls of higher learning: "A lady has penetrated to the core of our hospital system and is determined to effect a permanent lodgement. The advanced guard of the Amazonian army which has so often threatened our ranks . . . entered the camp."[65] This description may seem humorous, but women are still barred from becoming doctors in various locations around the world. Given this fierce defense against women entering the medical ranks, it is understandable that some feminist historians would want to argue that a woman—Dr. Barry—had already "penetrated to the core" of not just one but two all-male institutions: medicine and the military.

Barry's story was so infamous that a little over a decade after his death, in 1877, a Massachusetts newspaper ran an article that read: "Our woman physicians ought to hunt up the record of Dr. James Barry, who died in the English army in 1865, and make a biography. He was an army surgeon for fifty years, an inveterate smoker, and of so testy a temperament that he was always in trouble, and once fought a duel. He was an unusually skillful and bold surgeon, and at his death was first inspector general of hospitals. Dr. Barry was a woman, a fact discovered and officially announced the day after his (or her) death."[66]

It is understandable that people interested in researching and writing the histories of marginalized groups want to claim Dr. James Miranda Barry as an example of a brilliant and successful woman pioneer. It is crucial, however, that we look at the ways that Barry presented himself. From the age of eleven or twelve, he presented himself to the world as male. His reported fit of rage when the nurse stormed into his room unexpectedly, our lack of any record of his intimate physical relationships, and his last wish not to be stripped before burial all point to a person who was assigned female at birth but who identified as a man. In light of all his work and his obvious wishes, isn't it disrespectful to write about him as a woman? We now have so many histories of women pioneers. Perhaps, instead of considering Barry the "first female British physician," it would be more appropriate to consider him to be one of our first transgender physicians and social justice advocates.

One Last Image

How recently did you take a selfie? How many photographs of you exist? With the many ways to take photos today and to share moments from our day-to-day lives, any one photograph can easily fall to the wayside. Although you may still get dressed up for special photo opportunities, you probably have many more casual images of yourself than formal ones. In the nineteenth century, however, when photography was an exotic and new invention, very few people were photographed in casual clothes. Finding a photographer, dressing carefully, and then sitting for a long time to have your photo taken were seen as marking a special occasion.

FIGURE 8.4 "Frances Thompson in Front of the Congressional Committee," by Cameron Rains. This image of Frances Thompson, unlike the images of the three other historical figures in this chapter, illustrates the ways that her story was nearly completely silenced. Here, as a freed slave and a trans woman, she sits with her back to us and is placed below the white congressional leaders as she courageously calls out the white men in Memphis, Tennessee, who brutalized, raped, and murdered people in the African American community during the Memphis Massacre in 1866.

Only two photographs of Barry are known to exist. One was taken at Adolph Duperly & Son at 85 King Street in Kingston, Jamaica, and it is readily available online.[67] For this photo shoot, Barry chose to include his dog and his manservant. As mentioned earlier, these were also the only two beings that Dr. Barry allowed into his personal chambers. What does it mean that Barry included them in this formal photo?

Defending Her Community/Defending Herself: Frances Thompson

What can we learn about the thirty-six years of a person's life when we have only brief glimpses into moments of two of those thirty-six years? In 1866, a year after Dr. James Barry's death in London, Frances Thompson (figure 8.4) sat before a congressional committee and shared the following information about herself:

Q. What is your occupation? A. I sew, and take in washing and ironing.

Q. Have you been a slave? A. Yes, sir.

Q. Where were you raised? A. I was raised in Maryland. All our people but mistress got killed in the rebel army.

Q. Have you been injured? A. I am a cripple. [The witness used crutches.] I have a cancer in my foot.[68]

Unlike Dr. James Barry or the Chevalier/Chevalière d'Éon, Thompson was not a professional who held a government position. Nor was she a global traveler and adventurer like de Erauso. Yet Frances Thompson's journey from slavery on a Maryland plantation to living as a freedwoman in South Memphis, Tennessee, is no less extraordinary, given her historical context.[69]

Frances Thompson did not leave a diary or a journal discussing her gender identity or her gender presentation, as d'Éon and de Erauso did. In fact, there is a good chance that, having been a slave, she did not know how to read or write, because slaves were usually forbidden to do so.[70] Like Barry, however, Frances Thompson was written *about* because she also stood up to people in power and spoke out about injustice. In Frances Thompson's case, she was speaking up to defend her community, to defend herself, and to ask for justice.

A Short History of Memphis and the Civil War

Before the Civil War in the United States (1861–1865), Memphis, Tennessee, was home to a thriving slave market. A few free African American people lived in Memphis, along with numerous African American slaves, but Memphis did not have a centralized African American neighborhood, and community activities often had to operate underground.[71] In June 1862 the Union Army occupied the former Confederate stronghold. Almost instantly, thousands of African Americans migrated to Memphis because, with the occupation, slavery instantly became illegal within the city. With the Union occupation, the city became, relatively speaking, a safe space for former slaves.[72] Suddenly, a slave who could make it safely to Memphis could live there as a free person. Although freed people did not have any political rights in Memphis, they were no longer slaves.[73] Think about the experience of slaves who suddenly gained their freedom. At the same time, think about how local people who supported the Confederate Army reacted to the swiftly changing political and cultural landscape.

In a relatively short amount of time, South Memphis, which had been home to large numbers of upwardly mobile white residents, became a booming and bustling area for newly freed African Americans. The socioeconomic status of that part of the city changed rapidly with the influx of recently freed slaves, who were poor and unskilled.[74] Churches were built. Schoolhouses were established. Freed African American men and women started building a community, training for employment opportunities, and creating homes for themselves. Many of the men had arrived in South Memphis as the rank and file of the ten thousand African American Union soldiers stationed at Fort Pickering in Memphis.[75] But the white, predominantly Irish police force in South Memphis and the African American Union soldiers were often in conflict. Irish immigrants were frequently treated badly; in many cases, Irish people and African American people competed for unskilled labor jobs. The racial tensions reached a climax during the first week of May 1866.

The Memphis Massacre

Soon after dark the red glare of fire shot up in the southern part of the city. . . . Some thirty houses, occupied by negroes, every school-house for colored children, and every place of worship for the freedmen were given to the devouring element.

"THE MEMPHIS RIOTS," *HARPER'S WEEKLY*, 26 MAY 1866 [76]

What started out as yet another fight between the police and the soldiers blew up into a full-scale massacre throughout South Memphis (figure 8.5). By the time the fighting stopped, much of South Memphis was in ashes. All twelve schools that had served African American children were gone; ninety-one houses and cabins of newly freed people were destroyed; at least forty-eight African American people were killed, and nearly eighty more were wounded.[77] The police had randomly shot African American men, women, and children as they tried to flee.

Numerous African American women were home alone when the violence broke out. Many of them were widowed or single. In one case, a pregnant woman's husband was out of town on military duty. For three days, a group of white men composed of police officers, store owners, and other white male residents of South Memphis went from house to house terrorizing and raping the women. One of the houses they invaded was occupied by twenty-six-year-old Frances Thompson and her roommate, Lucy Smith. Smith was sixteen and had been a slave in Memphis before the Union Army's occupation.[78] The following is Frances Thompson's statement to the congressional committee regarding what happened on that fateful night:

> Between 1 and 2 o'clock, Tuesday night, seven men, two of whom were policemen, came to my house; I knew they were policemen by their stars . . . they said they must have supper, and asked me what I had, and said they must have some eggs and ham and biscuit; I made them some biscuit and some strong coffee, and they all sat down and eat; a girl lives with me; her name is Lucy Smith; she is about sixteen years old; when they had eaten supper they said they wanted some woman to sleep with; I said we were not that sort of women, and they must go. . . . One of them laid hold of me and

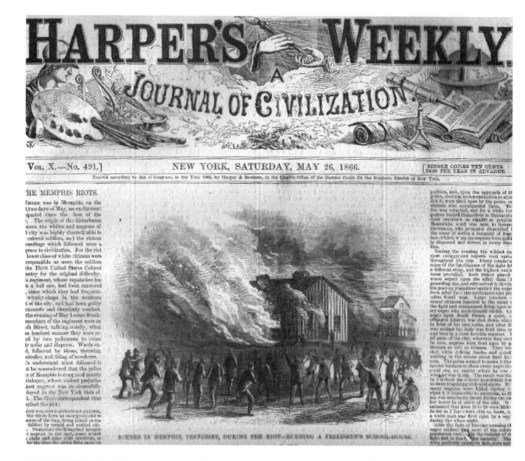

FIGURE 8.5 An African American schoolhouse burning in the Memphis Massacre, 1866, from *Harper's Weekly*. This image depicts the firebombing and destruction of the African American schoolhouse during the Memphis Massacre in 1866. *Harper's Weekly* was a pro-abolition northern newspaper focused on getting the truth of racial violence out to its readership.

hit me on the side of my face, and, holding my throat, choked me; Lucy tried to get out of the window, when one of them knocked her down and choked her; they drew their pistols and said they would shoot us and fire the house if we did not let them have their way with us; all seven of the men violated us two; four of them had to do with me, and the rest with Lucy.[79]

Before the men left, in a further fit of rage against Frances and Lucy specifically, and the Union Army more generally, they stole quilts that the two women had been making for the Union soldiers. Lucy Smith could not talk for two weeks because her throat and neck were damaged from the choking, and Frances Thompson was in bed sick with a fever for several days.[80]

Congressional Testimony

A group of Radical Republicans in Washington, D.C., horrified by the events, wanted to give the freed people in Memphis a public forum in which they could make formal complaints about the violence that they had suffered and survived. So, a month after the Memphis Massacre, in a conference room at Memphis's Gayoso House hotel on June 1, 1866, Frances Thompson, Lucy Smith, and several other women who had been raped and brutalized during the attack testified before three white U.S. congressmen. The historian Hannah Rosen discusses the importance of this event: "The more than 250 African Americans who came before these bodies to testify exercised a key right of citizenship still denied them in city and state courts. . . . African American women testifying that they had been raped was a radical act within the context of southern state law and tradition."[81]

Think about how nervous those women must have been. In their lifetimes, no white person with any real power had ever cared to hear what Frances Thompson, Lucy Smith, or, with a few exceptions like Frederick Douglass, any African American person had to say. Now three men from Congress were listening carefully and taking notes. After the congressional committee heard the accounts of the massacre, they made public pronouncements against the attackers. The newspapers in New York and other northern cities printed articles calling the attackers inhuman. Despite the congressional committee's findings, though, no legal charges were brought against the rapists. Memphis laws protecting the white police officers and store merchants were strong; but few, if any, Memphis laws protected the African American community. The Memphis Massacre and its aftermath captured national attention in the press during May and June 1866. Ten years later, in 1876, an unusual arrest made the Memphis Massacre front-page news across the United States again.

Frances Thompson's Arrest

In 1876 Frances Thompson was arrested on masquerading charges. There are conflicting stories about how the authorities came to the conclusion that she was cross-dressed. One of the stories is that a Memphis doctor *suspected* that she might be cross-dressed, and the suspicion validated her arrest and the subsequent strip search of her body.[82] A newspaper account claims that "suspicions of the officers" were the reasons for the arrest and that "several physicians were called in" and agreed that "Thompson was a man. He was made to don male garb and sentenced to the chain gang for 100 days."[83] Other southern newspapers, all of them white-owned, with a conservative white readership (in contrast to Radical Republican southern and northern newspapers and the emerging African American press), ran articles claiming that Thompson was a known local crook and had run **assignation houses** (brothels). Whether or not Thompson worked in the sex-work industry in Memphis is not the important point here. Claiming that she did provided a way for the conservative press to further denigrate her.

During her hundred-day sentence, Thompson was subjected to many forms of abuse. She was threatened with force if she did not let a team of medical men examine her body to prove to the public that she was a man dressed as a woman. The physicians went directly to the local newspapers to report their findings. With all the publicity, crowds gathered at the jail to catch a glimpse of Frances Thompson. One of the jail keepers even set up a show and took money by allowing spectators to see her wearing her men's prison outfit. She reported that the guards repeatedly sexually abused her.[84]

Political Fallout

The conservative press used Frances Thompson's arrest for cross-dressing to dig up the testimony given to the congressional committee ten years earlier. Even though none of the rapists from the Memphis Massacre was charged, conservative parties remained furious that their crimes had been made public. They used Thompson's genitals/anatomy instead of her clear gender identity to argue that she had lied to the public about being a woman. Therefore, they said, she must also be lying about having been raped and abused. Thompson's arrest for cross-dressing was used against *all* the women who testified. In other words, the conservatives used Frances Thompson's trans identity as a sign that everything she (and anyone associated with her) said was false. As a result, the conservative establishment argued that the African American women had not been raped ten years earlier. Underlying their argument was the wrong idea that men cannot be raped (because they were reading Thompson as a man). In some cases, the conservative Democratic newspapers "used these charges to condemn their Republican opponents" because the Republicans had supported the African American women who testified against their rapists.[85]

This leap in logic may seem ridiculous to us now, but the underlying argument is clear: *because* Frances Thompson cross-dressed and lived her life as a woman, she was a deceitful, untrustworthy, bad person. Even in 1876, the stereotype of the transgender person as a liar was evident, and many trans people continue to face this stereotype even today.

A Clearly Articulated Gender Identity

De Erauso and d'Éon wrote down their reasons for and their thoughts about cross-dressing and gender identity. As far as we know, Dr. Barry never wrote explicitly about his cross-dressing, although he clearly lived every day of his life from enrollment in medical school onward as a man. Even without a formal education, Frances Thompson still found a way to make public her ideas about her gender identity. She stood up in the face of ridicule and opposition in order to fight for her community and for herself.

Upon Frances Thompson's death shortly after her release from jail, her body, like d'Éon's, was stripped and examined, and the Memphis coroner reported that she was "anatomically male."[86] In other newspaper accounts, Thompson reportedly claimed that she was "double sexed," or someone with differences of sex development (DSD), and that she had worn girls' clothing since she was a child.[87] Frances Thompson clearly understood something about herself that we still grapple with in the twenty-first century: that her genital makeup had nothing to do with her gender identity. Frances Thompson saw herself as a woman. Frances Thompson was a woman.

It seems that Frances Thompson was respected and honored as an important member of the community of African American freed people in South Memphis. The moment she was released from jail, she moved to a cabin in North Memphis, presumably to get away from reporters. Members of the African American freed community found her sick and alone and took her to a hospital. She died there of dysentery on 1 November 1876.

If you consider the obstacles facing her, it seems miraculous that Frances Thompson's story can reach us now. As a trans woman of color—a freed slave—who found the strength to speak out against injustice, Frances Thompson left a legacy that can reach out to us now and help empower trans people.

How Are Incarcerated Trans People Treated Now?

Frances Thompson's treatment in 1876 is, sadly, not much different from the treatment of incarcerated trans people today. In the United States, trans people are forced into jails and prisons that match their sex assigned at birth and not their gender identity. In particular, trans women are often put into men's prisons, where they suffer at the hands of male prisoners and male guards. You may recall from Chapter 6 that the activist and pioneer Miss Major Griffin-Gracy is an African American trans woman who has been, in the twentieth and twenty-first centuries, subjected to the same treatment as Frances Thompson.[88]

What Is Written on the Body?

A birthmark, a scar on your knee, and the curve of your fingernails are all parts of your body, but they usually do not define you. They may help tell your story, but they do not encompass your entire being. Why, then, do we often use people's genitals to define them? For all four of the people we discussed in this chapter, their genitals wound up being *exactly* what defined them to a larger audience. It is clear, however, that their genitals did *not* define who they were to themselves. It is highly reductive to define someone solely on one physical characteristic. Of course, many cultures around the world do precisely that, defining persons on the basis of skin tone, any sort of physical difference, and, of course, their genitals.

Of the four people discussed in this chapter, Catalina/Don Antonio de Erauso had the most agency in revealing genitalia. The revelation was coerced; the choice was to show his genitals and submit to a full exam to prove virginity or face execution. De Erauso made the choice to reveal to a group of women in order to stay alive. To reward de Erauso for bravery and for remaining a virgin, the pope allowed de Erauso to choose to live fully as a man or as a woman. De Erauso lived out his later years as a mule driver and small merchant in Mexico. For d'Éon, Barry, and Thompson, though, the revelation of their genitals happened after they were dead.

Sadly, for both the Chevalier/Chevalière d'Éon and Frances Thompson, their bodies were disrespectfully violated after their deaths. In the case of d'Éon, several "men of science" and "medical experts" came to view and measure d'Éon's genitalia where the Chevalier/Chevalière's body was laid out.

Frances Thompson's body was violated in both life and death. From birth, Thompson's body was not her own because she was born into slavery in Maryland. Her body was put on display and ridiculed after her arrest. Frances Thompson was a trans woman. Frances Thompson was African American. Frances Thompson was poor. These parts of her life lined up in such a way that we can think of her as having no agency. Yet we need to remember her strength when she said she and Lucy Smith were "not that sort of women." After she died, Frances Thompson's body was, like d'Éon's, examined by authorities who found her to be "perfectly male."

The examination of d'Éon's and Thompson's bodies after their deaths in the name of scientific discovery dehumanizes them both. For Thompson, in particular, we are reminded that some trans women today, especially trans women of color, are still brutally violated in life as well as in death.

These four figures provide more historically complex case studies of gender variance before the twentieth century. D'Éon's and Thompson's stories suggest how the gender binary and inherent sexism still play out in the twenty-first century. After their deaths, they were ridiculed in ways that de Erauso and Barry were not. Crossing gender boundaries is still seen as a sensational topic for the tabloids. De Erauso and Barry, who were both assigned female at birth, traded up on the power ladder by dressing and living as men. Their decisions leave them open to ridicule, but they do not receive the same public condemnation that d'Éon and Thompson do. Underlying these reactions is the idea that it is understandable for a person assigned female at birth to want to be a man but deplorable for a person assigned male at birth to want to be a woman. These perceptions go directly back to the gender hierarchies that are deeply woven into the fabric of Western culture.

WRITINGS FROM THE COMMUNITY

MS. BOB DAVIS

How Do You Know What You're Seeing?

Ms. Bob Davis began writing about transgender history in community publications such as Lady Like, Transgender Community News, *and* Transgender Tapestry. *Many of these articles are available in the tgforum.com archive. Her article "Using Archives to Identify the Trans* Women of Casa Susanna" appeared in the "Archives and Archiving" issue of* Transgender Studies Quarterly, *published by Duke University Press. The short essay presented here is based on her illustrated lecture "Do the Clothes Fit? — Searching for Transgender Identity in Archival Images of Cross-Dressing," which premiered at the University of Victoria's "Moving Trans* History Forward" conference and was the opening keynote address at the Fortieth Annual Fantasia Fair. A collector of transgender publications and ephemera for almost forty years, Ms. Bob Davis is the founder and director of the Louise Lawrence Transgender Archive in Vallejo, California, lltransarchive.org.*

Finding archival photographs of cross-dressing isn't difficult. With a little perseverance, everything from posed nineteenth-century studio portraits or informal early twentieth-century Kodak Brownie snaps to midcentury color Polaroids are available at flea markets, paper fairs, and online. More challenging is deciding what you're seeing. Many of these gender transformations are no more than pleasant diversions, memories of a festive masquerade or community talent shows. But, undoubtedly, some are expressions of transgender identity.

Below are some guidelines that may be helpful when trying to identify transgender identity in archival images of cross-dressing. These guidelines were deduced by examining the photographic collections of self-identified transgendered women. There are common themes in these collections and, if enough of these themes are evident in the archival photos under examination, it may be that some form of transgender identity is being expressed.

Indications of Transgender Identity in Archival Photographs of Cross-Dressing

- Efforts to appear genuine in the gender of choice, even to the extent of being able to pass in public unnoticed.

- Personal collections of exclusively cross-dressing images.
- Collections or photo albums that include multiple images of cross-dressing done on multiple occasions and/or featuring multiple outfits, even if cross-dressing is not present in the majority of images.
- Solo portraits taken in a safe, private space.
- Group portraits taken in a safe, private space.

These common themes are evident in the personal photo collections of three self-identified, mid-twentieth-century transgender women. First is Susanna Valenti, who with her wife, Marie, owned a succession of small Catskill Mountain resorts, Chevalier d'Eon Resort, and later Casa Susanna, where men could cross-dress and safely express their feminine identity. A portion of Susanna's photographic archive was published as *Casa Susanna* in 2005.[89] Many of the photos in the book were taken at the resorts, but many were not. Those were sent to Susanna by people she met through the resort or her column, "Susanna Says," which ran for ten years, 1960–1970, in Virginia Prince's magazine *Transvestia*.[90]

The second archive was assembled by Bobbie Thompson, who appears on the cover of *Transvestia* no. 22, August 1963. Bobbie was a member of Phi Pi Epsilon (also known as the Foundation for Personal Expression, or FPE), the national male sorority. The third archive considered is contained in five scrapbooks compiled by a cross-dresser I can identify only as "Denise."[91] All three collections include photos shot at one of Susanna and Marie's resorts, as well as many taken elsewhere. Before the advent of the Internet, cross-dressers exchanged photographs of themselves in their trans identities through the mail. This exchange, this sharing of "the secret," was key to building trust in the early transgender community.

One striking element of Susanna's and Bobbie's collections is the dozens of photographs they have of themselves, photos taken over many years on multiple occasions and, of course, modeling many different outfits. Besides a large gender-transgressive wardrobe, these images demonstrate a continuity of transgender presentation and a desire to document it, for both themselves and others. Bobbie's collection includes several poses of her in an off-the-shoulder dress, but there's one pose she must have liked in particular because she had an eight-by-ten-inch enlargement and over a dozen five-by-seven-inch copies. The smaller photos she shared with her trans women friends, and they in turn shared their images with her.

In her collection Bobbie has twenty-two photographs of her friend Sheila Norris, *Transvestia*'s longtime literary editor. In them Sheila models a variety of outfits. The photos are in several different formats and were taken at different locations, which implies they were taken on different occasions. Multiple images of multiple outfits on multiple occasions taken over an extended period is a clear indication of transgender identity in photographs. It's true of Bobbie, Sheila, and Susanna. It's true of me.

Another key element that separates these images from those of the Halloween masquerader or Mardi Gras reveler is the desire to "pass," to be authentic in the gender of choice. In all three collections, clothing styles are conservative and color-coordinated; all is consistent with the norms of dress for middle-class women in the mid-twentieth century. The shoes match the purse and the purse matches the gloves. Needless to say, the clothes fit well and often appear tailored. Every effort is made so they could pass unnoticed while window shopping on a sunny afternoon or walking in the park. The intention is to express gender, not burlesque it.

There's only one person in the vast majority of these photographs, a lone cross-dresser, sometimes in an anonymous motel room, with the drapes drawn. Even when the room appears many times in the collection, a place where transgender photos were posed again and again, the drapes are drawn. These are safe spaces, private spaces, where inner lives are revealed. Bobbie and another cross-dresser, Betty Wharton, rented a room in a Rochester, New York, boardinghouse, a place where they felt safe enough to explore their feminine selves. Susanna and Marie created several transgender safe havens. Besides their succession of resorts, they also ran the Chevalier d'Eon Club out of their six-room apartment in New York City, where men could unpack the secret suitcase they kept hidden in the trunk of their cars and dress for a night on the town *en femme*.[92]

The guidelines above can be tested by applying them to a collection of photos where the original owner/compiler is unknown as well as photo collections of cross-dressed women. If enough of the guidelines are met, will it make a convincing case for the possible presence of the subject's transgender identity? The collection we'll examine was purchased at a paper fair in 2013. It's made of 104 unbound pages from a hundred-year-old photo album from Nebraska. There are three hundred photos remaining; many were removed before the sale. Over half of the photos are of children. Forty are portraits, probably friends and family members. The next-largest category is eighteen photographs of cross-dressed women. That's more than photos of fishing (sixteen), a train wreck (seven), or a flood (twelve).

The cross-dressing photos divide into four sets. The first is two photos of three women wearing men's hats, jackets, and shirts without ties. One sports a derby and smokes a cigar. The other two wear caps. The caption reads, "Pickled," which explains the cross-dressing as a harmless, inebriated masquerade. On the other side of the page begins a ten-photo series titled "A Mock Wedding Feb. 6th 1916 Ithaca Neb."

FIGURE 8.6 Nebraskan cross-dressed couple, circa 1916. Credit: Louise Lawrence Transgender Archive. The two people portrayed in this archival photograph were, presumably, assigned female at birth. They are both depicted here, however, as young men dressed in dapper clothing and posing for the camera. This photo is from an album that is part of a collection of trans archival images from rural Nebraska taken in the early twentieth century. We have no information about the photographer or about the people posing for the images.

The cigar-smoking woman from the previous shots is the groom, now sporting a paper moustache and goatee. Two photos are of the ceremony posed with a third, much taller woman as minister. There are five shots taken after the ceremony; the bride is in a dark jacket and hat, both trimmed in white, and the groom is wearing his derby. The groom gleefully engages in traditional male behavior. In one shot the bride is seated in an armchair; the groom, sitting above her on the chair's arm, is pawing her jacket. In another she's sitting on his lap.

The third set is four exterior shots. The cigar-smoking groom is whittling in one, posed with the tall woman, the former minister, in two others. Both are wearing suits and men's caps, but no neckties. In one they're under an umbrella and the groom tenderly lays her cheek against the taller woman's hand (figure 8.6).

The last is a set of two, also exterior and possibly shot on a different day. Certainly, they are exposed very differently from the other photos. The groom, the focus of our inquiry, is cross-dressed. She's with a woman dressed in long plaid skirt and wearing a shawl. Perhaps it's the taller woman from the other photos? The groom continues the traditional male/female relations. In one

FIGURE 8.7 Tall cross-dresser, circa 1930s. Credit: Louise Lawrence Transgender Archive. This image, which also lacks the photographer's and the subject's names, depicts someone presumably assigned male at birth but who is cross-dressed in a white dress for the occasion of the photo opportunity. What can we learn about someone's identity by archival images like these?

photo he's tickling the taller woman's chin. In the other, the taller woman is sitting on the groom's lap.

Because the groom is a woman who cross-dresses on multiple occasions and was photographed in multiple outfits, and because of the relatively large number of cross-dressing photos in the collection, I believe that cross-dressing was more than a comic masquerade to the woman who played the groom. And, though it is impossible to know, the guidelines suggest a transgender identity.

Sometimes, when an entire collection of photos isn't available, even one or two can convey a sense of identity, though the judgment is, of course, more subjective. I have a set of three small black-and-white images, three poses of a tall cross-dresser, possibly from the 1930s, wearing a white dress that looks homemade (see figure 8.7). The cuffs are trimmed with black ribbons, which match her black hat, black belt, and black open-toed shoes. Around her neck there's a pendant on a delicate chain. She expresses femininity awkwardly, but that doesn't appear to be how she feels about being able to express it. She looks like she is enjoying herself. There aren't any windows or exterior doors in the images and no sense that she is going anywhere. She's not dressed for the ball or for the stage. She's dressed to enjoy her femininity in a safe and private space.

Key Concepts

assignation house (p. 302)
holistic medicine (p. 293)
pass (p. 270)
sumptuary laws (p. 270)
surtout (p. 289)

Activities, Discussion Questions, and Observations

1. Ms. Bob Davis's "Writings from the Community" piece works with photographic archives that depict cross-dressing in different situations. What are your thoughts about the various ways she has broken them down into categories? Would her categories work for the four persons whose histories we discussed in this chapter? Why or why not?

2. Closely examine the two photographic images included with Ms. Bob's selection and compare them to Ms. Bob's argument. What else do you see in the images? If you came across these images in a different context, what would you notice without having read about them in this book? Now see if you can find a photo that you are unfamiliar with in an old family album. If you do not have an old family album, you can find a random image online or at a garage sale. What do you see there?

3. Historians who have written about Catalina de Erauso, the Chevalier/Chevalière d'Éon, Dr. James Miranda Barry, and Frances Thompson have made different choices concerning gender and pronouns. For example, Hannah Rosen, a historian who has researched extensively the life of Frances Thompson, states clearly that she refers to Thompson with the pronoun "she" because that was how Thompson identified. Because Frances Thompson's story has only recently been discovered, we do not yet see modern-day scholars contradicting Rosen. With regard to the other three persons, though, historians disagree on pronoun usage. D'Éon is almost always referred to as "he." Barry and de Erauso are more often than not referred to as "she." Which pronoun(s) would you use when writing about each of these people? Why?

4. This chapter discusses four individuals who cross-dressed to express their gender identity to themselves and to the world. The following is a list of other people throughout history who cross-dressed. Pick one of them to research. What did you find out? Did they cross-dress at a specific time in their lives for

a specific purpose? Was their cross-dressing more permanent, a daily occurrence? At what point did cross-dressing for a specific time and purpose become more permanent? At what point does the cross-dressing indicate what today we would call a trans identity?

- Valerie Arkell-Smith/Colonel Barker
- Joan of Arc
- Thomas Ernest Boulton (Stella) and Frederick Park (Fanny)
- Willmer Broadnax (Little Ax)
- Charley Parkhurst
- Wong Ah Choy
- Mary Read
- Peter Sewally (Mary Jones)
- Mary Anne Talbot
- Hannah Snell

5. Below are two excerpts from pieces published in 1876. In the first, George Thomas, Earl of Albemarle, recounts his meeting with Dr. James Barry. Albemarle's memoir was written after the general public learned about the char-woman's discovery when she undressed Barry to prepare his body for burial. The second is a portion of a newspaper article originally published in the *Memphis Appeal* regarding Frances Thompson after she was arrested on masquerading charges. Conduct a close reading of the two pieces. Be sure to look up any words that are confusing because they can help you better understand the tone and context of the pieces. How do the authors view Barry and Thompson? What words are used to describe them? Are they positive or negative? What stereotypes about trans people are being established? In the Thompson piece, what are some of the intersecting identities described? How are these identities used? What is your overall impression of the two pieces? Which one is more damaging? Why? How could each be rewritten in a more respectful way?

From Albemarle's *Fifty Years of My Life:*

There was at this time at the Cape a person whose eccentricities attracted universal attention—Dr. James Barry. . . . I . . . sat next to him at dinner at one of the regimental messes. . . . I beheld a beardless lad, apparently about my own age, with an unmistakable Scotch type of countenance—reddish hair, high cheek bones. There was a certain effeminacy in his manner, which he always seemed striving to overcome. . . . While at the Cape he fought a duel, and was considered to be of a most quarrelsome disposition. He was frequently guilty of flagrant breaches of discipline. . . . The Times one day announced the death of Dr. Barry, and the next day it was officially reported to the Horse Guards that the doctor was a woman. It is singular that neither the landlady of her lodging nor the black servant who had lived with her for years, had the slightest suspicion of her sex.[93]

"Under False Colors"
A Colored Man Who Has Successfully Passed as a Woman for Twenty-seven Years

Frances Thompson (colored) better known as "Aunt Crutchie," who for the past twenty-seven years has gone about this city in female garb, was arrested yesterday, and after medical examination was pronounced a member of the male sex. The quartette of medical experts who worked upon the case also discovered that the dusky Thompson's lower limbs were as crooked as a young dogwood tree or a ram's horn. This deformity served as an excuse for the pretended female cripple to promenade the streets on crutches. Thompson is well known to the people of this city as a low minded criminal of the most revolting character. The recorder imposed a fine of $50 upon the prisoner. Not being able to pay the fine a lot of male toggery was put upon the impecunious Thompson, and he was sent out on the chain gang to work the streets. An immense crowd of curious idling people collected about to see the changed figure of the thick lipped, foul mouthed scamp, and finding it impossible to drive them off, Thompson was sent to the lock up again. Known then as Miss Frances Thompson, this person testified before the Washington Congressional Committee to have been outraged a number of times during the Memphis riots soon after the war. Her evidence appears at length in the official report. It is just probable that Mr. Thompson lied.[94]

6. Think back to times you've been asked to tell your "story" for a particular audience—for example, (a) a personal statement for college or a scholarship; (b) an interview with a new or potential roommate; (c) a first date. What you talk about depends on your audience. Chances are, you presented a "you" that emphasized certain strengths. How did you actively select your details and shape your story? What did you leave out? Why? Now, think back to de Erauso and d'Éon and what we know about their reasons for publishing their memoirs. How do you think their audiences influenced the details they included? How did the audience influence the framing of their stories? In d'Éon's case, you have more than one memoir to consider.

Film and Television of Interest

Amazing Graces—Dr. Barry, the Female Doctor in the All-Male British Army (2014, Ireland, 12 minutes)

This YouTube video from the Irish Audio Project covers the life of Dr. James Miranda Barry with historic facts and excellent visuals. Although the video does sensationalize the charwoman's claims about Barry's genitals, it focuses more on the fact that Barry made major and lasting medical reforms in South Africa.

Catalina de Erauso, La Monja Alférez (Año 1592) (2016, Spain, 23 minutes)

Catalina de Erauso's life is explored in this short YouTube video. The video is in Spanish.

Le Chevalier d'Eon (2006, Japan, TV, 28 minutes per episode)

D'Éon's life has captured the imagination of Japanese writers in the twenty-first century, and this twenty-four-episode anime television series follows d'Éon's adventures as a spy and a hero.

Memphis Massacre 1866 Panel 2 (2016, U.S., 80 minutes)

This outstanding YouTube video captures an academic panel at a conference exploring the ramifications of race riots in the nineteenth century in the United States. The presentations are given by African American historians and scholars. This video is an outstanding place to hear about the current academic work being done on reexamining this hidden history.

Memphis Massacre: We Remember with Antonio Neal (2016, U.S., 7 minutes)

The modern Memphis historian Antonio Neal discusses the history of the massacre of African Americans in 1866 in this YouTube video.

Memphis Riots of 1866 (2013, U.S., 5 minutes)

This YouTube video contains excellent archival images of Memphis and the 1866 riots as well as photographs of the African American community in the city at that time. The photos are accompanied by music, but there is no dialogue.

La Monja Alférez (1944, México; U.S. release 1945, 88 minutes)

In this dramatization of the life of Catalina de Erauso, the filmmaker focuses on the sensational aspects of de Erauso's life story. It is filmed in black and white and is in Spanish.

Rebel (2013, U.S., 73 minutes)

This documentary explores the life of Loreta Janeta Velázquez, a nineteenth-century figure who cross-dressed in order to fight in the Civil War as a Confederate soldier. The film looks at the ways that history is erased because, until recently, her writing was seen as merely a hoax.

Le Secret du Chevalier d'Éon (1959, France, 96 minutes)

This French film explores the life of d'Éon as a comedy and sensationalizes d'Éon's life. It is a good film to compare to the sensationalized film focusing on de Erauso (*La Monja Alférez*) because it underscores a stereotype: when people understood to be men are cross-dressed, it is comedy; but when women are cross-dressed, it can be not only comedy but also adventure.

NOTES

1. Faiza Zerouala, "Headscarf Ban Turns France's Muslim Women towards Home-working," *Guardian,* 3 October 2014, https://www.theguardian.com/world/2014/oct/03/france-muslim-women-home-working (accessed 13 January 2017).

2. For excellent analyses of these sumptuary laws, see Marjorie Garber's *Vested Interests: Cross-Dressing and Cultural Anxiety* (1991; repr., New York: HarperPerennial, 1993), 392–393.

3. In the French language, as with all Romance languages, the spellings of words fall within a binary of masculine and feminine. D'Éon's name is spelled both ways in various newspaper accounts throughout d'Éon's life as well as after d'Éon's death. The masculine is Chevalier. The feminine is Chevalière. When I refer to d'Éon with the more formal moniker, I use both: Chevalier/Chevalière. I also use the neutral pronoun "they" when referring to d'Éon because that has been the pronoun used by present-day writers wishing to convey respect for d'Éon and because d'Éon clearly embraced masculinity and femininity. In the case of de Erauso, I use masculine pronouns because it becomes obvious that de Erauso fully chose to be male; he did not find comfort in identifying as a woman.

4. Catalina de Erauso, *Lieutenant Nun: Memoir of a Basque Transvestite in the New World,* trans. Michele Stepto and Gabriel Stepto (Boston: Beacon Press, 1996), 4.

5. Ibid., 4.

6. Ibid., 6.

7. Ibid., 19.

8. Ibid., 64.

9. Ibid., 65.

10. Ibid., 66.

11. Ibid., 78.

12. Heidi Zogbaum, *Catalina de Erauso: The Lieutenant Nun and the Conquest of the New World* (North Melbourne: Australian Scholarly, 2015), 121.

13. Eva Mendieta, *In Search of Catalina de Erauso: The National and Sexual Identity of the Lieutenant Nun,* trans. Angeles Prado (Reno: Center for Basque Studies, University of Nevada, 2009), 195–196.

14. De la Valle quoted ibid., 199–200.

15. Ibid., 200.

16. Nicholas Cullinan, *Director's Trail* (brochure) (London: National Portrait Gallery, 2016), 2.

17. Havelock Ellis, *Studies in the Psychology of Sex,* vol. 7, *Eonism and Other Supplementary Studies* (Philadelphia: F. A. Davis, 1928), 26–27.

18. "Charles, Chevalier d'Éon de Beaumont," https://www.britannica.com/biography/Charles-chevalier-dEon-de-Beaumont (accessed 26 February 2017).

19. Charles d'Éon de Beaumont, *The Maiden of Tonnerre: The Vicissitudes of the Chevalier and the Chevalière d'Eon,* ed. and trans. Roland A. Champagne, Nina Ekstein, and Gary Kates (Baltimore: Johns Hopkins University Press, 2001).

20. Ibid., xiii.

21. Ibid.

22. D'Éon's two letters appear in Frédéric Gaillardet, *Memoirs of the Chevalier d'Éon,* trans. Antonia White (London: Anthony Blond, 1970), 220–221; emphasis in original.

23. "London, Saturday June 22," *Reading (England) Mercury and Oxford Gazette,* 24 June 1771, 3.

24. D'Éon de Beaumont, *The Maiden of Tonnerre,* xv.

25. Gaillardet, *Memoirs of the Chevalier d'Éon,* vii.

26. D'Éon de Beaumont, *The Maiden of Tonnerre,* 3.

27. Ibid., xviii.

28. "Duellists in Petticoats," *Leeds (England) Times,* 25 May 1895, 4.

29. "For One Night Only," *Chester (England) Chronicle,* 27 March 1795, 3.

30. Gaillardet, *Memoirs of the Chevalier D'Eon,* xx–xxi.

31. "Postscript," *Norfolk Chronicle; or, The Norwich (England) Gazette,* 26 May 1810, 2.

32. "Chevalier d'Eon," *Cheltenham (England) Chronicle and Gloucestershire Advertiser,* 31 May 1810, 89.

33. D'Éon de Beaumont, *The Maiden of Tonnerre,* x.

34. Ibid., xix. The editors have translated the entire text, which appears as the third section of their English translation and publication of D'Éon's autobiographical writings.

35. Ibid.

36. Ibid., 142; emphasis added.

37. Percy Ward Laidler and Michael Gelfand, *South Africa: Its Medical History, 1652–1898* (Cape Town: C. Struik, 1971), 132.

38. Archived material from Edinburgh Medical School, "James Barry," https://www.ed.ac.uk/medicine-vet-medicine/about/history/women/james-barry (accessed 11 April 2018).

39. Isobel Rae, *The Strange Story of Dr. James Barry, Army Surgeon, Inspector-General of Hospitals, Discovered on Death to Be a Woman* (London: Longman's, Green, 1958), 2.

40. June Rose, *The Perfect Gentleman: The Remarkable Life of Dr. James Miranda Barry, the Woman Who Served as an Officer in the British Army from 1813 to 1859* (London: Hutchinson, 1977), 17.

41. Ibid., 22.

42. Rae, *Strange Story of Dr. James Barry,* 10–13.

43. Rose, *The Perfect Gentleman,* 27.

44. "Hospitals," *London Lives, 1690 to 1800—Crime, Poverty and Social Policy in the Metropolis,* https://www.londonlives.org/static/Hospitals.jsp (accessed 6 March 2017).

45. Rose, *The Perfect Gentleman,* 27–28.

46. Rachel Holmes, *Scanty Particulars: The Life of Dr James Barry* (London: Viking, 2002), 4.

47. Laidler and Gelfand, *South Africa,* 140.

48. Ibid., 153.

49. Ibid.

50. Ibid., 140.

51. Ibid., 152.

52. Ibid., 157.

53. Rose, *The Perfect Gentleman,* 40.

54. Ibid., 38. These terms all refer to various groups of people of color from several Indigenous tribes and groups racially categorized by the Dutch and the British in South Africa.

55. Laidler and Gelfand, *South Africa,* 159.

56. Holmes, *Scanty Particulars,* 118–119.

57. Quoted ibid., 112–113.

58. Laidler and Gelfand, *South Africa*, 160; emphasis added.

59. Holmes, *Scanty Particulars*, 214.

60. Ibid., 214.

61. Ibid., 326.

62. Ibid., 3.

63. Bessie Knox Fenton (Mrs. Fenton), *The Journal of Mrs. Fenton: A Narrative of Her Life in India, the Isle of France (Mauritius), and Tasmania during the Years 1826–1830* (London: Edward Arnold, 1901), 323.

64. Ibid., 324; emphasis in original.

65. Holmes, *Scanty Particulars*, 261. Holmes is quoting from an article in the *Lancet*.

66. "Our Woman Physicians Ought to Hunt Up the Record of Dr. James Barry," *Lowell (Mass.) Daily Citizen*, 3 December 1877.

67. Holmes, *Scanty Particulars*, 254–255.

68. "Under False Colors," *Memphis Appeal*, reprinted in *St. Louis Globe-Democrat*, 15 July 1876, 5. The newspaper reprinted some of the congressional transcript from the previous decade. Although the 1876 article is quite derogatory, the newspaper did publish the record of the proceedings. In many cases with the people discussed in this chapter, crucial biographical information is included in derogatory writings. Marginalized groups often have to find their stories within derogatory pieces written by people from the dominant culture.

69. Hannah Rosen, *Terror in the Heart of Freedom: Citizenship, Sexual Violence, and the Meaning of Race in the Postemancipation South* (Chapel Hill: University of North Carolina Press, 2009), 61.

70. It is possible that after she was freed, she was able to learn to read and write. Her level of literacy is one of the details of her life that has been lost to history.

71. Rosen, *Terror*, 29.

72. Hannah Rosen, "'Not That Sort of Women': Race, Gender, and Sexual Violence during the Memphis Riot of 1866," in *Sex, Love, Race: Crossing Boundaries in North American History*, ed. Martha Hodes (New York: New York University Press, 1999), 269.

73. Ibid.

74. Rosen, *Terror*, 62.

75. Ibid., 29.

76. "The Memphis Riots," *Harper's Weekly*, 26 May 1866, 322. Note that today some of the terminology referring to African American people here is offensive and certainly outdated. *Harper's* was a northern magazine that was supportive of the Union and of the abolition of slavery. At the time this was published, the term *Negroes* was actually seen as the respectful one; even the term *colored* was not as offensive as it is now.

77. Rosen, *Terror*, 62.

78. Rosen, "'Not That Sort of Women,'" 275.

79. "Under False Colors," 5.

80. Ibid.

81. Rosen, *Terror*, 76–77.

82. Ibid., 235.

83. "A Sensation at Memphis," *St. Louis Globe-Democrat*, 12 July 1876, n.p.

84. Rosen, *Terror*, 237.

85. Ibid., 236. See also Susan Stryker, "To Appear as We Please," *Aperture* 229 (2017): 32–35.

86. Rosen, *Terror*, 238.

87. Ibid.

88. TGI Justice, http://www.tgijp.org/mission-and-staff.html (accessed 15 February 2017).

89. Michel Hurst and Robert Swope, *Casa Susanna* (Brooklyn, N.Y.: powerHouse Books, 2005).

90. Susanna Valenti's photos are now part of

the collection of the Art Gallery of Ontario in Toronto, Canada. Over three hundred can be viewed at the Digital Transgender Archive, www.digitaltransgenderarchive.net.

91. Bobbie Thompson's archive and Denise's scrapbooks are in the collection of the Louise Lawrence Transgender Archive.

92. Susanna Valenti, "Susanna Says," *Transvestia* 2 (March 1960): 15–19.

93. George Thomas, Earl of Albemarle, *Fifty Years of My Life* (New York: Henry Holt, 1876), 144.

94. "Under False Colors," *Pulaski (Tenn.) Citizen,* 20 July 1876.

BIBLIOGRAPHY

Bevan, Margaret. *Dr. James Barry, 1795?–1865, Inspector-General of Military Hospitals: A Bibliography.* Johannesburg: Johannesburg Public Library, 1966.

"Chevalier d'Eon." *Cheltenham (England) Chronicle and Gloucestershire Advertiser,* 31 May 1810.

Cullinan, Nicholas. *Director's Trail.* Brochure. London: National Portrait Gallery, 2016.

De Erauso, Catalina. *Lieutenant Nun: Memoir of a Basque Transvestite in the New World.* Translated from the Spanish by Michele Stepto and Gabriel Stepto. Boston: Beacon Press, 1996.

D'Éon de Beaumont, Charles. *The Maiden of Tonnerre: The Vicissitudes of the Chevalier and the Chevalière d'Eon.* Edited by Roland A. Champagne, Nina Ekstein, and Gary Kates. Baltimore: Johns Hopkins University Press, 2001.

"Duellists in Petticoats." *Leeds (England) Times,* 25 May 1895.

Ellis, Havelock. *Studies in the Psychology of Sex,* vol. 7, *Eonism and Other Supplementary Studies.* Philadelphia: F. A. Davis, 1928.

Fenton, Bessie Knox (Mrs. Fenton). *The Journal of Mrs. Fenton: A Narrative of Her Life in India, the Island of France (Mauritius), and Tasmania during the Years 1826–1830.* London: Edward Arnold, 1901.

"For One Night Only." *Chester (England) Chronicle,* 27 March 1795.

Gaillardet, Frédéric. *Memoirs of Chevalier d'Éon.* Translated by Antonia White. London: Anthony Blond, 1970.

Garber, Marjorie. *Vested Interests: Cross-Dressing and Cultural Anxiety.* 1991. Reprint. New York: HarperPerennial, 1993.

Hamish. "Dr. James Miranda Barry." *The Drummer's Revenge: LGBT History and Politics in Canada,* 2 December 2007. https://thedrummersrevenge.wordpress.com/2007/12/02/dr-james-miranda-barry/. Accessed 15 February 2017.

Holmes, Rachel. *Scanty Particulars: The Life of Dr James Barry.* London: Viking, 2002.

"Hospitals." *London Lives 1690 to 1800—Crime, Poverty and Social Policy in the Metropolis.* https://www.londonlives.org/static/Hospitals.jsp. Accessed 6 March 2017.

Hurst, Michel, and Robert Swope. *Casa Susanna.* Brooklyn, N.Y.: powerHouse Books, 2005.

"James Barry." Edinburgh Medical School. https://www.ed.ac.uk/medicine-vet-medicine/about/history/women/james-barry. Accessed 11 April 2018.

Laidler, Percy Ward, and Michael Gelfand. *South Africa: Its Medical History, 1652–1898.* Cape Town: C. Struik, 1971.

"London, Saturday June 22." *Reading (England) Mercury and Oxford Gazette,* 24 June 1771.

"The Memphis Riots." *Harper's Weekly,* 26 May 1866, 322.

Mendieta, Eva. *In Search of Catalina de Erauso: The National and Sexual Identity of the Lieutenant Nun.* Translated by Angeles Prado. Reno: Center for Basque Studies, University of Nevada, 2009.

"Our Woman Physicians Ought to Hunt Up the Record of Dr. James Barry." *Lowell (Mass.) Daily Citizen,* 3 December 1877.

"Postscript." *Norfolk (England) Chronicle; or, The Norwich Gazette,* 26 May 1810.

Rae, Isobel. *The Strange Story of Dr. James Barry, Army Surgeon, Inspector-General of Hospitals, Discovered on Death to Be a Woman.* London: Longman's, Green, 1958.

Rose, June. *The Perfect Gentleman: The Remarkable Life of Dr. James Miranda Barry, the Woman Who Served as an Officer in the British Army from 1813 to 1859.* London: Hutchinson, 1977.

Rosen, Hannah. "'Not That Sort of Women': Race, Gender, and Sexual Violence during the Memphis Riot of 1866." In *Sex, Love, Race: Crossing Boundaries in North American History,* edited by Martha Hodes, 267–293. New York: New York University Press, 1999.

———. *Terror in the Heart of Freedom: Citizenship, Sexual Violence, and the Meaning of Race in the Postemancipation South.* Chapel Hill: University of North Carolina Press, 2009.

"A Sensation at Memphis." *St. Louis Globe-Democrat,* 12 July 1876.

Stryker, Susan. "To Appear as We Please." *Aperture* 229 (2017): 32–35.

TGI Justice. www.tgijp.org/mission-and-staff.html. Accessed 15 February 2017.

Thomas, George, Earl of Albemarle. *Fifty Years of My Life.* New York: Henry Holt, 1876.

"Under False Colors." *Pulaski (Tenn.) Citizen,* 20 July 1876.

"Under False Colors." *St. Louis Globe-Democrat* [reprinted from the *Memphis Appeal*], 15 July 1876.

Upton, Emily. "The First British Surgeon to Perform a Successful C-Section Was a Woman Disguised as a Man." *Today I Found Out: Feed Your Brain,* 1 November 2013. www.todayifoundout.com/index.php/2013/11/first-british-surgeon-perform-successful-c-section-woman-disguised-man/. Accessed 2 February 2017.

Zerouala, Faiza. "Headscarf Ban Turns France's Muslim Women towards Homeworking." *Guardian,* 3 October 2014, https://www.theguardian.com/world/2014/oct/03/france-muslim-women-home-working. Accessed 13 January 2017.

Zogbaum, Heidi. *Catalina de Erauso: The Lieutenant Nun and the Conquest of the New World.* North Melbourne: Australian Scholarly Publishing, 2015.

CHAPTER 9

Cross-Dressing and Political Protest
Parasols and Pitchforks

Key Questions

1. The combination of the festival, carnival, and protest has existed for centuries around the world. How has this combination changed over the centuries? How has it remained the same?

2. How can we understand gender and gender roles, as well as the role of cultural context, in cross-dressed protests and riots? What similarities do we see between times and places as diverse as rural western England in the seventeenth century and urban Tehran, Iran, in the twenty-first century?

3. How have riots or protests with a cross-dressing component helped change or reinforce laws and social policy?

4. What is the role of humor in protests featuring cross-dressing?

Chapter Overview

The first section of this chapter explores the protests and riots throughout England and Wales over the course of three centuries. The poor farmers, artisans, and manual laborers who planned and took part in these protests and riots often used aspects of folk customs that were specific to their village or region—for example, "rough music" or "skimmingtons" in rural England and *ceffyl pren* in Wales. These small villages and communities often governed and policed their own moral and ethical codes. Most of the people in these communities, however, had no voting rights (they did not live in a democracy) and therefore no political power. Protests and riots became their only recourse for achieving social and economic justice. Protesters often cross-dressed to express their disapproval of policies, such as inflated grain, food, and housing prices,

Haefele-Thomas, Ardel, *Introduction to Transgender Studies*
dx.doi.org/10.17312/harringtonparkpress/2019.01.itts.009
© 2019 by Harrington Park Press

that threatened them with starvation and homelessness. These policies were often put in place by royalty or the landed gentry.

In these cross-dressing riots, gender transgressions had a specific purpose and occurred for a limited amount of time. The working-poor rioters and protesters donned clothing that was not "appropriate" to their gender. But the men did not wear women's nightdresses and bonnets in order to pass as women, nor did the women who wore men's coveralls do so in order to pass as men. In fact, the protesters wanted to look outlandish and humorous; they were not interested in passing, but they *purposefully* transgressed the gender binary. Their specific reasons for crossing the binary were unique to each protest.

The second section of this chapter moves into the late twentieth and early twenty-first centuries to explore protests that used cross-dressing and humor to make a political point. In Boulder, Colorado, in the 1990s a group of cross-dressing protesters known as "The Ladies" or "Ladies in Support of the President" (LISP) appeared over a two-year period at various events, ranging from antiwar protests to rallies in support of LGBTQ+ rights and women's rights. These peaceful protestors used cross-dressing satirically to point to social inequalities. In the twenty-first century, a group of men in Iran have launched a social media campaign in which they take selfies and videos of themselves in their wives', sisters', or mothers' hijabs to protest Iran's rigid clothing restrictions, which have been in place for the last few decades. Their actions protest not only the clothing itself, but also the restrictions on women's rights in Iran.

The protests and riots explored in this chapter have one thing in common: the cross-dressing took place to protest and/or riot against political and socioeconomic power being exerted over groups of disempowered people. The cross-dressing in these riots used, or uses, humor to raise awareness about serious issues of social inequality and injustice.

Introduction: Inverting the Social Order

It is crucial for us to understand the *situation* and *context* as we explore various reasons for cross-dressing. In all cases of cross-dressing, even if the goal is sheer entertainment, the gender binary gets transgressed. Of course, not all cross-dressing points to trans identity, but the gender disruptions caused by cross-dressing can be subtle and complex. The four historic figures discussed in Chapter 8 cross-dressed because this was the only way they could live from day to day in the gender with which they identified. The clothing really did make the person. In this chapter, however, the cross-dressing is not permanent; it is meant, very specifically, to be disruptive and to make a political point.

Let's say you are reading an assigned book on English politics and the working class for your history course. Somewhere in the middle of this long text, you read a short paragraph that grabs your attention. The author discusses a working-class revolt in which men used sledgehammers to destroy new machinery, which factory owners had purchased to replace the laborers. The workers destroying the machines were wearing their wives' or mothers' clothing, and they called themselves "General Ludd's wives." Suddenly, you are wide awake and rereading to make sure you understood the passage. These industrial laborers cross-dressed as part of their protest against the machines and the factory owners. Why? You continue reading to see if your questions will be answered, but they are not. When you ask your history professor about General Ludd's wives, he dismisses your question with a quick answer: "Oh, they were probably disguised as women because the law was not as harsh on women." Never mind the fact that in England women could also be hanged for crimes against property.

In hir groundbreaking book, *Transgender Warriors,* Leslie Feinberg addresses situations like the one above:[1] "Many historians dismiss the female attire the male peasants wore as simply a convenient disguise. It's frustrating to me that historical examples of cross-dressing are so casually dismissed. When women military leaders like Joan of Arc cross-dressed, some historians claim men's clothes were most suited for warfare. Then why would male peasants choose women's clothes for battle? And since when is a dress an effective disguise? Cross-dressing is a pattern in rebellions in far-flung countries. And most importantly, this tradition appears to have ancient roots."[2] Feinberg points to the fact that cross-dressing was a common element of rebellion. It was not specific to any one country or region, but rather a global phenomenon taking place over the course of human history. It is also clear that the clothing worn by the protesters was not necessarily a disguise, especially because the protesters were not trying to pass as a different gender. Feinberg builds on a point made by the feminist historian Natalie Zemon Davis, one of the first writers to examine the nuances of cross-dressing and protest.

Historians who have written about cross-dressed protests and riots have argued that the **inversion** of men wearing women's clothing and women wearing men's clothing ultimately reinforced hierarchies and the gender binary. In other words, these inversions were brief ruptures in the social order, but once the cross-dressing event was over, the social order returned to normal. In fact, this idea of "normal" needed the disruption to remind people what was correct.

Davis has suggested, however, that "inversion could *undermine* as well as reinforce" and that cross-dressing could "widen behavioral options for women within and even outside marriage" and "sanction riot and political disobedience for both men and women in a society that allowed the lower orders few formal means of protest."[3]

You may be wondering if this use of the term *inversion* is the same as the sexologists' use of the term to denote same-sex desire. The answer is no. Many early sexologists understood same-sex desire as a gender or sex inversion. The cross-dressing that accompanied protesting and rioting, however, was not necessarily indicative of homosexuality. And at many of these cross-dressed protests, clothing was not the only inversion—often the rioters blackened their faces. (Today it is difficult to think about this tradition without assuming a racist element or agenda. In ancient Greek culture, however, blackening of the face meant that people were in mourning. The blackening of the face could also underscore workers' hard labor, especially the work of miners.) Other inversions at the protests were the mixing of human and animal, or human and supernatural beings like fairies. How and why did these customs of inversion begin? To answer that question, we need to go back a few hundred years and explore village festivals and carnivals.

Is This a Carnival or a Protest?

Carnival's mockery, chaos, and transgression have always threatened the sobriety and seriousness of the state, which is why it was often banned or heavily controlled.
NOTES FROM NOWHERE, ED., *WE ARE EVERYWHERE*[4]

When was the last time you attended a festival, carnival, or parade? What was the occasion? What costumes did you see? Although you may have seen people in costume, or you may have been in costume yourself, you may not have thought about how the costumes display inversions. As the quote above points out, festivals are often heavily controlled because the revelry can become unpredictable. Think for a minute about the tradition of Mardi Gras in New Orleans or carnivals in cities like Venice (Italy) and Rio de Janeiro (Brazil). These celebrations are famous for their costumed street parties, drinking, eating, and festive atmosphere. Here is a description of carnival: "Throughout history, carnival has been a time for inverting the social order, where the village fool dresses as the king and the king waits on the pauper, where men and women wear each other's clothing and perform each other's roles. This inversion exposes the power structures and illuminates the processes of maintaining hierarchies—seen from a new angle, the foundations of authority are shaken up and flipped around."[5] This social shake-up is precisely why the celebrations are closely monitored; and, once the festival is over, it is back to normal life.

Carnivals need not take place on a scale as large as Mardi Gras celebrations. Around the world, small towns sponsor parades and festivals that celebrate their unique cultures and locations. The reasons for the celebrations differ. Some are religious celebrations, whereas others are harvest festivals, Pride Parades, or celebrations of a local sports team. Going back four hundred years, the festivals that took place throughout rural regions in Europe and Great Britain were often tied to agrarian rituals relating to harvests and fertility, but the festivals also allowed the people living in these villages to deal with moral and ethical problems that had arisen.

In England and Wales, until the mid-nineteenth century, when rail lines were built, rural villages were isolated from city centers. In each region, one or two of the larger villages served as a central meeting place on market days. Most people traveled no farther than the local market town in their entire lifetimes. For example, the majority of farmers and artisans living in rural western England, and the miners and farmers in Wales, would never have made it as far as London, which was the seat of government and the monarchy. In London the laws created were *meant* to govern all English and Welsh people. Villagers in remote places, however, often took the law into their own hands, setting up and enforcing their own codes of conduct.

For example, agrarian villages used localized methods of dealing with the social issues concerning citizens. Domestic violence, adultery, and other social problems became the entire community's problem. Therefore, villages found ways to discipline those offending the moral or ethical code, and they often administered such discipline through carnival rituals.

As Mikhail Bakhtin, a Russian philosopher, noted, "Carnival . . . is *syncretic pageantry* of a ritualistic sort. As a form it is very complex and varied, giving rise . . . to diverse variants and nuances depending upon the epoch, the people, the individual festivity."[6] In western England, several villages engaged in a disciplinary practice known as a **skimmington.** In 1843 a London newspaper article defined this type of protest as "in vogue in less refined times, as a mode of punishing, or holding up to contempt without having recourse to law."[7] The historian Buchanan Sharp describes a typical skimmington in which a male community member was disciplined: "The community assembled in a loud and raucous procession carrying fowling-pieces and beating drums or suitable domestic substitutes such as pots and pans, and then marched on the house of the offender. In the procession would be included some symbolic representation of the offender—either an effigy, or a person appropriately garbed, such as a man in women's clothes."[8] Women who transgressed the ethical code received a similar punishment. Skimmingtons were specific to particular regions of the English countryside and were a combination of ritual and pageantry (as Bakhtin notes) as well as community-based disciplinary practices. Farther west, in Wales, a similar local practice known as *ceffyl pren* took place. Cross-dressing the offender and parading that individual through town was part of the ritual, along with tying the offender to a wooden frame.

Skimmingtons involved the entire village, as people banged pots and pans, creating what was known as "rough music." Everyone came out to make sure the person violating the village's moral or ethical codes was put in check. In other words, a skimmington was a village shaming. One historian notes that these events also had aspects of protest: "A protest Skimmington involving male cross-dressing distinctly emerged in the early 1600s. The festive culture . . . created a tie that bound communities and community members together. It provided a discourse and vocabulary through which they could express their outrage, anxiety, and understanding of justice."[9] The villagers' localized understandings of justice became a crucial component of larger protests and riots when they faced unjust laws. The villagers resorted to the one type of justice that they knew: the use of the festival or the carnival to call out and punish violations of their ethical and moral codes. The authority figures who appeared from outside the communities did not know what hit them.

Can we claim that these groups of cross-dressed people were trans in our modern understanding of the term? Probably not. We can, however, look at the ways they politicized gender and transgressed gender binaries in ways that made people in positions of social and political power very uncomfortable. And it is possible that their overt flying in the face of gender binary conventions was a large part of their success in protest.

Fences, Machines, and Toll Gates: Three Hundred Years of Protest

From the 1600s through the 1800s, a number of cross-dressed protests took place across England and Wales. In each of these cases—the Enclosure Riots, the Luddite Riots, and the Rebecca Riots—workers donned clothing deemed inappropriate to their gender to highlight the power imbalances between the wealthy and the working poor. These riots were all in response to either government or factory owner actions that were seen as unjust to everyday working people trying to make ends meet.

You're Putting a Fence Where? Lady Skimmington and the Enclosure Riots

Within the context of the enclosure riots, cross-dressing engaged the power of clothing to enhance the impact of destroying property while subverting the gender hierarchy.
CHRISTINA BOSCO LANGERT[10]

Imagine that you lived and worked on a farm in rural England in the 1600s. Your family had been farming the land for generations, but they did not own the land. Rather, the lord of the manor (landed gentry) owned the land. On occasion, he might ride by and check on you or collect your rent. For holidays, you and your family might be invited to a celebration at the manor house or, at the end of the year, the lord might bring you a present. Although neither you nor the other villagers owned any land, everyone managed to live sustainably from it. As the historian Christina Bosco Langert has noted, "Within a village community, commonly used land was a combination of manorial waste land, manor lands after the harvest, forests, or unowned land. Common land supplemented the income of poor villagers by serving as a place to glean, graze their few animals, hunt, fish, or collect timber for housing and heat."[11] Even though the land was not technically yours or anyone else's within the village and surrounding area, there was an unspoken understanding about the common use of public land, which benefited everyone in the community. Residents had right of way to the roads, fields, and forests.

When King Charles I ascended to the throne in 1625, he immediately began causing trouble. From marrying a Catholic in 1626 (not acceptable in Protestant England) to dissolving Parliament in 1629 because it did not agree with him, the monarch wreaked havoc on existing governmental structures. Ultimately, he was beheaded for treason in 1649.[12]

King Charles I also ran the Crown into deep financial debt. To dig himself out of the increasing deficit, the king set his sights on the forests in rural western England as places of untapped wealth for his kingdom: "It was by disafforestation that the Crown . . . tapped this resource. Each forest was declared no longer subject to the forest law."[13] In other words, the farmers' and artisans' freedom to use the surrounding forests as places to hunt and fish for supplemental food, and gather wood to heat their homes, came to an end. Charles I demanded that the forests be enclosed and access denied. In some cases, the villagers were paid a small sum to compensate them for their loss, but they completely lost their rights to use the land that their families had used for generations. Suddenly, the working poor people could not feed their families, and they could not heat their homes because the king wanted more wealth. Within a short time, village residents who had enjoyed right of way to the forests, roads, and pastures had become trespassing criminals.

The villagers did not passively accept the new laws. The series of Enclosure Riots known as the Western Rising took place from 1626 to 1632. At the heart of all the riots was Lady Skimmington, a "leader clad in female garb [to] raise the call to rebellion."[14] "Lady Skimmington" was not one individual, but the name taken up by the leaders of the protests. The village custom of cross-dressing and carnival protest to keep individual community members in line had suddenly expanded to protest the actions of a greedy king. The local villages' traditions of cross-dressing and skimmingtons were an engrained part of these agrarian communities; however, when the working-class politics of peasant farmers and artisans clashed with the politics of the Crown, the community leaders who took on the role of Lady Skimmington rose to legendary status: "Dressed in women's clothing, John Williams alias Lady Skimmington became a symbol of disorder to the state and a symbol of justice to members of the rural communities affected by enclosure. Women . . . dressed in men's clothing and adopted male titles, such as captain, to protest enclosure. . . . Cross-dressing provided a battleground for the contestation between individuals, communities, and the state over the ownership of land, one's social and gendered identity, and even ownership of the title Lady Skimmington."[15] Although the Luddite ("General Ludd's Wives") Riots took place two hundred years after the Western Rising, we can see similarities in the combination of cross-dressing and protest, most notably with the idea that one person takes a special title such as "Lady Skimmington," after which hundreds of people adopt the identity when taking part in working-class riots.

The two main areas of rioting were in the Forest of Dean in Gloucestershire and Braydon Forest in Wiltshire. The following is a description of the large number of people who turned out for the protest in the Forest of Dean: "On 25 March 1631 riots broke out in the Forest of Dean—about 500 people led by men dressed in women's clothing assembled and destroyed the enclosures. The success of this riot and the potent presence of skimmington brought six times the number of people the following month. On 5 April, 3,000 people assembled to destroy the enclosures, fill ore pits, and damage houses in other parts of the forest. By the end of the month all the enclosures that had been part of the decree extinguishing common rights had been destroyed."[16] In the case of the Western Rising, the protestors were only partially successful. They tore down the fences and hedges meant to keep them out of what had been communal land, but they "could not attack enclosure's underlying causes—capitalist influences and changing royal parliamentary regulations."[17]

Four years later, in 1635, the Braydon Forest rioters were all sentenced and fined for their participation. Three men deemed the leaders of the uprising were fined £500 each, a huge sum of money at that time, and then "ordered set in the pillory at the Western assizes dressed in women's clothes—their disguise in the riots—with papers on their heads describing the offense."[18] Note that their cross-dressing—their gender transgression—went from a point of public empowerment to a point of public shame and ridicule, which underscores the importance of *why*, *how*, and *when* cross-dressing gets used for political purposes.

You're Replacing Me with a Machine? General Ludd's Wives

The intensity of Luddism, its geographical spread, and the panicked if not severe response of the authorities, gave the agitation of 1811–12 a peculiarly compelling character and legacy.
KATRINA NAVICKAS[19]

Do you know someone who still uses a landline instead of a mobile phone? Or someone who prefers to write and mail a birthday card instead of sending wishes on Facebook or Twitter? Today you might jokingly think of the landline user or the letter writer as a "Luddite." Today, when we use the term **Luddite** or *Ludd,* we are usually referring to someone who is old-fashioned or a technophobe. Now you know, however, that this term comes from "General Ludd's wives" and the early nineteenth-century English riots in which manual laborers destroyed new machinery intended to replace them.

Whereas Lady Skimmingtons protested in rural areas, the Luddite Riots often took place "on the edge of arable land on the fringes of industrial villages or on the turnpike over pastoral moors."[20] The locations of the Luddite Riots, however, were neither completely rural nor completely urban; geographical landscapes were changing and transforming rapidly with the rise of the Industrial Revolution. Just as the boundaries between rural and urban were in constant flux, so too were the gendered presentations of many Luddite protesters.

To understand the Luddite Riots of 1811–1812, we need to look at the larger socioeconomic climate in England at this time. The years 1811–1812 were marked by a major economic downturn, and the machine workers, farmers, and other laborers suffered. A series of bad harvests had inflated prices, causing the purchasing power of the workers' wages to plummet.[21] Even as food prices skyrocketed, landlords continued to raise the rent, and churches demanded more tithe money. (Church tithes were mandatory for everyone at this time.)

In the middle of this economic crisis, several textile factory owners purchased new technology, including steam-powered looms and other machines that would replace shearmen or croppers in cloth-finishing shops. The increased rent, higher church tithes, inflated food prices, and factory layoffs created a perfect storm: "On 14 April 1812, men wearing women's clothing and calling themselves 'General Ludd's wives' led a crowd of men, women, and boys on a rampage through the market area of Stockport, destroying food shops, and resetting prices for bread and potatoes. The event culminated in the destruction of steam-powered looms in a factory."[22]

Frank Peel, a Yorkshire historian writing in the early twentieth century, noted "several instances of transvestism, such as the February 1812 Luddite attack on wagons carrying shearing frames on Hartshead Moor, carried out by shearmen, several of whom wore women's frocks."[23] Interestingly, Peel specifically uses the sexologist Magnus Hirschfeld's relatively new term, *transvestite,* to describe the cross-dressed rioters. In this case, too, note that the men wearing women's clothing led a mixed crowd of other men, women, and boys. This report of the Stockport riot depicts the rioters' gender and age diversity as they moved through the market to reset food prices and destroy the looms. The spontaneity of the carnival and the highly charged political atmosphere are exemplified by the people parading behind the cross-dressed Luddite leaders, as they made their voices heard by wreaking havoc through the marketplace.

The wave of rioting by Luddites across England became so much a part of popular culture that numerous songs and stories were created to celebrate those seeking socioeconomic justice. The cross-dressing was almost always present in the songs and the retellings because it had become an integral part of the protest. In one novel, reproduced in a third edition between the years 1898 and 1905, the fictional narrator comments, "Late of a Saturday night a number of men with faces blacked and their dress disguised, some wearing women's gowns and others strange head-gear, broke into the dressing shop of Mr. Joseph Hirst, of Marsh, destroyed the dressing frames, the shears, and other furniture of a gig-mill."[24] All the inversions and the "strange head-gear" are reminiscent of the skimmingtons' carnival tone.

Not only did the cross-dressed Luddites transgress the gender binary, but, as one modern historian points out, it was often the most overtly masculine men who cross-dressed: "In small cloth-finishing shops in . . . West Riding, which typically employed three to four shearmen or croppers, the radically masculinist workers [were the ones] who were perhaps the most determined Luddites (and those most frequently reported to use women's attire)."[25] Why did the more stereotypically masculine men tend to cross-dress during the protests? Is there an underlying notion that if you are hypermasculine, you can take the risk of looking more outlandish? Does the masculinity underscore the inversion? In what ways are masculinity and femininity transformed during the riots? As the same historian notes, the hypermasculinity goes back to the tradition of "rough music" and the skimmingtons in the seventeenth century. Although the Luddite Riots took place nearly two hundred years later and in different locations, the fact that they resembled the skimmingtons attests to the enduring power of local working-class folk traditions.

What Is This in the Middle of Our Road? The Rebecca Riots

The leaders of the mob were disfigured by painting their faces various colours, wearing horse-hair beards and women's clothes.
PAT MOLLOY[26]

The series of events known as the "Rebecca riots" has made a more permanent and positive mark on history than many other nineteenth-century protests.
RHIAN E. JONES[27]

The skimmingtons and the Luddites exemplify the ways that local communities whose residents had no social or political power used folk customs and inversions, specifically cross-dressing, to protest against governing powers. Though their stories are legendary, their political movements were ultimately shut down by authorities. The Rebecca Riots in Wales had a different outcome. Note that even though we will now be exploring Welsh riots, many Welsh traditions were exactly the same as the traditions in rural England. The Welsh *ceffyl pren* is basically the same as "rough music" or a skimmington.

The Forest of Dean and Braydon Forest, where the skimmington riots took place, were far from London. Wales, however, was even more remote. Western Wales, the location of the Rebecca Riots, is close to neither Cardiff (the Welsh capital) nor London. Wales is separated from England by the Severn Estuary, which makes it even more isolated. The new Great Western Railway did not go anywhere near western Wales; London was more than a day's travel away. Stagecoaches could be hired, but the terrain and weather could be treacherous. It is possible that the remoteness of the location helped make the Rebecca Riots a success.

Like the Western Rising in the 1600s and the Luddite Riots in the early nineteenth century, the Rebecca Riots, which started in 1839, were a response to the authorities' abuse of power. The enduring stereotype of the Luddite Riots holds that the protests were solely about breaking the machines; however, as noted earlier, many other socioeconomic factors added to the workers' grievances. In the popular imagination, the Rebecca Riots were solely about destroying tollgates that sprang up on public roads. In reality, many other social and cultural factors led to the protests. As the industrial and capitalist system expanded from urban centers like London and Manchester, English lawmakers denigrated the Welsh, their customs, and their language. (Only in recent decades has the Welsh language returned to the public sphere; Wales is a bilingual country.) And though the English authorities had little respect for the Welsh people, they definitely were interested in the Welsh coal mines and the profits that could be had there.

On top of the English disregard for the Welsh, the same socioeconomic factors that motivated the Luddites were in full force in Wales. The years 1839–1841 brought too much rain, which was followed by poor harvests and falling prices for dairy products and cows.[28] Rents were rising. Churches were demanding more tithes. The New Poor Law gave more power to landowners, owners of large farms, and clerics. In the middle of the economic downturn, the wealthy decided to make more money by setting up tollgates across public roads that the workers had to travel daily, either with their loads from the coal mines or lime kilns or with their cattle. Each tollgate had a tollhouse and a gatekeeper whom travelers had to pay to continue on the road. The following is a London newspaper's description of the difficult terrain and a tollgate: "Imagine a turnpike road on which a traveller has to pay heavy tolls, worse than any lane leading to a farmhouse in England, full of deep holes at almost every step, covered here and there with large loose stones and so thoroughly bad that a traveller who would venture faster than a walk after nightfall would do so with the certainty of either breaking his own neck or his horse's leg, or perhaps both."[29] These toll gates, placed along the already treacherous roads, were the last straw for the struggling miners and farmers. As had the protesters led by Lady Skimmingtons and the Luddites, they resorted to their ancient folk customs, including inversions and the protest carnival. As the historian Pat Molloy writes, "The Rebecca Riots were a classic example of mass protest against a logjam of inequity."[30] In response to this logjam, Rebecca and her daughters were born.[31]

On Monday, 13 May 1839, the quiet rural village of Efail-wen in western Wales was disrupted by hundreds of cross-dressed protesters yelling that they were Rebecca's daughters. They banged drums, blew horns, and waved sledgehammers, axes, and sticks in the air on their way to destroying the tollgate and the gatekeeper's house. Local officials hired more constables to police the situation; however, "the constables fled for their lives, pursued by Rebecca and a number of other female-garbed horsemen."[32] As the protests continued over the next four years, the groups got bigger and more outlandish in their cross-dressing and pageantry. The cross-dressed rioters took the name Rebecca or Rebecca's daughters, and they used high-pitched voices to act out skits in front of the gates and the tollhouses *before* they tore them down. This elaborate ritual of music, song, and playacting underscored ideas of inversion and carnival.

An Irish newspaper reporter recounted that a large crowd had gathered specifically in the hope of seeing Rebecca and her daughters on parade. They were not disappointed: "The multitude declar[ed] their intentions to parade the town to show their numbers and declare what they would do unless their alleged grievances were removed. They then read a list of their complaints and the changes they desired, which included, not only the removal of all the turnpike-gates in the country, but also the abolition of all tithe and rent charge in lieu of tithes, the alteration of the present poor-law, towards which they expressed the most bitter hostility, abolition of church rates, and an equitable adjustment of their landlord's rents."[33]

The image in figure 9.1 appeared in *Punch,* a satiric British periodical, in 1843. Note that the cross-dressed rioters are armed with saws and sledgehammers as they destroy a tollgate; various laws and political issues are written on the boards: the Poor Laws (which did *not* protect the poor) and the church rates (the increased tithes). The startled gatekeeper peers around his door in his nightcap.

The Rebeccas' protests transgressed gender boundaries even more than the Skimmingtons' or the Luddites' had. In the newspaper accounts of the earlier English riots, the reporters indicated that the men were cross-dressed, and they used masculine pronouns when writing about them. As the modern historian Rhian E. Jones notes throughout her book on the Rebecca Riots, *Petticoat Heroes,* something very different happened with the newspapers' descriptions of the **Rebeccaites**. The following excerpt comes from the *Derby Mercury,* an English newspaper: "On Tuesday, Rebecca, and a great number of her daughters, assembled at Mydwin, about four o'clock in the afternoon, and stopped there some hours. They were nearly all dressed in women's clothes, and Rebecca was on horseback, elegantly attired. . . . They assembled at St. Clear's from all parts of

REBECCA AND HER DAUGHTERS.

Tolltaker . . . Sir R. P—l.   Irish Rebecca . . D— O'C—l.   Rebecca's Daughters by Members of the Repeal Ass——n.

FIGURE 9.1 "Rebecca and Her Daughters," from *Punch*, 1843. In this humorous depiction of the Rebecca Rioters, the artist at *Punch* has included the various men dressed in women's clothing as they are wielding axes, swords, and saws. The rioters are shown literally sawing down the wooden toll gate set up by the British government. Listed on the pieces of wood are some of the issues burdening the working class: the New Poor Laws, inflated church tithes, and other forms of inflation.

the country; most of them arrived with guns and other destructive weapons, and immediately leveled with the ground the gates leading to St. Clear's from both ends."[34] Notice that, in the first sentence, the reporter refers to Rebecca and *her* daughters; the feminine pronoun is used. In the next sentence, though, the reporter writes about the rioters being dressed in women's clothing and notes that Rebecca was on a horse in a fine outfit. The female pronoun underscores the fact that Rebecca and her daughters were a group of men crossdressed. Why did the press begin to use "she" and "her" for Rebecca while also going into great detail about men wearing women's clothing?

Five days after the report above, a London newspaper printed an article about the Rebeccaites giving fair warning to a gatekeeper. Take a close look at the gendered complexities:

> Very early on Thursday morning, a party on foot, of Rebeccaites, in number about twenty, dressed in white frocks, and headed by one horseman, made their appearance at the New Lun gate, near Llandilo, and politely requested the toll collector (a female) to leave the place. She instantly complied with their request and removed her goods and chattels from the house, the party gallantly rendering her every assistance, regretting that their sense of public duty obliged them to act as they did. They then commenced the work of tearing down the tollhouse, gate, & c., amidst shouts and the discharge of fire-arms. All was destroyed within a very short period.[35]

What are some of the more unusual details in this account? The cross-dressed Rebeccaites made a show of riding up in their white frocks, but they also displayed stereotypically masculine behavior with their chivalry. According to Jones, instances like these were quite common, and the pageantry of the men's behavior makes it clear that the cross-dressing was not meant to be merely a disguise. Jones notes that on many occasions, the protesters not only carried parasols and wore women's nightgowns and outlandish wigs, but also sported large horsehair beards, meaning that they were simultaneously hyperfeminized *and* hypermasculinized. As Jones notes, "Rebeccaite costume had less to do with one gender adopting the clothing of the other, and more with the attempt to convey an altered state of being. By presenting a transitional identity . . . individuals could become invested with the heightened power and abilities customarily accruing to such liminal spaces and figures."[36] Here Jones notes the power that marginalized spaces and figures can embody. The mixture of joy, carnival humor, and direct riotous action paid off. In 1844 the prime minister, Robert Peel, and his government passed the Turnpike Act, which rid Wales of all the remaining tollgates.

FIGURE 9.2 "Rebecca and Her Daughters Kissing the Hand of the Prince of Wales," from *Punch*, March 1843. Courtesy of the Department of Special Collections, Stanford University Libraries. In another satiric depiction of the Rebecca Rioters, *Punch* magazine published this image of the cross-dressed rioters, who are also blackened up (possibly because of their work with coal or possibly as a racial inversion), going to kiss the hand of the Prince of Wales, who looks disgusted at the prospect of having to interact with everyday working people.

In another satiric depiction from *Punch* (figure 9.2), the artist makes fun of Parliament's abolition of tollgates. The cross-dressed and grimy Rebeccaites are shown kissing the hands of royalty, which also suggests that the Crown might not have approved of Parliament's move.

Although we cannot claim that these groups were trans, it is important to note that gender transgression was a crucial part of their political protest. Given the history of many anti-cross-dressing and anti-masquerading laws, these already rebellious protestors were adding another layer of radical rebellion to their actions. Crossing gender binaries, regardless of century, has been and still can be a way to trouble the gender binary and to help point out social inequities.

It is noteworthy that the skimmingtons, Luddites, and Rebeccaites used gender transgressions as a major component of the protest. What did these gender transgressions signal? And how did these transgressions empower poor farmers, miners, and manual laborers? Whose attention were they trying to get?

In the next section, we examine two examples from the twentieth and twenty-first centuries in which the protesters, like the skimmingtons, Luddites, and Rebeccaites, transgressed gender lines as an integral part of the protest. They were not trying to pass as anything but outraged.

No Protections, Only Protest

This section looks at two forms of cross-dressed protest employed in the twentieth and twenty-first centuries. Whether these protestors knew it or not, they were actually carrying on a very old tradition in social and political protest: that of cross-dressing. In both cases that you will read about here, cross-dressing was employed by the protestors to help underscore inequality. In one case, however, the protestors themselves were violating both civic and religious laws and were putting themselves in danger of facing extreme consequences such as imprisonment.

Ladies in Support of the President (LISP)

Boulder, Colorado, is home to the University of Colorado's flagship campus, which was established in 1876. Many university towns are politically liberal, sometimes even radical, compared to towns that do not house college or university campuses; and Boulder ranks high on that list, alongside Berkeley, home to the University of California. The politics and cultural climate of Boulder, however, are complex. If you find yourself in Boulder and are interested in the Beat poet Allen Ginsberg, who wrote against militarism and industrial capitalism, you can visit the library named after him at Naropa University, which is the Buddhist institution he cofounded with the Tibetan scholar Chögyam Trungpa in 1974. Boulder is also the birthplace of one of the most successful U.S.–based fundamentalist Christian men's groups, the Promise Keepers, which was founded by the University of Colorado's head football coach, Bill McCartney, in 1990.

In the 1980s Boulder and the university were home to a political, robust, and growing LGBTQ+ community. At the university, student coalitions working together included the Black Student Alliance, the Chicanx and Latinx group UMAS Y MEChA, Gays and Friends, the Lesbian Caucus, and the Feminist Alliance. The 1980s also saw the beginning of the AIDS epidemic and its ever-increasing number of victims. There would be no long-term treatment options until 1996, and AIDS was still considered a "gay disease." Boulder and Denver both established support groups as well as political protest groups like ACT UP (AIDS Coalition to Unleash Power), which is often credited with pressuring the government to allow the release of new AIDS and HIV medications to the market more quickly. ACT UP often used street theater, such as "die-ins" in public spaces, to make the nation aware of the inequities facing people living with HIV and AIDS.

The 1980s and early 1990s also saw three Colorado towns prohibiting discrimination in housing and employment on the basis of sexual orientation: Aspen, a wealthy ski resort town in the mountains; Boulder, the liberal college town; and Denver, the state capital. Once Denver's ordinance passed, however, more conservative cities and towns throughout the state, including Pueblo and Colorado Springs, became worried that they, too, would have to accept a nondiscrimination ordinance. At this turning point, CU Boulder's head football coach, Bill McCartney, and other political and religious conservative leaders began a six-year political and legal battle that would end up in the U.S. Supreme Court in 1996. A state referendum, Amendment 2, was slated to be on the November 1992 ballot. A "yes" vote meant that Colorado would pass laws against protection ordinances and that Aspen, Boulder, and Denver would have to overturn theirs. A "no" vote meant that the ordinances would remain in effect and that other cities and towns could also pass nondiscrimination laws.

As the Promise Keepers achieved huge success with their first convention (which filled the CU football stadium—about 50,000 seats) and the number of pro-LGBTQ+ supporters grew, the first Gulf War broke out. In Boulder, on any given weekend, you might have encountered fundamentalist Christian rallies, LGBTQ+ marches, and antiwar protestors blocking the entrances to military recruiting stations. With protests looming around every corner, a group composed of predominantly gay men took matters into their own hands by appearing all over Boulder at various political gatherings wearing outlandish secondhand dresses,

FIGURE 9.3 "LISP," by Cameron Rains. This image of members of Ladies in Support of the President at the University of Colorado, Boulder, in the 1990s shows the outlandish costumes that the men wore to bring attention to various local social justice and political issues. The men are depicted with hairy legs and beards while they wear secondhand dresses. Their cross-dressing was meant to look ridiculous in order to bring humor and satire to their protest.

wigs, hats, and shoes: the Ladies in Support of the President (LISP) (figure 9.3) were born. The group decided on LISP as a satiric name that purposefully made fun of cultural stereotypes that gay men lisp and have limp wrists. This embracing of a homophobic stereotype was a form of inversion that goes back to the idea of the carnivalesque.

Whether they knew it or not, the members of LISP had a great deal in common with the skimmingtons, Luddites, and Rebeccaites. Like Rebecca and her daughters, the members of LISP took part in theatrical displays that included cross-dressing and skits. In doing so, they tapped into some of the humorous and satirical aspects of carnival and protest.

Have you ever watched *Saturday Night Live*? This show, which often uses satire in its sketches and stand-up comedy, has been one of the most successful late-night television shows of the past four decades. In the late 1980s, the actor Dana Carvey created the character of Enid Strict, better known as the iconic "Church Lady." Responding to the rise of the Christian right in national politics, Carvey's character used inversion and satire to critique the "moral majority." When LISP formed in 1990, it took inspiration from Carvey's character to create a group of pious "church ladies" who appeared at numerous and diverse protests.

In March 1991, for example, a lesbian choir director at the First Presbyterian Church was "ousted from her position . . . after she revealed that she is a lesbian." The *Boulder Daily Camera* noted that "churches are not exempt from the human rights ordinance."[37] For several weeks, LGBTQ+ community members protested the church's policy. Within that period, the members of LISP attended church services fully cross-dressed, speaking in high falsetto voices about "those dreadful homosexuals" and the need to run them out of town. The church's membership, despite displaying homophobic behavior toward their former choir director, did not want to be seen as agreeing with the inflammatory and hateful language coming from the Ladies in Support of the President. At the same time, some members of the LGBTQ+ community who were protesting in earnest did not quite understand LISP's tactics. Every time LISP showed up, however, potentially volatile situations calmed down.

This combination of humor, satire, and confusion made LISP a group favored by the Boulder Police Department. During some of the most violent clashes between antiwar demonstrators and military recruiters in Boulder, the police came to rely on LISP to defuse the situation. Time after time the group of bearded men appeared in their flower-print dresses, wigs, heavy makeup, hose, and heels to yell: "We want our men to go kill all of those evil people! Let them sign up for the army!" The antiwar protestors would stop and stare in wonder: Were these cross-dressed men serious? Were they being satirical? Meanwhile, the military recruiters and people enlisting often became uncomfortable with the idea that these cross-dressed gay men were supporting them and underscoring the idea that war is about killing people. Neither side knew what to do with LISP, and so, as confusion reigned, violence de-escalated. This is why the Boulder Police Department appreciated their appearance.

For more than two years, LISP showed up at protests that covered a wide range of issues: the war, the firing of the lesbian choir director, and the Promise Keepers' big push to pass Amendment 2. In one instance, LISP showed up in full cross-dressed splendor to a rally against the Promise Keepers at one of the university's largest lecture halls. In this case, although they were always known as LISP, they changed their name to match the occasion: "Ladies against Nasty Homosexuals." With their ladylike pseudonyms and clothing, they brought an important sense of both humor and purpose to the people working to save the protection ordinances.

Amendment 2 passed in November 1992, so the protection ordinances that had covered LGBTQ+ people in Aspen, Boulder, and Denver were undone. It took a four-year legal battle, but in 1996, the U.S. Supreme Court of the United States made a landmark decision that declared Amendment 2 unconstitutional.

An interesting fact about LISP is that its members were all LGBTQ+ people. We have no way of knowing how many of the skimmingtons, Luddites, or Rebeccaites were LGBTQ+ (remember, too, that this abbreviation did not exist during those periods), but most scholars believe that the cross-dressers during the working-class protests were heterosexuals who borrowed either their wives' dresses or their husbands' coveralls. In the case of LISP, the protestors took cross-dressing to a new level. They were predominantly gay men who wanted to look outlandish in their "church lady" outfits, with their female aliases and their falsetto voices. But they were not trying to pass as anything but outraged by an unjust political and legal system that had granted them basic protections and then, for four years, took them away.

#MenInHijab: Cross-Dressing to Support Their Wives

In the past few years, some Iranian men have been cross-dressing by wearing hijabs (headscarves) and posting their pictures on social media in support of their wives and other women relatives who are required to wear a hijab in public.[38] It is illegal for women in Iran to appear in public without their heads covered; however, for many, this law feels just as confining as the French laws that ban the hijab in public. In both cases, women's rights and freedoms are not respected because the women do not get to choose what to wear on their heads.

Women led the initial protest in Iran by shaving their heads and posting the images on social media, which is viewed as blasphemous in the face of the strict morality laws. Masih Alinejad, a journalist and activist from Iran who lives in New York, started a campaign entitled "My Stealthy Freedom" to ask the public to question the morality laws and to argue that women should have the freedom to choose their clothing.[39] She started the campaign *outside* her home country, but she reports that she has received photos of several men who have taken their pictures in a hijab and posted these photos to their own Instagram accounts.[40] In many of the men's photos, a woman, whether she is a wife or another female relative, stands next to the man with her head uncovered.

In Iran these protests are taken very seriously; the morality police are outraged over the images. Although the gay men in Boulder who cross-dressed to make a political point were out and visible in public, it is probably much more dangerous for these presumably heterosexual men in Iran to appear on social media in women's clothing because doing so directly violates both religious and governmental policy. The only thing worse than the men appearing cross-dressed are the women appearing with their heads uncovered. Both the men and the women are violating strict dress codes and laws that define gender normativity.

RHIAN E. JONES

Writing *Petticoat Heroes*

Rhian E. Jones grew up in southern Wales and now lives in London, where she writes fiction and nonfiction about history, politics, popular culture, and the places where they intersect. She has written for the Guardian, Salon, McSweeney's Internet Tendency, *and the Royal Shakespeare Company. She is the author of* Clampdown: Pop-Cultural Wars on Class and Gender *(Zero Books, 2013);* Petticoat Heroes: Gender, Culture and Popular Protest in the Rebecca Riots *(University of Wales Press, 2015); and, with Daniel Lukes and Larissa Wodtke,* Triptych: Three Studies of Manic Street Preachers' The Holy Bible *(Repeater Books, 2017). She is coeditor of the collection* Under My Thumb: Songs That Hate Women and the Women Who Love Them *(Repeater Books, 2017). She blogs at* Velvet Coalmine *(www.rhianejones.com) and is currently at work on a new novel set during the Rebecca Riots.*

When writing *Petticoat Heroes*, I was unable to avoid both the political and the personal. At school I had been captivated by the history of radical popular movements, which guided my decision to study history as a degree. Although I subsequently managed to escape an academic career, my enduring interest in both historical and contemporary popular protest eventually led me, over years of independent writing and research in the gaps between my day jobs, to finish a book on the subject. *Petticoat Heroes*, an examination of the often fascinating forms that popular responses to political changes can take, also provides useful examples of how the past can illuminate the present.

To grow up somewhere like the South Wales coalfield is to be conscious of how heavily *then* weighs on *now*. Long before I thought about becoming a historian, I was aware of being a historical case study. The early economic historians J. L. Hammond and Barbara Hammond, for instance, had described my part of the world as giving "perhaps the most complete picture of the worst features of the Industrial Revolution." While nineteenth-century industrialists, settling in South Wales, formed a socially and politically privileged layer, workers in their mines and ironworks were subject not only to hard and dangerous toil but also to job insecurity and dread of incurring sudden expense through illness, accident, or the death of a wage earner. But South Wales was also exemplary for the struggles for workers' rights and living standards that sprang up in response to these conditions, from the rudimentary proto–trade union organizing of the Scotch Cattle [coal miners] to the Chartists' sophisticated campaign for popular democracy. What was obvious about this history of struggle, unfortunately, was how much of it had ended in failure, loss, and defeat: the leaders of these movements had been arrested, imprisoned, and transported, but the exploitation and inequality they sought to challenge remained characteristics of industrial capitalism long into the twentieth century.

The only exception I could find to this melancholy rule was the 1840s disturbance known as the Rebecca Riots, which have gone down in Welsh and British history as a successful popular campaign against charging tolls for the right to travel by road. The story of Rebeccaism as it was generally told was one of single-issue revolt, but, when I began to look in greater depth at these events, it became clear that the movement had more interesting features—many of them relevant to today—which had been forgotten, ignored, or downplayed. Some of the aspects of Rebeccaism I found most fascinating—the use of costume, symbol, and ritual, the media attention given to the movement, and the way the figure of "Rebecca" captured the public imagination—had been considered too obscure or simply irrelevant to analyze. My own research looked at newspaper archives, government records, individual memoirs, and correspondence covering the events, and at the politics and culture of the time, in an attempt to fill in these gaps.

The Rebecca Riots, like many protests in nineteenth-century Britain, were produced by the dislocation, conflict, and resistance generated as an older society regulated by paternalism, the authority of popular custom, and what E. P. Thompson called a preexisting "moral economy" was replaced by an economy, politics, and society informed by industrial capitalism. "Rebeccaism," looking at times like a Victorian version of Occupy, was a wide-ranging and not always coherent social movement that called attention to the negative impact of political change and the lack of attention by local elites to those they governed. Rather than a single-issue campaign against road tolls, it was a broad and multifaceted reaction that sought to defend the established rights of rural communities on several economic, social, and cultural fronts.

Traditional narratives of nineteenth-century history have tended to portray the social transformation wrought by industrialization, and the popular response to it, in terms of the organizational and institutional aspects of working-class development—notably the growth of trade unions and Labour Party politics. From this perspective, the nineteenth century is a period in which older, spontaneous, and disorderly forms of particularized violence diminished in frequency, intensity, and reach, in favor of more openly organized, rational, restrained, and constitutional forms of conflict. However, the development of cultural history over the past few decades, making it possible to explore parts of history that previously looked impenetrable, has done much to challenge this picture. E. P. Thompson's brilliant *Customs in Common* used anthropological techniques to explore the links between eighteenth- and early nineteenth-century protest and popular culture, and to attempt to reconstruct what such protest meant for participants. Work by Eric Hobsbawm, Natalie Zemon Davis, Robert Darnton, James Epstein, and Nicolas Rogers made use of similar methods, distinguishing itself from previous labor history through shifting its attention from the accomplishments of political vanguards to those of "primitive rebels" whose consciousness traditional Marxist historiography might have labeled backward or unenlightened. In this less teleological outlook, early industrial popular movements appear broader and more eclectic than previously acknowledged, rooted in and appealing to diverse preindustrial forms of cultural expression and ways of seeing and presenting the world. Participants could integrate the techniques of preindustrial protest and local oral-visual culture into a modern industrial context in dynamic and innovative ways that belie their superficially incomprehensible or anachronistic appearance. Movements like Rebeccaism combined physical-force tactics and folk culture with more modern forms of protest, such as petitioning and marching, challenging overly simplistic models that stress "progressive" and "reactionary" ways of protesting.

An important part of this approach involves studying the use of ritual and symbol in popular political activity, in order to better understand how protestors expressed themselves and the frames of reference to which they appealed for legitimacy. In this respect Rebeccaism is a valuable case study, especially the use made by male Rebeccaites of female dress and accessories. Even though this played a significant part in characterizing and establishing the movement within the popular imagination, historians have tended to recognize ritual cross-dressing as part of Rebeccaism without making any more detailed attempts to explore its meaning. Indeed, the regularity of ritual cross-dressing within protest in general has received little analysis, beyond its similarities to local forms of carnival and festival or the speculation that it functioned as a method of disguise. The latter explanation looks particularly inadequate in the case of Rebeccaite protestors, who often chose female dress that was impractical, theatrical, and highly stylized—up to and including ornate gowns, wigs, and jewelry—making it unlikely that disguise was their main concern. Moreover, the preoccupation with feminine signifiers also fails to explain Rebeccaites' frequent—and invariably overlooked—inclusion in their costumes of masculine signifiers like false beards and swords, which suggests that whatever they were trying to do involved more than simply female imitation.

So what was actually going on? My argument is that theories that concentrate only on the use of female dress leave unexplored a further possibility: that protestors were deliberately referencing and drawing on tropes of inversion, already established in local festival, carnival, and popular custom, in order to attempt the representation of a dual identity, in which fixed categories were visibly destabilized and boundaries transgressed. Why do this? Perhaps to enable their actions to take place in what was perceived to be a liminal and transient state. When in this kind of liminal space—whether during protest or play—participants could carry out extraordinary actions, liberated from the responsibilities that their everyday roles and identities imposed within a more restrictive social structure. From this perspective, female guise was a strengthening and enabling signifier for male protestors, but it derived its fundamental strength from being deliberately combined with masculine signifiers to produce an unstable or neutral identity that functioned as a ritual enabling device. This argument sees the use of female costume as neither disguise nor attempts by male protesters to pass as women, although it may have contained secondary elements of both.

The study of Rebeccaism also has insight to offer on the historical development of images and ideas about both women and men. In the press, popular culture, and even political discourse, "Rebecca" was rapidly adopted as a heroine or antiheroine, compared as much to legendary national outlaws like Robin Hood as to more specialized precedents like the Luddite movement's mythical figurehead, General Ludd. In this process, contemporary attitudes and anxieties about gender were projected onto the particular example of Rebecca. On the ground, meanwhile, the figure of Rebecca was influenced by the images of women prominent in the communities from which her followers arose. Finally, the traditional and overly simplistic concentration on Rebecca rioters as "men dressed as women" ignores or underplays the mixed demographics of the movement. Although the physically demanding work of destroying tollgates fell overwhelmingly to men, women took part in Rebeccaism as supporters, observers, organizers, and agitators. Women as well as men were prominent in attempts to defend the rights of single mothers and illegitimate children against the strictures of the New Poor Law—another front on which Rebeccaism tried to uphold older, more permissive attitudes and customs—which helps show how gender roles appropriate to patriarchal capitalism were introduced, established, and resisted.

Although Rebeccaism quickly faded from national consciousness after its flashpoint of 1843–1844, the name and image of the movement remained locally embedded. "Rebecca" has been continuously referenced in twentieth- and twenty- first-century Welsh protests by groups or individuals wishing to express opposition to one or many perceived injustices, generating action often far removed from its original purposes. Its endurance and evolution mean that it could be described as a kind of meme. This concept came to mind when I was in the very early stages of putting *Petticoat Heroes* together, at a point that coincided with the sudden upsurge in Europe and the U.S. of popular oppositional and pro-democracy movements following, and often inspired by, the 2011 Arab Spring. These movements seemed to signify a return to the protests of preindustrial history, which, like them, were largely spontaneous, anonymous, leaderless, and made significant use of an oral-visual repertoire. Protestors in 2011 obscured their own identities and proclaimed their allegiance using Guy Fawkes masks rather than bonnets and petticoats, and they called themselves "the 99%" rather than "the children of Rebecca," but there were striking similarities in how these groups were guided, as the Rebeccaites were, by the feeling that they had increasingly little control over their working and living conditions, and that remote, incompetent, or corrupt political and economic elites paid little attention to their plight.

The reasons for these similarities seem obvious enough. Many Western societies currently feel not only postindustrial but also almost post-democratic. When those in power appear uninterested in and impervious to constitutional protest, direct action will inevitably have greater appeal, as it did to the followers of Rebecca. My own part of South Wales was once defined by its heavy industry, but, following the destruction of its manufacturing sector in the 1980s, the area is now defined by structural unemployment and the consequences of this: extensive poverty, precariousness, and psychological trauma. In June 2016 the U.K.'s narrow vote to leave the European Union was driven in many such post-industrial areas by a sense of abandonment by political authorities and of an unbridgeable distance between the individual citizen and those with decision-making power. On a wider scale, the international financial crisis of 2008 has inspired a broader resentment of corporate, financial, and political establishments, also generated by the fact that many problems familiar to our Victorian ancestors—poverty, high rents, unemployment, privatization of common space—have either never gone away or are making a stark return.

The choice of how to address these difficulties has been further limited by the twenty-first-century decline of mass-membership political parties or trade unions through which change or redress may be sought on a constitutional level. This intensely bleak situation has very recently spiraled into the election of populist leaders and parties on outright anti-establishment tickets, in addition to the slightly earlier resurgence of Rebeccaism-like mass movements. The two are not mutually exclusive and may overlap and intertwine, but they seem to represent different ways of dealing with similar circumstances—on the one hand retaining faith in a central political hierarchy under a change of personnel, on the other seeking to devolve and decentralize decision-making power to local communities. In a political situation that seems increasingly fraught and volatile, the study of historical responses to comparable developments is one of our few remaining ways to make sense of things.

Key Concepts

inversion (p. 324)
Luddites (p. 330)
Rebeccaites (p. 334)
skimmington (p. 326)

Activities, Discussion Questions, and Observations

1. Discuss Rhian E. Jones's very personal reasons for wanting to research the history of the Rebecca Riots. Does any event in political history feel highly personal for you? Explain.

2. Study the two images depicting the Rebecca Riots from *Punch* (figures 9.1 and 9.2). Which specific details strike you as you look at these images? If you did not know anything about the Rebecca Riots, would you be able to understand some of the issues by examining one or both of these images? If so, how and why?

3. One of the key questions at the beginning of this chapter asked you to consider the ways that humor operates in cross-dressed protests. Now that you have read about several political issues and protests, explain what gets made fun of in each of the protests. What social, economic, and/or political structures do the protests reinforce?

4. "According to the records, it seems that no more than seven men cross-dressed out of the thousands who participated in the Forest of Dean and Braydon Forest riots but the alias Skimmington repeatedly makes its way into the court documents." This quote comes from one of the newspaper accounts of the skimmington protests. At this point, we know it is likely that many more than seven men cross-dressed. Why might a suppression of numbers in the press be important? In which other historic events that involved mass protest have the numbers been suppressed? Why do you think they were suppressed? (You may need to conduct some research to answer these questions.)

5. For this activity, you will be researching and writing about the history of festivals and carnivals. Starting from various festivals that were agrarian in focus—harvest festivals in particular—to spiritually and religious-based festivals, you will trace the history of the creation of the festival and the ways it has changed over time. Are there also ways that these festivals and carnivals became tied to protest at one point or another? Here is a list of the festivals you might research:

- El Día de los Muertos—Mexico/global

- Lunar New Year and Spring Festival (also known as Chinese New Year)—China/global

- The Chinese Ghost Festival—China/global

- Samhain or Winter Night—Druid festival—U.K.

- Beltane or May Eve—Druid festival—U.K.

- Summer Solstice—Stonehenge/global

- Winter Solstice—Stonehenge/global

- Mardi Gras—U.S.

- Rio de Janeiro Carnival—Brazil

- Carnevale di Viareggio—Italy

6. Here is a quote from the book *We Are Everywhere:* "If you look hard enough, you can find carnival between the cracks of many of history's unpredictable moments of rebellion." With this quote in mind, research a protest of your choosing. What kinds of clothing did the protesters choose to wear? Did the protest have a theme? How did the clothing aid the protesters in getting their message across? What aspects of those costumes made them powerful or effective?

Film and Television of Interest

Border Café (Café Transit) (2005, Iran, Greece, 105 minutes)
Although there is nothing trans about this feature-length drama, it is still a radical and outstanding exploration that provides cultural and political context for anyone wanting to study the ways that women are confined in Iran. When a widow takes over her husband's restaurant, it is illegal and unsafe for her to be in the dining room serving customers, many of whom are men, because the road is on a major trucking route. In Farsi, Greek, Turkish, and Russian with English subtitles.

Facing Mirrors (Aynehaye Rooberoo) (2011, Iran, 102 minutes)
This feature-length film in Farsi with English subtitles explores the life of Eddie, an Iranian trans man, and his friendship with an Iranian woman, Rana, who drives a taxi to support her family, which is forbidden by Iranian law. The film beautifully explores the similarities in their oppressions.

The History of the Luddites (2010, U.K., 4 minutes)
This very short video is an excellent place to start researching the Luddite Riots. It is a fun and accessible video with factual historic information.

Sisterhood: A Look at the Sisters of Perpetual Indulgence, Inc. (2015, U.S., 5 minutes)
The Sisters of Perpetual Indulgence do drag for a cause. Over the years, the sisters have raised thousands of dollars for HIV and AIDS programs, and they have always been dressed in their unique drag for various political actions. This short film looks at the organization as a performance and political group.

Stop, Look, and Listen: Tales from Wales—The Rebecca Riots (2001, U.K., 6 minutes)
This short video gives some of the background on the Rebecca Riots. It is narrated through the experience of one family's struggle.

NOTES

1. If you have read Chapter 1, you might recall learning about Leslie Feinberg, a trans writer and activist, who tried to come up with pronouns that did not reflect the gender binary. One set of pronouns that Feinberg came up with and used was zhe and hir. Now the neutral pronoun they is most commonly used to show a gender identity outside or beyond the binary. Because Feinberg used zhe and hir, those are the pronouns used for Feinberg in this book.

2. Leslie Feinberg, *Transgender Warriors: Making History from Joan of Arc to RuPaul* (Boston: Beacon Press, 1996), 78; this is a revised edition of *Transgender Warriors: Making History from Joan of Arc to Dennis Rodman.*

3. Natalie Zemon Davis, *Society and Culture in Early Modern France* (Stanford: Stanford University Press, 1975), 131.

4. Notes from Nowhere, ed., *We Are Everywhere: The Irresistible Rise of Global Anticapitalism* (London: Verso, 2003), 177.

5. Ibid., 174–175.

6. Mikhail Bakhtin, "Carnival and the Carnivalesque," in *Cultural Theory and Popular Culture: A Reader,* ed. John Storey, 2nd ed. (Athens: University of Georgia Press, 1998), 250.

7. "Skimmington," *Times* (London), 28 September 1843.

8. Buchanan Sharp, *In Contempt of All Authority: Rural Artisans and Riot in the West of England, 1586–1660* (Berkeley: University of California Press, 1980), 104.

9. Christina Bosco Langert, "Hedgerows and Petticoats: Sartorial Subversion and Anti-enclosure Protest in Seventeenth-Century England," *Early Theatre* 12.1 (2009): 120.

10. Ibid., 121–122.

11. Ibid., 122.

12. "King Charles I Executed for Treason," This Day in History, 2010, www.history.com/this-day-in-history/king-charles-i-executed-for-treason (accessed 11 June 2017). If you visit London, check out the Horse Guards — there is a clock tower with the numbers blackened on the hour that Charles I lost his head.

13. Sharp, *In Contempt of All Authority,* 84.

14. Langert, "Hedgerows and Petticoats," 124.

15. Ibid., 119.

16. Ibid., 126.

17. Ibid., 125.

18. Sharp, *In Contempt of All Authority,* 108.

19. Katrina Navickas, "Luddism, Incendiarism and the Defence of Rural 'Task-Scapes' in 1812," https://www.academia.edu/535604/Luddism_incendiarism_and_the_defence_of_rural_task-scapes_in_1812, 1 (accessed 16 May 2017).

20. Ibid., 2.

21. Malcolm I. Thomis, *The Luddites: Machine-Breaking in Regency England* (Newton Abbot, U.K.: David and Charles, 1970), 70.

22. Kevin Binfield, "Industrial Gender: Manly Men and Cross-Dressers in the Luddite Movement," in *Mapping Male Sexuality: Nineteenth-Century England,* ed. Jay Losey and William D. Brewer (Madison, N.J.: Fairleigh Dickinson University Press, 2000), 29.

23. Peel quoted ibid., 30.

24. D. F. E. Sykes, *Ben o' Bill's, the Luddite,* 3rd ed. (Huddersfield, U.K.: "The Worker" Press, n.d.), 53. Available at Stanford Special Collections, Stanford University.

25. Binfield, "Industrial Gender," 32.

26. Pat Molloy, *And They Blessed Rebecca: An Account of the Welsh Toll-Gate Riots, 1839–1844* (Llandysul, Wales: Gomer Press, 1983), 39.

27. Rhian E. Jones, *Petticoat Heroes: Gender, Culture and Popular Protest in the Rebecca Riots* (Cardiff: University of Wales Press, 2015), 1.

28. Ibid., 19.

29. Molloy, *And They Blessed Rebecca*, 25, quoting a footnote from the *Times*, 28 September 1843.

30. Molloy, *And They Blessed Rebecca*, 20.

31. There are several theories about why the name Rebecca was chosen for the rioters. Many accounts say that it was selected because it is biblical; other accounts claim that a protestor's wife was named Rebecca; and there are other ideas about the origin of the name. Several excellent books on the history of the Rebecca Riots are available, as well as several online sources.

32. Molloy, *And They Blessed Rebecca*, 4.

33. "Alarming State of Wales—Rebecca Riots—Attack on the Carmarthen Workhouse and Capture of the Rioters," *Freeman's Journal and Daily Commercial Advertiser* (Dublin), 23 June 1843.

34. "The Rebecca Riots in Wales," *Derby (England) Mercury,* 5 July 1843.

35. "The Rebecca Riots," *Morning Chronicle* (London), 10 July 1843.

36. Jones, *Petticoat Heroes,* 70.

37. Emily Narvaes, "Church's Firing of Lesbian May Violate City Ordinance," *Boulder (Colo.) Daily Camera,* 14 March 1991, 2C.

38. "Iranian Men Wear Hijabs to Protest against Headscarf Law," *Middle East Eye,* 3 August 2016, www.middleeasteye.net/news/iranian-men-wear-hijabs-women-protest-headscarf-law-645609373 (accessed 16 July 2017).

39. "Iranian Men Wearing Hijabs to Support Wives," MSN, https://www.youtube.com/watch?v=y8llPOvY0WI (accessed 15 June 2018).

40. "Iranian Men Wear Hijabs to Protest against Headscarf Law."

BIBLIOGRAPHY

"Alarming State of Wales—Rebecca Riots—Attack on the Carmarthen Workhouse and Capture of the Rioters." *Freeman's Journal and Daily Commercial Advertiser* (Dublin), 23 June 1843.

Bakhtin, Mikhail. "Carnival and the Carnivalesque." In *Cultural Theory and Popular Culture: A Reader,* edited by John Storey, 250–259. 2nd edition. Athens: University of Georgia Press, 1998.

Binfield, Kevin. "Industrial Gender: Manly Men and Cross-Dressers in the Luddite Movement." In *Mapping Male Sexuality: Nineteenth-Century England*, edited by Jay Losey and William D. Brewer, 29–48. Madison, N.J.: Fairleigh Dickinson University Press, 2000.

Davis, Natalie Zemon. *Society and Culture in Early Modern France.* Stanford: Stanford University Press, 1975.

Feinberg, Leslie. *Transgender Warriors: Making History from Joan of Arc to RuPaul.* Boston: Beacon Press, 1996.

"Iranian Men Wear Hijabs to Protest against Headscarf Law." *Middle East Eye*, 3 August 2016. www.middleeasteye.net/news/iranian-men-wear-hijabs-women-protest-headscarf-law-645609373. Accessed 16 July 2017.

"Iranian Men Wearing Hijabs to Support Wives." MSN, 5 August 2016. https://www.youtube.com/watch?v=y8llPOvY0WI. Accessed 15 June 2018.

Jones, Rhian E. *Petticoat Heroes: Gender, Culture, and Popular Protest in the Rebecca Riots*. Cardiff: University of Wales Press, 2015.

"King Charles I Executed for Treason." This Day in History, 2010. www.history.com/this-day-in-history/king-charles-i-executed-for-treason. Accessed 11 June 2017.

Langert, Christina Bosco. "Hedgerows and Petticoats: Sartorial Subversion and Anti-enclosure Protest in Seventeenth-Century England." *Early Theatre* 12.1 (2009): 119–135.

Molloy, Pat. *And They Blessed Rebecca: An Account of the Welsh Toll-Gate Riots, 1839–1844*. Llandysul, Wales: Gomer Press, 1983.

Narvaes, Emily. "Church's Firing of Lesbian May Violate City Ordinance." *Boulder (Colo.) Daily Camera*. 14 March 1991, 2C.

Navickas, Katrina. "Luddism, Incendiarism and the Defence of Rural 'Task-Scapes' in 1812." https://www.academia.edu/535604/Luddism_incendiarism_and_the_defence_of_rural_task-scapes_in_1812. Accessed 16 May 2017.

Notes from Nowhere, ed. *We Are Everywhere: The Irresistible Rise of Global Anticapitalism*. London: Verso, 2003.

"The Rebecca Riots in Wales." *Derby (England) Mercury*, 5 July 1843.

Sharp, Buchanan. *In Contempt of All Authority: Rural Artisans and Riot in the West of England, 1586–1660*. Berkeley: University of California Press, 1980.

"Skimmington." *Times* (London), 28 September 1843.

Sykes, D. F. E. *Ben o' Bill's, the Luddite*. 3rd edition. Huddersfield, U.K.: "The Worker" Press, n.d. [between 1898 and 1905].

Thomis, Malcolm I. *The Luddites: Machine-Breaking in Regency England*. Newton Abbot, U.K.: David and Charles, 1970.

CHAPTER 10

Gender Diversity in Artifacts, Art, Icons, and Legends from Antiquity to the Middle Ages
Classically Trans

Key Questions

1. What can we learn about gender identity and gender diversity from artifacts that are thousands of years old?

2. How do ancient artifacts, legends, and icons reflect contemporary social issues and concerns?

3. What stereotypes and issues have not changed much over the course of millennia?

Chapter Overview

The ancient civilizations of Egypt, Greece, China, Mesopotamia, Rome, and India created artifacts, art, and spiritual or religious icons depicting gender diversity and gender expansiveness. Some legendary figures from ancient and medieval history even crossed the gender binary. From the sacred to the everyday, this chapter explores gender diversity from ancient times to the Middle Ages.

The chapter begins in Egypt, where recent excavations from the bottom of the Nile have recovered a religious statue of Hapy (sometimes spelled Hapi), a deity who was both male and female. After discussing gender diversity in ancient Egypt, the chapter goes on to explore the gender-diverse iconography and art of several world religions. Next, it offers insight into two powerful women who adopted male descriptors: Pharaoh Hatshepsut and General Mulan. The chapter closes with an examination of ancient Greek and Roman culture and their often uneasy relationship with gender diversity.

Haefele-Thomas, Ardel, *Introduction to Transgender Studies*
dx.doi.org/10.17312/harringtonparkpress/2019.01.itts.010
© 2019 by Harrington Park Press

Introduction: From the Depths of the Nile

Imagine you are flying in an airplane over the point where the Mediterranean Sea meets the Nile River. It is a clear day, and as you look down into the depths below, the sun hits the murky water in a perfect way. Suddenly, you discern the forms of stone buildings and statues deep below the surface. Are you imagining things? Maybe you've read too many stories about the mythical city of Atlantis.

This "hypothetical scenario" happened in real life. In 1933 Captain Cull of Britain's Royal Air Force flew his airplane over the tip of the area known in ancient times as Lower Egypt. Captain Cull reported his observations to the authorities. In response, Prince Omar Toussoun of Egypt used the tools available at the time to explore underwater. Thirty feet down, the Egyptian explorers found columns and statues covered in Nile River silt and mud.[1]

Over 1,200 years ago, two thriving cities, Canopus and Thonis-Heracleion, sank to the bottom of the Nile. Thonis-Heracleion was a major trading hub, and Canopus was a religious center. These port cities were centers of commerce for centuries because of their location at the mouth of the Nile River and on the Mediterranean Sea. Because the rich land of the Nile Delta was not solid enough, however, both cities sank.[2] Archaeologists have speculated that Canopus and Thonis-Heracleion could have disappeared into the Nile for many reasons: earthquakes, tsunamis, rising sea levels, the marshy, unstable ground, and the heavy stone used in the construction of the beautiful buildings that proved too heavy for the ground on which they sat.[3]

These cities, whose histories point to a complex and rich relationship between ancient Greece and ancient Egypt, simply disappeared. As stories about the cities were passed from generation to generation, they took on a legendary, almost mythical quality. After Captain Cull and Prince Toussoun verified that the remains of ancient cities rested at the bottom of the Nile, archaeologists, classical scholars, and historians began looking for ways to recover the near-perfect ruins (the Nile's mud and silt acted as excellent preservatives). By 2000 advanced excavation technology allowed the French marine archaeologist Franck Goddio to lead a team of underwater archaeologists into the depths of the Nile and the Bay of Aboukir.[4]

Over the past two decades, the excavators have retrieved many stunning artifacts from Thonis-Heracleion and Canopus.[5] In 2016 the British Museum held a special exhibition entitled *Sunken Cities: Egypt's Lost Worlds*. Visitors entered darkened rooms that simulated viewing the two cities underwater.

One of the statues retrieved from the sandy riverbed of the Nile is that of the deity Hapy, the God of the Nile. A London newspaper, the *Guardian,* reported: "The pink granite statue of Hapy, a personification of the Nile flood that was crucial for the country's fertility and wealth . . . [is] the tallest object ever to come to the [British Museum] on loan, and the tallest ever discovered of an Egyptian god."[6] This statue of Hapy, which weighs six tons and is eighteen feet tall, suggests Hapy's importance to the citizens of Canopus and Thonis-Heracleion.

Hapy embodied both the masculine and the feminine. Though Hapy is usually described as a male deity and wears a typical Egyptian male beard, he has female breasts, and he is depicted with the symbols of the lotus for Upper Egypt and the papyrus for Lower Egypt.[7] Hapy embraces the binaries of the masculine and the feminine as well as the binary between Upper Egypt and Lower Egypt, which had a history of warring with each other. Hapy became a metaphor for a united Egypt. Hapy's breasts symbolized the god's association with fertility and nourishment. Hapy was the god of the Nile River, and there is nothing more important in the desert than water.

What does this colossal statue, recovered from the Nile River floor, tell us about gender diversity in the ancient world? Hapy depicted a divine androgyny, a mix of the masculine and feminine as something to be celebrated and worshipped. Androgynous religious figures were not unusual in the ancient world; many, though not all, ancient religions and spiritual beliefs honored gender diversity.

Sacredly Trans: Gender Diversity in Religious Artifacts, Icons, and Legends

The combination of two sexes into one that the two-spirit had undergone was spiritual, an inner transformation or union . . . the cross-dressing that often, but not always, accompanied two-spirit status was a physical, external symbol of their nonphysical inner state.
JIM ELLEDGE[8]

Given the statue's size and original location at the mouth of the Nile, Hapy was clearly an important deity to the residents of Canopus and Thonis-Heracleion. Within the larger ancient Egyptian context, however, Hapy was a lesser god. Does the fact that Hapy was a lesser deity mean that gender fluidity was uncommon and relegated to minor deities? Or, might the prevalence of gender fluidity in even minor Egyptian deities suggest that gender diversity was present at many levels of myth, spirituality, and folklore? Let's explore some possible answers to these questions.

Indigenous Americas

The ancient Egyptians were not alone in worshipping gender-diverse deities. Many tribes throughout the Indigenous Americas and Pacific Islands sang songs and chants recounting creation stories that featured what we would understand today as Two-Spirit or *Māhū* figures. In Hawai'i, many of the ancient hula dances focused on gender fluidity or third-gender identities rather than a gender binary. It can be difficult to find the histories of ancient Indigenous peoples, especially in the Americas, where centuries of colonization nearly obliterated the ancient stories that had been passed from generation to generation through an oral tradition. Nonetheless, some of these histories are now being recovered. The following is an example from the ancient Mohave "Song of the Hwame":

> *he dances*
>
> *back and forth, back*
>
> *and forth.*
>
> *He feels it.*
>
> *Even if he's a girl,*
>
> *he dances that way.*[9]

This "Song of the Hwame" is one part of a three-part initiation chant for young people who begin their journey as Two-Spirit. For the purposes of translation into English, the he/she pronoun binary is still there, but you can imagine the intention behind the translation: one of gender fluidity not encompassed within a binary. The "Song of the Hwame" is only one example of Two-Spirit songs and chants, which were common to Indigenous cultures in the Americas.

Vodou and Diaspora

You have probably heard of Vodou, more commonly spelled Voodoo. If you are a fan of Disney animation films, you may remember *The Princess and the Frog* (2009), based in New Orleans. One of the sinister characters is Dr. Facilier, better known as Shadow Man, who is a Vodou practitioner. Disney has a long history of depicting Vodou as an ancient, evil religion. If you visit the Voodoo Museum in New Orleans' famous French Quarter, you will find eerie and sensationalistic depictions. Only when you study Vodou's history do its complexities become obvious.

Vodou is a Creole tradition that "embraces elements of African, indigenous American, European esoteric, and Christian origins. . . . The distinct form of

Vodou that emerged in New Orleans has tended to emphasize eclectic, magical, divinatory, and Catholic elements."[10] In other words, Vodou is a culturally diverse and complex religion. It is practiced mostly in Haiti and within Creole populations in New Orleans, but it is also related to Hoodoo, which has deep African cultural roots that encompass healing and magic. The various forms of Vodou indicate the flexibility of the Vodou tradition. It has evolved and changed over the centuries, and it has long been associated with an empowering resistance to oppression from the reality of slavery. In response, some white Protestant forms of Christianity have classified it as satanic. In fact, particularly in the Americas, religions that embrace multiple and shifting deities—religions that traverse gender, racial, or ethnic boundaries, or even the crossroads between the living and the dead—are often demonized.

Vodou specifically symbolizes the African *diaspora,* which is a term used for people who have been forced out of their homeland for various reasons. For instance, the slave trade in the Americas forced Africans out of their homeland. Numerous gender-diverse divinities are found in African-diasporic Vodou in the Americas. Mawu-Lisa, a patron saint of artists, is associated with both male and female twins as well as a *gynandrous* (another antiquated term for hermaphrodite) or transgender divinity who "created the first humans from clay."[11] Legba, often understood to be androgynous or transgender, is a powerful intermediary between the living and the dead. Legba rules the crossroads so that there are no binaries with regard to gender, age, life, or death.[12] Obatalá is an androgynous divinity of peace and a lawmaker. Obatalá embodies father and mother, king and queen. In the Catholic tradition, Obatalá becomes Our Lady of Mercy,[13] pointing to the fact that Catholicism has marginally embraced some divine figures in Vodou (while changing them a bit).

Trans Deities at the British Museum

The British Museum in London houses thousands of ancient artifacts, including the Rosetta Stone. If you ever decide to tour the museum, several guidebooks are available to help you. *A Little Gay History,* by R. B. Parkinson, offers an excellent introduction to looking at gender diversity and trans icons in the British Museum. Although the book's title may suggest that it focuses solely on gay men, the term "gay" in Britain is also shorthand for LGBTQ+.[14]

From Mesopotamia around 1750 BCE, the museum has a baked clay panel, the Burney Relief, depicting a figure known as "The Queen of the Night." The image is a naked woman with a horned headdress, wings, and talons for feet. As Parkinson notes, "She could be an aspect of Ishtar . . . [who] could even be shown with a beard in her more warlike forms. She had the power to assign gender identity and could 'change man into woman and woman into man.'"[15] Ishtar, the goddess of war and love in ancient Mesopotamia, embodied gender flexibility as well as fluidity between human and animal (which are also aspects of many Vodou and Indigenous American deities).

A beautiful copper alloy statue from 800 CE in India depicts Shiva, the Hindu dancing god or the lord of the dance. As Parkinson notes, "In Hindu mythology gender is often fluid, with the divine transcending any mortal categories of male and female."[16] Shiva's gender fluidity is subtle, and you will need to examine the earrings on this figure to see that they are different from each other. One symbolizes masculinity and the other femininity. Interestingly, Shiva is not the divine figure revered by *Hijras* in India. Rather, many *Hijras* revere Bahuchara Mata, who is often identified with self-mutilation. (As noted in Chapter 7, a **penectomy**, or removal of the penis, is one of the *Hijras*' sacred practices.[17])

From seventeenth-century Nepal, you can find a gilded bronze figure with beautiful inlaid turquoise and gems. This figure represents the Hindu deity Lakshminarayan, who "represents the male god Vishnu and his female consort Lakshmi . . . sometimes shown as a single figure whose body is half male and half female."[18] On this bronze figure, the gendered earrings are different, as they are on the Indian statue of Shiva. Interestingly, Lakshminarayan's elaborate combination of the masculine and the feminine is not uncommon in Nepal, where "Hinduism and Buddhism have been practiced side by side, often in distinctive and combined forms."[19] In other words, Nepal's religious figures seem to reflect the country's acceptance of religious and gender fluidity. As noted in Chapter 6, Nepal was one of the first countries in the world to recognize a third gender identity on government documents; perhaps this religious and historic context helps explain why.

There are numerous religions around the world, past and present, that have not only tolerated but even accepted and embraced various ideas of gender fluidity or gender diversity. Whether there are deities depicted as a more androgynous combination of male and female, which still remains within a gender binary, or whether there are numerous gender possibilities, it is clear that in many cultures, part of the power of the deities was precisely the ability to encompass and embrace all gender representations as sacred.

FIGURE 10.1 Jeanne d'Arc, by Cameron Rains. In 1429, at the age of seventeen, Jeanne d'Arc received a message from God to dress as a man and lead French peasants to defend France against the English. Her military battles were successful; however, her power threatened the French royalty, which claimed she was a heretic because of her cross-dressing and burned her at the stake.

A Legend Burned at the Stake: Jeanne d'Arc and Shifting Religious Attitudes

Whether as a saint or a nation-maker, Jeanne's place in world-history is assured.
T. DOUGLAS MURRAY [20]

The famous French trans ambassador, the Chevalier/Chevalière d'Éon, died in London in 1810. At the time, d'Éon had been writing a book on the history of saints who crossed the gender binary to fully embrace their religion. A devout Catholic, d'Éon focused on people assigned female at birth who, in order to fully embrace the divine, dressed and lived as men. D'Éon saw these saints as heroes and role models because d'Éon's own religious devotion was truly realized only when d'Éon lived as a woman. (For more on d'Éon's fascinating history, see Chapter 8.) At the time, one trans religious figure was so well known that d'Éon deemed her inclusion in the history unnecessary: Jeanne d'Arc, or, as we more popularly know her, Joan of Arc (figure 10.1).

In 1429 the seventeen-year-old Jeanne, dressed in men's military attire, went to Prince Charles, the heir to the French throne. The English were once again invading France, and Joan promised to lead an army of peasants to drive the English out of France. She stated that her masculine clothing and her mission to fight the English were a directive from God. The prince supported the teenager and sent her off with an army of 10,000 peasants.[21] During her time as a military leader, Jeanne remained devoutly religious and demanded the same of her soldiers. Here is a description of Jeanne d'Arc: "Her name and fame brought levies of ardent volunteers, from all sides, eagerly contending for the glory of serving under such a leader. Her frame was hearty and enduring. She wore armour night and day for a week at a time."[22]

The French were victorious against the English, and Jeanne d'Arc was a major influence in France's transformation into a free nation-state. Just after victory, she "was abducted by English sympathizers (who called her 'homasse,' or 'man-woman'); they turned her over to the Inquisition in England."[23] The new French king, Charles VII, could have paid a "king's ransom" to the English for her safe return, but he was envious of her military success and feared her ability to organize large and loyal numbers of peasants.[24] In other words, the king, who became the monarch in large part *because* of Jeanne d'Arc's bravery, chose to leave her at the mercy of the English.

In the English prison at Rouen, Jeanne d'Arc was "chained, mocked at, threatened, and insulted," but her faith in the French cause and her faith in God never failed.[25] When her trial began in April 1431, the initial charge was witchcraft because she had been raised in a part of France that held on to ancient pagan beliefs, of which the Catholic Church was deeply suspicious. (England would not become Protestant for another century.) Clearly, though, Jeanne d'Arc was so devoutly Catholic that the witchcraft charges had to be dropped. Ultimately, the judges sentenced her to death because of her refusal to dress in women's clothes and act in the ways they thought women should act. Jeanne d'Arc never wavered in the claim that her masculine gender expression came as a directive from God. Until the moment of her execution, she refused women's clothing and refused to act in any way that was deemed proper for a woman.[26] Jeanne d'Arc was burned at the stake on May 30, 1431.

Eighteen years after Jeanne d'Arc's excruciating and public execution, the Catholic Church carried out a new set of inquiries into her original sentencing. In 1456 the Church completely recanted the original sentencing: "To-morrow, at the Old Market-Place, in the same place where the said Jeanne was suffocated by a cruel and horrible fire, also with a General Preaching and with the placing of a handsome cross for the perpetual memory of the Deceased . . . we . . . honor her memory."[27] Jeanne d'Arc, originally put to death for heresy because of gender nonconformity, was later canonized as a saint. In thinking about the pope's allowing Catalina de Erauso, the "lieutenant nun," the choice between living as a man and living as a woman (see Chapter 8), one wonders if the famous and tragic story of Jeanne d'Arc informed his decision.

Egyptian Reality/Chinese Folklore: Pharaoh Hatshepsut and General Mulan

Jeanne d'Arc was burned at the stake for gender nonconformity. In 1456 the verdict was nullified, and in 1920 she was canonized (declared a saint). To this day, Jeanne d'Arc remains a religious icon. She was a real person caught in a time when the Catholic Church and warring nations were trying to figure out if God really had spoken to the young warrior. Was her violation of Old Testament anti-cross-dressing laws a sign of her heresy? Or was she one of the chosen few whom God directed to transgress the gender binary and become a warrior? The two stories in this section explore the ways that women in power—one real and the other most likely fictional—flourished by presenting themselves as male: Pharaoh Hatshepsut and General Mulan.

For centuries, it was believed that Pharaoh Hatshepsut (1508?–1458 BCE) was merely a mythical figure. Then, in the early nineteenth century, her nearly obliterated history and shattered artifacts were discovered. Pharaoh Hatshepsut (figure 10.2) had been a living, breathing monarch who ruled over two decades of peace and prosperity in Egypt. It is most likely that General Mulan from China was not any one person; she is probably a compilation of stories about brave young women who honored their families. Mulan's legend, "despite its journey across time, geography, and cultures, continues to be about a young woman's successful transgression."[28] Their stories offer examples of situational cross-dressing, but they also exemplify the fluctuation and evolution in a person's gender identity over time, not only in their own lifetimes, but also as their stories are discovered, rediscovered, and handed down through the centuries.

Because Pharaoh Hatshepsut was a real person and General Mulan is most likely a folkloric figure, you may want to consider the following question as you read about them: How do we view a real legendary person differently from the way we view a fictional legendary person?

In the Twenty-first Century, a Pharaoh on Display

On 15 October 2005, a long line of people snaked through a section of Golden Gate Park in San Francisco. They were waiting for the reopening of the de Young Museum, which had undergone a major renovation. Although anticipation and excitement were high for the museum's grand reopening, the curators knew

FIGURE 10.2 Pharaoh Hatshepsut, by Cameron Rains. Hatshepsut lived from circa 1508 to 1458 BCE. During that time, Pharaoh Hatshepsut ruled for two decades of prosperity and moderate peace in the Nile Valley. Refusing to be called Queen Hatshepsut, she donned the fake beard worn by male pharaohs and during her period in power shifted all her imagery and iconography to that of a masculine ruler.

they had to wow visitors with the museum's first special exhibit. King Tut is always a crowd pleaser, but the curators chose to take a risk. Working with a team from the Metropolitan Museum of Art in New York, the Kimbell Art Museum in Fort Worth, Texas, and a traveling entourage of delegates and ambassadors from Cairo, Egypt, the de Young launched the world premiere of the exhibition "Hatshepsut: From Queen to Pharaoh."

The Hatshepsut exhibition was a risk for the museum because it celebrated Egypt's little-known, nearly forgotten trans ruler: "Having achieved kingship, she was officially acknowledged as a female pharaoh, although in conformity with the Egyptian ideology of rulership she was often represented in art as a man. After her death, Hatshepsut's monuments were destroyed and her name omitted from subsequent Egyptian king lists."[29] This description of Hatshepsut's history presents us with more questions than answers. Couldn't an Egyptian woman ruler be a queen? Cleopatra comes to mind. Why did Hatshepsut become a pharaoh and not a queen? Who was in charge of the art depicting Hatshepsut? Why were the monuments destroyed? And, if the monuments were destroyed, how do we have any history or evidence of Hatshepsut (figure 10.2)?

A Pharaoh Nearly Erased: Hatshepsut's Rediscovery

Jean-François Champollion, a French scholar who focused on deciphering Egyptian hieroglyphics, went to Egypt in 1828–1829, where he visited the temple at Deir el-Bahri. Imagine his confusion and surprise as he studied ancient texts on the wall that used "female gender endings with depictions of a male king."[30] Champollion decided that the hieroglyphics must have referred to Amessis, sister to Pharaoh Thutmose II. Champollion assumed that she succeeded her brother to the throne upon his death and remained there until she married, which would explain some of the feminine gender endings on the cartouche.

As we now know, Champollion was wrong. His discovery, however, ultimately gave voice to a woman pharaoh whose story had nearly been obliterated. In the 1920s and 1930s, researchers from the Metropolitan Museum of Art in New York discovered two huge pits filled with statues from Hatshepsut's temple. It took years to piece these relics together because they had been smashed and desecrated. The popular working theory at the time was that Thutmose III so hated his stepmother for usurping his power that he ordered everything she had built to be destroyed.[31] Now, in the twenty-first century, the scholarly debate focuses on Hatshepsut's extraordinary decision to become a pharaoh rather than remain a queen; and speculation continues about why Thutmose III ordered all evidence of Hatshepsut's life be shattered.

The rediscovery of Pharaoh Hatshepsut offers us a complex counterpoint to other narratives of Western imperial and colonial violence that erased the gender-diverse histories of so many Indigenous cultures around the world. In this case, the European explorers helped recover the lost history of a ruler who, it turns out, carefully transitioned across the gender binary by way of the masculine statues and other monuments she commissioned to be built to honor her as a king and not as a queen.

Mr. Pharaoh Herself: Hatshepsut's Transition from Queen to Pharaoh

Hatshepsut ruled Egypt for nearly twenty years in the mid-fifteenth century BCE. Although some military battles were fought during those two decades, and Hatshepsut led some of the fights herself, her reign is generally considered to have been peaceful and prosperous. In fact, some scholars believe that Egypt had a renaissance during this time that positively affected Egyptian art and culture for the next thousand years.[32]

Recall that the Egyptian gender-diverse god Hapy embraced the binaries of masculine and feminine. The large statue of the deity is adorned with the lotus and the papyrus, representations of Upper Egypt and Lower Egypt, symbolizing the union of the geographic binary. Pharaoh Hatshepsut's reign was also marked by the union of Upper and Lower Egypt, another indicator of the relative peace of those two decades.[33]

Hatshepsut first came to power when Thutmose II died at a young age. Thutmose II and Hatshepsut had a daughter together; however, Thutmose II's son, Thutmose III, had been born to a secondary wife. Because Hatshepsut was Thutmose II's primary wife and the aunt to Thutmose III, the boy was crowned, but Hatshepsut, in fact, ruled as his regent.[34] Obviously, a very young child cannot rule a country.

In the second year of the child Thutmose III's reign, while Hatshepsut was acting as regent, she began to move toward becoming a king herself. At Semna temple in Nubia, Hatshepsut commissioned reliefs to be carved depicting her in the company of the gods, and "the description of her actions—as an heir, as a builder, as a ritual officiate—are those of a masculine king."[35] In ancient Egypt, as today in many countries with a monarchy, the king or queen holds what is called a **divine right.** In other words, the monarch is believed to be the human form of god, or at least the monarch perpetuates the idea that he or she rules as a result of a god's will. And so, over the course of her twenty years in power, Hatshepsut gradually moved from having artists and temple builders depict her as a queen—a ruler standing in long skirts with her feet close together—to a king with a beard, standing in masculine hunting clothes with legs apart.

The following is a modern historian's account of the change in Hatshepsut's presentation on statues: "Early on in her kingship, Hatshepsut attempted to add a layer of masculinity to her feminine forms. . . . This life-size limestone statue from her Temple of Millions of Years . . . shows [her] without a shirt, wearing only a king's kilt, but she retains . . . delicate facial features, and even the generous hint of feminine breasts. Eventually, Hatshepsut opted for a fully masculinized image in her statuary, showing herself with wide and strong shoulders, firm pectoral muscles, and no sign of breasts."[36] You can compare two statues of Hatshepsut at the Metropolitan Museum of Art's website. Here are the links: www.metmuseum.org/art/collection/search/544450 and www.metmuseum.org /art/collection/search/544446. These two statues show Hatshepsut's obvious gender transformation from queen to king.

Most people in ancient Egypt could not read—certainly not the common people. So, in her earliest reliefs and obelisks, Hatshepsut had the artists portray her as feminine, but she also had writing (hieroglyphics) chiseled into the stone that portrayed her in a masculine light. Unbeknown to most Egyptians, the masculine and the feminine were already beginning to meld together. It would not have been unusual for the ruler to wear a fake beard. In ancient Egypt, men did not wear facial hair, which was seen as dirty. All pharaohs literally tied a specific type of royal beard onto their chins.[37]

One specific piece of evidence tells us about the way Hatshepsut wanted to be remembered after her death and into eternity. On the facade of her Temple of Millions of Years, where she depicted herself as a mummified version of the god Osiris, "the first skin color she chose for these statues was yellow ocher, the traditional color of a woman. As time went on, she opted for orange, an androgynous blend. Finally, she decided to fully masculinize her imagery . . . the latest statues [were] the red ocher of masculinity."[38] Over the course of twenty years, the changing colors in the statues of Hatshepsut show a full transition across the gender binary. This was the transition that she wanted future generations to see. After her death, though, Thutmose III had very different ideas.

Erasing a Legend

If Thutmose III had destroyed all Pharaoh Hatshepsut's obelisks, statues, and temples (of which there were many, commemorating and memorializing her as a great ruler) immediately after her death, then his motive might be clear. After all, Hatshepsut was his regent, who was supposed to help him as a child and then transfer power to him when he came of age. Pharaoh Hatshepsut, however, forced Thutmose III to remain in the proverbial backseat until after her death. It is understandable that Hatshepsut's refusal to transfer power would have upset Thutmose III. Why, then, did he wait until twenty years after her death to command the destruction of every one of Hatshepsut's images, statues, temples, and obelisks? Why did he wait so long? Nobody knows. As one scholar has noted, "While the obliteration of her memory was once explained as an act of retribution on the part of her successor, and more current theories propose that the motive was safeguarding the royal succession, the reasons . . . are still not entirely clear."[39]

A striking example of Hatshepsut's erasure occurred in the Karnak temple, where chisel bearers, on the orders of Thutmose III, "so carefully chiseled out her human form that the shadow of her former kingship still haunts Amen's temple walls."[40] Although Thutmose III attempted to erase Hatshepsut from history, he was not successful. Many of the broken artifacts have now been put back together, restoring Pharaoh Hatshepsut's history.

FIGURE 10.3 General Mulan, by Cameron Rains. The famous Chinese legend of the brave girl who went to war in place of her sick and aging father has been in the popular imagination for around 1,500 years. "The Ballad of Mulan" notes the warrior's complex gender identity. Mulan's story has been the inspiration for film and literature.

China's Most Honorable Girl: The Legend of Mulan

For love of her elderly father
she will dress in warrior's clothes,
walking and talking like a man,
so no one ever knows.
CHARLIE CHIN, *CHINA'S BRAVEST GIRL*[41]

If you have seen Disney's animated feature *Mulan* (1998), or the less successful *Mulan II* (2004), you are familiar with the legend of the brave young woman from China who went into the military in place of her aging and ailing father. The story of *Mulan* comes from an ancient Chinese poem, "The Ballad of Mulan." The many legends of Mulan (figure 10.3) share the same background story. War is imminent, and upon seeing a draft notice listing all the men from her village who must report for duty, Mulan is devastated to see her father's name on the list. Mulan has no brothers, so her father must report to the front. Mulan decides to dress as a male soldier and take her sick father's place. Here is a portion of the ballad:

"I want to buy a saddle and horse,

And serve in the army in Father's place."

In the East Market she buys a spirited horse,

In the West Market she buys a saddle,

In the South Market she buys a bridle,

In the North Market she buys a long whip.[42]

The directions beautifully invoke traditional epic Chinese themes that are prevalent, for example, in the ancient tile game Mahjong, which is still played around the world today; they symbolize the compass points of the journey she is about to make. Not only will Mulan literally journey across a vast landscape as a soldier, but she will also journey from her position as a girl in her village to a man who becomes a decorated military general.

Searching for Mulan's Origins

Historians of folklore are not sure when the story of Mulan first appeared, but it is likely that her ballad began with an oral tradition. Scholars believe that the earliest written form of her ballad appeared in *Gujin yuelu,* which is a Chinese musical collection compiled sometime around 568 CE.[43] This compilation has been lost for a long time, but it is cited in numerous sources from the thirteenth century until its disappearance in the nineteenth century. If we assume the citations are correct, then we also know that the editor of the lost collection was Zhijiang, a Buddhist monk who lived during the Chen Dynasty of 557–588 CE.[44]

Mulan's ballad originated during a time of civil war and violence in China's northern regions. At the time, China was not one unified country, but rather a large geographic area rife with various warring tribes. As one scholar has noted, "Representation in the 'Ballad' of the masculine spirit as a characteristic of northern women resembles some northern folk songs that portray heroic women as skilled archers and horse riders."[45] So the tale of the brave young woman who takes her father's place in the military comes from a tradition of strong tribal women who fought for their communities.

Even the ancient "Ballad" makes it clear that gender and gendered spaces are transgressed. Although gender roles in China centuries ago were not exactly the same as they are in modern-day China or in today's Western culture, women were in charge of inside spheres (domestic) and men were in charge of outside spheres (public). Gender is not the only boundary transgressed within the story: the "Ballad" reflects a "social blending of different ethnic traditions through the heroine's ability to perform feminine duty at home as well as to wield masculine prowess in the frontiers."[46] Ethnic traditions and gender boundaries blend in Mulan's story, which has continued to evolve over 1,500 years. The core theme of Mulan's legend remains constant regardless of its location; it is the story of a brave, honorable, patriotic young woman who cross-dresses and joins the military to spare her sick father.

Mulan in Popular Culture

One modern example of the evolution of Mulan's legend is Maxine Hong Kingston's 1976 novel, *The Woman Warrior.* Kingston combines ancient Chinese folk tales with Mulan's fictionalized autobiography as she explores what it means to be a Chinese American woman and feminist in the United States in the late twentieth century. Some speculate that Kingston's novel may have been the seed for writers at Disney.

In the 1998 Disney film *Mulan,* the young warrior stares into a pool and questions when the reflection will show the true person inside. Mulan's song can resonate with trans people who feel that the person whom the world sees—and specifically the gender identity that the world assumes—does not reflect who they are on the inside. For trans people who have seen the film or heard the music, Mulan's song allows a place of identification, safety, and comfort in the middle of a mainstream popular film. Although popular culture is becoming more inclusive of trans characters in mainstream shows like *Orange Is the New Black* and *The Fosters,* many trans people, particularly trans youths, continue to have difficulty finding cultural representations that do not portray the trans person as the butt of a joke or as a monstrous shape-shifter. (You will read more about these two stereotypes in Chapter 11.)

Though the Disney film takes risks by hinting at a trans identity for Mulan, the film reverts to a cisnormative and heteronormative ending when Mulan returns home, throws off the warrior's outfit, embraces her femininity, and gets engaged to a man. The ancient "Ballad" leaves the reader with a much more ambiguous ending: "How can they tell if I am he or she?"[47]

Another film version of Mulan's story is the 2009 Chinese movie *Mulan: Rise of a Warrior* (original title *Hua Mulan*), directed by Jingle Ma and Wei Dong. In this film Hua Mulan cross-dresses, leaves her village to fight in her father's place in the military, and over the course of twelve years becomes a general. In many ways, this modern telling stays true to the original ballad. Unlike the Disney version, which often makes fun of or sensationalizes Mulan's cross-dressing, this film considers the warrior's need to pass as a man in the military, but cross-dressing is not the film's focal point. Rather, over the course of this two-hour epic that depicts the harsh realities of continued warfare, viewers begin to forget that they are watching a young woman cross-dressed. They gradually transition to the idea that Mulan is the general and a man. The conclusion to Ma and Dong's film is true to the "Ballad" in that Mulan's gender identity upon her return home remains ambiguous. Neither the viewer nor Mulan knows if the warrior is he or she. And perhaps the point is that the gender binary no longer holds.

Trans Cornerstones of Western Civilization: Ancient Greece and Rome

Greek mythology tells many stories about gods and goddesses becoming upset with one another or with mortals. Often the stories involve someone who is male being turned into a female or vice versa.

One famous Greek story is alive and well in our contemporary popular culture: *Hedwig and the Angry Inch* (2001). The film did relatively well at the box office, particularly at smaller independent LGBTQ+ film festivals. The Tony Award–winning musical starring Neil Patrick Harris, however, has brought the story to a much wider audience. If you have seen the film or the live production, think back to the song "The Origin of Love." If you have not seen either version, it is easy to find the song and its lyrics online.

Why are you reading about a contemporary trans rock musical when the heading for this section clearly indicates that you are going to be learning about ancient Greece and Rome? "The Origin of Love" comes from *The Symposium,* written in the fourth century BCE by the Greek philosopher Plato. *The Symposium* looks at love in its various forms. Imagine a group of people sitting around eating good food, drinking good wine, and talking through the night on the topic of love. That is precisely the scenario for *The Symposium.* This work, which has been read, taught, and discussed for well over two thousand years, includes stories of what we would understand today as same-sex desire, love between a man and a woman, and love that has no erotic component. Each guest at Plato's all-nighter has a chance to speak on the nature of love.

When it is Aristophanes' turn to discuss love, we get a bittersweet story of the first human beings who embodied at least two genders, perhaps more. These gender-diverse figures were happy. In fact, they were too happy in the eyes of Zeus, who was often a jealous god. Zeus sent down a lightning bolt that literally cut the humans up and tore their genders apart so that they roamed around without all their parts. This piece of mythology is an interesting way to think about the creation of a gender binary. As Plato wrote Aristophanes' story, numerous Indigenous cultures around the world embraced the gender-diverse people whom the mythical Zeus tore apart.

You may remember that *differences of sex development* (also sometimes referred to as *intersex*) is relatively new terminology. For centuries, the word *hermaphrodite* had been used for people whose sex at birth might not have been completely clear. But where did the word *hermaphrodite* come from? The Roman poet Ovid wrote the most well-known version of the tale of Hermaphroditus, the beautiful son of Hermes and Aphrodite. One day Hermaphroditus was bathing in a spring, where a nymph, Salmacis, fell in love with him. He rejected her. In her heartbreak, she cried to the gods to never separate her from her beloved. That is when their bodies melded together:

> *So these two joined in close embrace, no longer*
>
> *Two beings, and no longer man and woman,*
>
> *But neither, and yet both.*
>
> *Hermaphroditus*
>
> *Saw that the water had made him half a man,*
>
> *With limbs all softness.*[48]

Although having differences in sex development and being transgender are not the same thing, you can see the gender stereotypes in Ovid's story. When Hermaphroditus and Salmacis are joined together as one, his masculinity becomes "soft" and the waters where he bathed become cursed. For a closer look at gender identities and attitudes toward gender expression in ancient Rome, read Cheryl Morgan's essay below, "Trans Lives in Rome."

CHERYL MORGAN

Trans Lives in Rome

Cheryl Morgan is a writer, editor, broadcaster, and publisher. In addition to being passionate about trans history, she is also the first openly trans person to have won a Hugo Award from the World Science Fiction Society. Follow her on Twitter as @CherylMorgan.

It is 204 BCE. In response to a prophecy, Rome has sent a delegation to the city of Pergamon, in what we now call Turkey, to beg for divine aid against Hannibal. Their ship was returning up the Tiber carrying a representation of a mighty goddess called Cybele. Then disaster: the ship became stuck on a sandbank. Thinking quickly, a noblewoman called Claudia Quinta prayed to the goddess and, by a miracle, was able to pull the ship free by herself.

Much of this is myth, of course. The Roman army already had the threat of Hannibal fairly well under control by that time, and no one knows if Claudia Quinta really existed. But Rome did import a goddess called Cybele from Turkey. The Romans called her Magna Mater, the Great Mother. Virgil gave her a starring role in *The Aeneid,* his tale of the founding of Rome by Trojan refugees. Her temple was on the Palatine Hill itself, and the annual games held in her honor were one of the great events of the year. All this was very odd.

Cybele wasn't a standard part of the Olympian pantheon that formed the bedrock of Roman religion. In addition, her cult had some very un-Roman practices. Cybele was served by a group of people called galli. They were assigned male at birth but underwent ritual castration and lived their lives as women.

Roman society was highly patriarchal. Women could not vote, hold public office, or act on their own behalf in a court of law. Roman men were obsessed with their virility. The very word *virile* is derived from the Latin word *vir,* meaning a manly man. That doesn't mean that they frowned on same-sex relationships. Sex with other men was perfectly okay provided that you took the manly, penetrative role. What a Roman man should never do was seem effeminate.

The origins of the cult of Cybele are lost in prehistory. Two thousand years before her arrival in Rome, the Sumerians worshipped a goddess called Inanna who, according to a royal priestess called Enheduanna, could turn a man into a woman and a woman into a man. Inanna's cult may have included people assigned male at birth who lived as women. In a colorful festival, the whole city crossed-dressed in celebration of the goddess's powers.

Down the centuries many other peoples in the Near East worshipped similar goddesses. There was Ishtar in Assyria and Babylon, Astarte in Phoenicia, Atargatis in Syria, Tanit in Carthage, and many more. The exact relation between these belief systems has been a topic for endless debate among archaeologists.

By Roman times writing was commonplace, so we know that the galli existed. We know some of their names and likenesses because a few were rich enough to have expensive tombs. They are mentioned, though not usually favorably, by numerous well-known Roman writers.

We also know that they were castrated. The mythological basis for their practice came from the legend of Attis, Cybele's consort, who was said to have castrated himself while overcome by divine frenzy. Catullus, in poem 63, tells the whole story and makes brilliant use of the gendered aspects of Latin to mark Attis's transformation from man to woman.

Rome was full of eunuchs. In Matthew 19:12 Jesus mentions three types, all of whom he was happy to accept as followers. There were those forcibly castrated, often upon entering slavery. There were those born eunuchs, an ancient term meaning anyone apparently male who had no interest in sex with women. And there were those who castrated themselves for religious purposes. Years later, Christian monks would take this as an instruction for becoming more holy, but when Jesus was alive the only people who castrated themselves for religious purposes worshipped a goddess.

It is unclear what surgery the galli would have had. Because of their feminine lifestyle, and perhaps from the graphic description of self-castration in Catullus, historians have assumed that they were fully castrated. However, a few castration clamps used in initiation ceremonies have been found. One was discovered in the Thames and is now in the British Museum. A paper in the *Journal of the History of Medicine* describes it as a device for ensuring that the patient does not bleed to death when the testicles are removed, and additionally for keeping the penis safely out of the way during surgery. The author notes that the device is very efficient and was very well used.

It seems likely that most galli would only have had their testicles removed. Roman medicine was good, but not good enough to guarantee survival after removal of the penis. Some galli may have been moved to take the risk of additional surgery because of a stronger feminine identity. Modern trans women have a variety of personal attitudes toward surgery, and there is no reason to suppose that the galli were any different.

The legal status of the galli was complicated. When Cybele first arrived in Rome, citizens were forbidden to join the cult because a eunuch could not be a Roman citizen. We have records of legal cases showing discrimination against trans people.

The most interesting is the story of Genucius, a gallus in the first century BCE who had been left an inheritance by a friend. Valerius Maximus tells us the court ruled that Genucius could not receive the money because under Roman law only men and women could be beneficiaries of wills. A gallus was neither male nor female.

The magistrate seems to have disliked the galli. He forbade Genucius to testify on her own behalf, saying that he did not want his court polluted by her "obscene presence and corrupt voice." This suggests that Genucius had a high-pitched, effeminate voice. She probably used vocal techniques similar to those used by modern trans women.

We don't know exactly what religious functions the galli performed. There are stories of noisy musical displays involving flutes, timpani, and castanets. They were often mendicant beggars. Cicero says that the galli were uniquely given exemption from the laws against begging, which shows how important Cybele was to the Romans.

The big question is how the galli saw themselves. Apuleius, in *The Golden Ass,* caricatures a group of galli as highly effeminate drag queens who call each other by feminine names and are eager to find handsome young men they can seduce. While satire has to be assumed to be an exaggeration, there must be some truth in this portrayal. Varo describes the galli as being very feminine and attractive. Philo of Alexandria refers to "those of them who . . . have desired to be completely changed into women and gone on to mutilate their genital organs." Some scholars have suggested that the galli went to extreme lengths in order to be able to live a homosexual lifestyle. Same-sex relations were common among Roman men, however. Even if one's preference was to be penetrated, there were plenty of roles in Roman society that would allow that without the need to be castrated or to live as a woman.

What marks the galli out is their wholehearted commitment to femininity in the face of a misogynistic society. That's something modern trans women can identify with.

The emperor Claudius, who ruled in the middle of the first century CE, was particularly fond of the Magna Mater. If Claudia Quinta was a real person, she would have been one of his ancestors. Because of this, Claudius made the rites of Attis an official part of the Roman religious calendar. This meant that Romans now had an annual Castration Day on which initiations were performed. It was a form of legal recognition.

Sadly, it wasn't to last, as successive emperors clamped down on what were starting to be seen as immoral practices. Domitian, entirely reasonably, prohibited the castration of children, who, we must assume, were rarely asked for consent. At the end of the first century Nerva toughened up the law by making the penalties apply to anyone who sold a slave for the purpose of being castrated. Neither of these laws applied to the galli. Several decades later, however, Hadrian widened the net yet again. His new edict included a statement that no one could "offer himself voluntarily for castration . . . on pain of capital punishment."

What effect this had on the cult of Cybele is unclear. Not long after Hadrian's reign, the cult adopted a new ceremony, the taurobolium, in which a bull was sacrificed to the goddess. It has been suggested that this was a form of substitution sacrifice whereby the chief gallus, and perhaps some of her followers, could undergo symbolic castration without actually breaking the law.

It also appears that one could, after payment of a suitable fee, obtain a license to be castrated. In the second century Justin Martyr, in a letter to Antonius Pius, Hadrian's direct successor, mentions a Christian who applied for such a license. Justin was trying to persuade the emperor that Christians were not one of those sex-mad mystery cults and would go to extraordinary lengths to avoid sinning sexually. One has to assume that pagans such as the galli could apply for a license to be castrated too.

Perhaps the most significant event of the entire story came in 218 CE, when a fourteen-year-old called Elagabalus became emperor. He had been born in Emesa (modern-day Homs) in Syria and had expected to be a local ruler. He was already high priest of a local sun god when he unexpectedly inherited the throne. His city was also home to the Cybele-like goddess Atargatis.

Elagabalus scandalized the Romans, partly through his attachment to foreign gods, but mainly because of his effeminacy. He made no secret of his attraction to men, demanded sexual favors from his guards, and married his charioteer. Then there is this tale from Cassius Dio: "He carried his lewdness to such a point that he asked the physicians to contrive a woman's vagina in his body by means of an incision, promising them large sums for doing so." So many terrible things were written about Elagabalus that Sir W. S. Gilbert included a reference to "the crimes of Heliogabalus" (using an alternative spelling) in the Major General's song from *The Pirates of Penzance*. It is hardly surprising that a child who became emperor of much of the known world aged just fourteen would prove an inept ruler, but Elagabalus may have been deeply troubled before ascending to the throne.

Martijn Icks in his recent book on the young emperor suggests that all the lurid tales about Elagabalus are made-up gossip. It is certainly true that Cassius Dio and Herodian, the other contemporary historian to write a life of Elagabalus, both published their works during the reign of his successor, Severus Alexander. The new emperor may well have had a hand in the brutal murder of his predecessor. It would have been unwise for either historian to describe Elagabalus favorably. However, it is not the fact of the character assassination that is interesting; it is the way in which it was done. Elagabalus was constantly attacked for his femininity.

We will never know if Elagabalus was the first trans woman to become ruler of most of the known world. What we do know is that the idea that someone assigned male at birth could undergo surgery and live as a woman for the rest of their life was well known to Romans. The cult of Cybele was popular throughout the empire, from Turkey to Britain and North Africa. The galli celebrated their goddess noisily, happily, and very publicly.

When Saint Augustine of Hippo, recalling his youth in Carthage, writes in *City of God* of "these effeminates . . . going through the streets . . . with anointed hair, whitened faces, relaxed bodies, and feminine gait," he is simultaneously harking back to the carnival atmosphere of the Sumerian festival of Inanna and providing a fairly accurate description of a modern Pride Parade. Those who partook in such ceremonies, and particularly those who took on female roles to better serve the goddess, were often looked down on by the rest of society. Nevertheless, they existed and lived their lives outside the gender binary.

REFERENCES

Abusch, Ra'anan. "Eunuchs and Gender Transformation: Philo's Exegesis of the Joseph Narrative." In *Eunuchs in Antiquity and Beyond*, edited by Shaun Tougher, 103–122. London: Gerald Duckworth, 2002.

Cantarella, Eva. *Bisexuality in the Ancient World*. Translated by Cormac Ó Cuilleanáin. 2nd edition. New Haven: Yale University Press, 2002.

Francis, G. "On a Romano-British Castration Clamp Used in the Rites of Cybele." *Journal of the History of Medicine* 1 (January 1926): 95–110.

Hales, Shelley. "Looking for Eunuchs: The Galli and Attis in Roman Art." In *Eunuchs in Antiquity and Beyond*, edited by Shaun Tougher, 87–102. London: Gerald Duckworth, 2002.

Icks, Martjin. *The Crimes of Elagabalus*. New York: I. B. Tauris, 2013.

Morgan, Cheryl. "Evidence for Trans Lives in Sumer." *Notches,* 2 May 2017. http://notchesblog .com/2017/05/02/evidence-for-trans-lives-in-sumer/.

Richlin, Amy. "Not before Homosexuality: The Materiality of the Cinaedus and the Roman Law against Love between Men." *Journal of the History of Sexuality* 3.4 (1993): 523–573.

Roller, Lynn E. *In Search of God the Mother: The Cult of Anatolian Cybele*. Berkeley: University of California Press, 1999.

Rowlands, Rhiannon M. "Eunuchs and Sex: Beyond Sexual Dichotomy in the Roman World." PhD dissertation, University of Missouri–Columbia, 2014.

Stevenson, Walter. "Eunuchs and Early Christianity." In *Eunuchs in Antiquity and Beyond*, edited by Shaun Tougher, 123–142. London: Gerald Duckworth, 2002.

———. "The Rise of Eunuchs in Greco-Roman Antiquity." *Journal of the History of Sexuality* 5.4 (1995): 495–511.

Williams, Craig. *Roman Homosexuality.* 2nd edition. New York: Oxford University Press, 2010.

Key Concepts

diaspora (p. 358)
divine right (p. 365)
gynandrous (p. 358)
penectomy (p. 359)

Activities, Discussion Questions, and Observations

1. What ideas in Cheryl Morgan's essay do you find the most compelling? Had you heard about Elagabalus before you read the essay? Refer to Chapter 7, which mentions the surgical procedures that the *Hijras* of India have undergone for thousands of years. What are some of the similarities between them and the ancient Roman galli?

2. The first part of this chapter provides examples of gender fluidity, gender diversity, and gender transgressions in spiritual and religious artifacts and iconography, but there are many more. For an individual or small-group project, or an in-class presentation, conduct more in-depth research on the examples discussed in this chapter, or research other cultures and deities that exhibited gender diversity. In what part of the world and during what period are these artifacts and/or stories found? Are these spiritual practices still active? If so, how have they changed over time? Were the changes the result of outside pressures? Or have some of these spiritual and religious practices remained constant? What has enabled these practices to remain unchanged?

3. For this assignment, you can either consider your own religious beliefs or research a religion that is different from yours. Think of some of today's major world religions. Or think about your own religion. It is often believed that many religions are against gender diversity or trans identity, especially the Abrahamic religions, the largest of which are Judaism, Islam, and Christianity. Conduct some research on one of these three religions (or another modern world religion) to determine its stance on gender diversity, cross-dressing, transgender identity, and trans expression, including medical approaches to gender affirmation. Remember that most religions have various forms, so you cannot

assume that if one branch of the religion is supportive, then all branches will be supportive. For example, the Episcopal Church (a Protestant religion) does not necessarily hold the same views as the Lutheran Church (another Protestant religion). Orthodox Judaism may not treat trans people the same way that Hassidic Judaism does. Even within one branch, opinions can vary widely.

4. Conduct research on the various legends of Mulan. Whether in children's book form, in poetry, in film, or in some other version, how is Mulan represented?

5. Watch both versions of *Mulan*, the Disney version and *Mulan: Rise of a Warrior*. What are the differences between the two films? How is gender addressed in each film? How is Mulan's passing as a male soldier depicted? In *Mulan: Rise of a Warrior*, the story is told by a Chinese director. How is the Eastern version of the film (the Chinese version) told? How is the Western version of the film (the Disney version) told? How is Mulan's gender portrayed in both films? The endings of the two films are very different. Discuss the nuances and differences concerning Mulan's future. How has being a general in the army affected Mulan's relationships? Do the films' depictions of these relationships reinforce traditional gender roles for women? Do they trouble gender? If so, how?

6. Pharaoh Hatshepsut has been recovered from the sands of time. How do we "read" this Pharaoh? In other words, can we read Hatshepsut as occupying a space along the trans spectrum? If so, how? Do you read Hatshepsut as someone who was hungry for power as the ruler of both Upper and Lower Egypt, which made it necessary for her to be a man?

7. In China (and beyond) the legend of Mulan has been passed from generation to generation. Now we have examples in the twentieth and twenty-first centuries in film. In contrast, Pharaoh Hatshepsut's memory was nearly erased thousands of years ago but rediscovered in the nineteenth century. China and Egypt are very different places with different cultures. What aspects of Mulan's story have endured throughout the centuries? Why was the story of Hatshepsut not recounted through the ages?

8. Historically, Elagabalus has been considered one of Rome's worst emperors. His lavish femininity and decadence have also contributed to historians' reading him as homosexual. However, some recent reflections on this emperor, who ruled for only four years, see Elagabalus as someone who may have been assigned male at birth but identified as a woman. How do homophobia and transphobia play out in the ways that we have learned about Elagabalus?

How is the response to Elagabalus as someone whom today we would probably identify as a trans woman similar to the responses in the nineteenth century to both the Chevalier/Chevalière d'Éon and Frances Thompson (see Chapter 8)?

9. Look at the website for gender diversity at the British Museum and choose a piece to examine. What intrigues you about the piece? Go online and do some extra research about either the artifact or the story behind the artifact. You may want to check out this British Museum website, which looks at gender identity and gender diversity: http://britishmuseum.org/explore/themes/same-sex_desire_and_gender/gender_identity.aspx#2.

Film and Television of Interest

Hedwig and the Angry Inch (2001, U.S., Germany, 95 minutes)
This cult classic, which is now a Broadway musical, explores the complexity of love and gender diversity. Most notably, the song "The Origin of Love," which talks about ancient people embodying multiple genders, is directly out of Plato's *Symposium*.

Joan of Arc (1999, television miniseries, U.S., 180 minutes)
This made-for-television film dramatizes the life of the famous cross-dressing saint.

The Messenger: The Story of Joan of Arc (1999, France, 92 minutes)
A dramatic depiction of the life and devotion of Joan of Arc.

Mulan (1998, U.S., 88 minutes)
Disney's animated musical loosely follows "The Ballad of Mulan." Though it is replete with the usual Disneyesque characters, there are still some songs within the film that are particularly heartrending and pertinent to trans viewers.

Mulan: Rise of a Warrior (originally Hua Mulan) (2009, China, 115 minutes)
This live-action feature won the lead actor, Zhao Wei, two major Chinese film awards. The movie is beautifully filmed and is a meditation on war and men in war. Mulan goes into the service in place of her sick father, but unlike the more sensationalized U.S. Disney version, this film winds up being a spectacular study of gender and nationalism. In Chinese with English subtitles.

Secrets of Egypt's Lost Queen (2007, U.S., 120 minutes)
This historic documentary takes a look at the discovery of Pharaoh Hatshepsut's tomb. The film focuses on the importance of the discovery and discusses Hatshepsut as a

NOTES

1. Kate Sparrow, Esther Aarts, and the British Museum, *Secret Treasures of Ancient Egypt* (London: Nosy Crow, 2016), 6–7.

2. Richard Gray, "Lost City of Heracleion Gives Up Its Secrets," *Telegraph*, 28 April 2013, www.telegraph.co.uk/news/earth/environment/archaeology/10022628/Lost-city-of-Heracleion-gives-up-its-secrets.html (accessed 16 June 2017).

3. Sparrow et al., *Secret Treasures of Ancient Egypt*, 26–27.

4. Aurélia Masson-Berghoff, "Secrets of the Sea," *British Museum Magazine* 84 (Spring/Summer 2016): 25.

5. Ibid.

6. Maev Kennedy, "Egyptian Statues from Lost City Are a Tall Order for British Museum," *Guardian*, 25 March 2016, https://www.theguardian.com/culture/2016/mar/26/egyptian-statues-lost-city-tall-order-british-museum (accessed 1 June 2017).

7. Richard Deurer, "Hapi: Father of the Gods," *Egypt Art*, http://egyptartsite.com/hapi.html (accessed 5 June 2017; page no longer live).

8. Jim Elledge, *Masquerade: Queer Poetry in America to the End of World War II*, ed. Jim Elledge (Bloomington: Indiana University Press, 2004), xxvii.

9. "Three Songs of Initiation—2. Song of the Hwame," ibid., 11.

10. Randy P. Conner with David Hatfield Sparks, *Queering Creole Spiritual Traditions: Lesbian, Gay, Bisexual, and Transgender Participation in African-Inspired Traditions in the Americas* (New York: Harrington Park Press, 2004), 21.

11. Ibid., 56.

12. Ibid.

13. Ibid., 68.

14. You can use this link to take a look at art and artifacts at the museum that exemplify gender diversity: http://www.britishmuseum.org/explore/themes/same-sex_desire_and_gender/gender_identity.aspx#1.

15. R. B. Parkinson, *A Little Gay History: Desire and Diversity across the World* (London: British Museum Press, 2013), 37.

16. Ibid., 57.

17. Amba J. Sepie (née Morton), "Gender Twists: Mythology and Goddess in Hijra Identity," May 2015, https://www.researchgate.net/publication/276205190_Gender_Twists_Mythology_and_Goddess_in_Hijira_Identity (accessed 19 April 2017).

18. Parkinson, *A Little Gay History*, 69.

19. Ibid.

20. T. Douglas Murray, ed. and trans., *Jeanne d'Arc, Maid of Orleans, Deliverer of France* (New York: McClure, Phillips & Co., 1902), xxiv.

21. Leslie Feinberg, *Transgender Warriors: Making History from Joan of Arc to RuPaul* (Boston: Beacon Press, 1996), 32.

22. Murray, *Jeanne d'Arc*, xv.

23. Mercedes Allen, "Transgender History: The Rise of Hatred (The Middle Ages)," *Bilerico Project*, 19 February 2008, http://bilerico.lgbtqnation.com/2008/02/transgender_history_the_rise_of_hatred_t.php (accessed 22 March 2017).

24. Murray, *Jeanne d'Arc*, xix.

25. Ibid.

26. Feinberg, *Transgender Warriors*, 35–37.

27. Murray, *Jeanne d'Arc*, 327.

28. Lan Dong, *Mulan's Legend and Legacy in China and the United States* (Philadelphia: Temple University Press, 2011), 1.

29. Harry S. Parker III, Philippe de Montebello, and Timothy Potts, foreword to *Hatshepsut:*

From Queen to Pharaoh, ed. Catharine H. Roehrig, Renée Dreyfus, and Cathleen A. Keller (New Haven: Yale University Press, 2005), vii.

30. Cathleen A. Keller, "Hatshepsut's Reputation in History," in Roehrig et al., *Hatshepsut,* 294.

31. Roehrig et al., introduction to *Hatshepsut,* 4.

32. Parker et al., foreword to Roehrig et al., *Hatshepsut,* vii.

33. Roehrig et al., introduction to *Hatshepsut,* 3.

34. Ibid.

35. Kara Cooney, *The Woman Who Would Be King* (New York: Crown, 2014), 101.

36. Ibid., photo insert between 144 and 145.

37. This fact was part of an explanation of the beard at the Hatshepsut exhibition at the de Young Museum in San Francisco, October 2005.

38. Cooney, *The Woman Who Would Be King,* photo insert between 144 and 145.

39. Parker et al., foreword to Roehrig et al., *Hatshepsut,* vii.

40. Cooney, *The Woman Who Would Be King,* photo insert between 144 and 145.

41. Charlie Chin, with illustrations by Tomie Arai, *China's Bravest Girl: The Legend of Hua Mu Lan* (Emeryville, Calif.: Children's Book Press, 1993), 6.

42. Hans H. Frankel, *The Flowering Plum and the Palace Lady: Interpretations of Chinese Poetry* (New Haven: Yale University Press, 1976), 69.

43. Dong, *Mulan's Legend and Legacy,* 52.

44. Ibid.

45. Ibid., 53.

46. Ibid., 57–58.

47. Frankel, *The Flowering Plum and the Palace Lady,* 69.

48. Ovid, *Metamorphoses,* translated by Rolfe Humphries (Bloomington: Indiana University Press, 1958), 4:374–379.

BIBLIOGRAPHY

Allen, Mercedes. "Transgender History: The Rise of Hatred (The Middle Ages)." *Bilerico Project,* 19 February 2008. http://bilerico.lgbtqnation.com/2008/02/transgender_history_the_rise_of_hatred_t.php. Accessed 22 March 2017.

Chin, Charlie, with illustrations by Tomie Arai. *China's Bravest Girl: The Legend of Hua Mu Lan.* Emeryville, Calif.: Children's Book Press, 1993.

Conner, Randy P., with David Hatfield Sparks. *Queering Creole Spiritual Traditions: Lesbian, Gay, Bisexual, and Transgender Participation in African-Inspired Traditions in the Americas.* New York: Harrington Park Press, 2004.

Cooney, Kara. *The Woman Who Would Be King.* New York: Crown, 2014.

Deurer, Richard. "Hapi: Father of the Gods." *Egypt Art.* http://egyptartsite.com/hapi.html. Accessed 5 June 2017; page no longer live.

Dong, Lan. *Mulan's Legend and Legacy in China and the United States.* Philadelphia: Temple University Press, 2011.

Elledge, Jim, ed. *Masquerade: Queer Poetry in America to the End of World War II.* Bloomington: Indiana University Press, 2004.

Feinberg, Leslie. *Transgender Warriors: Making History from Joan of Arc to RuPaul*. Boston: Beacon Press, 1996.

Frankel, Hans H. *The Flowering Plum and the Palace Lady: Interpretations of Chinese Poetry*. New Haven: Yale University Press, 1976.

Gray, Richard. "Lost City of Heracleion Gives Up Its Secrets." *Telegraph,* 28 April 2013. www.telegraph.co.uk/news/earth/environment/archaeology/10022628/Lost-city-of-Heracleion-gives-up-its-secrets.html. Accessed 16 June 2017.

Keller, Cathleen A. "Hatshepsut's Reputation in History." In *Hatshepsut: From Queen to Pharaoh,* edited by Catharine H. Roehrig, Renée Dreyfus, and Cathleen A. Keller. New Haven: Yale University Press, 2005.

Kennedy, Maev. "Egyptian Statues from Lost City Are a Tall Order for British Museum." *Guardian,* 25 March 2016. https://www.theguardian.com/culture/2016/mar/26/egyptian-statues-lost-city-tall-order-british-museum. Accessed 1 June 2017.

Masson-Berghoff, Aurélia. "Secrets of the Sea." *British Museum Magazine* 84 (Spring/Summer 2016): 24–27.

Murray, T. Douglas, ed. and trans. *Jeanne d'Arc, Maid of Orleans, Deliverer of France*. New York: McClure, Phillips & Co., 1902.

Ovid. *Metamorphoses*. Translated by Rolfe Humphries. Bloomington: Indiana University Press, 1958.

Parker, Harry S., III, Philippe de Montebello, and Timothy Potts. Foreword. In *Hatshepsut: From Queen to Pharaoh,* edited by Catharine H. Roehrig, Renée Dreyfus, and Cathleen A. Keller, vii. New Haven: Yale University Press, 2005.

Parkinson, R. B. *A Little Gay History: Desire and Diversity across the World*. London: British Museum Press, 2013.

Roehrig, Catharine H., Renée Dreyfus, and Cathleen A. Keller, eds. *Hatshepsut: From Queen to Pharaoh*. New Haven: Yale University Press, 2005.

Sepie, Amba J. (née Morton). "Gender Twists: Mythology and Goddess in Hijra Identity," May 2015. https://www.researchgate.net/publication/276205190_Gender_Twists_Mythology_and_Goddess_in_Hijira_Identity. Accessed 19 April 2018.

Sparrow, Kate, Esther Aarts, and the British Museum. *Secret Treasures of Ancient Egypt*. London: Nosy Crow, 2016.

"Three Songs of Initiation." In *Masquerade: Queer Poetry in America to the End of World War II,* edited by Jim Elledge, 10–12. Bloomington: Indiana University Press, 2004.

Wilde, Robert. "The Elgin Marbles/Parthenon Sculptures." *ThoughtCo.,* 13 February 2016. https://www.thoughtco.com/the-elgin-marbles-parthenon-sculptures-1221618. Accessed 22 June 2017.

CHAPTER 11

Trans Literature, Performing Arts, Music, and Visual Arts
The Art of Resistance/The Art of Empowerment

Key Questions

1. How have representations of trans people in art and culture changed over the past two hundred years?

2. Why is it important for people who do not identify as trans to create trans characters?

3. Why is it important for trans artists and writers to create their own images of trans identity?

4. Is cross-dressing in performance always a sign of gender transgression?

Chapter Overview

This chapter begins by looking at the ways trans figures have been depicted in Gothic horror over the past two hundred years. As a marginalized genre itself because it was not deemed a "high" form of literature, Gothic horror offers an excellent way to study how representations of trans people have evolved and developed over two centuries in art and the popular imagination. Art is not only aesthetic—something pleasurable to see. Quite often art resists cultural norms and stereotypes. Art also empowers. This chapter examines how trans topics appear in literature, the performing arts, music, and visual art. Now, in twenty-first-century art, many trans artists are creating and depicting their own truths to share with audiences.

Haefele-Thomas, Ardel, *Introduction to Transgender Studies*
dx.doi.org/10.17312/harringtonparkpress/2019.01.itts.011
© 2019 by Harrington Park Press

Introduction: It Was a Dark and Stormy Night . . .

I will burn this building down before I let anyone touch that beautiful brain!
AMANITA TO NOMI IN *SENSE8* [1]

It was *not* a dark and stormy night. In the early morning hours on 16 June 1816, the light of a bright moon shone through eighteen-year-old Mary Godwin's window at Villa Diodati on Lake Geneva. She would later recall that the mixture of the moon and earlier conversations with her lover and future husband, Percy Shelley, and their friend Lord Byron (the Romantic poet) gave her the "waking dream" that would turn into a classic Gothic horror story: *Frankenstein*, first published in 1818. [2]

Have you ever sat around with your family or friends and told scary tales? Maybe you were on a camping trip and there was no WiFi, so you resorted to the age-old tradition of telling ghost stories around a campfire. There was certainly no WiFi in 1816, when the group of five friends vacationed at Lake Geneva, where it rained for most of the trip. One evening, as the group sat around the fireplace, they decided to take part in a writing competition. Whoever came up with the best ghost story would win, and "Mary's ghost story of her hapless Monster took the prize." [3]

Frankenstein is an iconic horror story in part because it is frightening, but it also touches on deeper cultural anxieties and themes. Dr. Frankenstein creates a monster, but this monster is not merely an evil being that roams the country-side causing destruction. Rather, Shelley's monster is someone who is marked as different. He is a lonely outcast who does not look or talk like other people. He is a "freak." At the end of the day, Dr. Frankenstein's creation wants companionship; he wants to be understood. The novel forces us to ask: *Who* is the actual monster—Dr. Frankenstein or his creation? We often, mistakenly, think of the monster as "Frankenstein" when, in fact, the monster has no name; Frankenstein is the name of the doctor. Why do we socially and culturally turn people who are different from us into "monsters"?

Trans Identification with Frankenstein

Frankenstein has been continuously in print since its original publication. Over the course of two centuries, it has proven to be ripe for numerous interpretations. Several trans writers have considered *Frankenstein* in terms of trans struggle and trans empowerment. For example, Ali Cannon, an American Jewish author, uses Frankenstein as part of his poem "A Trilogy of Horror and Transmutation" to discuss his gender transition:

The monster lies waiting on the slab

dull and lifeless

at the moment of infusion

the bolt cracking

all the tissue igniting

the body raised from the dead

when I get my first testosterone shot

I'm lying like the creature on the slab

. . . .

Frankenstein is gentle and fragile

even while prone to rages.[4]

The first testosterone shot, like the bolt of lightning, will bring Cannon to life. Many trans people do not feel fully alive until they come out and take whatever steps they can to fully embrace their gender identity. Cannon's understanding about himself through the idea of Shelley's monster is empowering.

The transgender historian, scholar, and filmmaker Susan Stryker, like Cannon, discusses the monster's rage. She compares her rage against the transphobia she encounters in our world with the rage that Dr. Frankenstein's monster must have felt: "I find a deep affinity between myself as a transsexual woman and the monster in Mary Shelley's *Frankenstein*. Like the monster, I am too often perceived as less than fully human due to the means of my embodiment."[5] Stryker is not necessarily claiming that Mary Shelley's creation was transgender as we understand the term today. Rather, Stryker is making the point that, socially and culturally, we often make those who are different "monstrous" on a personal level and on much larger cultural levels. For both Cannon and Stryker, Mary Shelley's Gothic monster from 1818 offers ways of considering trans resistance and trans empowerment.

Mary Shelley's monster was demonized because he was different, but that does not mean that Mary Shelley believed that Dr. Frankenstein's creation was monstrous. In fact, one way to read this classic story is to see Dr. Frankenstein as the monster, or even more broadly, to label as "monstrous" a culture and society that permit those who are different to endure such suffering.

Tracing Trans through the Gothic

Gothic horror may seem like an odd genre to start a chapter on resistance and empowerment in trans literature, art, and culture. In many ways, though, Gothic is the perfect place to study how trans people have been portrayed in popular culture over the past two centuries. *Frankenstein* is an excellent example of how one Gothic story continues to resonate over time.

Have you watched a vampire or zombie movie or television show lately? What makes the vampires or the zombies so scary? What often frightens viewers is the fact that these Gothic monsters can show up anywhere at any time. Imagine you are rushing across campus between classes, minding your own business, when, suddenly, a zombie comes at you. Your normal, everyday reality is shattered in this Gothic moment. This transgression of the boundaries between reality and fantasy is exactly why the Gothic genre is not always taken seriously.

From its beginnings in the eighteenth century, Gothic has been a rogue genre. Critics have denigrated it, but Gothic horror should not be dismissed because it always troubles the boundaries between what is normal or proper and what is not.[6] Because Gothic was (and still is) marginal, it has been the perfect genre for allowing authors to write about controversial topics. The Gothic genre serves as a microcosm through which to explore the broader ways that public perceptions of minority communities have been created. Gothic offers a lens into perceptions of gender variance and gender transgression. It also shows how popular sentiment concerning trans bodies has developed over two centuries.

Victorian Gothic and Trans Bodies

Visualize the stereotype of the "sweet granny" or the "proper married Victorian wife and mother." She cares for the children, cooks delicious food, and runs a household. In the case of Elizabeth Cleghorn Gaskell (1810–1865), she was also someone who created radical Gothic stories exploring gender issues and women's rights. Gaskell, often referred to as Mrs. Gaskell, was a vicar's wife, mother, and writer. Gaskell was deeply Christian (not just because she was married to a vicar) and a member of the Unitarians, who were, even then, liberal and open-minded.[7]

Her most famous novels deal with the socioeconomic and cultural ramifications of the Industrial Revolution in England.[8] Gaskell made enough money from writing that she was able to buy a house for her husband; sadly, just before they were to move in, she had a heart attack and died. Legend has it that she was telling one of her new stories out loud when she died in mid-sentence. Charles

Dickens, probably the best-known Victorian writer, commissioned several short stories from her for his literary magazines, *Household Words* and *All the Year Round*.

In one story, "The Grey Woman," Gaskell uses the Gothic to explore gender transgressions. Anna, a young and naive German woman, is married off to an evil French man who imprisons her in his castle. One night, Anna sneaks out of her isolated chambers to find out if her husband has been withholding letters from her father. She has to hide under a table covered by a long cloth when her husband comes home early. To her horror, she hears her husband and his gang talking about the neighboring family they have just murdered.

Anna gets out of the situation alive with the help of Amante, a clever older woman who has been hired as the younger woman's companion. Anna and Amante have to escape the dark and isolated castle, which is located on a steep cliff, in the middle of the night. To disguise themselves, Amante dresses as a male tailor, and then she and Anna pass as a tailor and his wife. As the story continues, they travel across the country but live in constant fear that Anna's husband will find them and kill them.

Once they are in a safe place, Amante continues to pass as Anna's husband and the father of Anna's newborn baby. One day, while Amante is working outside the home, a member of Anna's husband's gang figures out her identity and kills her. After the doctor has retrieved and examined Amante's body, everyone in the village is shocked by the cross-dressing revelation, but they are also deeply saddened by the murder. Possibly the most interesting and radical part of this mid-nineteenth-century story is the dignity and empathy with which Gaskell portrays Amante. Many Victorian writers would have made the trans figure monstrous or freakish. During this same period, sideshows (today we would call them freak shows) were popular in London and other cities. The public flocked to these shows to stare at gender-diverse people like Julia Pastrana from Mexico (Chapter 3) and Madame Clofullia from Switzerland, who was displayed as a "bearded lady."[9]

Elizabeth Gaskell was an avid newspaper reader, and she certainly would have been aware of all the press surrounding the London sideshows. We also know that she went to the library often to research extensively for her writing, so it is highly likely that she read about the infamous Chevalier/Chevalière d'Éon and earlier newspaper accounts of the doctors examining d'Éon's body after death. The final scene in "The Grey Woman" harkens back to the reality of doctors stripping d'Éon's body after death.

Another Victorian story that provides a more stereotypically monstrous Gothic view of a trans character is Richard Marsh's *The Beetle*, written in 1897. *The Beetle* was initially more popular than the other big Gothic novel published that same year, Bram Stoker's *Dracula*.

The Beetle takes place in London, but it is a cautionary tale about what happens to proper English gentlemen who travel to "exotic" locales like Egypt or India and do things that are not gentlemanly. In this novel, a member of Parliament has returned from Egypt, where he had an illicit affair with a woman. As it turns out, he has been cursed by an ancient Egyptian symbol: a scarab, or beetle. This beetle turns into a human shape that is sometimes a man, sometimes a woman, and sometimes a gender presentation that is both or neither. It also attacks men and women in very sexually suggestive ways. Not only does the monster fluctuate across gender and species lines, but it is also a person of color. In other words, the monster roaming the streets of London is an Egyptian gender-transgressing person/bug who is ultimately exterminated by a male character who is working on a scientific formula that will help him carry out mass genocide of Indigenous people in South America.[10]

One component of *The Beetle*'s popularity was the scene in which the Egyptian gender-variant monster gets squashed—literally like a bug—in a train car on the London Underground. How do we see stereotypes at work in what we read or watch? How often are trans people depicted as shape shifters, like the scarab in *The Beetle*? Gothic horror depictions like Marsh's helped popularize these stereotypes. And the stereotypes continued into the twentieth century, in some of the most popular horror films of all time.

Checking in at the Bates Motel: Trans Killers

What is your favorite scary movie? If you had to list the top five horror films of all time, or, more to the point, the top five classic horror *scenes* in film, chances are that you would include Alfred Hitchcock's *Psycho* on your list. Robert Bloch's 1959 crime novel, *Psycho,* adapted for film by Alfred Hitchcock in 1960, became one of the most popular crime/horror films of the twentieth century.[11] The story focuses on Norman Bates, a fidgety, effeminate man played by Anthony Perkins. (Remember Richard von Krafft-Ebing, the sexologist, from Chapter 3? The title of the book and film alludes to *Psychopathia Sexualis,* and Norman Bates could easily have walked out of one of Krafft-Ebing's case histories.)

Norman manages the Bates Motel in a creepy location off a main highway in Fairvale, California. Norman's crime—at least the one that leads investigators to the motel door—is the stabbing murder of a female guest in *the* shower scene that forever transformed horror film. Norman's deeper crime, however, revealed in the movie's climax, is that he has taken on his mother's persona, in both mind and body, after murdering her. In the film Norman Bates is a killer *because* he lives with multiple personality disorder, and more specifically because he is transgender—or, perhaps more accurately, because he has gender dysphoria. Regardless of Bloch's or Hitchcock's intent, the conflation of the sissy mama's boy and the trans woman is complete in the film's final scene, where Norman is escorted out of the room in a straitjacket talking in a high feminine voice.[12] *Psycho* helped perpetuate the stereotype that trans people, and trans women more specifically, are mentally ill criminals who have to be contained.

Thomas Harris's 1988 psychological thriller, *The Silence of the Lambs,* pits a rookie woman FBI agent, Clarice Starling, against a transgender woman serial killer who skins her victims.[13] The novel became a blockbuster film for director Jonathan Demme in 1991. Upon release, the movie encountered public outcry from LGBTQ+ groups such as GLAAD (Gay and Lesbian Alliance against Defamation), which focuses on LGBTQ+ representation in the media. Demme, who considered himself an LGBTQ+ ally, was stunned.[14] What was shocking and hurtful to many in the community was Jodie Foster's defense of her starring role in the film. Although Foster did not hint that she was a lesbian until 2007 and did not fully and publicly come out until 2013, her sexuality was already well known in the LGBTQ+ community.[15] So to have a lesbian defend starring in a transphobic film felt like a betrayal. The popularity of *The Silence of the Lambs,* however, far outweighed the protest. It garnered five Oscars, one Golden Globe, and other international awards.[16]

"Buffalo Bill," the serial killer at the heart of the story, kidnaps large women, takes them to a dungeon, starves them, murders them, and then skins them to fashion a dress made from female skin. In other words, the serial killer's road to gender transition is the murder of cisgender women, which underscores the cultural stereotype that trans people are sick, criminal, and dangerous. The movie has several terrifying scenes, including one in which the camera lingers on a private moment when Buffalo Bill is at home in a silk bathrobe, dancing slowly and backing away from the camera as the shot lingers on her pubic triangle—without a visible penis. The transgender body creates shock and horror just by being visible.

Norman Bates and Buffalo Bill represent a merging of criminality, gender nonconformity, and insanity. They are stock figures in both Gothic and criminal narratives. They are criminals within their fictionalized worlds, but because images of transgender women in popular culture are so few and far between (until the past five years or so), we need only look to real-life statistics regarding hate crimes, often murder, perpetrated against transgender women to see the power these stories carry. Often, when a suspect is questioned about why he brutalized or murdered a trans woman, he claims he felt threatened because she was masquerading (and somehow fooled him) or that she was mentally ill. The trans woman, by her very being, is seen to pose a threat.

"My Name Is Nomi":[17] *A Reading of the Wachowskis'* Sense8

As if to answer these popular transphobic depictions, the trans writers and directors Lana and Lilly Wachowski (who wrote *The Matrix* and *V for Vendetta*) created the 2015 Netflix Original Series *Sense8* with J. Michael Straczynski. *Sense8* combines elements of the Gothic, science fiction, and fantasy genres to create a story that delves into the lives of eight different people around the globe. Through their mental, emotional, and spiritual connection, these "sensaters" have the ability to occupy each other's bodies, minds, and hearts regardless of their physical location. They are, in a sense, one another. Nomi Marks, one of the eight, played by the transgender actress Jamie Clayton, portrays a white trans lesbian living in San Francisco. There is no explanation, nor is there anything sensational about her "coming out" as either lesbian or transgender; rather, she embodies a proud queer and trans identity that enables her character to "get on" with the business of being human like everyone else. Nomi's partner, Amanita (played by Freema Agyeman) is cisgender and African American. The hybrid framework for *Sense8* embraces Nomi's character. It is the antidote to narratives like *Psycho* and *The Silence of the Lambs,* where Nomi would probably have appeared as a monstrous killer. This is not to say, though, that monstrosity and criminal behavior do not pervade Nomi's story line.

In an early scene in Episode 2, "I Am Also a We," Nomi writes the following on her blog: "I was taught by my parents that there's something wrong with me. Something that you could never love." She goes on to talk about the ways that LGBTQ+ people are often disowned by their families of origin, and she encourages her audience to find strength in chosen family. She finishes writing her blog post and leaves for the San Francisco Pride Parade, where she falls off Amanita's motorcycle and is rushed to the hospital unconscious. When Nomi wakes up, she is in a hospital bed hooked up to monitors. Her mother approaches the bed and calls her Michael, her **deadname.** (This is a term many trans people use for the name they were given at birth that does not represent the name with which they identify. It is hurtful and disrespectful to use someone's deadname.)[18] Nomi looks at her mother with abject terror and says, "My name is Nomi." Her mother laughs callously and replies, "Nomi—what kind of name is that? You were Michael when they took you out of me. And will be until I am in my grave."[19] Nomi looks around the room desperately in search of Amanita. Her mother says, "This hospital only allows family into critical care." Nomi responds by saying, "She is my family." Finally, with disgust, her mother says, "Michael, this isn't your blog; this is your life."[20]

It soon becomes apparent that Nomi is not in the hospital simply because she fell off a motorcycle. The Western medical authority Dr. Metzger comes in to tell Nomi that her brain scan is abnormal and that she needs immediate surgery or she will die. He puts up images of brains, telling Nomi, "This is what a normal brain looks like." Then he proceeds to show Nomi her own supposedly abnormal brain. Nomi attempts to defend herself and her brain, but the doctor refuses to listen. Nomi experiences a moment of sheer terror when she begins to realize that Dr. Metzger wants to perform a lobotomy on her.[21] In historic Gothic tales as well as in real life, trans people were often thought to be criminally insane; it was not unusual for trans and queer people to undergo shock treatments and partial lobotomies at the hands of men of science attempting to normalize them. In this scene, the Wachowskis place viewers in Nomi's position to depict the Western cisgender man of science, and not the trans lesbian, as the true criminal, the true monster.

The science of nineteenth-century sexology reaches out of the past to terrorize Nomi in her twenty-first-century San Francisco hospital bed. In one scene Nomi tells the nurse, "You can't keep me here against my will." The nurse replies: "I'm afraid we can. Dr. Metzger and your family have signed the papers." Nomi comments to the nurse, "I cannot believe that this is happening to me in the twenty-first century."[22]

Just at the moment that Nomi begins to think she is insane, Amanita sneaks a call into her from one of the hospital phones in a nurses' lounge. She tells Nomi, "I will burn this building down before I let anyone touch that beautiful brain."[23] Note that the Wachowskis redistribute the power to those people whom the Victorian scientists would have seen as less than human. Amanita is African American, and so is her friend who works at the hospital who sneaks her into a private staff room so that she can use the hospital phone to call Nomi. As women of color, and more specifically as queer women of color, Amanita and her friend work together against Western white medical systems of power that have historically (and sometimes still do) dictate who is fully human and deserving of human dignity and who is not.

In the third episode, we see Nomi in the operating room being readied for anesthesia. When the fire alarms begin to go off, the surgery is aborted. In her drugged state, Nomi hears the nurse say, "Some lunatic set fire to the visitors' lounge." Amanita will stop at nothing to free her partner from the evil clutches of Dr. Metzger and his goal of killing Nomi for her own well-being. By the fourth episode, one of the other sensaters, Will, a police officer in Chicago, is able to fully occupy Nomi's body as Dr. Metzger is, yet again, putting Nomi under anesthesia. Nomi groggily sneaks out of the operating room and falls into the arms of

Amanita, who is dressed as a nurse. Amanita puts her in a wheelchair and rushes her out of the hospital doors, followed by the furious hospital authorities—those people meant to keep monstrosity and criminality in check—and into a waiting cab. As they leave the scene of Nomi's near murder, Amanita holds her and continually says, "I got you. I got you."[24] Nomi's escape with the help of the other sensaters and her lover, Amanita, serves as the Wachowskis' antidote and answer to Hitchcock's and Demme's portrayals of monstrous trans women.

The Gothic genre offers us a lens through which we can see the trajectory of the portrayals of trans people over the past two hundred years. From *Frankenstein* to *Sense8,* you can study the evolution of the ways that gender-variant people have been portrayed, from societal outcast to victim to monster. With the Wachowskis, the trans person finally has agency and is empowered to tell her own story.

Trans Literature: Definitely Queer/Trans, Too?

In a sense, every author has to be transgender in order to get into the minds and hearts of all of the characters.
ARMISTEAD MAUPIN[25]

In this section we explore three women writers who lived and worked during the same period: the American Pulitzer prize–winning author Willa Cather (1873–1947); the English author who endured an obscenity trial for one of her novels, Radclyffe Hall (1880–1943); and the English feminist and center of the Bloomsbury Group, Virginia Woolf (1882–1941). These three authors were queer, although they may never have used that word for themselves; both Willa Cather and Radclyffe Hall were openly in relationships with women throughout their adult lives, and Virginia Woolf and Vita Sackville-West, an English poet, notoriously had a love affair.

As we discussed in Chapter 2, the term *queer* is often used as an umbrella term for LGBTQ+ people, although there is a shift toward the use of the word *trans* separately as another umbrella term to help explore many different gender transgressions, particularly in a historic context. These words, *queer* and *trans,* are also used in literary theory to explore meanings within texts—sometimes overt meanings, but often covert meanings. Remember, too, that the early sexologists conflated gender identity and sexual orientation. For example, they used the word *bisexual* for two types of people: a person who was sexually attracted to both men and women *and* a person who equally embraced the characteristics of a man and a woman. For our purposes here, it is critical to remember that Cather, Hall, and Woolf wrote during a period when society did not really distinguish between gender identity and sexual orientation.

FIGURE 11.1 Willa Cather, by Cameron Rains. Willa Cather was an American writer who, in her teens and twenties, often went by the name William Cather. Biographers have argued that in many of her novels she fashioned the male protagonists after herself.

Willa Cather

Though she won the Pulitzer Prize for her World War I novel, *One of Ours,* Willa Cather (figure 11.1) is probably most famous for her novels depicting rural life in Nebraska.[26] Cather was romantically involved with women, and her novels and short stories offer covert lesbian subtexts during a time when she could not have been out publicly. As part of the argument that lesbianism plays a role in Cather's novels, biographers point to the fact that Cather often writes in the person of a male narrator.[27] The problem with this idea is that it imposes a heteronormative model onto a lesbian identity, if, in fact, Cather identified as a lesbian.

We do know that starting in 1888, at the age of fourteen, Willa Cather spent the next few years as William Cather. Cather cut her hair short and wore boys' clothing. During this time, Cather took great pains to make sure that a professional photographer photographed her as William Cather.[28] In the late 1800s, photography was still a new and expensive way to capture a moment in time. The fact that Cather went to the trouble to get a professional photograph as William suggests that "William" was a public persona. It is also interesting to note that Cather had the "William" photo taken in her home in Red Cloud, Nebraska. (You may recall from Chapter 8 that one of Ms. Bob Davis's treasured finds was a photo album containing eighteen photos of cross-dressed people in the early 1900s somewhere in Nebraska.) As Cather's biographer Sharon O'Brien argues, Cather's male public image became even more pronounced when Cather took to the stage in male roles.[29]

In private correspondence, Cather often signed letters as William. Some of these letters present an interesting gender fluidity. For example, on 31 May 1889 Cather wrote to her friend Helen Louise Stevens Stowell. She signed the letter, "Yours Truly Wm. Cather Jr." Then she added a "P.S." to the letter, which she signed, "Yours truly Willa Cather."[30] Of course, Cather could have been playing with gender in these letters to her friend, but the dual signature does indicate that she was experimenting with gender identity and gender expression in her outward persona as well as in her writing. The possibility of trans as well as queer readings of Willa Cather enriches our approach to her writing.

Radclyffe Hall

Radclyffe Hall (figure 11.2) was dyslexic and struggled with reading, so her lover, Lady Una Troubridge, often read books out loud to her. You may be wondering what Hall enjoyed hearing. Mysteries? Romances? No. Radclyffe Hall enjoyed listening to Richard von Krafft-Ebing's *Psychopathia Sexualis* and Havelock Ellis's *Studies in the Psychology of Sex*.[31] She then used these two sexologists' theories of inversion to create what became one of the most controversial novels of the twentieth century: *The Well of Loneliness*. Hall even convinced Havelock Ellis to write a commentary for the beginning of the novel so that readers would begin the story with the notion that the book could serve as a case history in sexology.

The Well of Loneliness follows the life of Stephen Gordon, a girl born into a wealthy family in England. From birth up to the novel's conclusion, the reader follows Stephen as she begins to recognize that she is attracted to women. Early in life, her sympathetic father dies, and she is left with her mother, who wanted more of a princess for a daughter. As soon as she can live independently, Stephen moves to Paris, where she encounters a community of artists and gay, lesbian, bisexual, and transgender people who flocked to Paris's liberal Left Bank in the 1920s. *The Well of Loneliness* was published in 1928 in Great Britain and the United States. The English courts immediately began proceedings to prosecute Hall, calling the book obscene and declaring that all copies should be burned.[32]

Hall's book remains *the* lesbian novel of the twentieth century. Even after it was banned, the book found its way into underground loan programs in England and in America; the book became a powerful tool for lesbian community building. For example, in Alexandria, Louisiana, in the 1950s, the public library carried Hall's book, but you had to speak to the librarian to check it out. You also had to sign your name on a card. While doing so was scary, the people who went through this process were able to read the library card and see the names of other

FIGURE 11.2 Radclyffe Hall, by Cameron Rains. Radclyffe Hall wrote one of the most important novels in the history of LGBTQ+ literature, *The Well of Loneliness*. Often understood to be the classic lesbian novel of the twentieth century, Hall's book can also be read through a trans lens. Hall often went by the name John.

people in the community who had read the book. Thus, an underground lesbian community was formed, even though lesbians were at risk of losing their jobs, their homes, and their families.[33]

The power of *The Well of Loneliness* is still evident today. It does not fit in the Gothic genre, but, like *Frankenstein,* it lends itself to trans interpretations because it is a social outcast's coming-of-age story. Before Stephen Gordon is born, the reader is told Stephen's father, Sir Philip, desperately wants a boy, which is why the baby is named Stephen. The newborn baby is "a narrow-hipped, wide-shouldered little tadpole of a baby, that yelled for three hours without ceasing, as though outraged to find itself ejected into life."[34] From the baby's first moments until Sir Philip's tragic death, he understands his child's innate masculinity and is supportive of Stephen.

Radclyffe Hall often signed her letters as "John." If you search for images of Hall, you will see someone who might be defined as butch, nonbinary, or both. In 1928 a person assigned female at birth who appeared to transgress gender boundaries would have been read as homosexual and not necessarily as trans. Also remember that butch identities may not be transgender, *but* they do always present gender transgressions because butch is exactly what women are not supposed to be. For example, Leslie Feinberg's 1993 novel, *Stone Butch Blues,* explores a butch identity as something outside the gender binary. Feinberg would certainly have been familiar with Hall's classic.

Suggesting that *The Well of Loneliness* is open to trans interpretation does not take away from its reputation as *the* lesbian novel of the twentieth century. There is ample room for multiple reader responses and reader interpretations. Indeed, opening up Radclyffe Hall and this pioneering novel to new interpretations only helps it retain its place in the queer and trans literary canon.

FIGURE 11.3 Virginia Woolf, by Cameron Rains. Virginia Woolf was one of the most important writers of the Modernist period in English literature. She was also at the center of the famous group of artists, writers, and thinkers known as the Bloomsbury Group. Her novel *Orlando* is the story of a person who, over the course of 300 years, lives as a man for 150 years and then, after a long sleep, wakes up as a woman and continues living for another 150 years.

Virginia Woolf

In 1928, the year that Radclyffe Hall published *The Well of Loneliness* and was later taken to court, Virginia Woolf (figure 11.3) published an overtly trans novel with no legal consequences. Why?

Orlando tells the story of a person who lives the first half of life as a man and the second half as a woman, over a three-hundred-year span. Like Gothic novels, Woolf's novel goes outside the bounds of realistic fiction, asking the reader to suspend belief about the way time moves forward. The story begins in the Elizabethan age with a nobleman named Orlando. As the novel moves forward and follows the young Orlando, the reader notices that decades pass, yet the protagonist never seems to age. Orlando becomes an ambassador, and, about 150 years into his life, he is sent on a trip to Turkey. While he is there, he falls into a trance for several days and then wakes up as a woman: "Orlando remained precisely as he had been. The change of sex, though it altered their future, did nothing whatever to alter their identity."[35] Notice that Woolf struggles with Orlando's pronoun because, at this point in the novel, Orlando occupies a nonbinary gender category. In the next sentence, Woolf states, "His memory—but in future we must, for convention's sake, say 'her' for 'his,' and 'she' for 'he.'"[36]

Woolf takes on the sexologists and popular ideas and stereotypes about gender variance. Here is a critical passage in the book: "The change seemed to have been accomplished painlessly and completely and in such a way that Orlando herself showed no surprise at it. Many people, taking this into account, and holding that such a change of sex is against nature, have been at great pains to prove (1) that Orlando had always been a woman, (2) that Orlando is at this moment a man. Let biologists and psychologists determine. It is enough for us to state the simple fact; Orlando was a man until the age of thirty; when he became a woman and has remained so ever since."[37]

The novel has a fairy-tale quality to it because Orlando lives for over three hundred years, which may explain why Woolf was not taken to court. In England at the time, men who cross-dressed were assumed to be homosexual and were arrested. Perhaps Woolf had read some of Magnus Hirschfeld's early writings and thought about gender identity and sexual orientation as two different concepts. Perhaps Woolf, a bisexual, regarded herself in the dual way that bisexual meant at that time: someone who was both male and female or someone who was attracted to both men and women. She dedicated the book to Vita Sackville-West. *Orlando* was published two years before the first known modern gender-affirmation surgery was performed, on Lili Elbe in 1930.

Less than forty years after these three writers pushed gender boundaries, there was an explosion of literature written by, for, and about trans people. These works include autobiographies, biographies, children's books, novels, poems, and short stories. At the end of this chapter you will find a project that asks you to find and read a recent trans book in a genre of your choice.

Trans on the Stage

But every artist has to express the truth as she sees it, and that gives us a power to change the world in subtle ways.
JO CLIFFORD[38]

If you are interested in classical Greek theater, you can find gender transgressions dating back to the comedies of Aristophanes (ca. 446–ca. 386 BCE). Many high school curricula do not include Greek plays; however, most do include William Shakespeare (1564–1616 CE) and his contributions to the popularity of the Elizabethan stage (1562–1642 CE). How many of Shakespeare's plays have you read? Have you seen a performance of one of his plays, and if so, which type of play was it? A comedy? A tragedy? One of the history plays? High school favorites include *Romeo and Juliet, A Midsummer Night's Dream,* and *Hamlet*. As you were considering Shakespeare, did you think about all of the trans possibilities his works offer?

Shakespeare's comedies, in particular, are often full of gender boundary crossings. In *As You Like It,* for example, the female characters disappear into the Forest of Arden and become men; the gender and romantic confusion results in plenty of laughs. On the Elizabethan stage, the jokes about crossing gender boundaries included an extra layer of complexity. Women were not allowed to perform onstage. So, during Shakespeare's time, the women who went into the Forest of Arden and became men were actually teenage boys acting as women who were acting as men. Audiences loved the gender hopping, and Shakespeare (along with other playwrights of his era) often played with **double entendre,** or a hidden, often sexual, connotation lurking underneath the spoken lines.

Famous for the Breeches Parts

A little over four hundred years after the Bard's death, Shakespeare companies around the world continue to experiment with cross-dressing and gender roles. In 2003 an all-women's company produced *The Taming of the Shrew* as the first play of the summer season at the Globe Theatre in London. The Globe's theme that year was "Season of Regime Change."[39] It was significant that the first play chosen by the women's troupe was the one that many critics have considered Shakespeare's most misogynous.

By the nineteenth century, it was legal for women to act on the stage. A stigma was attached, however, and actresses were often stereotyped as "loose women." When women were on the stage, they were there to play women's roles, though there were a few exceptions. One of these was Charlotte Cushman, the American Shakespearean actress who played the **breeches parts**—that is, the "britches parts" or men's parts. Women cross-dressing onstage in Shakespeare's comedies was quite common in the nineteenth century; however, many were suspicious of a woman playing a man in the tragedies.[40] Early in her career, Cushman played women's roles. But after she became famous for playing Hamlet in the United States, she continued to play men in costumes previously worn by male actors.[41] In contrast, many women who played men's roles often feminized the costume by adding a shawl or another piece of clothing that would soften their masculine appearance.

While cross-dressing onstage certainly exemplifies gender transgression, the acclaim that Cushman received for her roles as the male leads in Shakespearean tragedies exceeds that of her female contemporaries. On both the American and English stage, she was most famous in her role as Romeo: "Unlike actresses who played up the possibility of titillating the predominantly male audience by displaying shapely bodies and legs, Charlotte Cushman, who by most accounts neither excited passions of men nor wished to be seen as desirable to them, could actually attempt to *personify* male characters."[42]

Several theater critics noted in their reviews that they forgot they were watching a woman play a man. Thus, Cushman crossed the gender binary and passed as a man on the stage. Interestingly, too, Cushman was not at all in the closet about having different women lovers throughout her lifetime. Nineteenth-century ideas about lesbianism were, generally speaking, not as harsh as they became in the twentieth century. In many instances, theater critics, particularly in England, were relieved that such a passionate Romeo was played by a woman, because the scenes of love and passion between Romeo and Juliet would have been too sexual and too scandalous with a man in the role: "A human being—not a caricature or a freak; this passionate woman publicly professing erotic love for another woman was regarded as superior to other *male* British actors as Romeo."[43]

A Famous Japanese Finishing School

If you were asked to imagine the curriculum at a girls' music and finishing school, what would come to mind? Would you imagine the girls learning how to do domestic tasks like cooking and cleaning while singing? Would you imagine them learning to speak different languages? And, upon graduation from this girls' finishing school, what kind of girl would be prized as the best material for an outstanding wife? The young lady who can sew the most beautiful dress? The young woman who can cook the tastiest meal? The young lady who had been a young man for the past year or two? Welcome to Japan and the famous and historic Takarazuka Revue, which, when established in 1914, "sparked a heated debate in Japan on the relationship of gender, sexuality, popular culture, and national identity."[44]

Over a century old now, Takarazuka Revue is still a point of national pride in Japan, and, as a continuing global cultural phenomenon, its popularity has never waned. The city of Takarazuka is near Osaka, Japan. In 1914 Ichizo Kobayashi, the father of Takarazuka Revue, wanted to create musical entertainment that would be suitable for the whole family. His motto for his earliest students, all female, was "modesty, fairness and grace."[45] This motto still holds throughout the performances, which thrill audiences with their music, melodrama, and gender transgressions on and off of the stage. Since 1914, all the musicals' story lines have depended on heterosexual romance as a main theme; however, Takarazuka is composed of only young women, which means, of course, that women must play the male roles.

Cross-dressing parts for both men and women have been common on the

Japanese stage throughout the centuries. What differentiates Takarazuka is the fact that the cross-dressing component is not limited to the stage. Each year, at the beginning of a new season, the school holds auditions to select one woman who will play the leading male role in every production. The competition is grueling, and the winner is seen as the star of the whole school. For the entire year, the winner not only plays the male lead on the stage in the musical revues, but she also dresses, acts, and is treated like a man by everyone at Takarazuka for that full year. Interestingly, whoever is selected to be the man for a year is also considered the best marriage material for a man. Why? The idea is that because she has been a man for a year, she understands what it is like to be a man and that, having been a man, she will make a better wife.[46]

Out as Trans on the Stage

Jo Clifford courted major controversy with her play *The Gospel According to Jesus, Queen of Heaven*. When it premiered in Scotland in 2009, angry picketers protested the depiction of Jesus as a trans woman. Clifford, who has been a successful playwright for decades, did not fully come out as trans until her fifties. She recalls that, when she was fourteen, she played the role of a girl in a school play and she loved being a girl; however, the idea also terrified her because she knew that a boy wanting to be a girl was not socially or culturally acceptable.[47]

Clifford has performed the play for small audiences in local churches so that she can work within a sacred Christian space to get her message across. She has been picketed, threatened, and called blasphemous, but as Clifford has noted in interviews, most of the protesters have not seen the play. Clifford's play uses Jesus's teachings from the New Testament to look at the ways that he would have been open to all people. Along these same lines, Clifford sees Jesus as the embodiment of all people, including trans women. This is a powerful message, particularly for various communities, including queer and trans Christians, who have often felt left out or even been abused by religious leaders. The play has been Clifford's way of giving love and empowerment to her community. As of 2017, the play was being performed by trans women in other countries, including Argentina and Chile, where it has been translated into Spanish, and Brazil, where it has been translated into Portuguese.

Sean Dorsey created Sean Dorsey Dance, a transracial queer and trans masculine dance troupe. Dorsey's group aims to present the fluidity and diverse possibilities of masculinity onstage. At the 2017 Fresh Meat Festival, another performance art venue started by Dorsey for queer and trans artists, the dance troupe gave the audience a preview of their next full show, *Boys in Trouble,* with a piece titled "Is This Butch Enough?" The show takes on various cultural and societal stereotypes about masculinity, exploring stereotypes about black cisgender male masculinity, gay cis male masculinity, and trans male masculinity. Through dance, music, and humor, Sean Dorsey Dance points to some of the absurdities of our societal stereotypes.[48]

Sean Dorsey and his dance group often use archival materials; they also conduct interviews as part of their research for upcoming shows. For example, Sean Dorsey Dance won several awards for their show *Uncovered: The Diary Project*, which used the GLBT Historical Society of San Francisco's archival materials to discover the diaries of Lou Sullivan, a gay trans man who died from AIDS in 1991. (For more information on Lou Sullivan, see Chapter 3.) Similarly, the dance group conducted hours of interviews with early survivors of the AIDS pandemic in the United States. From these stories the award-winning show *The Missing Generation* was created. A part of Sean Dorsey Dance's *Missing Generation* appears in Season 1 of *Sense8*.

Charlotte Cushman and the performers in Takarazuka may not be transgender by today's definitions. Their crossings of the gender binary both on and off the stage, however, allow us to explore trans possibilities underneath their performances. With Jo Clifford and Sean Dorsey, being transgender takes center stage; trans awareness and understanding are at the core of the messages that these groundbreaking artists want their audiences to see and feel. Jo Clifford continues to perform in venues where she faces hatred, but she feels strongly about getting the message of the possibilities of all-inclusive Christian love out to the public. And, in July 2017, Sean Dorsey and his dance group became the first openly transgender performing arts group to perform in the state of North Carolina after that state passed a bill requiring people to use the bathroom that corresponded with their biological sex appearing on their birth certificate. You can see how this new state law could cause all sorts of problems given that states vary in their rules about changing sex on a birth certificate. And, of course, you are also probably wondering what would happen to people who have differences in sex development (DSD) who come from a state that recognizes this on a birth certificate. Jo Clifford and Sean Dorsey are there to make sure that people see the richness and complexity of trans artists and trans cultural production.

Historic and Modern Trans Music

Last night I dreamed we stole a car and smashed through the gates of heaven. The
goddamned place was ready to blow in a gender Armageddon.
SHAWNA VIRAGO[49]

In 2016 Laura Jane Grace of the punk band Against Me! burned her birth certificate onstage at a concert in North Carolina in protest of that state's notorious
transphobic laws.[50] Laura Jane Grace is one of numerous out and proud trans
musicians around the world at this time. Trans people have always been part of
the music industry; however, it is only relatively recently that musicians have
been able to be out and proud.

Their Audience Did Not Know They Were Trans

When Billy Tipton (1914–1989) was born in Oklahoma City in 1914, doctors identified the baby as a girl, and Tipton was raised as a daughter until 1933. In 1933,
at the age of nineteen, Billy rejected his gender designation and fully embraced
his identity as Billy Lee Tipton, which he retained until his death, in 1989.[51] In
Spokane, Washington, in 1989, an ambulance was called to Tipton's home because
he was gravely ill; as the paramedics undressed him, they asked his son, "Did
your father have a sex change?"[52] In this case, the paramedics had the presence
of mind to consider that their patient was trans.

From the well-received Tipton biography written by Diane Middlebrook to the
New York Times article "One False Note in a Musician's Life," Billy Tipton is regu-
larly described as someone who deceived his wives and adopted children. He is
often depicted as someone who cross-dressed solely for the purpose of getting a
job as a jazz musician. According to Middlebrook, Tipton "occupied an undefin-
able space. She was someone who worked creatively in the gap between biology
and gender."[53] On the one hand, Middlebrook makes an important point about
people who cross the gender binary or remain somewhere in the middle of or
outside it. Like many historians studying trans people, however, Middlebrook genders Tipton as "she" even though Tipton lived fifty-six years of his life as a man.

Billy Tipton was a white trans man who was a moderately successful jazz
pianist. His two albums on vinyl, *Sweet Georgia Brown* and *Billy Tipton Plays Hi-Fi*
on Piano, are collector's items. You can do a simple online search to find and
listen to his songs. Some videos show him playing piano in the background
while photos from his life scroll across the screen.[54]

Most biographical information about Tipton uses terms like *deception* and focuses on his former wives and children who all, at least publicly, deny knowing he was trans. At this point, though, we should think about the ways that people are interviewed and what their answers might mean. Why might ex-wives and children say in a public forum that they never knew their husband or father was trans? What does it matter if Billy Tipton originally cross-dressed to become a jazz musician? Some biographers have focused on his need for privacy and unwillingness to appear undressed, even at home, as a sign of deception. (In this regard, Billy Tipton may remind you of Dr. Barry, who also guarded his privacy. See Chapter 8.) The underlying assumption here is that Tipton was being private in order to deceive. What's missing is an understanding that any public display of their bodies can feel dangerous to trans people because it often is dangerous.

Two years after Billy Tipton's birth in Oklahoma City, the African American gospel singer Wilmer "Little Axe" Broadnax (1916–1992) was born in Houston, Texas. Billy and Wilmer were both from the same geographic region. They were both born in late December, two years apart. They were both trans men in the music industry. Their stories, however, are radically different.

According to the short documentary *Wilmer and Willie Broadnax: "Little Axe" & "Big Axe,"* even though Wilmer "was pronounced a female at birth, he and his family knew he was a boy. When he was thirteen, a census taker came by the Broadnax home and recorded him as male and that was that."[55] Note Wilmer's family's support of him from an early age. In the early twentieth century, the general public had no knowledge about gender diversity, and yet Wilmer's family knew their child was a boy, and they proceeded to love him and support him. Even today, despite the wealth of available information, trans kids often do not receive love and support like this from their families.

Wilmer's successful career as a gospel singer started when he and his brother, William, performed as part of the St. Paul Gospel Singers in Houston. Shortly afterward, in 1939, they went to Los Angeles to sing with the Southern Gospel Singers. The brothers soon started their own group, the Golden Echoes, which became one of the most successful gospel touring groups in the 1940s. "Little Axe" had a pure and amazing tenor voice that was the highlight of the Golden Echoes, which he led for over two decades. He was also a member of the Spirit of Memphis Quartet, the Fairfield Four, and the Five Blind Boys of Mississippi.[56] Online you can find various songs featuring Broadnax, including "Make More Room for Jesus," "If You Make a Start to Heaven (Don't Turn Around)," "Glory, Glory," and a gospel rendition of "You Are My Sunshine."

Wilmer died in 1992 as a result of domestic violence; his girlfriend stabbed him. He was discovered to be trans on the autopsy table, so, as was the case with many other successful trans people, a medical intervention led to a public revelation.[57] In Broadnax's case, though, his family knew he was trans, and so did those most intimately involved with him. It was only the general public that did not know.

Gospel, which is a rich and religious musical genre, may not have been open to a trans artist in the 1940s; Broadnax was not out among his musical peers because being out could have been dangerous. His brother "Big Axe" knew and often helped protect him in work situations. If we fast-forward to the twenty-first century, you may be surprised to learn that a trans gospel group, Transcendence Gospel Choir, made musical and religious history in 2003 when it performed at a General Synod meeting at the United Church of Christ in Minneapolis. Following the group's performance and its members' testimonies to the congregation, the United Church of Christ voted to openly welcome trans people. The United Church of Christ became the first mainstream Christian group in the United States to vote to expand its ministry to the transgender community.[58]

Tipton and Broadnax present two examples of the different ways the histories of trans people get told. People who were not part of the trans community often chose to depict Tipton as a musician as "deceptive" and his life as a "masquerade." In contrast, a short documentary on Broadnax by the trans artist Rhys Ernst and the trans historian and blogger Monica Roberts's *TransGriot* post about Broadnax as an African American trans pioneer both underscore the importance of marginalized communities' being able to tell their own stories. As Roberts states on *TransGriot*, "Wilmer 'Little Axe' Broadnax is another fascinating story from our Black trans history and another concrete example of Black trans people being an integral kente cloth part of our Black community."[59]

Tipton and Broadnax exemplify the difficulty of being out as trans in the music industry, and in broader culture, in the twentieth century. Although their lyrics did not present audiences with themes about gender identity or gender transgressions, these two trans musicians leave us with a rich musical legacy.

"I Met Her in a Club Down in North Soho": Mainstream Musical Trans Representation

The British rock band the Kinks released their single "Lola" in June 1970. The song begins with these lyrics: "I met her in a club down in North Soho where you drink champagne and it tastes like Coca-Cola."[60] The song goes on to chronicle the story of a young man who picks up a trans woman of color, Lola, at the club. As the story unfolds, he is intrigued by her walking "like a woman" but talking "like a man." Then, in one of the most interesting twists to the song, the lyrics, as sung by Ray Davies, say something unexpected: "Girls will be boys, and boys will be girls/It's a mixed up, muddled up, shook up world except for Lola."[61] In other words, the trans woman, Lola, is not mixed up; but the other people, who can be read as either gender-fluid, crossing the binary, or symbolic of the new sexual revolution and changes in male and female gender roles, are confused or confusing. The young man falls in love with Lola.

The BBC (British Broadcasting Corporation) forced the Kinks to return to the studio and rerecord the song, but not for the reasons you might think. It was against BBC policy to mention specific products in a song, so "Coca-Cola" had to be replaced with the more generic "cherry cola."[62] The original vinyl 45, with "Coca-Cola" in the lyrics, is now a collector's item.

Let's place "Lola" in historical perspective. When the Kinks, a major British Invasion band, broke into the Top 10 in both the United States and the United Kingdom in 1970, England was only three years past decriminalizing same-sex relations between men.[63] So the lyrics "I know what I am, and I'm glad I'm a man/ and so is Lola," clearly describe sex between men. However, the lyrics also demonstrate the conflation of sexual orientation and gender identity.[64] In the United States the anti-homosexuality laws, known as sodomy laws, were not repealed in all fifty states until June 2003, yet the Kinks' song seems to have flown under the radar and was never banned from American radio.[65]

Given the time it was written and recorded, "Lola" can be read as a relatively open-minded song for a mainstream rock band. The song hit the Top 10 on both sides of the Atlantic, so it is clear that people enjoyed the message.[66] And the fact that Lola, the trans woman of color, is *not* demonized is extremely important.

Two years later, in 1972, Lou Reed (1942–2013), a guitarist and songwriter with the Velvet Underground, wrote and recorded a song about New York City's nighttime subculture of sex workers, hustlers, and gender radicals, "Take a Walk on the Wild Side." This is the first verse:

> *Holly came from Miami F.L.A.*
>
> *Hitch-hiked her way across the U.S.A.*
>
> *Plucked her eyebrows on the way*
>
> *Shaved her legs and then he was a she*
>
> *She said, hey babe, take a walk on the wild side.*[67]

The song is slow and sultry. Upon its release, many radio stations across the United States cut certain verses out because they were seen as too overtly sexual or too overtly queer (or both).

Reed's song has continued to be controversial. In May 2017 newspapers and social media were abuzz with discussions about the song's being transphobic. A Canadian newspaper, the *Independent,* reported that the University of Guelph in Ontario had released an apology for including "Take a Walk on the Wild Side" at a campus event because it depicts trans people as "wild." Friends of the late singer were shocked and appalled. They defended Lou Reed as someone who respected the people in the song.[68] A number of people made subsequent posts on Facebook, Twitter, and other social media outlets debating whether the song is offensive. Some history may be helpful here. Lou Reed was writing about specific people in New York in the late 1960s and early 1970s. Holly in the above quote refers to Holly Woodlawn, a trans woman artist who made a career of working in Andy Warhol's films along with Candy Darling, who is also mentioned later in the song. Some women of color find the song's chorus offensive, but that does not mean that Lou Reed meant any disrespect or harm when he wrote and recorded the song—terminology has changed over the decades. What was not necessarily offensive in the 1970s may be now.

Many have argued that Ray Davies and Lou Reed meant no offense and, indeed, approached the subject matter with respect. Nonetheless, what stereotypes might these two songs put forward about trans women? Both songs can be said to fetishize trans women. What are some of the problems with that? Although "Lola" and "Take a Walk on the Wild Side" have some problematic features, are there any benefits to studying them? In mainstream culture, are these songs helpful or hurtful in constructing social and cultural ideas about trans women? And how do intersecting identities play out within "Lola" and "Take a Walk on the Wild Side"?

"I'm Calling Out a War Cry to Guide Me to My Hero":[69] *Trans Musicians Becoming Our Heroes*

Iceis Rain is a member of the Mikisew Cree First Nation and makes her home in both Fort MacKay, Alberta, and Vancouver, British Columbia. Iceis Rain is also Massey Whiteknife: "Living his two-spirit identity means that by day he is an openly gay male business owner . . . and at night, she is Iceis Rain."[70] As someone who keenly understands how it feels to be bullied for being different, Iceis Rain also does youth advocacy work; each year she puts on a national antibullying show in Canada to educate Canadians and empower bullied youth.[71] As she explains in the introduction to her music video *The Queen:* "Growing up as a boy, I was bullied daily. I was abused. I was taken advantage of. And so I started to dress up as Iceis. Iceis has never been bullied, molested, or abused. She showed me that I could be just who I want to be and live my life and follow my dream."[72]

Iceis Rain's strength and power come from being Two-Spirit *and* being Mikisew Cree First Nation. In an interview for PowWows.com, her interviewer asks, "How does being Native impact your life and music?" Iceis answers, "I believe in the creator very much. . . . I try to incorporate our cultural sounds to my music in subtle ways to showcase our culture but also wanting the music to be universal."[73] Her song "Warrior (War Cry)" begins with traditional drums and a war cry that then becomes a love song.[74] Iceis Rain says that she wrote the song "thinking people would listen to it while driving to a pow-wow."[75] By embracing traditional music and infusing it with a mixture of rock and country, Iceis Rain blends multiple musical styles in a way that symbolizes her life.

Like many trans musicians today, Iceis Rain seeks to entertain, but her music also carries a powerful message for people who struggle with being bullied for being different, whatever that difference is. When she produces her annual antibullying show in Canada, which attracts top talent from all over the country, she makes sure that 100 percent of the proceeds go to various organizations that work to empower youth.[76]

Like Iceis Rain, StormMiguel Florez embraces the richness of his identities. He is "a queer Chicanx trans man who came out and identified as a dyke in 1987" in Albuquerque.[77] Both Florez and Iceis Rain honor their queer sexual orientation and their trans identities. Neither sees these identities as mutually exclusive, but rather as a part of the continuum of who they are as queer and trans people of color living in a mainstream white society that often attempts to silence them.

In his song "Legend," Florez explores the deep wounds of racism and the cultural diaspora felt by Chicanx people in the United States. In this haunting folk melody, played on acoustic guitar, StormMiguel sings, "Wash this brown out of us, it's the only way we'll make it."[78] His songs often examine the immense pressure to fully assimilate, leaving parts of culture and identity behind to die. Through his music Florez captures the complexity of simultaneously embracing and crossing numerous boundaries as a queer, trans Chicanx artist. He performs nationally, bringing a sense of the history of struggle and empowerment to his audiences. You can also see his work in the documentary film *Major!* about the life and work of Miss Major Griffin-Gracy.

Earlier you read about Wilmer "Little Axe" Broadnax's gospel song "If You Make a Start to Heaven (Don't Turn Around)." Shawna Virago's amalgamation of blues, punk, and folk in her song "Gender Armageddon" could almost be her reaching through time and space to answer the late gospel singer. In her brassy lyrics, Virago sings about stealing a car and smashing through the gates of heaven.[79] "Gender Armageddon" is just one song on her critically acclaimed album, *Heaven Sent Delinquent*. In her lyrics, Virago is unapologetic in her exploration of queer and trans themes. She does not write her music to explain or ask for acceptance from mainstream audiences. Rather, like the car smashing through the gates of heaven, her lyrics and her style are empowering in their "take no prisoners" approach.

Trans Visual Art: A Look at Two Visual Art Installations

I have dared to step out into the light.

CHARL MARAIS[80]

More and more visual art displays highlighting trans artists and trans themes are appearing around the world in various museums and galleries. Recent trans visual art installations have included collaborative photographic and interview pieces by Jess T. Dugan and Vanessa Fabbre, Yishay Garbasz's film and photography focusing on trans diaspora, and Micha Cárdenas's work that looks at trans people of color within digital media and art. Though trans artists are enjoying more visibility on a global level, it is also important to remember that for many trans artists, it can still be very dangerous to be out as trans and to explore a trans identity within art.

"Trans: Body Maps of Transgender South Africans": *Johannesburg, South Africa, 2007*

Compared to the majority of other countries in Africa where being transgender is illegal, South Africa's post-apartheid constitution, which protects all people, is progressive. There is, however, a great disparity between the law and reality. In 2007 a three-day workshop for transgender and gender-variant people included the creation of an art exhibition. Each participant was asked to trace their body onto cardboard and then, with words and paint, create representations of themselves and their lives. The exhibition was titled "Trans: Body Maps of Transgender South Africans." The goal of the exhibition, which was shown at Constitution

Hill ("a living museum that tells the story of South Africa's journey to democracy"[81]) in Johannesburg in April 2007, was to show the everyday lives of trans people living in South Africa.[82]

This powerful gathering of trans people from many different racial, ethnic, religious, and socioeconomic backgrounds in the historic prison-turned-museum would have been illegal in apartheid South Africa on at least two levels: the intermingling of people from different racial and ethnic groups, and people being out as transgender or gender variant. Even though South African laws have changed, the outlined images and lives rendered through art showed that trans people still face day-to-day discrimination and violence in South Africa.

Chantelle, a white trans woman who owns a successful business, depicted herself in red, with images around her of her house being burned down and her business being fire-bombed because she is transgender.[83] Charl, a trans man of color, depicted his two selves in blue: the darker blue the old closeted self and the lighter blue moving toward the sunlight.[84] Charl's piece and many of the other pieces also used religious symbols, most of them Christian, to depict how their religious upbringing made it very difficult for them to come out.

"Twilight People": London, United Kingdom, 2016

The issue of religion and transgender identity is one that many trans artists grapple with. Are you religious? Were you raised in a religious environment? If so, how does your religion view trans people?

Nine years after the Johannesburg exhibition "Twilight People: Stories of Faith and Gender Beyond the Binary" became "the first source of faith and transgender history in Britain."[85] After opening in the London neighborhood of Islington in February 2016, this vibrant installation of photographs and people's stories began traveling throughout the United Kingdom, and part of the show was featured in the United States at the University of Arizona in October 2016.

The title of the exhibit, "Twilight People," refers to a prayer that was written by Rabbi Reuben Zellman of the United States. The prayer is often read as part of Transgender Day of Remembrance.[86] The exhibit focuses on people from the Abrahamic religions (mostly Christianity, Judaism, and Islam) and how they have worked with their trans identity *and* their faith, which is not always trans friendly. At the "Twilight People" website, you will be able to download the exhibition booklet for free and check out the various photographs and stories: https://www.twilightpeople.com/the-project/. Given the tensions among Christianity, Judaism, and Islam as reported in the mainstream media, "Twilight People" serves another purpose: uniting these religions through trans themes.

WRITINGS FROM THE COMMUNITY

SEAN DORSEY AND SHAWNA VIRAGO

Interview on Trans Art

Sean Dorsey is an award-winning San Francisco–based choreographer, dancer, writer, and activist. Recognized as the first acclaimed transgender modern U.S. dance choreographer, Dorsey has toured his work to over twenty-five cities. Dorsey's work The Missing Generation *toured twenty cities; Dorsey created the work after recording seventy-five hours of oral history interviews with transgender and LGBTQ+ longtime survivors of the early AIDS epidemic. In April 2018 Sean Dorsey Dance's* Boys in Trouble *had its world premiere in San Francisco before going on the road.* Boys in Trouble *focuses on the intersections of race, class, and queer and trans masculinity. Dorsey tours and travels the United States performing, teaching, lecturing, and hosting community residencies. You can visit his website at www.seandorseydance.com.*

Shawna Virago is a transgender music pioneer and cult solo acoustic artist. She is celebrated for her striking lyric-based songs. Her music has been profiled in No Depression, *the* Huffington Post, Paste, Louder Than War, *the* Advocate, Bitch, Rumpus, Curve, NPR, PBS, *and left-of-the-dial radio. She is artistic director of the San Francisco Transgender Film Festival, and her own films have been screened at more than fifty festivals around the globe. You can visit her website at www.shawnavirago.com.*

Q: How long have you been working together?

SEAN: Shawna and I have been partners for fifteen years, and we've been working together just as long. We've collaborated on many artistic projects, and have co-curated, co-organized, and co-produced many trans arts events together. I'm the founder and artistic director of Fresh Meat Productions and Shawna is general manager. Together, we've provided opportunities for over five hundred trans and gender-nonconforming and queer artists since 2002! Shawna is the artistic director of the San Francisco Transgender Film Festival—she has supported and screened films by more than four hundred transgender filmmakers from twenty-one countries around the world! Shawna is a brilliant singer-songwriter . . . her music is soul-stirring, insightful, moving. And I get to hear it every day! I'm blessed that Shawna has also composed original music for my dance company, Sean Dorsey Dance.

SHAWNA: Sean and I have been together for fifteen years, and I am still constantly blown away by the extraordinary intelligence, skill, and integrity he brings to his choreography and his writing. I believe his work challenges the hetero- and gender-normative world of dance. We're also very fortunate to be two working artists in a relationship. We get to support each other and create a private sanctuary in this transphobic world.

Q: What does it feel like to both be leaders of a trans artistic revolution?

SHAWNA: I have many gender expressions that operate on several spectrums. I have no allegiance to a single pronoun or gender to identify myself by, but I do identify as a songwriter. Songwriting is my vocation and I'm grateful for just the fact that I'm still here making music. When I started performing as an out gender-expressive person twenty-five years ago, it was lonely. There was a lot of transphobia from the various music scenes, even here in San Francisco.

SEAN: I feel so very blessed to be alive at this time in history—and I am also very mindful that I can be out and active as a transgender artist today because of the hard work, activism, art-making, and struggles of my elders and ancestors. I am inspired by these elders and ancestors; as a community leader, it is my calling and joyous responsibility to honor and name and remember these people. I do this through my work, my art-making, and my choreography (my last three full-length shows were a trilogy of works exploring buried or censored aspects of trans and LGBTQ history), and I do it with Fresh Meat Productions.

Q: Where do you get your inspiration to move forward with this work?

SEAN: I am inspired by many things: I am inspired by my elders and ancestors; I am inspired to make dances because of the beauty and strength of trans/queer people; I am inspired to keep my heart open in this work by my beloved Shawna Virago; I am inspired to lovingly fight for justice because of continued racism, white supremacy, transphobia, ableism, homophobia, misogyny, ageism, and sizeism in America; I am inspired by my fellow leaders, artists, activists; I am driven to cultural activism because of the extreme underrepresentation and lack of support and opportunities for trans people.

Q: What was the motivation for starting the Transgender Film Festival?

SHAWNA: The San Francisco Transgender Film Festival was started in 1997, and we are the longest-running transgender film festival in the world. My friends

Christopher Lee and Alex Austin started it and brought me in as codirector in 2003. I've been artistic director since then. We prioritize films made by gender-expressive people outside mainstream media culture.

Q. How did Fresh Meat Productions come about? And how did Sean Dorsey Dance form?

SEAN: In 2002 there was this groundswell—an emergence of really exciting trans and gender-nonconforming artists and performers. But no one was supporting our art, or putting us onstage. Funders wouldn't fund trans art. The media wouldn't cover trans artists. Professional and emerging trans dance, theater, and music artists had no opportunities—but were creating amazing art! So I brought together a group of trans and queer artists and activists, and we organized what we thought would be a onetime festival of trans and queer performance: that was the first Fresh Meat Festival in June 2002 at ODC Theater in San Francisco. The performances were standing room only, there was an extraordinary response—and the community wanted MORE. So we transformed it into an annual event and then into a full organization. Today we are celebrating our fifteenth anniversary, and we're the first organization in the U.S. to create, present, and tour year-round trans arts programs.

As for Sean Dorsey Dance (this is our eleventh season): I create dance-theater that is rooted in trans and queer lives, experiences, history, and community. I've been blessed to have received national recognition and support for my work and have toured to twenty-six cities. I'm the nation's first acclaimed transgender contemporary dance choreographer and dancer. I'm the first openly transgender artist to be awarded support from the National Endowment for the Arts.

Q: How has your work been received outside the San Francisco Bay Area?

SEAN: Incredibly well! I've been presented in theaters in twenty-six cities in the U.S. (and Canada), and most of these theaters were not LGBT theaters or presenters—and in some cases it was the first time they'd ever presented LGBT-themed work. In every case, we had full houses and incredible, enthusiastic, emotional audience response. It's extraordinary!

Q: Talk about the dance training you've had. What did you do before Sean Dorsey Dance?

SEAN: Growing up and then as a young adult, I absolutely loved dance. And music. And theater. But I didn't see ANYONE else like me in dance. So I never even thought about the possibility that I could be a dancer or choreographer. I studied piano for many years, and did a lot of youth theater, and writing. But I did not "grow up at the ballet barre." In fact, I did almost no training as a child or teen. It wasn't until I was in my twenties that I dared to begin beginner training—and then took the plunge, dropped out of grad school, and did a full-time training program. I started dancing with some companies right away and also began making my own work. Here in San Francisco, I danced with the amazing Lizz Roman and Dancers for six years—it was really intense, physical work and site-specific, daring, gorgeous projects.

It's very powerful to put a trans body onstage, and to bring trans experience and embodiment into dance. I love what I do.

Q: Who are some of the artists who have influenced you?

SEAN: As a transgender professional choreographer and dancer, I don't have any peers. So I have to get inspiration in creative ways—certainly from queer dance artists, but also trans and queer theater artists, sculptors, visual artists, filmmakers. I'm also a writer (and write my soundscores, which are all text-based), so writing and visual art are both very important to me. I am always inspired by Shawna Virago.

I created my last show, *The Missing Generation,* by traveling the U.S. and recording oral history interviews with trans and LGBTQ longtime survivors of the early AIDS epidemic. The audience hears these real-life voices and remarkable stories in the show's multilayered soundscore—layered with gorgeous original music by my team of composers, and my own writing/narration. The twenty-five survivors I met all across the U.S. deeply influenced me, changed me, and inspired everything about the show. I created the work based completely on their lives and experiences. We're now touring this work to twenty cities across the U.S.

SHAWNA: I have too many influences to name. Musically I was influenced by early punk rock, politically by leftist political organizing. My gender expressions were formed by life before the Internet, by various queens in out-of-the-way bars and salacious magazines I'd find in adult bookstores.

Q: What do you see as the influence of trans art on society?

SHAWNA: Reality shows exploiting transgender people are not going to secure our civil rights. I think the trans civil rights movement or trans revolution, if it's not attached to the struggles of people of color, and dismantling white supremacy, and if it's not attached to dismantling prisons, then it has no legs to stand on. All our struggles are intersected.

Q: What do you see as the benefits (and challenges) of being a trans artist?

SHAWNA: There is nothing better than being a transgender, or gender-expressive artist. I have so much permission and space to create the kind of songs I want to, and also I get to keep challenging myself to keep smashing binaries and margins and to build something with other gender revolutionaries, a more just society.

SEAN: I love being trans. I am proud that I am trans. And I am proud that I have had the courage and strength and endurance to be openly trans in a profoundly gendered field, contemporary dance. Every day I give thanks and feel deeply blessed that I make my living being a trans artist; it is a great blessing to perform and teach and operate a trans arts nonprofit. Some of the benefits of being a trans artist are the connection and community of other trans activist-artists; the blessing of being a "pioneer"; the profound reward in talking to trans and gender- nonconforming audiences who come up after a show or a workshop in tears, moved, changed by the experience of finally seeing themselves reflected onstage, or finally feeling good about their body, or finally feeling like they COULD dance—in one of my workshops.

Some of the challenges include discrimination, stereotyping, being dismissed, the glass ceiling, being pigeonholed, having to "prove" myself that much more to mainstream funders and presenters.

Q: What motivates your work?

SEAN: I am passionate about making art that transforms people—that offers insight, healing, education, connections between generations, the soothing balm our broken hearts need after death or loss. I believe it my joyous responsibility as a dance maker to create dances that people can actually understand, that people are deeply moved by, and that transform or create communities. This is my job. And I think it's the most exquisite job in the world.

SHAWNA: Avoiding a real job. Seriously, that's why I do most of what I do.

GLORIA

The following story is from Jess T. Dugan and Vanessa Fabbre's collaborative project To Survive on This Shore: Photographs and Interviews with Transgender and Gender Non-Conforming Older Adults. *Jess T. Dugan's art explores "gender, sexuality, identity, and community."*[87] *Dugan received an MFA in photography from Columbia College Chicago and an MA in museum studies from Harvard University. Vanessa Fabbre is a professor in the Women, Gender, and Sexuality Studies Department at Washington University in St. Louis, Missouri. Her focus is on gender identity and aging.*

Gloria, 70, Chicago, IL, 2016.
Photo by Jess T. Dugan.

I identify myself as a female. I've always identified myself as a female. From a little tot, I knew who I was then, you know? And people say how do you, at the early age, know who you are? I've always felt that way so that's who I am. The men in my family, they were sort of apprehensive about me, but the women were strong; they wore the pants in my family. My mother would tell them, this is your child, this is our baby and you're going to love my baby because you love me. And that's the way it was.

My grandmother, my mother's mother, that woman was amazing. She was there for me all the time. And my mother. My mother was a *Jet* centerfold model, and a dancer, and she was beautiful. I came up in a household with beautiful women. My great aunt Fannie lived to be 103. She taught school in slavery days when they weren't supposed to learn how to read. But she went on and she taught school, she became a teacher . . . and I would go to her house and sit up in her house and we would talk. She would give me words of wisdom. She would tell me, "Baby, you are you and don't let nobody change you." And I would sit there and look at her in amazement.

The inspiration for the Charm School, I would have to say, was between my grandmother, my mother, and my aunt Fannie. All these women were amazing. They wore gloves, slips up under their dresses. My grandmother would teach me how to sit down at a table, how to break bread. Being raised by these amazing women and learning the techniques to life, that gave me the inspiration when I went to the Center on Halsted and saw these wild women, you know, trans young people, acting a fool and cutting up, and I thought well, maybe they need some help. And they appreciated me so they came up with the word Momma Gloria. And I said ok, I accept that. That was them being respectful, calling me their mother. They'll say, oh yeah, "This is my gay mother, Momma Gloria."

Being a senior citizen, I made it to seventy and a lot of them won't make it, they won't make it at all. Because most of them die from drugs, from sexual disease, or they're murdered. They ask me questions like "Well, Momma Gloria, how did you get through?" I say, "I got through with love from my family and the grace of God." That's how I got through. You have to have some stability and you have to have some kind of class, some charm about yourself. I never was in the closet. The only time I was in the closet was to go in there and pick out a dress and come out of the closet and put it on.

DALLAS DENNY AND JAMISON GREEN

We Control the Transmission

Dallas Denny is a leader in the transgender rights movement. Her work as a writer, editor, speaker, and community builder has played a significant role in the advancement of rights for transsexual and transgender people in North America and around the world. The entirety of Dallas's work is available at her website: www.dallasdenny.com.

Jamison Green is a trans author, speaker, educator, and activist from Oakland, California. For more than twenty years, he has also been a director or advisory board member for many nonprofit organizations working to improve health, safety, and civil rights for gay, lesbian, bisexual, transgender, and DSD/intersex people. His activism work has helped provide legal protection, medical access, safety, civil rights, and dignity to transgender and transsexual people. He is also the author of the award-winning book Becoming a Visible Man. *He also has written essays, articles, and a column for PlanetOut.com. In 2009 Jamison became the first trans person to receive a Distinguished Service Award from the Association of Gay and Lesbian Psychiatrists for his contributions to LGBTQ+ mental health. He received the Transgender Advocate Award from the LGBT Bar Association, and the Vanguard Award from the Transgender Law Center (also in 2009). He has joined the staff at the Center of Excellence for Transgender Health at the University of California, San Francisco.*

We are on the front end of an incredible revolution in human communication. The ways we spend our time, the ways we interact with one another, the very ways we behave and think have been changed and are being changed by our interactions with intelligent electronic devices. And if things are so very different already, just remember: it's only the beginning!

Over the centuries and then decades and now years and even months, the pace of change has accelerated in logarithmic fashion. These days not only new products but new methods of communication can be invented, developed, marketed, sold, and massively adopted in mere months. Consumer electronic devices have made all this possible.[88] Consider: the first iPhone was announced on January 9, 2007. Other smartphones had been marketed, but had not come into wide use, and for most people around the world texting was difficult and rare, and cellphone photos and video were of low quality or nonexistent. In 2007 social media—as we know it now—did not exist. There was no Facebook, no Twitter, no Instagram, no Skype, no Reddit. Those under twenty years old when this book is published probably won't remember the days without smartphones—but as we write this they have been around for only ten years! And can you imagine living without one?[89]

The effect has been profound. We can search for, find, and retrieve information—vast amounts of it—with only a few clicks of a mouse.[90] We can locate and purchase obscure books in an instant and have them in our hands in days, listen to music before we make purchases, submit a paper for publication without having to use the mail, or read the history of Ernest Shackleton's expedition to the South Pole without leaving our seat.

The Internet, and for that matter computing devices themselves, are still in their infancy—but their effects on business and everyday life have been profound. Newspapers and magazines are in decline, and many mastheads are no more. CDs, which rendered vinyl records obsolete, have become obsolete themselves as customers download purchased music files.[91] DVDs are following as more video content becomes available online. Just as streaming video is impacting broadcast and cable television, electronic and audio books are having a significant impact on the publishing industry.

Most important, the Internet has facilitated entirely new types of interactive communication. Weblogs and video blogs have empowered hundreds of thousands of people by giving them a voice. Bloggers write about anything and everything and publish with a click. Readers—and some blogs have tens or hundreds of thousands of readers—can subscribe to newsfeeds that ensure they'll be notified of new content and can respond to the blogger's posts by leaving comments. Any individual can share their feelings, opinions, photos, or surroundings in, essentially, real time.

All this has had a huge effect on politics and culture. Individuals are able to break news stories sooner than media organizations or dig up and distribute news distressing to individual politicians. For instance, in 2007 Josh Marshall, a blogger, was the first to alert the public to the Bush administration's politically motivated firing of U.S. attorneys.[92]

The Internet facilitates organizing around issues such as discrimination and hate crimes. Even more important, it gives any individual with a computing device and the will to write a platform an opportunity to be seen and heard. This empowers individuals and has a robust impact on LGBTQI community building.

The ability to send messages via text on cell phones has become a critical means of communication. Already, changes in the cognition and behavior of college students are being remarked on by academics. Today's students come to class with their computers and handheld devices and tend to multitask, dividing their attention among the lecture, Twitter, instant messages to friends, running apps, booking appointments, browsing websites for course-related research, and shopping: "College students used their laptops for frequent multitasking during classes, generating, on average, more than 65 new screen windows per lecture, 62% of which were unrelated to the courses they were taking, say James M.

Kraushaar and David C. Novak of the University of Vermont. Students who allocate more cognitive resources to bringing up non-course-related material on their computers show lower academic performance. Instant messaging seems 'especially virulent' as a distraction, the researchers say."[93]

In the late 1980s and early 1990s, when we first became active as activists and authors, most trans and gender-nonconforming people were isolated and alone. Those fortunate enough to live in big cities like New York, San Francisco, Los Angeles, London, Berlin, or Paris, or who managed to make their way to those cities, could sometimes find community, and trans people in smaller cities could seek understanding and acceptance of a sort in gay bars, but for most of us there was no easy way to connect with one another. Books were scarce and often depressingly defamatory. There were some newsletters and magazines produced about and by us, but they were not in commercial distribution and were found mostly by word of mouth—and there is no word of mouth if you know no one else who is trans. There were support groups for cross-dressers and there were a few doctors who treated transsexuals, but they were similarly hard to find. Most trans and gender-nonconforming people absolutely lived for the occasional movie, television show, or newspaper or magazine article that depicted us, even negatively.

In the face of such adversity, by about 1990 enough of us somehow managed to connect and form a nationwide network of support groups, sympathetic helping professionals, sellers of clothing and cosmetics and prosthetic devices, and supportive allies. This community welcomed newly arrived individuals and worked to orient them, formed alliances and support groups, produced self-help books, operated electronic bulletin boards,[94] produced and exchanged newsletters, and held an increasing number of regional and national conferences. The focus was education, but around 1993 this community reached a sort of critical mass, and many within it turned their focus to political activism. This activism, which was initially looked on with skepticism by more than a few trans people, gave us a new term—transgender—and started a revolution that increased our visibility and eventually led us to the legal protections, insurance coverage, political gains, and allies we enjoy today.

It isn't coincidental that these changes evolved with the public availability of the Internet. USENET, online chatrooms and websites, and, later, social media allowed trans people to find one another readily. Once connected, we shared ideas and terminology, and our fears, hopes, and aspirations. For the first time, we were visible—not only to one another, but to the world at large, and especially to those who became our allies.

Amazingly (and also not coincidentally), for the first time we took control of our own narratives. Soon we were producing our own literature, our own media. We had previously been locked out of the very literature that described and defined us. Today we control the narrative. We control the transmission.[95]

Historically, material about transgender identities has been produced and published by cisgender people. We were the subjects of the media that referenced us, but not the authors, not the playwrights, not the directors, not the photographers or filmmakers. Just as we were rigorously and systematically excluded from political office and employment opportunities, we were denied publication in the medical and psychological literature and popular media. Our novels were not published, our films not released. This is not to say we aren't still stigmatized—we certainly are—but before the 1990s, for us to contribute in any meaningful way to literature, television, or motion pictures (other than as subjects, of course) was as unthinkable as our not contributing is today.

The purported reason, laughable as it may now seem, was that we were too biased by our identities to have anything of importance to say about them.[96] The truth, of course, was this: it wasn't *we* who were biased.[97]

The first crack in this dam occurred in 1986 with the publication of Allucquére Rosanne (Sandy) Stone's essay "The *Empire* Strikes Back: A Posttranssexual Manifesto." *Empire* is, justifiably, widely considered the first salvo in what would eventually develop into the discipline transgender studies.[98]

The year 1993 saw the publication of Leslie Feinberg's semiautobiographical novel *Stone Butch Blues*. It resonated with a wide variety of people who colored outside the lines of binary gender norms.[99] A year earlier, Feinberg's booklet *Transgender Liberation: A Movement Whose Time Has Come* had been published by World View Forum Publishers. In 1996 Gary Bowen published an erotic FTM story in Cecilia Tan's anthology *S/M Pasts*. Two years earlier, Bowen had produced an anthology of LGBT science fiction.[100] And Loren Cameron's groundbreaking 1996 photography book, *Body Alchemy: Transsexual Portraits,* shook both the world of art photography and the world of possibilities for transgender pride.

Dallas Denny's 1994 *Gender Dysphoria: A Guide to Research* was arguably the first book-length non-autobiographical contribution to the scientific literature written by an out transperson. The publication of this 650-page annotated bibliography was facilitated by the late Vern Bullough, who asked Denny if he could contact Garland Publishing on her behalf.[101]

Collectively, these works from the 1990s can be held (barely) under one arm. Before the turn of the century, however, something remarkable was happening: we were becoming thoroughly integrated in academia and other areas of American society.

What has happened for trans people in the first eighteen years of this century so far has been remarkable. Today we are not only taking the lead in representations of us in print, onstage, on film, and in music—we are defining those representations, and we are doing so in multitudinous ways. We are lawyers, doctors, artists, researcher/scholars, teachers, social workers, and engineers who are using our professional skills to win litigation and civil rights, to establish trans-inclusive healthcare protocols, to turn hearts and minds away from the misinformation and prejudice about trans people, to help trans people navigate the systems that threaten to (and often do) abuse us.

Everything isn't perfect yet for all trans people, but we have made amazing progress. New communications technologies have opened channels that have forever changed the trans community and trans identities themselves. Today, we are proud to say, *we* control the transmission.

WORKS CITED

Bornstein, Kate. *Gender Outlaw: On Men, Women, and the Rest of Us*. New York: Routledge, 1994.

Bowen, Gary. *Queer Destinies: Erotic Science Fiction*. Cambridge, Mass.: Circlet Press, 1994.

———. "Saddlesore." In *S/M Pasts,* edited by C. Tan, 37–49. Cambridge, Mass.: Circlet Press, 1996.

Cameron, Loren. *Body Alchemy: Transsexual Portraits*. San Francisco: Cleis Press, 1996.

Denny, Dallas. "All We Were Allowed to Write: Transsexual Autobiographies in the Late XXth and Early XXIst Centuries." Workshop presented at Fantasia Fair, 19–26 October 2014, Provincetown, Mass. Presentation slide show at http://dallasdenny.com/Writing/2014 /10/29/all-we-were-allowed-to-write-2014/.

———. *Gender Dysphoria: A Guide to Research*. New York: Garland, 1994.

Feinberg, Leslie. *Stone Butch Blues*. Ithaca, N.Y.: Firebrand Books, 1993.

———. *Transgender Liberation: A Movement Whose Time Has Come*. New York: World View Forum Publishers, 1992.

———. *Transgender Warriors: Making History from Joan of Arc to RuPaul*. Boston: Beacon Press, 1996.

———. *Trans Liberation: Beyond Pink or Blue*. Boston: Beacon Press, 1998.

Gabriel, Davina A. "Interview with the Transsexual Vampire: Sandy Stone's Dark Gift." *TransSisters* 1.8 (1995): 14–27.

Middendorf, Joan, and Kalish, Alan. "The 'Change-up' in Lectures." *National Teaching and Learning Forum* 5.2 (1996): 1–12.

Raymond, Janis. *The Transsexual Empire: The Making of the She-Male*. Boston: Beacon Press, 1979.

Rothblatt, Martine. *The Apartheid of Sex: A Manifesto on the Freedom of Gender*. New York: Crown Publishers, 1994.

Stone, Sandy. "The *Empire* Strikes Back: A Posttranssexual Manifesto." In *Body Guards: The Cultural Politics of Sexual Ambiguity,* edited by Kristina Straub and Julia Epstein. New York: Routledge, 1996.

Williams, Cristan. "TERF Hate and Sandy Stone." *TransAdvocate*, 16 August 2014. http://transadvocate.com/terf-violence-and-sandy-stone_n_14360.htm. Accessed 20 July 2017.

Key Concepts

breeches parts (p. 399)
deadname (p. 391)
double entendre (p. 399)

Activities, Discussion Questions, and Observations

1. View Jess T. Dugan's four photographs from Dugan and Vanessa Fabbre's *To Survive on This Shore: Photographs and Interviews with Transgender and Gender Non-Conforming Older Adults.* You have now read all four of the stories attached to these photographs (see "Writings from the Community" in Chapters 1, 3, 5, and 11). What do you see in the images? Which one is your favorite? Why? Which elements of the image capture your attention? The stories are all about trans elders whose lives and experiences are vastly different. If you enjoyed these images and stories, visit this website to see and read more: https://www.tosurviveonthisshore.com/.

2. Dallas Denny and Jamison Green write about the ways that technology, in particular, has helped the trans community. What other communities has technology helped? Does it seem unusual that marginalized communities could be strengthened by technology? What barriers does technology still hold? How easy is it for you to find out information about trans people and trans history on the Internet?

3. Shawna Virago discusses the Transgender Film Festival. Why is there a need for a Transgender Film Festival separate from LGBTQ+ film festivals?

4. Think about the different media of performing arts: theater, spoken word, dance, film, music, and so on. How is trans embodiment presented in different media? What are some of the differences between seeing a live performance and seeing a filmed one? What are the differences in terms of audience, community, reach, and potential influence?

5. Kent Monkman is a world-renowned Cree Two-Spirit artist living in Canada. In 2018, at the "Moving Trans History Forward" conference at the University of Victoria in British Columbia, Monkman gave a presentation titled "Trans as the New Frontier." Monkman's vibrant art focuses on the intersections of colo-

nization, genocide, gender expression, sexual orientation, Indigenous history, and nationalism. For this assignment, visit his website, choose one of his art pieces, and then conduct your own close reading and interpretation of the piece. What action is taking place in the art? What point is Monkman trying to get across to the audience? If you have chosen a piece that is a revision of a classic landscape painting, be sure to note which original painting Monkman is critiquing. What are some of the ways that Monkman has reenvisioned the original? How do humor, anger, and sadness play out in the art piece you have chosen? How does Monkman's use of color underscore the point of the piece of art? Here is Monkman's website: www.kentmonkman.com/.

6. One important artistic and cultural phenomenon not discussed in this chapter is *The Rocky Horror Picture Show,* originally released in 1975. It started with a cult following. Now, over the course of four decades, thousands (perhaps even millions) of people around the world have seen it. Have you been to a public showing of *Rocky Horror*? If so, what was your experience ? Even if you have not been to a showing, you have probably heard about the film. What have you heard? *Rocky Horror* still shows in many places for a midnight showing at least once a month. You could go with a group of friends. Be sure to take a spray bottle, a newspaper, and some toast, and get ready to do the Time Warp! Why does *Rocky Horror* remain so popular? At the heart of the film is a trans character who seems to reach out and entrance almost everyone regardless of their sexual orientation or gender identity. Why? What about this film makes it "safe" for people to enjoy a trans figure? And what parts of the film are subversive even today?

7. Suppose you are writing a character who is a different gender from you. How do you go about writing this character? What stereotypes about this other gender do you have? How is writing a character with a gender other than your own the same as or different from writing a character of a different race or ethnicity? Nationality? Age?

8. Pick a country and research a trans artist in that country. What are the laws in that country regarding trans people? Is the artist's art political? What message is the artist trying to convey?

9. Go to YouTube and check out the Kinks' "Lola" or Lou Reed's "Take a Walk on the Wild Side." Next, check out a song from one of the trans artists mentioned in this chapter, or find another trans artist and song online. As you listen to the lyrics and to the story of the song, what has changed over time?

Both the Kinks and Lou Reed have been accused of being transphobic, but is that a fair critique of songs from the early 1970s? What do these two older songs still offer us culturally now? What might they have offered to trans people at the time?

10. Go to this website for the exhibition "Twilight People": https://www.twilight-people.com/the-project/. Choose two of the stories and photos. Analyze and discuss the stories.

11. Cross-dressing does not necessarily mean trans. In other words, sometimes cross-dressing, particularly in film, is used for comedic purposes or to reinforce the gender binary. Consider one of these films that employs cross-dressing and/or drag as humor (these are mainstream films that are easy to find): *Big Momma's House; Mrs. Doubtfire; Tootsie; To Wong Fu; Hairspray; Priscilla, Queen of the Desert; Some Like It Hot*. Does the film have any trans elements?

12. Suppose you have been asked to curate a trans art exhibition. You get to choose the location of the exhibition. Choose up to eight artists who work in any genre or medium to include in your show. The overarching theme is trans artists, but you might want to focus your exhibition on a specific period or a particular world region. Those choices are yours. You will be walking your visitors through the show, so the placement of the different artists is important for the overall effect. Which artists have you chosen? Why? What will visitors see at your exhibition?

Film and Television of Interest

The Believers (2006, U.S., 80 minutes)

This film won the audience award for best documentary at the 2006 Frameline San Francisco LGBT film festival. Focusing on the Transcendence Gospel Choir, a transgender Christian chorus, the film follows the members through their day-to-day lives as well as their journey to winning a music award. The intersections of transgender identity, race, and religion take center stage in this film.

Dance to Miss Chief (2010, Canada, Germany, 5 minutes)

The Cree Two-Spirit artist Kent Monkman's music video humorously critiques Germany's fascination with Indigenous people in the Americas. Monkman's alter ego, Miss Chief Eagle Testickle, uses a mix of archival and current images depicting First Nations people.

Dream Girls (1994, U.K., Japan, 50 minutes)

Takarazuka Revue is the focus of this documentary about the girls' finishing school in Japan where only the best student in the class gets to be the man for a year of performance. The film does an excellent job of studying cisgender heterosexual women who fall at the feet of their masculine performing idols. Although some of the terminology is now outdated, this film includes interviews with the performers and gives the viewer a look into this unique school.

Frankenstein (1931, U.S., 70 minutes)
The iconic horror film looks at the mad doctor Victor Frankenstein and his monstrous creation. The scenes of the monster's being an outsider speak metaphorically and broadly about being a marginalized figure.

Glen or Glenda? (1953, U.S., 68 minutes)
It is difficult to pin down exactly what genre Ed Wood's experimental trans film belongs to. On the one hand, this 1950s movie attempts to give a sympathetic portrayal of a trans woman. On the other, the film has a split narrative, as Bela Lugosi narrates a semi-Gothic story. Unlike *Rocky Horror,* which was released twenty years later, it is not clear if *Glen or Glenda?* is meant to be satiric or serious. It is most likely that it did influence the creation of *Rocky Horror,* however, and it is still a film worth watching for people wanting to trace the history of the depictions of trans people in film.

I Am Divine (2013, U.S., 85 minutes)
The quirky and iconic U.S. film director John Waters worked for years with Harris Glenn Milstead, more famously known as Divine. Divine was featured in numerous films, most popularly *Hairspray,* in which she played Edna Turnblad. This documentary follows the life story of Divine as she empowered so many gender transgressors through her art.

I've Been to Manhattan (2012, U.S., 6 minutes)
This is StormMiguel Florez's first short film and music video. It is a comic film that features trans zombies in San Francisco.

Little Axe (part of the We've Been Around docuseries; 2016, U.S., 30 minutes)
In this series of trans documentaries, the director and artist Rhys Ernst looks at historic trans figures who have nearly been forgotten. This short film focuses on the gospel singer Little Axe Broadnax and his family, who were fully supportive of him as a trans man. The film looks at the intersections of being poor, African American, and transgender in the early twentieth century.

Lou Sullivan (part of the We've Been Around docuseries; 2016, U.S., 30 minutes)
In this short documentary, part of the *We've Been Around* series, the trans filmmaker and historian Rhys Ernst explores the life and legacy of Lou Sullivan, a gay trans man, AIDS activist, and founder of FTM International.

Orlando (1992, U.K., 93 minutes)

The director Sally Potter takes Virginia Woolf's *Orlando* and turns it into this visually stunning film. The depiction of gender fluidity throughout the film is underscored by Tilda Swinton's portrayal of Orlando and by Quentin Crisp, one of Britain's most iconic gay men, as he portrays Queen Elizabeth I.

Princess Knight (1967–1968, television, Japan, approximately 50 minutes per episode)

This animated Japanese television show follows Princess Knight on escapades that are not deemed appropriate for a young girl. This groundbreaking and gender-binary-breaking television show paved the way for current Japanese anime that often focuses on gender variance in adventure stories.

Queen Christina (1933, U.S., 99 minutes)

Greta Garbo is classic in this film based on the real Queen Christina of Sweden, who ruled in the seventeenth century. Queen Christina was famous for her cross-dressing, and Garbo's performance is spectacular.

The Rocky Horror Picture Show (1975, U.K., U.S., 100 minutes)

This film adaptation of the stage musical has broken the world record for longest-running film in history. This iconic audience-participation film stars Susan Sarandon and Tim Curry in a campy and satiric look at gender diversity, gothic horror, and late-night B movies. It is also another trans take on *Frankenstein*. For many young people in more conservative areas, *Rocky Horror* was the one place that offered safety to experiment with gender diversity, even if only for the film's duration.

Sense8 (2015–2018, television, U.S., approximately 60 minutes per episode)

Directed by the trans siblings Lana and Lilly Wachowski, this Netflix original series follows eight people around the world who are all able to be in each other's minds and hearts regardless of location. Nomi, played by the trans actress Jamie Clayton, is in a relationship with her cisgender African American partner, Amanita. More to the point, the series intelligently and deftly looks at the ways that all genders and characters can be part of each individual.

Shabnam Mousi (2005, India, 150 minutes)

For fans of Bollywood film, this musical will not disappoint. Although the film is a fictionalized musical, it is based on the life of a *Hijra* who became a successful politician in India.

Shinjuku Boys (1995, U.K., Japan, 53 minutes)

The documentary focuses on Japanese trans men who work as hosts at a popular nightclub in Tokyo.

Some Like It Hot (1959, U.S., 122 minutes)

Although this film was made during the time of the infamous Hays Code in the United States (a time when films that hinted at homosexuality and/or transgender identity were banned in Hollywood), this romantic comedy went under the radar because it was seen simply as a cross-dressing madcap comedy. Although the film certainly does use cross-dressing for humor, there are many layers of cross-dressing that include Tony Curtis cross-dressing as both a millionaire (he is a penniless musician running from the mob) and as a woman in an "all girls" traveling band. It is Jack Lemmon's cross-dressed character, "Daphne," though, that truly pushes the gender boundaries. The final two minutes of the film are not to be missed.

Still Black: A Portrait of Black Trans Men (2008, U.S., 78 minutes)

This artistic and experimental documentary is a meditation on being African American and a trans man in the United States. It is an outstanding look at intersecting identities in an experimental film.

The Strange Story and Remarkable Life of Billy Tipton (2010, U.S., 9 minutes)

This short documentary has some excellent archival footage of Billy Tipton. The interviews with family members, however, are invasive and show the sensationalized nature of the ways that trans people and their families are treated. This short film is good to contrast with the film about Little Axe Broadnax (Little Axe), which is done in a respectful manner.

Twelfth Night, or What You Will (1988, U.K., 165 minutes)

Most of Shakespeare's comedies (and some of his tragedies and histories) tend to have elements of cross-dressing. During the Renaissance period when he wrote, women were not allowed on the stage, so cross-dressing was required for male actors. This 1988 filmed version of the stage play has the famous Shakespearean actor and director Kenneth Branagh directing a stage production that was filmed. It is not lavish like other productions of Shakespeare's comedies that have made it to the silver screen, but it does remain true to the script.

NOTES

1. Lana Wachowski, Lilly Wachowski, and J. Michael Straczynski, "Smart Money's on the Skinny Bitch," *Sense8,* Season 1, Episode 3, release date 15 June 2015, Netflix Original Series.

2. Gregory William Mank, "Man-Made Monsters," in *The Art of Horror: An Illustrated History*, ed. Stephen Jones (Milwaukee: Applause Theatre & Cinema Books, 2015), 66.

3. Ibid., 74.

4. Ali Cannon, "A Trilogy of Horror and Transmutation," in *From the Inside Out: Radical Gender Transformation, FTM and Beyond*, ed. Morty Diamond (San Francisco: Manic D Press, 2004), 40–41. Also note that Cannon calls the monster Frankenstein. This conflation of the doctor and his creation has almost always been the case with Shelley's story.

5. Susan Stryker, "My Words to Victor Frankenstein above the Village of Chamounix: Performing Transgender Rage," in *The Transgender Studies Reader,* ed. Susan Stryker and Stephen Whittle (New York: Routledge, 2006), 245.

6. William Hughes and Andrew Smith, "Introduction: Queering the Gothic," in *Queering the Gothic,* ed. William Hughes and Andrew Smith (Manchester, U.K.: Manchester University Press, 2009), 1.

7. Ardel Haefele-Thomas, "'Those most intimately concerned': The Strength of Chosen Family in Elizabeth Gaskell's Gothic Short Fiction," in *Gothic Kinship,* ed. Agnes Andeweg and Sue Zlosnik (Manchester, U.K.: Manchester University Press, 2013), 30–47.

8. If you enjoyed the history of the labor protests in Chapter 9, you might enjoy her two most famous novels, *Mary Barton* and *North and South.* They are long Victorian novels, but you will find that many of the struggles working people faced in the nine-

teenth century are issues that we still grapple with today.

9. Ardel Haefele-Thomas, *Queer Others in Victorian Gothic: Transgressing Monstrosity* (Cardiff: University of Wales Press, 2012), chaps. 1 and 2.

10. Ardel Thomas, "Queer Victorian Gothic," in *The Victorian Gothic: An Edinburgh Companion,* ed. Andrew Smith and William Hughes (Edinburgh: Edinburgh University Press, 2012), 150.

11. Robert Bloch, *Psycho* (New York: Simon & Schuster, 1959).

12. Joseph Stefano, *Psycho,* directed by Alfred Hitchcock, Universal Studios, 1960.

13. Thomas Harris, *The Silence of the Lambs* (New York: St. Martin's Press, 1988).

14. Jeffrey Bloomer, "When Gays Decried *Silence of the Lambs,* Jonathan Demme Became an Early Student of Modern Backlash," *Slate, Outward: Expanding the LGBTQ Conversation,* www.slate.com/blogs/outward/2017/04/28/director_jonathan_demme_faced_down_silence_of_the_lambs_gay_backlash.html (accessed 6 July 2017).

15. Kiki Von Glinow, "Jodie Foster Gay: Actress Comes Out at Golden Globes 2013," *Huffington Post,* "Queer Voices," 13 January 2013, www.huffingtonpost.com/2013/01/13/jodie-foster-gay-golden-globes_n_2469439.html (accessed 6 July 2017).

16. IMDb, "*The Silence of the Lambs:* Awards," www.imdb.com/title/tt0102926/awards (accessed 6 July 2017).

17. Lana Wachowski, Lilly Wachowski, and J. Michael Straczynski, "I Am Also a We," *Sense8,* Season 1, Episode 2, release date 15 June 2015, Netflix Original Series.

18. Loved ones of trans people often slip and use the deadname, particularly if their

loved one's gender identity is something they are still getting used to. Using the deadname on purpose to hurt someone, however, is not only disrespectful but also violent.

19. Wachowski, Wachowski, and Straczynski, "I Am Also a We."

20. Ibid.

21. Ibid.

22. Ibid.

23. Wachowski, Wachowski, and Straczynski, "Smart Money's on the Skinny Bitch."

24. Lana Wachowski, Lilly Wachowski, and J. Michael Straczynski, "What's Going On," *Sense8*, Season 1, Episode 4, release date 15 June 2015, Netflix Original Series.

25. Armistead Maupin, guest presentation, 10th Annual One City One Book, San Francisco, City College of San Francisco, 14 October 2014. Armistead Maupin's best-selling *Tales of the City* books contain one of the earliest and most positive depictions of a trans character, the iconic landlady of 28 Barbary Lane, Anna Madrigal.

26. Willa Cather, *One of Ours* (New York: Alfred A. Knopf, 1922). The Pulitzer Prize information is from the Willa Cather Foundation website: https://www.willacather .org/ about/willa-cather/timeline (accessed 3 July 2017).

27. See Sharon O'Brien's groundbreaking biography, *Willa Cather: The Emerging Voice* (Oxford: Oxford University Press, 1987).

28. Ibid., 96.

29. Ibid.

30. Willa Cather, *The Selected Letters of Willa Cather*, ed. Andrew Jewell and Janis Stout (New York: Alfred A. Knopf, 2013), 8–10.

31. Diana Souhami, *The Trials of Radclyffe Hall* (New York: Doubleday, 1999), xix.

32. Ibid., xvii.

33. My mother, who was on a medical school residency in Alexandria, Louisiana, told me about this. She always talked about how depressing the novel was, but that it was the only novel to discuss love relationships between women.

34. Radclyffe Hall, *The Well of Loneliness* (New York: Doubleday, 1928), 13.

35. Virginia Woolf, *Orlando: A Biography* (1928; repr., London: Hogarth Press, 1933), 127.

36. Ibid.

37. Ibid., 127–128.

38. Lyn Gardner, "'I want to be a threat': Jo Clifford on Her Transgender Christ and Overcoming Fear," interview with Jo Clifford, *Guardian,* 2 March 2016, https://www.theguardian.com/stage/ 2016/mar/02/jo-clifford-transgender- christ-overcoming-fear-every-one-bac- london (accessed 30 June 2017).

39. Program for *The Taming of the Shrew,* Globe Theatre, July 2003.

40. Anne Russell, "Tragedy, Gender, Performance: Women as Tragic Heroes on the Nineteenth-Century Stage," *Comparative Drama* 30.2 (1996): 135.

41. Ibid., 147.

42. Lisa Merrill, *When Romeo Was a Woman: Charlotte Cushman and Her Circle of Female Spectators* (Ann Arbor: University of Michigan Press, 2000), 111.

43. Ibid., 115.

44. Jennifer Robertson, *Takarazuka: Sexual Politics and Popular Culture in Modern Japan* (Berkeley: University of California Press, 1998), xi.

45. "The Takarazuka Revue's Allure," http:// kageki.hankyu.co.jp/english/about/index .html (accessed 14 July 2017).

46. Kim Longinotto and Jano Williams, *Dream Girls* (film), Twentieth Century Vixen/Women Make Movies, 1994.

47. Gardner, "'I want to be a threat.'"

48. Fresh Meat Festival, Sean Dorsey Dance, "Is This Butch Enough?" Performed at Z Space in San Francisco, 15 June 2017.

49. Shawna Virago, "Gender Armageddon," on *Heaven Sent Delinquent,* Tranimal Records, 31 August 2016.

50. Jennifer Maerz, "Laura Jane Grace on New Memoir, Why She's Not a Trans Spokesperson," *Rolling Stone,* 15 June 2016, https://www.rollingstone.com/music/news/laura-jane-grace-on-new-memoir-why-shes-not-a-trans-spokesperson-20160615 (accessed 20 March 2018).

51. Diane Wood Middlebrook, *Suits Me: The Double Life of Billy Tipton* (Boston: Houghton Mifflin, 1998), 12.

52. Ibid., 3.

53. Middlebrook is quoted in Dinitia Smith, "One False Note in a Musician's Life; Billy Tipton Is Remembered with Love, Even by Those Who Were Deceived," *New York Times,* 2 June 1998, www.nytimes.com/1998/06/02/arts/one-false-note-musician-s-life-billy-tipton-remembered-with-love-even-those-who.html (accessed 30 June 2017).

54. Tipton playing the piano can be heard at www.bing.com/videos/h?q=films+about+Billy+tipton&view=detail&mid=5E0D854F48AAC72D6D365E0D854F48AAC72D6D36&FORM=VIRE (accessed 23 April 2018).

55. Rhys Ernst, *Wilmer and Willie Broadnax: "Little Axe" & "Big Axe,"* part of Ernst's *We've Been Around* docuseries, 2016, https://ew.com/article/2016/03/01/little-axe-transgender-gospel-singer-short-film/ (accessed 15 June 2018).

56. Monica Roberts, "Black Trans History:

57. Ibid.

58. Rona Marech, "Singing the Gospel of Transcendence/Nation's First All-Transgender Gospel Choir Raises Its Voices to Praise God and Lift Their Own Feelings of Self-Love and Dignity," *SF Gate,* 18 April 2004, www.sfgate.com/bayarea/article/SAN-FRANCISCO-Singing-the-gospel-of-2791956.php (accessed 4 July 2017). Metropolitan Community Church (MCC) and Dignity Catholic are both LGBT Christian groups. Although there are numerous congregations worldwide that welcome anyone and everyone, they are not considered mainstream.

59. Roberts, "Black Trans History."

60. The Kinks, "Lola," on *Lola versus Powerman and the Moneygoround, Part One,* prod. Ray Davies, Pye Records, 1970.

61. Ray Davies, "Lola," www.bluesforpeace.com/lyrics/lola.htm (accessed 28 June 2017).

62. Raul, "The BBC Made the Kinks Change Their Lyrics to 'Lola' in Order to Get Airplay," *FeelNumb,* 30 November 2009, www.feelnumb.com/2009/11/30/the-bbc-made-the-kinks-change-their-lyrics-to-lola-in-order-to-get-airplay/ (accessed 28 June 2017).

63. Caryn E. Neumann, "The Labouchère Amendment (1885–1967)," *glbtq Encyclopedia,* www.glbtqarchive.com/ssh/labouchere_amendment_S.pdf (accessed 7 July 2017).

64. This is the original British wording. Later, the words were changed to "I know what I am in bed, I'm a man, and so is Lola."

65. Lawrence et al. v. Texas, Supreme Court of the United States, no. 02-102, argued 26 March 2003, decided 26 June 2003,

Wilmer 'Little Axe' M. Broadnax," *Trans-Griot,* 16 July 2013, http://transgriot.blogspot.com/2013/07/black-trans-history-wilmer-little-axe-m.html (accessed 30 June 2017).

www.law.cornell.edu/supct/html/02-102 .ZS.html (accessed 7 July 2017).

66. "The Kinks Bio," *Rolling Stone,* www.roll ingstone.com/music/artists/the-kinks/ biography/ (accessed 28 June 2017).

67. Lou Reed, "Take a Walk on the Wild Side," https://www.bing.com/search?q=take%20 a%20walk%20on%20the%20wild%20 0004D010716A316A5D3C6E&form= CONBDF&conlogo=CT3210127 (accessed 23 April 2018).

68. Roisin O'Connor, "Lou Reed Song 'Take a Walk on the Wild Side' Accused of Includ-ing Transphobic Lyrics by Canadian Student Group," *Independent,* 22 May 2017, www .independent.co.uk/arts-entertainment/ music/news/lou-reed-walk-on-the-wild-side-transphobic-guelph-university-stu dents-canada-transformer-album -a7748686.html (accessed 1 July 2017).

69. Iceis Rain, "Warrior (War Cry)," on *The Queen,* Iceis Media, 2014, www.iceisrain .com/work.html (accessed 15 June 2017).

70. Iceis Rain, "Bio," www.iceisrain.com/bio .html (accessed 15 June 2017).

71. Dawn Karima, "Double Blessing: A Visit with Iceis Rain," PowWows.com, 4 November 2014, www.powwows.com/double-blessing-a-visit-with-iceis-rain/ (accessed 7 July 2017).

72. Iceis Rain, *The Queen,* introductory remarks to the music video: www.bing.com/videos /h?q=ICEIS+Rain&&view=detail&mid =9CC320DC14AFED0864159CC320DC14 AFED086415&rvsmid=7996AAFB6C78FF6 09A557996AAFB6C78FF609A55&fsscr =0&FORM=VDQVAP (accessed 15 June 2017).

73. Karima, "Double Blessing."

74. Iceis Rain, "Warrior (War Cry)."

75. Karima, "Double Blessing."

76. Ibid.

77. StormMiguel Florez, "Albuquerque Dyke Youth in the 80s!" www.stormflorez.com/ the-whistle.html (accessed 7 July 2017).

78. StormMiguel Florez, "Legend," www .stormflorez.com/lyrics/legend (accessed 7 July 2017).

79. Jen Dan, "Shawna Virago—'Gender Arma-geddon,'" *Delusions of Adequacy,* 20 April 2017, www.adequacy.net/2017/04/shawna -virago-gender-armageddon/ (accessed 23 April 2018).

80. Words on Charl Marais's drawing from the exhibition "Trans: Body Maps of Trans-gender South Africans," Constitution Hill, Johannesburg, April 2007, in Ruth Morgan, Charl Marais, and Joy Rosemary Wellbe-loved, eds., *Trans: Transgender Life Stories from South Africa* (Auckland Park, South Africa: Jacana, 2009), insert between 124 and 125.

81. "Constitution Hill," https://www.constitu tionhill.org.za/ (accessed 21 March 2018).

82. Morgan et al., *Trans,* insert between 124 and 125.

83. Chantelle's drawing, ibid.

84. Charl's drawing, ibid.

85. "Twilight People: Stories of Faith and Gender beyond the Binary," https://www .twilightpeople.com/the-project/ (accessed 15 June 2016).

86. Ibid.

87. Jess Dugan, "Artist Statement," www.jess dugan.com/to-survive-on-this-shore/ statements/ (accessed 27 March 2018).

88. Before the mid-1970s, computers were huge and hugely expensive machines that filled entire rooms and cost millions of dol-lars. Computers in the home? Unthinkable!

89. We would like to emphasize how very new this modern online world is. Consider that Google—now a huge multinational corporation—was founded only in 1998.

Yahoo and Amazon were launched in 1994, eBay in 1995, Netflix in 1999, Wikipedia in 2001, and YouTube in 2005. Facebook was launched in 2004, Twitter in 2006. None of these companies, of course, immediately became the juggernauts they are today; most achieved their full impact only in the last few years before this book was published.

90. We can't begin to tell you what a boon the World Wide Web was in the preparation of this essay. It was easier, most of the time, to find a citation online than it was to walk across the room and snatch a book from a shelf.

91. Interestingly, vinyl is having a resurgence with audiophiles and millennials who like the warmer sound.

92. This does not mean the information we receive or retrieve is of worth or even true. The deleterious effects of false news stories were readily apparent during the 2016 U.S. presidential campaigns and election.

93. *Daily Stat (Harvard Business Review)*, 17 February 2011. On the other hand, even before computers became ubiquitous in the classroom, studies showed that the students' attention spans were far shorter than the typical college lecture, so perhaps students are actually attending to lectures as much as they ever did. See Joan Middendorf and Alan Kalish, "The 'Change-Up' in Lectures." *National Teaching and Learning Forum* 5.2 (1996): 1–12.

94. Bulletin boards were hosted on computers owned by individuals and accessed by individuals who dialed the board's dedicated telephone line. Once logged in, users could read news, read and leave messages, and download or upload articles—but only one person could log on at a time. Although a few bulletin board operators could afford two or three phones lines, most had only a single line, and often that was used for both voice communication and data exchange. Busy signals were common.

95. "There is nothing wrong with your television set. Do not attempt to adjust the picture. We are controlling transmission. If we wish to make it louder, we will bring up the volume. If we wish to make it softer, we will tune it to a whisper. We will control the horizontal. We will control the vertical. We can roll the image, make it flutter. We can change the focus to a soft blur or sharpen it to crystal clarity. For the next hour, sit quietly and we will control all that you see and hear. We repeat: There is nothing wrong with your television set. You are about to participate in a great adventure. You are about to experience the awe and mystery which reaches from the inner mind to *The Outer Limits*." Initial television voice-over, 1963.

96. We illustrate this point with an anecdote told to one of us by the anthropologist Anne Bolin. Bolin, who has long been an opponent of the medical model, received a rejected journal manuscript in the early 1990s; one of the reviewers had scrawled on the cover, "Obviously a transsexual." Bolin isn't transsexual; her critic simply assumed she was, and that was enough to rate a rejection (Bolin, personal communication to Dallas Denny). There were exceptions, of course. For instance, in the 1970s Virginia Prince coauthored a series of articles in medical journals with cisgender physicians, using her male and female pseudonyms together, and she presented at the International Symposia on Gender Identity, using her female pseudonym.

97. Sadly, we were so far down the chain of human rights that our humanity didn't register to others, and sometimes not even to ourselves. It didn't matter how intelli-

gent or how well-educated or well-spoken we were, we were locked out of our own discourse. There was an exception to this, however. We were encouraged to tell our personal stories. We did so as the subjects of newspaper articles about our transitions and about the obstacles we encountered in our visibly trans lives, and in memoirs and autobiographies. We obliged by producing autobiographies—hundreds were published. See Dallas Denny, "All We Were Allowed to Write: Transsexual Autobiographies in the Late XXth and Early XXIst Centuries," workshop presented at Fantasia Fair, 19–26 October 2014, Provincetown, Mass.; you can view a presentation slide show at http://dallasdenny .com/Writing/2014/10/29/all-we-were -allowed-to-write-2014/2014.

98. Stone's essay was in large part a response to Janis Raymond's virulent and highly personal attack on her in the 1970s. See Janis Raymond, *The Transsexual Empire: The Making of the She-Male* (Boston: Beacon Press, 1979); Davina Gabriel (1995), "Interview with the Transsexual Vampire: Sandy Stone's Dark Gift," *TransSisters* 1.8 (1995): 14–27; and Cristan Williams, "TERF Hate and Sandy Stone," *TransAdvocate,* 16 August 2014, http://transadvocate.com/ terf-violence-and-sandy-stone_n_14360 .htm (accessed 20 July, 2017).

99. As did Kate Bornstein's *Gender Outlaw: On Men, Women, and the Rest of Us* (New York: Routledge, 1994) and Martine Rothblatt's *The Apartheid of Sex: A Manifesto on the Freedom of Gender* (New York: Crown Publishers, 1994), which appeared a year later. Feinberg published a history of transgender

people in 1992 and an argument against binary gender norms in 1998.

100. Erotic fiction has a long tradition in the transfeminine transgender community. Even relatively staid magazines like *Transvestia* have erotic content (erotic, at least, for cross-dressers), and there have been hundreds of books with names like *Destined for Dresses, Fated for Femininity*, and *Tales from a Pink Mirror*. A famed illustrator of such early books was named Stanton, and books with his illustrations bring high prices. We would be interested in hearing from anyone who knows Stanton's history. Vicky West was another illustrator of transgender erotica (and nonerotic stories; she was the primary artist for Lee Brewster's *Drag* magazine). West's legal name was Dirk Luykx. The photojournalist Mariette Pathy Allen, who inherited West's works, exhibited them at Fantasia Fair in the mid-2000s; a number of West's illustrations were featured in issue no. 111 of *Transgender Tapestry* (Winter 2006–2007). Bowen's work was an early example of transmasculine erotic fiction.

101. In 1998 the psychiatrist and attorney Richard Green wrote, in his chapter in Denny's edited text *Current Concepts in Transgender Identity*, "Startling as it is for me to think it, I wrote the conclusion to *Transsexualism and Sex Reassignment* about 25 years ago. It's been a long time since I re-read it. As I handwrite my reflections (I still do not type or word process), I am struck at the outset that the biggest change with this new text may be that it is edited by a transsexual."

BIBLIOGRAPHY

Bloch, Robert. *Psycho*. New York: Simon & Schuster, 1959.

Bloomer, Jeffrey. "When Gays Decried *Silence of the Lambs*, Jonathan Demme Became an Early Student of Modern Backlash." *Slate, Outward: Expanding the LGBTQ Conversation*, www.slate.com/blogs/outward/2017/04/28/director_jonathan_demme_faced_down_silence_of_the_lambs_gay_backlash.html. Accessed 6 July 2017.

Cannon, Ali. "A Trilogy of Horror and Transmutation." In *From the Inside Out: Radical Gender Transformation, FTM and Beyond*, edited by Morty Diamond, 40–47. San Francisco: Manic D Press, 2004.

Cather, Willa. *One of Ours*. New York: Alfred A. Knopf, 1922.

———. *The Selected Letters of Willa Cather*. Edited by Andrew Jewell and Janis Stout. New York: Alfred A. Knopf, 2013.

Chantelle. Untitled drawing. In *Trans: Transgender Life Stories from South Africa*, edited by Ruth Morgan, Charl Marais, and Joy Rosemary Wellbeloved. Auckland Park, South Africa: Jacana, 2009.

"Constitution Hill." https://www.constitutionhill.org.za/. Accessed 21 March 2018.

Davies, Ray. "Lola." www.bluesforpeace.com/lyrics/lola.htm. Accessed 28 June 2017.

Drucker, Zachary, and Rhys Ernst. *Relationship*. Munich: Prestel, 2016.

Ernst, Rhys. *Wilmer and Willie Broadnax: "Little Axe" & "Big Axe."* Part of *We've Been Around* docuseries. 2016. https://ew.com/article/2016/03/01/little-axe-transgender-gospel-singer-short-film/. Accessed 15 June 2018.

Feinberg, Leslie. *Stone Butch Blues*. Ithaca, N.Y.: Firebrand Books, 1993.

Florez, StormMiguel. "Albuquerque Dyke Youth in the 80's!" www.stormflorez.com/the-whistle.html. Accessed 7 July 2017.

———. "Legend." www.stormflorez.com/lyrics/legend. Accessed 7 July 2017.

Gardner, Lyn. "'I want to be a threat': Jo Clifford on Her Transgender Christ and Overcoming Fear." Interview with Jo Clifford. *Guardian*, 2 March 2016. https://www.theguardian.com/stage/2016/mar/02/jo-clifford-transgender-christ-overcoming-fear-everyone-bac-london. Accessed 30 June 2017.

Globe Theatre. Program guide for *The Taming of the Shrew*, by William Shakespeare, July 2003.

Goldstein, Dana. "Summer Reading Books: The Ties That Bind Colleges." *New York Times*, 1 July 2017. https://www.nytimes.com/2017/07/01/us/college-summer-reading.html. Accessed 3 July 2017.

Haefele-Thomas, Ardel. *Queer Others in Victorian Gothic: Transgressing Monstrosity*. Cardiff: University of Wales Press, 2012.

———. "'Those most intimately concerned': The Strength of Chosen Family in Elizabeth Gaskell's Gothic Short Fiction." In *Gothic Kinship*, edited by Agnes Andeweg and Sue Zlosnik, 30–47. Manchester, U.K.: Manchester University Press, 2013.

Hall, Radclyffe. *The Well of Loneliness*. New York: Doubleday, 1928.

Harris, Thomas. *The Silence of the Lambs*. New York: St. Martin's Press, 1988.

Hughes, William, and Andrew Smith. "Introduction: Queering the Gothic." In *Queering the Gothic*, edited by William Hughes and Andrew Smith, 1–10. Manchester, U.K.: Manchester University Press, 2009.

Iceis Rain. "Bio." www.iceisrain.com/bio.html. Accessed 15 June 2017.

———. *The Queen*. Introductory remarks to the music video. www.bing.com/videos/search?q=ICEIS+Rain&&view=detail&mid=9CC320DC14AFED0864159CC320DC14AFED086415&rvsmid=7996AAFB6C78FF609A557996AAFB6C78FF609A55&fsscr=0&FORM=VDQVAP. Accessed 15 June 2017.

———. "Warrior (War Cry)." On *The Queen*, Iceis Media, 2014. www.iceisrain.com/work.html. Accessed 15 June 2017.

Ikeda, Riyoko. *The Rose of Versailles*. [Original Japanese title: *Berusaiyu no Bara*.] Tokyo: Shueisha, 1972.

Karima, Dawn. "Double Blessing: A Visit with Iceis Rain." PowWows.com, 4 November 2014. www.powwows.com/double-blessing-a-visit-with-iceis-rain/. Accessed 7 July 2017.

The Kinks. "Lola." On *Lola Versus Powerman and the Moneygoround, Part One*, produced by Ray Davies. Pye Records, 1970.

"The Kinks Bio." *Rolling Stone*. www.rollingstone.com/music/artists/the-kinks/biography. Accessed 28 June 2017.

Lawrence et al. v. Texas. Supreme Court of the United States. No. 02-102. Argued 26 March 2003, decided 26 June 2003. https://www.law.cornell.edu/supct/html/02-102.ZS.html. Accessed 7 July 2017.

Maerz, Jennifer. "Laura Jane Grace on New Memoir, Why She's Not a Trans Spokesperson." *Rolling Stone*, 15 June 2016. https://www.rollingstone.com/music/news/laura-jane-grace-on-new-memoir-why-shes-not-a-trans-spokesperson-20160615. Accessed 20 March 2018.

Mank, Gregory William. "Man-Made Monsters." In *The Art of Horror: An Illustrated History*, edited by Stephen Jones, 66–85. Milwaukee: Applause Theatre & Cinema Books, 2015.

Marais, Charl. Untitled drawing. In *Trans: Transgender Life Stories from South Africa*, edited by Ruth Morgan, Charl Marais, and Joy Rosemary Wellbeloved. Auckland Park, South Africa: Jacana, 2009.

Marech, Rona. "Singing the Gospel of Transcendence/Nation's First All-Transgender Gospel Choir Raises Its Voices to Praise God and Lift Their Own Feelings of Self-Love and Dignity." *SF Gate*, 18 April 2004. www.sfgate.com/bayarea/article/SAN-FRANCISCO-Singing-the-gospel-of-2791956.php. Accessed 4 July 2017.

Maupin, Armistead. Guest presentation. 10th Annual One City One Book, San Francisco. City College of San Francisco, 14 October 2014.

Merrill, Lisa. *When Romeo Was a Woman: Charlotte Cushman and Her Circle of Female Spectators*. Ann Arbor: University of Michigan Press, 2000.

Middlebrook, Diane Wood. *Suits Me: The Double Life of Billy Tipton*. Boston: Houghton Mifflin, 1998.

Neumann, Caryn E. "The Labouchère Amendment (1885–1967)." *glbtq Encyclopedia.* www.glbtqarchive.com/ssh/labouchere_amendment_S.pdf. Accessed 7 July 2017.

Newhall, Barbara Falconer. "Armistead Maupin: The Man Who Wrote the Quintessential San Francisco Novel—on a Newspaper Deadline." *Barbara Falconer Newhall: Riffs on Life from a Veteran Journalist,* 23 January 2014. http://barbarafalconernewhall.com/2014/01/23/armistead-maupin-the-man-who-wrote-the-quintessential-san-francisco-novel-on-a-newspaper-deadline/. Accessed 7 July 2017.

O'Brien, Sharon. *Willa Cather: The Emerging Voice.* Oxford: Oxford University Press, 1987.

O'Connor, Roisin. "Lou Reed Song 'Take a Walk on the Wild Side' Accused of Including Transphobic Lyrics by Canadian Student Group." *Independent,* 22 May 2017. www.independent.co.uk/arts-entertainment/music/news/lou-reed-walk-on-the-wild-side-transphobic-guelph-university-students-canada-transformer-album-a7748686.html. Accessed 1 July 2017.

Raul. "The BBC Made the Kinks Change Their Lyrics to 'Lola' in Order to Get Airplay." *Feel-Numb,* 30 November 2009. www.feelnumb.com/2009/11/30/the-bbc-made-the-kinks-change-their-lyrics-to-lola-in-order-to-get-airplay/. Accessed 28 June 2017.

Roberts, Monica. "Black Trans History: Wilmer 'Little Axe' M. Broadnax." *TransGriot,* 16 July 2013. http://transgriot.blogspot.com/2013/07/black-trans-history-wilmer-little-axe-m.html. Accessed 30 June 2017.

Robertson, Jennifer. *Takarazuka: Sexual Politics and Popular Culture in Modern Japan.* Berkeley: University of California Press, 1998.

Russell, Anne. "Tragedy, Gender, Performance: Women as Tragic Heroes on the Nineteenth-Century Stage." *Comparative Drama* 30.2 (1996): 135–157.

Sean Dorsey Dance. "Is This Butch Enough?" Fresh Meat Festival, performed at Z Space in San Francisco, 15 June 2017.

"*The Silence of the Lambs*: Awards." IMDb. www.imdb.com/title/tt0102926/awards. Accessed 6 July 2017.

Smith, Dinitia. "One False Note in a Musician's Life; Billy Tipton Is Remembered with Love, Even by Those Who Were Deceived." *New York Times,* 2 June 1998. www.nytimes.com/1998/06/02/arts/one-false-note-musician-s-life-billy-tipton-remembered-with-love-even-those-who.html. Accessed 30 June 2017.

Souhami, Diana. *The Trials of Radclyffe Hall.* New York: Doubleday, 1999.

Stefano, Joseph. *Psycho.* Directed by Alfred Hitchcock. Universal Studios, 1960.

Stryker, Susan. "My Words to Victor Frankenstein above the Village of Chamounix: Performing Transgender Rage." In *The Transgender Studies Reader,* edited by Susan Stryker and Stephen Whittle, 244–256. New York: Routledge, 2006.

"The Takarazuka Revue's Allure." http://kageki.hankyu.co.jp/english/about/index.html. Accessed 14 July 2017.

Tally, Ted. *The Silence of the Lambs.* Directed by Jonathan Demme. Strong Heart/Demme Production, Orion Pictures, 1991. www.imdb.com/title/tt0102926/. Accessed 6 July 2017.

Thomas, Ardel. "Queer Victorian Gothic." In *The Victorian Gothic: An Edinburgh Companion,* edited by Andrew Smith and William Hughes, 142–155. Edinburgh: Edinburgh University Press, 2012.

Tipton, Billy. *Billy Tipton Plays Hi-Fi on the Piano.* Vinyl. Tops, 1956.

———. "Sweet Georgia Brown." Piano audio with photographs. http://www.bing.com/videos/search?q=films+about+Billy+tipton&view=detail&mid=5E0D854F48AAC72D6D365E0D854F48AAC72D6D36&FORM=VIRE. Accessed 30 June 2017.

———. "Sweet Georgia Brown." Vinyl. Tops, 1955.

"Twilight People: Stories of Faith and Gender beyond the Binary." https://www.twilightpeople.com/the-project/. Accessed 15 June 2016.

Virago, Shawna. "Gender Armageddon." On *Heaven Sent Delinquent.* Tranimal Records, 31 August 2016.

Von Glinow, Kiki. "Jodie Foster Gay: Actress Comes Out at Golden Globes 2013." *Huffington Post,* "Queer Voices," 13 January 2013. www.huffingtonpost.com/2013/01/13/jodie-foster-gay-golden-globes_n_2469439.html. Accessed 6 July 2017.

Wachowski, Lana, Lilly Wachowski, and J. Michael Straczynski. *Sense8.* Season 1. Release date 15 June 2015. Netflix Original Series.

Willa Cather Foundation. https://www.willacather.org/. Accessed 3 July 2017.

Woolf, Virginia. *Orlando: A Biography.* 1928. Reprint. London: Hogarth, 1933.

"Zackarhys." http://zackarhys.tumblr.com/about. Accessed 3 July 2017.

CHAPTER 12

The Importance of Archives
Hearing Our Own Voices

Key Questions

1. Why is history important? Why is trans history important?

2. How do archival materials differ from other research sources?

3. Ephemera refers to printed materials like fliers, postcards, and announcements that are usually seen as useful only in the short term. Why is it important to keep various types of ephemera?

4. Why is it important to have archives that focus on specific topics or specific groups?

Chapter Overview

This concluding chapter is different from the other chapters in this textbook. It begins with my own voice and an example of a brief newspaper article that mentions my summer visit to my grandparents' farm in the Ozark Mountains in Arkansas. The chapter then offers examples of how we can use archival materials to uncover stories and histories. The chapter ends with a look at specific transgender archives and the importance of keeping trans history alive.

Introduction: A Small Local Notice

A brittle and yellowed clipping from the *Madison County Record,* the local newspaper serving rural northwestern Arkansas since 1879, notes that I visited my maternal grandparents for two weeks in July 1972. This short notice, just three sentences long, stated that I visit my grandparents annually and that I came from Oklahoma City. Aside from the fact that news may have been slow in northwestern Arkansas that week, what does this short article of "local interest" tell you about me as an eight-year-old staying with my grandparents in the Ozarks?

Haefele-Thomas, Ardel, *Introduction to Transgender Studies*
dx.doi.org/10.17312/harringtonparkpress/2019.01.itts.012
© 2019 by Harrington Park Press

The word *annual* tells readers that I visited the Ozarks every summer. Readers also learn that I came from Oklahoma City, so if you look at a map app, you can see that it was not a long trip—about 250 miles. The notice also identifies me as my grandparents' granddaughter, so the paper identified me as a girl (although that never felt quite right to me). My grandparents' names are in the notice, and so is mine, so you could go online and begin a family search. From a three-sentence newspaper clipping, you have the tools to learn quite a bit about my family and my background.

What other parts of my childhood story lie within this old newspaper notice? In other words, what other elements of my past are hinted at? It was July 1972. What was happening in the United States at that time? The Watergate scandal in Washington, D.C., had broken the previous month. The United States was still heavily involved in the Vietnam War. You might wonder if either of these national events affected my family. Were my grandparents and I, tucked away in the safety of those beautiful old hills, worried about my cousin who had been drafted and was in Vietnam? Conducting online research by searching my grandparents' names, you could find a genealogy that might lead you to other articles from the newspaper that covered the Madison County residents who were on active duty in the war. You could discover my cousin's name there (he had the same last name as my grandfather). Further research might show you that he survived to come home, get married, and have children. It will not tell you about his permanent disability or his body-wracking bouts of sickness from being sprayed with Agent Orange, a poisonous defoliant used in the jungles of Vietnam. It will not tell you about his posttraumatic stress disorder (PTSD) or his sleeplessness because he feels he needs to keep watch and protect his family through the night.

Furthermore, my cousin's history does not tell you that I loved emulating my grandfather. I wore Big Smith overalls that were just like granddad's; I followed him and did chores with him all over the hills that made up their farm. He taught me to milk cows. My two favorites were Tiny (a funny name for a cow) and her daughter, Ginger, who was the only cow at the farm who still had her horns. He taught me that the best place to keep the watermelon we had just cut off the vine was in the large and near-freezing water cooler that held the milk cans until the dairy truck came to collect them. Nothing was more sweet than sitting outside and eating that cold fruit in the thick and heady Ozark summer evening air.

The article does not tell you that on hot afternoons I loved sitting in the cool musty cellar carved into the limestone hill behind the house, snapping green beans with my grandmother. She taught me the art of canning fruits and vege-tables. On really special days, when there was not an afternoon chore, she and I would sit in the living room with the fan on high as we played a board game. Her favorite was *Shakespeare,* in which you moved around the board gathering the Bard's quotes. For the most part, my grandmother read only the Bible, but Shakespeare was her guilty pleasure.

The newspaper clipping doesn't say how much I hated being stuffed into a scratchy dress to go to church on Sundays. I used to sit on that hard wooden pew, itchy and sweating, because the church was a former one-room schoolhouse without air conditioning or a fan. I would stare into the corner, fascinated at the spider building a web. And just as it kept getting hotter and hotter, the preacher seemed to get more warmed up to the topic of that day's sermon. The newspaper clipping doesn't tell you how I jumped into the bed of my grandfather's truck for the nine-mile ride over the dirt road home, catching dust and the breeze in antic-ipation of exchanging the dress for my T-shirt and overalls.

The article doesn't mention my sense of myself as different because I wanted to be just like my granddad, but everyone expected me to be like my grand-mother. I loved them both, so why couldn't I emulate the best parts of each one of them?

These recollections and feelings are not something you can learn from a brief, old newspaper article. Those three sentences are a beginning, however, an opening into a past, if you are ready to ask questions and do some research.

Go Ahead, Get Dusty!

When was the last time you completed a research project? You may even be worried about one due soon. Do you conduct your research online? Do you go to the library, check out books, and research articles in the academic databases?

By way of an example, let's assume you will be researching the famous Mexican artists Frida Kahlo and Diego Rivera. You will find a lot of information online about their rocky relationship, their art, and their lives. If you go into a library and check out some books on them, you will probably find even more detailed information about their art and their relationship. Now, what hap-pens if you have access to a library **archive** that has a collection of letters from Frida to Diego?

Imagine the difference between a published book of their letters (sorted and selected by an editor, and then typeset for the book) and actually holding (with a gloved hand) a letter from Frida to Diego. You are holding a piece of paper that

FIGURE 12.1 "Archives" by Cameron Rains. In the final image they created for this book, Cameron Rains has envisioned what an archival space that holds information about various people and events discussed in this book might look like.

Frida Kahlo once held. You can see where her pen made a heavier indentation and where she crossed one word out and wrote another. At the bottom of the letter, there is a lipstick kiss. Decades after her death, the red of the lipstick still looks bright and glossy on the paper, as though it was placed there yesterday.

What are some of the differences between a published book of the authors' letters and the letter you are holding? The published book provides more material and more information. And, if you do not read Spanish, then a book that includes translations will be easier to understand. Think beyond the information and consider how the two different sources *feel* to you. Archives are often about the combination of feeling and gathering information. A printed book's typeset version of the letter's content provides the same information as the handwritten letter. But when you hold the letter, Frida's small drawings in the margins and her lipstick kiss give you a sense of the love and playfulness she may have been feeling at the time. The archival letter provides more emotional depth; it might even make Frida Kahlo come more intensely to life for you.[1]

Dancing Archives?

The San Francisco–based Sean Dorsey Dance troupe (discussed in detail in Chapter 11) often uses historic archives as the raw material for dance projects. In the troupe's 2009 award-winning show, *Uncovered: The Diary Project,* a section entitled "Lou" was dedicated to the life of Louis Graydon Sullivan. Chapter 3 provides more information about Lou Sullivan and his tireless work on behalf of trans men, including his efforts to help get the Standards of Care (SOC) changed. He was also one of the first people to discuss the problems with assuming that a trans identity automatically meant a heterosexual orientation after transition. These biographical facts about Sullivan are important, but for Sean Dorsey it was more important to know how Lou Sullivan *felt* as a gay trans man in a world that told him no such thing existed. What were Lou's deepest feelings about himself? What were his desires and his dreams?

Dorsey had already looked at some of his own childhood diaries, in which he was attempting to work out ideas about his gender identity. The first part of *Uncovered,* "Lost/Found," combines parts of his diary entries with music and dance to portray his own coming-out process. From this deeply personal place of reading his own writing, Sean started to wonder what it would be like to read Lou Sullivan's diaries, if any existed. With some quick research, Sean discovered that the San Francisco GLBT Historical Society has Lou Sullivan's diaries. In fact, Lou Sullivan had bequeathed thirty journals from childhood into early adulthood *precisely* so that other people—but particularly trans people desperately looking for role models—could visit the archive, read his words, sit with his thoughts and feelings, and leave with a sense that they are not alone.

Sean Dorsey spent hours poring through Sullivan's journals, and as he did so, he began to imagine parts of the dance choreography. Lou Sullivan died in 1991 at the age of thirty-nine, but his words, his thoughts, and his feelings touched Sean Dorsey in 2008. The power of Lou Sullivan's diaries spoke to Sean Dorsey and his dance troupe. Beyond that, though, each and every night that Sean Dorsey Dance performed *Uncovered: The Diary Project* in sold-out venues around the United States and Canada, every person seeing that show also experienced the *archives* of Louis Graydon Sullivan's life. In the show, Lou was alive again, telling us his story.[2]

Don't Throw That Away!

Are you part of a student group at your college? Have you attended any events on campus? If you have gone to a dance performance, art show, or campus movie night, how did you find out about it? Or, if you joined a student group or are thinking about joining one, how did you find out about it? Although social media are an excellent means for reaching out to people, there are still plenty of good old-fashioned posters, postcards, and fliers up on campus billboards, lampposts, and kiosks. If you look at campus kiosks closely, you will see the bones of thousands of staples (some of them rusty) from years of public posts. And what usually happens when an event is over? The notices come down and are thrown away.

Picture this: in 1987, at the University of Colorado, Boulder, colorful fliers were posted all over campus announcing a drag show at the campus venue, Quigley's. The entry fee was five dollars because the show was a fund-raiser for several different student groups. Why would someone keep a copy of this flier to look at thirty, forty, or even a hundred years later? Most of the fliers were taken down and discarded after the show. Some of the fliers were taken down before the show because people had written homophobic things on them. But what can this flier tell you about a student fund-raising event in 1987?

If you look at a list of the student groups that cosponsored and benefited from the show, you might see something interesting. The first group on the list was Gays and Friends (not terribly surprising for a drag show). The next group was the Lesbian Caucus. Now, you might be curious: Why was Gays and Friends different from the Lesbian Caucus? Weren't they all gay? Why were there two different groups in 1987, and there is one large group on campus now? Other sponsors of the show included the Black Student Alliance, MEChA (Movimiento Estudiantil Chicano de Aztlán), and a few other student groups focused on historically marginalized communities. Just from this flier you might infer that these different student groups, which represented different marginalized communities on the university campus, came together for a fund-raising event. And you would be right. In fact, this was the first event on which all these student groups worked together. This was an example of intersecting identities before that phrase was coined.

Not only did the event sell out (which many believed would never happen), but the collaboration between the sponsoring groups also created important working bonds between student groups that, despite representing marginalized parties, might not necessarily have considered supporting other groups.[3]

The Importance of Transgender Archives

The Louise Lawrence Transgender Archive (LLTA, figure 12.2) is in the process of being built. The LLTA is named in honor of the Northern California transgender pioneer Louise Lawrence, who began living full-time as a woman in 1942. Lawrence was responsible for publishing, along with Virginia Prince (another trans pioneer), one of the earliest underground and longest-running trans publications, *Transvestia,* beginning in 1952.[4]

FIGURE 12.2 Louise Lawrence Transgender Archive, logo created by Robyn Adams. The Louise Lawrence Transgender Archive opened in Vallejo, California, in 2018. The archive was founded by Ms. Bob Davis and is named after the trans pioneer Louise Lawrence.

For well over forty years, the founder of and collector for the archive, Ms. Bob Davis (see "Writings from the Community" in Chapter 8) has been painstakingly collecting newspaper clippings, underground trans magazines, historical photographs, and other pieces of **ephemera**. The LLTA will be housed in a remodeled and climate-controlled building in her backyard in Vallejo, California. The archive Ms. Bob is building is a grassroots effort because she does not have a major institution (such as a university) supporting her efforts. Nonetheless, she is already hosting scholars who want to look through forty years' worth of trans materials that could have wound up in the garbage. Through grant support and community fund-raising, the LLTA is coming to life. The nearby GLBT Historical Society in San Francisco has also been supportive.

Another trans-specific archive is the University of Minnesota's Tretter Collection's Transgender Oral History Project, whose director is Andrea Jenkins; the University of Victoria, in British Columbia, Canada, holds the world's largest transgender archive. Dr. Aaron Devor is Chair in Transgender Studies and founder and academic director of the Transgender Archives at the University of Victoria.

What if you have no way of traveling to these archives and yet you want to be able to study trans history? First of all, these archives are increasing their online presence. At this time, for example, you can go to the Transgender Oral History Project and read the transcripts of Jenkins's interviews, which are available in PDF format. There is also the Digital Transgender Archive, which is solely online and was created by K. J. Rawson, professor at the College of the Holy Cross. This ever-expanding archive offers links to trans materials from around the world. Finally, it is important to remember that any local public library, museum, or college or university library has archival material. Harrison Apple's writing at the end of this chapter discusses the local archive in Pittsburgh where they were able to find historic material on a local trans figure. Within these local museums and libraries, you, like Harrison, can find trans histories. It may take some digging, but trans people have always been in all communities everywhere in the world.

Why are transgender archives so important? Andrea Jenkins and Aaron Devor give their answers in "Writings from the Community" at the end of this chapter. For my answer, I would like to leave you with an *imagined* scenario. What if, somewhere in a dusty London attic, someone uncovered the diaries of a young doctor in training? He was looking forward to going abroad to work as a British army surgeon in South Africa. The diaries recount the hours of physical discomfort from binding his breasts and the oppressive heat and smells from the operating theater where he worked twelve-hour shifts with his mentor. He didn't dare faint for fear of his clothing being stripped off in an effort to revive him. He did not go out drinking with the other medical students because he always had to keep his guard up, and yet he knew he was as much a man as any of the other medical students. What would happen if diaries like these existed and found their way into a mainstream archive? In the best of all possible worlds, of course, the archive would have the integrity to respect Dr. James Miranda Barry as the man he was. (See Chapter 8 for Dr. Barry's full story.) In a transgender archive, we are assured that his modern-day community would embrace his history as a trans man. Imagine if Dr. Barry had kept a diary. Imagine what his life story could have done for someone like Lou Sullivan. Trans people have a long and rich history, and we owe it to future trans people to curate it well so that they do not feel as alone as Lou Sullivan did, or as Dr. James Barry must have.

ANDREA JENKINS

The Transgender Oral History Project: Huge Undertaking

In 2017 Andrea Jenkins became the first African American transgender woman to be elected to the city council of a major city. She now proudly represents Ward 8 of Minneapolis, Minnesota. Andrea is an artist-activist and award-winning poet and writer. She has been awarded fellowships from the Bush Foundation, Intermedia Arts, and the Playwrights Center and has won writing and performance grants and scholarships from the Givens Foundation, Intermedia Arts, the Loft, the Napa Valley Writers Conference, and Pillsbury House Theater. Andrea is the co-curator of Queer Voices at Intermedia Arts (the longest-running series of its kind in the nation) and, in 2018, completed several years' worth of work collecting oral histories from hundreds of people in the upper Midwest transgender community as an oral historian in the Jean-Nickolaus Tretter Collection in Gay, Lesbian, Bisexual, and Transgender Studies.

Andrea is the author of three chapbooks of poems and a full-length book of poetry, The "T" Is NOT Silent: New and Selected Poems. She has been published in several anthologies, including Gender Outlaws Two: The Next Generation; When We Become Weavers: Queer Female Poets on the Midwestern Experience, edited by Kate Lynn Hibbard; The Naked I: Wide Open and The Naked I: Inside Out, edited by 20% Theater; and most recently Gay, Lesbian, Bisexual, and Transgender Civil Rights: A Public Policy Agenda for Uniting a Divided America, edited by Wallace Swan. She was also a contributor to the widely acclaimed anthology Blues Vision, edited by Alexs Pate, Pamela Fletcher, and J. Otis Powell! (Minnesota Historical Society Press, 2015), as well as the anthology A Good Time for the Truth, edited Sun Yung Shin (Minnesota Historical Society Press, 2016). To learn more about her, visit http://andreajenkins.webs.com.

The Tretter Collection Transgender Oral History Project at the University of Minnesota

It has been an amazing time since the Transgender Oral History Project began in April 2015. It has been a tremendous learning experience for me. After spending the first three months setting up the project, attending workshops to learn the intricacies and ethics of developing an oral history project, recruiting and organizing a great advisory committee, researching and purchasing the appropriate equipment, and hiring a transcriptionist, I began to interview members of the trans and gender-nonconforming community in Minnesota and around the country. The Transgender Oral History Project has completed sixty-eight interviews across a wide variety of identities, ages, and ethnicities.

"Big Mama"

Our oldest interviewee so far is an eighty-three-year-old trans woman named Donna "Big Mama" Ewing. Her story is fascinating. Born on a farm in southern Minnesota, she states that she felt like and was treated as a little girl from the age of eighteen months. She asserts that she began working in the farm kitchen as early as five. She served food to the farmhands and other workers, and they all treated her like the little girl that she believed she was.

At nineteen she moved to the Twin Cities and began to truly express and embrace the woman she was. She later became one of the first people to access gender-confirmation surgery at the famed Program in Human Sexuality at the University of Minnesota. She worked for twenty-one years after her surgery as the self-described coat-check girl at the Gay 90s, a club in downtown Minneapolis. She was one of the first transgender persons that many members of the Twin Cities gay and lesbian community had ever met. She served as an ambassador for the community as someone who was able to successfully transition and create a new life for herself.

Her story reflects the type of compelling oral histories that I've been so honored and humbled to collect for this project. Some of the luminaries thus far include Kate Bornstein, Chrishaun "CeCe" McDonald, Roxanne Anderson, and Ignacio Rivera. While these may not be household names in the broader community, these are folks who have shaped the modern movement for transgender equality here in Minnesota and throughout the country through advocacy, writing, and the arts.

Why is this important? The project is critical to countering the negative narratives that are being espoused by mean-spirited politicians and others who wish to ban transgender folks from using the bathroom of their choice, as we have witnessed in North Carolina. This project is important because there were twelve trans people of color murdered in the United States in 2016 and twenty-four murdered in 2015. This project is important because the rates of trans suicide calls have doubled in 2016, and unemployment and homelessness rates continue to grow in trans communities throughout the country.

Beyond the amazing oral histories that I've been able to the collect, the project has provided me a platform to travel throughout Minnesota and the country to discuss issues facing the community. I've been a panelist and keynote speaker in places like Augsburg College, Macalester College, Hamline University, State University of New York at Geneseo, University of Massachusetts at Amherst, and a meeting of the Organization of American Historians in Providence, Rhode Island. I've also served as a contributor on multiple publications and events in many of those locations. I even attended and presented at the "Moving Trans History Forward" conference in Victoria, British Columbia, at the University of Victoria—home to the largest transgender historical archives in the world—with the local actress and participant in the Trans Oral History Project, Erica Fields.

These stories that I've been privileged to witness are fascinating in their everydayness but also inspiring in their messages of triumph over adversity. One participant stated, "The Trans Oral History Project humanizes and connects the transgender narrative through space and time in an unprecedented compilation of personal and collective stories. Growing up, I felt isolated because I did not see my trans identity reflected in the broader cultural discourse around gender. I wish I would have had a resource like this when I was younger. I am honored to contribute my story to the collection so that future generations of trans folks know that we have always been here, and we aren't going away."

AARON DEVOR, PHD

The World's Largest Transgender Archives: The Transgender Archives at the University of Victoria

Dr. Aaron Devor, FSSSS, FSTLHE, holds the world's only research chair in transgender studies and is the founder and academic director of the world's largest transgender archives, both at the University of Victoria in British Columbia, Canada. Studying and teaching about transgender topics for more than thirty years, he is the author of numerous frequently cited scholarly articles and the author of the widely acclaimed books FTM: Female-to-Male Transsexuals in Society *(1997, 2016); the Lambda Literary Awards finalist* The Transgender Archives: Foundations for the Future *(2014); and* Gender Blending: Confronting the Limits of Duality *(1989). He has delivered more than twenty keynote and plenary addresses to audiences around the world. He is a national award–winning teacher, an elected member of the International Academy of Sex Research, and an elected fellow of the Society for the Scientific Study of Sexuality, and he has been a member of the World Professional Association for Transgender Health's (WPATH) Standards of Care committee since 1999. Dr. Devor is overseeing the standards' translations into world languages.*

The Transgender Archives

The most effective way to destroy people is to deny and obliterate their own understanding of their history.
GEORGE ORWELL

Study the past if you would define the future.
CONFUCIUS

What Are the Transgender Archives and Why Are They Important?

Many of the things that people do also leave behind some kind of record. In some cases, it is only what resides in the memories of people who were there when something happened. Many times there are documents that record some version of what happened. These records may exist in computer files; on paper; embedded in DVDs, CDs, vinyl, film, or magnetic tape; as works of visual art; as poetry or music. The documentation for what has happened may be a kind of formal "official" version, or it may represent alternative views and experiences. When historians want to understand how something happened, they turn to records from the past and try to reconstruct as true a version as possible by using as many different sources as they can. The job of archives is to collect, organize, safely store, and make accessible records from the past so that people can know how we got to where we are today, which, in turn, can help us build a better future.

The Transgender Archives, held at the University of Victoria in British Columbia, Canada (figure 12.3), are the world's largest collection of original materials documenting the work of transgender activists and researchers about trans, nonbinary, and Two-Spirit people. The collection is composed of thousands of books; hundreds of newsletter and magazine titles from eighteen countries on five continents; newspaper clippings files reaching back to the 1920s; hundreds of short books of trans fantasy fiction; activist organizational records; informational pamphlets; personal papers of trans, nonbinary, and Two-Spirit activists; historic court case records; audio recordings on magnetic tape, vinyl, and CDs; mass culture, specialty, bootleg, and conference videos on magnetic tape and DVDs; art and amateur photographs; erotica; original works of visual art; and ephemera including items such as T-shirts, matchbook covers, business cards, trophies, and plaques. The collection documents nearly 60 years of activism and traces more than 125 years of research. If you put all the books and bankers' boxes on one long shelf, it would stretch the length of one and a half football fields (approximately 533 linear feet or 162 linear meters).

FIGURE 12.3 "Do Not Destroy! This material is NOT junk": sticker, Transgender Archives, University of Victoria. The Transgender Archives at the University of Victoria is the largest trans archive in the world. This sticker is a reminder of the importance of ephemera in archival collections.

The University of Victoria is a large Canadian research-intensive, publicly funded university. It serves over 20,000 students, including a large component of graduate students, and has been repeatedly rated among the world's top 1 percent of universities by the Times Higher Education World University Rankings. It is also located in a quiet, midsized city on the southernmost tip of a large island (larger than the state of Israel) off the west coast of Canada that is best known as a bucolic tourist destination—not the kind of place that one would immediately think of as a magnet for trans research and activism. When most people first hear of the Transgender Archives, they assume that they are small and limited to Canadian content. When they understand its size and scope, the first thing that that they generally say is "How did it end up there?"

The Beginnings of the Transgender Archives

The start of the Transgender Archives was not planned. One day I was having lunch with Rikki Swin, the founder of the Rikki Swin Institute (RSI) of Chicago, which had closed in 2004, and I asked her what the status of the RSI was. She told me she was contemplating relocating it to Victoria, and I somewhat impetuously asked her if she might consider donating it to the University of Victoria.

To my great pleasure and astonishment, she agreed to consider the idea. I immediately contacted the university librarian to find out if UVic Libraries actually wanted the collection that I had already solicited. After learning more about the RSI and its archival collections, the university librarian was completely in support, and the entire institute ended up coming to the University of Victoria as a gift.

The next major donation came about as a result of the research work I had then been doing for over a decade on the life of the activist, philanthropist, and trans man Reed Erickson (1917–1992), founder and funder of the Erickson Educational Foundation (1964–1984). Over the years, I had become friends with his daughter. When she had decided that it was time to donate his papers to an archive, she chose the University of Victoria. Up until this point, none of us thought of ourselves as amassing a transgender archive. However, with the acquisition of the Reed Erickson papers, we realized that we then had two large and historically significant trans collections. We started to think that we were developing a transgender archive as we added a few small collections to what we already had. Near the end of 2011, we officially launched the Transgender Archives.

Word got out through our publicity and networking efforts. As it did, more small and medium-sized collections were donated to the Transgender Archives. Whenever I was in contact with people whom I knew from working with trans activists and researchers, I would ask them about their plans for their papers. Many of them held cherished collections going back decades. They understood that they and their colleagues had been doing activist and research work of historical importance that needed to be recorded and preserved. Many of the items in their collections often also reminded them of times when such things acted as lifelines for trans people during a period when the isolation and loneliness of being trans was profound. These were not collections that would be parted with lightly, both because of their personal significance and because of the moral obligations that the collectors felt to past and future generations of trans, nonbinary, and Two-Spirit people.

However, many of the people with whom I spoke were old enough that they were considering their mortality, or simply downsizing. We talked about ensuring that their collections did not end up in the trash because of inattention or neglect. At the same time, they knew that most trans community organizations were fragile and transitory. Many people holding collections were wary that community groups might not have the resources to safely preserve their documents over the long term. The University of Victoria offered them an ideal home for their collections: a publicly funded and publicly accessible institution with high-quality facilities, an exceptionally strong institutional commitment to trans studies, and the prospect of long-term stability. The Transgender Archives continue to grow steadily.

What the Transgender Archives Do for Trans People

First and foremost, the Transgender Archives preserve raw materials from which the history of trans activism and research may be written. Brave people have been working for over one hundred years to increase social understanding, acceptance, and integration for gender-variant people. All people today and in the future—trans, cis, nonbinary—need to know and appreciate the work done by these pioneers. The original records of their work need to be safely held and made available to the public at no cost to users. The Transgender Archives do this and more.

Every year, high school, college, and undergraduate university students from the region around the University of Victoria make use of the Transgender Archives as part of the courses that they take and the papers that they write. Every year, masters and doctoral students from around the world travel to the Transgender Archives to do research for research papers, theses, and dissertations on topics as diverse as science policy, political theory, pop music performance, pulp fiction, queer archives, and prison policy. Many professors and librarians also visit us. Some of the areas that they have been researching include Japanese trans publications, trans culture before the Internet, the history of trans rights for adults and children, and how to build a queer archive. Other people come to the Transgender Archives just because they want to know more about history, or because they want to learn how to do something similar in their location, or they come to borrow some things to show as part of an exhibition back home.

Every two years, the Transgender Archives and the Chair in Transgender Studies sponsor Moving Trans History Forward conferences. They span several days and attract hundreds of people, teens to octogenarians, from all across Canada and the United States, as well as from Latin America, Europe, and Asia. The conferences are designed to be of interest to a mix of students, academics, and community-based people, a place where people from the entire spectrum of trans life—transsexual, transgender, nonbinary, drag, cross-dresser, families, and cis allies—can interact in a positive and respectful environment. We also make many speeches and arts events open to the public for free. After the conferences, we post online as much of the proceedings as we can.

The Transgender Archives and the Chair in Transgender Studies also work to communicate with the interested public through a variety of means. We run a Facebook page with a stream of relevant news and information about modern and historical trans life. We also run a Twitter feed about our collections and about general trans events and activities. Almost every day we post new images from the Transgender Archives to our Instagram account. Our YouTube channel runs videos from the Moving Trans History Forward conferences and our other events. You can also download for free our Lambda Award finalist book, *The Transgender Archives: Foundations for the Future*.

The Future

The Transgender Archives will continue to grow and serve. As our collections grow, we hope to fill some of the gaps in what we now hold. The materials in our archives have come to us as gifts from private collectors. Private collections reflect certain realities about their collectors. To amass a significant collection of historical materials, one must have enough money to purchase items, enough space to store them, and enough housing stability to preserve them. Furthermore, people collect what interests them and what is available to them. In the trans world, as in much of the rest of society, this means that what has been created in the first place, and what has subsequently been collected, largely reflects the experiences of middle-class white people assigned as males at birth. Thus, one of our projects is to acquire holdings that better reflect the diversity of trans, nonbinary, and Two-Spirit lives.

Although the Transgender Archives are completely free and open to the public, we recognize that few of the millions of people who might want to visit us will be able to do so. Therefore, we will continue the work already begun, both in partnership with the Digital Transgender Archive and on our own, to make larger portions of the Transgender Archives available online for free public access. Fund-raising is also ongoing to provide subsidies to assist visitors with travel expenses.

As the largest collection of transgender archival materials in the world, the Transgender Archives are a unique and invaluably rich resource from which to learn about the complexity of human gender variation. Our collections bear witness to the courage, vision, and perseverance of our elders and forebears. They had the wisdom to see that there was much important work to be done to make the world a more just place for all. Each, in their own ways, took on a piece of the job of making the world safer and more hospitable for people who do not easily fit within prevailing simplistic binary and hierarchical systems and structures of gender. They all took risks in doing this. Some suffered significantly for their boldness. All contributed to advancing gender freedoms. We owe them more than we can know.

The Transgender Archives stand as a testament to those brave souls who risked so much to forge a pathway for today's advances. By keeping their names alive, and by preserving the records of the work they have done, we can repay some of our debt to our pioneers. Thus, those who have had the foresight to do the work of collecting and preserving also do the work of advancing social justice. All people need to know their history; this is even more true for people who have been so abject that, through much of our history, our very survival has depended on our ability to keep our gender variance hidden.

We welcome community members, scholars and independent researchers, activists and allies to come to the Transgender Archives to explore our diverse collections, and thereby to learn about who we are and how we got to where we are today. Open to the public, free of charge, and accessible to all, the Transgender Archives safeguard a broad spectrum of trans heritage so that the work that our pioneers have done will not be forgotten. We remember. We respect. We preserve. We persevere. We invite you to join us.

HARRISON APPLE

Finding Trans Context in Everyday Newspaper Archives

Harrison Apple is the founding codirector of the Pittsburgh Queer History Project (PQHP) and a PhD student of gender and women's studies at the University of Arizona. Their work on the PQHP documents the emergence of a queer after-hours nightclub community in Pittsburgh between the 1950s and 1990s and its influence on contemporary community politics. Since 2012 they have been collecting oral histories and ephemera that offer divergent and complementary accounts of gendered and sexual practices in the Steel City. Their doctoral work combines transgender studies and archival science to critically engage the criteria of "evidence" when presented with radically conflicting accounts of shared histories.

The Most Livable City: A Reading of Pittsburgh's 1976 Massage Parlor War

Renaissance II—a civic and corporate partnership campaign to restrict air and river pollution, construct public parks, and demolish decrepit buildings in Pittsburgh's downtown between 1944 and 1984—was simultaneously responsible for the regulation of gender and sexuality of the population of Pittsburgh. Specifically, the rise in violence over control of the massage parlor and pornography industry, located on downtown's Liberty Avenue, is a well-documented historical moment in which city officials and the press circumscribed an abject corner of its population and expelled it with full support of public opinion.

Pittsburgh's downtown, also known as the Golden Triangle, is located where the Allegheny and Monongahela Rivers meet to form the Ohio. It is a historic juncture for river transportation, and for that reason it has been a consistently documented site of power struggle since at least the eighteenth century. The triangle was controlled by the French military in 1754, seized by the British in 1758 during the French and Indian War, later used as a fort for the Union Army during the American Civil War, and, at the start of the twentieth century, it was a site of impoverished dwellings among mixed industrial warehouse space. This Gateway to the West, as it came to be known, has been inscribed repeatedly with imperialist practices of domination, and by the 1950s it was the center for Pittsburgh's post–WWII Renaissance.[5]

Pittsburgh's Renaissance was the work of a public-private partnership known as the Allegheny Council for Community Development. Since 1944, the Allegheny Council has designed and funded projects to lift Pittsburgh out of its industrial past, echoing urban planning philosophies that revere wide green spaces and hygienic urban landscapes.[6] The Allegheny Council began with projects to reduce air and water pollution, addressing the infamous smog that was so thick it required street lamps to be on all hours of the day.[7]

By 1976 the Pittsburgh Convention Center (which didn't open for another five years), planned as one of the final gems of downtown urban renewal, promised to attract reinvigorated industrial investment, but it faced the conundrum of being only blocks from the stretch of Liberty Avenue that had been home to a cluster of massage parlors and porn theaters, serving a diverse nightlife and sex-work economy. This stretch of Pittsburgh was strategically circumscribed, demonized, and exorcised from the city's history and replaced with a monument to public culture aptly named the Cultural District.[8]

The Massage Parlor War

The Massage Parlor War is in large part a story drawn from the headlines of two daily newspapers, the *Pittsburgh Press* and the *Pittsburgh Post-Gazette*. Both publications had followed the career of a former "rub parlor" kingpin George Lee and his empire of sex-for-pay businesses. However, after his murder in 1976, the coverage of the massage parlor industry transitioned from a moral quandary to austere politics of public safety.[9] Until this moment, the historical narrative of Pittsburgh's Golden Triangle had been structured on invasion and defense, architecturally memorialized in the brick outlines of Fort Duquesne, Fort Pitt, and the preservation of the block house still standing on Point State Park. However, the Massage Parlor War demonstrates a shift in historical narrative from defense against invasion to the management of life through Pittsburgh's Renaissance II. The deployment of "war" in the coverage of the massage parlors illustrates the French philosopher Michel Foucault's concept of biopolitics, whereby modern power primarily and pervasively works to regulate the "health" of populations. For Foucault, modern power is exercised, in other words, through discourses and disciplines (e.g., urban planning, criminology, sexology, medicine, and journalism) that delimit which subjects can be known and discussed. In this theoretical framework, power becomes relational, discursive, and enacted through the disciplining of knowledge and management of life.

The Massage Parlor War began on 23 December 1977, as a yellow cab pulled away from the Gemini Spa at 641 Liberty Avenue, owned by Nick DeLucia—a former employee of George Lee and inheritor of a handful of his businesses. The driver had been instructed to deliver a white Christmas package, addressed to the parlor's star masseuse, Joanna "Sasha" Scott. Only moments later, the package exploded, sending glass, blood, and debris out of the second-floor parlor and onto Christmas shoppers below. In the blast, gold calling cards for the Gemini Spa flew into the street with the words "twelve beautiful girls to serve you, private and intimate," along with the names of their many clients.[10] As paramedics tended to victims of the blast, police collected evidence from the parlor, and journalists rushed from their downtown office buildings to document the beginning of the Massage Parlor War.

The parlor explosion came at an opportune time for the Allegheny Council and ancillary committees, which were focused on the construction of the Pittsburgh Convention Center. With plans in place since the early 1970s, there were hopes for the Convention Center to attract new industries to make their home in the Steel City. However, their construction plans had begun to push against the nightlife that had made its home in downtown since the 1960s. The cover of a 1976 issue of the *Pittsburgh Gay News* features a photograph of one of the many porn theaters with the caption "Massage parlors were under attack—are we next?"[11] In a two-part report, Jonathan Bowden followed the popular opinion of city planners and invested parties that the strip of massage parlors on Liberty Avenue must be eliminated to execute their vision of a hygienic postindustrial landscape.

For the council, the rebirth of Pittsburgh depended on excising the massage parlors, which despite their long-term residency were not the kind of "historic charm" the city could sell to investors. In response to the explosion, Mayor Richard Caliguiri—whose mayoral term inaugurated Renaissance II—told the press, "Every law abiding citizen has reason to be as outraged as I am by [this] vicious bombing . . . *aside from the death and destruction it dealt to those in the massage parlor,* the explosion endangered the lives and property of the innocent people in the area."[12] Though it would remain unclear who was responsible for this particular act of violence for many years, the mayor's statement arranged the event as an internal assault on the population of Pittsburgh. He directed public outrage not toward the single perpetrator but toward the industry of the city's criminal underbelly, their profane sexual industry becoming conflated with an indictment of reckless endangerment.[13]

Caliguiri's multilayered public comment and its framing with a photograph of the blast zone by the *Pittsburgh Press* initiated a panic beyond the crime itself and toward the business owners and employees whom the reporter casually defined as "flesh merchants."[14] Lisa Duggan and Nan Hunter's 1989 essay "Sex

Panic" takes on the National Endowment for the Arts scandal, in which the public expressed similar outrage that taxpayer dollars supported the creation of "pornographic images" by Robert Mapplethorpe, gnawing at the tenets of American national culture. What Duggan and Hunter salvage from the uproar is that sex panic, along with witch hunts and red scares, are in fact staples of American history. The American tradition of moral outrage and subsequent acts of "moral reform" had become an effective tool for disregarding systemic issues of racism, sexism, and poverty.[15] Their argument suggests that public sex scandals most often reinforce social hierarchies rather than shed light on social inequities, and that moral reform becomes nothing more than political theater.

Mayor Caliguiri's call to action revealed the neoliberal urban redevelopment plans that demanded the positioning of the massage-parlor industry as an internal threat to the Pittsburgh population and gathered public support for its ejection from the Golden Triangle. As reported in the newspapers, the blast turned Pittsburgh's sex-work communities from something "private and intimate" into something "public and violent," which had to be destroyed without a trace to ensure the continued life of the population. This narrative emerges as a regulation of public sexuality and gender—and transgender bodies in particular—in order to turn an "industrial wasteland" into an attractive, productive, and lively service-industry metropolis. In so many words, a portion of the population would have to die to facilitate the city's rebirth.

Tex Gill's Killer Publicity

Over an eight-year investigation, Dante "Tex" Gill, a white trans-masculine massage parlor owner, was indicted on charges of fraud, ranging from the juridical to the gendered. He emerged in the Massage Parlor War narrative as a criminal element whose various fronts for processing income from sex work—a paintable pottery shop and various health spas—declared him criminally inauthentic.[16] The narrative of his professional deception is echoed in the stock language used to describe him in nearly every article among more than sixty published as "a woman who dresses as a man and prefers to be known as Mr. Gill." In piecing together the Massage Parlor War, we see that his alleged *inauthenticity* as both a man and a parlor owner positioned him as a threat to the sexual moralism expounded by Renaissance II and the fantasy of postindustrial Pittsburgh.

Tex's masculinity was taken to task repeatedly while his substantial tax evasion was investigated. Unlike his parlor peers, who were cisgender heterosexual married men and who retained an unexplained distance between their personal life and their life of crime, Tex is identified as a lesbian in a scare-quoted "marriage" to another woman, who despite having legally changed her name, is not reported as Cynthia Gill but as Cynthia Bruno.[17] In contrast to George Lee and Nick DeLucia, Tex did not participate in heterosexual reproduction; he did not have children or a normative family structure to balance his pornographic career. His gender nonconformity was part and parcel of his criminality in the eyes of the law and court of public opinion.

Though Tex would never be convicted for sex work, U.S. District Court Judge Gustav Diamond, who oversaw Tex's sentencing, went so far as to ask the jury to consider Tex's "line of work" (a thinly veiled reference to sex work) in his trial for tax fraud. Despite the lack of evidence to charge Tex with prostitution, the specter of sexual immorality was intentionally attached to Tex's legal experience and the city's war on massage parlors. To quote Judge Diamond, the state's investigation into Tex Gill promised to "pierce the sham" of his career in deception.[18]

This language of exposure, veneer, and representation of the Massage Parlor War entangled pornography, sex work, and trans bodies into a discourse of *authenticity* versus *inauthenticity*. Tex's case migrated from an insinuation of public safety hazard to an inquisition of economic and gendered deception. What's more, his public image of fraudulent business and fraudulent masculinity was publicized by being awarded both the Year's Most Dubious Man and Most Dubious Woman by the Pittsburgh Press in 1984.[19]

Tex's publicity positioned him as a distinct foil to the language of moral integrity, sexual conservatism, and nuclear family structure written into Pittsburgh's Renaissance. In newspaper accounts, Tex's criminality and gender became fused as a pornographic representation of sex out-of-place, the legal consequence of which is to padlock the massage parlors, and padlock Tex in federal prison. In this logic, the city had to lock up the pornographic in order to contain its threat to the postindustrial rebirth of Pittsburgh, always on the horizon.

Devoid of Life . . . All Uninhabited Seemed Totally Ours

The Gateway area on the "town" side of the freeways, for all its office towers, seems to be essentially suburban in tone. The placing of the buildings among the ornamented open spaces has been handsomely accomplished, but there is a little too much openness. From the Liberty Avenue entrance of the quarter, one has a sense of tremendous sweep and verve that is entirely pleasing but even at noonday there seems to be a kind of busy emptiness about these spaces. After five o'clock, when the office workers, like homing pigeons, head for the distant suburban hills, the gardens become really vacant. We, in the past, have dined al fresco on summer Sunday evenings at the Hilton, and the great spaces stretching away from the terrace were often quite devoid of life. Those green pleasances stretching out, all uninhabited, seemed totally ours. How grand and how sad!

JAMES D. VAN TRUMP, "AN ANTIPHON OF STONES" (1983)

The above quotation from the founder of the Pittsburgh History and Landmarks Foundation describes the Golden Triangle in the early years of Pittsburgh's Renaissance. Van Trump's poignant essays included in *Life and Architecture in Pittsburgh* express the sentiment of development as it assigns life to some places and "busy emptiness" to others. In his sentimental vignettes of Pittsburgh's landscape, he expresses the desire to inscribe the triangle with life. These spaces, evacuated by suburban office workers, appear as a tabula rasa, inscribable without consequence. Through a strategic use of moral outrage, the development teams for Renaissance II reinscribed the downtown landscape of sex-for-pay businesses as a blank slate for the rebirth of a postindustrial metropolis. While Pittsburgh continues to brand itself as the "most livable city," the contestable record of Tex Gill and the Massage Parlor War poses the question, "Most livable for whom?"

REFERENCES

"About Us." Allegheny Conference on Community Development. www.alleghenyconfer ence.org/AboutUs.php. Accessed 1 January 2015.

Ackerman, Jan. "Jurors Being Chosen for 'Tex' Gill Trial." *Pittsburgh Post-Gazette,* 3 October 1984.

Alberts, Robert C. *The Shaping of the Point.* Pittsburgh: University of Pittsburgh Press, 1980.

Berrey, Lester V., and Melvin Van den Bark. *The American Thesaurus of Slang: A Complete Reference Book of Colloquial Speech.* New York: Thomas Y. Crowell, 1942.

Bowden, Jonathan. "Gays and Liberty Avenue: Establishment's Next Target?" *Pittsburgh Gay News,* April 1976.

Byrd, Jerry. "Miss Gill's Ceramics Low-Profile." *Pittsburgh Press,* 23 May 1979.

Donalson, Al. "Reputed Rub Parlor Chief Tex Gill Gets 13-Year Term for Tax Evasion." *Pittsburgh Press,* 3 January 1985.

Duggan, Lisa, and Nan D. Hunter. "Sex Panic." In *Sex Wars,* edited by Lisa Duggan and Nan D. Hunter, 71–75. New York: Routledge, 2006.

Foucault, M.. *Society Must Be Defended: Lectures at the Collège de France, 1975–76.* Edited by Mauro Bertani and Alessandro Fontana. Translated by David Macey. New York: Picador, 2003.

Harbrecht, Doug. "Massage King's Heritage Bloody, Estate Small." *Pittsburgh Press,* 25 December 1977.

"Huge 'Gateway Center' Planned in Pittsburgh." *Pittsburgh Star-News,* 22 September 1949.

"Name Change Asked." *Pittsburgh Post-Gazette,* 20 September 1979.

Post-Gazette Staff. "The Blockhouse, Point State Park." *Pittsburgh Post-Gazette,* 6 October 2008.

Rotstein, Gary. "'Most Livable City' Took Its Lumps over Tag." *Pittsburgh Post-Gazette,* 27 February 2010.

"Smoke Control Lantern Slide Collection." *University of Pittsburgh Digital Libraries*. http://historicpittsburgh.org/collection/smoke-control-lantern-slides. Accessed 25 April 2018.

Tierney, John. "How the Arts Drove Pittsburgh's Revitalization." *Atlantic*, 11 December 2014, www.theatlantic.com/business/archive/2014/12/how-the-cultural-arts-drove-pittsburghs-revitalization /383627/.

"Tracing the Trends from AIDS to Yuppie." *Pittsburgh Post-Gazette*, 25 December 1989.

Van Trump, James D. "An Antiphon of Stones." In *Life and Architecture in Pittsburgh*. Pittsburgh: Pittsburgh History and Landmarks Foundation, 1983, 13–20.

Wisser, William, and Rich Gigler. "4 Rub Parlors Shut Down after Fatal Blast." *Pittsburgh Press*, 24 December 1977.

Key Concepts

ephemera (p. 444)
archive (p. 440)

Activities, Discussion Questions, and Observations

1. Library archives have historically collected written materials and ephemera that give us a rich sense of communication and the material culture of a specific period. Today many events are publicized online and might even take place entirely online. How do you think our "wired world" will change the nature of archives and future research? What needs to be saved? How will these items be saved? What might be worth saving for future researchers to get a sense of today's culture?

2. Harrison Apple provides a terrific example of what happened when they decided to delve into a local newspaper archive in Pittsburgh. There Apple found a rich and complex history about the ways that gender identity, and more specifically trans embodiment, gets tied to a "less desirable" side of a city and the ways that urban development gets tied into conversations about gender identity. What Harrison discovered in their research into the Massage Parlor Wars is similar to the conditions found in the specific locations of some of the early trans riots in the United States, Cooper's Donuts and Compton's (see Chapter 4). For this exercise, check out your local newspaper archives. No matter what size town you live in or near, there will be a local newspaper, and there will be an archive. Pick a random date, preferably before you were born, and start reading various stories in the newspaper from that day. Instead of national news, choose a local story, photograph, or informational item. What did you learn from it? What information does it give you? What information can you infer from it? What other questions do you have?

3. Andrea Jenkins is working painstakingly to record oral histories for the trans-gender oral history archives. Although not all the stories from her interview-ees' lives are online in transcript form yet, several are now available. For this project, go to the oral history website (https://www.lib.umn.edu/tretter/transgender- oral-history-project) and choose someone's history that is avail-able to read. What did you learn about the person? How did they tell Andrea their story? You may wish to compare two of the stories, which will also pro-vide insight into the different ways people respond to the interviewer. Why is it important to have both an oral history and a written record of the person telling their life story?

4. It might not be convenient for you to get to the Transgender Archives in Vic-toria, British Columbia. (If you can get there, I highly recommend it; the staff are very welcoming to everyone wanting to look through the archive.) Several pieces of the collections are available for viewing on the archives' website: www.uvic.ca/transgenderarchives/index.php. If you click on "Our collec-tions," you will see a sidebar menu. Have some fun clicking around in the various collections. From items such as underground trans gatherings and newsletters (which you will find in the Stephanie Castle and the Zenith Foun-dation's pages), to informational pamphlets like the one Lou Sullivan worked on for trans men (found in the Reed Erickson pages), to archival photographs in the Fantasia Fair section, you can click through the various pieces of the collection and study them. What did you find, and what interested you? What did you learn? Most of all, just have fun going through the materials.

Archives Websites

Digital Transgender Archive
     https://www.digitaltransgenderarchive.net/

A Gender Variance Who's Who
     https://zagria.blogspot.com/p/index.html#.WVf-Brvyu34

GLBT Historical Society, San Francisco
     www.glbthistory.org/

Hoover Institution Library and Archives
     www.hoover.org/library-archives

Louise Lawrence Transgender Archive
     http://lltransarchive.org/

Online Archive of California
     www.oac.cdlib.org/

Transgender Archives at the University of Victoria
    http://transgenderarchives.ca

TransGriot Archive and Blog by Monica Roberts
    http://transgriot.blogspot.com/

Tretter Transgender Oral History Project at the University of Minnesota's Tretter Collection
    https://www.lib.umn.edu/tretter/transgender-oral-history-project

University of Michigan, Labadie Collection: Transgender Items
    http://guides.lib.umich.edu/c.php?g=282858&p=1884819

NOTES

1. Many of Frida Kahlo's letters are held at the Hoover Archives at Stanford University in Stanford, Calif. The Hoover Archives were first established by President Hoover and are dedicated to collecting anything and everything from around the world that has something to do with war, peace, and revolution. The Hoover Archives are free and open to everyone. You do not have to be affiliated with Stanford to research in the archives. You can go online and check out some of the holdings at www.hoover.org/library-archives.

2. Heidi Landgraf, "Uncovered: The Diary Project: Sean Dorsey's Fifth Home Season," *dancersgroup*, 1 January 2010, http://dancersgroup.org/2010/01/uncovered-the-diary-project-sean-dorseys-fifth-home-season/ (accessed 30 June 2017).

3. In 1987 I was the president of the Lesbian Caucus at CU Boulder. It was the first time that the Lesbian Caucus joined together with Gays and Friends to put on a fundraiser. At the time, I caught a lot of flack from many of the women in the Lesbian Caucus because they felt that it was not okay to work with Gays and Friends. They were also opposed to a drag show on feminist principles. I realize in hindsight that this event was the beginning of the two groups' working together, and I am still very proud of that. I was often much more comfortable around the members of Gays and Friends, so it is ironic that I was president of the Lesbian Caucus, where I never felt I really fit in. Of course, given that I identify as nonbinary trans and given my love of many things that are associated with gay male culture, it is not surprising that I wanted to work on a drag show.

4. The Louise Lawrence Transgender Archive homepage, http://lltransarchive.org/ (accessed 16 July 2017).

5. Robert C. Alberts, *The Shaping of the Point* (Pittsburgh: University of Pittsburgh Press, 1980), 21, 25.

6. "About Us," Allegheny Conference on Community Development, www.alleghenyconference.org/AboutUs.php (accessed 1 January 2015).

7. "Smoke Control Lantern Slide Collection," University of Pittsburgh Digital Libraries, http://historicpittsburgh.org/collection/smoke-control-lantern-slides (accessed 25 April 2018). Pittsburgh's reputation for smog was so prevalent that a 1942 English slang dictionary included an entry for shouting "PITTSBURGH!" to alert someone that the toast was burning; Lester V. Berrey and Melvin Van den Bark, *The*

American Thesaurus of Slang: A Complete Reference Book of Colloquial Speech (New York: Thomas Y. Crowell, 1942).

8. John Tierney, "How the Arts Drove Pittsburgh's Revitalization," *Atlantic*, 11 December 2014, www.theatlantic.com/business/archive/2014/12/how-the-cultural-arts-drove-pittsburghs-revitalization/383627/.

9. Doug Harbrecht, "Massage King's Heritage Bloody, Estate Small," *Pittsburgh Press*, 25 December 1977.

10. William Wisser and Rich Gigler, "4 Rub Parlors Shut Down after Fatal Blast," *Pittsburgh Press*, 24 December 1977.

11. Jonathan Bowden, "Gays and Liberty Avenue: Establishment's Next Target?" *Pittsburgh Gay News*, April 1976.

12. Wisser and Gigler, "4 Rub Parlors Shut Down after Fatal Blast"; emphasis added.

13. Ibid.

14. Ibid.

15. Lisa Duggan and Nan D. Hunter, "Sex Panic," in *Sex Wars*, ed. Lisa Duggan and Nan D. Hunter (New York: Routledge, 2006), 71–75.

16. Jerry Byrd, "Miss Gill's Ceramics Low-Profile," *Pittsburgh Press*, 23 May 1979.

17. "Name Change Asked," *Pittsburgh Post-Gazette*, 20 September 1979. Cynthia has since contacted the author and is collaborating on a project to revisit the Massage Parlor Wars from the position of some-one inside the business and close to Tex. Besides confirming how frequently the papers misrepresented events (both public and private), she also confirmed that her marriage to Tex was legal and occurred during a trip to Hawaii.

18. Al Donalson, "Reputed Rub Parlor Chief Tex Gill Gets 13-Year Term for Tax Evasion," *Pittsburgh Press*, 3 January 1985.

19. "Tracing the Trends from AIDS to Yuppie," *Pittsburgh Post-Gazette*, 25 December 1989.

BIBLIOGRAPHY

"Frida Kahlo and Diego Rivera Materials in the Hoover Institution Archives." Hoover Institution Archive at Stanford University, 13 August 2008. www.hoover.org/news/frida-kahlo-and-diego-rivera-materials-hoover-institution-archives. Accessed 1 July 2017.

Landgraf, Heidi. "Uncovered: The Diary Project: Sean Dorsey's Fifth Home Season." *Dancersgroup*, 1 January 2010. http://dancersgroup.org/2010/01/uncovered-the-diary-project-sean-dorseys-fifth-home-season/. Accessed 30 June 2017.

Louise Lawrence Transgender Archive. http://lltransarchive.org/. Accessed 16 July 2017.

Transgender Archives at the University of Victoria. www.uvic.ca/transgenderarchives/index.php. Accessed 20 July 2018.

Tretter Transgender Oral History Project at the University of Minnesota's Tretter Collections. https://www.lib.umn.edu/tretter/transgender=oral=history=project. Accessed 20 July 2018.

INDEX

Page numbers in *italics* refer to illustrations and their captions

and hermaphrodites, 5
legal identification in, 211
see also Hijras
Indigenous Americans
and cultural empowerment, 250–253,
265n4
and European colonialism, 241–244, 249,
259
spiritual practices and, 14, 357
Industrial Revolution, 328–330, 341
Instagram, social protest and, 340
Institut für Sexualwissenschaft, 101–103
International Powerlifting Federation, 187
intersecting identities, 10
intersex, as term, 5
Intersex Society of North America (ISNA), 6
Intersex South Africa, 184
interviews, as archival material, 442–443,
444–446
inversion, 322, 323
Iran, conditions in, 127n25, 321, 340
Ishtar, 357, 371
"Is This Butch Enough?" (Dorsey), 400

Jacob syndrome, 4
Jamaica, anti-homosexuality laws in, 49
Jamal, personal narratives of, 13–14, 23
Janus Society, 143
Japan, trans stage in, 398–399
jazz, 401–402
Jeanne d'Arc (Joan of Arc), 358–360, 358
Jenkins, Andrea, 71–73, 442, 443, 44r–446
Jenner, Caitlyn, 21, 22, 23, 114, 117–118, 120,
183, 186
Jennings, Jazz, 118
Jesus Christ, 371, 399
Jim Crow laws, 172
Johannesburg, South Africa, trans images in,
407–408
Johnson, Lyndon Baines, 132
Johnson, Marsha P., 149, 152, 215, 243

Jones, Cleve, 153
Jones, Rhian E., 330, 332, 334, 341–346
Jorgenson, Christine, 19, 20
Journal of American Psychology, 63
Journal of the History of Medicine, 371
journals, 79–80, 439–440
Justin Martyr, 373

Kahlo, Frida, 438–439
Karnak temple, 364
Kato, David, 69
Kellerman, Stewart, 16
Kelly Kelly, personal narratives of, 24, 51, 207
Kimbell Art Museum, 361
King, Billie Jean, 185
King, Martin Luther, Jr., 132
Kingston, Maxine Hong, 367
Kinks (rock band), 403–404
Kinsey, Alfred, 52–56, 52
Kinsey Scale, 53
Kladney, Mat, 221–223
Klinefelter syndrome, 4
Knights of the Clock, 140
Kobayashi, Ichizo, 398
Krafft-Ebing, Richard von, 96, 97–100, 97, 387,
393
Kraushaar, James M., 417
kuchu, 68–70
Kumu Hina, 253, 253

Labat, Jean-Baptiste, 245
labels. *See* pronouns, personal; terminology
Ladies in Support of the President (LISP),
336–340, 338
Lady Skimmington, 326–328
Laidler, Percy, 288
Lakshmi, 357
Lakshminarayan, 357
Lambda Legal, 211–212
land, public access to, 326–328, 331–336